Locke and Law

I0890845

**Philosophers and Law**
*Series Editor: Tom Campbell*

**Titles in the Series:**

**Cicero and Modern Law**
*Richard Brooks*

**Aristotle and Modern Law**
*Richard O. Brooks and James Bernard Murphy*

**Plato and Modern Law**
*Richard O. Brooks*

**Locke and Law**
*Thom Brooks*

**Rousseau and Law**
*Thom Brooks*

**Kant and Law**
*B. Sharon Byrd and Joachim Hruschka*

**Marx and Law**
*Susan Easton*

**Hobbes on Law**
*Claire Finkelstein*

**Hume and Law**
*Ken Mackinnon*

**Gadamer and Law**
*Francis J. Mootz III*

**Nietzsche and Law**
*Francis J. Mootz III and Peter Goodrich*

**Wittgenstein and Law**
*Dennis Patterson*

**Hegel and Law**
*Michael Salter*

# Locke and Law

*Edited by*

Thom Brooks

*University of Newcastle, UK*

Routledge
Taylor & Francis Group
LONDON AND NEW YORK

First published 2007 by Ashgate Publishing

2 Park Square, Milton Park, Abingdon, Oxfordshire OX14 4RN
711 Third Avenue, New York, NY 10017

*Routledge is an imprint of the Taylor & Francis Group, an informa business*

First issued in paperback 2018

Copyright © 2007 Thom Brooks. For copyright of individual articles please refer to the Acknowledgements.

All rights reserved. No part of this book may be reprinted or reproduced or utilised in any form or by any electronic, mechanical, or other means, now known or hereafter invented, including photocopying and recording, or in any information storage or retrieval system, without permission in writing from the publishers.

Notice:
Product or corporate names may be trademarks or registered trademarks, and are used only for identification and explanation without intent to infringe.

Wherever possible, these reprints are made from a copy of the original printing, but these can themselves be of very variable quality. Whilst the publisher has made every effort to ensure the quality of the reprint, some variability may inevitably remain.

**British Library Cataloguing in Publication Data**
Locke and law. – (Philosophers and law)
1. Locke, John, 1632-1704 2. Law – Philosophy
I. Brooks, Thom
340.1'092

**Library of Congress Control Number**: 2007925930

ISBN 978-0-7546-2678-7 (hbk)
ISBN 978-1-138-37845-2 (pbk)

# Contents

# Acknowledgements

The editor and publishers wish to thank the following for permission to use copyright material.

American Journal of Jurisprudence for the essay: Suri Ratnapala (1993), 'John Locke's Doctrine of the Separation of Powers: A Re-Evaluation', *American Journal of Jurisprudence*, **38**, pp. 189–220.

Blackwell Publishing Limited for the essays: A. John Simmons (1991), 'Locke and the Right to Punish', *Philosophy and Public Affairs*, **20**, pp. 311–49; Paul Bou-Habib (2003), 'Locke, Sincerity and the Rationality of Persecution', *Political Studies*, **51**, pp. 611–26. Copyright © 2003 Political Studies Association.

Cambridge University Press for the essays: Jeremy Waldron (2005), 'Nozick and Locke: Filling the Space of Rights', *Social Philosophy and Policy*, **22**, pp. 81–110. Copyright © 2005 Social Philosophy and Policy Foundation; Brian Calvert (1993), 'Locke on Punishment and the Death Penalty', *Philosophy*, **68**, pp. 211–29. Copyright © 1993 Cambridge University Press.

Canadian Journal of Philosophy for the essay: David C. Snyder (1986), 'Locke on Natural Law and Property Rights', *Canadian Journal of Philosophy*, **16**, pp. 723–50.

Sage Publications for the essay: Martha C. Nussbaum (2006), 'Radical Evil in the Lockean State: The Neglect of the Political Emotions', *Journal of Moral Philosophy*, **3**, pp. 159–78.

Seattle University Law Review for the essay: David L. Wardle (2002), 'Reason to Ratify: The Influence of John Locke's Religious Beliefs on the Creation and Adoption of the United States Constitution', *Seattle University Law Review*, **26**, pp. 291–308.

University of California for the essay: Donald L. Doernberg (1985), '"We the People": John Locke, Collective Constitutional Rights, and Standing to Challenge Government Action', *California Law Review*, **73**, pp. 52–118.

University of Nebraska for the essay: Donna M. Byrne (1999), 'Locke, Property, and Progressive Taxes', *Nebraska Law Review*, **78**, pp. 700–38. Copyright © 1999 Nebraska Law Review.

Vermont Law Review for the essay: John M. Kang (2004), 'John Locke's Political Plan, Or, There's No Such Thing as Judicial Impartiality (And It's A Good Thing, Too)', *Vermont Law Review*, **29**, pp. 7–31.

Yale Law Journal for the essay: Benjamin G. Damstedt (2003), 'Limiting Locke: A Natural Law Justification for the Fair Use Doctrine', *Yale Law Journal*, **112**, pp. 1179–221.

Every effort has been made to trace all the copyright holders, but if any have been inadvertently overlooked the publishers will be pleased to make the necessary arrangement at the first opportunity.

# Series Preface

The series *Philosophers and Law* selects and makes accessible the most important essays in English that deal with the application to law of the work of major philosophers for whom law was not a main concern. The series encompasses not only what these philosophers had to say about law but also brings together essays which consider those aspects of the work of major philosophers which bear on our interpretation and assessment of current law and legal theory. The essays are based on scholarly study of particular philosophers and deal with both the nature and role of law and the application of philosophy to specific areas of law.

Some philosophers, such as Hans Kelsen, Roscoe Pound and Herbert Hart are known principally as philosophers of law. Others, whose names are not primarily or immediately associated with law, such as Aristotle, Kant and Hegel, have, nevertheless, had a profound influence on legal thought. It is with the significance for law of this second group of philosophers that this series is concerned.

Each volume in the series deals with a major philosopher whose work has been taken up and applied to the study and critique of law and legal systems. The essays, which have all been previously published in law, philosophy and politics journals and books, are selected and introduced by an editor with a special interest in the philosopher in question and an engagement in contemporary legal studies. The essays chosen represent the most important and influential contributions to the interpretation of the philosophers concerned and the continuing relevance of their work to current legal issues.

TOM CAMPBELL
*Series Editor*
*Centre for Applied Philosophy and Public Ethics*
*Charles Sturt University*

*For Miles and Ella*

# Introduction

John Locke (1632–1704) is easily one of the most influential figures in the history of philosophy. He wrote on many areas, but is primarily known as a towering figure in epistemology and political thought. Although Locke himself was not a legal philosopher, his ideas have great relevance for our thinking about law. This fact has not been lost on many legal philosophers working today, more than three centuries after Locke's death.

In this collection, I have carefully selected essays that best explore Locke's contributions to contemporary work in legal and political theory, covering a wide range of issues, such as natural law, natural rights, property, abortion, constitutional law, the relationship between law and society, punishment, tolerance and civil disobedience. These essays bring together both excellent scholarship and clear insights into Locke's many contemporary contributions, including some speculative work pointing ahead to where future contributions may lie (see Donna Byrne, Chapter 5; Benjamin Damstedt, Chapter 2; Donald Doernberg, Chapter 14; Kimberly Sharron Dunn, Chapter 7; Martha Nussbaum, Chapter 11).

Before turning to these essays, I believe it is worthwhile to say a few words about Locke's legal and political theory before considering how it might contribute to contemporary work in legal and political theory. This is especially the case given that the particular details of Locke's legal and political theory may be less well known amongst contemporary legal theorists than that of more conventional figures in the history of legal thought.

John Locke was originally a medical doctor who did not write professionally until he was nearly 60 years old. None of these writings were subsequently on medicine: all concerned various philosophical topics. Locke was Anthony Ashley Cooper's physician, becoming famous for treating Cooper's advanced liver condition. Locke and Cooper soon became best friends. This led to Locke's exposure to political and legal affairs, as Cooper would become the first Earl of Shaftesbury and the Lord Chancellor. The two men discussed all ideas concerning legislation and politics. Locke's writings began as policy documents for Cooper. One such document was Locke's now famous *A Letter Concerning Toleration*. His most well-known work in political philosophy is his *Two Treatises of Government*.

In the next sections, I will discuss important background themes in both his *Letter* and *Two Treatises*.[1]

### The State of Nature and Natural Rights

In his *Second Treatise of Government*, Locke's examination of political philosophy begins with a look at how people would relate to one another in a state of nature: a world where there are no political institutions. The thought is that we can know best the most perfect form of government if we understand human nature. Locke calls the state of nature 'a State of perfect

[1] My purposes for this Introduction mirror those of my Introduction to *Rousseau and Law* (Brooks, 2005a).

Freedom' (§4).[2] We are all free to do as we like. Our equal freedom forms the basis of our equality: 'A State [of Nature is] also of Equality, wherein all the Power and Jurisdiction is reciprocal, no one having more than another' (§4). We are all equally free.

This freedom is not a freedom without restraints, however. Famously, in words echoed later in the American Declaration of Independence, Locke says:

> The State of Nature has a Law of Nature to govern it, which obligates every one; And Reason, which is that Law, teaches all Mankind, who will but consult it, that being all equal and independent, no one ought to harm another in his Life, Health, Liberty, or Possessions. (§6)

In a state of nature, we are constrained by nature's law – reason. Reason's constraint is minimal and negative: it does not tell us what we can do, but only what we cannot do – namely, injury to another's life, health, liberty or possessions.

There are a few important points arising from the above quotation worth highlighting. First, in a state of nature, we are each in possession of valuable individual rights. We do not need to be citizens of a state in order to enjoy the free exercise of our lives or possessions. States may come to regulate our conduct with others, but they may not infringe upon our natural rights. These rights are 'natural' insofar as we possess them naturally in virtue of our common humanity.

Second, although previous writers (such as Hobbes) have defended natural rights, Locke expands on Hobbes's natural right to self-preservation fairly considerably. We retain this natural right not only to life, but also to our health, liberty and property. This was significant as at the time the idea of natural rights was widely contested by those who adhered to the divine right of kings perspective.

The divine right of kings to absolute monarchical power is most clearly spelled out in Sir Robert Filmer's *Patriarcha*, published in 1680. Just as God instructs us to 'honour thy father', Filmer claims God's command is effectively to honour our king. Disobeying our king is like disobeying our father; both are rightly condemned by God. A king is very much like a father to his people: 'all the duties of a king are summed up in an universal fatherly care of his people' (Filmer, 1991, p. 12). All kings are direct descendants of Adam. As Adam held dominion over the world, this right to rule all creatures on this earth is handed to Adam's sons. Their right to rule comes directly from God. Moreover, God does not sanction democracies: we are told that the Bible nowhere mentions democracies. Therefore, those who favour democracy over monarchy move away from godly rule.

Locke's criticisms of the divine right of kings are devastating. First, he reminds us that Filmer is selectively choosing passages. We are to honour not only our fathers, but our mothers as well. If this passage helps us understand our obedience to kings, we equally should obey queens. There cannot be one and only one person in charge of a monarchy: there must be two. Second, Locke argues that the paternal power of a king as the son of Adam has no force. Adam did not have a right to rule based upon his birth: he was not born, but created. Adam could never have had a fatherly right to rule *before* he became a father. He had no such power and could never have given this to his descendants. Third, kings are thought to be direct descendants of Adam. This gives them rule over all of us. However, if Adam and Eve were

2 Unless noted otherwise, all references pertain to Locke (1988).

the first human beings, then *everyone* is a direct descendant of Adam. A king is no more a descendant than you or me.[3]

Finally, Locke conclusively rejects the claim that, since Adam was given dominion over the world, he and his heirs had the right to rule over all people. Locke says:

> And if God made all Mankind slaves to Adam and his Heirs, by giving Adam Dominion over every little thing that moveth on the Earth, Chap. I. 28. as our A— would have it, methinks Sir Robert should have carried his Monarchical Power one step higher, and satisfied the World, that Princes might eat their Subjects too, since God gave as full Power to Noah and his Heirs, Chap. 9. 2. to eat every Little thing that moveth, as he did to Adam to have Dominion over them. (Locke, 1988, p. 28)

No one would say that kings have the right to eat their subjects, even if Noah was given the right to eat all that moves. By analogy, it is then not clear that dominion over the earth means dominion over all human beings as the right over all people (to eat them) does not seem granted here. Filmer is stretching the meaning of a phrase to make it suit his purpose, but it is not clearly solid evidence on which to build his case.

In his *First Treatise of Government*, Locke dismantles the divine right of kings theory on every score. His *Second Treatise of Government* presents a picture of political life independent of the divine right of kings. This new vision of political life has natural rights at its core. Our rights are not privileges granted to us at the discretion of our king, but given to us naturally at birth by God.

**Punishment**

We may next wonder – what if we violate natural rights? Locke admits that laws mean little without enforceability. The problem is that, in a state of nature, enforceability is determined by the capabilities of the victim. That is, if someone violates my natural rights, I have a right to punish him in the state of nature. It is a right I have independently of the state. Locke says:

> In transgressing the Law of Nature, the Offender declares himself to live by another Rule, than that of reason and common Equity, which is that measure God has set to the actions of Men, for their mutual security: and so he becomes dangerous to Mankind, the tye, which is to secure them from injury and violence, being slighted and broken by him. (§8)

The problem with criminals is that they act unreasonably: they are not thinking properly. If they did, they would discern that all people have natural rights that protect and promote the mutual security of all. By infringing the rights of others, criminals make plain that they are a danger to the mutual security of us all. In effect, we play by the rules of natural reason and the criminal is playing a different game.

The punishment we may legitimately inflict on criminals must be proportionate. Locke adds:

> Each Transgression may be punished to that degree, and with so much Severity as will suffice to make it an ill bargain to the Offender, give him cause to repent, and terrifie others from doing the like. (§12)

3 This criticism is my own, although suggested in Locke's account.

Locke seems to adhere to the benefits theory of retributivism – namely that criminals earn illegitimate benefits from their crimes. Punishment must remove this benefit. Thus, if a criminal profits £550 from a deceitful contract, then the punishment must ensure the loss of this £550. Lockean punishment has further goals, too. In addition, the punishment must endeavour to enable the criminal to take ownership of his wrongdoing and seek the forgiveness of others. Finally, punishment must act as a deterrent to others.

Of course, Locke gives us no particular examples that help flesh out how this should work. For instance, he does discuss capital punishment, but this violates the need to 'give [criminals] cause to repent'. We might offer two criticisms. First, it is unclear how criminals can be said to 'benefit' from their crimes. Perhaps the embezzler has extra cash. Perhaps the murderer removes a rival to his lover, better ensuring his marriage to her. However, it is unclear if any murderer truly benefits from an act of evil: if anything, we might think it a burden as it permanently damages his character. Furthermore, it is unclear that cannibals 'benefit' from eating human beings or rapists 'benefit' from sexually violating others. Benefit often carries with it the connotation of improvement. All these acts are not marks of improvement, but detriment. Beyond more obvious metaphors with money and contracts, the benefit theory of retributivism seems an odd theory to defend.

The second criticism, is that even if we accept the benefit theory, it seems wholly incompatible with Locke's further features. The degree that one might 'benefit' from a crime ($x$) may not be commensurable with a sufficient level of pain enabling repentance ($y$) nor general deterrence ($z$). Locke's view seems to think that we can set punishment as $x = y = z$. Without clear examples, this is unsatisfactory as such.

These criticisms do not betray his project. Many other philosophers have attempted so-called 'mixed' theories of punishment, bringing together retributivism, deterrence, and rehabilitation (see Bosanquet, 1965, pp. 201–17; Brooks, 2003; 2004; 2005b; Green, 1986, pp. 138–59).[4] The problem is not in justifying the need for a mixed theory: after all, if a theory did give criminals what they deserve, rehabilitated them and deterred others, then we might all *prima facie* agree that such a theory is better than a theory that only performed one or two of these tasks.[5] The problem is in working out how two tasks or more can be brought together into a single, consistent theory. This is a project that we have perfected little better than Locke, although he rightly sees the need to begin developing such a theory.

Interestingly, it is the problem of punishment that sets up the need for a political state. When our natural rights are infringed, we have the right to punish those who harm us. This is true in a state of nature and is itself a natural right. Locke says:

> Want of a common Judge with Authority, puts all Men in a State of Nature: Force without Right, upon a Man's Person, makes a State of War, both where there is, and is not, a common Judge. (§19)

The state of nature is a state of war. We rely on ourselves to protect ourselves and uphold our natural rights. Of course, the problems with this are several. If someone violates our rights, we have a right to punish him. The problems are the following:

---

[4] I consider the problems with each major single theory of punishment in Brooks (2006), highlighting the need for a theory that can accommodate the strengths of each while overcoming their many weaknesses.

[5] For theories that combine two of these tasks, see Hart (1968, pp. 1–27) and Rawls (1955).

- We might punish the wrong person.
- We might punish the wrong crime.
- We might be unable to punish the criminal.
- Our punishment may be disproportionate to the violation of our rights.
- Our attempt to punish may encourage the criminal to commit further violations of our rights.

These problems lead us to create a political society. In political society, each one of its members gives up his private right to punish. This right is transferred to our community. The referee of when rights violations occur and their appropriate punishment is our community, rather than ourselves. Instead of individual guesswork and intuition, the community will decide these matters 'by settled standing Rules, indifferent, and [act] the same [towards] all Parties' (§87). With this rule of law, we leave the state of nature and enter into political society. We are governed by the rule of law, which gives force and substance to the law of reason. This is thought to best secure our natural rights. These are ideas that many defend today and they are explored in several essays in this collection (see Benjamin Damstedt, Chapter 2; John Kang, Chapter 10; Suri Ratnapala, Chapter 8; on punishment, see Brian Calvert, Chapter 13 and A. John Simmons, Chapter 12).

## Property

Locke's political philosophy is perhaps best known for its view of property rights, most particularly its theory of property acquisition. This is reflected in many of the essays found in this collection (see Donna Byrne, Chapter 5; Jeremy Waldron, Chapter 6; Leif Wenar, Chapter 4). Locke claims that everything found on the earth was given to human beings by God for our common sustenance. All the earth and its creatures are held by humans in common.

This is surprisingly *not* to say that you and I must possess equal shares of the world's resources. It only means that you and I are *entitled* to make equal use of the world's resources. Locke famously says:

> The Labour of his Body, and the Work of his Hands, we may say, are properly his. Whatsoever then he removes out of the State that Nature hath provided, and left it in, he hath mixed his Labour with, and joined to it something that is his own, and thereby makes it his Property. (§28)

We do not need the consent of others to appropriate our labour and take ownership of an object. Our act of labour – an act where we invest ourselves in something – removes this object from a common state, a domain where anybody could have come along and employed their labour into making this object their property. When we invest ourselves in the acquisition of an object, by 'mixing' our labour with it, this object becomes our property. We take ownership in this way.

How we 'mix' our labour with an object is greatly contested. One general way of understanding this is in our actions of acquisition. An example might make this clear. Suppose we are in a field that is owned by no one. This field is in a 'common state': all the resources before us are effectively up for grabs to the first person seeking their ownership. In this field, we find a fruit tree where we spot a ripened pear. If we 'mix' our labour with this pear, we may own it and consume it. How do we this? By simply climbing the tree and plucking the fruit from it. This aspect of work, of toil, transforms the pear into an object that is attached to a tree in a natural state into an object of more immediate use for me. It has been literally plucked from its common state and becomes my property. It is my property in virtue of my work in acquiring it.

When we take possession of an object, our labour gives that object its primary value. This is not to suggest that, for instance, a tree is not itself an object of value. But it is to say that a wooden desk has a given value, the better part of which is due to our labour in making that desk from a tree. Likewise, the greater value of a piece of land emerges from the use of our labour – say, when we turn an unprofitable meadow into a maize field. One field will be more valuable than the other mostly because of the industry a person has invested in claiming the field as *hers*. Our labour gives natural objects their worth. When we use our labour to acquire objects no one else possesses, our labour transfers possession to us.

Of course, we can only have as much property as we can enjoy: there are limits on our ownership. Locke says:

> But how far has [God] given [all things in nature] to us? *To enjoy*. As much as any one can make use of to any advantage of life before it spoils; so much he may by his labour fix a Property in. Whatever is beyond this, is more than his share, and belongs to others. Nothing was made by God for Man to spoil or destroy. (§31)

Locke takes as an article of faith that there are enough resources globally to go around: that there is enough for everyone to use and possess. However, while we have a right to remove objects from a common state and take possession of them, we have no right to waste them. If we waste what we take possession of, we then ruin what was held in common. If God created resources for us to use and we ruin them, we effectively act contrary to God's will. Thus, possessing more than we can use is an affront to God and to natural law and rights. The world was created with enough for all. In wasting resources, we potentially disadvantage others. As a result, we have the right to take possession of pears in a common field, but we do not have the right to gather more pears than we can consume or sell.

## Consent

In political society, our obedience stems from our consent. We obey our state because we consent to its authority. We do not obey the state for other reasons, such as the divine right of kings theory discussed above. We consent in virtue of agreeing with our fellow human beings to form a community for the following reasons:

> The only way whereby any one devests himself of his Natural Liberty, and *puts on the bonds of Civil Society* is by agreeing with other Men to joyn and unite into a Community, for their comfortable, safe, and peaceable living amongst another, in a secure Enjoyment of their Properties, and a greater Security against any that are not of it. (§95)

When we consent to do just this, we consent to create one community, 'one Body Politick', whereby the majority have the right to act on behalf of all. The thought is that if society only acted if *everyone* agreed to a certain course of action, society would find it terribly difficult to make decisions. Thus, when we consent to form a political society, we consent to rule by the majority.

Locke makes a well-known distinction between express and tacit consent. My express consent is given when I sign a contract or openly declare my agreement. Tacit consent is more subtle and difficult to discern. His understanding of tacit consent is controversial and revealing. He says:

> And to this I say, that every Man, that hath any Possession, or Enjoyment, of any part of the Dominions of any Government, doth thereby give his *tacit Consent*, and is as far forth obliged to Obedience to the Laws of that Government, during such Enjoyment, as any one under it; whether this his Possess be of Land, to him and his Heirs for ever, or a Lodging only for a Week; or whether it be barely travelling freely on the Highway; and in Effect, it reaches as far as the very being of any one within the Territories of that Government. (§119)

The first half of this quote suggests that tacit consent is limited: we are obliged to obey laws insofar as we have some possession or enjoyment within the territory of the community. The thought seems to be that if we lack possessions or enjoyment, then we are not obliged to obey the laws. Further, it might be suggested that those who have less may be less obliged to follow the law than those who have more. But the second half of the statement clarifies this situation right away. In essence, we tacitly consent to the laws of a political society simply by virtue of our being in their midst – by existing within their boundaries. Locke suggests that to satisfy this condition of 'enjoyment' we need do no more than walk along a path within the community. We can then be said to 'enjoy' the land of the community and, hence, we are bound by its laws. If we do not want to enjoy the goods of the community, then we should not be found anywhere within it.

Ultimately, Locke's thought seems a bit more than simply the claim that we must obey the laws of wherever we live as he argues that we are bound only to what we consent to. However, he has a broad notion of consent and, further, he suggests that we are always free to shuffle off and join a different political society at will. Not only is it not true that we can always pick up our bags and leave our political society – perhaps for lack of money, inability to travel, ignorance of other languages and so on – but it is unclear that in every case the political society we choose to join will let us in as new members.

All this said, political societies can abuse our consent. If they do, then the people have the right to revolution and may overthrow their political leaders. In particular, if those in power violate the people's natural rights, they then lose the right to rule. We possess natural rights in virtue of our common humanity. We give up the right to make decisions on law and punishment for ourselves when we join a political society. We never (and can never) give up our natural rights. If these become infringed, our political society loses our consent and its right to govern us.

Needless to say, Locke's views on revolution were defended widely by Thomas Jefferson and others. This so-called 'right to revolution' was a particularly major difference between Locke's political philosophy and what had been written before. For example, we see no such right in Hobbes's *Leviathan* (see Hobbes, 1996). Curiously, we have no doubt today that Locke is the author of the *Two Treatises of Government*. However, Locke himself never admitted publicly to being its author. For one thing, associates and friends of his were being arrested and executed for acts of treason – Locke had already been in trouble with authorities himself, having been expelled from Christ Church College at the University of Oxford because of his political leanings. A book claiming a right to revolution (albeit in highly circumscribed cases) was bound to be received poorly by the authorities of his time. In fact, Locke named the book *de Morbo Gallico* – strictly, 'the French disease' and slang for syphilis – in order to avert prying eyes studying its contents (see Locke, 1988, p. 62).

### Tolerance

The second famous work Locke wrote in political and legal philosophy was his brief *Epistola de Tolerantia* of 1689, translated as 'A Letter Concerning Toleration' (Locke, 1983). The essay is primarily about demarcating a space for the proper business of government separate from that of religion. He understands government, or the commonwealth, in the following way:

> The Commonwealth seems to me to be a Society of Men constituted only for the procuring, preserving, and advancing of their own *Civil Interests*.
>
> *Civil Interests* I call Life, Liberty, Health, and Indolency of Body; and the Possession of outward things, such as Money, Lands, Houses, Furniture, and the like. (Locke, 1983, p. 26)

Given this understanding, Locke believes it is clear that the business of the state does not extend 'to the Salvation of Souls' (ibid.). He offers the three following reasons why this is the case:

1. Governments rule through consent. They do not have the authority or right to make people believe one thing or another. This authority for what one believes lies with each individual person.
2. Governmental power extends to external actions only. It cannot persuade our conscience, at least not in a way 'acceptable to God' (Locke, 1983, p. 27). That is, the government may make us go to Methodist services, but whether we become a true member depends on our own change of heart and faith. We decide this matter of conscience individually. No state can compel our conscience.
3. Different governments profess different beliefs. It cannot be up to the ruler to tell the people which path is *the* single way to heaven because they often disagree.

Locke next considers what a church is, as opposed to a government. He defines a church in the following way:

> A Church then I take to be a voluntary Society of Men, joining themselves together of their own accord, in order to the publick worshipping of God, in such a manner as they judge acceptable to him, and effectual to the Salvation of their Souls. (Locke, 1983, p. 28)

In essence, the government can regulate our material goods and well-being. Churches are societies with views on spiritual goods, as it were. Given this, it follows that churches have the right to excommunicate members. However, given the division of labour Locke envisions, excommunicated persons can be kicked out of a church, but they cannot be deprived of their worldly possessions. What happens to these is not for the church to decide. Only the government decides such matters. This division of labour is stated well by Locke. He says:

> For Churches have neither any Jurisdiction in Worldly matters, nor are Fire and Sword any proper Instruments wherewith to convince men's minds of Error, and inform them of the truth. (Locke, 1983, p. 32)

A few passages later he says something that seems obvious:

> Let them not call in the Magistrate's Authority to the aid of their Eloquence, or Learning; lest, perhaps, whilst they pretend only Love for the Truth, this their intemperate Zeal, breathing nothing but Fire and Sword, betray their Ambition, and shew that what they desire is Temporal Dominion. For it will be very difficult to persuade men of Sense, that he, who with dry Eyes, and satisfaction of mind, can deliver his Brother unto the Executioner, to be burnt alive, does sincerely and heartily concern himself to save that Brother from the Flames of Hell in the World to come. (Locke, 1983, p. 35)

Those who seek to punish unbelievers and the like are not really displaying devotion to God, but rather the desire to dominate other human beings. The two projects are not the same. Thus: 'The Care thereof of every man's Soul belongs unto himself, and is to be left unto himself' (ibid.). In essence, the job of the state is to punish crimes, not sin. Political leaders should be mindful of this distinction.

This picture has as its primary object the divorce of political from religious affairs. However, there are clear implications for a case in favour of toleration. Toleration on matters of conscience seems necessary provided that the natural rights of others is respected. The government lacks a right to restrict matters of conscience as such matters are beyond its authority and legitimate scope. Locke will set clear limits for toleration: we ought not tolerate actions that endanger our society's preservation, and so on (see Locke, 1983, pp. 49–51). Yet, the point about toleration is that it is not something we adhere to out of charity, but instead something we respect because it is right. These views on toleration, too, have won many admirers and provoked critical comment today, including several essays in this collection (see Paul Bou-Habib, Chapter 16; Donald Doernberg, Chapter 14; James Tully, Chapter 15).

## Conclusion

The main purpose of this volume, *Locke and Law*, is not only to stimulate greater attention amongst legal theorists and practitioners to the many interesting peculiarities distinctive to Locke's legal and political thought. Rather, it is my great hope that this volume will make clear how Locke's legal and political ideas have influenced the way we think today about natural law, natural rights, property, abortion, constitutional law, the relationship between law and society, punishment, tolerance and civil disobedience, amongst many other issues. In addition, it is hoped that the essays in this volume help point us towards several fruitful avenues where Locke's insights might be applied in future, such as with abortion, intellectual property, punishment and tolerance. In these areas and many others, there is much more important work to be done. I hope this volume inspires others to help in this great endeavour.

## Acknowledgement

My sincere thanks to the many teachers of Locke's philosophy from whom I have studied and the many students to whom I have taught Locke's legal philosophy since. I must also thank Tom Campbell and John Irwin for their support of this project from its beginning. Finally, this collection is dedicated to Miles and Ella: I would not smile half as much without them.


## References


Bosanquet, Bernard (1965), *The Philosophical Theory of the State*, London: Macmillan.

Brooks, Thom (2003), 'T.H. Green's Theory of Punishment', *History of Political Thought*, **24**, pp. 685–701.

Brooks, Thom (2004), 'Is Hegel a Retributivist?', *Bulletin of the Hegel Society of Great Britain*, **49–50**, pp. 113–26.

Brooks, Thom (2005a), 'Introduction', in Thom Brooks (ed.), *Rousseau and Law*, Aldershot: Ashgate, pp. xiii–xxv.

Brooks, Thom (2005b), 'An Idealist Theory of Punishment', *Social Science Research Network*, at: http://ssrn.com/abstract=869444.

Brooks, Thom (2006), 'Rethinking Punishment', *International Journal of Jurisprudence and Philosophy of Law*, **1**.

Filmer, Robert (1991), *Patriarcha and Other Writings*, ed. J.P. Sommerville, Cambridge: Cambridge University Press.

Green, Thomas Hill (1986), *Lectures on the Principles of Political Obligation and Other Writings*, eds. Paul Harris and John Morrow, Cambridge: Cambridge University Press.

Hart, Herbert L.A. (1968), *Punishment and Responsibility*, Oxford: Oxford University Press.

Hobbes, Thomas (1996), *Leviathan*, ed. Richard Tuck, Cambridge: Cambridge University Press.

Locke, John (1983), *A Letter Concerning Toleration*, ed. James Tully, Indianapolis: Hackett.

Locke, John (1988), *Two Treatises of Government*, ed. Peter Laslett, Cambridge: Cambridge University Press.

Rawls, John (1955), 'Two Concepts of Rules', *Philosophical Review*, **64**, pp. 3–32.

# Part I
# Natural Law and Natural Rights

# [1]

# *Locke on Natural Law and Property Rights**

DAVID C. SNYDER
Calvin College
Grand Rapids, MI 49506
U.S.A.

Whether John Locke's *Two Treatises* is a justification of revolution or a demand for revolution, it is a book about political revolution. Yet it is also a book about property. This is so not only because of the obviously central place that Locke's discussion of property holds in the *Second Treatise* but also because his account of when revolution is justified hinges, in three crucial respects, on his account of how private, or, exclusive, rights to property arise.

* This paper was presented at a colloquium on the historical study of John Locke, held at Rutgers University on June 13-17, 1983. I wish to thank Paul Marshall, Fred Schick, James Tully, John Yolton and the referees of *The Canadian Journal of Philosophy* for their helpful comments on earlier versions. I am also indebted to Martha Bolton, Doug Husak and Gordon Schochet for valuable discussions of related matters.

The first of these respects concerns Locke's notion that there can be no injustice where there is no property.[1] Revolution is justified only, of course, when civil government is unjust. But if for Locke injustice is just a denial of property rights, then he needs a theory of property rights to satisfactorily establish when revolution is justified. Thus a theory of legitimate property ownership is necessary for Locke to give an account of revolution.

Now it must be remembered that Locke's definition of 'property' is a wide one indeed. For although he often uses the term to signify material goods he defines it as 'Lives, Liberties and Estates.'[2] Consequently we must not assume that for him exclusive ownership of goods is necessary for injustice to occur. Denial of liberty, for example, can also constitute injustice. However, since goods are part of what he means by 'property,' he needs an explanation of why one is entitled to one's goods to give a complete justification of revolution.

Second, Locke needs a theory of property to show why free men would obligate themselves to civil government. His answer is that they do so to protect their property, part of which is goods (II, 127). And since property protection is the reason men consent to be governed in the first place, when their government no longer fulfills that task revolution is justified.

---

1 *Where there is no Property, there is no Injustice,* is a Proposition as certain as any Demonstration in *Euclid*: For the *idea* of *Property*, being a right to any thing; and the *Idea* to which the Name *Injustice* is given, being the Invasion or Violation of that right; it is evident, that these *Ideas* being thus established, and these Names annexed to them, I can as certainly know this Proposition to be true, as that a Triangle has three Angles equal to two right ones' (*An Essay Concerning Human Understanding*, Book IV, chapter III, section 18). All references in this paper to Locke's *Essay* will be taken from the Nidditch edition (New York: Oxford University Press 1975) and will be indicated in notes by book, chapter and section.

2 *Second Treatise*, section 23; all references in this paper to either the *First* or *Second Treatise* will be taken from *Two Treatises of Government*, Peter Laslett, ed. (New York: Cambridge University Press 1960), and hereafter will be indicated in the text of the paper by either 'I' or 'II,' referring to the *First* or *Second Treatise*, respectively, and by section number. Besides the ambiguity already mentioned in Locke's use of the word 'property' there is another problem as well. For whether he uses it to refer to goods, or in its wider application, to 'lives, liberties and estates,' in both of those senses 'property' refers to things one owns. However, in the passage quoted in the first note, Locke defines 'property' as a right to anything. There it does not refer to the thing owned but to the right to own a thing, or an entitlement.

Third, Locke needs a theory of property to explain why political authority is legitimate. One cannot say when political authority exceeds its proper bounds if one cannot say what those bounds are. And for Locke part of what constitutes the limits to government is the limits of men's willingness to be governed. In other words, men consent only to that which betters their lot (II, 168), and if government is legitimate it must be a good bargain for the governed. But it will not be a good bargain if the government itself systematically violates property rights or allows them to be violated. Thus even though the basis for property ownership in the state of nature changes to some extent once civil society is instituted, if government exists to protect property rights in its extended sense, and if government is legitimate only if it is sufficiently successful in carrying out its task so that the governed continue to extend their consent, then Locke's explanation of how exclusive property rights arise is an important ingredient in his theory of civil authority and obligation.

It has recently become increasingly apparent that Locke's theory of property cannot be understood apart from his view of natural law.[3] Although this makes his justification of property acquisition a bit more complex than is recognized by some commentators,[4] as well as, given Locke's assumptions, much more interesting, nonetheless I do not think we presently have an adequate understanding of how for him exclusive property ownership is possible. One purpose of this paper is to attempt, then, a further exploration of the relationship between his doctrine of natural law and his justification of property acquisition in the state of nature. Second, my analysis of this relationship uncovers new problems with Locke's view. In carrying out this task I argue that some other attempts to criticize him will not do. My account seeks to avoid these pitfalls by being sensitive both to Locke's assumptions and to his successes and failures in argument.

3 Probably the best account to date of Locke's theory of natural law and property is James Tully, *A Discourse on Property: John Locke and His Adversaries* (New York: Cambridge University Press 1980).

4 Cf. Laurence Becker, 'The Labor Theory of Property Acquisition,' *The Journal of Philosophy* 73 (1975) 653-64; Robert Nozick, *Anarchy, State, and Utopia* (New York: Basic Books 1974), 174-82.

*David C. Snyder*

**I Locke's Theory of Natural Law**

Locke pointedly rejects the view that bases property rights on consent (II, 25, 28, 29). In his eyes the right to property is natural, or precontractural; it antedates not only civil society but also other types of social arrangements. So to show that individual property ownership is morally justified he must appeal to some other prescriptive principle or set of principles. In Locke's scheme these principles turn out to be the laws of nature. So to understand why he thinks that persons have property rights it is important to first consider his view of natural law.

John Yolton has claimed that Locke's 'use of the law of nature must be viewed in the context of the doctrine of innate knowledge.'[5] This is true because to understand his concept of natural law it is important to note not only what Locke argues against in his attack on the dogma of innate knowledge but what he accepts. If this is not done one might mistakenly conclude that Locke's acceptance of a doctrine of natural law is inconsistent with his well-known rejection of innate knowledge in the *Essay*.[6]

Now this possibility of confusion is abetted by Locke's own language. In the *Second Treatise* he refers to the law of nature as 'writ in the Hearts of all Mankind' (II, 11). Moreover, in his *Essays on the Law of Nature* he claims that this law is 'innate.'[7] On the face of it Locke's use of such language to describe his own doctrine of natural law is inconsistent with his polemic in the *Essay* against innate knowledge, the latter of which he describes as 'primary Notions, Characters, as it were stamped upon the Mind of Man.'[8] However, this apparent contradiction is only superficial.

5 John Yolton, 'Locke on the Law of Nature,' *The Philosophical Review* **67** (1958) 479

6 Peter Laslett makes this mistake in the 'Introduction,' (94-5) to his edition of the *Two Treatises*. There he says that 'the *Essay* has no room for natural law and that in the *Two Treatises* 'Locke uses language on the subject of natural law which seems inconsistent with his own statements about innate ideas in the *Essay*.' Laslett also suggests that Locke 'realized his dilemma, but was unable to find a solution.' For a defense of the consistency of Locke's political and epistemological views see S.B. Drury, 'John Locke: Natural Law and Innate Ideas,' *Dialogue* **14** (1980) 531-45.

7 *Essays on the Law of Nature*, W. von Leyden, ed. (New York: Oxford University Press 1954), 117; hereafter I will refer to this volume as ELN.

8 Locke, *Essay*, I, II, 1

Although Locke argues that we do not have truths imprinted upon our minds from birth – indeed, he rejects the claim that we do as not merely false, but nonsensical – he never says that we have no innate capacity of reason or that there are no principles discoverable by the understanding alone. Self-evident truths are self-evident not because they are innately impressed upon the mind but because it is impossible to believe to the contrary.[9] Moreover, although the doctrine of innate knowledge of principles must be rejected, if those who support this view mean merely that we have an innate rational capacity for knowledge, then their point is true but trivial.[10] Thus even though Locke attacks the doctrine of innate knowledge, he does believe that the mind has the capacity to gain knowledge of some principles through reason alone.

Second, in the ELN he states that his conception of natural law as known via the light of nature does not commit him to embracing the doctrine of innate knowledge. In his third essay, entitled 'Is the Law of Nature Inscribed in the Minds of Men? No,' he considers and rejects the view that the laws of nature are innate.[11] Since Locke takes an entire essay to tell us that on his view natural law is not innate in the objectionable sense it should be clear that according to him, anyway, there is no inconsistency here. This makes Laslett's comment, that Locke seemed to be aware of his inconsistency on this point, somewhat curious and most certainly incorrect. Moreover, as von Leyden has demonstrated, the arguments in the ELN against the idea that the law of nature is innate are incorporated into Book I of the *Essay* itself.[12] Locke is arguing in the same way against a single view in both the *Essay* and the ELN. Consequently, if the ELN and the *Essay* are inconsistent, the inconsistency is within the ELN itself and not primarily between it and the *Essay*.

Lastly, there is one passage in which Locke unequivocally and clearly distinguishes his view of natural law from innate knowledge. As this passage settles the issue, I quote it in full.

9 Locke, *Essay*, I, II, 21

10 Locke, *Essay*, I, II, 5

11 Locke, ELN, 137

12 Von Leyden, 'Introduction' to ELN, 60-82

> We do not maintain that this law of nature, written as it were on tablets, lies open in our hearts, and that, as soon as some inward light comes near it (like a torch approaching a notice board hung up in darkness), it is at length read, perceived, and noted by the rays of that light. Rather, by saying that something can be known by the light of nature, we mean nothing else but that there is some sort of truth to the knowledge of which a man can attain by himself and without the help of another, if he makes proper use of the faculties he is endowed with by nature.[13]

It is not inconsistent for Locke to hold on the one hand that the notion of innate knowledge is a myth and on the other that there are self-evident principles to which the rational man will readily assent, for it is the ability to discover these truths, not the truths themselves, that is innate.

There is much more to natural law, however, than simply being known by man. Throughout the ELN Locke also calls it the law of reason, and for two reasons this should not be taken to refer to its epistemic status. First, when he discusses the origins of our knowledge of the law of nature he asserts that reason cannot be that origin.[14] Second and more important, near the beginning of the first essay he equates moral good with the law of right reason, stating that these and other terms all refer to the law of nature. At this point he distinguishes between reason as a faculty of the mind and as a moral law which decrees principles of action and obedience to which is rational.

> By reason, however, I do not think is meant here that faculty of the understanding which forms trains of thought and deduces proofs, but certain definite principles of action from which spring all virtues and whatever is necessary for the proper moulding of morals. For that which is correctly derived from these principles is justly said to be in accordance with right reason.[15]

Now as Yolton points out, 'Locke was seeking to justify a system of morality by grounding the moral law in something objective.'[16] But what is this 'something objective' upon which the law of nature is

13 Locke, ELN, 123

14 Locke, ELN, 125

15 Locke, ELN, 111

16 Yolton, 'Locke on the Law of Nature,' 483

founded? Locke contends that it is simply the divine will. Natural law is part of the decree of God who, being entirely rational, only decrees those moral principles that are in conformity with himself; i.e., those in conformity with rational nature.[17] Furthermore, although this law is known by the mind, it is called the law of reason primarily because it ordains principles of action that are morally right and, at the same time, rational. Since all men are created rational, Locke argues, the law of nature is universally binding.[18]

Locke is seeking to ground right action upon a natural law which is part of the will of God. This law is discoverable by the human mind, but more importantly it prescribes moral, rational action. Any action not in accordance with its precepts is in defiance of the divine will and hence contradicts reason itself. But actions in accordance with natural law are right, moral and rational.[19]

## II Natural Law and the Two Treatises

Locke begins the *Second Treatise* by describing the state of nature, which is human society as it exists apart from the civil state. Although there is no government in this natural condition, that does not mean that

---

17 'Hence this law can be described as being the decree of the divine will discernible by the light of nature and indicating what is and what is not in conformity with rational nature, and for this very reason commanding or prohibiting' (Locke, ELN, 111).

18 Locke, ELN, 199

19 My account of Locke's view of natural law is quite different from that of Leo Strauss. Strauss, in *Natural Right and History* (Chicago: University of Chicago Press 1953), argues that although Locke apparently goes along with the traditional view of natural law, he actually conceals his true Hobbesean inclinations out of caution. Now besides the fact that Strauss's reading is marred by his failure to consider the ELN, his general notion of writing under persecution is troublesome because it renders his own interpretation of any historical text virtually unfalsifiable. For he can always explain away recalcitrant passages by saying that they are inserted to conceal the author's true intentions. Moreover, this way of reading historical documents is particularly inapplicable to Locke, since its result is to reduce his view of natural law to utter mystery and nonsense. For a critique of Strauss see Yolton, 'Locke on the Law of Nature.'

there is no moral law which ought to be obeyed. Indeed, 'the *State of nature* has a Law of Nature to govern it, which obliges everyone' (II, 6). Furthermore, this law of nature wills 'the Peace and *Preservation of all Mankind* (II, 7). Later we are told that the preservation of man is '*the Fundamental Law of Nature*' (II, 16).[20]

One ambiguity occurring throughout the *Two Treatises* is that on the one hand Locke identifies natural law with God's will in general, and on the other he sometimes speaks of certain laws of nature as prescribing specific actions, such as the duty to preserve others. That is, sometimes he writes as if the law of nature is singular and other times as if it encompasses many different laws. There is no problem here, however, if we pay attention to the contexts within which these words occur. Natural law is part of God's will, but what God primarily wills is the peace and preservation of mankind. Thus these are the fundamental precepts of this law. Any actions that promote peace and preservation are also laws of nature in the sense that since they do aid in the fulfillment of God's law, or since they may even be necessary for the fulfillment of God's law, they are derivable from natural law and so are properly called laws of nature.

Now the state of nature is, for Locke, a condition of equality and freedom; at least it is initially. Since no one enjoys legitimate political power over another, all men 'order their Actions, and dispose of their Possessions, and persons as they think fit' (II, 4). But even this state of freedom is limited, for the rational law which governs it decrees principles of action which promote peace and preservation. One may not simply do as one wishes, if what one wishes to do is contrary to the law of nature, for everyone is morally bound by that law. One principle derivable from the law, for example, is that 'no one ought to harm another in his Life, Health, Liberty, or Possessions' (II, 6). Since this principle is derivable from the law of nature – it is necessary for peace and preservation – and so is a part of that law, observing it is obedience to the rational will of God and is one expression of human rationality.

So far I have described Locke's law of nature as a rule which

---

20 The duty of preservation includes both self-preservation and preservation of others (II, 6). Here Locke is simply repeating the traditional concept of preservation as basic to natural law, for not only is preservation fundamental, but at times Locke speaks of man's desire for self-preservation as if it is an expression of God's will, directing human reason (e.g., I, 86).

prescribes moral, rational action, and it is that. But it also should be pointed out that it grants certain rights to persons and requires certain duties of them. Locke has no worked-out theory of rights. However, by examining his examples we can learn some things about the rudimentary theory to which he seems committed.

I will point out only one of those things here. For Locke, rights and duties are correlative; wherever the law of nature prescribes a rule of conduct (duty) it describes a right. For instance, parents have a duty to preserve their children. Locke derives this duty from the fundamental precept of preservation because if parents did not provide for their children the children would die. Now from this general parental duty Locke further derives the duty of parents to share their goods with their children, which extends even to the duty of parents to bequeath their goods to their children. As a result children have a right to the goods owned by their parents. 'Men being by a like Obligation bound to preserve what they have begotten, as to preserve themselves, their issue come to have a Right in the Goods they are possessed of' (I, 88). Similarly, since parents are under an obligation to nourish and educate their children, the children have a right to receive these things. In this case the parents' duty is logically prior to the children's right, and as far as I am aware Locke always grounds rights, even the right to possessions, as we shall see, on duties, whether owed to other people or to God. Thus rights and duties are correlative for Locke, although in making duties logically prior to rights Locke differs from the contemporary correlativity thesis as it is usually described, in which a right to X and a duty to provide X are each merely partial descriptions of the same thing, neither being logically prior to the other.[21] And as we will see, Locke sometimes derives a right to X from a duty one has to God to do or have X. For example, as I will argue, men have a right to property because natural law requires it, and everyone is obligated to the law of nature. This notion of an individual having a right to X because he has a duty to do or have X further distinguishes Locke's doctrine from the contemporary correlativity thesis, as for him my right to something can arise out of my duty (to God) to do or have that thing.[22]

21 David Lyons, 'The Correlativity of Rights and Duties,' *Nous* **4** (1970) 45-55

22 The literature on Locke's doctrine of rights is surprisingly thin, but for other discussions of aspects of his theory see Tully, 62-3; Frederick Copleston, *A*

*David C. Snyder*

There is a good deal of looseness in Locke's notion of correlatively, which is to be expected since he employs the language of rights but does not work out a theory. For Locke various rights and duties are correlative for various reasons: some duties are necessary to fulfill natural law, and these give rise to correlative rights; others, such as the duty not to commit suicide (II, 6) are correlative with God's right of ownership, and still other rights and duties grow out of agreements. Locke's idea of correlativity is just that rights and duties occur together; he is vague about the reasons for this.

This doctrine is obviously important later for Locke's justification of revolution, for when magistrates fail in their duties towards citizens, when the citizens' rights are systematically violated, revolution is justified. And since we sometimes have a duty to protect the rights of ourselves or others (II, 6), this implies that for Locke revolution may sometimes be a duty. This is especially so since the obligations of natural law are 'drawn closer' in civil society (II, 135).

Of course he recognizes that there are some who will not obey the law of nature. He implies, however, that such a person is the exception to the harmonious rule, describing him as 'degenerate,' and declaring 'himself to quit the Principles of Human Nature, and to be a noxious Creature' (II, 10). But because such individuals do exist, and because Locke seemingly realizes that similar tendencies tempt all men at least occasionally, to uphold natural law and deter future transgressions the rational man has the right to punish criminals. For if no one had such a right the law of nature would be in vain (II, 7). In order for the law not to be in vain, then, punishment of its transgressors is required, and its existence mandates that some have a right to punish. Although it would be odd to say, and Locke does not, that criminals, therefore, have a duty to be punished, I think that on his view it is true nevertheless that they are obliged to submit to punishment. The law requires that criminals be punished, and even criminals are duty-bound to obey the law, so therefore it seems that Locke is committed to the view that they have the duty to submit to punishment.

---

*History of Philosophy*, volume 5, part 1, (New York: Image Books 1964), 139; A. John Simmons, 'Inalienable Rights and Locke's "Treatises",' *Philosophy & Public Affairs* **12** (1983) 175-204; Paul Marshall, 'John Locke: Between God and Mammon,' *Canadian Journal of Political Science* **12** (1979) 73-96; J.J. Jenkins, 'Locke and Natural Rights,' *Philosophy* **42** (1967) 149-54.

## III Natural Law and Property

After Locke establishes the state of nature as a condition of equality founded on God's normative order of peace and preservation, which prescribes both natural rights and natural duties, he discusses the right to property. The context of the problem he sets out to solve was determined by two factors. First, Locke's primary target in the *Two Treatises*, Robert Filmer, had argued that since God gave the world to Adam and his heirs in succession (not to everyone simultaneously), only those who acquire property through some legitimate transference of entitlement (bequest, gift, exchange, etc.) are morally entitled to it. In opposing this theory (for if true it would support the divine right of kings view of civil government, and could be used, and was used, to undermine a justification of revolution, at least given the theistic assumptions Filmer and Locke share) Locke argues, in the *First Treatise*, that God has granted the world to Adam and all his posterity in common, holding that all have an original equal right to property but that no one has an original exclusive right to anything.

But such an approach creates a new problem. How can it be shown that individuals have (private) property rights when God has given the world and everything it contains to all in common? Or as James Tully so nicely puts it, how do exclusive property rights arise from inclusive ones?[23] One answer, adopted by Grotius, Pufendorf and others,

23 Tully does not think, however, that exclusive property rights are the same as private property because he accepts Macpherson's definition of private property in which it is both alienable and held independently of the owner's performance of any social function, while for Locke an exclusive right to property meets neither of these conditions, according to Tully, p. 99. But the distinction is not relevant for Locke. If one has exclusive rights to a thing then one can legitimately exclude others from its use. And the concept of private property need mean nothing more than this. Moreover, for Locke clearly property rights, even in land, are alienable, and although such rights usually do serve a social function, they need not. They would exist even if their only function was to preserve the individual who possesses them. From the fact that according to Locke the function of property rights is to preserve persons, Tully makes the unwarranted inference that the function of any particular property right is to preserve mankind as a whole. However, although property rights do serve to preserve the race, they are justified merely because they preserve the individual. Thus serving a social function is not necessary to Locke's notion of exclusive property rights. Note, too, that Locke does use the term 'private Possessions' (II, 35).

is that universal consent is necessary and sufficient to justly claim anything as one's own.[24] Various schemes were accordingly developed to explain how this could be achieved, but Locke is not willing to undergo the intellectual gymnastics required to substantiate any such view, and he avoids this alternative. As a result his task is to demonstrate 'how Men might come to have a *property* in several parts of that which God gave to Mankind in common, and that without any express Compact of all the Commoners' (II, 25).

Immediately after stating the problem Locke begins his justification of property acquisition in the state of nature. This occurs before the well-known passages on mixing one's labor with things (II, 27, 28, 34, 40) and suggests that his argument is much more complex than we might suppose if we concentrate too heavily on those passages. For before Locke shows *how* property rights arise he demonstrates *why* these rights are necessary for God to work his will for his creatures. Only after establishing this point does he tell us how one appropriates, or excludes others from, goods in the state of nature. And if we miss the former point we are likely to misconstrue the latter. As I will argue, before he even discusses mixing labor with things Locke shows that the right to property exists. If this interpretation is correct, it turns out that the passages on mixing labor are not intended as an argument for the existence of property rights, as is commonly supposed, but are designed to show how an individual may exercise his property rights under certain conditions. Locke's prior goal, however, is to show that men *must* have exclusive rights to property if God's will is to be fulfilled. This, in turn, serves his primary ideological task in writing the *Two Treatises*, which is to justify revolution (not to refute Filmer, although that was socially necessary to carry out the former task) when the government intentionally and systematically violates those or other rights and, by implication, the will of God.

In the following passage Locke explains why property rights must exist.

> God, who hath given the World to Men in common, hath also given them reason to make use of it to the best advantage of Life, and convenience. The

24 For a discussion of the relationship between Locke, Grotius and Pufendorf, see Tully, 68-94. See also Karl Olivecrona, 'Appropriation in the State of Nature: Locke on the Origin of Property,' *Journal of the History of Ideas* **35** (1974) 211-30.

> Earth, and all that is therein, is given to Men for the Support and comfort of their being. And though all the Fruits it naturally produces, and Beasts it feeds, belong to Mankind in common, as they are produced by the spontaneous hand of Nature; and no body has originally a private Dominion, exclusive of the rest of Mankind, in any of them, as they are thus in their natural state: yet being given for the use of Men, there must of necessity be a means *to appropriate* them some way or other before they can be of any use, or at all beneficial to any particular Man. (II, 26)

Here he squarely grounds the right to appropriation upon God's will, the law of nature. His argument is that since God has given the earth to man for his support and comfort he means for man to use it. But to use most things an individual must appropriate them. In other words, preservation demands that persons use objects, but to use them they must first appropriate them, must own them. This is just Locke's point in this passage. In another passage he explains that the food I eat is indisputably mine (II, 28), but in order for me to legitimately exclude others from its use there must be a point at which it becomes mine, as it was originally part of the common. To live I must exclude others from some goods, and to exclude others I must appropriate. Often, such as with food, this appropriation must be by an individual. So preservation requires appropriation. Moreover, since preservation is a fundamental precept of God's will, it follows that in order for God's will to be obeyed appropriation is necessary. And if appropriation is necessary, it must be the case that persons have a right to appropriate. Finally, since appropriation is one means for establishing exclusive ownership, if one has a right to appropriate things one has a right to own them. So for Locke exclusive ownership of property, which can begin, and in the state of nature does begin, when certain conditions are met, by appropriation, is justified because it is necessary for the fulfillment of God's will and is a duty owed to God (II, 32).

Now that he has shown that exclusive property rights exist, Locke next addresses the different question of how an object becomes one's exclusive possession. How does an object become mine? The answer, of course, is when I mix my labor with the object. However, there is another question involved as well. *Why* does my labor mark off an object as mine? Locke spends a considerable amount of effort answering that one, giving essentially two different responses to it.

It is important to see, however, that having shown *that* property rights exist in general, Locke now addresses the different question of *how* it is possible for an individual to have property in any particular object. This is an essential part of his complete justification of property rights, to be sure, but he tells us *how* we can have exclusive property rights only after he has shown *that* it must be the case that we have them.

The first response that he gives to the question of why one's labor distinguishes labored-on objects as one's own is something of a slippery slope argument. Yet his apparent intention is not to offer a tautly compelling argument for his conclusion but to invite his readers to consider whether the conclusion is reasonable. He that picks and eats some apples, Locke observes, has clearly appropriated them, for the nourishment they provide is undeniably his and no one else's. He continues, 'I ask then, When did they begin to be his? When he digested? Or when he eat? Or when he boiled? Or when he brought them home? Or when he pickt them up?' (II, 28). Locke's point here is simply that there is no good reason to deny that objects become one's own when one labors on them. Everyone grants that the nourishment one gets from an apple is rightfully one's exclusive property; it would be absurd to deny that. Similarly, just as the apple when digested is one's exclusive property, it is also one's property when one eats it, and so on. Therefore it seems that one's labor in picking up the apple marks it as one's own, or at least, there is no good reason to deny that it does.

Locke's second response to the question of why one's labor marks off an object as one's own is found in several passages. In one he says that a man owns his labor, and whatever he mixes that labor with is properly his (II, 27). In another he claims that labor adds value to a thing; as much as 99/100 of the value of the '*Products* of the Earth useful to the Life of Man' (II, 40) is owing to man's labor. And in yet another he tells us that if anyone other than the laborer desires to 'meddle with' an object improved by that labor, he desires, 'the benefit of another's Pains, which he had no right to' (II, 34). Although each of these passages gives a slightly different explanation of how labor makes appropriation possible, they are not, contrary to Becker, three separate attempts to justify property acquisition.[25] As I have argued, prior to these passages Locke gives that argument.[26] Rather they are all part of a single attempt to show that it is possible for appropriation to occur, given that appropriation must occur because preservation demands

25 Becker, 'The Labor Theory of Property Acquisition,' 653

26 Cf. Tully, 95-130 and Alan Ryan, 'Locke and the Dictatorship of the Bourgoisie,' *Political Studies* **13** (1965) 225.

it. Here he merely shows how an individual exercises those rights granted him by the law of nature.

This interpretation considerably reduces the force of Nozick's objection that Locke fails to justify property acquisition because in mixing one's labor with a thing one might simply lose one's labor.[27] For one thing, the notion of mixing one's labor with a thing is only part of one of Locke's two reasons for thinking that labor makes appropriation possible. But more importantly, Nozick has not taken into account Locke's entire argument. For in having previously shown that property rights exist, Locke argued that everything on earth is put here for man's use. Things do not exist for themselves but are always and only for man. However, in their natural state most things are not particularly useful or valuable, and they must be improved by man before they can be an object of use. Especially when it comes to land, the most important of God's gifts, Locke supposes that at least 9/10 of the value of a piece of land is the result of human improvements (II, 40). But no one has a right to 'another's Pains,' so no one other than the laborer has a right to an object labored on, since the improvements now are attached to the object – are a part of the object – and the improvements cannot be owned without the object coming with them. Therefore no one other than the laborer has a right to the object. So since each object is created for man's use, and since no one other than the laborer has a right to them, it follows that if God's will is to be obeyed the laborer must have a right to the objects. 'That was his *Property* which could not be taken from him where-ever he had fixed it. And hence subduing or cultivation [of] the Earth, and having Dominion, we see are joyned together. The one gave Title to the other. So that God, by commanding to subdue, gave Authority so far to *appropriate*' (II, 35).[28] So mixing one's labor with a thing does not by itself enti-

---

27 Nozick, 174-5; Thomas Mautner ('Locke on Original Appropriation,' *American Philosophical Quarterly* **19** [1982] 259-70) gives similar objections which are also generated, I believe, by failing to pay sufficient attention to the complexity of Locke's complete justification of property rights.

28 Tully's claim that for Locke a laborer creates a new object out of material provided by God, rather than simply modifying an already existing object by adding value and improvements to it is, it seems to me, both unwarranted and an unnecessary device for answering Nozick. Moreover, this interpretation may not even satisfy Nozick's objection. For why should the mere fact that I create something serve as my entitlement to that thing?

tle one to an object, contrary to what Nozick thinks. Rather, it excludes others and as a result entitles the laborer to the labored-on object precisely because any object which must be owned to be useful is potentially ownable by some individual because ownership is necessary for the law of nature to be fulfilled.

Still, it might be objected that some things – the ocean, for example – cannot be owned even if I mix my labor with them, and other things already owned, such as your garden, are likewise unavailable for my appropriation. Locke recognizes this, and I fail to see that it is a telling objection to his view. Of course I may not appropriate the entire ocean, unless I need it to survive. But even then I would run afoul of one of Locke's limits to appropriation. Similarly, I may not appropriate the fruits of your garden because I have no right to the benefits of your labor. You have already legitimately excluded me from that. Locke's argument is not designed to show that *anything* with which I might mix my labor thereby becomes mine, but that there *are* things from which I may exclude others by mixing my labor with those things.

Whatever our evaluation is of the success of Locke's argument, and I think it is better than is often thought, Locke believes he has shown that labor does indeed provide a means for appropriating objects that God has intended for us to enjoy. But if his arguments are plausible they are so only if considered within the natural law framework he employs. As he himself asserts, it is the law of nature 'that does by this means give us property' (II, 31).

Moreover, since God, on Locke's view, commanded man to labor, it is by carrying out the divine will that property is possible. For the law of nature demands that property rights exist, and labor is the method of exercising those rights, at least in the state of nature. Thus exclusive property rights and appropriation are derived from natural law. Of course it is clear from the structure of Locke's argument that for him the law of nature requires appropriation. But he also explicitly acknowledges that labor is commanded by God and that possession of property is the natural result.

> God, when he gave the World in common to all Mankind, commanded Man also to labour, and the penury of his Condition required it for him. God and his Reason commanded him to subdue the Earth, *i.e.* improve it for the benefit of Life, and therein lay out something upon it that was his own, his labour. He that in Obedience to this Command of God, subdued, tilled, and sowed any part of it, thereby annexed to it something that was his *Property*, which another had no Title to, nor could without injury take from him. (II. 32)

The establishment of private possessions through labor is thus required by God's law. As such it is an expression of the rationality of man: appropriation through labor is a rational activity.[29] Just as obedience to any other precept of natural law is rational, so is labor and appropriation. After all, God gave the world 'to the use of the Industrious and Rational' (II, 34).

## IV Limits to Appropriation

Locke anticipates an objection to his theory of property rights: Why cannot someone labor on and appropriate as much as he wants and far more than he needs, perhaps depriving others of satisfying their needs, and so hindering preservation, since his labor is that which makes appropriation possible? He answers that the law of nature, which requires that men own property, also limits the amount they may rightfully possess. For the earth is given to man to enjoy but not to spoil or destroy. Therefore one may not appropriate more than one can use. If a man takes so much that some spoils in his possession, he has taken more than his share and has therefore robbed others (II, 31).

The interesting feature here is that Locke places no limits on the amount appropriated as long as nothing spoils. The law of nature is violated only by waste and not by large amounts of possessions in themselves. It is not 'the largeness of his Possession, but the perishing of any thing uselessly in it' (II, 46) that determines whether a man has unjustly hoarded anything.

A second limit to appropriation is that enough and as good must be left over for others to appropriate (II, 33). Even though Locke does not explicitly state that this is a limit to appropriation, he does say that if one 'leaves as much as another can make use of, [one] does as good

29 C.B. Macpherson, *The Political Theory of Possessive Individualism: Hobbes to Locke* (New York: Oxford University Press 1962), 233; Macpherson's claim, however, that Locke limits rationality to the property-owning class is not supported by the text. Appropriation is only one way of expressing one's rationality. Locke never suggests that land owners alone are rational.

as take nothing at all' (II, 33). So it does appear that if this provision is not met there has been an unjust assumption of ownership.[30]

These two limits are designed to insure that the law of nature is not violated. Appropriation is required to fulfill the law, but waste or greed would, if unchecked, prevent the law of nature from being fulfilled. Therefore the law itself requires these limits, and Locke reserves his harshest language for those who violate the law by taking what they have no right to, either what someone else had labored on or more than they could use. In one place, for instance, he calls such persons 'Quarrelsome and Contentious' (II, 34). But he nowhere says or implies that merely desiring things is itself evil or covetous. He always uses such terminology to refer to the desire for things *to which one is not entitled*. For example, in the educational writings he asserts that 'the Root of all Evil' is 'Covetousness, and the Desire of having in our Possession, and under our Dominion, more than we have need of.'[31] Now if we desire more than we need we run a risk of harming others by attempting to fulfill such a desire and depriving others of satisfying their needs. Such actions naturally are violations of the law of nature and constitute, for Locke, theft. But we should note that 'the Root of all Evil' here is not merely desiring possessions, but desiring more than we need, or in other words, desiring things to which we are not entitled.

Locke does not end his discussion of property at this point. If he had, two problems would have remained. First, he would have given no account of money, an important element in any concept of property. Second, his two limits to property ownership would have appeared to be currently operational. Both of these would be problems for Locke, given that money obviously exists and that the limits to ownership are obviously ineffective. So as Macpherson claims, Locke in effect if not in intent, solves both of these problems by introducing money into

---

30 J.J. Waldron ('Enough and as Good Left for Others,' *Philosophical Quarterly* **29** (1979), 319-28) and Mautner (260) claim that Locke's 'enough and as good' provision is not a moral limit to original appropriation but is simply a fact about appropriation in the early ages of man, there being plenty to go around. I think Locke's view is perhaps best characterized as a contrary to fact hypothetical condition: if there is not enough and as good left for others (which there was in the state of nature), then appropriation is unjustified.

31 *The Educational Writings of John Locke*, James L. Axtell, ed. (New York: Cambridge University Press 1968), paragraph 110, p. 213.

his account as a way of transcending both limits to property ownership.[32] Anything that will not spoil, and which men agree to use as a common medium of exchange, functions as money. Its value is purely conventional, but it does allow man to transcend the spoilage limit because once money is introduced property can be hoarded as cash for an indefinite period of time without spoiling. Since it is not the 'largeness of his possessions' but allowing something to spoil which determines whether one transgresses the law of nature, once this first limit is superseded it no longer effectively functions to regulate the amount of property one may own, and hence in terms of the spoilage limit unlimited appropriation is allowed in principle and in cooperation with natural law. Furthermore, the same consent to introduce money is also consent to unequal distribution of property, a situation which the existence of money exacerbates (II, 50).[33]

The second limitation, the sufficiency provision, is also transcended by the use of money. As in the case of the spoilage limit it still exists, but money renders it inapplicable. To show that this is the case, Locke argues diligently that labored-on land is much more valuable to everyone than it would be otherwise. With the establishment of a system of commerce, even a rudimentary one, he assumes that the increased wealth will be distributed to the benefit of all. That is at least part of the reason 'a King of a large and fruitful Territory' in America, where most land, in Locke's day, was unappropriated, 'feeds, lodges,

32 Macpherson, 204-11. Locke says, 'That the same *rule of Propriety, (viz.)* that every Man should have as much as he could make use of, would hold still in the World, without straitning any body, since there is land enough in the World to suffice double the Inhabitants had not the *Invention of Money*, and the tacit Agreement of Men to put a value on it, introduced (by consent) larger Possessions, and a Right to them' (II, 36). Tully claims that Locke's intention here is not to justify unlimited acquisition but to replace these limits with 'other conventional rules, based on consent' (153), and he is surely right to think that removing the original limits causes an intolerable situation that can be alleviated only by creating government and positive law. However, until that civil law is enacted – until the state is formed – money does, for Locke, transcend the original limits to appropriation and, in the interim, justify unlimited acquisition.

33 But it is not necessarily the case that the existence of money causes inequality of possessions. Locke merely says that in agreeing to use money men agree to unequal possessions. Unequal possessions could exist before money is introduced as a result of unequal capacity for usage or unequal industriousness.

and is clad worse than a day Labourer in *England*' (II, 41). 'Thus, although more land than leaves enough and as good for others may be appropriated, the greater productivity of the appropriated land more than makes up for the lack of land available for others.'[34]

In transcending the sufficiency limitation the market serves as a means for distributing wealth to everyone, although all that is required to facilitate such a distribution is a simple market economy. Since all men benefit from greater productivity of appropriated land, the law of nature is more completely fulfilled if all land is appropriated. And the fulfillment of that law is that from which the limitation was derived in the first place. So the use of money overcomes the sufficiency provision because by so doing the reason for the existence of the provision is more fully realized.

It might be objected to my account that Locke is not recommending the use of money but merely describing its effects. Moreover, as Tully claims, the objection continues, Locke disapproves of covetousness and 'identifies the emergence of covetousness as an outgrowth of barter' (147), and money is only an extension of barter. Not only does Locke think that 'the only change which money explains is the enlargement of possessions,' but he 'shows that the consequences of work and industry he wishes to endorse accrue to mankind without the use of money' (148). Thus according to this objection Locke thinks that at best a market economy is a necessary evil, at worst simply an evil, contrary to my analysis.

The objection involves three different claims. First, Locke is not recommending the use of money but describing its effects. Second, for Locke money serves only one purpose, enlargement of possessions, and he disapproves of this purpose. Third, according to Locke a market economy is unnecessary and undesirable since it increases covetousness, or at least the opportunities to covet.

In support of the first claim Tully argues that Locke groups together objects often used as items of exchange, such as shells, diamonds or pebbles, and calls then 'things' as opposed to useful goods. This is supposed to show that he disapproves of acquiring these things. Money is introduced as a continuation of this practice, a practice Locke stigmatizes but allows.

---

34 Macpherson, 212. As Tully (149) shows, however, the passage to which Macpherson appeals to support this evaluation does not support it. But others do.

The problem with this interpretation is that it simply is not supported by Locke's text. It is true that he calls gold, shells, diamonds and pebbles 'things' which are not useful as such, but it does not follow that he morally disapproves of barter or the use of money. Rather, he is merely contrasting these things with intrinsically useful goods. As things, gold, shells, diamonds and pebbles derive their value from someone's taking a fancy to them but are not inherently useful for either preservation or convenience, although goods are. Locke calls these items 'things' merely to mark this distinction. Similarly, he sometimes describes the acquisition of such things as 'hoarding' or 'heaping up' not because he wishes to demonstrate his disapproval of enlarging one's possessions (which would have contradicted his own practice of judicious investment), but because he wishes to emphasize the distinction between intrinsically useful goods and things useful only as a medium of exchange or to satisfy someone's fancy. Thus Locke does not stigmatize the use of money, and so the claim that he merely describes the effects of money without recommending its use is unjustified.

In addition, as I have indicated above and will argue for in greater detail below, the market economy plays an important role for Locke in securing peace, preservation and convenience. This conclusively demonstrates, if I am right, that he does recommend the use of money, for he surely thinks that the fulfillment of these fundamental tenets of natural law is good, and since money and the market economy aid in their fulfillment, he must approve of money as well. It will also answer the objections that for Locke money serves only the undesirable purpose of enlarging one's possessions and that a market economy is undesirable since it increases covetousness.

In section 41 of the *Second Treatise* Locke argues that the value of goods is due primarily to the effects of labor. To prove this contention he appeals to the difference between the amount and quality of possessions enjoyed by the Americans and by the English. For although the Americans have land and raw materials, they have few of the conveniences the English have. 'And a King of a large fruitful Territory there feeds, lodges, and is clad worse than a day labourer in *England*' (II, 41). Locke's idea here is that laborers enjoy better goods and more of them as a result of the effects of labor. But whose labor creates this difference in quality and quantity of possessions? It cannot be that of the English laborer himself, for there is no reason to think that he works harder than the Americans do. Rather, he enjoys more and better possessions because he is part of a society that includes other laborers (among other things), and the benefit of everyone's labor accrues in part to him. But he can only benefit from others' labor if there is some sort of market system, for otherwise there would be no means by which the benefits of others' labor could be available to him. So in this passage Locke apparently assumes that some sort of market economy exists and that it is beneficial, although, of course, this need not be a capitalist economy. Furthermore, obviously a market economy did exist in Locke's day, so it is not surprising that he indicates no moral disapproval of the effects of such a market but on the contrary implicitly approves of it.

The second passage to which I appeal to support my claim that the marketplace plays a useful role for Locke in promoting preservation and convenience occurs in section 36. There he says, 'Nay, the extent of *Ground* is of so little value, *without labour*, that I have heard it affirmed, that in *Spain* it self, a Man may be permitted to plough, sow, and reap, without being disturbed, upon Land that he has no other Title to, but only his making use of it. But, on the contrary, the Inhabitants think themselves beholden to him, who, by his industry on neglected, and consequently waste Land, has increased the stock of Corn, which they wanted.' Now he does go on to say that even without money there would be enough land to support twice the number of the present inhabitants of the earth, but in this passage he assumes that a benevolent market economy exists. For why would the people of Spain think themselves in debt to a man for growing corn if there were no means for them to acquire some of it? And how could they legitimately acquire it apart from barter or money? I can make no sense of this passage unless it is granted that Locke again assumes and morally approves of the operation of the marketplace and implicitly approves of barter and money.

Of course I am not claiming that a market economy is sufficient to insure that one is better off with one than without one. I am simply pointing out that for Locke a functioning marketplace is necessary for one to be well off, and so money and the marketplace are necessary for, or conducive to, preservation and convenience being more fully realized by greater numbers of individuals. Locke does think that the rule that everyone should have as much as he can make use of would still hold without money, and would hold 'without straitning anybody' (II, 36), but that does not imply that money is detrimental to the attainment of preservation and convenience. He is merely saying there that people could still get by if money had not been introduced.

What we need is an account of Locke's implicit distinction between the use and abuse of money. Clearly the use of money to pile up wealth is permissible for Locke. Indeed, the ability to 'lay up for the future,' an ability 'the Wisdom of the great Creatour' has given to man, should be exercised, according to Locke, to provide for one's children (II, 80). Acquisitiveness, or the desire to accumulate things, is not wrong in itself. Covetousness, however, or the desire to accumulate things *to which one is not entitled*, is.

As a result I think the objections fail. Locke does recommend the use of money in the sense that it plays an important and positive role in his theory of property and in that it serves to promote peace and preservation. Money and the marketplace are benevolent because they help to fulfill the law of nature.

## V Ambiguities in Locke's Concept of Natural Law and Property Rights

I wish to take up one remaining issue. Macpherson argues that Locke's state of nature is ambiguous.[35] At times, he claims, Locke contrasts the state of nature with war, but at other times it appears that there is no difference between the two. Is Macpherson's claim correct?

Early in the *Second Treatise* Locke does contrast the state of nature with war. Men living together on the earth according to reason without a common earthly superior with authority to judge between them is properly the state of nature (II, 19). War, however, is the use of force, or the intent to use force, where there is no effective judge to settle the issue, and it can occur in the state of nature or in political society (II, 226).

But later a far different picture emerges of the state of nature, for it comes to be warlike. The natural state is described as 'unsafe and uneasie' (II, 131), and enjoyment of freedom outside of civil society 'is very uncertain, and constantly exposed to the Invasion of others' (II, 123). Moreover, 'For all being Kings as much as he, every Man his Equal, and the greater part no strict Observers of Equity and Justice, the enjoyment of the property he has in this state is very unsafe, very unsecure. This makes him willing to quit a Condition, which however free, is full of fears and continual dangers: And 'tis not without rea-

35 Macpherson, 238-47

son, that he seeks out, and is willing to joyn in Society with others...' (II, 123).[36]

It is no longer the few who disobey the law of nature, but now the 'greater part' fail to observe 'Equity and Justice.' Later we read the rebellion which dissolves civil government brings 'back again the state of war' (II, 226). But why does it not bring back the peaceful natural state? The answer is that the peaceful state of nature has disappeared, and even if civil government is dissolved it will not reappear.

Macpherson calls this change from a peaceful to a warlike condition Locke's 'ambiguous state of nature' and declares that it is 'the central contradiction in the explicit postulates on which Locke's political theory is built.'[37] He recognizes, however, that it could be argued against his interpretation that Locke's theory simply requires development, or better, degeneration, in the natural state, the change occuring roughly when money was introduced. On this view the premonetary phase is peaceful while the postmonetary phase becomes increasingly warlike.

Macpherson rejects this scheme because, he claims, 'Locke presents both the pleasant and the unpleasant versions as pictures of the state of nature immediately preceding the establishment of civil society, i.e., of the second stage of the state of nature.'[38] He cites one passage to substantiate this contention, found in section 135 of the *Second Treatise*. Here Locke argues that since the legislator has no legitimate power but that delegated to him by the citizens, and since no citizen ever had absolute arbitrary power over anyone, the legislator cannot have arbitrary power either.

> For no Body can transfer to another more power than he has in himself; and no Body has an absolute arbitrary Power over himself, or over any other, to destroy his own life, or take away the life or Property of another. A Man, as has been proved, cannot subject himself to the Arbitrary Power of another; and having in the State of Nature no Arbitrary Power over the Life, Liberty, or Possession of another, but only so much as the Law of Nature gave him for the preservation of himself; and the rest of Mankind; this is all he doth,

36 Locke also describes the state of nature in warlike terms in sections 124, 125, 131 and 137.

37 Macpherson, 241

38 Macpherson, 242

> or can give up to the commonwealth, and by it to the *Legislative Power*, so that the Legislative can have no more than this. (II, 135)

It is curious that Macpherson cites this passage to support his claim that Locke sometimes equates the peaceful state of nature with the post-monetary stage. For if he is correct, the passage must be a description of the state of nature. But that is just not the case. Actually this passage only discusses what the law of nature decrees, irrespective of what men really do, and hence is not a description of the state of nature but of the reasons why political authority is limited. Locke simply asserts here that no one *rightfully* has absolute arbitrary power over himself or anyone else in the state of nature, and so no political ruler may have such power. It is not meant to be a statement about what actually happens but what natural law decrees. Hence a few lines down Locke adds, 'The Obligations of the Law of Nature, cease not in Society but only in many cases are drawn closer, and have by Humane Laws known penalties annexed to them, to inforce their observation' (II, 135). This is not to postulate, as Macpherson would have it, 'that the state of nature from which men enter civil society is one in which men do on the whole follow the law of nature.'[39] Rather it is simply to state that under the normative law of nature men may not *legitimately* arbitrarily invade the lives of others, whether or not they really obey that law.

So Macpherson's claim that Locke's state of nature is ambiguous, and not simply divided into two stages, is undocumented. As a result I think he is mistaken in his claim that there is a contradiction here in Locke's political theory. Nevertheless, I do think that there is a central structural ambiguity in Locke's theory, but it rests in his notion of natural law and its relationship to property rights instead of in his concept of the state of nature.

Apparently the turning point in the state of nature occurs with the introduction of money.[40] The premonetary natural state is pleasant while after men consent to use money it begins to grow increasingly unpleasant until finally they seek a remedy in the civil state. This is so because money allows them to satisfy their desires above and be-

39 Macpherson, 242

40 Cf. Tully, 152-4.

yond their needs (II, 37). Just as money gives them 'the opportunity to continue to enlarge' their possessions (II, 48), it follows that it also increases the opportunity to covet another's goods. In fact as far as I am aware Locke describes the state of nature in Hobbesean warlike terms only when referring to its latter stages, after money has been introduced. Indeed we find in the *Second Treatise* a progression from a peaceful to a warlike state of nature, a progression which becomes greatly accelerated once money is introduced. But the only theoretical device Locke has at his disposal to explain this change is the invention of money. For these reasons the basis for degeneration can only be found in the features of the consent to establish a monetary system, even though Locke clearly thinks that money also serves to fulfill the peace and preservation required by natural law.

The most obvious result of the introduction of money is that it allows individuals lawfully to increase their holdings. Once the boundaries of appropriation are transcended there are no theoretical limits to what one may rightfully own, so long as it is held as currency, and so large estates are possible. And given that appropriation by labor is rational behavior, because it is commanded by God, and that man is rational, it is likely that the more industrious and rational individuals will achieve large estates. Of course, because many individuals do not obey the law of nature, they will be envious of the ones who lawfully accumulate vast holdings. This is especially so since money makes land, for instance, scarce (II, 45). It is not difficult to imagine, and this is what Locke seem to have in mind, that the strife to which this state of affairs leads would be comparable to a state of war, where everyone would feel unsafe and insecure, especially the ones with much to lose. To unite and form a civil society would be advantageous in such a situation. So it does not seem unreasonable to conclude that it is the great and disproportionately unequal amount of possessions owned by individuals which causes the peaceful state of nature to degenerate into war.

But there is another important feature of the consent to use money: as I have argued it also allows a more complete fulfillment of natural law by promoting preservation and convenience. By transcending the scarcity limitation it permits individuals to appropriate as much as they want, beyond their mere needs, sell whatever they cannot use before it spoils, and so assist in providing for others' needs as well. In this way money gives individuals incentive to help satisfy others' needs and so promotes peace, preservation and convenience. And since men are rational, circumventing this limit creates the possibility of greater, or at least repeated, expressions of rational behavior. So transcending the scarcity limits creates the possibility for a more complete fulfillment of the law of nature because it allows men more often to engage in a rational activity and that activity results in, Locke assumes, increased quality of life for everyone.

Furthermore, we saw that the sufficiency limitation is also transcended through the operation of a commercial economy because Locke (falsely) assumes that the greater benefit of appropriated land, no matter who owns it, will be distributed to all, as long as that land is worked. The economy is the instrument through which the benefit of productive land is distributed, and since all do benefit, the law of nature is more completely fulfilled. Thus with the introduction of money the sufficiency limit is transcended, and scarce goods can be accumulated in any amount, although, of course, not so that they spoil.

But now an important ambiguity emerges in Locke's doctrine of natural law with respect to property. On the one hand property is justified because without appropriation the fundamental law of nature cannot be fulfilled, and the consent to use money, which transcends the limits to appropriation, is justified because it makes possible a more perfect realization of the law of nature. But on the other hand consent to use money, in that it results in large inequalities of holdings, causes widespread envy, covetousness and strife, and this disintegrates the peaceful state of nature and ushers in a state of war.[41]

So although natural law requires property rights, and the consent to use money increases the amount of property one may lawfully own and is justified because it promotes peace and preservation, this increase in possessions causes the peaceful state of nature to degenerate into war, in which peace and preservation, the law of nature, is not observed. In other words, Locke needs natural law to justify property rights, but when this justification is fully drawn out to in-

41 I find it remarkable that John Dunn (*The Political Thought of John Locke* [New York: Cambridge University Press 1969], 118) realizes that for Locke property serves both of these purposes, yet he fails to notice, or at least does not mention, the conceptual incoherence involved. In successive sentences Dunn asserts that money 'leads to economic progress and betters the conditions of all members of the population,' and that it also causes 'differentiation in wealth [which] leads to greater social conflict and to a decline in the moral quality of social life under stress of increasing motives for envy.' However, Dunn passes over this uneasy juxtaposition in silence.

clude money, it leads to the destruction of peace and preservation, and the law of nature is no longer followed. So to be fulfilled the law of nature requires property rights, but property rights, when fully analyzed, destroy the peaceful state of nature and endanger preservation, the most important tenet of natural law. This is a central tension in Locke's analysis of natural law and property rights, generated by his ambiguous attitude towards money. Insofar as Locke's inhabitants of the state of nature follow the law of nature, ultimately they cause, by those actions, the endangerment of peace and preservation and the elimination of convenience, until at last they find relief in the remedial civil state.

For Locke appropriation is a right because it expresses obedience to God. But this obedient, rational action creates a situation in which the fundamental tenet of God's will cannot be upheld. This tension in Locke's doctrine of natural law is pivotal to his political theory because it motivates the shift in his account of the state of nature, and without the warlike natural state there would be no need for men to form a civil society. And one central question Locke seeks to answer in the *Two Treatises* is why men are willing to submit themselves to political authority. Locke is able to answer this question only because of the tension involved in his concept of natural law and property rights.

*Received January,. 1984*
*Revised July, 1984*

# [2]

# Limiting Locke: A Natural Law Justification for the Fair Use Doctrine

**Benjamin G. Damstedt**

## INTRODUCTION

Focusing a discussion of intellectual property on a 300-year-old text may seem unusual, but John Locke's *Two Treatises of Government*[1] has an uncommon place in American intellectual property theory. Historically, Lockean natural rights informed the Framers' understanding of intellectual property law.[2] Courts also have a long history of using natural law justifications in intellectual property cases.[3] The Lockean perspective has been particularly appealing to theorists because of its ability to justify

---

1. JOHN LOCKE, TWO TREATISES OF GOVERNMENT (Peter Laslett ed., Cambridge Univ. Press 1988) (1690). Locke's original purpose was not to provide a comprehensive justification for private property rights but to refute Sir Robert Filmer's opposing theory in *Patriarcha* that all property rights were contingent on the king, who inherited them from Adam. JOHN LOCKE, THE FIRST TREATISE OF GOVERNMENT, *in* TWO TREATISES OF GOVERNMENT, *supra*, §§ 1-6; JOHN LOCKE, THE SECOND TREATISE OF GOVERNMENT, *in* TWO TREATISES OF GOVERNMENT, *supra*, § 25 [hereinafter LOCKE, SECOND TREATISE]; *see also* ALAN RYAN, PROPERTY AND POLITICAL THEORY 27-36 (1984) (arguing that Locke's aim was "primarily to sabotage the idea that patriarchal authority had been absolute and that rulers still possessed it"). One of the most enduring portions of Locke's argument, however, has been his support for private property in chapter 5 of the *Second Treatise*.

2. *See* THE FEDERALIST NO. 43, at 239-40 (James Madison) (Clinton Rossiter ed., 1999); Letter from Thomas Jefferson to Isaac McPherson (Aug. 13, 1813), *in* BASIC WRITINGS OF THOMAS JEFFERSON 708 (Philip S. Foner ed., 1944).

3. Diane Leenheer Zimmerman, *Information as Speech, Information as Goods: Some Thoughts on Marketplaces and the Bill of Rights*, 33 WM. & MARY L. REV. 665, 690-703 (1992) (discussing the strong Lockean influences on early intellectual property law in the United States and England).

widely varying property systems,[4] ranging from expansive communitarianism to subsistence-worker-based capitalism.[5] Although modern intellectual property doctrine has attempted to disavow its association with natural law justifications, some debate the ability of courts to adjudicate intellectual property claims without consulting natural law principles.[6]

Revisiting Locke for a theory of intellectual property has become vital because of two important recent shifts in doctrine and scholarship. First, statutory and doctrinal innovations have continued to expand private intellectual property rights.[7] Second, academics have increasingly advocated the importance of the public domain as a way of limiting the expansion of private property rights.[8] One recent example of the conflict between private intellectual property rights and the public domain is *Eldred v. Ashcroft*,[9] upholding the Sonny Bono Copyright Term Extension Act, which extended the duration of a copyright to the life of the author plus seventy years. While the government's brief advocating for the copyright extension emphasized the need for fairness to authors,[10] the petitioners' brief highlighted that "[p]etitioners are various individuals and businesses that rely upon speech in the public domain for their creative work and livelihood."[11] These arguments were mirrored by amici, including the Recording Industry Association of America (RIAA) on the government's side, which emphasized the importance of "fair compensation of authors,"[12] and a group of fifty-three law professors, who stated that "[a]mici are in

---

4. *See* RYAN, *supra* note 1, at 18-22 (describing interpretations of Locke from "modern and revolutionary" to "positively old-fashioned in 1680").

5. *Compare* JAMES TULLY, A DISCOURSE ON PROPERTY: JOHN LOCKE AND HIS ADVERSARIES 99 (1980) (presenting a communitarian interpretation), *with* C.B. MACPHERSON, THE POLITICAL THEORY OF POSSESSIVE INDIVIDUALISM: HOBBES TO LOCKE 217, 250 (1962) (presenting a capitalist interpretation).

6. *See* Jeremy Waldron, *From Authors to Copiers: Individual Rights and Social Values in Intellectual Property*, 68 CHI.-KENT L. REV. 841, 856 (1993); Alfred C. Yen, *Restoring the Natural Law: Copyright as Labor and Possession*, 51 OHIO ST. L.J. 517, 521 (1990) (arguing that because judges seem to incorporate natural law principles, the natural law should not be ignored when enacting intellectual property statutes).

7. *See, e.g.*, Sonny Bono Copyright Term Extension Act of 1998, Pub. L. No. 105-298, 112 Stat. 2827 (extending the length of a copyright to the life of the author plus seventy years); Uruguay Round Agreements Act, Pub. L. No. 103-465, 108 Stat. 4809 (1994) (extending patent duration to twenty years).

8. *See, e.g.*, James Boyle, *The Second Enclosure Movement and the Construction of the Public Domain*, 66 LAW & CONTEMP. PROBS. 33 (2003) (contrasting the undesirability of the recent encroachments on the public domain with the economically sensible historical privatization of land).

9. 123 S. Ct. 769 (2003).

10. Brief for Respondent at 30-33, *Eldred* (No. 01-618).

11. Brief for Petitioners at 3, *Eldred* (No. 01-618).

12. Brief of Amici Curiae Recording Industry Association of America at 19, *Eldred* (No. 01-618).

particular concerned about the recent, rapid expansion of copyright scope and duration, at the expense of the public domain."[13]

Scholars have seen Lockean theory as an essential tool in reconciling these arguments because the main thrust of Locke's theory is the reconciliation of strong private property rights with a common of materials available to all. Locke argues that laborers have a private property right in the products of their labor because individuals mix their labor with materials from the common that are free for all to use. The private property right in an individual's labor is mixed into the product of labor, and thus the private property right also attaches to the product of labor. He supports this argument by adding natural law principles that must be followed to maintain exclusive property rights. The natural law principle that has been most commonly considered by scholars is the sufficiency proviso, which requires that the laborer not take too many materials out of the common.

Two substantial criticisms are often directed at Lockean theory. First, scholars argue that even though Locke claims to reconcile a robust common with strong private property rights, his property rights swallow the common.[14] Thus, the object of Lockean theorists, as mirrored in the title of this Note, is often concerned with limiting the scope of the Lockean property right. Second, scholars argue that the sufficiency proviso cannot be fulfilled in a morally compelling way because the common of tangible goods is inherently scarce.

Previous scholarship concerning Lockean theories of property rights in intangible goods has focused on the ability of the nonrivalrous characteristic of intangible goods to eliminate the scarcity problem. This scholarship began with the publication of two influential articles, one by Justin Hughes in 1988[15] and another by Wendy Gordon in 1993,[16] and has been refined in the last decade.[17] A fundamental difference between

13. Brief of Amici Curiae Intellectual Property Law Professors at 1, *Eldred* (No. 01-618).

14. ROBERT NOZICK, ANARCHY, STATE, AND UTOPIA 174-78 (1974).

15. Justin Hughes, *The Philosophy of Intellectual Property*, 77 GEO. L.J. 287 (1988).

16. Wendy J. Gordon, *A Property Right in Self-Expression: Equality and Individualism in the Natural Law of Intellectual Property*, 102 YALE L.J. 1533 (1993).

17. *See* PETER DRAHOS, A PHILOSOPHY OF INTELLECTUAL PROPERTY 41-72 (1996); Lawrence C. Becker, *Deserving To Own Intellectual Property*, 68 CHI.-KENT L. REV. 609 (1993); William Fisher, *Theories of Intellectual Property*, *in* NEW ESSAYS IN THE LEGAL AND POLITICAL THEORY OF PROPERTY 168 (Stephen R. Munzer ed., 2001); Edwin C. Hettinger, *Justifying Intellectual Property*, 18 PHIL. & PUB. AFF. 31 (1989); Linda J. Lacey, *Of Bread and Roses and Copyrights*, 1989 DUKE L.J. 1532; Adam D. Moore, *Intangible Property: Privacy, Power, and Information Control*, 35 AM. PHIL. Q. 365 (1998) [hereinafter Moore, *Intangible Property*]; Adam D. Moore, *A Lockean Theory of Intellectual Property*, 21 HAMLINE L. REV. 65 (1997) [hereinafter Moore, *Lockean Theory*]; Tom G. Palmer, *Are Patents and Copyrights Morally Justified? The Philosophy of Property Rights and Ideal Objects*, 13 HARV. J.L. & PUB. POL'Y 817 (1990); Joan E. Schaffner, *Patent Preemption UnLocked*, 1995 WIS. L. REV. 1081; Seana Valentine Shiffrin, *Lockean Arguments for Private Intellectual Property*, *in* NEW ESSAYS IN THE LEGAL AND POLITICAL THEORY OF PROPERTY, *supra*, at 138; Horacio M. Spector, *An Outline of a Theory Justifying Intellectual Property Rights*, 8 EUR. INTELL. PROP. REV. 270 (1989); Stewart E. Sterk,

tangible goods and intangible goods, however, is that intangible goods are nonrivalrous, which means that they can be used by an infinite number of people in an infinite number of ways without harming the use value of any other person, including the initial producer.[18] Previous scholarship has persuasively argued that because intangible goods are nonrivalrous, the common of intangible goods contains materials that are not subject to a scarcity problem and thus that Lockean theory does not fail when it is applied to intangible goods. Scholars have tended to overemphasize the importance of this claim, however, by conflating the Lockean common with a public domain. The Lockean common contains undeveloped materials, whereas a public domain is composed of developed goods. Although the Lockean common is quite useful for independent production, the nonrivalrous nature of intangible goods means that a public domain can be used to foster incremental innovation, which is much more valuable.

This Note takes a different direction than previous scholarship by focusing on another of Locke's natural law principles, the waste prohibition. The waste prohibition forbids a laborer from wasting products of labor or portions of such products, with the violation resulting in the loss of private property rights in the portion of the product wasted. I define Lockean waste in the following way: Waste occurs where a unit of a product of labor is not put to any use. When scholars have considered the application of the waste prohibition to intangible goods previously, they have arrived at polar conclusions, with some asserting that waste rarely occurs and others claiming that waste always occurs.[19]

The waste prohibition is of negligible importance for tangible goods, but is immensely important when constructing a Lockean theory of intangible goods. The waste prohibition is largely a nonissue for tangible goods because one can exchange money—by definition a nonwasting good—for units of a product of labor that may be prone to waste. Laborers will thus have incentives to sell all the units they possess that they will not use and violations of the waste prohibition will be rare. The nonrivalrous

---

*Rhetoric and Reality in Copyright Law*, 94 MICH. L. REV. 1197 (1996); Waldron, *supra* note 6; Lloyd L. Weinreb, *Copyright for Functional Expression*, 111 HARV. L. REV. 1150 (1998); Yen, *supra* note 6; Barbara Friedman, Note, *From Deontology to Dialogue: The Cultural Consequences of Copyright*, 13 CARDOZO ARTS & ENT. L.J. 157 (1994); R. Anthony Reese, Note, *Reflections on the Intellectual Commons: Two Perspectives on Copyright Duration and Reversion*, 47 STAN. L. REV. 707 (1995).

These articles often mirror arguments made previously by authors dealing with the application of Lockean theory to tangible goods. *See* MACPHERSON, *supra* note 5; NOZICK, *supra* note 14; RYAN, *supra* note 1; JEREMY WALDRON, THE RIGHT TO PRIVATE PROPERTY (1988).

18. *See* Paul M. Romer, *Endogenous Technological Change*, 98 J. POL. ECON. S71, S73-S78 (1990) (explaining the attributes of rivalry and nonrivalry).

19. *Compare* Hughes, *supra* note 15, at 328 (claiming a more narrow potential for violation), *with* Hettinger, *supra* note 17, at 44-45 (asserting a broad violation of the waste prohibition). In her analysis, Gordon barely considers the waste prohibition. *See* Gordon, *supra* note 16, at 1550-51.

nature of intangible goods can be characterized as the production of an unlimited number of "intangible units" at the initial creation of any intangible good. Although the limited number of units of a tangible good can usually be converted into nonwasting money, the unlimited number of intangible units suggests that the laborer will not be able or willing to convert all of the intangible units into money whenever any intangible good is produced. The combination of nonconversion and nonuse constitutes a violation of the waste prohibition. As the waste prohibition is enforced through the loss of property rights in the wasted intangible units, the waste prohibition creates what I call a Lockean fair use right. Price discrimination allows greater conversion of intangible units into money but is an imperfect solution due to practical difficulties in attaining perfect price discrimination.

This Note also examines the implications of government regulation on Lockean intellectual property rights and compares a Lockean regime with current U.S. intellectual property doctrine and theory. The establishment of a government allows much more variety in the scope of private property rights under Lockean theory, but the Lockean fair use right binds civil governments in much the same way that it binds individuals in the state of nature. Although the theory and doctrine of copyright fair use shares many characteristics with Lockean fair use, the current U.S. fair use right is more limited than the Lockean right. One example considered in this Note is that strong government support for anticircumvention measures may violate Lockean principles if the ability to police the waste prohibition is not protected. An even larger difference is that there is no coherent patent fair use right in the United States, although such a right would be demanded under a Lockean regime.

This argument will be fleshed out in the remainder of this Note. Part I introduces general Lockean concepts, focusing on the impacts of the nonrivalry of intangible goods on the common and the waste prohibition. Part II applies Lockean concepts in an economic framework, demonstrating a fair use right in a Lockean state of nature. Part III considers the transition of society into a civil government, with its attendant changes in the scope of property rights in intangible goods. Part III also applies the Lockean analysis of this Note to two areas of current intellectual property debate—the anticircumvention provisions in the Digital Millennium Copyright Act (DMCA) and the enforcement of drug patents in developing countries. Part IV concludes.

## I. ELEMENTS OF A LOCKEAN THEORY OF INTELLECTUAL PROPERTY

> Though the Earth, and all inferior Creatures be common to all Men, yet every Man has a Property in his own Person. . . . Whatsoever, then, he removes out of the State that Nature hath provided, and left it in, he hath mixed his Labour with, and joyned to it something that is his own, and thereby makes it his Property. . . . For this Labour being the unquestionable Property of the Labourer, no Man but he can have a right to what that is once joyned to, at least where there is enough, and as good left in common for others.[20]

This single paragraph, section 27 in the *Second Treatise of Government*, outlines nearly all of Locke's natural law justification for private property rights. Stated simply, each individual has a property right in her own labor. When the individual combines her labor with materials from the common, this property right extends to the items she has removed from the common due to the mixing of her property-laden labor with the items.[21] This individual may continue to remove items from the common so

---

20. LOCKE, SECOND TREATISE, *supra* note 1, § 27.

21. Scholars have described the normative appeal of Locke's labor-mixing argument in the following way. Hughes finds that Locke has "immediate, intuitive appeal: it seems as though people do work to produce ideas and that the value of these ideas . . . depends solely upon the individual's mental 'work.'" Hughes, *supra* note 15, at 300. Lloyd Weinreb adds that this intuition is stronger for intangible goods because creation is "more plainly and completely the product of the author's labor." Weinreb, *supra* note 17, at 1222.

There are a number of interpretations supporting the Lockean labor concept of which I will briefly describe four. *See* Fisher, *supra* note 17, at 184-85 (describing six Lockean arguments to justify private ownership). First, Locke relies heavily on the commands of God to justify the concepts of his natural law theory. *See* RYAN, *supra* note 1, at 25-32 (describing Locke's theistic justifications for natural law principles). Second, Adam Moore argues that the combination of labor and the sufficiency proviso creates a "Pareto-based" moral principle: Once an individual expends labor, she has a "weak presumptive claim" to the work that turns into a strong exclusionary right if the sufficiency proviso is fulfilled. Moore, *Intangible Property*, *supra* note 17, at 368-70. Third, Hughes suggests that Lockean theory may be premised on an "avoidance" view of labor. Hughes, *supra* note 15, at 302-05. He then describes normative and instrumental arguments supporting this view. The normative argument states that the "unpleasantness of labor should be rewarded with property," whereas the instrumental argument rewards labor with property "because people must be motivated to perform labor." *Id.* at 303. The normative argument can be used to support a natural law right, whereas the instrumental argument is framed as a utilitarian argument. *Cf.* ALAN RYAN, PROPERTY 69 (1987) ("The point of thinking in proprietary terms is to avoid utilitarian considerations, not to succumb to them."). Fourth, Robert Nozick is most famous for emphasizing a libertarian theory of rights. NOZICK, *supra* note 14, at 333-34. This justification shares much with the theistic conception, but relies on each individual's ownership of himself (rather than ownership by God) to provide the initial justification for property rights.

For purposes of this Note, I assume that labor mixing is coherent and sufficient to justify the private property right that Locke suggests, although numerous scholars have offered various counterarguments against basing private property rights on one's labor. First, in a somewhat

long as she adheres to three independent conditions: the no harm principle, the independent production principle, and the waste prohibition.

First, the natural law broadly prohibits an actor from harming another in his "Life, Health, . . . [or] Possessions."[22] Rather than examining the "no harm" principle in the abstract, however, Locke narrowed it to a discussion of two specific provisos: the sufficiency proviso and the taking prohibition.[23] The sufficiency proviso requires the laborer to leave "enough, and as good" for others to take from the common as well.[24] The sufficiency proviso also lends the theory much of its normative appeal because the laborer who asserts a property right but "leaves as much as another can make use of, does as good as take nothing at all"[25] from the common. The taking prohibition proscribes another from taking a good that a laborer has removed from the common.[26] In order to violate the taking prohibition, an

complicated argument, Jeremy Waldron contends that the idea of labor mixing itself is incoherent. *See* WALDRON, *supra* note 17, at 184-89. Second, scholars debate about what amount of labor and how much mixing is required to create a property right. Edwin Hettinger is content with a property right based on a minimal amount of labor and labor mixing. *See* Hettinger, *supra* note 17, at 37. Nozick argues that a minimal amount of labor will be insufficient to justify a property right, suggesting that if someone labors on the sea by dumping a single can of tomato juice in it, he hasn't gained a property right in the sea but has "foolishly dissipated" his tomato juice. NOZICK, *supra* note 14, at 174-75. Alan Ryan approaches this concern from the mixing perspective, arguing that harvesting an apple provides the laborer a right in the apple and not the tree from which it was plucked. RYAN, *supra* note 1, at 32-35. Third, labor mixing does not necessarily justify a right to the whole value of the good, as opposed to the value related to the effort expended. *See* WALDRON, *supra* note 17, at 205; *see also* Reese, *supra* note 17, at 714-15 (setting a "fair return on investment" as the appropriate scope). Fourth, postmodern theories describing the deconstruction of the author undermine the ability to assert author-based entitlements and, therefore, also undermine the ability to rely on an author's labor to justify a property right. *See* Waldron, *supra* note 6, at 878-79. Finally, if one follows Hughes's avoidance theory as the true normative justification for labor providing a property right, enjoyable labor might not be rewarded with a property right. *See* Hughes, *supra* note 15, at 302-04, 313-14 (describing arguments that enjoyable labor should not be rewarded with a property right and finding that these arguments justify the idea-expression dichotomy in copyright law).

22. LOCKE, SECOND TREATISE, *supra* note 1, § 6.

23. *Cf.* RYAN, *supra* note 21, at 64 (explaining that a theory of natural rights begins in a minimal way, but must be supplemented by case-by-case interpretations of what the no harm principle means).

24. LOCKE, SECOND TREATISE, *supra* note 1, § 27. Scholars disagree on the appropriate interpretation of Locke's sufficiency proviso. *Compare* Hughes, *supra* note 15, at 297 (strong sufficiency proviso), *with* WALDRON, *supra* note 17, at 210-11 (weak sufficiency proviso).

25. LOCKE, SECOND TREATISE, *supra* note 1, § 33; Gordon, *supra* note 16, at 1565 (stating that the sufficiency proviso "serves as Locke's bedrock response to the complaints of the nonpropertied"); Hughes, *supra* note 15, at 297-98 (arguing that the sufficiency proviso "protects Locke's labor justification from any attacks"). A recent interpretation of Locke focuses on the command to make full use of God's grant of the commons and finds that the inherent characteristics of intangible goods require that no property rights be allowed in order to make full use of the initial common. Shiffrin, *supra* note 17, at 144, 151-53, 166-67.

26. LOCKE, SECOND TREATISE, *supra* note 1, §§ 32-34; Gordon, *supra* note 16, at 1543 (describing the taking prohibition as a duty not to interfere). Waldron's deconstruction-of-the-author argument may suggest that users can never actually take a work. Because *Hamlet* is "in effect rewritten or reconstructed every time it is read," people are not merely taking but are coauthors. *See* Waldron, *supra* note 6, at 878. This argument seems limited to a person's

actor must not only take a good, but this taking must also harm the other party.[27] Consensual trades and the giving of gifts do not violate the taking prohibition.[28]

Second is the right to independent production, which Locke explicitly describes, stating, "[T]hough Men had a Right to appropriate, by their Labour . . . [y]et this could not be [so] much, nor to the Prejudice of others . . . who would use the same Industry."[29] The ability to independently produce a good is restricted when the sufficiency proviso is violated or when the ability to labor is controlled.[30] In order to claim a property right in the state of nature, therefore, individuals must not violate the sufficiency proviso or control the ability of another to labor.[31] Finally, Lockean theory prohibits the waste of goods removed from the common. The waste prohibition will be considered in detail throughout this Note.

Locke relates these property-creating elements to three societal arrangements, which represent a rough progression in the development of property rights and are legitimated by consent and continued adherence to the natural law.[32] Locke describes a "State of Nature," which he then divides into a state of nature before trade is introduced and one after trade is established.[33] Locke's third societal arrangement envisions civil government regulation of property.[34] To move from the initial state of nature to one incorporating a trade system requires the consent of the

relationship to the intangible good itself because it would be much harder to argue that a person cannot take a tangible embodiment of an intangible good, for example through stealing a CD.

27. If the taking prohibition absolutely barred taking without regard to the harm to the owner, the waste prohibition could not be enforced in the state of nature. Additionally, independent production is not only permitted but protected even though it harms the owner's competitive advantage. Independent production does not violate the taking prohibition because an independent producer harms but does not take.

28. LOCKE, SECOND TREATISE, *supra* note 1, §§ 46-48; *see also id.* §§ 17-19 (prohibiting coerced action).

29. *Id.* § 37. The independent production principle is strengthened by Locke's views on equality in the state of nature. *See id.* § 4.

30. *Compare* NOZICK, *supra* note 14, at 178-82 (focusing on the sufficiency proviso's implications for independent production), *and* Gordon, *supra* note 16, at 1582 (same), *with* Moore, *Intangible Property*, *supra* note 17, at 367-71 (tying the right to independently create to the importance of personal autonomy in Lockean theory), Palmer, *supra* note 17, at 829-35 (arguing against intellectual property rights as a "restriction on the liberty of everyone"), *and* Sterk, *supra* note 17, at 1234-35 (discussing the importance of freedom of action).

31. LOCKE, SECOND TREATISE, *supra* note 1, §§ 27, 33-37.

32. *Id.* § 135; MACPHERSON, *supra* note 5, at 210-11; RYAN, *supra* note 21, at 62; WALDRON, *supra* note 17, at 163.

33. LOCKE, SECOND TREATISE, *supra* note 1, §§ 4-6, 47-51.

34. *Id.* §§ 77-243.

trading parties and the consent of society to introduce money.[35] Specific consent by individuals is required to transition into a civil government.[36]

Scholars have debated the importance and logical coherence of the Lockean elements throughout the centuries, largely concluding that Lockean theory is either inapplicable or morally unpersuasive. The most damning arguments for Lockean theory have generally centered on Locke's sufficiency proviso. If the proviso is interpreted strongly to mean that the laborer must leave for the next laborer exactly the same opportunity to appropriate from the common, any scarcity in the common will cause Lockean theory to fail in its effort to justify property rights.[37] It is not difficult, therefore, to demonstrate that Lockean theory fails for tangible goods because scarcity is an inherent quality of tangible goods.[38] The sufficiency proviso has also been interpreted in two weak ways, each of which robs the theory of its moral appeal. The first interpretation narrows the scope of the common; the second narrows the group of persons who have access to the common. First, the scope of the enough-and-as-good requirement is narrowed to a level of subsistence.[39] Thus, weak sufficiency does not provide a right to use of the common, but merely provides a right to use whatever has not yet been appropriated from the common so long as all laborers can at least maintain subsistence.[40] Second, C.B. MacPherson has argued that Locke actually intended to narrow the group of people to

35. *See id.* §§ 46-50. *But see* WALDRON, *supra* note 17, at 224-25 (arguing against the need for societal consent to the money system).

36. LOCKE, SECOND TREATISE, *supra* note 1, § 14 (stating that the consent required for trade is insufficient to establish a civil government); *id.* §§ 15, 22, 95 (requiring the individual's "own Consent" to move to civil government).

37. In the ongoing debate between Filmer and Locke, Filmer argued that private property rights cannot be created when a strong no harm requirement is combined with a scarce common for tangible goods. *See* RYAN, *supra* note 1, at 16-17. Either the no harm proviso would be violated or the people "must sit back and starve." WALDRON, *supra* note 17, at 212-13. Locke put forth three arguments in an unsuccessful attempt to support a theory incorporating the strong sufficiency proviso. First, Locke introduced a subsistence proviso, stating that an individual has a right to subsistence that transcends others' rights to property removed from the common. LOCKE, SECOND TREATISE, *supra* note 1, § 25. Second, in America (at least in 1689) and during other periods of history, land was so abundant as compared to the number of people that even a strong sufficiency proviso would be upheld. *Id.* §§ 36-38. *But see* WALDRON, *supra* note 17, at 214 (arguing that property acquired through initial appropriation may violate the right for later persons to appropriate). Third, Locke argued that the people can bind themselves together through common consent in a civil government, where they can divide up the common. LOCKE, SECOND TREATISE, *supra* note 1, §§ 2-3. Unfortunately, these arguments fail to provide a morally compelling justification because they merely allow private ownership in historical times, provide a subsistence right in the modern era, or eliminate the natural law justification for private property rights independent of a civil government altogether.

38. It is in this situation that Lockean theory becomes subject to Ryan's objection that it "goes terribly wrong when applied to any goods whose supply cannot be expanded indefinitely." RYAN, *supra* note 21, at 69.

39. *See* WALDRON, *supra* note 17, at 153-57.

40. Under this interpretation, Locke's theory becomes a "First Labour" theory. *Id.* at 173-76.

whom the sufficiency proviso applies.[41] MacPherson claims that members of the laboring class were not seen as full members of society and therefore they could be ignored when considering the sufficiency proviso. To sum up, Lockean theory applied to tangible goods is thus ineffective under a strong interpretation of the sufficiency proviso and morally unappealing under a weak interpretation of the sufficiency proviso.

### A. *Fundamental Differences Between Tangible and Intangible Goods*

Fundamental differences between tangible and intangible goods have significant ramifications for the scope of private property rights justified by Lockean theories of property. Consider three types of goods: tangible goods, intangible goods, and tangible embodiments of intangible goods. The first difference is in the physical or nonphysical nature of the good. Tangible goods are composed of, and defined by reference to, tangible, physical materials. At the other extreme, intangible goods are composed of intangible, nonphysical materials and are defined conceptually rather than physically. Tangible embodiments of intangible goods are combinations of tangible and intangible goods, with the tangible good being used to communicate and store the intangible good.

A second difference between tangible goods, intangible goods, and tangible embodiments of intangible goods is the rivalrous or nonrivalrous nature of the goods. As defined by Paul Romer, "A purely rival good has the property that its use by one firm or person precludes its use by another; a purely nonrival good has the property that its use by one firm or person in no way limits its use by another."[42] Due to their physical nature, both tangible goods and tangible embodiments of intangible goods are rivalrous and thus can only be used by one person at a time. Intangible goods, however, are nonrivalrous, which means that at the same time different people may use the same intangible good in the same way or in different ways without affecting any other person's ability to use the intangible good.

A third difference is that only intangible goods may be obtained without harming the original holder's use value in the good. Tangible goods may be obtained in one of two ways: independent production or acquiring a tangible good from someone else. Intangible goods may also be obtained in those two ways: independent production or acquiring a tangible embodiment of an intangible good from someone else. The acquisition of a tangible good or a tangible embodiment of an intangible good from someone else deprives the initial holder of the use of that good. Intangible goods are different, however, in that an individual may make a copy of the

41. *See* MACPHERSON, *supra* note 5, at 222-24, 247.
42. Romer, *supra* note 18, at S73-S74.

intangible good using her own materials to create the tangible embodiment without depriving the initial holder of his use value in the good.[43]

These characteristics make intangible goods at once unlimited and singular. There are three ways in which an intangible good has unlimited qualities. First, a single intangible good may be used by an unlimited number of people at the same time. Second, an intangible good may be used in an unlimited number of ways at the same time. Third, once an intangible good has been created, it need never be produced again but can be copied. The initial productive labor is therefore expandable without limit. An intangible good is also inherently singular; each individual can have multiple tangible copies but can have only one unit of a single intangible good. Suppose one person has ten apples and ten copies of the movie *Gladiator*. If asked the question "Do you have an apple?" the person could reply "Yes. I have ten apples." If asked the question "Do you have the movie *Gladiator*?" the person could reply "Yes. I have ten copies of the movie *Gladiator*." The person could not, however, reply that he has ten copies of an apple or that he has ten movies called "*Gladiator*." The inability to state that one has ten movies called "*Gladiator*" shows the singularity of intangible goods in that each individual may only have one unit of an intangible good but may have multiple tangible embodiments of an intangible good, each of which is a "copy" of the others. Intangible goods are therefore quantified by their relation to individuals, but tangible embodiments of intangible goods are quantified by the number of physical copies.

The unlimited and singular characteristics of intangible goods can be modeled as a multidimensional space. I will consider two dimensions, the first of which is the unlimited number of potential users. The second dimension is the unlimited number of uses of the intangible good. Although other dimensions could also be considered,[44] each set of coordinates will define an "intangible unit" in this Note. The infinitely expandable initial productive labor also means that the whole intangible good space—the sum of the unlimited number of intangible units—is formed at the initial creation of an intangible good. Copying the intangible goods into tangible embodiments of intangible goods is the only labor that remains after the initial creation; independent production is not necessary.

Although intangible goods have always been nonrival, digital technology and the Internet have changed the ability to conceptualize the unlimited nature of intangible goods. First, use of the digital medium makes tangible embodiments of intangible goods much less tangible. John Perry

43. The initial holder of the intangible good may also make a copy, creating a tangible embodiment that she can convey to others.

44. An example of such an additional dimension would be time.

Barlow has argued that intangible goods in an Internet era are like wine without bottles, i.e., that tangible embodiments are no longer necessary, but that people can transmit "pure thought or something very much like thought: voltage conditions darting around the Net at the speed of light."[45] Second, it is also easier to envision an unlimited number of intangible units because it is not difficult to imagine a single copy of a popular song quickly multiplying into a million copies through the use of file-sharing programs at virtually no cost. Finally, the digital medium shows the high "plasticity" of intangible goods, which refers to the ability to use an intangible good in any number of adaptive ways.[46]

The conception of nonrivalry employed in this Note will be relatively thin, thereby avoiding many philosophical debates on the concept of the intangible good. I will assume that the intangible good can be defined independently of any human who possesses it.[47] An example of such a fungible intangible good might be a mathematical formula, whereas a Rorschach inkblot test is a paradigm example of an intangible good that is highly dependent on its relationship to specific individuals. Additionally, a thicker conception of intangible goods might include the requirement of some effort on the part of the recipient in order for an intangible unit to be created and transferred.[48] However, because this requirement does not influence the conclusions from the analysis in this Note, this thicker conception will not be considered.[49]

### B. *The Utility of a Lockean Common of Intangible Goods*

Locke's common of tangible goods consists of undeveloped tangible materials that are available to all and created by the "spontaneous hand of Nature."[50] Locke characterizes the undeveloped materials in the common as

45. John Perry Barlow, Selling Wine Without Bottles: The Economy of Mind on the Global Net, *at* http://www.eff.org/IP/idea_economy.article (last visited Nov. 12, 2002) (highlighting that "[d]igital technology is detaching information from the physical plane").

46. Pamela Samuelson, *Copyright, Digital Data, and Fair Use in Digital Networked Environments*, *in* THE ELECTRONIC SUPERHIGHWAY: THE SHAPE OF TECHNOLOGY AND LAW TO COME 117, 121-22 (Ejan Mackaay et al. eds., 1995).

47. Philosophical debates associated with the concept of an author are one example of where this assumption might not hold for all intangible goods. *See, e.g.*, Waldron, *supra* note 6, at 878 (arguing that deconstruction-of-the-author theories suggest that intangible goods aren't fungible across different people).

48. For example, if the intangible good is a scientific concept, such as the law of gravity, a thicker conception might posit that the intangible good has not been transferred unless the user of the good actually understands the concept.

49. If one considers a transaction between a seller and a buyer of an intangible good, the understanding requirement only adds costs to the buyer's side; it does not create an additional seller-side expense. Thus, the marginal cost of distributing these partially completed intangible goods is still zero, and the analysis of the Note holds.

50. *See* LOCKE, SECOND TREATISE, *supra* note 1, §§ 25-26, 34-36, 47-48.

"unassisted Nature,"[51] which have little immediate value but can be greatly enhanced in value through labor.[52] Examples of undeveloped materials in the common include land, animals, and wild fruit.[53] The fact that these are tangible goods means that they are rivalrous and that only one individual may use them at a time. Universal access to the common facilitates an "equality of opportunity"[54] to independently produce.

A Lockean "common of intangible goods"[55] differs in important respects from the Lockean common of tangible goods. The most important similarity, however, is that the common of intangible goods also consists only of undeveloped materials that are a product of the spontaneous hand of nature. Just as the common of tangible goods is characterized by Locke as "unassisted nature," one might characterize the common of intangible goods as "uncomprehended nature." Although it is difficult and somewhat unnecessary for purposes of this Note to determine what materials are contained in the common of intangible goods, these might include natural facts or mathematical proofs.[56] The most important difference between the common of intangible goods and the common of tangible goods is the nonrivalrous nature of the undeveloped intangible materials in the former. Nonrivalry means that there is infinite allocative capacity of materials contained in the common of intangible goods.[57] The result of the infinite

---

51. *Id.* § 42.

52. *Id.* § 37 ("For the provisions serving to the support of humane life, produced by one acre of inclosed and cultivated land, are . . . ten times more, than those, which are yielded by an acre of Land, of an equal richnesse, lyeing wast in the common.").

53. *Id.* §§ 25-26.

54. *See* Sterk, *supra* note 17, at 1234-35.

55. *See* Gordon, *supra* note 16, at 1555 (coining this phrase); *see also* Hughes, *supra* note 15, at 323 (describing a "common of potential ideas").

56. *See* Fisher, *supra* note 17, at 186 (discussing materials that might be included in a Lockean common of intangible goods). It might be easier to consider three types of intellectual labor and then work backward to determine whether the underlying materials can be characterized as uncomprehended nature. First, consider the intellectual labor of observing the natural world to obtain facts. Facts produced by observing the natural world certainly seem to be elements of a Lockean common. Second, consider logical reasoning. Explanations of natural phenomena derived by reasoning from known facts may seem to contain an intangible material that is a product of the "spontaneous hand of nature," but creative thought experiments about phenomena that have never occurred in nature are much less obviously a spontaneous product of nature. Third, one may combine observable facts with logical reasoning to produce what one might call an invention. These three types of labor correlate loosely with Shiffrin's description of three types of commons, which consist of mere discovery of existing intangible goods, a combination of human uniqueness with the subject matter of intangible goods, and creation ex nihilo, i.e., an empty common with human labor alone responsible for the creation of intangible goods. Shiffrin, *supra* note 17, at 158-66.

57. Provisioning refers to producing a good, whereas allocation refers to distributing an existing good to individuals. The common of intangible goods is surely expandable in the allocative sense. *See* Yochai Benkler, *Coase's Penguin, or, Linux and* The Nature of the Firm, 112 YALE L.J. 369, 438 (2002) ("Information production entails only a provisioning problem. Because information is nonrival, once it is produced no allocation problem exists."). A more difficult question is whether the common is infinitely expandable in the provisioning sense, i.e., whether there are an infinite number of potential intangible goods.

allocative capacity of undeveloped intangible goods is a much more robust ability to independently produce.

The emphasis that previous scholars have placed on the common of intangible goods and, by association, on the sufficiency proviso has been misplaced.[58] For example, Hughes noted that "ideas fit Locke's notion of a 'common' better than does physical property" because "the inexhaustibility condition is more satisfied; each idea can be used by an unlimited number of individuals."[59] As shown above, the nonrivalrous character of the common of intangible goods merely produces a strong ability to independently produce. The ability to independently produce is important, but it is much less important than the potential ability to use already developed intangible goods as inputs in the development of further intangible goods.[60] As examples, the nonrivalrous nature of a mathematical equation describing a physical law is useful not because everyone can figure it out on his or her own, but because everyone can use the law directly after one person has discovered it, and the nonrivalrous nature of books allows them to be used indirectly as inspirations for further works. The potential gains from using previously developed intangible goods in the development of further intangible goods may be larger for different types of intangible goods.[61]

Intellectual property scholars advocate more strongly for a robust public domain than for a Lockean common, but those scholars who have previously considered Lockean theory have largely conflated the two. A regime that would facilitate the use of developed intangible goods as inputs in the production of additional intangible goods is a public domain, which is a set of developed intangible goods that may be freely used by a set of individuals. A public domain is not equivalent to the Lockean common, however, because the Lockean common contains undeveloped materials, whereas a public domain contains developed goods. Gordon's analysis fails because she conflates the Lockean common with a public domain.[62] Barbara Friedman has described Gordon's conflation this way: "For Locke, the common property was an inheritance from God . . . . Gordon, by

58. *See, e.g.*, Gordon, *supra* note 16, at 1563 (emphasizing the Lockean proviso); Sterk, *supra* note 17, at 1235 (same).

59. Hughes, *supra* note 15, at 315.

60. *See generally* Suzanne Scotchmer, *Standing on the Shoulders of Giants: Cumulative Research and the Patent Law*, 5 J. ECON. PERSP. 29 (1991) (analyzing the importance of previous innovation on the scope of patent protection).

61. *See* Julie E. Cohen & Mark A. Lemley, *Patent Scope and Innovation in the Software Industry*, 89 CAL. L. REV. 1, 39-42 (2001) (arguing that the software industry is especially characterized by the reuse of previously developed code).

62. *See* Gordon, *supra* note 16, at 1559; *see also* Schaffner, *supra* note 17, at 1094, 1106-10.

contrast, in speaking of culture as a common of intangibles, is referring to works and ideas that are manifestly the product of human labor."[63]

To summarize, the nonrivalrous nature of intangible goods creates a robust common that can be used for independent production, but this common does not include intangible goods developed through human effort. As we shall see in the next Section, however, the nonrivalrous nature of intangible goods has important ramifications for Locke's waste prohibition, which does provide access to developed intangible goods.[64]

## C. *The Primacy of the Waste Prohibition*

Locke describes the waste prohibition as follows:

> Nothing was made by God for Man to spoil or destroy.
>
> . . . .
>
> . . . [H]e who gathered as much of the wild Fruit . . . by placing any of his Labor on them, did thereby acquire a Propriety in them: but if they perished, in his Possession, without their due use . . . he offended against the common Law of Nature, and was liable to be punished . . . .
>
> The same measures governed the Possession of Land too . . . . [I]f either the Grass of his Inclosure rotted on the Ground, or the Fruit of his planting perished without gathering, and laying up, this part of the Earth, notwithstanding his Inclosure, was still to be looked on as Waste, and might be the Possession of any other.
>
> . . . .
>
> . . . The exceeding of the bounds of his just Property [does not lie] in the largeness of his Possession, but the perishing of any thing uselessly in it.[65]

Various justifications for the waste prohibition have been posited. The only justification independent of the no harm principle, and the one that I

63. Friedman, *supra* note 17, at 166. Gordon claims that everyone has a Lockean natural right to the public domain, in which she includes "creations whose period of protection has expired." Gordon, *supra* note 16, at 1559. Her analysis conflates actions available under a civil government with those available in the state of nature because expiration of property rights in unabandoned property requires a forced taking, which only a government can legitimate.

64. The transition to civil government establishes the ability to create a public domain. *See infra* notes 156-159 and accompanying text.

65. LOCKE, SECOND TREATISE, *supra* note 1, §§ 31, 37-38, 46; *see also* WALDRON, *supra* note 17, at 161 (arguing that waste amounts to abandonment of the property).

adopt for this Note, is that the waste prohibition is an objective moral criterion, i.e., waste is wrong, or, in Lockean terms, "Nothing was made by God for Man to spoil or destroy." Alan Ryan claims that this independent justification for the waste prohibition was Locke's primary intention.[66] Compelling moral support for this interpretation can be found in the patent drug debate that is discussed in more detail in Subsection III.C.2. Two additional justifications, however, can be gathered from Locke's discussion. First, the waste prohibition seems to recognize a scarcity of resources, as Locke argues that the waste prohibition prevents a person from "ingross[ing] as much as he will."[67] Second, wasted goods harm the laborer herself because she has wasted her labor that was mixed into the good.[68] These additional justifications will not be considered in this Note; the first because it does not apply to a common of intangible goods, and the second because the no harm principle can be largely alienated from the individual in a transition to a civil government, but the objective moral criterion remains binding even after a transition.

The waste prohibition is violated if the laborer does not take advantage of the use value that he has added through his labor for both easily spoilable and relatively nonspoilable goods. First, the individual may allow a good prone to spoil, such as wild fruit, to rot in his possession. Second, the individual may waste a good that is not prone to spoil, such as land, if he does not take advantage of the use value that he has added through his labor. The second type of waste can be discerned from the above quotation in that it is not only the grass or the fruit but also the land that is lost when the products of labor are not put to their due use. The use value may be directly related to the property, such as the consumptive value of owned fruit, or it may be indirectly related to the property, such as the use value of crops grown on owned land.

I posit the following definition of waste under Lockean theory: Waste occurs where a unit of a product of labor is not put to any use. This definition focuses on Locke's concern that goods be put to their due use. The rivalrous nature of tangible goods means that questions of divisibility—i.e., determining what constitutes a unit—will be difficult but important in ascertaining violations of the waste prohibition. For example, allowing one tract of a farmer's land to lie fallow for a time in order to preserve its later productiveness might not violate the waste prohibition, whereas letting some portion of a farmer's harvested crop spoil would violate the waste prohibition. The nonrivalrous nature of intangible goods

66. RYAN, *supra* note 1, at 37 (finding that the waste prohibition teaches that "things have certain natural and proper uses, such that it would be perverse to use them otherwise").

67. LOCKE, SECOND TREATISE, *supra* note 1, § 31.

68. Hughes, *supra* note 15, at 327-28.

means that intangible goods are divisible without limit, with the fundamental unit being the intangible unit defined above.[69]

The penalty associated with a violation of the waste prohibition is the loss of exclusionary property rights in the good, but the prohibition does not create an affirmative duty to prevent waste.[70] If only part of the good is wasted, property rights are only lost for that portion of the good that is wasted.[71] An example is a landowner who harvests ninety percent of the land but is unable to use the remaining ten percent of the crops. The way in which this penalty is enforced will depend on whether the laborer is acting in the state of nature or under a civil government. In the state of nature, enforcement of natural law rights is left up to individuals, or in Locke's words, "in the State of Nature, every one has the Executive Power of the Law of Nature."[72] In the state of nature, therefore, the waste prohibition is enforced by individuals who act in individual self-interest in seeking the property. Although Lockean theory normally forbids individuals from taking the property of another, the enforcement mechanism for the waste prohibition is that the wasted good may "be the Possession of any other."[73]

Just as Locke can claim for private property rights that a person who appropriates from a nonscarce common "does as good as take nothing at all"[74] from the common, an individual who polices the waste prohibition can be said to have done as good as take nothing at all from the owner. Only where the laborer obtains no use value from a good must he allow

69. Hughes describes a more limited scope for the applicability of the waste prohibition for intangible goods. *See id.* at 327-29. He argues that, unlike food, ideas are not perishable because they always retain some inherent future value as compared to the absolute loss associated with food spoilage. He also argues that so long as there is no harm to the laborer—i.e., that the labor produced an overall benefit to the laborer—limiting distribution of intangible goods does not violate the waste prohibition. Hughes's analysis is flawed for two important reasons. First, he ignores the nonrivalrous characteristic of intangible goods. Due to the unlimited number of intangible units, limiting the ability of users to obtain copies of the intangible good does result in the kind of absolute loss that he describes for food. Second, waste to the individual is only one of three alternative ways of conceiving of the waste prohibition. He misses the fact that although an individual might be perfectly satisfied with the level of use to which the good has been put, if the intangible units are not put to their due use, a violation of the waste prohibition has occurred.

Hettinger comes closer to the analysis presented in this Note. He argues that placing a nonzero price on intangible goods is "clearly wasteful," stating that "[h]ow wasteful private ownership of intellectual property is depends on how beneficial those products would be to those who are excluded from their use as a result." Hettinger, *supra* note 17, at 44-45. He fails, however, to draw any conclusions from this analysis, to consider the important relationship of money to the waste prohibition, or to recognize the importance of the waste prohibition applying to a portion of the goods rather than the use of the good being partially wasteful.

70. LOCKE, SECOND TREATISE, *supra* note 1, §§ 36-37.

71. *See id.* § 46 (arguing that a laborer can avoid violating the waste prohibition by giving "away a part to any body else").

72. *Id.* § 13. Problems associated with self-bias and limited enforcement power will be considered in more detail in Section III.A, which discusses enforceability as a reason to move into a civil government.

73. *Id.* § 38.

74. *Id.* § 33.

others access to it under the waste prohibition. Conversely, if the laborer receives no use value from the good, another will do no injury to the laborer—and thus, will not violate the taking prohibition—by taking the good.[75] In other words, only where the laborer violates the waste prohibition can another take the good without violating the taking prohibition. Therefore, justified taking can be seen as a natural way to police the waste prohibition.[76]

## II. A LOCKEAN THEORY OF FAIR USE IN THE STATE OF NATURE

Property rights are maintained if one uses the products of labor, but Locke argues that trading a good for money, which I will call "money substitution," also avoids the waste prohibition. Locke asserts that the invention of money effectively eliminates violations of the waste prohibition because perishable goods can be exchanged for nonperishable money.[77] This argument holds so long as Locke's assumption that laborers are willing and able to limit their production to goods that they can use or sell is plausible, which it is for tangible goods.[78] As this Part will show by applying Locke's waste prohibition in a modern economic framework,[79] this assumption fails for intangible goods. In fact, a producer of intangible goods acting in her self-interest will purposely violate the waste prohibition. The primary distinction is that a laborer can limit the number of copies of a tangible good, whereas the creation of an intangible good produces an unlimited number of intangible units.

75. In some cases, the good cannot be taken without harming the owner. Here, the owner's refusal to allow taking can be seen as avoiding a harm. Thus, it can be argued that he is obtaining some value because a harm is being avoided. Preventing arbitrage may be an example of a reason to prevent copying even where the intangible good is ostensibly being wasted. For a more systematic treatment of these arguments, see *supra* notes 115-116 and accompanying text.

76. For a discussion of situations where the laborer and the enforcers have conflicting natural rights, see *supra* notes 119-120 and accompanying text.

77. LOCKE, SECOND TREATISE, *supra* note 1, §§ 46-47 (explaining that money is "some lasting thing that Men might keep without spoiling" as compared to the "greatest part of things really useful to the Life of Man" that are "generally things of short duration"); MACPHERSON, *supra* note 5, at 204 (arguing that the waste limitation "seemed to Locke to be obviously transcended by the introduction of money"). Locke also claims that the introduction of money opens up the world to greater appropriation. LOCKE, SECOND TREATISE, *supra* note 1, §§ 48-50. Although Locke is correct to some extent that money acts as a magnifier or release valve, the introduction of money is just one portion of the gains from a market system.

78. Locke's reliance on both the ability and desire to limit production can be implied from the following statement: "Supposing an Island . . . [w]hat reason could any one have there to enlarge his Possessions beyond the use of his Family, and a plentiful supply to its Consumption . . . ?" LOCKE, SECOND TREATISE, *supra* note 1, § 48.

79. The application of Lockean principles in an economic framework does not change the natural rights character of the argument into a utilitarian analysis. Scholars who have similarly applied Lockean principles in a modern economic framework include Nozick and John Stick. *See* NOZICK, *supra* note 14, at 178-82; John Stick, *Turning Rawls into Nozick and Back Again*, 81 NW. U. L. REV. 363, 396-99 (1987) (considering the implications of the sufficiency proviso primarily on the transfer of tangible goods).

The waste prohibition requires that each unit either be put to some use or sold to retain a property right in the good. In other words, property rights are lost to the extent that the laborer does not achieve "total money substitution," which I will define as the conversion into money of all units of a product of labor that an individual will not personally use. External factors, including the demand curve for the good, will determine the maximum price that the laborer can charge to achieve total money substitution. External factors also determine whether the laborer is a price taker—meaning that the amount of goods that the laborer offers to sell does not influence the price that the laborer can charge—or, at the other extreme, whether the laborer can act as a monopolist.

This Part will begin by considering only two ideal-type market situations: price taking or monopoly power. Additionally, it will be limited to considering two potential choices by the laborer: how many goods to produce and at what price to sell the goods. Although the analysis in this Note is similar to Locke's own argument in sections 46 to 51, I set out Locke's assumptions more explicitly and consider more carefully a laborer's likely pricing decisions. The assumption that all goods are sold at a single market price is followed in Section II.A but will be relaxed when price discrimination is considered in Section II.B. Enforceability will be assumed throughout this Part, but will be considered in the analysis of Part III. The demand curve for the good will be assumed static and known. I will assume, following Locke, that laborers generally act in their self-interest.[80]

## A. *Waste-Prohibition-Based Lockean Fair Use*

### 1. *Nonviolation of the Waste Prohibition in Markets of Tangible Goods*

In a market for a tangible good, the laborer can limit the number of units of a specific good produced and can set the price of the units.[81] Although the laborers are able to set their prices freely, their choice will be influenced by the valuation that individual buyers place on the good. The most common method for analyzing this valuation is the estimation of a

80. This assumption coheres with the self-interested rationality evident throughout Locke's treatment. *See, e.g.*, LOCKE, SECOND TREATISE, *supra* note 1, §§ 123-124; *see also* Moore, *Intangible Property*, *supra* note 17, at 369 (describing laborers as "rational project pursuers" with a "wide range of value theories"). This weak rationality requirement does not incorporate the concept of opportunity cost, which would require the laborer not only to produce the optimum amount of a specific good, but would require the laborer to choose the good that would bring her the greatest aggregate wealth.

81. There may be certain constraints on the ability of laborers to limit production of tangible goods. A famous example from literature occurs in *The Grapes of Wrath* where oranges are destroyed in order to keep up the price despite the existence of a "million people hungry." JOHN STEINBECK, THE GRAPES OF WRATH 473-77 (Viking Penguin 1989) (1939).

demand curve, which is an aggregation of the heterogeneous valuations of a specific good by the individual potential buyers. A demand curve does not vary in relation to changes in price but does vary for different goods.[82]

First, consider a laborer who is a price taker. As a price taker, such a laborer may continue to produce goods without considering whether he will violate the waste prohibition. So long as the laborer sells his goods at or below the market price, all the goods will be sold, resulting in total money substitution and no loss of property rights. Within these limits, a laborer acting in his self-interest will continue to produce units until the marginal cost of producing the last unit equals the market price and will set a price equal to, rather than below, the market price.

Second, consider a monopolist laborer. By limiting the number of goods produced, the laborer can charge a higher price and obtain the monopoly rent. Although monopolies are inefficient from a social-economic perspective, they do not violate the Lockean waste prohibition. In common economic analysis, the economic loss associated with monopolistic pricing is called a deadweight loss. As an opportunity cost, this is a real economic loss; however, Locke's waste prohibition does not apply directly to all opportunity costs. For example, one does not violate the waste prohibition by removing too little out of the common. Additionally, no punishment can be justified under Locke's theory if one chooses to gather apples rather than oranges, even if oranges have a higher tradable value.

The preceding analysis showed that for all practical purposes the waste prohibition will never be violated for tangible goods. Although the price at which the laborer sells the good is dependent on external factors such as the demand curve and the type of pricing available to the laborer, laborers acting in their self-interest will have no incentive to produce goods that they do not sell. Laborers may sell at or below the efficient market price if they are price takers and may sell at or below the monopoly rent-maximizing price without violating the waste prohibition.

---

82. Factors that may cause a shift in the demand curve include a change in the price of substitutable goods, shifts in tastes, or increased income levels among the potential purchasers. PAUL A. SAMUELSON & WILLIAM D. NORDHAUS, ECONOMICS 38-42 (15th ed. 1995) (describing demand curve basics). The creation of a robust Lockean fair use right may shift the demand curve downward because a downward move in the price of a substitutable good will create a downward shift in the demand of the original good, and the creation of a vibrant fair use right adds a set of intangible goods that the user can get for free. The magnitude of this shift will depend on the substitutability of the intangible goods, which depends on a variety of factors. On the other hand, some intangible goods might actually become more valuable as the set of goods available to an individual increases. *See* Benkler, *supra* note 57, at 415-23 (demonstrating that there are increasing returns to scale when the set of available informational resources is increased). This downward shift may influence the profitability of any single intangible good but will not eliminate the existence of low-value users and uses.

### 2. *A Lockean Fair Use in Markets of Intangible Goods*

Recent technological changes have facilitated the ability to imagine a market for an intangible good rather than a market for a tangible embodiment of an intangible good. A paradigm example of a money-based transfer of a tangible embodiment of an intangible good is the purchase of a CD, which includes the purchase of both an intangible unit and a corresponding tangible embodiment. A market for an intangible good, however, would involve trade of only the intangible good. On the Internet, one no longer needs to purchase a CD in order to purchase a song, but a buyer and seller each connected to the Internet can transmit "pure thought or something very much like thought."[83] Even though individual copies—tangible embodiments—are being traded on the Internet, the conceptual jump to a true market for intangible goods is smaller than it has historically been.

Another important implication of recent technological changes is the decreasing marginal cost of creation and transmission of such goods. The marginal cost of producing an intangible unit is zero, whereas the marginal cost of producing a tangible copy embodied in a CD is some positive amount.[84] The marginal cost of producing an intangible unit is zero because an inherent quality of nonrivalrous goods is that a very large number of intangible units have already been produced. Returning to the Internet example, if the buyer and seller each have access to the Internet, the marginal cost of producing a copy—a tangible embodiment—of the song also approaches zero. Neglecting costs associated with transaction costs, such as collecting payment, a seller incurs virtually no additional cost whether a single person or a million people copy the music.

Applying Locke's waste prohibition to intangible units also makes changes to baseline framework considerations. First, the determination of how many units must be sold in order to achieve total money substitution is altered. For tangible goods, one must use or sell all units of the good. For intangible goods, there are as many intangible units as there are potential

83. Barlow, *supra* note 45.

84. Mark Lemley and David McGowan explain:

> The "marginal cost" of a new copy of Microsoft Windows is the cost of the disk (a few cents), the labor required to copy it (essentially none), and the cost of the manuals, packaging, and distribution of the box itself to consumers (by far the largest portion). Software distributed on the Internet has *essentially no marginal cost*, as it can be downloaded by consumers on their own time, albeit with some commitment of computer resources by the supplier.

Mark A. Lemley & David McGowan, *Legal Implications of Network Economic Effects*, 86 CAL. L. REV. 479, 595 n.484 (1998) (emphasis added); *see also* Robert M. Weiss & Ajay K. Mehrotra, *Online Dynamic Pricing: Efficiency, Equity and the Future of E-Commerce*, 6 VA. J.L. & TECH. 11, ¶ 17 (Summer 2001), *at* http://www.vjolt.net/vol6/issue2/v6i2-all-Weiss.html (finding that the "digital economy is filled with numerous firms defined by a structure of high fixed costs and low marginal costs").

users, but only a portion of those users will place a nonnegative value on the intangible unit. Although waste occurs whenever an intangible unit is not put to any use, the waste prohibition is enforced by individuals in the state of nature, and no individual who values the good at less than zero will exert effort to obtain a copy. If a property right is defined as the ability to exclude and one is able to exclude all persons who would potentially want to purchase or use the good, then, effectively, no property rights have been lost. Therefore, total money substitution for intangible goods is best defined as all nonnegative demand being fulfilled. Second, a laborer in intangible goods may still choose the price at which to sell, but a laborer cannot limit the number of units of an intangible good that he produces. This is unlike a laborer in tangible goods, who can control whether he makes five cars or ten thousand.

Again consider a price-taking laborer, this time in a market for an intangible good. A laborer's inability to influence the price is primarily due to competition in the market. Competition occurs in a market for a distinct intangible good if a number of people are selling the same good.[85] Competition is more likely to result if the intangible good is not relatively unique—that is, others are easily able to independently produce the good. Assuming negligible transaction costs, as may be achievable on the Internet, the price set in a competitive market for an intangible good will be zero[86] because the marginal cost of producing an additional unit of the nonrivalrous good is zero. Therefore, a competitive market for an intangible good destroys the laborer's profitability. This ex post destruction of profitability also removes the ex ante incentive to produce the good when viewed from a dynamic perspective.[87]

If the intangible good is relatively unique—difficult to independently produce—the laborer might be able to act as a monopolist. If the laborer can act as a monopolist and set a positive price, she may be able to garner

85. While not defined as competition, the demand curve, and therefore the price of the good, will also be influenced by the existence of substitutable goods in other markets. *See supra* note 82.

86. *See* Kenneth J. Arrow, *Economic Welfare and the Allocation of Resources for Invention*, *in* NAT'L BUREAU OF ECON. RESEARCH, THE RATE AND DIRECTION OF INVENTIVE ACTIVITY: ECONOMIC AND SOCIAL FACTORS 609, 614-15 (1962).

87. The argument generally proceeds in the following manner. Unless some kind of a "monopoly" can be obtained for the intangible good, the good will not be ex post profitable to the laborer. If the laborer does not anticipate ex post rewards, then she will not devote the ex ante effort to produce it. Therefore, the intangible good will not be produced in the first instance.

One way in which this problem might be partially solved is to consider competition gradually increasing over time. For example, a laborer might initially be able to demand a monopoly price, which will be dissipated over time as additional market entrants force the price to zero. In such a case, the initial sale of the good will generate money substitution in some finite portion of the units of the intangible good, which may be sufficient to create the necessary ex ante incentive to produce. As time goes on, competition will increase until the market price reaches a level at which it is no longer profitable for the laborer to trade in the good.

profits from the venture.[88] However, the establishment of a monopoly price excludes those persons who value the intangible good at above the marginal cost of production but below the price set by the laborer. Such a person will be called a "low-value user" in this Note. As the intangible units have already been produced, the choice to refuse to sell units of the intangible good violates the waste prohibition and results in the loss of property rights in those specific units. This violation can be enforced by the corresponding low-value users.[89] The quantity of this loss coincides with the amount of the deadweight loss described in the previous Section, although unfulfilled demand for intangible goods is more than a mere opportunity cost because the intangible units have already been produced.

The application of these ideal-type pricing mechanisms to intangible goods demonstrates that the goal of a self-interested laborer is not to obtain total market substitution, even at the cost of a loss of property rights in a portion of the units of the intangible good. In fact, in order to gain any revenue in a single-price market, the laborer must violate the waste prohibition. The problems generally associated with monopolies may even be more acute for intangible goods because the loss associated with monopolistic behavior may be higher for intangible goods.[90]

The result of the laborer's decision not to set the price at zero in order to effectuate total market substitution, reasonable though it may be, creates a fair use right. All those persons who value the good above zero but below the laborer's price can justifiably copy the good without reimbursing the laborer, although these low-value users must make the copy at their own cost, not the cost of the laborer.[91] Just as the laborer's actions in producing

88. In fact, a cost of copying equal to zero suggests that a monopolist might be able to garner significant profits from the sale of an intangible good.

89. Potential purchasers—those who value the good at above the monopoly price—would violate the taking prohibition if they made an illicit copy because they would impose a harm on the laborer: the lost profits. However, taking by low-value users cannot violate the taking prohibition because the laborer will lose no profits from the sale.

90. *See* Yochai Benkler, *An Unhurried View of Private Ordering in Information Transactions*, 53 VAND. L. REV. 2063, 2066-69 (2000) (citing factors such as high uncertainty, positive externalities, and budget constraints that increase deadweight losses and are often pronounced for intangible goods).

91. The fair use right in turn may influence the ability to determine true valuation because it allows an individual to gain access to the good without actually revealing the level at which the individual values the good. Although economists might be able to predict reasonably accurate demand curves, even where demand has not been explicitly revealed, this aggregate information will not be helpful in determining which specific individuals are low-value users on a case-by-case basis. An underlying concern here is that individuals will then have an incentive to disguise their true valuation. Although this type of system gaming can be cabined into an enforceability concern and saved for Part III, the concern may be more problematic than mere enforceability because an individual's true valuation might not be knowable except as a revealed preference. If one has the alternative of either paying a price for a good or getting the good for free (through the fair use right), one will "reveal" the fact that one prefers free use. In other words, it may not be that individuals will lie in bad faith about their valuation, but that they will be unable to determine their actual valuation of the intangible good without having to choose between alternatives.

the good create a moral, natural-law-based property right in the good, the laborer's pricing actions may create a moral, natural-law-based fair use right in others. Gordon's conclusion that "[a]voiding 'deadweight loss' is a natural right only if the public has a right to free copying" and that the public "has no such right"[92] is incorrect. First, a laborer has no right to exclude individuals from unused or unsold intangible units because she has no property right in such goods. Therefore, a focus on the public's right may be deceiving because the laborer herself does not have a property right in those intangible units. Second, even if the public as a whole does not have a right to free copying, some individuals within the public, the low-value users, will have a right to enforce the waste prohibition against the property owner.

### 3. *Nonmarketed Intangible Goods and Nonmarketed Uses of Intangible Goods*

Some intangible goods do not directly fit the market model of the preceding Subsection. First, consider intangible goods that are indirectly, not directly, valuable to the laborer. These "enabling intangible goods" are valuable for the way that they enable the production of other goods, intangible or not. A Lockean example of such a good in the waste prohibition context is land harvested for fruit.[93] Other examples of such goods include a chemical process that creates a tangible chemical product, a compression technology used to store a tangible embodiment of intangible digital photographs, and an intangible cast of characters used in a movie sequel. In order to determine the scope of a waste prohibition violation in relation to these enabling intangible goods, one should look at whether the end product is being wasted. If the laborer has a monopoly in the end product, then the waste prohibition will be violated for the underlying enabling good. One reason that these enabling goods might be used to develop monopolies rather than licensing the use of the enabling goods to other producers was described by Kenneth Arrow, who argued that

Solutions to these two problems are likely to take the form of the methods of price discrimination described in Section II.B. For example, one might develop a postpurchase objective test that measures the amount of time and attention that one devotes to the good, such as how often one listens to the CD. Violations of privacy, however, may prohibit the ability and desirability of using this type of postpurchase value determination. *See* Julie E. Cohen, *A Right To Read Anonymously: A Closer Look at "Copyright Management" in Cyberspace*, 28 CONN. L. REV. 981 (1996).

92. Gordon, *supra* note 16, at 1549. Others who have argued against a Lockean fair use right have also largely ignored the waste prohibition. *See, e.g.*, Lacey, *supra* note 17, at 1564 (asserting that the fair use doctrine is "totally unjustifiable" because of the "absolutist proposition" required by Lockean property rights, without, however, considering the waste prohibition); Moore, *Lockean Theory*, *supra* note 17, at 98 (arguing, without citing the waste prohibition, that there "should be no mandatory government legislated policy of fair use").

93. LOCKE, SECOND TREATISE, *supra* note 1, § 38.

information will not be purchased until it is known, but if it is known, it cannot be sold.[94] In other words, it may be that some intangible goods cannot be effectively sold in a market. As compared to directly copying the intangible good, enforcement of the waste prohibition for enabling intangible goods will be accomplished through what is commonly called reverse engineering. In other words, a user will examine the end product in an attempt to determine the process by which it was developed—that is, the underlying enabling intangible good.

Second, there will be specific intangible goods or specific uses of intangible goods[95] that are not valuable enough to make trading in the good worthwhile, either in a market or through direct contracting.[96] As the good or use of the good is not marketed at all, the user would maintain a full fair use right to enforce the waste prohibition. A common example of an intangible good for which there is not likely to be enough aggregate demand to justify negotiating between laborers and users is an out-of-print book. Analogously, there will also be certain uses for which there is such little aggregate demand that negotiation costs would actually be greater than the value of the use. These will be called "low-value uses" in this Note. An example of a low-value use might be the use of a poster as part of the background in a theatrical set.[97]

### B. *Perfect Price Discrimination as a Means of Eliminating Fair Use*

A laborer may be able to limit the scope of the fair use right through price discrimination. Price discrimination occurs when the seller charges "different prices to buyers when the price difference cannot be explained by a cost difference in supplying" the good.[98] Although the social and economic merits of price discrimination for intangible goods are contested,[99] there are definite implications for the Lockean waste

94. Arrow, *supra* note 86, at 609, 614-16.

95. Property rights to use intangible goods in specific ways can be individually marketed. A laborer may market the ability to use an intangible good in one way at a certain price and another way at a different price. For example, the owner of a Broadway musical might sell the rights to listen to the music on a CD for a relatively small amount and sell the rights to perform the musical for a relatively large amount.

96. Although the impetus is on the laborer to offer the good for sale in order to avoid violating the waste prohibition, a user who values the good at a high enough level to offset negotiation costs may be under a duty to self-identify as a potential purchaser of a relatively low-value use.

97. *But cf.* Ringgold v. Black Entm't Television, Inc., 126 F.3d 70 (2d Cir. 1997) (holding that the use of a poster of a quilt as set decoration on a television program did not qualify as fair use).

98. Michael J. Meurer, *Copyright Law and Price Discrimination*, 23 CARDOZO L. REV. 55, 58 (2001). For a detailed analysis of price discrimination, see JEAN TIROLE, THE THEORY OF INDUSTRIAL ORGANIZATION 133-68 (1988).

99. *Compare* Meurer, *supra* note 98, at 90-102 (describing distributional and allocative efficiency problems with price discrimination), *with* William W. Fisher III, *Property and Contract*

prohibition. Perfect price discrimination is defined as the case where the seller sets an individual price for each buyer that is equal to the buyer's valuation of the good. In this situation, each buyer who values the good at a positive amount will purchase the good, resulting in total money substitution, no violation of the waste prohibition, and no free use by individuals (except perhaps those individuals who value the good at exactly zero).[100] Yochai Benkler argues, however, that in practice all price discrimination will be "lumpy."[101] Imperfect price discrimination, where some but not all of the demand is satisfied, may lower the amount of the waste-prohibition violation but does not eliminate it entirely.

In order to price-discriminate, a seller must be able to link different prices to buyers with different valuations.[102] Economists have classified methodologies into three categories: first-, second-, and third-degree price discrimination.[103] First-degree price discrimination is the ideal case where the value of the buyer is known without effort—i.e., under the assumption of perfect information. First-degree price discrimination is also equated with perfect price discrimination.[104]

Second- and third-degree price discrimination correlate objective factors with a buyer's valuation and therefore result in imperfect price discrimination. Second-degree price discrimination uses product differentiation to sort users with different valuations. Three objective product distinctions are common when performing second-degree price discrimination: time, quantity, and quality. A seller who releases an initial high-cost version of a good, such as the sale of CDs in a music store, followed by subsequent low-cost distribution, such as the sale of CDs in a music club, uses time to accomplish second-degree price discrimination. A seller who controls the number of times a user may use the good, such as admission to a movie, accomplishes second-degree price discrimination through quantity. Finally, a seller might also offer lower-quality goods to users who value the good less.

Third-degree price discrimination employs objective buyer characteristics to differentiate potential valuation. Characteristics of

*on the Internet*, 73 CHI.-KENT L. REV. 1203, 1234-40 (1998) (claiming distributional and allocative efficiency gains from price discrimination).

100. Although under perfect price discrimination the seller gets to appropriate all of the surplus, an alternate pricing scheme could achieve total money substitution. Consider an example with three potential buyers: *A* values the good at $V_a$, *B* values the good at $V_b$, and *C* values the good at $V_c$. Assume that the marginal cost of production is the same for these three goods and is equal to $c$. If $p_n$ is the price of the good offered to each user, total money substitution will result so long as $c < p_a < V_a$, $c < p_b < V_b$, and $c < p_c < V_c$, whereas perfect price discrimination demands that $p_a = V_a$, $p_b = V_b$, and $p_c = V_c$.

101. Benkler, *supra* note 90, at 2072.

102. Other requirements include the existence of market power and the ability to prevent arbitrage. Meurer, *supra* note 98, at 59.

103. *See* TIROLE, *supra* note 98, at 135; Meurer, *supra* note 98, at 67-75.

104. TIROLE, *supra* note 98, at 135.

individuals or entities that might be relevant in determining their valuation include socioeconomic status, which is likely to correlate roughly with the ability to pay for goods and may itself also be correlated to other objective factors such as student or senior status. The type of use might also indicate differences in valuation, such as differential pricing for commercial, as compared to personal, use of software packages. Additionally, differential valuation may be correlated to some extent with geographical boundaries.

A Lockean waste prohibition perspective on price discrimination yields two results. First, it suggests an inversion of the common relationship between price discrimination and user rights. Michael Meurer argues that the "relationship between [user] rights and price discrimination is simple—broad user rights impede price discrimination."[105] Under a Lockean analysis, however, it is the choice or the inability to obtain perfect price discrimination that creates the fair use right in the first instance. Second, although first-degree price discrimination will completely fulfill the requirements of the waste prohibition, second- and third-degree price discrimination violate the waste prohibition to some extent due to their lumpiness. Some methods of price discrimination, especially second-degree price discrimination, also violate the waste prohibition to a greater degree. If price discrimination is accomplished through marketing an inferior good, the waste prohibition has been violated as to the difference in quality between the two goods in addition to the violations pertaining to low-value uses and users.

### C. *Culture as a Basis for a Lockean Fair Use Right*

This Section will consider culture as an alternative means of justifying a Lockean fair use right. Lockean theorists, most notably Wendy Gordon, have argued for a Lockean right to cultural fair use.[106] Gordon emphasizes access to a common of intangible goods and the public domain as well as compliance with the strong sufficiency proviso.[107] First, she argues that restricted access to those developed intangible goods that are part of the society's culture constitutes a harm because culture is a part of the Lockean

105. Meurer, *supra* note 98, at 61.

106. A postmodern Lockean argument for a right to cultural fair use identifies the public as a collective identity that participates in the authorship of intangible goods. Steven Wilf, *Who Authors Trademarks?*, 17 CARDOZO ARTS & ENT. L.J. 1, 6-10 (1999). *But see* Waldron, *supra* note 6, at 862 (claiming that natural law theory focuses on individuals). In a discussion of trademarks, Steven Wilf emphasizes the dynamic communication between the public and the trademark owner. In order for the trademark to be owned, it must have acquired secondary meaning, defined as recognition by the public. Wilf, *supra*, at 32-36. Therefore, Wilf argues that because the public participates in authoring the trademark, it should be granted a partial natural law property right in the good as a coauthor. *Id.* at 1-6.

107. Gordon, *supra* note 16, at 1563 ("The proviso . . . lies at the center of this Article's thesis.").

common.[108] As explained earlier, Gordon's argument fails, however, because she conflates the Lockean common of intangible goods, which is limited to undeveloped intangible goods, with culture, which is composed of developed intangible goods.[109] Second, Gordon argues that a person who independently produces an intangible good may harm another by making that person's holdings less valuable.[110] Given the existence of the independent production right and Locke's explicit allowance for great disparities in talent and wealth, this type of relativistic no harm principle does not cohere with Locke's theory.[111]

A cultural fair use right may be analyzed more appropriately through Locke's removal requirement and by consulting the independent production principle in a different way than Gordon. Locke requires that the laborer remove the good from the common in order to exclude others.[112] Removal of tangible goods in an abundant common consists of (1) physically separating a rivalrous good out of the common and (2) using methods of exclusion to maintain separation. Although physical removal is impossible for intangible goods, one can exclude others by controlling access through secrecy.[113] Finally, the exclusion must be maintained, which can be accomplished, for example, through agreements for postpurchase nondisclosure.[114] Loss of exclusivity may involve several stages, whereby the intangible good progressively becomes less and less secret.[115]

---

108. *Id.* at 1559, 1562-63, 1593.

109. *See supra* notes 62-63 and accompanying text.

110. Gordon, *supra* note 16, at 1567-68; *see also* Waldron, *supra* note 6, at 876-82 (arguing that because "we constantly compare ourselves to others," a relative difference in wealth may cause emotional harm).

111. *See* Sterk, *supra* note 17, at 1234 (describing Lockean theory as an "equality of opportunity theory" rather than a theory of relative equality). A relativistic notion that Locke does use is a comparison between individuals in the state of nature and under civil government. *See* LOCKE, SECOND TREATISE, *supra* note 1, § 137.

112. LOCKE, SECOND TREATISE, *supra* note 1, § 27. Emphasizing the removal requirements, Robert Bone concludes that natural rights theory is a "formalistic theory of property rights that equates property with factual exclusivity." Robert G. Bone, *A New Look at Trade Secret Law: Doctrine in Search of Justification*, 86 CAL. L. REV. 241, 304 (1998).

113. *See* Andrew Beckerman-Rodau, *Are Ideas Within the Traditional Definition of Property?: A Jurisprudential Analysis*, 47 ARK. L. REV. 603, 627-31 (1994) ("The requirement that a trade secret must not be generally known is merely another way of determining whether the trade secret owner has possession of the know-how comprising the trade secret."); Bone, *supra* note 112, at 252-58 (describing the emergence of trade secret law in the United States under a natural rights theory that follows generally the structure outlined in this Note).

Hughes mischaracterizes the process of removal. He implicitly asserts that removal of an idea or fact also removes the ability to independently produce it. *See* Hughes, *supra* note 15, at 314. Controlling access to the intangible good through secrecy does not allow others to appropriate it immediately, but it also does not keep others from independently discovering the same idea.

114. *See generally* Steven Cherensky, Comment, *A Penny for Their Thoughts: Employee-Inventors, Preinvention Assignment Agreements, Property, and Personhood*, 81 CAL. L. REV. 595 (1993) (discussing the importance of such nondisclosure agreements).

115. *But see* Schaffner, *supra* note 17, at 1127 (claiming that Lockean theory is limited to property exclusive against the world or to a common exclusionary against no one).

Alternatively, one can view the secrecy requirement through the lens of the independent production principle. For an easily communicated intangible good, merely showing the good may be enough to transfer the good, as "some inventions 'infect' one immediately with knowledge of their workings."[116] One result of such an immediate infection is that the person would not subsequently be able to independently produce the idea. As the independent production right is a requirement of Lockean theory, a laborer must not reveal an intangible good before a purchase agreement has been made or else he loses his property rights in that good.

Property rights in widely disseminated cultural goods are not tenable under Lockean theory because elements of a culture cannot be kept secret. For example, the right to describe one's surroundings, an example used by Gordon, would fit into this category.[117] As advocated by Jeremy Waldron, where a privately held intangible good is "thrust out into the cultural world to impinge on the consciousness of all of us," the owner could be seen as having abandoned the good into the public domain rather than having removed it from the common.[118]

The removal requirement also highlights an important tension in the state of nature. Labor mixing provides a right for laborers to exclude others from the good. This exclusion can be enforced by what Locke calls an "Inclosure"[119]—analogous to a wall or fence for tangible goods—instead of merely relying on others to obey the natural law. The waste prohibition, however, allows a rightful user to break through this enclosure in order to get at the wasting goods.[120] The tension lies in determining the appropriate strength of the enclosure. At one extreme, the owner's creation of an impermeable enclosure eliminates the ability to enforce a violation of the waste prohibition. At the other extreme, a fair user who decimates the owner's enclosure such that anyone can steal as much of the good as he wants can be seen as contributorily violating the owner's property right in the good. Although the principles of the state of nature do not provide a clear way to resolve this tension, this tension should be reexamined in light of Part III, where the government as a single entity can internally balance the competing interests.

---

116. Gordon, *supra* note 16, at 1582; *see also* Reese, *supra* note 17, at 720-23 (arguing that known inventions lessen the chance for actual independent production).

117. *See* Gordon, *supra* note 16, at 1556-58.

118. Waldron, *supra* note 6, at 883 (analogizing to the doctrine of trademarks becoming generic).

119. LOCKE, SECOND TREATISE, *supra* note 1, § 38.

120. *See id.*

## III. LOCKEAN FAIR USE UNDER A CIVIL GOVERNMENT

This Part addresses the societal transition to a civil government. Locke argues that the principle of majority consent largely replaces individual consent under a civil government. The shift to majority consent has important implications for the potential scope of the private property right under a civil government. Of the three independent principles that bind action in the state of nature, I argue in this Part that only the waste prohibition continues to bind a civil government. The state, therefore, takes over the duty to police violations of the waste prohibition, which it may accomplish in alternative ways that are not available in the state of nature, such as establishing a public domain.

This Part also compares a Lockean regime to current U.S. intellectual property theory and doctrine. The functional application of copyright fair use is similar in that fair use is an all-or-nothing privilege that inheres in individuals in both the Lockean regime and under U.S. copyright law. Differences are also demonstrated, including the absence of a patent fair use doctrine and a more limited scope of fair use under current U.S. copyright doctrines than would be provided under a Lockean regime. Finally, the moral implications of wasted intangible goods are considered in the drug patent context.

### A. *The Transition to Civil Government*

Locke devotes a vast majority of the *Second Treatise* to a discussion of civil government.[121] Locke begins by claiming that expediency drives people together into civil governments[122] and that the consent of these people legitimates the governments.[123] Upon entering a civil government, they subject themselves to supreme power in the legislature,[124] which retains this power until individual members decide to leave the society or the government acts outside the bounds of its authority and the people as a whole revolt.[125]

Locke provided a number of principles to guide the legislature in pursuing lawmaking authorized by the natural law. The first set of requirements deals with the rulemaking power. Rules must be general,

121. The discussion of the transition into civil government constitutes the bulk of chapters 7-19, as compared to the discussion of property, which is limited to chapter 5.

122. LOCKE, SECOND TREATISE, *supra* note 1, § 127.

123. *Id.* §§ 15, 22.

124. *Id.* §§ 149-150.

125. *Compare id.* §§ 149, 243 (explaining that supreme power is in the legislature), *with id.* §§ 211-221 (describing which actions by the government justify revolt and dissolution of the common government).

known by the community, and made by the legislative power.[126] The second set of requirements deals with the scope of the rulemaking power. The scope of the law is limited in that the law cannot contain more power than the parties had to give in the state of nature,[127] cannot take property without majority consent,[128] cannot harm the society,[129] and cannot constrain a person's freedom to act as she wishes in the absence of a prescribed rule.[130]

As the legislature remains bound by the natural law,[131] the major difference relating to trade in the state of nature and under civil government is the aggregation of consent. In the state of nature, consent is given from individual to individual, whereas under civil government, consent is given from the individual to the state, which may then act and compel individuals to act under a theory of majority consent. Although semantically the right to exclude remains—nobody "hath a right to take their substance, or any part of it from them, without their own consent"[132]—a civil government may act in a wide variety of ways that may limit the right to exclude because consent is redefined as majority consent[133] acting "only for the Publick Good."[134]

Locke lists three reasons why groups of individuals transition from a state of nature into a civil government: a scarce common,[135] enhancement of the public good,[136] and, most importantly, enforcement of property rights.[137] In order to enforce a property right, one must be able to exclude and choose

126. *Id.* § 3.

127. *Id.* § 135.

128. *Id.* § 138.

129. *Id.* § 166.

130. *See id.* §§ 128-129.

131. *Id.* § 135 (declaring that the "Law of Nature stands as an Eternal Rule to all Men, Legislators as well as others").

132. *Id.* § 138.

133. *Id.* § 140. Despite the tension between individual and majority consent, Locke strongly asserts the need to submit to majority consent. He argues that "[w]hen any number of Men have so consented to make one Community or Government, . . . the Majority have a Right to act and conclude the rest." *Id.* § 95. This right is required because "that which acts any Community, being only the consent of the individuals of it, and it being necessary to that which is one body to move one way; it is necessary the Body should move that way whither the greater force carries it, which is the consent of the majority." *Id.* § 96. If the right is not recognized, Locke argues, "where the majority cannot conclude the rest, there they cannot act as one Body, and consequently will be immediately dissolved again." *Id.* § 98.

134. *Id.* § 3; *see also id.* §§ 88, 96, 140. The legislature is bound to act in the people's interest, in addition to acting within the confines of the natural law, because the members would not have entered into, or remain in, a society where they were going to be harmed. *See id.* §§ 137, 166.

135. *Id.* § 45 (claiming that when people obtain more goods through the use of a money system, the land becomes scarce and the people organize themselves together). This reason is unimportant when considering the nonrivalrous common of intangible goods.

136. *Id.* § 3.

137. *See, e.g., id.* § 124 ("The great and chief end . . . is the Preservation of their Property.").

to exclude others.[138] Exclusion is protected by a natural right to punish a party who violates the natural law,[139] whether the violation occurs through ignorance of or ignoring the natural law.[140] The practical difficulties associated with enforcing one's own property rights against others do not confound the natural law but merely suggest a reason why men typically move out of the state of nature and into a civil government.[141]

The problem of maintaining exclusion is more pronounced for intangible goods, and thus the incentives for transitioning into a civil government are also more pronounced for owners of intangible goods. Many definitions of intangible goods qualify them as public goods, namely that they are nonrivalrous and that they are physically nonexcludable.[142] Hughes argues that intangible goods are nonexcludable in part because a person cannot be prevented from privately using an idea.[143] Even if exclusion can initially be maintained, the framework must also prevent arbitrage from the persons who obtain a fair use right or who pay a lower price to those who are obligated to pay a higher rate.[144] Exclusion can be enforced through technical means, such as digital-rights-management provisions, or through legal means, such as statutes like the No Electronic Theft Act, which imposes criminal sanctions for large-scale violations of intellectual property rights.[145] In addition to establishing an impartial arbiter, a civil government may also be able to establish clear categories of

138. For example, Locke defines property as that which cannot be taken from a man without his consent. *Id.* § 193; *see also* WALDRON, *supra* note 17, at 158-60 (arguing that Locke maintains a clear distinction throughout the *Second Treatise* between "property in" items and items that are the "property of" a person, with the second allowing for exclusion).

139. *Compare* LOCKE, SECOND TREATISE, *supra* note 1, §§ 7-11 (allowing for full restitution and preventing offenses), *with id.* § 126 (explaining that men will often lack the power to enforce their own property rights).

140. *See id.* § 124.

141. *See id.* §§ 13, 123-127.

142. *See, e.g.*, Lacey, *supra* note 17, at 1553-55. Mechanisms are evolving, however, for the protection of intangible goods, such as encryption and password requirements that may allow greater enforceability than that which exists for tangible goods. Benkler, *supra* note 90, at 2065.

143. Hughes, *supra* note 15, at 315-16 (arguing that "thought-police" would be required to make intangible goods fully excludable, but that these thought-police are technologically infeasible and would violate privacy rights); *see also* Moore, *Intangible Property*, *supra* note 17, at 371-75 (discussing privacy considerations).

144. The arbitrage problem is likely to be less pronounced for low-value uses due to the lack of any market in which to conduct the arbitrage. *See* Maureen A. O'Rourke, *Toward a Doctrine of Fair Use in Patent Law*, 100 COLUM. L. REV. 1177, 1188-89 (2000).

145. No Electronic Theft (NET) Act, Pub. L. No. 105-147, 111 Stat. 2678 (1997) (codified as amended at 17 U.S.C. §§ 101-803 (Supp. IV 1998) and at 18 U.S.C. § 2319 (2000)); *see also* Karen J. Bernstein, *The No Electronic Theft Act: The Music Industry's New Instrument in the Fight Against Internet Piracy*, 7 UCLA ENT. L. REV. 325 (2000) (discussing in detail the evolution of the willful infringement requirement under the statute).

individuals or uses that may act as proxies for permissible and impermissible intrusions on property rights.[146]

### B. *The Existence and Scope of the Fair Use Right*

If society has transitioned out of the state of nature and into a government,[147] what can Lockean theories of civil government teach us about the intricacies of intellectual property theory? That a government should act "for the publick good," or even "only for the publick good,"[148] is a tautology so thin that it provides little to no help in determining the actual scope of intellectual property rights. This deflating question may lead to problematic conclusions. Gordon's Lockean theory of intellectual property is incorrect because she does not carefully distinguish limitations and opportunities that are different between the state of nature and a civil government.[149] Other, more cynical arguments suggest that Locke was mostly unconcerned with his natural rights theory of property, and thus his deontological justifications for property should be ignored.[150]

As described earlier,[151] Lockean theory contains three independent principles from the state of nature that could potentially continue to limit property rights in a civil government: the independent production principle, the no harm prohibition, and the waste prohibition. The independent production principle is intimately tied to individual consent. Even though autonomy cannot be alienated fully,[152] individual consent in the state of nature can largely be replaced by majority consent in a civil government.

146. Governmental regulation may take the form of traditional laws—"East Coast Code"—or technical requirements, such as those embedded into the architecture of the Internet—"West Coast Code." LAWRENCE LESSIG, CODE AND OTHER LAWS OF CYBERSPACE 53-54 (1999).

147. The question of whether the interactions of nation-states constitute a state of nature, or whether, through treaty or custom, the state of nature no longer exists is beyond the scope of this Note.

148. LOCKE, SECOND TREATISE, *supra* note 1, § 3.

149. *See* Friedman, *supra* note 17, at 165 ("Gordon focuses on Locke's deontological state-of-nature theory without considering that Locke liquidates natural property rights when civil society is founded."). Gordon bases her ability to impose the scope of property developed in the state of nature to a civil government on Locke's claim that the natural law must be fulfilled at all times. Gordon, *supra* note 16, at 1554-55. Gordon argues that other than rights of enforcement, the "individual retains virtually all the other rights and duties of the law of nature in civil society." *Id.* As described previously, a vital problem with Gordon's argument is that it conflates the public domain and the Lockean common.

Wilf does not conflate the two societal systems, arguing that different property rules are obtained in the state of nature and under civil government. Wilf, *supra* note 106, at 31-32 (concluding that no intellectual property is cognizable under the state of nature).

150. *See, e.g.*, Friedman, *supra* note 17, at 164 ("Locke's property theory is a digression made necessary only to challenge the absolutist politics advanced by Filmer. Hence it should not surprise us that Locke is willing to undo private property rights once they have served his polemical purpose . . . .").

151. *See supra* notes 22-29 and accompanying text.

152. *See* LOCKE, SECOND TREATISE, *supra* note 1, § 23 (arguing that natural law forbids a man, even by consent, to enslave himself).

This alienability suggests that the independent production principle and the Lockean fair use right to culture are largely inapplicable under a civil government. The no harm principle is also largely alienable under majority consent in a civil government. Therefore, Locke can argue that legislative actions that impose benefits on some individuals and harms on other individuals are legitimate because the individual harmed by one statute is benefited by other statutes, such that the overall effect on the individual is a benefit.[153] So long as the government generally acts in a way that benefits society as a whole, the no harm principle is not violated.

The consent given from the governed to a civil government does not, however, affect the applicability of the waste prohibition. In other words, a private action or governmental regulation that violates the waste prohibition in the state of nature will still violate the natural law under a civil government and is null under Lockean theory.[154] As an owner does not have a right to violate the waste prohibition in the state of nature, his consent cannot justify such a violation under a civil government. Even consent by those who enforce the waste prohibition in the state of nature cannot alienate this right under a civil government. In the state of nature, individuals enforced the waste prohibition by taking the spoiling good, but under a civil government, the government itself enforces the natural law.[155] This suggests that the state has a duty to determine what constitutes a violation of the waste prohibition and "punish" such violations.

In addition to increasing enforceability of property rights in intangible goods, a transition to civil government opens up opportunities for alternative ways of avoiding a violation of the waste prohibition. An important implication is that a government could use its power of majority consent to establish a public domain—a set of developed intangible goods that are available freely to all potential users. There are a number of ways in which the government could establish a public domain, including the current U.S. system whereby the government provides enforcement of intellectual property rights in exchange for the mandatory donation of the intangible good to the public domain after a set period of time. Recently, a number of alternate proposals for establishing more universal access to intangible goods using government-provided prizes have been offered.

153. This argument can be pieced together from the following. First, Locke claims that unless we allow the consent of the majority to bind all individuals in civil government, the "variety of Opinions, and contrariety of Interests" will limit the ability of the government to survive. *Id.* §§ 95-99. Second, Locke requires that a civil government must provide enough benefits to propel a man to "quit the freedom of the state of Nature." *Id.* § 137; *see also* Moore, *Intangible Property*, *supra* note 17, at 369-71 (discussing the appropriate baseline of comparison).

154. *See* LOCKE, SECOND TREATISE, *supra* note 1, § 135.

155. *See id.* § 87.

Although implementing the policies may be difficult,[156] these proposals can be used to highlight the different methods available to a civil government in satisfying the waste prohibition. First, consider an initial proposal that the government's eminent domain power could be used to "take" the property rights in an intangible good for just compensation.[157] The government would thus use general tax revenue in order to purchase the intangible good for the free use of society as a whole. This idea was later spun in a somewhat different fashion, suggesting that it would be more efficient to provide rights-holders with an option either to keep the intellectual property rights or to sell the government the rights to the good for an amount that can be determined either ex ante, as with the initial proposal, or could be determined ex post by correlating sales incorporating the intangible good to a prize function.[158] Finally, one might use the government funds to facilitate purchases by low-value users, providing subsidies to facilitate purchase at the prevailing market price.[159]

### C. *Application to U.S. Intellectual Property Theory and Doctrine*

#### 1. *Copyright Fair Use and the DMCA*

The fair use doctrine in U.S. copyright law is similar in function and economic justification to the Lockean fair use right developed in this Note. A copyright is obtained in "original works of authorship fixed in any tangible medium of expression"[160] and provides broad-reaching property rights to copyright holders, including the ability to exclude others from copying the work, distributing copies, or performing the work publicly.[161] Under copyright law, the property rights are enforceable through preliminary and permanent injunctions, as well as through statutory and actual damages.[162]

The functional application of the fair use doctrine in copyright law mirrors Lockean principles. The scope of an owner's copyright is limited by

156. For an excellent overview and critique of existing patent prize proposals, see Michael Abramowicz, *Perfecting Patent Prizes*, 56 VAND. L. REV. (forthcoming 2003).

157. Robert C. Guell & Marvin Fischbaum, *Toward Allocative Efficiency in the Prescription Drug Industry*, 73 MILBANK Q. 213 (1995).

158. Steven Shavell & Tanguy van Ypersele, *Rewards Versus Intellectual Property Rights*, 44 J.L. & ECON. 525 (2001).

159. *See* Douglas Gary Lichtman, *Pricing Prozac: Why the Government Should Subsidize the Purchase of Patented Pharmaceuticals*, 11 HARV. J.L. & TECH. 123 (1997).

160. 17 U.S.C. § 102 (2000). Works that do not exhibit sufficient originality do not get copyright protection. *Id.* Examples of these types of works include mere data compilations, Feist Publ'ns v. Rural Tel. Serv. Co., 499 U.S. 340 (1991), short phrases and slogans, 37 C.F.R. § 202.1 (2002), and scenes à faire, Williams v. Crichton, 84 F.3d 581 (2d Cir. 1996).

161. 17 U.S.C. § 102.

162. *Id.* §§ 502-504.

section 107, which establishes a four-factor test to determine whether a use is a fair use.[163] Fair use is a "privilege in others than the owner of the copyright to use the copyrighted material in a reasonable manner without his consent."[164] The functional result of the fair use privilege is in most cases an "all-or-nothing choice"[165] between an injunction against the use or use without compensation by the infringing party. The application of the fair use doctrine comports with the Lockean application of the waste prohibition to monopolist pricing in a single-price market for an intangible good in two significant ways. First, the ability to transcend the broad property rights of the owner of the intangible good is centered in specific individuals rather than in specific intangible goods. The fair use doctrine allows only some individuals the right to use the copyrighted material for free, while everyone else must pay a fee. Similarly, the Lockean waste prohibition grants a right of free use to only some individuals and not to others. Second, the "all-or-nothing" dichotomy of fair use law mirrors the Lockean waste prohibition because a violation of the waste prohibition produces a total loss of property rights—i.e., fair use—in that specific intangible unit.

Although a variety of justifications for the fair use doctrine exist, such as promoting First Amendment considerations,[166] this Subsection focuses on the economic element of the theoretical framework for the fair use doctrine based on potential market failures associated with transaction costs.[167] The framework for economic considerations was established by

---

163. *Id.* § 107. The four factors are:

> (1) the purpose and character of the use, including whether such use is of a commercial nature or is for nonprofit educational purposes;
>
> (2) the nature of the copyrighted work;
>
> (3) the amount and substantiality of the portion used in relation to the copyrighted work as a whole; and
>
> (4) the effect of the use upon the potential market for or value of the copyrighted work.

*Id.*

164. Harper & Row, Publishers v. Nation Enters., 471 U.S. 539, 549 (1985) (citation omitted).

165. Wendy I. Gordon, *Fair Use as Market Failure: A Structural and Economic Analysis of the* Betamax *Case and Its Predecessors*, 82 COLUM. L. REV. 1600, 1623 (1982). Some courts have even suggested that compulsory licensing regimes might be appropriate. *Id.* at 1623-24 & nn.127-28.

166. *See, e.g.*, Jed Rubenfeld, *The Freedom of Imagination: Copyright's Constitutionality*, 112 YALE L.J. 1, 3-5 (2002) (arguing that current copyright doctrine's "insulation from the First Amendment" should be reconsidered using the "freedom of imagination" as a framework). *But see Harper & Row*, 471 U.S. at 558-60 (construing First Amendment rights to fair use narrowly). *See generally* Zimmerman, *supra* note 3 (arguing for a greater First Amendment limitation on copyright law).

167. The parody exception allows users to "conjure up" a copyrighted work in order to comment or criticize the original. *See* Campbell v. Acuff-Rose Music, Inc., 510 U.S. 569, 588 (1994). Although market-related, the economic justification for parody as a fair use right is different than the justification I am considering here. This Note largely considers the problem of transaction costs, whereas the parody exception exists largely because the owner of the property

Gordon,[168] has been expanded upon by others, such as Maureen O'Rourke,[169] and was important in congressional consideration of the 1976 Copyright Act.[170] Gordon argues that the fair use doctrine is a judicial response to market failures, some of which are created by transaction costs.[171] Working from first principles, Gordon's fair use theory begins with basic market assumptions including the absence of transaction costs. Granting a copyright allows the establishment of markets for a wide array of intangible goods and their uses.[172] Transaction costs may, however, limit the ability of buyers to engage with sellers who would be willing to purchase the good at above the marginal cost of production (which marginal cost is zero in the case of markets for intangible goods). A complete market failure occurs when there is no exchange of an intangible good for a specific use—an intangible unit—when there are buyers who value the good at above the cost of copying. In such a case, fair use by the potential buyer is a Pareto superior move because the potential buyer is able to gain utility without diminishing any monetary reward that the seller could have gained.[173]

Gordon's theoretical justification for the fair use doctrine largely coheres with the Lockean description in this Note. The easy case for comparison is complete market failure, such as the absence of a market for an out-of-print book. The failure of the market to effectuate socially efficient uses of out-of-print books by scholars and others has often motivated courts to provide fair use rights.[174] This is also an easy case for the Lockean waste prohibition. Due to the waste prohibition, the laborer cannot maintain property rights in the intangible units of the book that she does not sell. The complete lack of a market is by its nature a complete violation of the waste prohibition and consists of a total abrogation of rights in the intangible good (except as to the single intangible unit used by the laborer herself).

The Lockean waste prohibition, however, creates a fair use right that is much more robust than the current fair use doctrine. Although Gordon includes the market assumption of competition, she then ignores the

has incentives not to license parodies that are not aligned with society's value in obtaining the parodies. *See* Gordon, *supra* note 165, at 1633.

168. Gordon, *supra* note 165 (arguing that fair use should be allowed where market failures prevent efficient trading).

169. O'Rourke, *supra* note 144, at 1177, 1180, 1188-89 (arguing that fair use is socially desirable in some cases of market failures).

170. Gordon, *supra* note 165, at 1603.

171. *Id.* at 1602-14.

172. *Id.* at 1612-13.

173. *Id.* at 1618-22.

174. *See, e.g.*, Triangle Publ'ns v. Knight-Ridder Newspapers, 626 F.2d 1171, 1176 n.14 (5th Cir. 1980) ("[I]f the copyrighted work is out of print and cannot be purchased, a user may be more likely to prevail on a fair use defense.").

implications of the fundamental nature of granting a copyright on this assumption. The grant of an intellectual property right in an intangible good limits competition and is frequently referred to as a monopoly grant that is acceptable only to the extent that it is necessary to provide ex ante incentives for intangible good producers. Stated another way, monopoly pricing above the efficient level is itself a market failure.[175] When a monopolist seller establishes a price, she divides the world into three groups: those who value the good at or above the market price, those who value the good below the market price but at or above zero, and those who put a negative value on the good. Due to the nonrivalry of intangible goods and Locke's waste prohibition, the seller loses the right to exclude all those who are in the latter two groups under a Lockean regime, but not necessarily under U.S. copyright law. This suggests that for the U.S. copyright law to align itself with Lockean principles would require a much more expansive fair use right.

Lockean analysis also provides an interesting perspective on the relatively recent anticircumvention measures enacted by the Digital Millennium Copyright Act,[176] specifically the provisions codified into section 1201 of the Copyright Act.[177] These provisions prohibit actions taken to circumvent access controls or other technological measures that protect a copyrighted work and provide relief independent of infringement actions.[178] Pamela Samuelson described the potential ramifications of such a privatized regime this way: "If works are protected against unauthorized copying by means of technology and contract law, there may be nothing for copyright to do . . . ."[179] The government holds a natural law duty both to protect private property rights and to police violations of the waste prohibition. One-sided government enforcement of private access controls that leaves the government with "nothing . . . to do" would represent a total abrogation of the government's duty to uphold the waste prohibition.

The DMCA may be viewed as an attempt by the government to reconcile the competing interests of self-enforcement and self-help for fair use discussed earlier.[180] The increasing digitalization of intangible goods creates an increased ability to erect enclosures that are unaccommodating to

175. This market failure may be a part of the category of "intermediate market failures," which Gordon defines as cases "where the market cannot be relied upon to generate all desirable exchanges, but where some such transactions would be possible." *See* Gordon, *supra* note 165, at 1618-22.

176. Digital Millennium Copyright Act, Pub. L. No. 105-304, 112 Stat. 2860 (1998) (codified in scattered sections of 17 U.S.C.); *see also* Jane C. Ginsburg, *Copyright Legislation for the "Digital Millennium*," 23 COLUM.-VLA J.L. & ARTS 137 (1999) (detailing the evolution and structure of the DMCA).

177. 17 U.S.C. § 1201 (2000).

178. *See id.*

179. Samuelson, *supra* note 46, at 117, 125.

180. *See supra* text accompanying notes 119-120.

fair use but also enables the laborer to price-discriminate in a more fine-grained manner, thereby allowing laborers to more fully avoid violating the waste prohibition. First considering low-value users, increasing digitalization enables sellers to offer product differentiation—second-degree price discrimination—on a much larger scale than ever before. In Jessica Litman's words, "Until very recently, a copyright holder had no means to instruct a book that it should sprout wings and fly back to its publisher after it had been read *N* times . . . ."[181] Increased digitalization also offers broad opportunities for third-degree price discrimination. An example of this is Amazon.com's temporary use of consumer information, such as geography, previous purchases, and past spending patterns to price-discriminate among consumers at its site.[182] In addition to the privacy implications such a regime entails, both second- and third-degree price discrimination also include some measure of lumpiness. Therefore, provisions that exempt additional classes of individuals from the anticircumvention prohibition are necessary from a Lockean perspective. Although DMCA provisions such as sections 1008 and 1201(a)(2) contain limited exemptions, they likely do not include all those that might be legitimate or required under Lockean theory.[183] The government would, therefore, need to balance its obligations under the natural law much more carefully to prevent violations of the waste prohibition for low-value users.

Low-value uses represent a much larger problem for the legitimacy of the DMCA anticircumvention provisions. The relatively large set of potential uses to which any intangible good may be put will far outstrip the newly enhanced ability to market different types of uses. As the increased barriers that prevent arbitrage and illicit copying of a good are also likely to impair significantly these legitimate uses, a potentially large violation of the waste prohibition will result from the enactment of anticircumvention provisions. This more seriously calls into question the legitimacy of the DMCA under a Lockean regime.

### 2. *Fair Use for Drug Patents*

The patent regime that currently exists in the United States is not cognizable in a Lockean state of nature but may be allowable with modification under a civil government. An impermissible aspect of such a patent regime in the state of nature is the right given to owners to prohibit

181. Jessica Litman, *Reforming Information Law in Copyright's Image*, 22 U. DAYTON L. REV. 587, 601 (1997). The deregulated airline industry is often cited as the primary example in recent economic history of extensive price discrimination, using product characteristics such as advance purchase, nonrefundability, and Saturday night stays to differentiate between high-value and low-value users. *See* Weiss & Mehrotra, *supra* note 84, ¶¶ 5-9.

182. Weiss & Mehrotra, *supra* note 84, ¶¶ 1-4, 10-14.

183. *See* 17 U.S.C. §§ 1008, 1201.

others from independently producing the intangible good.[184] Although the independent production principle is a requirement in the state of nature, under a civil government the independent production right may be alienated through majority consent.

A transition to a civil government does not, however, alter the waste prohibition's applicability because it does not operate on the consent of the laborer or the user. Therefore, a fair use right must be provided in both the state of nature and under a civil government. While the U.S. system allows for a fair use right in copyright, no coherent fair use right is allowed in patents. Although doctrines such as the experimental use provision may create a limited fair use right in certain situations,[185] a more refined patent fair use doctrine would be demanded by Lockean theory.

Although it is beyond the scope of this Note to operationalize such a patent fair use right, the currently intense drug patent debate provides a stark example of the morally compelling nature of such a right.[186] Even though Locke argues that the state of nature is a state of equality,[187] this equality is limited to equality of opportunity, not equality of wealth or ability.[188] The waste prohibition, however, does establish that low-value users have a fair use right to the intangible goods, which may import some measure of redistributional equity, because one characteristic that will tend to identify a low-value user is socioeconomic status.

The existence of a large class of low-value users can be substantiated by the numerous claims that have been made that many people in developing countries are unable to afford drugs at the price set by the patent holders. Regarding the AIDS pandemic in China, a local doctor stated, "I know how to treat these people, but I don't have the drugs, and the patients

184. *See* Hettinger, *supra* note 17, at 44 (finding that patents "clearly run afoul" of Lockean principles due to an improper restriction on independent production). Hettinger's analysis is flawed, however, because he does not consider important differences between the state of nature and civil government.

185. O'Rourke, *supra* note 144, at 1192-93. Although not relying on a Lockean perspective, O'Rourke has argued that a patent fair use doctrine should be developed because patents may be subject to the same market defects as those that create the need for copyright fair use. *Id.* at 1187. She suggests a five-factor test to operationalize a patent fair use doctrine. These factors incorporate social ideals that do not directly map onto the requirements of the waste prohibition, but might be a good start for determining how to operationalize a Lockean fair use right. She finds the following relevant to fair use:

> (i) the nature of the advance represented by the infringement; (ii) the purpose of the infringing use; (iii) the nature and strength of the market failure that prevents a license from being concluded; (iv) the impact of the use on the patentee's incentives and overall social welfare; and (v) the nature of the patented work.

*Id.* at 1205.

186. Another way in which a Lockean right to fair use of drug patents might be sustainable is through Locke's subsistence proviso. For a description of the subsistence proviso, see *supra* note 37.

187. LOCKE, SECOND TREATISE, *supra* note 1, § 4.

188. *See id.* §§ 34-36, 47-48; Sterk, *supra* note 17, at 1234 (describing Lockean theory as an "equality-of-opportunity theory").

can't pay."[189] A Nigerian representative has argued that his country has little money to help its three million people with HIV and so turns to Indian-made generic drugs that cost substantially less.[190] The concerns transcend the AIDS issue, as new malaria drugs create the ability to save hundreds of thousands of patients, but the cost of $1.30 per dose is sufficiently higher than the existing treatment's cost of $0.25 per dose that African health ministries continue to prescribe the cheaper but less effective treatment.[191] Jean Lanjouw has provided additional empirical support for the existence of a large class of low-value users, showing that the assertion of monopoly power provides little profits to the patent holder but creates a great loss to those who would be able to purchase the good at greater than the cost of producing the drug.[192]

Establishing the existence of low-value users also establishes a Lockean fair use right for those users. To the extent that patent holders are unable or unwilling to sell the patented drugs at affordable prices, these low-value users have a Lockean fair use right. Additionally, although affordable drug pricing is admittedly not a full solution to the problem, the developing countries' moral claim asserts that the patent drug issue is not one of incentives, but of rich against poor. An Ethiopian representative claimed that "[p]atents are a system to help the most powerful people who need the least protection, even while millions of poor AIDS patients are dying."[193] This claim seems particularly incisive after the United States government's near abrogation of Bayer's patent rights in the anti-anthrax drug Cipro after the terrorist attacks in late 2001.[194]

## IV. CONCLUSION

This Note has applied the principles set forth in Locke's *Two Treatises of Government* to determine the existence and scope of property rights in intangible goods. To this end, the *Treatises* have been treated as an authoritative text, but American intellectual property law has tended to

189. Peter S. Goodman, *In China, AIDS Crisis Is at the Mercy of Global Commerce*, WASH. POST, Dec. 5, 2002, at A1.

190. Sebastian Mallaby, Editorial, *Talking Cadillacs to Rickshaw Riders*, WASH. POST, Oct. 7, 2002, at A19.

191. Karl Vick, *Aid Group: Malaria Drug Need Is Ignored: Africans Still Rely on Inferior Therapy*, WASH. POST, Feb. 14, 2002, at A30.

192. Jean O. Lanjouw, A Patent Policy Proposal for Global Diseases (Apr. 2001), *at* http://econ.worldbank.org/files/1733_lanjouw.pdf. Although gaining fair use to drugs produced for developed nations benefits developing nations, there is almost no investment in treating diseases that primarily afflict developing nations. *Id.*

193. Mallaby, *supra* note 190.

194. Shankar Vedantam & Terence Chea, *Drug Firm Plays Defense in Anthrax Scare: For Now, U.S. Declines To Suspend Bayer's Patent and Authorize Generic Cipro*, WASH. POST, Oct. 21, 2001, at A14.

reject the natural law framework. Instead, the United States has adopted a utilitarian framework, focusing on the incentives that must be given to laborers to produce intangible goods. What, then, can a Lockean theory of property in intangible goods teach us about U.S. intellectual property?

First, the analysis demonstrates the need to consider carefully the special characteristics of intangible goods that make them so sharply different from tangible goods. The waste prohibition set out by Locke quickly becomes a nonissue for tangible goods when a money system has been introduced. As I have shown, however, this result changes dramatically when one considers the nonrivalrous nature of intangible goods. That a prominent theory justifying property rights produces such different conclusions when one considers the differences between tangible and intangible goods suggests that one must take care to consider the special characteristics of intangible goods when making intellectual property policy decisions.

Second, although U.S. doctrine has disavowed use of natural law concepts in determining the scope of intellectual property rights, proponents often use natural law arguments to justify expansion of intellectual property rights that should be balanced against the natural law arguments for the fair use right described in this Note. Take, for example, the RIAA's use of natural-law-type arguments to sway policy decisions regarding peer-to-peer music sharing, quoting Art Alexakis of Everclear as saying, "I think the fact that Napster is stealing recorded music is something that we have to stop. . . . That's the way I look at it. It's wrong. It's inherently wrong. It's stealing," and Alanis Morissette as claiming that the artist "should be the person who's ultimately in a position to decide when, where, and how something should be shared with whomever they choose to share it with."[195] Alexakis's claim against "stealing" and Morissette's claim for artistic control rights are natural law arguments rather than arguments about the socially optimal level of property rights. To the extent that they are used to provide additional justification for the existing regime of strong property rights for intangible goods owners or are presented as justification for additional rights, the Lockean theory developed in this Note can be used as a counterargument. In fact, the use of natural law arguments may work against marketers of intangible goods because the extensive nature of the Lockean waste prohibition may limit intellectual property rights even more than the incentives-based system currently in place, with one example being a mandatory patent fair use right.

Finally, the waste prohibition has moral appeal that is similar to the moral appeal that supports Locke's theory of private property rights. There

195. Recording Indus. Ass'n of Am., The Napster Lawsuit, *at* http://www.riaa.org/Napster.cfm (last visited Oct. 29, 2002).

is something intuitively appealing about giving a property right in controlling a good to the creator of that good, especially where no others have been harmed by this creation. By that same token, it is intuitively appealing to provide a fair use right where the owner is letting the good spoil and waste, especially if it can be done without harming the owner. Just as one might find the rock stars' argument that they ought to be compensated compelling, one would find compelling the claims by Third World governments that perfectly exclusive private property rights are inappropriate when the resulting waste—the deadweight loss—is actual human suffering and death.

# [3]

# THE SHAPE OF LOCKEAN RIGHTS: FAIRNESS, PARETO, MODERATION, AND CONSENT*

By Richard J. Arneson

## I. Introduction

The Lockean natural rights tradition—including its libertarian branch—is a work in progress. Thirty years after the publication of *Anarchy, State, and Utopia* (1974), Robert Nozick's classic work of political theory is still regarded by academic philosophers as the authoritative statement of right-wing libertarian Lockeanism in the Ayn Rand mold.[1] Despite the classic status of this great book, its tone is not at all magisterial, but improvisational, quirky, tentative, and exploratory. Its author has more questions than answers. On some central foundational questions, he refrains from taking a stand. There is spadework yet to be done on the project of developing the most plausible versions of Lockean and Lockean libertarian views. Prior to doing this work and articulating the sensible alternatives and what can be said for and against them, we are not yet in a position reasonably to opt for any particular version of Lockean theory, or for that matter to decide between the natural rights tradition and rival consequentialisms. This essay aims to explore hard and soft versions of Lockean theory. The exploration aims to persuade the reader to favor the soft versions.

Section II formulates four claims (all asserted by Nozick) and provisionally identifies the Lockean libertarian view with these claims. Section III notes that although Nozick in his 1974 book made scant progress toward providing a justification of his particular doctrine of rights, compared to advocates of rival doctrines, no rights theorist since then has made significant advances on that front, so Nozick's achievement has not been superseded. Section III also rehearses Nozick's view of rights as side constraints. Sections IV and V raise a question that Nozick first posed: Should rights be regarded as specifying ways individuals may not be treated, infringement of which is *never*, or *sometimes*, or *always* morally

* I thank Ellen Frankel Paul for helpful, constructive, and substantive comments on a prior draft of this essay. It goes without saying that her comments outstripped my ability to respond.

[1] Robert Nozick, *Anarchy, State, and Utopia* (New York: Basic Books, 1974). Further references to Nozick's book will take the form of parenthetical page citations in the text, using the abbreviation *ASU*. Nozick criticized arguments purporting to provide a moral foundation for capitalism that he located in Ayn Rand's writings. See Nozick, "On the Randian Argument," reprinted in Robert Nozick, *Socratic Puzzles* (Cambridge, MA: Harvard University Press, 1997), 249–64. This essay was first published in 1971.

acceptable, provided full compensation is paid to any victims? *Hard libertarianism* is defined as a version of Lockean libertarianism that replies "Never!" to this question along with offering strict interpretation and uncompromising affirmation of the four provisional claims detailed in Section II. Sections VI through VIII explore and criticize Nozick's own discussion of the question under review. An alternate phrasing of it is: Is every infringement of an individual natural right a violation of it? The discussion proceeds by raising several examples and interpreting them as counterexamples to hard libertarianism. Sections IX and X discuss examples that provide reasons to embrace a weak or soft interpretation of the Lockean norm of self-ownership. Sections XI and XII introduce further softening. Section XI proposes a Pareto constraint on the content of individual rights. Section XII proposes moderation, the idea that any natural moral right of any person should give way if the consequences for other people if one does not violate the right are sufficiently bad. Moderation says rights are side constraints that give way under pressure of consequences. In other words, people are inviolable, up to a point. Section XIII argues that the soft Lockean position at which we have arrived is not a repudiation but, rather, an intelligible development of the Lockean tradition, and in particular does not reject but only qualifies the claim of self-ownership. Section XIV summarizes the modifications to Nozick's version of libertarianism that this essay defends. Section XV notes that the considerations adduced in favor of soft as opposed to hard versions of Lockeanism consist entirely of descriptions of examples. But Nozick himself has rightly stressed that the evidence for a moral theory that consists in responses to puzzle cases is not to be sneered at.

## II. Basics

The fundamental Lockean libertarian view comprises four claims:

1. Each person has a moral right to do whatever she chooses with whatever she legitimately owns unless her actions would harm nonconsenting others in certain ways that violate their rights.
2. Each person has the right not to be harmed by others, whether by physical assault, interference with her liberty by coercion or force, physical damage to her person or property, extortion, theft or fraud, breach of contract, libel, or threat of any of these things.
3. Each adult person legitimately owns herself.
4. All of these moral rights are forfeitable by misconduct, transferable from their holder to another by mutual consent, and waivable by voluntary consent of their holder.[2]

[2] Not all Lockean libertarians accept the claim that one's right to self-ownership is fully transferable and waivable. This claim implies that voluntary slavery contracts may be

An important derivative element in Lockean theory is that from the premises above, given a world in which material resources are initially unowned, it follows that individuals can acquire extensive private ownership rights over material resources.[3] The exact specification of this derivation, the characterization of its outcome, and the assessment of its success are crucial and tricky issues for Lockean theory, and are much debated.[4] For the purposes of this essay, I simply assume that some version of this derivation does succeed and that within Lockean theory strong rights of individual private ownership of material resources are justifiable.[5]

## III. Why Side Constraints?

This bare-bones statement of the Lockean idea immediately prompts two closely related questions. The list of the ways in which people have a right not to be harmed is a motley set. One wonders, can ordering principles be found that explain and unify the items on the list and that justify each item's inclusion (or suggest revisions)? A second question is, what is the moral basis of individual rights so conceived? What are the

morally valid. Nozick takes this line, however, and it has the virtue of simplicity, so I include it in the statement of core Lockean libertarianism. See also John Simmons, "Inalienable Rights and Locke's Treatises," *Philosophy and Public Affairs* 12, no. 3 (1983): 175–204.

[3] Some readers may balk at my terminology here, on the ground that John Locke's initial premise is that the earth is communally owned. I believe my characterization in the text is correct as applied to Locke. Locke holds that initially the earth is unowned, and that all persons have provisional use rights, which can be supplanted by permanent bequeathable full private ownership rights, given certain conditions. See John Locke, *Second Treatise of Government* (1690), ed. C. B. Macpherson (Indianapolis, IN: Hackett Publishing Company, 1980), chap. 5. In this essay, I use the terms "Lockeanism," "Lockean theory," and "Lockean libertarianism" to refer to a family of views that develop doctrines of individual moral natural rights that are broadly similar to the basic position adumbrated by Locke. Although there are important libertarian strands in Locke's doctrines and arguments, his view is sufficiently different from the libertarianism of Rand and Nozick that it would be misleading to call Locke himself a libertarian. In this essay, "hard libertarianism" refers to an uncompromising version of libertarianism. Libertarianism also comes in softer versions. If one qualifies and weakens soft libertarianism sufficiently, eventually one arrives at the "soft Lockeanism" defended in this essay. To my mind, nothing essential hangs on the terminology, but the position I defend departs significantly from the doctrines standardly associated with libertarianism, so it is probably better to reserve the term "libertarian" for positions closer to the paradigm case. For the purposes of this essay, the paradigm libertarian is Nozick.

[4] For a recent discussion, see John T. Sanders, "Projects and Property," in David Schmidtz, ed., *Robert Nozick* (Cambridge: Cambridge University Press, 2002), 34–58. For skeptical discussions of the issue, see G. A. Cohen, *Self-Ownership, Freedom, and Equality* (Cambridge: Cambridge University Press, 1995). For discussions of John Locke's dealings with this issue, see A. John Simmons, *The Lockean Theory of Rights* (Princeton, NJ: Princeton University Press, 1992), chap. 5; and Jeremy Waldron, *The Right to Private Property* (Oxford: Oxford University Press, 1988). The literature on this topic is voluminous.

[5] I am assuming the correctness of the Lockean derivation of private property rights arguendo, in order to concentrate attention on other issues, and not because I believe the derivation is correct. For familiar reasons, I doubt it is correct.

reasons that should persuade reasonable persons to accept Lockean morality as correct?

In a review of *Anarchy, State, and Utopia,* Thomas Nagel reports with some impatience that Nozick does not make much progress in answering these questions:

> To present a serious challenge to other views, a discussion of libertarianism would have to explore the foundations of individual rights and the reasons for and against different conceptions of the relations between those rights and other values that the state may be in a position to promote. But Nozick's book is theoretically insubstantial: it does not take up the main problems. . . .[6]

I agree with Nagel that Nozick has not explored the foundations of individual rights, but I deny that this lack marks his book as theoretically insubstantial. Decades later, moral philosophers have made only slight advances in the understanding of the moral foundations of individual rights. Nozick's modest achievement in exposing the beams above the foundations looks more and more impressive with the passage of time.

At the most general level, a morality of individual rights denies that moral principles postulate goals, which all persons equally have reason to pursue, by whatever means would be most effective. Such goals might be agent-relative, in the sense that what specific goal is set for a given individual is relative to that individual. "Each person ought to seek to maximize her own happiness" is an example of an agent-relative goal-oriented principle. "Each person ought to seek to maximize aggregate human happiness" is an example of an agent-neutral goal-oriented principle. An agent-neutral goal-oriented principle postulates the same goal or goals for all persons.

In contrast, a morality of individual rights, as Nozick puts it, imposes side constraints on choice of a course of conduct by an agent. Among the available alternative actions a person might choose at a particular time, rights rule out some options; that is, rights render these options ineligible. The person who would respect rights confines her choice to the reduced set of options, the ones that do not violate anyone's rights. From the standpoint of an individual deciding what to do, rights are commands addressed to her, and moreover addressed to her at this particular time: "Do not now do anything that—now or later—violates anyone's rights!"[7]

[6] Thomas Nagel, "Libertarianism without Foundations," reprinted in Jeffrey Paul, ed., *Reading Nozick* (Totowa, NJ: Rowman and Littlefield, 1981), 191–93.

[7] The formulation in the text cannot be quite right as it stands. Suppose I wrongfully launched a slow missile attack at you in the recent past, and now I can choose to launch a countermissile that will prevent this attack from injuring you without violating anyone's rights. A Lockean morality will hold that I must now launch the countermissile that will block my previous attempted rights violation. Hence, against the statement in the text, it is

A right specifies a way that a person (or group of persons) should be treated or not treated—for example, not to be physically assaulted. Rights function not as goals to be promoted but as constraints to be respected. If A has a right not to be assaulted, that right does not tell me to act so as to minimize assaults on A. Rather, it tells me that I must not now choose any act that involves my assaulting A (or my inducing or assisting another to assault A). Rights belong to people, the right-holders. If A has a right not to be assaulted, this generates a duty on my part not to assault A, a duty that is owed to A, and one that is waivable by A and transferable by A to others.

As so far characterized, a morality of individual rights could consist entirely of agent-relative positive duties to help people in need and more generally to undertake specified sorts of actions toward specified other people.[8] The doctrine decisively does not go in that direction. The core content that fills the individual rights structure is the idea that the negative duty not to harm others in certain ways takes priority over any positive duties to give aid.[9] The libertarian versions of this moral theory are uncompromising in this regard: the moral rights that each adult person initially has are entirely negative—rights not to suffer interference or harm of certain sorts. No adult individual initially has any right to any sort of positive treatment or aid from others. No individual initially has any duty to provide such aid, though by voluntary acts such as binding oneself by contract or doing what brings about the birth of a child, or through inadvertence amounting to negligence, one may according to libertarianism come to have strict duties to provide others with aid, to which (under these circumstances) they have a right. This is the thesis

---

not enough that I choose actions that do not, now or in the future, violate anyone's rights. I must also choose actions that, to the greatest extent possible without introducing any new rights violations, undo the effects of past actions of mine that, left unchecked, will violate someone's rights in the future.

[8] This claim in the text might sound obviously false as a characterization of a morality of rights conceived as a morality of constraints, so some explanation is in order. A morality of goals postulates goals and directs the agent to undertake whatever means are necessary to reach the goals. A morality of constraints says the agent may pursue whatever goals she wishes provided that certain constraints on her choice of goals or courses of action to achieve the goals are respected. The constraints might either enjoin a positive act or direct the agent to refrain from a type of act. Thus, a morality of constraints might assert, "Don't harm your mother!" or "Whatever else you do, help your mother!" Just as the former, negative constraint does not say, "Do whatever is required to bring it about that your mother is not harmed (by another or by you)," the latter, positive constraint does not say, "Do whatever is required to bring it about that your mother is helped (by another or by you)." A positive constraint prescribes an action that must be done, not a goal that must be achieved. In a conciliatory spirit, I add that if the reader wants to insist that a morality of constraints can only consist of negative constraints, the reader is welcome to amend my text accordingly. Nothing I want to assert hangs on this point.

[9] This terminology of negative and positive duties is taken from Philippa Foot, "The Problem of Abortion and the Doctrine of Double Effect," reprinted in Philippa Foot, *Virtues and Vices and Other Essays in Moral Philosophy* (Berkeley: University of California Press, 1978), 27. This essay was first published in 1967. According to Foot, negative duties are duties not to harm, more generally to refrain from specified courses of action. Positive duties are duties to aid, to do something for somebody or other.

of self-ownership: Each adult person is the full rightful owner of herself, and possesses over herself the full rights to use and abuse that an owner of a piece of property has over that property. Since A owns herself, no other person B has any property rights in A, which would give B a right to dictate to some extent how A should use her own body (beyond the negative constraint not to harm others in certain ways).

Why should we accept that morality rightly construed has a side constraint structure, that it is constituted by side constraints? Also, why should we accept the further claim that the fundamental constraints are negative, not positive? Nozick tries to place this conception in an attractive light by clarifying some implications of one version of it and suggesting that these implications are plausible. In effect, Nozick tries to show that the Lockean structure is acceptable in reflective equilibrium.[10] Beyond that, he floats some suggestions about what the moral basis of Lockean rights theory might be, but I agree with Nagel that these suggestions do not advance the discussion very far.[11] However, this does not mean that Nozick's discussion has been superseded, since no one else has succeeded in advancing the discussion much further in the interim.[12]

This essay retreats from the large theoretical questions raised in the preceding paragraph. I shall instead follow Nozick's lead and explore variants of the particular side constraints and individual rights that Nozick espouses. The aim is to seek a position in the region of his version of libertarianism that, as it were, rounds off its sharp edges and brings us closer to a reflective equilibrium that considers and accommodates examples that tend to elicit nonlibertarian responses in many of us, even those of us who are initially sympathetic toward the spirit of Nozick's project.

[10] An individual is in a state of reflective equilibrium when she has critically examined pertinent arguments and affirms a set of general moral principles that explain and justify the moral judgments that she endorses about what to do in particular circumstances. The agent's particular and general moral judgments are in equilibrium. For this notion, see John Rawls, *A Theory of Justice*, rev. ed. (Cambridge, MA: Harvard University Press, 1999), 40–46.

[11] One suggestion that Nozick makes is that beings who have a capacity for rational long-term agency and meaningful life in virtue of those capacities acquire Lockean rights not to be harmed in specified ways, rightly deemed wrongful. See Nozick, *Anarchy, State, and Utopia*, 48–50. On its face, the suggestion is incomplete. Since persons whose Lockean rights are violated often succeed in leading meaningful lives, not suffering such violations cannot be a necessary condition for achieving a meaningful life. Anyway, why should possession of a capacity for meaningfulness bring it about that one is endowed with Lockean rights? Nozick recognizes this gap but does not hint at how one might fill it. For criticism of Nozick on this point, see Samuel Scheffler, "Natural Rights, Equality, and the Minimal State," reprinted in Paul, ed., *Reading Nozick*, 148–68.

[12] For the suggestion that rights confer the valuable status of inviolability (or at least limited violability) on every person and that this status is valuable, hence we have rights, see Frances Kamm, "Non-consequentialism, the Person as an End-in-Itself, and the Significance of Status," *Philosophy and Public Affairs* 21, no. 4 (1992): 354–89. Nagel seems to endorse Kamm's suggestion in Thomas Nagel, "Personal Rights and Public Space," *Philosophy and Public Affairs* 24, no. 2 (1995): 89–93. Kasper Lippert-Rasmussen refutes the suggestion in his "Moral Status and the Impermissibility of Minimizing Violations," *Philosophy and Public Affairs* 25, no. 4 (1996): 333–51.

One recurring suggestion is that within the side constraints framework, there are plausible candidates for the status of constraints other than those on which Nozick concentrated attention. Another is that perhaps morality has a hybrid structure that combines side constraints and goal promotion in some way. The most straightforward hybrid identifies moral goals that each person should pursue to some extent—the goals to be balanced off against constraints in deciding what to do in any case, with constraints having less than infinite weight (less than lexical priority). Another hybrid strategy suggests that for any right of any strength, if the consequences of abiding by it in any particular case would be sufficiently bad, one is morally permitted to do what the right, at the first level, prohibits.

## IV. Nozick's Chapter Four Questions

One significant foundational question that Nozick leaves unresolved is the topic of chapter four of *Anarchy, State, and Utopia*. To introduce the topic, Nozick has us suppose we have some understanding of the content of the moral rights that we naturally possess. Nozick states, "Individuals have rights, and there are things no person or group may do to them (without violating their rights)" (*ASU*, ix). People have rights, moral claims not to be treated by other people in certain ways. An individual's right is partly constituted by the obligations of others to constrain their behavior by refraining from doing what the right forbids. Nozick suggests that we think of the right as drawing a boundary in moral space. The question then arises, *"Are others forbidden to perform actions that transgress the boundary or encroach upon the circumscribed area, or are they permitted to perform such actions provided that they compensate the person whose boundary has been crossed?"* (*ASU*, 57). In another terminology, we might say that actions that do what a person's right specifies one should not do *infringe* the right. Infringements that are, all things considered, morally wrong (at least partly on the ground that they are infringements) are *violations* of the right. The issue then arises whether all infringements of rights are violations. Nozick's question then can be rephrased: Are some or all infringements of rights coupled with full compensation to the injured right-bearer morally permissible?[13] Or are any and all infringements of rights morally forbidden (unless the right-bearer consents to what is done, in which case there is no real infringement)?

To make sense of what Nozick is up to in his chapter four discussion, we must suppose that we are thinking through questions about what

[13] Nozick identifies full compensation with compensation that leaves the recipient neither glad nor sad that the combination of the rights violation and the compensation for it occurred—a subjective view. An objective version would hold that the individual is fully compensated when she is rendered neither better off nor worse off by the combination of suffering the rights violation and receiving the compensation for it.

rights people have and what exactly rights require of people, without already having committed ourselves firmly to principles that entail particular answers to these questions. In Rawlsian terminology, we have not attained reflective equilibrium and we know it. Reflection on some examples and cases persuades some of us that Lockean accounts are on the right track, that some position in this neighborhood is correct, but much remains unsettled. If we take it for granted at the start of the discussion that all people are endowed initially with a particular set of moral rights, of known content and character, and that it is always morally wrong to act against anyone's rights without obtaining the individual's prior consent, Nozick's chapter four questions, which presuppose that the content and character of rights are to some degree unsettled, will appear either trivial or incoherent. Nozick will be read as asking, "Under what circumstances is it morally permissible to do what it is never morally permissible to do, namely, violate rights?"

This essay explores these questions. I shall endeavor to assess the adequacy of the responses and suggestions adduced by Nozick in his pathbreaking discussion and to follow some of his insights to see where they lead. I shall proceed by describing examples, considering possible responses, and formulating principles that would explain and justify the responses and that seem independently plausible.

## V. Hard Libertarianism

The position I shall call "hard libertarianism" holds that Lockean natural rights (1) may never permissibly be infringed without the prior consent of the right-holder and (2) may always permissibly be infringed provided that the prior consent of the right-holder has been given. In addition, hard libertarianism affirms unequivocally and without any qualifications the four claims that make up the basics of Lockeanism as presented in Section II of this essay. Soft libertarian/Lockean positions substitute "sometimes" for "never" in (1) and "also" for "always" in (2), and in addition relax some or all of the four basic claims discussed in Section II. Beyond a certain point, substitution and relaxation of this sort renders the term "libertarianism" unapt.[14] Hard libertarianism is controversial both in what it allows and in what it prohibits. Consider some examples.

*Whim.* For no good reason A voluntarily requests that B saw off A's arm. B saws off A's arm. Provided that A is sufficiently morally competent to qualify as a right-bearer, he has the right to waive any right that he has and to set aside the protection to his interests (here, his intact arm) that his Lockean rights afford. If A is neither mentally retarded below an appropriate threshold nor so severely mentally ill that he is not reasonably

[14] See note 3 for my usage of the terms "Lockean" and "libertarian" and "soft."

deemed responsible for his choices, his moral rights include the right to waive any of his other rights.

*Hiker.* A is a hiker lost in a blizzard in the mountains. He stumbles upon a cabin that is privately owned by B and posted with "No Trespassing" signs. Although the door to the cabin is locked, A could break the lock, enter the cabin, build a fire using the cabin's furniture as fuel, eat the food from the larder, and save his life. Hard libertarianism holds that A is morally prohibited from taking B's property without B's permission even to save his life and even if he fully intends to provide full compensation for costs imposed on B by his taking.

In the face of these examples, the hard libertarian might stand fast by her position. If one were moved to alter hard libertarianism so that it yields a softer verdict on such cases, the next question would be, what sort of norms might be reasonable to embrace to give shape to the accommodations? In this connection it is helpful to pay attention to Nozick's insightful discussion that bears on these matters.

## VI. Nozick on the Factors that Might Determine Permissible Boundary Crossing

Nozick mentions several considerations that militate against the proposal to allow any boundary crossing without prior consent provided full compensation is paid to any person whose right is infringed by the boundary crossing and who is injured thereby. I list all that Nozick mentions:

a. A system that allows boundary crossings with full compensation "embodies the use of persons as means" (*ASU*, 71).
b. "[K]nowing they are being so used, and that their plans and expectations are liable to being thwarted arbitrarily, is a cost to people" (*ASU*, 71).
c. "[S]ome injuries may not be compensable" (*ASU*, 71).
d. An agent may not know that she will have the means to pay compensation if injury occurs and compensation is called for (*ASU*, 71).
e. Some boundary crossings tend to produce widespread fear and anxiety not only in actual victims, but also in people who identify themselves as potential victims (*ASU*, 65–71).
f. A system that allows boundary crossings with full compensation licenses an unfair distribution of the benefits of what would be voluntary exchange scenarios except that the prospect of involuntary takings renders negotiation toward voluntary exchange a comparatively unattractive prospect. Suppose A owns a car, which B covets. Rather than negotiate with A and pay the price they agree on, B under a system that allows takings in the absence of voluntary consent can simply take the car and pay A the lowest amount

of money that would induce A voluntarily to relinquish the car. Normally the price they would agree on would be somewhat higher than this, with the benefits that arise from the fact that B values the car more than A being split between A and B. Nozick points out that in this sort of case, permitting a taking rather than requiring B to negotiate to a voluntary agreement with A seems unfair (*ASU*, 63–65).

This list can be pared down. Regarding (c), one can just note that the principle that infringement of any right is allowed provided full compensation is paid to all injured victims does not on its face allow infringement of rights in any case when the infringement causes uncompensable injury. Also, the principle on its face forbids people from infringing a right and declining to pay full compensation because they lack the means to pay, so (d) on Nozick's list is otiose. The issue of compensation raises practical questions concerning what sorts of conditions on right infringement should be built into legal rules or social norms. But the theoretical question—what moral principles are correct?—is not touched by this sort of consideration. The proposal to allow all boundary crossings provided full compensation is forthcoming emerges unscathed from the worries about compensation expressed in (c) and (d).

The injunction in (a) against using people as means strikes me as not advancing the discussion and hence as eliminable from the list. Using people as means to one's ends cannot in itself be problematic. This occurs constantly in interactions we all would regard as innocuous. Kant's humanity formulation of the categorical imperative forbids using people (the humanity or rational agency in people) as *mere* means.[15] What is it to use a person *merely* as a means to one's ends? If I use you as a means to my ends, but only within limits prescribed by morality, I would say I am not using you *merely* as a means. Following this suggestion, let us say that the injunction against using people as means may be interpreted as the injunction never to use people as means to one's ends in ways that are unacceptable according to correct moral principles. Which principles are these? The slogan by itself does not say, and moreover, so far as I can see, does not point us toward any particular answer. So scratch entry (a) from the foregoing list of pertinent considerations.

Entry (b) should also be dropped. The worry that one's plans are liable to be interrupted by a boundary crossing is a cost to be compensated like any other. If the concern is that people who never actually suffer having their boundaries crossed might be troubled by anxiety that such things

[15] Immanuel Kant, *Groundwork of the Metaphysics of Morals*, ed. and trans. Mary Gregor, with an introduction by Christine Korsgaard (Cambridge: Cambridge University Press, 1998), 38. The principle states: "So act that you use humanity, whether in your own person or in the person of any other, always at the same time as an end, never merely as a means."

could happen to them, this anxiety is an aspect of the generalized fear consideration (to which I now turn).

Nozick makes the interesting suggestion (e) that certain harms such as assault tend to provoke generalized, widespread fear and anxiety, and that for this reason one should not treat the infliction of the harm along with full compensation as permissible. Of course, people's innocent activities that violate no one else's rights will sometimes cause harm to others, and people may fear suffering such harms. If it is permissible for A to inflict a harm on B, given that the infliction violates no right of B, then it can hardly be impermissible that A might also be inducing anxiety in C that a similar harm might befall him. For example, A might permissibly harm B by successfully wooing the person B ardently wants to marry, or by successfully applying for a job for which B, who is less well credentialed, also applied, and which he would have been granted but for A's application. But if one is inflicting harm by doing something that at the first level is forbidden by a moral right, the situation seems different.

One response that one might put in the mouth of the advocate of the proposal to allow boundary crossings with compensation is that the point about fear is not an objection to the proposal but, rather, indicates a complexity in the idea of paying full compensation. Suppose I assault B and as a consequence C, D, and E become fearful. We might hold that this sort of indirect harm is properly traceable to the infringer of the right, hence full compensation to victims should be understood broadly so that C, D, and E qualify as victims to be compensated. At this point, one might draw a line between reasonable and unreasonable fear responses. Suppose that C and D are in circumstances that are in relevant ways similar to B's, so that it is understandable and reasonable that they come to believe that there is some considerable probability they might be harmed in a way that is similar to what has happened to B. They become alarmed at this prospect. In contrast, E lives in Alaska, far away, or he has a moat with alligators around his house, or for some other reason the fact that I have assaulted B does not provide any grounds for E's altering upward his belief that he might be subject to assault (or provides grounds that reasonably raise the probability only below some threshold that should be tolerable). We might distinguish sharply between the reasonable fear experienced by C and D and the unreasonable fear experienced by E and require the boundary crosser to compensate fully the C's and D's of the world but not the E's. Alternatively, we might discount the cost of fear by the degree to which the person who experiences the fear of the boundary crossing should be held responsible for unreasonably becoming fearful and reduce the required compensation correspondingly. In any event, what Nozick seems to be calling attention to is a fact about appropriate compensation, not an objection to the proposal under review.

Nozick objects to this treatment of fear. He notes that it may in practice be very difficult to determine whether the vague anxiety E experiences is fear of assault or something else, and whether the fear is properly traceable back to any particular boundary crossing or aggregate of boundary crossings. He also notes that even if no boundary crossings of a certain type in fact occur, the bare fact that the rules in play allow boundary crossings of that type provided compensation is forthcoming might elicit fear. Here I am inclined to draw the line. If no boundary crossings of type X have ever occurred, how can I reasonably fear such attacks? This anxiety must be either de minimis or caused by my oversensitivity rather than by any actions of other persons. Or one might hold that B's fear of boundary crossing X in the absence of any instances of boundary crossings of type X, to the degree it is reasonable, must be caused by the fact that boundary crossings of other types occur, so that one should then hold the perpetrators of these other boundary crossings liable to pay for this extended but reasonable anxiety as well. The discussion in this and the two preceding paragraphs then leads to the conclusion that Nozick's consideration (e) also deserves to be eliminated from his list.

To recapitulate: Nozick cited six considerations, (a) through (f), as weighing against the proposal to allow any boundary crossing without prior consent provided that full compensation is paid to any person whose right is infringed and who suffers injury. The foregoing discussion has suggested grounds for dropping all but (f) from his list.

## VII. Fair Distribution of the Benefits of Exchange

I now turn to the sole remaining entry on Nozick's list, point (f), concerning the fair distribution of the benefits of voluntary exchange (versus unfair distribution in a system that allows boundary crossings with full compensation). Nozick's point is not that there is an independently determinable fair price for goods and services, which voluntary exchange tends to approximate. He disparages the medieval notion of "just price" as a possible basis for economic regulation. Nozick's point is that if one has full ownership rights in something, it is unfair that one is dispossessed of the something absent one's own voluntary choice to relinquish it. This is the norm that is directly challenged by the responses many of us have to the *Hiker* example introduced at the end of Section V above. There is more to be said about this example, but further examples may be useful. Consider the following.

*Holdout.* A proposes to use property he owns to start a widget-making factory, which would be profitable, and beneficial to many. The only feasible process for manufacturing widgets unfortunately spews a type of pollution that unavoidably inflicts small harm on a great many people, the millions of residents of a valley. Each resident suffers a one-dollar loss per year from this pollution. A proposes a scheme of compensation that involves establishing a park that will provide two dollars per year of benefit to each valley resident. Millions agree to this scheme, but one resident, B, refuses to relinquish his right not to be impinged on by harmful pollution unless virtually all of the profits of the factory's operation accrue to him.

Suppose the theorist responds that B has no right to gouge his cooperating and productive neighbors in this way. One might propose a "just price" intuition: If one's involvement in a productive activity amounts only to being slightly physically harmed by it, one has a moral right to be fully compensated for this inconvenience, no more and no less. But this principle sounds suspiciously ad hoc and tailored too specifically to the particular example to be very convincing.

One source of unease with the example might stem from concern that one's right not to be impinged on by others in ways that physically cause damage to one's person or property is not a full, tradable property right. After all, C should not be permitted to sell his right not to be harmed in specified ways in the future to D, who might wish to purchase such rights in the hope that their price might rise in the future. (Or should he? The hard libertarian might simply not blink in the face of any putative counterexample.) But the concern about gouging can arise when the rights at stake are ordinary property rights of an unproblematic sort, as in the following examples.

*Spite.* A installs a huge false chimney on the second story of his house. Its only point is to annoy his neighbor B by blocking B's view of the surrounding landscape. Or A might threaten to install such a chimney and agree to desist only if B pays A very close to B's reservation price, the maximum he would be willing to give to retain the unimpeded view.[16]

*Easy Rescue.* A is drowning. He is in a leaky boat that is slowly sinking, so there is ample time for negotiation. B happens to arrive on the scene in his boat, and offers to save A's life, a feat that can be accomplished at very small cost to B, if A agrees to transfer all of his financial assets to B in return for this easy rescue. (The example can be amplified with details such as that A is far wealthier than B or the reverse, or that A is far better off than B in aggregate lifetime well-being to this point or the reverse.)

Although Nozick does not discuss these two specific examples, it is clear that he would give no quarter to the position that B is under an enforceable duty to perform easy rescue and hence has no right to charge A whatever he is willing to pay for lifesaving service. However, Nozick discusses more sympathetically some pros and cons that might be applied to cases such as *Spite.* His thought is that the imperative of prohibiting boundary crossings without prior consent in order to ensure fair division of the benefits of exchange applies only to the category of productive

[16] This example is drawn from the 1855 French legal case *Keller v. Doerr.* I owe this reference to Gijs Van Donselaar, *The Benefit of Another's Pains: Parasitism, Scarcity, Basic Income* (Amsterdam: Department of Philosophy, University of Amsterdam, 1997), 2.

exchange. In the typical exchange, both parties benefit, and this sort of exchange is unproblematically productive. He defines an *unproductive exchange* as one that satisfies two conditions: (1) one party to the exchange is no better off as a result of it than if the other party did not exist at all, and (2) what this party who is no better off gets from the exchange is the other party's abstention from an activity she would not be motivated to engage in except for the possibility of selling abstention. Another test mentioned by Nozick is that one party to an unproductive exchange would be no worse off if the exchange were prohibited.[17] Where an exchange is in the offing that would be unproductive in this sense, morality does not insist on allowing the exchange to go forward. Depending on further circumstances, it might be right to forbid the activity by one party to the contemplated exchange that would become the object to be exchanged, and it might be right in some cases to require (and in others not to require) compensation accompanying the prohibition. If the first condition for unproductive exchange is satisfied but not the second, call the exchange *semiproductive*. Nozick suggests it may be morally acceptable to prohibit semiproductive exchange by prohibiting one of the parties from engaging in the activity, abstention from which is being exchanged, provided some compensation is given to the party whose favored activity is prohibited in this way.

Nozick applies this analysis to blackmail. In some cases, a blackmail exchange would be unproductive. In these cases, prohibition of blackmail with no compensation to the would-be blackmailer is appropriate. Other cases are mixed. Suppose A wants to publish secrets about B's life. Their inclusion in a book A is writing would improve the book. It is worth a thousand dollars to B to prevent the publication of these secrets. The value to A of his planned use of this information about B is $500. According to Nozick, A can legitimately charge at most $500 for declining to publish B's secrets. This latter case is one in which the first but not the second condition for unproductive exchange would be satisfied, but once B agrees to pay $500 to A, the latter's attempt to make a deal with B for further payment would be an attempt to bring about an unproductive exchange.

The problem with this line of analysis is that the hypotheticals it relies upon are unruly and cannot be tamed.[18] I would be better off if the party with whom I am negotiating an exchange did not exist at all in many circumstances in which this fact does not render the looming exchange in any way problematic or liable to special restriction or prohibition. I am being hired as a consultant to help write A's acceptance speech for the Nobel Prize in chemistry, but if A did not exist at all or had nothing at all

[17] Nozick, *Anarchy, State, and Utopia*, 84–87.

[18] In this connection, see the criticism of Nozick in Eric Mack, "Nozick on Unproductivity: The Unintended Consequences," in Paul, ed., *Reading Nozick*, 169–90.

to do with me, I would be better off, because I would then be next in line to receive the Nobel Prize for my chemistry achievements, which are good, but less good than A's. This fact does not render my exchange of my speechwriting services for A's cash on mutually agreeable terms a semiproductive exchange. The first condition as Nozick formulates it is satisfied, but this does not have the significance Nozick attributes to it. The same is true if I purchase A's abstention from entering a contest she is sure to win if she enters. My chances of winning are greater if A does not enter the contest, and better for that matter if A did not exist or had nothing at all to do with me.

For much the same reason, one cannot say that A wrongfully causes harm to B by physical interaction with B just in case A renders B worse off than would be the case if A did not exist. Nor can the condition be: just in case A renders B worse off than B would be if she had no interaction at all with A. Consider a case in which A has been B's trading partner for years. These interactions have brought a large profit to B. Today A viciously kicks B in the shin, seriously injuring his leg. B is still a net beneficiary of his interactions with A; nonetheless, A violates B's right not to be physically attacked when A kicks B in the shin.

Perhaps it is possible to revise Nozick's conditions on unproductive exchange while preserving the basic idea—or perhaps not. The judgment that in the *Spite* case A has no right to erect a false chimney on his own property and that it would not be wrong forcibly to prohibit A from harming B in this way need not wait upon the vicissitudes of further developments of Nozick's theory of unproductive exchange. In the example, A is being malicious. He is acting in a way he knows will harm B purely for the sake of harming B. (We can contrast *Spite* as specified in the text with an alternate version in which A is a lover of false chimneys and wants to erect this addition to the top of his house in order to improve its appearance by his lights. In the alternate version, A in some sense does the same thing as in the original version, but his intention and motivation are not spiteful, and this fact makes all the difference. In the alternate version, A has a moral right to act as he does and should not be prohibited from doing so.) A plausible interpretation of Lockean rights maintains that intention and motivation can affect the permissibility of what an agent does. An act might be permissible if done with a certain intention or with a certain motive, but the same act—the same physical movement leading to the same physical changes in the world—done with a different intention or motive might be impermissible.

One might object that *Spite* is a very odd case, from which no general normative implications flow.[19] In *Spite* there is no plausible motive except

[19] In this essay, I am concerned with what it is morally permissible and impermissible for people to do in various possible examples. I am not trying to devise a practical doctrine of laws and social norms, which might well be designed for ordinary cases, not extraordinary

malice that would likely explain the homeowner's desire to construct a false chimney on his house. But in the general case, it will not be possible to read off the agent's motive from his behavior. For this reason a regime of rights that rendered the limits of an agent's freedom sensitive to harmed-and-putatively-injured parties' hunches and guesses about the motives of the agent whose doings they find distressing would be an administrative chaos. So we should not understand the limits of people's moral rights in this way.

The objection makes a significant mistake. It fails to distinguish the theoretical question—"What rights do we have?"—from the practical question—"What sort of laws should be established in order to protect individual rights?" Epistemic and administrative difficulties will play a large role in answering the second question but not in answering the first. It will then sometimes make perfect sense for an advocate of individual rights to say, for example, that Smith has a perfect moral right to do X, but nonetheless it is morally correct that a just state should prohibit Smith from doing it, or that Smith has no moral right to do Y but nonetheless a just state should allow her to do it.[20]

## VIII. Why Ever Allow Infringements without Prior Consent?

The flip side of the question, "Why not always allow any border crossing coupled with full compensation?" is "Why ever allow such border crossings not licensed by prior consent?" Discussing this issue, Nozick suggests that transaction costs—the costs of negotiating deals—play a key role. The costs of reaching a deal might be large because the number of parties whose agreement is needed may be large. It may be difficult to locate the agents from whom agreement must be obtained, and difficult or expensive to set in place the communications technology needed for negotiation. The process of making a deal may consume resources in many ways. At the limit, it may be physically impossible to negotiate with someone.

---

ones. That said, if a hard-libertarian reader is disposed to think that this and other cases I discuss are practically resolvable by writing careful contracts, I recommend consulting the theory of incomplete contracting on the economic importance of the impossibility of writing a complete contract that deals with all contingencies that might arise. See Oliver Hart, *Firms, Contracts, and Financial Structure* (Oxford: Clarendon Press, 1995), and the additional literature Hart cites.

[20] Here I presume that an adequate Lockean morality will integrate considerations of mandatory moral goals to be promoted and required side constraints to be respected, and will not go whole hog for either alternative. The fact that if we tried to establish rules that would require the state to enforce people's subtle right to X, the result would be that people's more important rights would be frustrated is then a relevant consideration for the question, what conception of rights should the state enforce?

When transaction costs are high, insistence on prior consent to any boundary crossing might leave all affected parties worse off than they would be if a more permissive rule were accepted. The transaction-cost consideration also introduces a reason of a quite different sort for sometimes allowing boundary crossing provided compensation is forthcoming. Consider an example in which at the time a choice has to be made, prior consent is impossible to obtain.

*Coma.* A has suffered a serious injury and needs immediate medical care, including surgery. Deliberately touching a person without her consent fits the technical definition of an assault, and imposing medical care on a person—which can significantly affect the patient's well-being for better or worse—without her consent is a serious breach of her rights. In this case, A is in a temporary coma and can neither give nor withhold consent to the surgery she needs to save her life.

It would violate the letter but not the spirit of hard libertarianism to allow the surgeon to provide medical care to A without first obtaining A's prior consent in situations of this sort. Three features of the situation favor this judgment: the infringement being proposed would be of great benefit to A; she is not capable of giving or withholding consent without delay that would dissipate this benefit; and she would consent if she were capable of giving or withholding consent. (The hard libertarian who is strict on this point would insist that A is out of luck if she has not previously contracted for care that encompasses this contingency or delegated to a specific agent the authority to choose in this contingency.)

The *Coma* case, from one perspective, is the tip of an iceberg. The underlying difficulty is that insistence on no impingement without consent only imperfectly safeguards an agent's liberty and vital interests. The giving and withholding of consent even under favorable conditions sometimes reflects the agent's distorted assessment or weakness of will. At such times, the agent voluntarily consents to what is bad for self and others.

Notice that some of the cases described previously either do not on their face appear to involve transaction-cost concerns or can be redescribed so it is clear that transaction costs are not driving the judgment that favors permitting infringement. Consider just one of these cases: *Easy Rescue* requires only a negotiation between two people; the negotiation concerns only the price to be paid by one for a simple service offered by the other, and there is plenty of time to negotiate. True, in any thin market setting like this, if the gap between the buyer's and seller's reservation prices is large, agreeing on a division of the gain from trade can be a challenge.

## IX. Chipping Away at Self-Ownership

Easy rescue cases, interpreted as prompting the claim that people are under an enforceable duty to be minimally decent Samaritans, directly challenge the self-ownership thesis. Hard libertarians will resist this challenge, but so will others. To explore the moral basis of self-ownership, one should contrast easy rescue cases with another class of cases that they somewhat resemble. Nozick provides an example:

*Accommodation.* A is minding his business, harming no one. A allows B onto his property. A has no reason to be distrustful of B. However, B takes out a gun and shoots innocent people from A's window perch. Police arrive and attempt to apprehend B. A shouts to the police that he is simply going about his business and has a perfect right to be where he is, which happens to be in the way of the police as they seek to render B harmless.

Nozick raises the question, Does A in these circumstances have a duty to get out of the way of the police as they seek to incapacitate B, who is wrongfully threatening others?[21] One might hold that the police have the moral right forcibly to remove A from the premises so that he does not impede the urgent crime-fighting effort. One might also hold that if A has a duty to move out of the way of the police and does not, then it might be permissible, depending on further circumstances, for the police to shoot at B even if doing so risks harming A. Given that A is not accommodating in the way morality requires, it might be the case that the police, killing A foreseeably but unintentionally as they seek to stop B, do not violate any right that A possesses against them. We can perhaps simplify the complex issues the example raises by imagining a state of nature version of it.

*State-of-Nature Accommodation.* A is fleeing B, an evil aggressor who intends to kill A. Let us assume it would be morally acceptable for A to kill B in self-defense, but unfortunately A in the circumstances is unable to do anything that is likely to save his life by attacking B in self-defense. There is a small alcove in the rocks above, from which C is watching B's chase of A unfold. A can elude B and save his own life by jumping onto the alcove where C is standing. B, a heavy-set aggressor, will not be able to follow. C could move to the rear of the alcove to give A room to land safely. If C does not accommodate A in this way, A has no way to save his own life except by jumping to the alcove, landing where C now stands, and thereby killing him. In the circumstances, all the facts just described are mutual knowledge between A and C: A knows, C knows; A knows that C knows; C knows that A knows; and so on. C does not move to the rear of the alcove.

Consider the position that in these circumstances, C has a moral duty to accommodate by moving from the unowned land that he is currently using but which A now needs as a platform to land on, in order to save his life. If C does not make this accommodating move and A jumps to this

[21] Robert Nozick, "War, Terrorism, Reprisals—Drawing Some Moral Lines," reprinted in Nozick, *Socratic Puzzles*, 303. This chapter was initially a book review published in 1978.

spot, killing C, A is not violating any of C's rights. One might adhere to this position without rejecting the thesis of self-ownership. That is to say, each person fully owns herself, but this is of course compatible with there being limits on the rights anyone has to use unowned land. The moral basis for the requirement of accommodation is the proper understanding of the idea that in a state of nature any person is at liberty freely to use any unowned land. If one person wishes to use a particular piece of unowned land and this desired use is not in conflict with any use anyone else wishes to make of the land, the use is morally permissible. A limit on this right of free use is that if two or more individuals wish to use the same piece of land at the same time in conflicting ways, the one who begins using the land first has the right of way unless one would-be user has significantly greater need of it than the other. In the latter case, the person with the significantly greater need has the right to use. If A and B both wish to sunbathe on the same strip of unowned land, and A gets there first, A has the right to use the land in this way. But if C needs to lie down on this particular sunlit land in order to relieve her intense headache, A must give way to C. I suppose there is also a time-limit on the extent to which any individual can use and keep using any piece of unowned land. The longer one has used the land for one's own purposes, the stronger becomes the presumption that one must yield to give others a turn, if a queue of would-be users of the same land forms. I do not claim that free use rights so understood are clear and well defined: their inadequacies, which perhaps warrant their supersession by private property rights, include their unclarity and vagueness. My claim is that our understanding of the nature of free-use rights to unowned land, partial as it is, underwrites our understanding of the idea that in the example of *State-of-Nature Accommodation*, C's right to the unimpeded use of the alcove where she stands disappears when A arrives on the scene with a pressing need to use that same spot temporarily.

Seen in this light, the *Accommodation* case and the *State-of-Nature Accommodation* case, which might look similar, in fact raise different issues. The latter raises questions about how to interpret rights to free use of unowned property and the limits of those rights. (These limits might continue in force after appropriation and cast a shadow on private ownership rights.) The former introduces a rights violator and other persons (the police) who are acting at risk to themselves to apprehend the rights violator, stop him from threatening others, and perhaps punish him in order to deter others from seeking to trample on people's rights. Those persons who act in this way act to preserve the system of rights that all of us are morally bound to uphold. In this sense they act for us, and we owe them cooperation corresponding to the amount of cost and risk they incur in the efficient pursuit of this goal. Refraining from impeding their efforts when we can refrain at moderate cost and risk to ourselves is part of the fair return we owe to those who cooperate to uphold the system of human rights by preventing those who would violate rights to advance their own ends from succeeding in their efforts. Consider in this connection the following example:

*Free Rider*. A, B, C, D, and E cooperate to provide police protection in their neighborhood. These patrols significantly benefit everyone who lives in this area, including F, by deterring crime. Given the nature of this benefit, there is no question of accepting it or rejecting it; it falls on everyone in the area, willy-nilly. The cooperators demand that F pay one-sixth of the cost of the ongoing police patrols, but F refuses.

In these circumstances, F is dragooned into receiving the benefits of the cooperative scheme that supplies the public good of justice. Is it acceptable to dragoon F into paying his fair share of the costs? (The complication is that given that A, B, C, D, and E are going to provide the good, they have no choice but to provide it to F as well.) The hard libertarian answers "No." The hard libertarian holds that the individual should be left free to live as he chooses unless his actions harm nonconsenting other people in certain ways that violate their rights. Failing to reciprocate a benefit that another person has conferred on you, in the absence of any prior mutual agreement to reciprocate, does not constitute your harming the other, according to the hard libertarian, in any way that amounts to a violation of the other's rights.

One may appeal to two arguments, alone or in tandem, to support a "Yes" answer, that is, to hold that coercing F to pay his fair share of the scheme is acceptable. One is the Hart-Rawls principle of fairness.[22] When others cooperate to supply public goods that benefit a number of people, those who have cooperated have a right that the other beneficiaries pay their share of the costs—to refuse is to be a free rider, which one has no right to be.[23] I construe this principle to continue to apply when there is no voluntary acceptance of benefits received (because of the nature of the good, not because the cooperators have deliberately foisted the good on an unwilling recipient). The hard libertarian reply is that in the absence of some voluntary act that can plausibly be regarded as triggering an obligation, no duties or obligations beyond the negative duties not to harm ever arise for anyone.

[22] For a formulation of the Hart-Rawls principle of fairness, references to the relevant prior literature, and sharp skeptical discussion of the principle itself, see Nozick, *Anarchy, State, and Utopia*, 90–95; A. John Simmons, "The Principle of Fair Play," reprinted in Simmons, *Justification and Legitimacy: Essays on Rights and Obligations* (Cambridge: Cambridge University Press, 2001), 1–26; and A. John Simmons, "Fair Play and Political Obligation: Twenty Years Later," ibid., 27–42.

[23] The duty to refrain from being a free rider might be construed broadly, applying to any scheme that supplies significant public goods, or narrowly, applying only to public goods schemes that provide goods of justice (security of enjoyment of all people's natural rights). The rationale for holding to the narrow construal would be that one views the system of Lockean natural rights, properly understood, as of paramount moral importance, swamping other considerations in the determination of what we owe each other.

The second argument asserts straightaway that each person has a natural duty to promote justice—to do his part, when feasible and not excessively costly, to bring into existence and sustain schemes that protect people's moral rights. In the *Free Rider* case, the natural duty to promote justice applies to F and, in these circumstances, requires him to pay his fair share of the costs of police protection. The hard libertarian replies either by flatly denying the natural duty to promote justice or in a more subtle way by denying that the general duty to support justice anywhere and everywhere requires F (for example) to contribute to the particular local justice promotion enterprise that his neighbors have devised.[24]

In response one might argue that the natural duty to promote justice requires the individual to accept only modest risk and cost in the service of justice, but the contribution that is made must be an efficient use of his resources. Normally this efficiency requirement ties the general duty to promote justice to some local scheme that is operating or is on the horizon. One can more surely and easily promote justice nearby than from afar. This need not always be the case, so the natural duty of justice may allow some Oliver North's and Che Guevara's to be excused from local justice duties because they are contributing sufficiently to justice provision schemes elsewhere.[25] The important break from hard libertarianism occurs when one accepts the natural duty to promote justice along with the norm against free riding.

One issue is whether the individual has a moral duty to refrain from free riding in circumstances like the *Free Rider* case. A second issue is whether the duty is enforceable, whether it warrants coercive force. Hard libertarians tend to see coercion as a large evil. I disagree. Being coerced to refrain from acts one has a right to perform is morally odious, but coercion that prevents one from doing what one has no right to do is not so bad. If traffic laws are just, it is unfortunate if I am coerced to obey them, because it would be better if I willingly complied, so that I am not coerced (the state's threats directed at me being idle). But if I am disposed to disobey, and coerced not to do so by effective traffic law enforcement, the forcing of my will here is not a significant bad, and is definitely preferable to the state of affairs in which I am free of coercion and act wrongfully, violating significant rights of other people.

## X. Self-Ownership Revisited

Construed in a libertarian spirit, self-ownership asserts that each person fully owns herself and may do with herself whatever she likes so long as

[24] For this argument, see A. John Simmons, "Associative Political Obligations," in Simmons, *Justification and Legitimacy*, 65–92.

[25] I am imagining that Oliver and Che, each in his own way, are deemed to be doing enough to advance the cause of justice in a distant country that the natural duty to promote justice cannot be interpreted as ruling out their disobeying some laws of their home country. This is a concession to the Simmons point cited in the previous footnote.

she does not thereby harm others. This entitlement includes the right of each person to destroy herself or waste her own life. As such, this same entitlement strictly forbids restriction of a person's freedom for her own good.[26]

One might instead hold that each individual has over herself the full rights that a private property owner has over whatever things he owns. These rights might not be unlimited, even setting aside the harm-to-others issue. Locke flirts with a stewardship conception of private ownership rights. He claims that one's ownership over a piece of land lapses if one lets the land go to waste.[27] Pressed to its logical limit, the no-waste condition would have it that if anyone else would use your land more productively and efficiently than you would, your right to own it gives way to the right of the more efficient would-be user. Suppose the idea is, rather, that one's uses must meet some acceptable threshold standard of productivity in order to satisfy the no-waste proviso.

By this line of thought, each person's self-ownership rights are also limited by a no-waste requirement. Owning oneself, one has a moral duty not to waste one's life but to make good use of it. A human life is (barring catastrophe) a precious opportunity for good, which ought not to be squandered. This norm leaves each individual vast realms of freedom to live as she chooses, because there are boundless varieties of ways to make something good of one's life. Still, there are limits. The no-waste condition is flagrantly violated by the agent who consents to be mangled for no good reason in the *Whim* case. Another example would be a self-indulgent, petulant suicide. An agent may violate the no-waste condition deliberately or by mistake. If self-ownership is understood by analogy with land ownership constrained by the no-waste requirement, paternalistic restrictions of an agent's liberty for her own good in extreme cases of mistake or folly are consistent with self-ownership, not wrongful violations of it.[28]

[26] Familiar qualifications to this formulation are needed. I might sign a contract that authorizes you to coerce me to stop eating when I try to indulge in rich desserts, and you might agree to this contract from concern for my good. When I lunge for the fancy chocolate cake and you restrain me, you are restricting my freedom for my own good, but in virtue of the contract, you are not violating any right of mine. The libertarian will also qualify the formulation to allow at least temporary paternalistic restriction of liberty in order to block egregiously nonvoluntary choices, as when I am about to drink poison in the false belief that the glass contains wine.

[27] Locke, *Second Treatise of Government*, chap. 5.

[28] Some readers will wonder to whom the duty not to waste one's life might conceivably be owed, and who would be entitled to decide that an individual is violating the duty and to intervene forcibly on the individual's behalf. On the first question, the duty not to waste one's life is owed to those—oneself and others—who stand to benefit if no waste occurs. This is a diffuse group. On the second question, in a Lockean theory, anyone is morally entitled to act to enforce people's natural rights. By the same token, anyone should be morally entitled to act to enforce the natural duty of each person not to waste his own life. Attempts at enforcement might spark umbrage on the part of the person who is being judged a life-waster, and quarrels may ensue, so here as in other cases of conflict around the enforcement of rights and duties, there is need for an impartial, reliable, judicious umpire, if one can be found.

## XI. In Search of Principles: The Pareto Constraint

We need to search for principles that might unify some of the seemingly disparate responses to the various puzzle cases examined to this point. One possibility is that rights are subject to a Pareto constraint:

> *A state of affairs that can be improved by making someone better off without making anyone else worse off is morally unacceptable. The specification of individual rights should be adjusted (if possible) so that respecting everyone's individual rights does not produce such a state of affairs.*

This Pareto constraint varies in substance depending on the interpretation of "better off" and "worse off." On a subjective interpretation, one is better off just in case one's preferences are satisfied to a greater extent (with one's own ranking of preferences determining the priority of satisfying each of them). On an objective interpretation, one is better off if one's well-being, assessed by the correct standard, is greater. The objective interpretation obviously relies on controversial value-theory assumptions, but if it can be sustained, the Pareto constraint generates moral considerations of greater strength, and I adopt it here. The appeal of the Pareto constraint in the context of developing Lockean theory is evident in the following example:

*Benign Trespasser.* A is the absentee owner of a large estate with an orchard. B and C trespass on the land in the autumn, picking ripe fruit in the orchard that would otherwise rot. They do no damage. There is no feasible way to spread the benefits B and C receive to other people without dissipating them. A's absentee status renders it the case that no negotiation between A and B and C can occur that would fix a mutually agreeable price for this incursion on A's land. Here, the Pareto constraint on the interpretation of Lockean rights requires us to take the view that the right of private ownership allows benign trespassing.

Some of the examples discussed so far in this essay that suggest the need to qualify libertarian principles are not explained and justified by the Pareto constraint. Consider the *Easy Rescue* case. One might try to claim that some would be better off and none worse off in a society in which our conception of individual rights is adjusted so that all who find themselves in serious predicaments and need easy rescue have a right to easy rescue if anyone is in a position to provide it, and each person has a duty to provide easy rescue if he is in circumstances such that by easy rescue he can prevent a person's unwanted serious injury or premature death.

One might claim that from a suitable ex ante standpoint, before it is known who will be in the rescuer role and who will be potential beneficiaries of easy rescues, everyone gains by agreeing to a rule requiring easy rescue. But ex post, once it becomes evident who will in fact be playing what role on what occasions, it is no longer plausible to maintain that a rule mandating easy rescue renders everyone better off than he would be if the rules were not in place. Consider A, who is lucky enough never to need an easy rescue and unlucky enough to find herself sometimes in the rescuer role. She is ex post a net loser. Or consider B, who as it turns out finds himself in a position to extract a large monetary windfall by negotiating the terms of an easy rescue with Bill Gates, who happens to need this service and is extraordinarily flush with cash to pay for it. B is better off over the course of his life in a world in which Lockean natural rights are enforced and the rights are not adjusted by adding a duty of easy rescue. That way, he gains the windfall from Bill Gates, which he does not receive under the regime in which easy rescue is required.

So consider the proposal that initially Lockean rights should be adjusted in order to incorporate an ex ante Pareto requirement. The idea would be that the rules that specify the content of Lockean rights should be qualified as necessary to yield the result that, from an ex ante perspective (before it is known who will gain and who will lose from any rules alteration), one cannot alter the rules further in a way that would improve everyone's expected level of advantage from the operation of the system of rules.[29] To clarify the proposal, one would need to specify in a more determinate way the relevant ex ante standpoint. Even without clarification, it should be plain that the ex ante Pareto norm radically alters Lockean rights. This point becomes more vivid if attention is switched from *Easy Rescue* examples to examples that involve the forced utter sacrifice of some persons' interests to benefit others. Surely a Lockean rights perspective that retains its integrity must disallow killing one person when that would be a necessary means to saving two others. But from an ex ante perspective, not knowing whether one is the person to be sacrificed or one of the two to be saved, everyone's prospects are improved by acceptance of a policy that licenses an agency to kill one innocent whenever doing so saves more than one innocent. The ex ante Pareto norm, once accepted as qualifying a set of Lockean rights, transforms the "rights" perspective into something close to aggregative utilitarianism.

If the aim of the discussion in this essay is to explore the alternatives within the Lockean tradition rather than others that radically and brutally

[29] This example illustrates the ex ante Pareto norm: Suppose that 100,000 people live in an isolated valley and that each year each resident faces a 1 percent chance of suffering an automobile accident that will cost the individual, on the average, $20 if easy rescue is forthcoming and $100 if it is not. (Easy rescue will be forthcoming if and only if it is legally required.) If everyone in the valley is legally required to provide easy rescue if present at an automobile accident, each member faces a 1 percent chance per year of being required to perform this service at a cost to the rescuer, on the average, of $30. Money is linear with utility for valley residents and all have a neutral attitude toward risk. In these circumstances, the introduction of a legal requirement of providing easy rescue provides an ex ante Pareto improvement.

depart from it, we should interpret the Pareto norm as ex post rather than ex ante.

The ex post Pareto norm does not unequivocally ratify some of the judgments about examples that I am supposing soft Lockeans will want to ratify. *Easy Rescue* is one such case. *Hiker* is another. A rule allowing infringement in circumstances like those of *Hiker* could be devised that would improve everyone's welfare (compared to the hard-libertarian position that requires the hiker to perish), but if we vary the case by providing the lost hiker access to a pay telephone so negotiation with the cabin owner can occur prior to use of the mountain cabin, any rule that partially expropriates the property right to the cabin for the benefit of those who need emergency aid is worse for the cabin owner, who can benefit by selling temporary use of the cabin to those in need of it. If, given this amended version of the case, the judgment persists that the cabin owner's property right should give way in the face of the lost hiker's need, the basis of the judgment is not the Pareto constraint but a norm of fairness that prohibits gouging the needy in this sort of situation.

## XII. Moderation

One possible nonlibertarian response to the *Easy Rescue* case denies that what warrants the limitation of self-ownership rights in this case has anything specifically to do with self-ownership. The idea would be that any moral right, however sacred, gives way if the consequences of upholding it in a particular case are sufficiently bad. Rights on this view are nonrigid, spongy side constraints.[30] For any individual deciding what to do and faced with a set of available courses of action that might be chosen, rights are side constraints that rule out certain courses of action and render them morally ineligible for choice, but if the consequences of abiding by these constraints would be sufficiently bad, they relax, and options that would otherwise be ineligible become eligible.

In an interesting footnote, Nozick sets aside the issue of whether rights are rigid or nonrigid side constraints. He comments, "The question of whether these side constraints are absolute, or whether they may be violated in order to avoid catastrophic moral horror, and if the latter, what the resulting structure might look like, is one I hope largely to avoid" (*ASU*, 30). Nozick does not declare a commitment one way or the other on this issue.

An alternative picture that contrasts with the rights-as-spongy-side-constraints metaphor represents rights as rigid but sometimes reconfigured under pressure of consequences. Sufficiently bad consequences can

[30] The term "spongy side constraint" is borrowed from Judith Jarvis Thomson, who uses it to describe a moderate position on the stringency of moral rights in her *The Realm of Rights* (Cambridge, MA: Harvard University Press, 1990), 154.

reshape the requirements that rights impose, the resultant rights being sometimes rigid again and sometimes nonrigid. For example, each person has a right of self-ownership, and no duty to use one's body to provide aid to the needy, but if the consequences of insistence on self-ownership would be sufficiently bad, the right dissolves, and may become a strict duty to aid, and correspondingly a right on the part of the needy to be assisted.

Judith Jarvis Thomson has suggested a useful way to characterize the stringency of a right: the degree to which it resists being overridden by counterconsiderations.[31] She proposes that a right is more stringent the greater the harm that would ensue for the right-holder if the right is not upheld. This formulation by itself explains the plausible thought that even though I have a right not to be violently assaulted and a right that my extra shirt button not be taken from me without my consent, the two rights are not on a par. They are not on a par in the sense that a greater weight of reasons is required to justify overriding the right against violent assault. A great harm is less easily offset than a small harm. Note also that if by some chance you would suffer grievous injury if your extra shirt button were stolen, the right to retain your extra shirt button would become correspondingly more stringent.

Thomson's formulation needs some tweaking.[32] Suppose that I would not be harmed at all if you stole from me the hard drugs I own and prize, because without your intervention I would use the drugs to my detriment. My right to the hard drugs I own then has zero stringency according to the formulation of the previous paragraph. However, the theft in these circumstances might be deemed an instance of wrongful paternalism, restriction of a person's liberty against his will for his own good. The individual has an interest in personal sovereignty, in not being subject to such paternalism, even if frustration of the interest does not harm him or reduce his welfare. Also, a person might have an interest in pursuing a valuable goal, the fulfillment of which would not enhance her own welfare. (Call such interests *agency interests*.) If A steals B's rowboat, which she was about to use to rescue someone in distress, the net effect may be no harm at all to B, who now is able to enjoy her picnic lunch in peace. But the significant loss to B's agency interest, we plausibly suppose, renders B's right to undisturbed possession of her rowboat a stringent right in the circumstances.

[31] Thomson, *The Realm of Rights*, chap. 6. An earlier discussion is in Judith Jarvis Thomson, "Some Ruminations on Rights," reprinted in Paul, ed., *Reading Nozick*, 130–47. This section of my essay is heavily indebted to Thomson's writings on the issue.

[32] In my essay "Moderate Deontology, Aggregation, and Rights" (typescript available from the author), I consider how one may aggregate goods and bads of various amounts that would accrue to the right-holder and others if one respects a right or not. Some doubt that failure to respect a person's serious right, such as a right not to be killed, could be offset by any aggregation of tiny benefits to others, however numerous these others. I argue against this plausible claim.

To accommodate these possibilities, I shall simply stipulate that a right is more stringent the greater the loss to the right-holder, in terms of the fulfillment of her interests (including welfare, personal sovereignty, and agency interests) if the right is not upheld.

According to the moderate view of moral rights, the stringency of a right depends on what is at stake for the right-holder. If the net effect on other people of infringing the right (acting against it), compared to what would happen to them if the right were not infringed, is positive and sufficiently large, the right is overridden. When a right is overridden, it is at least permissible, and may be mandatory, to infringe it. The ratio of the loss-to-the-right-holder-if-the-right-is-infringed to the net-loss-to-others-if-the-right-is-not-infringed determines whether or not infringement in a particular case is permissible. If the numerical value of the ratio is sufficiently large, the right may permissibly be breached. The simplest view would hold that there is one numerical value of this ratio that always marks the point of permissible infringement of any right. Another view would hold that this numerical value might vary depending on the type of right under consideration. For example, a one-to-three ratio might suffice for relatively inconsequential rights, so that it is morally permissible to steal my extra shirt button in order to prevent three similar thefts. The required ratio might shift for more consequential rights, so that it is not morally permissible to attack and kill one healthy, innocent person even in order to save three other healthy, innocent persons from a similar fate.

A further complication is that considerations of responsibility or deservingness might discount or amplify the value of the losses and gains of affected parties that determine whether a right in given circumstances may be overridden. A limiting case that illustrates this point is a lone individual defending herself against attack by evil aggressors. It's her life or theirs. Given the culpability of the agents who would suffer if the individual's right not to be attacked is upheld, their numbers do not matter. Even if the evil aggressors are legion, their cumulative loss if the individual defending her life manages to kill all of them would not morally outweigh her loss if she were wrongfully killed.

## XIII. "Core" Self-Ownership: No Duty to Aid the Needy Per Se

None of the modifications to the Lockean individual rights doctrine that I have suggested contravenes the core of the libertarian self-ownership constraint, which I would formulate in this way: *The mere facts that one person is in a position to help another person who is in need of help and that the first person could provide assistance so that what she loses by providing aid is less than what the beneficiary gains are not sufficient to generate a duty to aid. Nor are matters changed if it is stipulated that nothing else the first person could do instead would help the needy to a greater extent (at lesser cost to herself than the gain to the beneficiaries). The mere fact that another is in need does not trigger an enforceable duty to aid.*[33]

This core self-ownership idea is consistent with the claim that one's ownership of things other than oneself is less than full. When the ratio of the good that one's possessions would do if used by others to the good those possessions would do if they remained entirely in one's own control exceeds a threshold, the right of ownership relaxes, as in the *Hiker* case.

Core self-ownership is also consistent with the claim that one has a natural duty to promote justice (the condition in which all people's natural rights are fully respected) to some extent. This duty can be understood so that it generates a duty to cooperate with citizens acting to uphold justice as in the *Accommodation* case. Core self-ownership is also compatible with the anti-free-rider norm suggested by the *Free Rider* case.

If core self-ownership is construed weakly as I have been suggesting, various other aspects of concern for fairness might be embraced without triggering conflict with this weak self-ownership constraint. One such aspect is that in thin market settings, where there are few buyers and sellers for a good or service, one does not have the right to charge whatever the traffic will bear. In particular, when the gap between the reservation prices of the would-be buyer and seller is very large, one does not have the right to force one party to an exchange at her reservation price even if one can do this by hard bargaining. This aspect of fairness colors the response to the *Holdout, Hiker,* and *Easy Rescue* cases. Notice that the rejection of the idea that in these examples the person in a strong bargaining position may legitimately charge whatever price she can negotiate does not rule out profit-taking in these settings by the person with the bargaining edge. Morality might accept profit-taking (beyond bare compensation for loss) but prohibit gouging or excessive profit-taking in such cases.

Objection: There is another element of self-ownership that equally merits designation as part of the core of the principle, and that straightforwardly conflicts with the judgments supposedly evoked (in my view) by *Holdout, Hiker, Free Rider,* and *Easy Rescue.* People are free to lead their lives as they choose (so long as they do not harm others) and may not be used against their will to advance the purposes of others.

Reply: It is wrong from the Lockean standpoint to force people against their will to advance other people's arbitrary ends, ends the coerced persons are not morally required to pursue anyway. The question then is, what ends are morally mandatory? The Lockean nonlibertarian holds that the promotion of justice for all—justice being identified with fulfillment of a Lockean set of rights—is an end that every person morally must

[33] Just for the record, I state that I do not myself endorse this statement of core self-ownership. In this essay I am exploring the natural rights tradition from within, not lobbing external criticisms at it.

adopt and pursue at least to a threshold reasonable extent. In like manner, the freedom to live as one chooses, within broad limits, is compatible with requiring individuals to comply with fairness norms in their dealings with one another.[34]

However, it should be noted that a problem is lurking in this neighborhood, one I shall not here attempt to resolve. Suppose one denies a duty to carry out easy rescues. Perhaps this is the point at which core self-ownership is thought to bite. With this denial in place, insistence on fairness conceived as ruling out charging whatever the traffic will bear in thin market settings will then be inconsistent with the Pareto constraint. To see this, note that A might be willing to rescue, but only if she profits by charging B his reservation price for this service, and B would prefer to pay this price rather than perish.

Even moderation (as introduced in Section XII), the norm that of those considered in this essay most radically alters the shape of natural rights theory, is strictly consistent with the core idea of self-ownership as I conceive it. The mere fact that a person is in need does not suffice to give the needy person a right to be assisted by anyone else, nor does it suffice to generate an enforceable duty to aid that falls on anyone else. But if someone is needy in the sense of being threatened with a loss that is excessive in relation to the cost that would have to be incurred by another individual who could avert the loss at least cost to herself, and if the threatened loss itself exceeds some threshold magnitude, then the moderation norm holds that a right to be aided and a corresponding duty to aid do arise.[35]

[34] For a contrary view, see Loren Lomasky, "Nozick's Libertarian Utopia," in Schmidtz, ed., *Robert Nozick*, 59–82. On p. 73, Lomasky writes, "Basic respect for autonomy enables pursuit of individual projects within a liberal order, but autonomy in any recognizable guise is the first casualty of a social arrangement in which everyone effectively owns a piece of everyone." To my ear this claim sounds wildly exaggerated. Consider a regime in which minimally decent Samaritanism is enforced: everyone has a minimal property right in everyone else that entitles each to command the aid of another in just those circumstances when (a) the aid will save a life well worth living, or bring about some comparably great benefit for its recipient, and (b) the aid can be provided at minimal cost to the giver. (If one likes, one can add a third condition: (c) the potential recipient of aid is not culpably responsible, beyond a certain threshold magnitude, for her dire predicament.) Whatever may be said for or against such a regime, it does not destroy autonomy in any recognizable guise (or in its most sensible guises). Much the same should be said of a regime in which each person has the following limited property right in the bodies of other persons: no one is permitted to be a free rider on cooperative schemes that provide important public goods of justice.

[35] There are two requirements here: the ratio between the benefit to the potential recipient of aid and its cost to the potential supplier must be sufficiently favorable, and the net magnitude of gain the recipient of aid would receive must be sufficiently large. One also wants the notion of "the person positioned to be able to supply aid at least cost to herself" to be sensitive to gains and losses over time. If Mother Teresa has already made huge sacrifices of her self-interest for the truly needy, whereas I have to this point in my life made nil sacrifices of this kind, and right now Mother Teresa could save a life at a cost of $10, whereas I could save the same life at the cost of $10.50 (suppose money here is linear with interpersonally comparable welfare), we want the moderate principle of Good Samaritanism to require me, not Mother Teresa, to provide the aid if anyone should in this instance.

## XIV. The Principles Considered

Moderation expresses the idea that people are inviolable, up to a point. Individuals have rights that constrain what others may do to them, but the constraints give way when too much evil will ensue if those rights are upheld.

The other revisionary principles that I have invoked to support the judgments about puzzle cases that seem compelling modify the idea of inviolability, or individuals' fundamental entitlements. These principles can all be regarded as partial explications of the idea of fair dealing. It is not fair to begrudge anyone a benefit when allowing that whatever brings the benefit is costless to all others (including oneself). It is not fair to hold out for the maximum possible benefit for oneself when circumstances of thin markets give one a bargaining edge over those with whom one might contract on mutually beneficial terms. It is never fair to act maliciously toward others, aiming at nothing except harm or evil for them. There is also fairness toward oneself. One may not act with malice toward oneself. One has a duty to make something good of one's life—utterly squandering it is unfair to oneself. It is not fair to free ride on the cooperative behavior of others that provides one the public goods associated with secure enjoyment of the system of rights. A closely related point is that it is not fair to shirk one's duty to assume one's reasonable share of the costs of promoting justice (the system of natural rights, modified by these fairness requirements and by the principle of moderation itself). What is unfair in these ways one does not have a moral right to do.

These revisions to Lockean libertarianism all raise the Goldilocks problem.[36] In each case, fairness is identified with a proper or appropriate or reasonable weighing of conflicting principles, but nothing has been said in this essay to identify these optimal balance points. More needs to be said here. A sketch is not a moral theory.

"Fairness" here is just a term that encompasses various moral considerations. Ideally, one would like to have a theory of fairness rather than a collection of intuitions. But lack of a theory does not by itself impugn the intuitions about puzzle cases.

A serious concern that would need to be addressed in a satisfactory treatment is whether or not the revisions proposed in the libertarian position can coalesce into a stable doctrine. Is soft Lockeanism an unstable compromise of what further investigation would reveal to be incompatible elements? Can side constraints and entitlements cohere with outcome-oriented moral concerns? A full answer to these questions would

[36] In the fable "Goldilocks and the Three Bears," Goldilocks wanders into the bears' house, encounters three chairs, three beds, and three bowls of soup with different features, and for each of the triples ponders which one is "just right." Given multiple moral values, each one varying by degree, a moral theory sets their relative value and so determines, for any states of affairs that combine the values in different combinations, which state of affairs is best, which second-best, and so on.

require the development of a complete moral theory. But pending the construction of such a theory, I do not see a deep problem here. "People are inviolable, up to a point" sounds paradoxical, but the underlying idea is coherent: "You may do whatever you choose so long as you do not harm others in ways that violate their negative rights, unless (a) doing what you choose while violating no such right would allow excessively large losses to others' interests, in which case you must cater to their interests, or (b) failing to violate a right of another would lead to excessively large losses to others' interests, in which case you must violate the right." This is a consequence-constrained side constraint view.

## XV. Conclusion

Throughout this essay, I have merely described examples and noted my own responses that take the form of judging the limits of people's rights in the situations as characterized. I have not advanced any argument supporting these responses except to note their inherent plausibility. The way is thus open for the hard libertarian to stand fast by her position and budge not. Against the assertion that the responses that contradict hard libertarianism are plausible, the hard libertarian can respond, "So what?" However, what Nozick says about the Randian position is relevant here:

> A large part of the attraction of the Randian view for people is the way it handles particular cases, the kind of considerations it brings to bear, its "sense of life." For many, the first time they encounter a libertarian view saying that a rational life (with individual rights) is possible and justified is in the writings of Miss Rand, and their finding such a view attractive, right, etc., can easily lead them to think that the particular *arguments* Miss Rand offers for the view are conclusive or adequate. Here it is not the argument which has led them to accept the view, but rather the way the view codifies, integrates, unifies, extends many of the judgments they want to make, feel are right, and supports their aspirations. If this is so, then one should hold the view so that it is open to challenge from just the sort of data that has provided its main support.[37]

I agree, and of course Nozick's own positive doctrine must answer to examples in just this same way. Libertarianism is open to challenge from the responses to cases that seem most compelling to us after scrutiny and reflection. On this basis my provisional conclusion is, "Down with hard libertarianism, up with soft Lockeanism."[38]

*Philosophy, University of California at San Diego*

[37] Robert Nozick, "On the Randian Argument," reprinted in Nozick, *Socratic Puzzles*, 249–64; see footnote 16 on p. 386.

[38] "Up with soft Lockeanism" means that this doctrine deserves to be regarded as a serious rival of the most plausible consequentialist morality. My own hunch is that consequentialism ultimately wins this competition.

# Part II
# Property

# [4]

# *Original Acquisition of Private Property*

LEIF WENAR

Suppose libertarians could prove that durable, unqualified private property rights could be created through "original acquisition" of unowned resources in a state of nature. Such a proof would cast serious doubt on the legitimacy of the modern state. It could also render the approach to property rights that I favour irrelevant. I argue here that none of the familiar Lockean-libertarian arguments for a strong natural right to acquisition succeed, and that any successful argument for grounding a right to acquire would have to use my favoured approach to property rights—the "vector-sum" approach. I conclude with some doubts about original acquisition theory and natural property rights.

## *1. Introduction: Rights and property rights*

The vector-sum approach is a component of the full justification of a right. It recommends that we first investigate the benefits to individuals that will flow from the right's being in effect; and that we make a similar tally of the costs to individuals' interests from recognising the right. With this information about costs and benefits, we calculate an "array of interests" that shows how well-off each individual would be were that right ascribed. We then calculate similar arrays of interests for alternative schemes in which slightly different rights are ascribed, and in which no such right is ascribed. Having assembled these arrays of interests, the vector-sum approach can pass the arrays to a larger normative theory. This larger normative theory explains why recognising the right in question is more reasonable, given its relative benefits and costs, than recognising slightly different rights or no right at all.

Different normative theories will of course have different ways of determining which selection of rights is more "reasonable". A theory may prefer the right which produces the array of interests where the sum of interests is greatest, or the array where the worst-off person is best off, or whatever. For our purposes here it is not important which of these larger theories is correct; all we will need is the relatively uncontroversial premise that it is more reasonable to recognise one scheme of rights than another if the one leads to greater benefits for every person than does the other, or if the one is better for some and worse for none.[1]

An example is the right that we ascribe to everyone against being touched without consent ("the right to bodily integrity"). On the one hand, this right protects several important individual interests: our interests in being free from pain and distraction, in being able to carry out complex plans of action, in being able to limit information about ourselves, and in being able to form intimate relationships. On the other hand, we pay the costs of respecting this right when another person's body is an object of aversion or desire, or an obstacle, or a threat. Recognising a general right to bodily integrity makes everyone better off than recognising no such right at all, or than, for example, recognising a general right that would be violated whenever one person came within ten feet of another. This is the justification of the general right to bodily integrity.

Yet the general right to bodily integrity that we recognise is also qualified in many ways. It may not be a rights-violation to strike an assailant, or to jostle through a crowd to catch a thief, or to pull a comatose victim to safety. The right to bodily integrity is intricately "shaped", and given even the sketch of rights-theory above we can see why this is so. A wide range of interests figure into the costs and benefits of recognising this right, and the relative importance of these interests will vary with circumstances. In some situations the costs of recognising the general right shoot up, while in others the benefits dwindle. The contours of a general right like the right to bodily integrity will be formed by the qualifications it admits for such situations.

Because several variable interests are relevant to most or all rights, we can expect that every right we ascribe will have some complexities to its shape. To use a metaphor from Nozick, every right will be "the (moral) vector resultant of the opposing weighty considerations, each of which must be taken into account somehow" (Nozick 1974, p. 146). One difficult task of a moral philosopher is to describe how these several interests should both ground and qualify a general right—that is, to explain exactly why a right of a certain shape is the "vector-sum" of all the interests at stake.[2]

Ownership is a three-place relation: some agent holds certain rights over some thing. Elsewhere (Wenar, forthcoming) I propose a conceptual analysis of ownership that focuses on the complex structure of the rights involved in this relation. Property, I claim, is any object of transferable

[1] Utilitarianism, contractualism, prioritarianism and traditional egalitarianism converge on the first part of this premise, and only egalitarianism dissents to the second part in some cases.

[2] A good example of an investigation of the qualifications to a general right is Sidgwick's study of promise-keeping (1907, pp. 303–11).

rights to exclusive use. One benefit of this analysis is that it fits well into the vector-sum approach. Bringing out the complexity of the property rights structure highlights the many ways that property rights—that is, rights to transfer, to exclude, and to use—can be strengthened or weakened so as to protect and advance different kinds of interests. The vector-sum approach as applied to this analysis of property says that the best way to discover which property rules are best for us is to examine how the large number of often countervailing interests put pressure on the contours of the property rights structure at different points.

This investigation of how various interests put pressure on the contours of property rights is more complex than an investigation into the right of bodily integrity would be, because *who* should be able to hold *which rights* of *what duration* over *what sorts* of property are in general more contentious questions than analogous questions about the body. Even cataloging the "vectors" relevant to property will require a lot of space.

The current paper argues against the type of libertarian theory that would say this space is not worth taking. Suppose it could be established that individuals have a natural right to appropriate unowned resources in such a way as to generate bequeathable and relatively unqualified property rights. It would then also be possible that the weighing of current costs and benefits would have no bearing on the question of what property rights we should recognise now. For appropriation in the state of nature could then create strong property entitlements that would persist to this day. Moreover, since the rights defining these entitlements could only be "reshaped" by the individual rights-holders, any general qualifications of property rights could come about only through an unlikely universal agreement to alter the ancient entitlements. Whether these inherited rights were isomorphic to the rights currently endorsed by the vector-sum approach would be irrelevant to their justification.

This challenge comes, of course, from original acquisition theory and the libertarian successors to Locke.[3] I will contend against such theorists that original acquisition theory, if it is to work at all, must use the vector-sum approach. My strategy is to corral acquisition theory toward this conclusion by closing off alternatives suggested by the Lockean tradition. Thus after an analysis and winnowing of possible pre-appropriation states of nature, I show that all arguments but one for ascribing a strong natural right of acquisition fall short. And this one remaining argument, I will claim, must fit within the vector-sum framework.

[3] I say "libertarian successors to Locke" because it seems unlikely that Locke would endorse the libertarian thesis that strong property rights are acquired in the state of nature. See for example Wolff (1991, pp. 24–7).

## 2. The structure of original appropriation theories

Specific arguments for a natural right to appropriate build on the assumptions of the surrounding theory, and particularly on the assumptions about what the state of nature is like before appropriation takes place. This section lays out the structure of original appropriation theories with special attention to the pre-appropriation states of nature that such theories might deploy. I argue that only one of these pre-appropriation states could be useful to the libertarian appropriation theorist, thereby establishing the context for the natural rights arguments examined later.

Original appropriation theories can be divided into five parts:

1. The first part of an original appropriation theory describes the rights enjoyed by the inhabitants of the state of nature before appropriation begins (I assume this includes normal bodily rights in all variations). I'll discuss three types of candidates for this initial state in a moment.
2. Second comes a description of what pressures the inhabitants to begin private appropriation, such as a looming tragedy of the commons (e.g. Schmidtz 1990) or as Pufendorf put it merely "innumerable conflicts ... from rivalry of many persons over the same thing" (Buckle 1991, p. 98).
3. Third is a specification of the circumstances in which appropriation is permitted, in the general form, "If *C* obtains, then *A* can appropriate *O*". Here we might find Locke's "enough, and as good left in common for others" (Locke 1689, p. 288), or Nozick's Lockean proviso: "A process normally giving rise to a permanent bequeathable property right in a previously unowned thing will not do so if the position of others no longer at liberty to use the thing is thereby worsened" (Nozick 1974, p. 178). Of course, a theorist may also (as Narveson 1988, pp. 84–5) place no circumstantial restrictions whatsoever on appropriation.
4. Fourth, an original appropriation theory states which acts give rise to private property entitlements. There are several familiar alternatives here, including labour-mixing, incorporation, and first occupation.
5. Finally, a theory must indicate the shape and duration of the rights of ownership that original appropriation generates. For example, Grotius qualifies the private right to exclude from land and water with a right in non-owners to "innocent use" of fields and rivers; and both Pufendorf and Locke provide that the (blameless) needy can expropriate the rich of their surplus. As to duration, Locke's spoilation proviso provides one type of qualification: a property right endures until it becomes clear that the property is going to spoil. Nozick's "historical shadow of the Lockean proviso on appropriation" fits here too: property rights over an object last only

> so long as non-owners are above some baseline situation with respect to that object (Nozick 1974, p. 180).

We are here engaged with original appropriation theories that seek to ground *strong* private property rights, which are the sorts of property rights that libertarians characteristically defend—that is, rights unqualified enough to call into question the legitimacy of the normal expropriative and regulatory powers of the modern state. These are the sorts of property rights that threaten to make the vector-sum approach to property irrelevant. It is as much the *duration* as the *shape* of these strong rights that threatens the vector-sum approach—because only durable naturally-generated rights would have implications for our current property practices. However, the duration of any individual's control over an appropriated resource must be neither too short *nor too long* if property rights are to play their role in libertarian theory.

Clearly, strong property rights must last beyond the time that the appropriator actually uses the appropriated thing. The duration of the rights must make it possible to own what is currently unused, just as the shape of the rights must make them somewhat resistant to the desires and even the needs of non-owners. Yet an appropriator cannot gain rights to control the appropriated thing for too far into the future, unless feudalism instead of capitalism is the desired result. A moment's reflection on the history of the entailed estate (true "absolute ownership" of real property) should convince the libertarian that the Law of Nature must include something like the Rule against Perpetuities. An appropriator may be granted strong rights to control an object during his lifetime, but he must not be allowed to determine the object's eternal fate.

We can now explore the options for the first part of original appropriation theory: the pre-appropriation state of nature. There are two species of pre-appropriation states of nature, and then a third species made up of hybrids of the other two.

The first species comprises the "no-ownership" states of nature, and the second the "common-ownership" states. In a no-ownership state, each person may initially use any object in any way she likes, within the limits of others's bodily rights. Each can possess, use, consume or destroy anything that she can grab or keep hold of. Moreover, anyone may unilaterally create private property rights in herself given that she is in the conditions that the theory specifies.

In a common-ownership state, on the other hand, theorising begins with everything owned by everyone. The task of the original appropriation theorist who starts from a common-ownership premise is to show how "privatization" as opposed to "acquisition" takes place.

Of course an original appropriation theorist may also choose an initial state that is a hybrid of these two basic types. Thus Rousseau famously (if not precisely) distinguishes original rights over different types of objects by declaring that "The fruits of the earth belong to all, and the earth itself to no one!" (Rousseau 1755, p. 60).

We want to discover which of these possible states of nature might be a viable starting point for the libertarian appropriation theorist. Modern theorists (e.g. Gaus and Lomasky 1990, p. 489) might think that the universal-ownership construals of the starting state cannot be motivated without an appeal to quaint theological premises. Or at the least the burden should be on the proponent of universal-ownership to say why it should be thought that everyone initially owns everything, rather than that everyone initially owns nothing.

Yet is it so obvious that this second assumption needs less justification than the first? None of the possible states of nature is, after all, a rights-vacuum. In the no-ownership scenarios each person has the natural right to create property rights in herself—is this less contentious than that each person should be vested with property rights from the start? Moreover the no-ownership variants give each inhabitant of the state of nature the right of using (even using up) what others may want or need, while the common-ownership states give each equal say in determining the disposition of the resources that all might use. When phrased in these terms—in terms of "equal freedom" versus "equal voice"—it seems less likely that no-ownership can win by default.

It is an entirely different matter, however, when we ask which of these feasible starting states might be useful to the theorist hoping to generate an extensive system of strong property rights. On this question, all other contrasts between no-ownership and common-ownership are overshadowed by one large difference. Within no-ownership states, appropriation is unilateral, while in the common-ownership states any appropriation of private property requires the consent of all non-appropriators. That is, acquisition from within no-ownership is do-it-yourself, while privatization from within common-ownership must be the result of a bargain among all parties.

There is one important advantage for the strong appropriation theorist who tries to generate private entitlements through universal consent. The rights that the strong appropriationist wants—unqualified, durable and transferable rights to exclusive use—are a simple and therefore a salient solution to the bargaining problem. A theorist attempting to use a unanimous consent justification for strong property rights would be well advised to highlight this salience by emphasising situations in which the pressures towards privatization are intense. Yet two types of asymmetries among the bargaining parties will scuttle a derivation of strong property from universal consent in any but the most extreme circumstances.

The first type of asymmetry is among the inhabitants of the state of nature with respect to the act that is supposed to generate strong property entitlements (see Gaus and Lomasky 1990, p. 499). Whatever act is proposed (first occupation, labour-mixing, etc.) some will be better at it, or better situated or more willing to do it. Those worse at the proposed act have incentives to hold out for qualifications to the property structure, such as usufruct rights, or perpetual side-payments, or something like the right of eminent domain. In Gibbard's example, the handicapped (who are worse at, say, first occupation) might hold out for mandatory welfare subsidies from the able-bodied (Gibbard 1976, pp. 80–1). Moreover Gibbard's example underestimates the complexities that follow from this type of asymmetry. For the possibility of coalitions makes it hard to say in advance how pressures to appropriate will bear on any individual.

Perhaps this first asymmetry could be overcome by bypassing the specification of an appropriative act and allowing the bargainers to agree simultaneously on a structure of strong property rights and on a distribution of particular entitlements. Such an agreement would still be a threat to the vector-sum approach to property. Yet even this solution cannot avoid the second type of asymmetry, which is the time of entry to the agreement (see Gibbard 1976, pp. 81–2). Children are born, and in unanimous consent theory they would not be bound to recognise pre-existing entitlements unless they agreed to respect them. Yet why would these latecomers agree to respect the existing structure and distribution of property rights? Either an original agreement must allow for continuous redistribution that placates latecomers, or the agreement must be renegotiated every time a child reaches maturity. In neither of these cases is a system of relatively unqualified, durable property rights in place.

The general difficulty facing the strong appropriation theorist who starts from a state where appropriation requires universal consent is that he is trying to create property out of contracts. What he needs to show is that there is a fairly well-defined structure of rights, good equally against all, that can be held over most objects. But what he has to work with in these scenarios is a group of contractors distinguished by their abilities, situations, desires, and generations. The nature of the bargaining situation works against him, tending to yield rights-structures that vary across time, that vary in strength, and that vary even according to what persons they relate. These tendencies make any proof of strong property from universal consent seem highly unlikely, and so should make any initial state of nature that involves common-ownership, including hybrids, unattractive to the strong appropriation theorist.[4]

## 3. The challenge to strong appropriation theory

I have tried to show that arguments for ascribing a right to create strong property entitlements must begin from a state of no-ownership. This conclusion should not discomfit Lockean-libertarians, since no-ownership is the context that they most often assume for their arguments. But now, when we examine a no-ownership state more closely, we will find that it contains a significant justificatory challenge for the strong appropriationist position.

In the no-ownership state before acquisition each person has broad rights to use natural resources, within the limits of the bodily rights of others. From this starting point all variants of strong appropriation theory grant to each person the right to create in herself property rights over some objects, by performing some specified action, under certain conditions, and without the consent of any other person.

It is specifically the grant of this power to create property rights that raises the justificatory challenge for original acquisition theory, because the exercise of this power causes such dramatic moral changes. Before acquisition, each inhabitant of the state of nature may use, consume, damage or destroy anything, just as she likes. After acquisition, every person but the acquirer has a duty not to disturb the acquired thing without the acquirer's permission. The acquirer in exercising her acquisitive right imposes a duty on each non-acquirer with respect to the acquired thing, and without any non-acquirer's consent. By the exercise of the acquisitive right, the acquirer unilaterally imposes duties on everyone else. Moreover, the acquirer typically imposes these duties intending only her own advantage, and since they are strong duties they may be burdensome to those who bear them.

[4] Nor will tacit consent help where actual consent theory is troubled. Tacit consent does not speak to any of the problems above, and it adds problems of its own. For the more tacit the consent, the less likely that people have tacitly consented to strong property rights. In every new situation, some person could always claim that she had not tacitly agreed to rights that were unconditional in that way (or that could be held over those objects, or that could last so long). Neither can the strong appropriation theorist improve his position by saying (with Pufendorf 1672) that the bargains that generate property begin locally, and only become more universal as groups expand and agree to respect each other's local agreements. None of the arguments above traded on the difficulties of getting all persons together to bargain; all turn on the difficulties that ensue once a group of any size is assembled.

Because of this unilateral imposition of potentially burdensome duties, the ascription of a right to acquire "cries out for a justification" (Waldron 1988, p. 271). Indeed, Waldron argues that the peculiar properties of a natural right to original acquisition are sufficient to consign it to a philosophical bestiary. Original acquisition, were it possible, would be the only act we recognise by which one person could create potentially burdensome duties in others without the others' consent (Waldron 1988, pp. 266–71).[5]

It is not merely the singularity of the act that is worrisome. Imagine an analogous right to impose potentially burdensome "contractaul" duties on another person for one's own advantage (say, a duty to perform at dinner-times, or to get out of Dodge). Such a right seems almost impossible to justify. How much more justificatory weight must there then be to ground a right to acquire property, by which one person can impose potentially burdensome duties on everyone else at once? This line of questions should be especially worrisome to libertarians, who generally treat involuntarily-imposed duties as anathema.

I will organise the Lockean-libertarian arguments in favour of the natural right to appropriate around this challenge of showing how potentially burdensome duties can be created in others without their consent. This organization will make the strong appropriation theorist appear to be giving what trial lawyers call a "four dog defense".[6] First I will consider arguments that original acquisition in fact creates no new duties in others; second, arguments that acquisition creates new duties in others but that these duties are not burdensome; third, that acquisition creates burdensome duties in others but that the acquirer deserves what he gets; and, fourth, that it creates burdensome duties in others without desert but that the burdens can be compensated for. As in a trial, the case will be won if any of these arguments succeeds. I aim to show that only the last dog will hunt, and then only if it pursues according to the vector-sum path.

## *4. Labour-mixing and incorporation*

A strong appropriation theorist might initially try to meet the challenge of justification by adapting two arguments of Locke. The first is that a person can come to have rights (our theorist says "strong rights") over unowned

[5] For debate over Waldron's thesis, see Gaus and Lomasky (1990) and Simmons (1994).

[6] "I own no dog"; "That's not my dog"; "My dog doesn't bite"; "My dog didn't bite him".

objects by mixing her labour with the objects.[7] The second is that a person can come to have rights over unowned objects by making the objects part of her body.[8]

These arguments are both notable for their attempt to generate property without creating any "new" rights. How this is supposed to work in labour-mixing is familiar. Labour is a substance over which the labourer has property-type rights, and this substance comes to be dispersed throughout the object laboured upon. Through mixing, rights previously confined to the labourer's body come to reside farther afield. The incorporation argument, on the other hand, is one that Locke applies only to food; but Samuel Wheeler (1980) provides the necessary extension for other types of resources. Any object, Wheeler claims, can come to be part of one's body when it becomes analogous to an actual or possible body part. Thus an artificial leg becomes a body part when it is used like a real leg; clothes qualify through analogy to fur, a mansion is analogous to a shell, and so on; in a very real sense "your property *is* your body" (Wheeler 1980, p. 184).[9] Here the incorporator's extant bodily rights are merely "stretched" to include more body, as they would stretch if he became more portly.

Both arguments have an air of sophistry to them, and it is not hard to compile a list of serious objections. To the incorporationist it may be pointed out that the rights we intuitively assign to our undetached body parts do not include rights of transfer; so even if, say, houses could be "incorporated" as suggested they would not become property strictly speaking. To the labour-mixing theorist the most obvious objection is that there is no "substance" that is both mixable with external objects and the object of personal rights (see Waldron 1988, pp. 180–3). Labour is an activity, not a substance; indeed, "mixing one's labour" may be incoherent in logical form, as it is the same form as "mixing one's mixing" (see Waldron 1988, pp. 184–7). And the extent of what one would acquire by labour-mixing is uncertain in any case (see Nozick 1974, p. 174).

Even if these objections could be overcome, both arguments can be shown to be poor responses to the justificatory challenge by an adaptation

[7] "Whatsoever then he removes out of the State that Nature hath provided, and left it in, he hath mixed his Labour with, and joyned to it something that is his own, and thereby makes it his Property .... For this Labour being the unquestionable Property of the Labourer, no Man but he can have a right to what that is once joyned to" (Locke 1689, p. 288).

[8] "The Fruit, or Venison, which nourishes the wild Indian, who knows no Inclosure, and is still a Tenant in common, must be his, and so his, i.e. a part of him, that another can no longer have any right to it" (Locke 1689, p. 287).

[9] See also T. H. Green: "These [appropriated] things, so taken and fashioned, cease to be external as they were before. They become a sort of extension of the man's organs, the constant apparatus through which he gives reality to his ideas and wishes" (Macpherson 1978, p. 115).

of Nozick's famous "tomato juice" argument (Nozick 1974, pp. 174–5). Nozick asks why when mixing one's tomato juice in the sea one should think that one is gaining the sea instead of losing one's juice. Similarly, we can ask the strong appropriation theorist why, even if bodily rights could be dispersed or stretched, we should construe the extensions as strong rights. As we saw with the right to bodily integrity, we acknowledge bodily rights because of the way these rights protect significant interests of the person whose body it is (in being free from pain and distraction, in being able to carry out complex plans of action, etc.). Yet the bodily rights we recognise are qualified, and many of the qualifications come in circumstances where recognising an unqualified right would be too costly to others (as when the rights-holder is an aggressor). Bodily rights that were mixed into or stretched over objects that are insensate, or detached, or not under the conscious control of the acquirer would be that much less connected to the acquirer's interests. Moreover bodily rights that extended to scarce goods or spaces would be that much more costly to others. So even an acquisition that created no "new" rights could not give rise to property rights that were strong rights.

## 5. *Value-creation and provisos*

A second strategy of the strong appropriation theorist would be to admit that acquisition creates duties in others, but to deny that these duties are even potentially burdensome. Authors defending original acquisition often use this strategy, if only in giving examples that draw the reader's attention toward acquisitions of trivial importance—such as Locke's "He" who gathers acorns under an oak (Locke 1689, p. 288), or Rothbard's sculptor moulding found clay (Rothbard 1974, pp. 109–10), or Nozick's grain of sand taken from Coney Island (Nozick 1974, p. 175).

A more serious version of this strategy could be drawn from other passages in Locke: "'Tis Labour indeed that puts the difference of value on every thing", a difference in value that he successively estimates at 9/10, 99/100, and 999/1000 of the total (Locke 1689, pp. 296–8). The thought here is that the duties created by acquirers are not onerous because the things acquired are of little value. No one can be made much worse off by being excluded from some marshland and a little seed, it might be said, and it is the labourer's own efforts that turn these into smiling fields.

Adding value to nature, in itself, seems too flimsy to support strong private property rights. For the possibility is always open that an improver is merely adding value to the commons. Moreover even if property were in the offing we can ask, as Nozick does, why an improver should get an entitlement over everything she works on instead of only the value she has created, and whether we can ever know what that value is (Nozick 1974, p. 175).[10]

Beyond these objections is the problem of keeping the value-creation argument from drawing its force from other arguments, which either admit that the imposition of property duties is onerous but say that the corresponding rights are deserved (perhaps because the labourer has created value), or admit that the duties are onerous but claim that the burdens on others will be compensated (perhaps when others gain access to the value the labourer creates).[11]

Once these arguments are separated out the value-creation strategy is without hope. For one thing, it can be burdensome to be excluded from materials with which one could create value oneself (Wolff 1991, pp. 104–5). For another, it can be hard to be excluded from a valuable good regardless of the origin of that value. One of the most notable features of strong property rights is their duration—the fact that they persist through changes in the value of their objects. The acquisition theorist can hardly declare a strong right trivial just because its object is not valuable today.

The strong appropriation theorist might instead try to reduce the burdensome nature of his favoured rights by altering parts of his original acquisition theory. Thus he might restrict the conditions in which acquisition is possible to those in which there is enough and as good left for others, or he might reshape the rights that acquisition generates.

As for "enough and as good" provisos, they will prevent potentially onerous duties being generated only at the price of prohibiting the acquisition of any scarce good. Or, to put it differently, the more scarce the goods that can be acquired under such a proviso, the more potentially onerous will be duties that acquisition can create. The point about duration carries through here too: the rights generated by acquisition may last forever, so the proviso will only acquit acquisitions of being burdensome if there will always be enough and as good.

[10] Worries such as this one lead Becker (1977) and Gaus (1989) to say that labouring cannot effect property rights over land and other natural resources, since these are not produced. For a detailed examination of Locke on value-creation and land, see Cohen (1986b).

[11] For example, another of Locke's quotes about value-creation:

> He who appropriates land to himself by his labour, does not lessen but increase [sic] the common stock of mankind .... He, that incloses Land and has a greater plenty of the conveniencys of life from ten acres, than he could have from an Hundred left to Nature, may truly be said, to give ninety acres to Mankind. (Locke 1988, p. 294)

In this argument it is not the "greater plenty of the conveniencys of life" that is doing the work, but the fact that non-enclosers are better off because the encloser no longer roams the other ninety acres. This is an implicit compensation argument, and so not the sort of argument we are looking for here. On the argument of this particular passage in Locke see also Wolff (1991, p. 104), Cohen (1986b).

The final version of this strategy would be to qualify the rights generated by original acquisition so as to limit the burdens that these rights impose on others. As noted above, the blameless needy might get a right to expropriate, or a right to harmless trespass might be granted. This tactic would reduce the pressure on strong appropriation from specific objections like those of Waldron (1988, pp. 267–8), who complains that the property duties imposed on non-acquirers can limit food supplies or make it hard to care for children.

Yet these sorts of qualifications underestimate the negative impact that strong property rights can have on what appear to be the legitimate interests of non-acquirers. Because of Locke (1988, p. 291) we tend to think of non-acquirers as lazy louts thwarted from pinching "the benefit of another's Pains". Yet non-acquirers faced with strong property rights would also have no recourse, for example, when land they could use went uncultivated, when sites of great natural beauty were whimsically destroyed, when huge pornographic balloons were floated nearby, or when the Old City was sold to the Other Side. The strong appropriation theorist cannot qualify acquired rights to mitigate all of the possible negative effects of strong rights, because after the qualifications no strong right would be left. Strong rights are pointless unless they thwart many seemingly unobjectionable desires of non-owners; for if other people do not care much about what you do with some thing, why shouldn't mere possession or a weak property right be enough?

## 6. Desert

The original appropriationist might now acknowledge that acquisition creates at least potentially burdensome duties, yet stake his claim on the acquirer deserving the corresponding rights. As Gaus and Lomasky (1990, p. 498) say, "a basic appeal of state of nature/original acquisition stories [is that] they fix a spotlight on the intuition that producers deserve to own the fruits of their labors".[12] Could desert be the basis of a natural right to strong property acquisition?

Once again we must work to get a clean intuition supporting the thesis. Certainly the mere expenditure of effort need deserve nothing (or nothing beyond bemusement or pity). To be a candidate for deserving property rights, the fruits of one's labour must be sweet. Yet to whom do we imag-

[12] Several theorists have opted for desert-based justifications for property rights in recent years, although they have also qualified both the conditions in which appropriation is allowed and the property rights generated. See Becker (1977, pp. 48–56), Munzer (1990, pp. 254–97), Gaus (1989).

ine the laboured-upon thing becomes more valuable? If one's labours produce something that will only ever be valuable to oneself (such as pink-enameled driftwood),[13] a reward of strong rights seems inappropriate if others will remain indifferent to it, there is no need for strong rights; and if others are averse to it, scorn seems more deserved than sanction. On the other hand, if the product is valued by others then we must again be careful to separate our intuitions about desert from the thought that non-acquirers may somehow be compensated for the duties imposed on them (for example, by gaining a chance to trade for the valuable good).

The intuition behind the desert argument seems most pure in the thought that a labourer is deserving when she expends effort to produce something that is objectively valuable, independent of the possible compensation that this value might provide for those who must render what the labourer deserves. (Perhaps Rothbard's sculptor working on found clay is an example.) There are threshold problems for making this intuition into an argument. The strong appropriation theorist wants to say that strong property rights are the appropriate reward for such effort, yet he must say why (or when) rights are deserved instead of, say, fame or gratitude. Also, he must fashion a correspondingly strong penalty for those who decrease the value of the commons (what happens if it is a very bad sculpture?) (see Becker 1977, pp. 48–56).

Yet the strong appropriation theorist's real problem is matching desert, which is a scalar magnitude, with his point-like set of favoured rights. We might wonder first whether any productive effort is so tremendous as to deserve rights to exclusive use that echo through the ages. Second, and more importantly, the desert theorist must explain why an improvement of greater value should not create a property structure that is more unqualified or that lasts longer. Even if Praxiteles could generate everlasting rights by his crafting, it is hard to see how my efforts would deserve more than a temporary reprieve from the kiln.

The strong appropriation theorist may be coming to a renewed appreciation of the states of nature that required universal consent to generate private property rights. For all of their difficulties, at least these states gave clear grounds for preferring a strong property structure (the salience of these rights as the solution to a bargaining problem). When the strength of the property structure cannot be taken for granted, it becomes harder to find arguments that point to exactly the right thing. But the strong appropriation theorist has one strategy remaining before he must take his chances with the vector-sum approach.

[13] Nozick's example of something made less valuable (Nozick 1974, p. 175).

## 7. Acquisition with compensation

The situation now stands as follows. The burden on the strong appropriation theorist is to justify the unilateral creation of relatively unqualified and durable private property rights. We have narrowed the possible strategies whereby this burden might be discharged to one that grants that non-acquirers must be compensated for the burdens that acquisition imposes on them. This is Nozick's (1974) strategy as indicated by the proviso on the principle of just acquisition:

> A process normally giving rise to a permanent bequeathable property right in a previously unowned thing will not do so if the position of others no longer at liberty to use the thing is thereby worsened … . Someone whose appropriation otherwise would violate the proviso still may appropriate provided he compensates the others so that their situation is not thereby worsened. (Nozick 1974, p. 178).

As explained above, each instance of strong appropriation renders someone potentially worse off in at least some respect; otherwise there would be no point to the creation of a strong right. This means that the strong appropriation theorist must potentially require compensation to non-acquirers for every act of acquisition. There are two ways that compensation could be effected, and only one is serviceable for generating the entitlements that the strong appropriation theorist desires.

The first way, suggested by Nozick's proviso and a few of his examples,[14] is to require that the burdens imposed by each act of acquisition be compensated by the acquirer—either directly through side-payments to the non-acquirers or indirectly though the benefits that flow to others from the acquirer's having private property rights (such as increased opportunity for trade). This first way is blocked by two practical obstacles.

First, the level of compensation required to bring each non-acquirer back to her pre-acquisition state will vary from person to person, according to how onerous the property duties imposed on each person turn out to be. It may be a real pain for one man to observe his neighbour's newly-acquired right to exclude from a plot, yet only an occasional inconvenience to another man. In fact these complexities may be even greater, since there is no reason to expect that any indirect compensation generated by property acquisition will correlate with the onerousness of that acquisition for any particular person.

Second, compensation must be ensured for each person for the entire duration of the property right, which (given the transferability of strong

[14] In particular, the examples of water in the desert, the newly discovered medicine, and the inventor's patent (Nozick 1974, pp. 178–80).

property rights) is essentially forever. This means that either some estimate of future burdens must be made for each person for each acquired resource and this compensation received instantly, or that the process of compensation will be ongoing as the relative onerousness for each person becomes apparent over time. Nor can ongoing compensation be avoided in any case, for latecomers will be owed compensation for the duties that acquisition imposes on them, and latecomers cannot be compensated in advance.

The practical difficulties surrounding the first way of effecting compensation should push the strong appropriation theorist toward a second way, which is suggested by Nozick's wider references to the overall benefits of capitalism.[15] By this argument, private acquisition that generates strong property entitlements is permissible because the operation of the system of property that emerges from individual acquisitions is not to the net detriment of anyone. The justificatory burden is discharged, that is, by showing that each person is on the whole no worse off in a world where strong property entitlements can be generated unilaterally. Compensation is handled not individually, but systematically.

This argument runs better where we have seen others stumble, because it includes a solid rationale for strong acquired rights. The stronger the system of rights, the fewer the qualifications and thus the fewer the rules that all must learn. And the lower a system's information costs, the more likely it is that it can provide adequate compensation.

Yet the justificatory foundation of this type of argument has not yet been located. At first, the argument seems to be grounded in some principle of natural freedom to engage in types of acts that are harmless. "One is free to pursue one's own good", such a principle might read, "so long as one's acts (perhaps when combined with similar acts of others) are not to anyone's detriment". If the system of property generated by strong appropriation does its work, then each individual acquisitive act will be part of a class of acts that together have no ill effects. It seems immaterial that it takes similar (predictable) acts of others to ensure that one's own act is permissible. My graffito might be by itself a defacement, but if others also take up a spray can the result may be pleasing to all.

Can this principle of natural freedom anchor an adequate justification of original acquisition? The economist's familiar admonition to respect opportunity costs makes it doubtful. There can only be one property system in effect at a time. If original acquisition is generating strong private property rights, it is not generating another possible property

[15] Especially the list of "the various familiar social considerations favoring private property" (Nozick 1974, p. 177), the footnote on Fourier (pp. 178–9), and the remark on about the "free operation of the market system" (p. 182). Wolff (1991, pp. 109–12) endorses reading Nozick in this second way.

system. But what if some other property system were better for everyone than a strong system? Or better for some people and not worse for others? Could it still reasonably be claimed that strong appropriation were acceptable, since a system of strong rights was adequate to compensate for its own burdens? To the contrary, isn't the relevant level of compensation for strong appropriation not the no-property state of nature baseline, but the baseline of the best property system that could be generated in the strong system's place?[16]

Once compensation "goes systematic" it is hard to see how this conclusion can be resisted. Consider the people living in a property system generated by original acquisition who could do better within some other system. They should be compensated, if compensation is possible, not only for the particular costs imposed by others' acquisitions, but for the opportunity costs of living in that property system instead of the system better for them. This implies that between two systems, if one is better for some and worse for none, then only that better system is acceptable.

The underlying justification for the systematic compensation argument now seems less like a principle of natural freedom, and more like the sort of benefit-cost reasoning with which this essay began. The strong appropriation theorist must prove that the system of strong property rights provides significant benefits, at a reasonable cost, and does so better than other systems that might be put into effect. He must show that a system of strong property rights is more reasonable than a weaker system of private rights, or a system of non-private rights, or a mixed system, or no property at all.

Moreover, the appropriation theorist must specify the interests against which benefits and costs are to be measured. It will not do simply to stipulate that people's interests are in the satisfaction of whatever desires they happen to have, nor to restrict the range of relevant interests artificially. The appropriation theorist must detail the interests that differently-shaped property rights protect and foster, in order to show that his favoured rights produce the array of interests that some larger normative theory would accept as most reasonable. If these rights turn out to be strong rights, so be it. Strong appropriation theory has been brought back to the vector-sum approach.

Perhaps this should not be surprising. The problem that laid the justificatory burden on the strong appropriation theorist was that property acquisition seems to be the only act by which one person can impose potentially burdensome duties on others without their consent, which duties are to the imposer's advantage. Yet property acquisition is not the

[16] For worries about setting the baseline for compensation, see also Cohen (1986a), Kymlicka (1990, pp. 112–7), Wolff (1991, pp. 112–5).

only act that can generate onerous duties in others simply without their consent. Such duties are generated by every human birth. You do not consent to the relatively strong duties to respect bodily integrity that are imposed on you whenever a child is born. Nor is it plausible to deny that such duties can be onerous—as anyone stuck aboard an airplane with a newborn can attest. Yet the vector-sum approach to rights works out well for the right to bodily integrity, so it should work for property rights too.

## 8. Conclusion

The strong appropriation theorist may balk at being singled out specially to face the challenge of showing that his preferred set of rights is one that could be generated from a state of nature. As Nozick says, "it is not only persons favoring private property who need a theory of how property rights legitimately originate" (Nozick 1974, p. 178). The same point could be made for strong private property. Doesn't everyone need to show how her favoured property system could originate, regardless of the property system she supports?

In general, I do not believe so. Were we to find the most reasonable system of property rights for us now using the vector-sum approach, the most important thing would be to move our rules of property toward that structure as smoothly as possible, relative to the various interests now at stake. It is only the strong appropriation theorist who believes that what happened in a state of nature, or what could legitimately happen there, might constrain our present choices about which property system to move toward. Other theorists (including those who merely believe that strong property rights are best for us now) do not need a theory of original appropriation, because their theories are compatible with any number of possible histories of legitimate property rules. What they need is a theory of transition.

Except, of course, that every theorist needs to say something about the original appropriation that is still possible for us (say, in Antarctica or on other planets).[17] For these cases every property theory will indeed need to face the problems of selecting a justifiable appropriative mechanism. But these cases will be ones that extend, not that create, a system of property rights, and so will be at the periphery not the core of a theory of property.

Finally, all of the objections to strong appropriation theory above might make it seem as though I am claiming that there could be no private rights

[17] The importance of contemporary appropriation is stressed by Schmidtz (1994) and Simmons (1994).

over resources whatsoever in a state of nature. And that claim seems counterintuitive, considering straightforward Lockean examples like the industrious farmer who has toiled to raise a crop. Wouldn't a brigand who carried this crop away violate some right in seizing "the benefit of another's Pains"?

There may well be a natural right to non-interference with resources that resembles a property right in many respects.[18] When a person in a natural state is engaged in an extended activity that uses or relies on some object, and when this activity is part of a plan to secure material sustenance, then (under certain conditions) it seems plausible to say that others ought not take that object to use it for their own purposes. It seems plausible to ascribe such a right because it seems plausible that people have strong interests in being able to engage in connected sequences of actions that are intended to sustain life and that require certain objects to remain undisturbed. The intuition that there are such interests and that they should be protected is a firm one, and it draws us when we think of the "Pains" that a person might take in Locke's state of nature. Yet this natural right of non-interference falls short of being a strong property right. The intuition that supports the right responds poorly when the "acquired" resource remains unused or is wasted, when it is used to insult or offend others, when it is part of a surplus of possessions, and in situations of general need. Nor does the intuition support a strong right of transfer. The interests that people have in being able to use a resource as part of an extended plan of action are important ones. Yet these interests constitute only one set of vectors that can influence the nature of the property rights that we should recognize.[19]

*Department of Philosophy* LEIF WENAR
*University of Sheffield*
*Sheffield S10 2TN*
*UK*
*l.wenar@sheffield.ac.uk*

## REFERENCES

Becker, Lawrence C. 1977: *Property Rights: Philosophic Foundations.* London: Routledge & Kegan Paul.

Buckle, Stephen 1991: *Natural Law and the Theory of Property.* Oxford: Oxford University Press.

[18] This point is derived from Scanlon (1987), from which Simmons (1992, pp. 273–4) also draws.

[19] Many thanks to Robert Nozick, T. M. Scanlon, Steven Gross and Miranda von Dornum.

Cohen, G. A. 1986a: "Self-Ownership, World-Ownership, and Equality", in Cohen 1995, pp. 67–91. Originally published in 1986 in Frank Lucash (ed.) *Justice and Equality Here and Now*. Ithaca: Cornell University Press.

——1986b: "Marx and Locke on Land and Labour", in Cohen1995, pp. 165–94. Originally published in 1986 in *Proceedings of the British Academy*, 71.

——1995: *Self-Ownership, Freedom, and Equality*, Cambridge: Cambridge University Press.

Gaus, Gerald F. 1989: " A Contractual Justification of Redistributive Capitalism" in J. W. Chapman and J. R. Pennock (eds.) *Markets and Justice: NOMOS 31*, New York: New York University Press, p. 13–58.

——1994: "Property, Rights, and Freedom". *Social Philosophy and Policy*, 11, pp. 209–40.

Gaus, Gerald F. and Lomasky, Loren E. 1990: "Are Property Rights Problematic?". *Monist*, 73, pp. 484–503.

Gibbard, Alan 1976: "Natural Property Rights". *Nous*, 10, pp. 77–85.

Green, T. H. 1885: *Lectures on the Principle of Political Obligation*. London: Longmans Green. Portions reprinted in Macpherson 1978, pp. 104–17.

Grotius, Hugo 1625: *The Rights of War and Peace*, F. W. Kelsey (trans.), New York: Oceana Publications, 1964.

Kymlicka, Will 1990: *Contemporary Political Philosophy: An Introduction*. Oxford: Clarendon Press.

Locke, John 1689: *Two Treatises of Government*. Cambridge: Cambridge University Press 1988.

Macpherson, C. B. (ed.) 1978: *Property: Mainstream and Critical Positions*. Oxford: Blackwell.

Munzer, Stephen R. 1990: *A Theory of Property*. Cambridge: Cambridge University Press.

Narveson, Jan 1988: *The Libertarian Idea*. Philadelphia: Temple University Press.

Nozick, Robert 1974: *Anarchy, State, and Utopia*. New York: Basic Books.

Pufendorf, Samuel 1672: *Of the Law of Nature and Nations*, C. H. and W. A. Oldfather (trans.), New York, Oceana Publications, 1964.

Rothbard, Murray 1974: "Justice and Property Rights", in Samuel L. Blumenfeld (ed.) *Property in a Humane Economy*, La Salle, Illinois: Open Court, pp. 97–116.

Rousseau, Jean-Jacques 1755: "Discourse on the Origin of Inequality", in his *Basic Political Writings*, Indianapolis: Hackett, pp. 25–109, 1987.

Scanlon, T. M. 1987: "Natural Wrongs and Institutional Rights I: Property" [unpublished].

Schmidtz, David 1990: "When is Original Appropriation Required?". *Monist*, 73, pp. 504–18.

——1994: "The Institution of Property". *Social Philosophy and Policy*, 11, pp. 42–62.

Sidgwick, Henry 1907: *The Methods of Ethics*. 7th ed. London: Macmillan.

Simmons, A. John 1992: *The Lockean Theory of Rights*. Princeton: Princeton University Press.

——1994: "Original-Acquisition Justification of Private Property". *Social Philosophy and Policy*, 11, pp. 63–84.

Waldron, Jeremy 1988: *The Right to Private Property*. Oxford: Oxford University Press.

Wenar, Leif forthcoming: "The Concept of Property".

Wheeler III, Samuel C., 1980: "Natural Property Rights as Body Rights". *Nôus*, 14, pp. 171–94.

Wolff, Jonathan 1991: *Robert Nozick: Property, Justice and the Minimal State*. Cambridge: Polity Press.

# [5]

# Locke, Property, and Progressive Taxes

Donna M. Byrne*

TABLE OF CONTENTS



---

* Associate Professor of Law, William Mitchell College of Law, St. Paul, MN. This essay had its genesis in the Summer of 1996. Before it was finished, I was diagnosed with breast cancer and underwent a series of treatments that made it difficult to work (to say the least). I would never have picked this up again if not for the love, support, and encouragement of my former colleagues at Widener Law School in Wilmington, Delaware, my new colleagues at William Mitchell College of Law in St. Paul, Minnesota, my family, and the many positive thinking folks I have encountered in the last two years. I owe a particular debt of gratitude to Natan Paradise, Alice Abreu, Phyllis Bookspan, Neil Hamilton, Dan Kleinberger, Denise Roy, and Spencer Tilmon for pushing me, putting up with me, and commenting on earlier drafts. I am also grateful to Nathan Kellett, Eric Fasking, Mark Berhow, and Liz Holland of William Mitchell and Maureen Middleton of Widener for research assistance. Of course, if the ideas are silly, the writing awkward, or the statements wrong, it's my fault, not theirs.

## I. INTRODUCTION

Although tax scholars have long scrutinized progressive taxation from a variety of vantage points,[1] most of my academic friends take it as given that progressive tax rates are fair. The recent popularity of the flat tax idea,[2] however, is testimony to the possibility that Americans are not as convinced of the fairness of progressive taxes as a sampling of leftist academics might suggest.[3] So what is fair about progressive taxation? Why have taxpayers accepted progressive rate structures for so long?[4] Are progressive taxes compatible with the philosophical underpinnings of our society?

A small, but swelling, wave of recent tax policy scholarship questions the assumptions on which our analytical approaches depend.[5]

1. *See generally* ROBERT NOZICK, ANARCHY, STATE, AND UTOPIA (1974); Calvin R. Massey, *Takings and Progressive Rate Taxation*, 20 HARV. J.L. & PUB. POL'Y 85 (1996); Jeffrey A. Schoenblum, *Tax Fairness or Unfairness? A Consideration of the Philosophical Bases for Unequal Taxation of Individuals*, 12 AM. J. TAX POL'Y 221 (1995).
2. By flat, of course, I refer to proportional taxes where the rate of tax is flat, although the amount certainly is not.
3. Although Steven Forbes often gets credit for the flat tax idea in the popular media, House Majority leader Dick Armey introduced a more complete version of this idea in the House. *See* H.R. 4585, 103d Cong. (1994), *revised and reintroduced as* H.R. 2060, 104th Cong. (1995) by Congressman Armey on July 19, 1995. Senator Richard C. Shelby, R-Ala., introduced a revised version in the Senate. The Armey-Shelby flat tax, as well as Steven Forbes's platform actually derived from an earlier work: ROBERT E. HALL & ALVIN RABUSHKA, THE FLAT TAX (2d ed. 1995). *See generally* Maria Recio, *Smaller Cuts, IRS Bill* 16.4(a) & (d) *Quiet Tax Reform Rallying Cry*, KNIGHT RIDDER TRIB. BUS. NEWS, Apr. 14, 1999; Gerald F. Seib, *Steve Forbes: Evolving Toward 2000 Decision*, WALL ST. J., Jan. 21, 1998, at A24 (crediting Steve Forbes, a Republican Presidential contender in 1996, with helping to make "Flat Tax" a household name by focusing his electoral platform on a flat tax proposal).

   The recent "flat tax" proposals would do more than change the tax rate structure. They would also significantly change the tax base and are actually consumption taxes, rather than true proportional income taxes. While this important distinction was reasonably clear to tax professionals, it was mostly invisible to the lay public. Most people seemed not to understand that only wage income, and not investment income, would be part of the tax base under the Armey-Shelby proposal (and similarly, under the Forbes flat tax). Under the USA tax, deposits and investments would have been deductible, resulting in the economic equivalent of a tax on consumed wage income.
4. I am grateful to Edwin S. Cohen for pointing out that the federal income tax has always exhibited some degree of progressivity and that progressivity itself seems not to have been at issue when the tax was originally enacted. (Actually, Professor Cohen, in true law professor form, raised the point as a question.)
5. *See, e.g.*, Alice G. Abreu, *Untangling Tax Reform: Simple Taxes, Complex Choices*, 33 SAN DIEGO L. REV. 1355 (1996); Patrick B. Crawford, *The Utility of the Efficiency/Equity Dichotomy in Tax Policy Analysis*, 16 VA. TAX REV. 501 (1997); Marjorie E. Kornhauser, *Through The Looking Glass with Alice and Larry: the Nature of Scholarship*, 76 N.C. L. REV. 1609 (1998); Martin J. McMahon, Jr. & Alice G. Abreu, *Winner-Take-All Markets: Easing the Case for Progressive Taxa-*

Sacred norms of economic efficiency, neutrality, and even fairness can (and should) be the subject of critical examination, both in legal and economic scholarship.[6] Recent scholarship has asserted that philosophically and as a matter of Constitutional law, progressive taxation is impermissible.

One recent article, for example, presents the argument that only a lump sum head tax (an "absolutely equal" tax) would be fair and consistent with liberal ideals of individual autonomy.[7] This unpopular position is a response to claims about the fairness of various "flat" tax structures voiced in recent political campaigns. While the lump-sum-head-tax suggestion is unusual, the assumptions and attitudes on which it rests are not. Many of the arguments against progressive taxation seem to rely on attitudes about the poor and assumptions about the rich that are, at best, discriminatory and that would tend to be exploitive if put into practice. Political rhetoric surrounding the tax system often obscures the underlying assumptions and motivations of the speakers.[8] In this essay I examine the often hidden assumptions, attitudes, and philosophical approaches to entitlement to property that appear to support the claims of the anti-progressivity movement.[9] Specifically, I consider the notions of entitlement deriving from the writings of John Locke. The essay responds most partic-

*tion*, 4 Fla. Tax Rev. 1 (1998); Nancy C. Staudt, *The Hidden Costs of the Progressivity Debate*, 50 Vand. L. Rev. 919 (1997); Nancy C. Staudt, *The Political Economy of Taxation: A Critical Review of a Classic*, 30 L. & Soc'y Rev. 651 (1996) (*reviewing* Henry C. Simons, Personal Income Taxation: The Definition of Income as a Problem in Fiscal Policy (1938)); Nancy C. Staudt, *Taxing Housework*, 84 Geo. L.J. 1571 (1996).

6. *See* Donna M. Byrne, *Progressive Taxation Revisited*, 37 Ariz. L. Rev. 739 (1995). *See generally* Staudt, *supra* note 5 (examining the tax theory focus on efficiency rather than fairness).
7. *See* Schoenblum, *supra* note 1, at 270-71.
8. *See* Marjorie E. Kornhauser, *The Rise of Rhetoric in Tax Reform Debate: An Example*, 70 Tul. L. Rev. 2345 (1996); *see also* Henry C. Simons, Personal Income Taxation: The Definition of Income as a Problem of Fiscal Policy 1 (1938) (appearance that fiscal policy is free of "mere ethical considerations" is an empty pretense); Anne L. Alstott, *The Earned Income Tax Credit and the Limitations of Tax- Based Welfare Reform*, 108 Harv. L. Rev. 533, 546 n.49 (1995). ("A critical evaluation of discourses about welfare and work might also question the social function of the work ethic and punitive treatment of nonworkers.").
9. Such as it is. Professor Schoenblum asserts that there really is no anti-progressivity movement. *See* Schoenblum, *supra* note 1, at 223 n.12 (noting that Marjorie Kornhauser, *The Rhetoric of the Anti-Progressive Income Tax Movement: A Typical Male Reaction*, 86 Mich. L. Rev. 465, 468 (1987), expresses concern over the increasing attacks on progressivity). Schoenblum states, "[t]his is difficult to discern in the academic literature, which almost, without exception, uncritically supports progressivity." Nevertheless, the various "flat" tax proposals of the last presidential campaign, the move to reintroduce substantial capital gains preferences, and the appearance of scholarly articles such as Schoenblum's suggest that the opponents of progressivity are more than a few. *See also* Massey, *supra* note 1.

ularly to Jeffrey Schoenblum's "absolutely equal" (lump sum) tax proposal because it is the most extreme of the anti-progressive proposals. My objections also apply to the milder forms of anti-progressivity, albeit less starkly.

Some tax scholarship, as well as much of the popular rhetoric, accepts as given a liberal philosophical approach to the world in which individuals are supreme and property is, and should be, owned absolutely by individuals.[10] In this view, individuals are entitled to all wealth that is justly acquired.[11] This idea goes back at least to the seventeenth century and is often attributed to John Locke (unnecessarily, as I argue below). Locke reasoned from the premise that individuals own their own labor,[12] and that mixing labor with a previously unowned resource entitles the individual to own the resulting product.[13] In this way, once upon a time, natural resources originally became subject to private ownership. For Locke, establishing this natural right to property was a necessary step in establishing a role for government in protecting property. Locke's theory of why we own property also sets up a framework within which to analyze the propriety of a government exacting some of that property. In certain extreme versions of the Lockean right to property, to tax land or its proceeds is to deny an individual some aspect of individual autonomy.

Moreover, when an individual makes an effort to produce that which society deems valuable, the individual should be entitled to the resulting accumulation. There are several possible justifications for this entitlement, some of which we explore below. The significance of the theory, however, is that different levels of labor mixing result in differences in wealth.

This approach seems to suggest that voluntary effort is the only reason (or substantially the main reason) that wealth accumulates

10. *See, e.g.*, RICHARD A. EPSTEIN, TAKINGS: PRIVATE PROPERTY AND THE POWER OF EMINENT DOMAIN (1985); NOZICK, *supra* note 1; Schoenblum, *supra* note 1.

11. In this view, taxation is a kind of attack on private property. *See* Marjorie E. Kornhauser, *The Morality of Money: American Attitudes Toward Wealth and the Income Tax*, 70 IND. L.J. 119, 128-31 (1994).

12. Locke was responding to Sir Robert Filmer, a contemporary who held that kings, by divine right, had total authority over their subjects. *See* JOHN LOCKE, *First Treatise of Government*, *in* TWO TREATISES OF GOVERNMENT § 3, at 160 (Peter Laslett ed., Cambridge Univ. Press 1960) (1690) [hereinafter LOCKE, *First Treatise*]; *see also* JOHN LOCKE, *Second Treatise of Government*, *in* TWO TREATISES OF GOVERNMENT, § 22, at 301 (Peter Laslett ed., Cambridge Univ. Press 1960) (1690) [hereinafter LOCKE, *Second Treatise*] (to the contrary, Locke responded, "[t]he *Natural Liberty* of Man is to be free from any Superior Power on Earth . . . .").

13. *See* LOCKE, *Second Treatise*, *supra* note 12, § 27, at 305-06. This argument was to fly in the face of notions such as divine right, absolutism, and patriarchy. Locke's predecessors such as Filmer and Hobbes believed that property was derived from divine authority or patriarchy and that, therefore, no property could exist in the state of nature.

and that by virtue of their efforts, people are entitled to their accumulations. While differences in talent and ability also affect accumulation of wealth, we must respect these differences in talent if we respect people as individuals. Thus, the argument proceeds, differences in talent and ability are not to be taxed away. Rather, if the market rewards an application of talent, respect for the individual means that we must respect the rewards to the individual's efforts.[14]

What are the implications of such a belief system for policy choices? At the extreme, a strong theory of private property including entitlement to all returns to labor precludes most taxation.[15] Under more moderate versions it precludes progressive taxation and may even require regressive taxation.[16]

In this essay, I argue that the version of liberal philosophy that opponents of progressive taxation espouse is not the only possible modern interpretation of Locke's respect for individual autonomy and, indeed, is not the best application of Lockean property rights to tax

14. *See* 1 F.A. Hayek, *The Fatal Conceit: The Errors of Socialism*, *in* 1 THE COLLECTED WORKS OF F.A. HAYEK 29, 29-31 (W.W. Bartley III ed., Univ. of Chicago Press 1988) (1899) (saying that misguided effort should not be rewarded).

15. A somewhat related argument is that progressive taxation constitutes a taking under the Fifth Amendment. *See* Massey, *supra* note 1. Although usually not taken seriously, the takings argument has resurfaced in a recent article by Professor Calvin Massey. Borrowing from Richard Epstein, Massey argues that the Takings clause requires that federal taxation satisfy the benefit theory of taxation, which says simply that taxes should be levied relative to the benefits the taxpayer receives from the government. Because the benefit theory does not conclusively require progressive tax rates, Massey argues, progressive rates must violate the Takings clause. Massey's analysis of the benefits derived from government is incomplete, poorly reasoned, and reveals typical anti-progressivist attitudes about wealth accumulation.

While the lump sum suggestion and the takings suggestion usually do not get serious attention, the suggestion that only a lump sum tax is consistent with the philosophical underpinnings of society should be taken very seriously. *See generally* Schoenblum, *supra* note 1. If Professor Schoenblum is correct, we have a real problem. We ascribe simultaneously to two mutually exclusive theories: First that all wealth obtained is morally deserved and should not be taken, and second that it is somehow unfair to expect someone who has landed in unfortunate circumstances to be able to contribute as much as someone who has experienced greater financial success.

16. *See, e.g.*, Walter J. Blum & Harry Kalven, Jr., *The Uneasy Case for Progressive Taxation*, 19 U. CHI. L. REV. 417 (1952), *reprinted in* WALTER J. BLUM & HARRY KALVEN, JR., THE UNEASY CASE FOR PROGRESSIVE TAXATION (1953) (claiming no need to make a case that progressive taxation is preferable to a regressive tax); *cf.* Nancy E. Shurtz, *A Critical View of Traditional Tax Policy Theory: A Pragmatic Alternative*, 31 VILL. L. REV. 1665, 1689 (1986) (presenting the choice of rate structure as between proportionate and progressive rates). *But see, e.g.*, Joseph Bankman & Thomas Griffith, *Social Welfare and the Rate Structure: A New Look at Progressive Taxation*, 75 CAL. L. REV. 1905, 1907 (1987) (concluding that optimal tax is a progressive one); Michael J. Graetz, *To Praise the Estate Tax, Not To Bury It*, 93 YALE L.J. 259, 274 (1983) (asserting that "the case for regressive taxation is surely wrong" but not citing any presentation of such a case).

rate discussions. Because I conclude that a philosophical middle ground is also defensible, I reject the suggestion that the only philosophically honest tax is a lump sum tax. Nevertheless, I applaud those who raise the question of how we decide what is "fair."

I argue here in favor of a philosophy derived from Lockean individualism but compatible with "unequal" taxation. I begin by outlining John Locke's theory of property and consider the possible justifications for that theory. Next I examine the implications of the theory and its usefulness for tax rate theory, emphasizing the failings of the traditional arguments in light of this discussion. Finally, I suggest a new model of "marginal deservedness of income" based on the justifications of Locke's theory of property.

## II. LOCKE

The purpose of this section is to outline John Locke's theory of entitlement to wealth and to examine two ways of justifying this theory. One of the main objections to unequal taxes is really an objection to mandatory redistribution of wealth, which in turn, is based on some sense of entitlement to that wealth.[17] To address the issue of unequal taxation, then, it makes sense to unpack the underlying theory of entitlement to wealth.

In Book II of his famous *Two Treatises on Government*,[18] John Locke addressed the question of how property came to be privately owned. He started from the premise that God had given all resources to all of humanity in common,[19] a position that was a rebuttal argument to another theorist of the time, Sir Robert Filmer.[20] According to Filmer, kings had a divine right to claim all property for themselves, and consent from the monarch was thus required for appropriation of hitherto unclaimed property.[21] Filmer's position on property derived from his belief that monarchs had absolute authority over

17. My colleague Dan Kleinberger points out that the objection could really be leveled at government choices affecting how wealth is redistributed.
18. LOCKE, *Second Treatise*, *supra* note 12.
19. As this starting point demonstrates, Locke was basically a natural rights theorist. While "natural law" may be somewhat out of vogue these days, "natural" notions of property seem to underlie much of modern thinking about markets, fairness, and entitlement to wealth.
20. *See* LOCKE, *Second Treatise*, *supra* note 12, § 1, at 285-86. For a more complete discussion of the theological aspects of Locke's argument, see John T. Sanders, *Justice and the Initial Acquisition of Property*, 10 HARV. J.L. & PUB. POL'Y 367, 369-71 (1987).
21. *See* LOCKE, *First Treatise*, *supra* note 12, § 3, at 160. *See generally, e.g.*, EDWARD RUTHERFORD, LONDON (Ballantine Publ'g Group 1998) (1997) (containing a fascinating account of the rise of modern London from its pre-Roman beginnings). According to Rutherford, "[K]ing James had somehow persuaded himself that since monarchs were anointed by God, they ruled by Divine Right—which meant that their subjects must obey them because they could do no wrong." *Id.* at 708.

their subjects. Under Locke's view, however, unclaimed resources belonged to all of humanity, not to the monarch, and were thus available to all for the satisfaction of subsistence needs.[22] In addition, unclaimed resources really were unowned and not commonly owned, so there was no need to seek permission from the community before appropriating such resources for private use.[23] Rather, anyone could appropriate as much of the common abundance as necessary for personal consumption by simply expending the effort to do so.[24]

In response to Filmer's claim that monarchs had total authority over their subjects, Locke argued in favor of a natural freedom. Locke argued that each individual owns, at a minimum, his or her own labor.[25] By mixing (personally owned) labor with unclaimed resources, one could establish private property rights in previously unowned resources and one could appropriate as much as necessary for personal survival.[26] No one was entitled to more than was necessary for subsistence, however, because the excess would spoil before it could be consumed. Locke saw this waste as a bad thing.[27] In addition to the no-waste limitation, Locke qualified his labor-mixing principle with the proviso that one must leave "enough and as good" for others.[28] For

---

This belief continued with Charles I who "believed implicitly in his Divine Right." *Id.* at 711.

22. Locke, *Second Treatise*, *supra* note 12, § 25, at 303-04; *see also* Justin Hughes, *The Philosophy of Intellectual Property*, 77 Geo. L.J. 287, 288-298 (1988) (outlining the Lockean property theory with the statement that individuals acquire goods held in common through a grant from God). God grants the bounty of nature to all of humanity with the requirement that individuals must mix their labor with the goods before converting them into private property. This labor thus adds value to the goods.
23. *See* Locke, *Second Treatise*, *supra* note 12, §§ 27-28, at 305-07.
24. *See id.* § 31, at 308.
25. *See id.* §§ 24-26, 31, at 302-05, 308; Geoffrey P. Miller, Comment: *Economic Efficiency and the Lockean Proviso*, 10 Harv. J.L. & Pub. Pol'y 401, 402-03 (1987).
26. *See* Locke, *Second Treatise*, *supra* note 12, § 37, at 312 ("Men had a Right to appropriate, by their Labour, each one to himself, as much of the things of Nature as he could use . . . .").
27. *See id.* §§ 37-38, 41, at 312-15. But this raises another question: in the pre-market state, does Locke see any limit to appropriation other than the fact that some wealth might go to waste? Is there something inherently morally wrong about overappropriating if it does not mean too little left for others? In other words, why should we have cared about waste in the first place if it did not hurt anyone? *See id.* § 46, at 318 ("[I]t was a foolish thing, as well as dishonest, to hoard up more than he could make use of.").

    Indeed, the reason hoarding of gold and silver is acceptable for Locke is that these metals "may be hoarded up without injury to any one, these metalls [sic] not spoileing [sic] or decaying in the hands of the possessor." *Id.* § 50, at 320.
28. This qualification, sometimes referred to as the "Lockean Proviso," has been the topic of much scholarly attention. *See, e.g.*, Sanders, *supra* note 20, at 373 ("Because there is a restriction on the whole notion of private property, one that involves the need of others, this restriction must be taken into consideration in the initial acquisition of property."); *see also* Hughes, *supra* note 22, at 297 ("The

Locke, the "enough and as good" proviso was not particularly limiting, since all of America seemed to be a vast source of unclaimed resources ripe for labor-mixing.[29] Modern scholars, however, have puzzled about how to apply the proviso in a world with relative scarcity.[30] As long as there is plenty to go around, there is nothing controversial about the labor-mixing principle,[31] but under modern conditions of relative scarcity, the contours of the labor-mixing theory are less clear.

Markets and money also complicate the applicability of Lockean labor mixing because money makes accumulation beyond subsistence possible without spoilage. One might gather extra acorns, for example, and trade them for another's extra venison. As long as only perishables are traded, the spoilage restriction remains operable; the total harvest will be the amount necessary for everyone to subsist. But if people trade for money, the spoilage limitation loses its force.[32] By using money, one may appropriate resources beyond immediate needs and trade the excess for something that doesn't spoil—gold. If some goods are scarce relative to the demand for them, their owner will be able to trade the scarce good for more than enough money to satisfy subsistence needs. The extra accumulation is a reward derived from the scarcity-driven demand for the product of the gatherer's labor. The use of money in a state of scarcity allows some first appropri-

---

enough and as good condition protects Locke's labor justification from any attacks asserting that property introduces immoral inequalities."); Carol M. Rose, *"Enough, and as Good" of What?*, 81 Nw. U. L. Rev. 417, 441 (1987) (discussing the controversy that lies in the conflicting goals of self-interest and cooperation in utilizing land to the benefit of all).

29. *See* Locke, *Second Treatise*, *supra* note 12, § 41, at 314 ("[S]everal Nations of the *Americans* are of this, who are rich in Land and poor in all the Comforts of Life . . . with the materials of Plenty . . . yet for want of improving it by labour, have not one hundredth part of the Conveniences we enjoy . . . .").

30. *See, e.g.*, Sanders, *supra* note 20, at 379 (criticizing Locke for his belief that America rendered questions of scarcity moot). One question this raises in my mind is why we care what Locke himself thought outside the context of initial acquisition. *See generally*, Rose, *supra* note 28, at 423-25 ("I have a pretty good idea that old John Locke wouldn't like it either"). In other words why is Locke God? For purposes of this discussion, however, Locke himself is as good a starting point as any. If the point I am rebutting is that liberal philosophy is fundamentally at odds with redistributive taxes, we have to look at some sort of liberal philosophy. Even more strongly, if Schoenblum calls Locke in as an expert witness, then Locke's views become relevant. *See* Schoenblum, *supra* note 1, at 266 ("[I]ndividuals are, in fact, justified in their claims to property derived from their labor or risk-taking.").

31. *See* Jeremy Waldron, Book Review, 102 Ethics 401, 403 (1992) (reviewing Stephen Munzer A Theory of Property (1990)) ("[T]alk of property makes little sense except against a background of scarcity . . . ."). *See also* Rose, *supra* note 28, at 424.

32. *See* Locke, *Second Treatise*, *supra* note 12, § 47, at 318-19 ("And thus *came in the use of Money*, some lasting thing that Men might keep without spoiling, and that by mutual consent Men would take in exchange for the truly useful, but perishable Supports of Life.").

ators to accumulate large amounts of wealth not only by appropriating more than they can use themselves, but also by reaping the rewards of scarcity-driven demand for the products of their labor.

Locke specifically allowed for excess accumulation in a money economy, noting that differences in "industry" would result in differences in the amount of money accumulated.[33] But some level of scarcity is nearly a prerequisite for currency to function.[34] In Locke's words, "where there is not something both lasting and scarce, and so valuable to be hoarded up, there Men will not be apt to enlarge their Possessions of Land were it never so rich, never so free for them to take."[35] The result is to allow excess accumulation when, by definition, at least one good is scarce. For Locke, money (a durable, non-spoiling, scarce good) explains how an individual could "fairly possess more land than he himself can use the product of." This inequality is fair, only because the scarce good is money, the accumulation of which harms no one.[36] But when something necessary for subsistence becomes scarce, the theory offers no justification for inequality. So in addition to questions about how to apply the "enough and as good" proviso, issues can be raised about how to view greatly unequal accumulations resulting from market forces, when the underlying property principle is the Lockean labor-mixing theory, and something needed for survival is scarce.[37] This is exactly the context in which liberal theory matters to us now, and if we want to discuss the fairness of government taking a portion of one's accumulation, the first question we have to ask is who holds what moral claim to the property.

Why exactly should the mixing of labor with a resource establish ownership? As Justin Hughes has pointed out, the labor-mixing approach can be viewed in two ways, depending on one's view of human nature. In both views, economic activity is a positive value that should be encouraged.[38] In the instrumentalist view, labor is unpleasant and people will be induced to perform labor only if they can be

33. *See id.* at 319 ("And as different degrees of Industry were apt to give Men Possessions in different Proportions, so this *Invention of Money* gave them the opportunity to continue and enlarge them.").
34. In theory, markets arise whenever there are advantages to specialization or when consumer preferences do not match the initial distribution of resources. From an individual perspective, some resource is scarce and must be purchased at a negotiated price. When a resource is in abundant supply, however, producers stop producing or leave the market until the product becomes scarce enough to bring a price that will sustain the producers. When that relative scarcity is absent, producers fail, as is now happening in certain agricultural sectors.
35. Locke, *Second Treatise*, *supra* note 12, § 48, at 319.
36. *See id.* § 50, at 319-20.
37. *See* Sanders, *supra* note 20, at 378 (noting interpretation questions revolving around "enough and as good").
38. Should this position be challenged? Consider environmental destruction, slavery, and cultural imperialism as products of the absolute value of economic activity.

assured of the right to keep the product of the labor.[39] So one possible justification for Locke's labor-to-private property result is that the possibility of accumulating property is an incentive to give up leisure in favor of labor, and the institution of private property (beyond subsistence needs) is necessary to induce economic activity.[40] In the more extreme versions of this approach, strong property rights are necessary to provide protection against the "limitless self-interest" of freeloaders.[41] Without adequate rewards, economic activity simply would not be worth the effort.

Market behavior supports the instrumentalist position only to a point. It is not necessarily true that people work more in response to higher after-tax wages, for example. Professor Robert Frank notes that over the last century the average real wage in this country has increased dramatically. Theoretically, this should have encouraged people to work more hours. Yet the length of the average workweek is now shorter than it was at the beginning of the century.[42] In the most recent part of that century, however, median after-tax wages have declined slightly over the last twenty years but the number of hours worked has been increasing over this period. Rather than responding to a lack of incentive, people seem to be trying to maintain a constant level of purchasing power in the face of lower wages.[43]

Professor Frank theorizes that a far more significant inducement to increased effort is the extent to which higher *relative* performance results in higher rewards.[44] The incentive to perform is the chance of coming out on top, rather than the promise of greater absolute re-

39. *See* Hughes, *supra* note 22, at 288 ("This [Lockean] labor justification can be expressed either as a normative claim or as a purely incentive-based, instrumental theory."); *see also* Margaret Jane Radin, *The Liberal Conception of Property: Cross Currents In the Jurisprudence of Takings*, 88 COLUM. L. REV. 1667, 1683 (1988) ("In this [Hobbesian] model of human nature, limitless self-interest and the consequent urgent need for self-defense require the most expansive possible notion of private property . . . .").

40. *See* Hughes, *supra* note 22, at 288-298 (advancing two theories to explain why property rights should be the reward for mixing labor with land).

41. *See* Radin, *supra* note 39, at 1683-84.

42. *See* ROBERT H. FRANK, PROGRESSIVE TAXATION AND THE INCENTIVE PROBLEM 4 (Office of Tax Policy Research Working Paper Series 98-8, 1998) (*citing* RONALD E. EHRENBERG & ROBERT S. SMITH, MODERN LABOR ECONOMICS (1994)); *see also* James J. Heckman, *What Has Been Learned About Labor Supply in the Past Twenty Years?*, 83(2) Amer. Econ. Rev. 116 (1993); ROBERT A. MOFFITT & MARK WILHELM, TAXATION AND THE LABOR SUPPLY DECISIONS OF THE AFFLUENT (National Bureau of Econ. Research Working Paper No. 6621, 1998).

43. *See* FRANK, *supra* note 42 at 5. This is the income effect in action.

44. *See id.* at 14 ("[I]ndeed, it is fair to say that virtually all top decile earners in the U.S. are participants in labor markets in which the rewards depend heavily on relative performance.").

wards.[45] Thus it is not even clear that as an empirical matter, absolute entitlement to economic rewards is necessary to induce economic activity.[46]

The second view of Lockean labor-mixing is that labor is virtuous and, therefore, deserves reward—a desert theory. This view has a much more moral overtone and may be reflected in current attitudes about wealth and virtue.[47] There are at least two variations on the desert theme. One is that labor is virtuous in its own right. Locke saw the plenitude of the natural world as a divine gift that could only be enjoyed through the application of labor; God intended that humankind prosper by using the abundance provided.[48] Thus, in a sense, labor fulfills divine design by making the riches of the natural world available. In addition, Locke saw labor itself as divinely commanded.[49] If labor fulfills some holy design, then it may be seen as virtuous in its own right and deserving of some reward.[50]

A second possible desert theory is that labor deserves reward because private property ultimately provides benefit to society.[51]

45. Professor Frank develops the concept of relative preferences in his book, CHOOSING THE RIGHT POND (1985); *see also* ROBERT H. FRANK & PHILIP J. COOK, THE WINNER-TAKE-ALL SOCIETY (1995); McMahon, Jr. & Abreu, *supra* note 5.

Comparison of median after tax wages and the number of hours worked is the conventional approach to measuring labor elasticity. Recent studies suggesting greater behavioral responses to changes in after-tax rewards have received considerable media attention. Indeed the issue of whether and how behavior changes in response to changes in after-tax wages has been called "one of the liveliest areas of debate of the last twenty years in public economics." AUSTAN GOOLSBEE, IT'S NOT ABOUT THE MONEY: WHY NATURAL EXPERIMENTS DON'T WORK ON THE RICH (American Bar Found. Working Paper No. 9716, 1998).

46. Some entitlement to reward is necessary to the extent that money functions as the "grades that grown-ups get." If money represents levels of prestige, then the existence of any difference in reward is more important than the magnitude of that difference. (Thanks to Dan Kleinberger for this analogy).

47. *See* Kornhauser, *supra* note 11, at 131 (stating that Americans are impelled to save money as a result of moral and economic virtues in order to help oneself and society); *see also* Marjorie E. Kornhauser, *Equality, Liberty, and a Fair Income Tax*, 23 Fordham Urb. L.J. 607, 614 (1996) (defining the principle of desert as when an individual "deserves" or merits the distribution because of some personal characteristic such as ability, effort, or talent).

48. LOCKE, *Second Treatise*, *supra* note 12, § 31, at 308 ("God has given us all things richly." (quoting *I Timothy* 6:17)).

49. *Id.* at § 32, at 308 ("God, when he gave the World in common to all Mankind, commanded Man also to labour, and the penury of his Condition required it of him."); *see also* Marjorie Kornhauser, *supra* note 47, at 125 (noting that American ideas about wealth and money stem partly from the notion of service to God through a vocation).

50. *See* Waldron, *supra* note 31, at 402 (stating that some account is needed of why productive labor is meritorious).

51. *See* Hughes, *supra* note 22, at 305 ("[W]hen labor produces something of value to others—something beyond what morality requires the laborer to produce—then the laborer deserves some benefit for it.").

Wealth is evidence of society's gratitude for value created. For Locke, uncultivated, non-productive land was practically worthless. Working the land added value in the form of produce which could be used for subsistence or for trade, ultimately to provide subsistence for others.[52] Even excess accumulation is beneficial in this view because it creates potential value for the rest of society.[53] In the case of land, productive use of privately owned land means that goods become available for purchase. Some theorists have interpreted the "enough and as good" proviso as applying to the market as a whole so that making goods available for purchase is somewhat analogous to leaving "enough and as good."[54] In addition, because labor is necessary for land to be productive, bringing land into productive use creates yet more demand for the labor of others.[55]

Thus, desert may also result from the value that those with high incomes have contributed to society.[56] The notion is related to Pareto optimality, the economics principle that suggests that a voluntary trade will only take place if both parties are as well or better off after the trade than they were before. In a voluntary trade, the two things traded have relatively equal value, since neither side would willingly pay more than the value of the good or service being received.[57] The

52. *See* Locke, *Second Treatise*, *supra* note 12, § 43, at 316 ("'Tis Labor then which puts the greatest part of Value upon Land, without which it would scarcely be worth any thing.").

53. "Thus the Lockean proviso is not violated if someone takes land out of the commons in excess of his or her pro rata share, so long as the benefits to others resulting from the excess land being placed in productive use exceed the value of the excess land which is taken." Geoffrey P. Miller, *Economic Efficiency and the Lockean Proviso*, 10 Harv. J.L. & Pub. Pol'y 401, 407 (1987); *see also* Hughes, *supra* note 22, at 305 (stating that labor-desert theory provides reward for labor because labor creates social value); *cf.* Sanders, *supra* note 20, at 393 (arguing that society should not prohibit labor that does not provide benefit to the community).

54. Locke, *Second Treatise*, *supra* note 12, § 40, at 314 ("[C]onsider, what the difference is between an Acre of Land planted . . . and an Acre of the same Land lying in common, without any Husbandry upon it, and he will find, that the improvement of labour makes the far greater part of the value"). So, for example, even if one country were to scoop up all the ocean floor manganese nodules, this would be far better than leaving this "common heritage" of mankind on the ocean floor. *See* Arvid Pardo, *An Opportunity Lost*, *in* Law of the Sea: U.S. Policy Dilemma 23 (Bernard H. Oxman et al. eds., 1983).

55. This is somewhat problematic. Under the labor-mixing theory, labor that makes land productive should result in ownership of the land or at least its produce.

56. *See* Barbara Fried, *Wilt Chamberlain Revisited: Nozick's "Justice in Transfer" and the Problem of Market Based Distribution*, 24 Phil. & Pub. Aff. 226, 245 n.39 (listing possible arguments for property rights in economic rents).

57. This assumption is reflected in the tax definition of fair market value: "The fair market value is the price at which the property would change hands between a willing buyer and a willing seller, neither being under any compulsion to buy or to sell and both having reasonable knowledge of relevant facts." 26 C.F.R. § 20.2031-1(b).

seller, then, is seen as providing value to the buyer, the extent of which value is measured by the amount the buyer is willing to pay. Accordingly, we can be confident that high incomes simply reflect the value that their recipients have contributed; the evidence is that others voluntarily paid the sums involved in return. In other words, one could argue that an individual is entitled to the marginal product of his or her labor.[58]

There are two fundamental problems with this form of desert argument. First, the fact that something has market value need not imply that providing it should create an entitlement to wealth in any moral sense. Anecdotal evidence suggests that there is a mismatch between what people deem to be important and what is highly compensated. For example, most parents would rate their children and their obligations to their children as of very high importance. But daycare workers command relatively low salaries. Similarly, the teachers who are entrusted with the education of the next generation of leaders and citizens receive only moderate salaries at best, notwithstanding the importance to society of the function they perform. Recent challenges to the quality of public school education notwithstanding, it is hard to argue that these jobs do not add considerable value to society. But this "value," apparently, is not something the market rewards. On the other hand, many people despise lawyers because they are seen as contributing to the unnecessary complexity of the law and as inducing people to be more adversarial and litigious. Yet lawyers are often very highly paid. Do lawyers create value in the same way that teachers create value? Some kinds of value do not translate well into market terms.[59]

Second, to the extent that markets are incomplete or imperfect, the price something reflects in the market may not be the equilibrium price that would result in perfect competition, but may represent some level of monopoly rent. How can value conferred on society, as measured by income, accurately determine desert when the producer or seller has monopoly power? This is a problem of scarcity. A scarce good commands a high price because consumers who value the good very highly will outbid other consumers for the limited quantities

58. *See* Fried, *supra* note 56, at 245 n.39 (defending individual entitlements to her marginal product of labor on Lockean and Hayekian grounds).

59. Those differences in pay may not trouble us from an instrumentalist perspective when we consider the intangible, psychic benefits of teaching that may be lacking in the practice of law such that the net utility of the one job is not so different from that of the other. From a *desert* perspective, however, focusing on the net benefit to the teacher is improper; our focus now is the benefit conferred on society.

In some cases, market values may reflect historical attitudes and values. For example, teachers and nurses may be undercompensated because these positions have typically been held by women.

available. Potential consumers who are outbid presumably do not value the good as highly as the successful bidders. But this analysis assumes that the only relevant question in determining price is willingness to pay. Ability to pay is simply assumed (or disregarded). It may be that poor individuals would derive even greater utility from the good if they had the means to purchase it. A concept of value that assumes across-the-board ability to pay, then, seems to be an inaccurate way of determining the moral brownie points that should accrue to provision of goods or services in an imperfect market. In addition, the market model only registers improvements in utility for the direct participants. The preferences of non-participants are ignored.

Thus the definition of value as it applies to economic market models is inadequate in describing desert. By definition, the market value of a good is the amount people are willing and able to pay. That definition of value may be fine for analyzing market incentives. But if our theory is that a seller is morally entitled to all of the proceeds from a sale because the seller has contributed value to society, a different understanding might be more appropriate. A utility-based concept of value, for all of its difficulty of measurement, might be more appropriate to a theory of desert than a value theory that is limited by ability to pay. Development of such a desert theory, however, is beyond the scope of this essay since it shifts the focus from the individual providing goods and services, whose autonomy we wish to respect, to a focus on those individuals acquiring the goods and services. A utility-based theory would require assumptions about the utility of goods and services to various purchasers independent of the price actually paid. The focus here, however, is whether the provider of the good/service is morally entitled to it.

We usually speak of income as if there were a direct correlation between income and effort—more effort means more income, and high income implies high effort. We would have a much more accurate picture if we recognized that a part of most incomes derives not directly from effort, but from luck, inheritance, or some other type of serendipity. Since both the desert theory and the instrumentalist theory of labor-mixing derive entitlement to wealth from the combination of labor (effort) and an unowned resource, neither form of the labor-mixing theory adequately explains our apparent belief in equal moral entitlement to all income.

Under either a desert or instrumentalist theory of labor-mixing (where desert is tied to the labor itself rather than to the market society's response to the product), it is possible to make a distinction between that part of the market returns that truly rewards an individual's efforts and that part of the returns that rewards luck, inheritance, or scarcity.[60] Yet this is a distinction that usually is not made. Indeed, the level of effort almost seems irrelevant.[61]

It seems clear that Locke had a high regard for individual effort as well as for individual autonomy, and to a large extent, effort is still a factor in desert.[62] Indeed, a frequent argument against redistribution of income is that someone who worked hard should not be penalized merely to benefit one who chose leisure over work.[63] Moreover, recent empirical studies show that people feel the most morally entitled to wealth they earn through personal efforts.[64] But even though on a conscious level we seem to believe that effort should matter,[65] as a society we do not reward effort. Rather, effort or exertion only *appears* to be the justification for accumulation of private property. Actually, the level of effort or exertion seems to be of minor significance when compared to the effectiveness of the effort. Actual achievement, rather than the labor that went into it determines desert to a greater extent than does effort.

The conclusion that effort matters little and outcome matters a lot is somewhat consistent with the basic Lockean labor-mixing theory. If a resource is unowned, then even a small amount of personal effort

60. This concept of value has been called the "social increment theory of valuation." *See* John J. Costonis, *The Disparity Issue: A Context for the Grand Central Decision*, 91 HARV. L. REV. 402, 415-416 (1977).

61. In some cases, even a value-added formula may be difficult to identify. For example, in 1996 the CEO of Green Tree Financial reportedly earned $102 million. Under a revised formula, he would have earned a meager $7 million plus stock options, according to the St. Paul Pioneer Press. *See* D.J. Tice, *What's the Answer on Skyrocketing CEO Pay?*, ST. PAUL PIONEER PRESS, July 23, 1997, at 6A.

62. *See* David Miller, *Distributive Justice: What the People Think*, 102 ETHICS 555, 562 (1992) (explaining that in studies where people judge an appropriate reward depending upon achievement, the notion of effort is also important because "it is possible for a person who achieves less but tries harder to deserve more than another who tries less but achieves more.").

63. *See* Kornhauser, *supra* note 11, at 139 (noting that income tax has been denounced as "rewarding the idle and the wastrel"); *see also* Elizabeth Hoffman & Matthew L. Spitzer, *Entitlements, Rights, and Fairness: An Experimental Examination of Subjects' Concepts of Distributive Justice*, 14 J. LEGAL STUD. 259, 273 (1985) (describing broad theories of distributive justice and empirically testing behavioral responses against these theories). Professors Hoffman and Spitzer showed that in an experimental setting, people behave as if effort is the most important factor in deciding how rewards should be distributed among participants. *See id.* at 266.

64. *See* Miller, *supra* note 62, at 562 (explaining that "effort does not obliterate achievement: with effort held constant, the one who achieves more deserves more, so presumably the view is that ability can count toward desert when it is combined with effort but not when it stands alone").

65. This is one of the arguments against high compensation for corporate executives. *See* Tice, *supra* note 61 ("People try to believe that skill, hard work and a decision to focus on monetary rewards (plus luck, usually) largely explain why some Americans are richer than others. Corporate America can't afford executive pay so extravagant and seemingly exploitive that it destroys this fragile confidence.").

will convert the resource to private property simply by establishing a right in the property that is stronger than any other right. One who is able to gather a lot of acorns with little effort is just as entitled to them as is someone who expends a lot of effort.[66] In the face of plenty, a lot of ineffective effort brings no greater reward than a little effective effort.[67] The effectiveness principle is even clearer, however, in a money economy. The use of money, as we noted above allows appropriation of scarce resources beyond an individual's personal needs. Scarcity creates demand at a relatively higher price, allowing even greater accumulation of wealth. So as a theoretical matter, Lockean regard for individuals results in rewarding effort, but in practice something else must be going on.

As noted above, money effects a fundamental change in the application of the labor-mixing theory because money does not spoil. The result is "disproportionate and unequal possession of the Earth."[68] Differences in "industry" result in unequal appropriations, and these differences can then be enlarged in the marketplace. The resulting distribution is unequal partly because of differences in effort but even more so because of differences in the market demand for different goods. In other words, wealth accumulates as a result of effort that is effective in producing market value. Ineffective effort, no matter how earnest, is simply not rewarded. Property ownership, then, is the reward of individual effort, to be sure, but it is greatly affected by the workings of the market as well. So what was forbidden in a state of abundance—appropriation beyond immediate needs—is perfectly acceptable and even rewarded in a money-driven market economy.

## III. SOCIAL INCREMENT APPROACH

As we have seen, a Lockean-derived respect for the autonomy of the individual does establish the appropriateness of some disparity of wealth or income. But it does not account for all of the disparity. Part of the disparity results from societal factors for which the individual is not responsible. To backstep just a bit, I have described how Locke's theory of property derives from individuals' ownership of their own labor. But how much property must necessarily be the reward for labor? Neither the instrumentalist nor the desert theory provides a clear answer. Under a desert theory—that property is a reward for

66. Consider *Pierson v. Post*, 3 Cai. R. 175, 2 Am. Dec. 264 (N.Y. Sup. Ct. 1805), which held that a dead fox belongs to the hunter who shot it, not to hunter who chased it all day and cornered it. The only labor that counts for anything is the labor that actually brings down the fox.

67. *See* Sanders, *supra* note 20, at 393 (arguing that not all labor is "successfully" invested, but that this is irrelevant to the labor-mixing criterion from a justice perspective).

68. LOCKE, *Second Treatise*, *supra* note 12, § 50, at 319-20.

virtue or a sign of virtue—if the virtue being rewarded is effort, wealth only needs to be proportionate to effort.[69] In fact, wealth is often (if not usually) vastly disproportional to effort. Thus, if effort is the virtue to be rewarded, a lot of wealth is not morally deserved, but is a windfall. Under the instrumentalist theory—that material reward is necessary to induce effort—only the material effort necessary to induce effort is justified. In fact, other factors also induce effort, and material compensation is likely to rise far beyond the level necessary to assure continued effort. These claims deserve closer examination.

## IV. DESERT THEORY

If effort is the virtue to be rewarded, a lot of wealth is not morally deserved. But we have said that we do not reward the virtue of effort so much as the virtue of efficacy.[70] Does the fact that we do reward efficacy mean that we respect it as a virtue? We also reward luck. Studies have shown that people regard effort as more virtuous and deserving of reward than luck. For example, in one study, subjects in one group were asked to play a short game that appears to require skill, but actually requires very little, the outcome generally depending on who gets to go first.[71] The winner of the game becomes the "controller" for a decision regarding how much money each player will be paid. Another set of subjects also had to make a decision regarding distribution of money, but the controller was chosen by coin toss. When the subject "earned" the right to be controller by winning the game, the distribution of money chosen was much more likely to be

69. But, the reader argues, not all effort is equal. Some effort amounts to just going through the motions, not real effort. Of course it is possible that some people would muck along making only half-hearted effort. A system that rewarded quantifiable effort rather than outcome would certainly have some free riders. The current system of rewarding outcome has the same effect, however, along with the failure to reward a lot of honest hard effort that produces little or that is abundantly available. If desert accrued to effort, everyone would at least have to go through the motions. The market could enforce the integrity of the effort. Those who did not really exert would find themselves without the opportunity to make an effort at all. In theory, this is already true. The problem is that we seem to assume that lack of effort is the only factor.

70. *See* Rose, *supra* note 28, at 437 (original appropriators seen to deserve reward "because they do a public service by starting a property system that encourages investment and care in the use of resources"); John Stick, *Renegotiating a RUM Deal*, 81 Nw. U. L. Rev. 443, 448 (1987) (stating that rational utility maximizer suggests that only property owners are productive members of society).

71. *See* Hoffman & Spitzer, *supra* note 63, at 268-69, 273. The game was very simple. Two players are shown a series of 17 vertical hash marks, which they must take turns crossing off. Each player in turn crosses off 1, 2, 3, or 4 hash marks. The person who crosses out the last hash mark loses the game. (Go ahead, try it. Great stuff for faculty meetings.)

/////////////////

disproportionate in favor of the controller. When the controller was chosen by coin toss, however, the distribution of proceeds was more even, the principle apparently being that effort and ability create desert but luck does not.[72]

How could it be then, that we would regard the lucky investor as more virtuous than the wage laborer? On its face, the question seems absurd, but higher incomes are likely to include investment income, while lower incomes are more likely to consist solely of wages. If high income is somehow a sign of virtue, then the lucky investor exhibits more evidence of virtue than the wage laborer. The failure to make a distinction between effort and outcome leads us to treat efficacy as a surrogate for effort,[73] and in our confusion, we assume that the greater output required the greater input. Opponents of progressive taxation often invoke images of idle poor and industrious wealthy people to support arguments against redistributive taxes.[74] But where Locke's theory starts with effort (labor) to explain an entitlement to wealth, our approach is backwards and circular. We take the existence of wealth and assume it all resulted from effort (labor) and then rely on that very effort to establish entitlement to wealth, an entitlement that resists taxation. Locke's theory does not explain an entitlement to all wealth, but only to that wealth that results from effort (labor). We add a first step of converting all wealth into the result of effort.

## V. INSTRUMENTALIST THEORY

Material compensation often exceeds the amount needed to induce effort. Under an instrumentalist approach to wealth the analysis is similarly inadequate. The instrumentalist rationale, again, is that the effective effort must be rewarded to induce people to engage in more productive effort. Yet this rationale for property does a poor job of justifying rewards that are disproportionate to effort. If the role of property is to encourage effort, then one should be entitled to as much property as is necessary to induce the desired effort, but not more. Yet when reward is based on efficacy of effort[75]—efficacy in terms of pro-

72. *See id.* at 282-283 (noting that subjects regarded position of controller as justified right after playing the hash mark game).

73. *See* Thomas Ross, *Taking Takings Seriously*, 80 Nw. U. L. Rev. 1591, 1601 (1986) (describing Epstein's argument that "providing welfare increases the number of people who will forego productive lives and choose to be supported by society" as at best "perfunctory and lethargic").

74. *See* Schoenblum, *supra* note 1, at 261 (presenting a situation where a person worked her way up from poverty to be a successful medical doctor while her old friends can now barely get by because of their "lack of willpower and determination").

75. *See* Hoffman & Spitzer, *supra* note 63, at 273. ("Lockean theory . . . has room within it for differences in efficacy of effort: even if two people spend the same

viding something that the market is willing to pay for—rather than the level of exertion,[76] the reward may go beyond that needed incentive. Individual levels of effort, like individual utility curves,[77] cannot be quantified. It is easy, however, to measure the amount that society is willing to pay for the results of that effort. It is only when the amount of a good or service is directly tied to the time spent providing it that we make any clear attempt to reward the effort itself. So hourly workers earn more if they work forty hours a week than if they work thirty. The hourly rate, itself, however, has little to do with the amount of effort involved in the task.[78] Rather, it is a measure of the "value" placed on the product of the labor, and only a very small portion of that value is tied to the actual effort expended.[79]

## VI. THE REST OF THE STORY—THE SOCIAL INCREMENT OF VALUE

There is room within Lockean property theory for a distinction between wealth that is the fair reward for engaging in productive labor and wealth that is the result of luck.[80] Locke's theory really only re-

amount of time or try as hard, the person who does a better job still deserves the resource.").

76. For a more vernacular statement of this principle, see Rosina B. Barker and Jasper L. Cummings, Jr., *Interview With Thomas F. Field*, 15 ABA Sec. of Tax'n Newsl. 13 (Summer 1996). Thomas Field, the founder of Tax Analysts, a major tax information publisher describes his start in tax publishing as "an illustration of the old adage, 'better lucky than smart'. . . . And step-by-step, little by little, very much to our surprise, we have found ourselves to be a factor in tax publishing. It is all an accident." *Id.* at 13-14.

77. The inability to make satisfactory comparisons of utility functions among individuals has long confounded the declining marginal utility of income theory. *But see* Mark S. Stein, *Diminishing Marginal Utility of Income and Progressive Taxation: A Critique of the Uneasy Case*, 12 N. Ill. U. L. Rev. 373, 374 (1992) (defending the concept of declining marginal utility of income).

78. Jennifer Hochschild interviewed people to determine their attitudes about income distribution and desert. She concluded that people believe that factors within the workers' control, such as effort, should create desert, but that they also believe that actual achievement should create desert. For example, a lazy janitor should receive less than a hardworking one, but even a lazy doctor should receive more than either. Jennifer Hochschild, What's Fair: American Beliefs About Distributive Justice 112 (1981), *cited in* Miller, *supra* note 62 (reviewing works in political theory on social or distributive justice and empirical studies of attitudes about distributive justice).

79. *See* Henry C. Simons, Personal Income Taxation: The Definition of Income as a Problem of Fiscal Policy 20 (1938) (noting the effect of market demand on wages over and above the amount of wages necessary to induce performance of services: "What competing firms must pay to get experts away from one another is vastly different from what society would be obliged to pay in order to keep the experts from being ditch-diggers").

80. *See* Hoffman & Spitzer, *supra* note 63, at 273; Margaret Jane Radin, *The Liberal Conception of Property: Cross Currents in the Jurisprudence of Takings*, 88 Colum. L. Rev. 1667, 1685 (1988) (stating that commitment to individual secur-

quires the conclusion that individuals are entitled to some return for their own labor or for the unpleasantness of having worked.[81] To the extent that wealth accumulation results not from labor, but from luck, inheritance,[82] or heredity, an individual's moral claim to that wealth is much weaker. Society, itself, may also have a role in the production of wealth even if only through the facilitation of markets that allow the trading that produces unequal accumulations of wealth.

Professor Barbara Fried makes this point with respect to natural talent, which can be seen as the result of pure luck.[83] If one mixes labor with that natural talent, the labor deserves to be rewarded, but because labor per se is not in short supply, the market price represents more than fair compensation for the labor. The part of the market price that exceeds the fair return to labor is more like monopoly rent[84]—the price is high not because of any virtue of the talented worker, but because there is more demand for the talent than there is supply of it.[85] Fried notes that there is an argument that society, which has supplied the demand for the talent, has just as good a claim on the surplus value generated by talent as does the athlete who simply has the good fortune to be born with that talent.[86] No amount of innate talent would have value if it did not match the preferences of some market segment.

Intellectual property offers another example that supports this point. Intellectual property scholars make a distinction between an idea and its expression.[87] There is no market for ideas without expression, just as there is no market for talent without effort and no

ity "moral as basis for property supports conservative and progressive conceptions of property"); Ross, *supra* note 73, at 1594 (stating that Locke's theory is consistent with redistribution).

81. *See also* Barbara H. Fried, *Fairness and the Consumption Tax*, 44 STAN. L. REV. 961, 1008 (1992) (extending Lockean theory to the act of saving because of the sacrifice involved).

82. Inheritance raises interesting cross-generational issues. Part of the incentive for parents to work may be to leave a legacy for their children, and that legacy should be treated as part of the parent's desert. But when we consider the child's income derived from that inherited wealth, it is appropriate to focus on the child's efforts rather than the parent's. Thus inherited wealth provides an income stream for which an individual does not labor.

83. Charles Fried, *The New First Amendment Jurisprudence: A Threat to Liberty*, 59 U. CHI. L. REV. 225, 251 (1992).

84. *See* DAVID N. HYMAN, ECONOMICS 386-87 (3d ed. 1994).

85. *See id.*

86. *See* Joseph Bankman & Barbara H. Fried, *Winners and Losers in the Shift to a Consumption Tax*, 86 GEO. L.J. 539, 545-46 (1998).

87. *See* CURTIS C. BERGER & JOAN C. WILLIAMS, PROPERTY, LAND OWNERSHIP AND USE 77-85 (4th ed. 1997); Justin Hughes, *supra* note 22, at 310. Professor Hughes notes, however, that courts have never developed a clear distinction between idea and expression, but goes on to develop the idea at least on a conceptual level. *See id.* at 312-13.

market for unappropriated natural resources. It makes sense that there should be no market for unexpressed talent and ideas. From an instrumentalist perspective, no amount of incentive can induce talent to appear where it does not exist, and to a certain extent, incentives cannot create "aha" experiences.[88] Although "aha" experiences may follow extensive research and thought, they are often serendipitous.

Once an idea is expressed, however, it becomes owned because of the expression. Thus it is only the effort involved in expressing the idea that creates entitlement to the idea and its proceeds.[89] Accordingly, that effort should be rewarded either to encourage more of it, or as a reward for having made a valuable product available.[90] But the price the market places on the expressed idea often reflects much more than the effort that went into expressing the idea. The market price also reflects society's response to the idea.[91] Thus it is the interaction between society and the fortunate talented individual that results in accumulation of wealth.

Similarly, actions of government in the public interest may result in private profit. For example, when a transportation authority plans rail routes to converge on a single train station, the owners of that station reap a windfall in higher rents. In the celebrated landmark preservation case, *Penn Central Transportation Co. v. City of New York*,[92] Justice Brennan, writing for the Supreme Court, acknowledged the contributions of society and government to the value of the Grand Central Station property in New York City. The state court opinion[93] relied on this reasoning to an even greater extent. The New York Court of Appeals asserted that "society as an organized entity especially through its government, rather than as a mere conglomer-

88. A recent issue of DISCOVER magazine highlighted the role of creativity in scientific advancement. One article focused specifically on discoveries that are made completely by accident.

    For example, Teflon was the result of an accidental polymerization of tetrafluoroethylene ("TFE") that was being stored in preparation for an unrelated experiment. *See* Robert Friedel, *The Accidental Inventor: Some Inventions Result from Unexpected Consequences*, DISCOVER, Oct. 1, 1996, at 58; *see also* Hughes, *supra* note 22, at 303 (explaining the instrumental argument for property that labor should be rewarded because people must be motivated to perform labor).
89. This discussion should not be interpreted to mean that there is little or no effort involved in expression. The effort can be considerable, as anyone who has written a law review article is well aware.
90. *See* Hughes, *supra* note 22, at 305.
91. Teflon, discovered quite by accident, was a valuable discovery because of its possible military and industrial uses. Scientists needed something that would resist the corrosive action of uranium hexafluoride that served as fuel for the atomic bomb in World War II. *See* Friedel, *supra* note 88.

    In addition, patent protection may also allow the inventor to enjoy monopoly rent for the duration of the patent.
92. 438 U.S. 104 (1978).
93. Penn Cent. Transp. Co. v. New York City, 366 N.E.2d 1271 (N.Y. 1977).

ate of individuals, has created much of the value of the terminal property."[94] Accordingly, the value that would require compensation in a takings case was something less than the full fair market value of the property. "A fair return is to be accorded the owner, but society is to receive its due for its share in the making of a once great railroad."[95]

It is thus possible to embrace a Lockean respect for individuals that rewards effort yet simultaneously to recognize a role for society in the production of wealth. Although some libertarian scholars would argue that personal freedom means we are entitled to all of the value that is generated by our own labor mixing,[96] it is difficult to see why we should be entitled to whatever the market will pay.[97] Because entitlement to wealth is justifiable only to varying extents even in a Lockean sense, it is not particularly surprising that American society embraces and has embraced seemingly conflicting attitudes about wealth.[98] In her article, *The Morality of Money*, Professor Marjorie Kornhauser traces American attitudes about wealth and its distribution.[99] She identifies a tension between a view that saving is more moral than spending so that unearned income somehow indicates deservedness and a view that labor is virtuous so that earned income is morally superior.[100] In addition, we hold competing views of the individual: we "extol individualism and the sacred right to property," but at the same time our regard for individuals leads to emphasis on equality.[101]

What does this have to do with tax rates? If the argument is that progressive rates are unfair because high income folks are entitled to their high incomes, then an argument that challenges the claim of entitlement may also help to establish the fairness of progressive (or at any rate "unequal") taxes. For example, in 1942, Congress enacted significant tax legislation. One of the debated issues was the appropriate rate of corporate income taxation. There was incentive to raise corporate taxes because corporations had become very profitable as a result of the war. Reported net corporate income had increased 146%

94. *Id.* at 332.

95. *Id.* at 333; *see also* Costonis, *supra* note 60, at 416 (defining social increment of value as "the portion of a property's value that is attributable to public investment and concomitant community growth").

96. *See generally* Nozick, *supra* note 1; Schoenblum, *supra* note 1, at 39-40.

97. *See* Fried, *supra* note 56, at 228.

98. *See generally* Kornhauser, *supra* note 11.

99. *See id.*

100. *See id.*

101. *Id.* at 120. Professor Kornhauser develops the roles of these attitudes in determining tax policy through the history of the U.S. income tax. *See also* Alexis De Tocqueville, Democracy in America (Henry Steele Commager ed., Henry Reeve trans., Oxford Univ. Press 1959) (pt. 1, 1835 & pt. 2, 1840) (asserting that these two views are antipathetic).

from 1939 to 1942, for example.[102] Senator La Follette testified that "these increased incomes can be considered as direct consequences of Government expenditures arising out of the national emergency" and concluded that it was not unjust for the government to "recover the additional net income."[103] At that time corporations were subject to a "normal" income tax, a surtax, and an excess profits tax.[104] The Treasury proposed a combined normal and surtax rate of 55%, which would have soaked up most of the additional profits.[105] The rationale behind the surtax was thus explicit recognition of the role of society as a whole in producing high incomes.

A similar concept appears in respect to the valuation of mobile homes. When mobile home sites are scarce, the market value of a mobile home in a park is much higher than the value of one not in a park. Karl Manheim discusses the concept of "placement value" and notes that courts have recognized this separate component of value but have disagreed about how to allocate it.[106] Certainly there are those who would argue that the "placement value" belongs clearly and only to the park owner,[107] but the scarcity of mobile home sites is often as much a result of very restrictive zoning laws that create virtual monopolies for the few mobile home parks allowed as it is a result of the landlord's foresight in choosing a good location.[108] Thus at least one court has found that legislation allocating the benefit of that placement value to the tenant does not violate any constitutional principles. No value has been taken *from* the landlord. Rather that value which the state has created, the state has now allocated.[109]

Barbara Fried has also described the ways in which a mere existence of government affects returns to investors. Increasing the money supply, for example, has an effect on interest rates, which in turn affects investors.[110] To the extent the effect is a positive one, government or society can be seen as playing a role in determining the

102. *See* Robert M. Follette, Jr., Individual Views, S. Rep. No. 77-131, pt. 2, at 6-7 (1942), *reprinted in* 108 U.S. Revenue Acts 1909-1950: The Laws, Legislative History and Administrative Documents (Bernard D. Reams, Jr. ed., 1979).

103. *Id.* at 7.

104. *See id.* at 8.

105. *See id.* at 7.

106. *See* Karl Manheim, *Tenant Eviction Protection and the Takings Clause*, 1989 Wis. L. Rev. 925, 964.

107. *See* Werner Hirsch & Joel Hirsch, *Legal-Economic Analysis of Rent Controls in a Mobile Home Context: Placement Values and Vacancy Decontrol*, 35 UCLA L. Rev. 399, 446-47 (1988) (characterizing "placement value" as merely a product of the landlord's right to set rents).

108. *See* Manheim, *supra* note 106, at 965.

109. *See id.* at 965 n.225 (discussing Eamiello *v.* Liberty Home Sales, 546 A.2d 805, 820 (Conn. 1988)).

110. *See* Fried, *supra* note 81, at 1007-1008.

rewards to investment activity.[111] This effect also serves to highlight the larger point that differences in rewards result from many factors other than differences in "industry."[112]

Finally, Ronald Dworkin has also identified market-generated returns that result from luck or inheritance, as opposed to effort.[113] Dworkin does not suggest that differences in effort would not generate differences in accumulation. Rather, he begins by describing the differences in accumulation that would quickly appear even in a closed economy where everyone starts out with the same level of ability and resources.[114] Differences in ambition and willingness to take risks result in differences in accumulation, but these differences are acceptable because they result purely from individual choice; everyone could accumulate as much as the person who accumulates the most, if they were willing to expend the effort or make the same sacrifices.[115] But when the inability to accumulate is due to "brute bad luck," Dworkin proposes a taxing scheme that would account for differences in income due to factors other than effort.[116]

## VII. APPLICATION TO TAX POLICY

Fundamental disagreements are likely to stem from underlying attitudes and assumptions, which usually are not the focus of debate.[117] But underlying attitudes should be the focus.[118] Opponents of progressive taxation argue that the usual theories of progressivity do not

111. *See generally* Duncan Kennedy & Frank Michelman, *Are Property and Contract Efficient?*, 8 HOFSTRA L. REV. 711 (1980) (arguing that any social structure "distorts" incentives relative to desert island economy).
112. This also is not quite the same as the more direct effects usually identified as "benefits" for purposes of the benefit theory, although advocates of progressivity do cite some indirect effects such as the availability of an educated labor force as factors in successful accumulation of wealth. *See, e.g.*, Kornhauser, *supra* note 9, at 484-85.
113. *See generally* Ronald Dworkin, *What is Equality? Part 2: Equality of Resources*, 10 PHIL. & PUB. AFF. 283 (1981). I have discussed Dworkin's Equality of Resources theory in greater detail elsewhere. *See* Byrne, *supra* note 6, at 778-782.
114. *See* Dworkin, *supra* note 113.
115. *See id.* at 292-93, 306; *see also* Byrne, *supra* note 6, at 778-79.
116. Dworkin, *supra* note 113, at 320-22. Dworkin sets forth a hypothetical model of social "underemployment" insurance whereby a person would be compensated in relation to the amount of insurance they would have bought had they not known what type of natural abilities they would possess. People would find it worth their while to buy at least the minimum amount necessary to ensure that they did not end up at the bottom of the employment ladder given the marginal utility of the policy. *See also* Byrne, *supra* note 6, at 778-779.
117. See my earlier article in which I presented in some detail the philosophical issues which inform the rate structure discussions. *See generally* Byrne, *supra* note 6.
118. Marjorie Kornhauser has made this argument in her articles on Tax Reform Rhetoric. *See* Kornhauser, *supra* note 9; Kornhauser, *supra* note 8; Kornhauser, *supra* note 47; *see also* Byrne, *supra* note 6; Schoenblum, *supra* note 1.

prove the fairness of redistributive taxes and that high income earners thus "have an especially compelling claim that there is no justice in being taxed more harshly than other taxpayers who do not earn as much."[119] Accordingly, there can be no ethical quality to differentiated rates of taxation; mere preferences for redistribution on equalitarian grounds are simply at odds with the value of individual autonomy.[120] In this section, I argue that a preference for individual autonomy as a normative value does not preclude redistributive taxes[121] and respond to arguments to the contrary.[122]

### A. Why Taxes Don't Interfere with the Instrumentalist Version of Lockean Respect for Individual Autonomy

Under the instrumentalist version of Lockean theory discussed above, the reason for allowing an individual to reap the rewards of effort is to provide an incentive for that effort. If enough incentive is left in place after taxation, the effort should still occur under this theory. Taxing the product of labor, however, reduces the incentive to engage in productive labor, at least in theory.[123] Thus taxes, which

119. Schoenblum, *supra* note 1, at 224.

120. I use the term "redistributive" loosely here to mean taxes that result in a transfer of benefit from the wealthy to the poor. A tax could also redistribute from the poor to the wealthy. For example, the absolutely equal tax that Schoenblum advocates could also be a redistributive tax if it is true, as benefit theory proponents suggest, that better-off people derive greater benefits from government than those less well off. If it is true at all that the wealthy benefit more (regardless of whether or not that disparity supports progressivity), then a lump sum tax would mean that poor folks, through their equal contributions, are paying for benefits that go only to the wealthy. *See* Schoenblum, *supra* note 1, at 249. For purposes of the discussion in this section, however, I will go along with the usual characterization of income taxes as redistributive in the sense of redistributive from high income to low income.

121. Schoenblum's proposal is not a pure head tax. He allows for a zero tax bracket and a phase-in range. Thus, under his proposal the poorest of the poor would not support the wealthy, although the fairly poor would. *See* Schoenblum, *supra* note 1, at 270.

122. In particular, Professor Jeffrey Schoenblum has argued that the only tax that is fair to all individuals is an "absolutely equal" tax—a lump sum head tax. *See* Schoenblum, *supra* note 1, at 271 (emphasizing that even if "equal" taxation is unattainable, it should serve as a standard by which tax models are evaluated for their fairness).

123. The extent to which this is true depends on the elasticity of labor. Studies have shown that the supply of labor provided by primary wage earners is inelastic with respect to income (and therefore taxes). *See* Jane G. Gravelle, *Behavioral Responses to Proposed High-income Tax Rate Increases: An Evaluation of the Feldstein-Feenberg Study*, 59 Tax Notes 1097, 1100 (May 24, 1993) (claiming that most studies find that labor supply elasticity for males is negative and small). There are several possible reasons for this phenomenon. First, upper income workers may work for reasons other than incremental salary increases. Nonmonetary considerations such as prestige and a sense of responsibility may be

remove some of the incentive, seem to be antithetical to the instrumentalist form of Lockean labor theory. This is only true, however, if there is no windfall inherent in the rewards to labor. Windfalls by definition are unexpected and unpredicted and should have no effect on incentives. The windfall portion of market prices is analogous to economic rent—that part of, say, an individual's salary that exceeds the price the individual could command in the next best activity.[124] If a lawyer is willing to work for $45,000 a year, the lawyer will probably be delighted to work for $200,000 a year. The additional $155,000 per year does not perform the instrumentalist function of inducing the lawyer to practice law; it is more like a windfall or a bonus.[125] To the extent that taxes are taken out of this "windfall" amount, there should be little or no effect on the lawyer's willingness to engage in the practice of law. Of course, at least some of the lawyers working for $200,000 would, at least in theory, not work for less.

In fact, there is considerable evidence to suggest that the motivation for working more or harder is not greatly dependent on the absolute monetary compensation for making the effort. The possibility of greater consumption is not likely to be a motivating factor, particu-

more important. At lower income levels, workers may not have the option of changing the amount of work supplied, since most jobs require a fixed time commitment. Finally, the "income effect" may operate at low income levels. The income effect is the tendency of some workers to work more hours as the after tax wage goes down in order to maintain a constant standard of living. *See* Bankman & Griffith, *supra* note 16, at 1922-26 (explaining that work helps determine social standing and self-esteem and reviewing studies of compensated elasticity of labor showing that elasticity of labor is generally lower, but higher for married women) (citing Gramm, *Labor, Work, and Leisure: Human Well-Being and the Optimal Allocation of Time*, 21 J. ECON. ISSUES 167, 175 (1987)); *see also* DAVID G. DAVIES, UNITED STATES TAXES AND TAX POLICY 68 (1986); Stein, *supra* note 77, at 388-89 & n.42 (1992) (presenting table showing hours worked at different income levels).

124. Economics textbooks define "economic rent" as the earnings that exceed the opportunity cost of an activity. *See* HYMAN, *supra* note 84, at 386; STEVEN M. CRAFTON & MARGARET F. BRINIG, QUANTITATIVE METHODS FOR LAWYERS 854-55 (1994); JOHN GOWDY & SABINE O'HARA, ECONOMIC THEORY FOR ENVIRONMENTALISTS 86 (1995) (defining economic profits as those profits over and above those obtainable in the best alternative in the economy). In the case of labor, however, opportunity cost may represent the value of foregone leisure, rather than some other salary-paying occupation. If a lawyer's best paying alternative pays only half as much as being a lawyer, but is more pleasant, then the lawyer's minimum price for legal work should include inducement to give up that pleasure. For purposes of my argument, it is the difference between the lawyer's minimum price for being a lawyer and what the lawyer actually receives that is relevant. This is only a portion of the "economic rent" that the lawyer receives if economic rent is calculated using only monetary compensation (as opposed to utility).

125. The market is supposed to work this way. The price increases until there are just enough lawyers. I do not mean to suggest that this function is inappropriate; rather, that for all except the very last lawyer to enter the market, the price received for services rendered is more than necessary to induce the performance of those services.

larly for very high income earners.[126] At some level of income, presumably, greater consumption is difficult at best. Christopher Carroll notes, for example, that Bill Gates would have to spend more than $10 million a day simply to avoid further accumulation.[127] Carroll also notes that very wealthy people make references to "having enough."[128] Although a diminished interest in greater consumption does not necessarily translate into a lack of interest in more money, it does suggest that the incentive to work more and earn more at some point comes from something other than the desire to eat more acorns.[129]

For example, in a study of affluent male workers, Robert Moffitt and Mark Wilhelm reported no change in hours worked in response to changes in marginal tax rates between 1983 and 1989.[130] Moffitt and Wilhelm speculate that these workers are working so many hours already that they cannot respond to lower tax rates by working more.[131] In other words, taxes did not seem to be depressing the number of hours these workers worked before rates were lowered. These findings are also consistent with the possibility that at least part of a high salary does not serve an ongoing incentive purpose. Carroll suggests several other motivations for work, namely, job satisfaction, philanthropic ambitions, and power-lust.[132]

Robert Frank has also argued that a primary incentive for market effort is relative performance. Relative standing in terms of income and wealth is more significant than one's actual absolute standard of living.[133] Further empirical evidence based on cross-cultural studies does not support the notion that higher tax rates result in less work effort.[134]

Thus as long as greater effort results in some improvement in position and in some increase in wealth after tax, imposition of tax does not confound the role of incentive as a motivator for productive effort. Of course, a tax that simply confiscated all income above some level would be inappropriate because it would completely eliminate incen-

126. *See* Christopher D. Carroll, Why Do the Rich Save So Much? 23 (National Bureau of Econ. Research Working Paper No. 6549, 1998).
127. *See id.* at 18.
128. *Id.*
129. In some cases, the challenge of earning more for its own sake may provide some incentive to increase productive activity.
130. *See* Moffitt & Wilhelm, *supra* note 42, at 41.
131. *See id.*
132. *See* Carroll, *supra* note 126, at 19.
133. *See* Robert H. Frank, Choosing the Right Pond: Human Behavior and the Quest for Status (1985). Professor Frank suggests that most people would be less than satisfied to move from a standard of living that is higher than that of their neighbors to a *higher* standard of living well below that of all of the new neighbors.
134. *See* Frank, *supra* note 42.

tives and would fail to reward high-income efforts at all. But some degree of progressivity would be acceptable so long as greater effort results in some after-tax increase.

### B. Why Taxes Don't Interfere with the Desert Version of Lockean Theory Either

The analysis under the desert view of property is similar. The emphasis is simply shifted from reward as necessary to induce effort to reward as moral desert. If effort deserves reward, then effort should be rewarded. But once we recognize the role of luck or of society in the accumulation of wealth, it is easy to see a fairness in taxing the returns that do not stem purely from effort, even while embracing the notion that effort deserves reward.

## VIII. TAX THEORIES

As we have seen, the imposition of tax does not interfere with the reasons for property as desert. Taxes that are not confiscatory do not unreasonably reduce the incentive to engage in productive effort and they do not eliminate the reward due to a virtuous worker. Income taxes, in other words, are not inconsistent with a Lockean property theory. One can respect individual autonomy and yet favor redistributive taxes.

We now shift perspective to the arguments that are used to support redistributive taxes, namely the benefit theory and the ability-to-pay or equal sacrifice theory. These theories have been subject to criticism from many corners, including my earlier work. I discuss them here, though, because when they are examined through a lens of Lockean property theory, the arguments against them seem less persuasive. There are two main problems with the usual theories. The first is that whether or not the benefit theory can produce a fair result depends partly on which version of Locke one starts with. A view that there is no social increment windfall to income produces a conclusion that the benefit theory does not justify graduated taxes. A view that takes luck and effort into account would redeem the benefit theory at least on this count. The second problem with the usual theories is largely an empirical one. Both sacrifice and benefit theories rely on internally subjective variables. The sacrifice/ability-to-pay theories depend on assumptions about the marginal utility of income curves of different taxpayers. The benefit theory depends on the value of government to the taxpayer. Because the value to the taxpayer of having government control or regulation of markets and infrastructure is almost impossible to measure and is probably somewhat subjective, the benefit theory uses income as a proxy for benefit received. But using income to determine the fairness of a tax on income is circular at best.

### A. The First Tax Theory Problem: Benefit Theory

This section will review representative arguments of the anti-redistributionist approach[135] and will show how they are colored by a philosophical position that makes no distinction between the rewards of effort and the rewards of luck. The benefit theory of taxation merely states that government should not be allowed to extract more from an individual in taxes than it provides in benefits.[136] The question thus becomes, how much benefit does government bestow, and upon whom? Proponents of progressive taxes have sometimes argued that high-income individuals receive more benefit from government than do low income individuals.[137] Extreme opponents of progressivity argue, however, that the benefit theory cannot justify any tax structure that requires high-income individuals to pay more tax than low-income individuals.[138] Thus, even many regressive rate structures would violate the benefit theory because the poor, could it only be proven, would be seen to receive more benefits than the wealthy.[139]

135. Although I focus on Professor Schoenblum's arguments, he is not alone in making them, although as he points out, law review articles are more likely to argue in favor of redistribution than against it. *See* Schoenblum, *supra* note 1, at 223 n.12 (stating that most of the academic literature uncritically supports progressivity).

136. *See* Byrne, *supra* note 6, at 769. *See generally* Radin, *supra* note 39.

137. As I have emphasized before, however, the benefit theory only justifies progressive taxes if the level of benefits rises *faster* than the level of income; in other words, if the wealthy receive not only more benefits, but *disproportionately* more benefits than the poor. The benefit theory would call for proportionate taxes (a "flat tax") if the wealthy receive proportionately more benefits, if the level of benefits rises proportionate to income. Note that it is possible for benefits to rise with income, but at a slower rate. The tax rate structure in such case would be regressive. High-income individuals would pay more taxes than low income folks, but the taxes would be a smaller part of that high income. *See* Byrne, *supra* note 6, at 770.

138. *See* Schoenblum, *supra* note 1, at 226. Less extreme opponents of progressivity argue only that the benefit theory cannot justify *progressive* taxes, although it could, presumably justify higher absolute taxes (whether regressive or proportionate) on higher incomes.

139. It is sometimes difficult to sort out the arguments against the benefit theory of taxation. Professor Schoenblum, for example, clearly does not believe the premise that rich people benefit more from government than poor people, but he does not exactly say what he would think *if* it could be proven empirically that such were the case (and of course that the amount of benefits rose faster than income). Philosophically, Professor Schoenblum seems to approach the benefit theory from a contractarian perspective. Taxation is justified as if individuals had contracted with the state for the provision of services. A problem arises with this justification for taxes to the extent that an individual prefers not to purchase some benefits. Professor Schoenblum acknowledges that it would be impossible not to provide benefits for which an individual did not wish to contract. Because some benefits must be provided, however, some taxation is appropriate. *See* Schoenblum, *supra* note 1.

The actual examples of benefit typically presented to show that the poor receive more benefit than the rich bear examination.[140] This view is consistent with a philosophy of entitlement to wealth that makes no distinction between wealth acquired because of exertion and wealth acquired because of one's natural endowments, or because of the luck of being in the right place at the right time. Since, in this view, society plays no role in income disparities, high income folks receive little or no indirect benefit as a result of social forces, the markets, or government. Rather, all differences in income are the result of differences in industriousness.

On the other hand, the great benefits that the poor receive are, by and large, empirically determinable transfer payments. Means-tested programs, public education, public transportation, and health care are all examples of the benefits that flow to poor people, but not to rich people.[141] Furthermore some government programs or policies are even detrimental to the interests of wealthy people. For example, foreign trade policies that are designed to protect domestic labor may be detrimental to the interests of high-income owners of business capital.[142] Finally, many government benefits, although available to rich and poor alike, are of greater benefit to the poor because the poor have no choice but to rely on government provision of some services. For example, rich people can pay for home security systems and are thus less dependent on local police protection.[143] Similarly, high income individuals are more likely to use private mailing services rather than the U.S. Postal Service.[144] Moreover, since the services provided to low-income people often are necessary for survival, they must surely have a higher utility value to the poor than they would to the rich.[145]

Thus, Lockean libertarians see only the direct benefits going to poor people, and not the indirect ones going to the wealthy. In part, they cannot see indirect benefits going to the wealthy because they believe as a philosophical matter that all income earned by the high

140. *See* Schoenblum, *supra* note 1, at 226.

141. *See id.* ("[M]any government programs are means-tested, thus limiting benefits that flow to the higher income earners.").

142. *See id.* at 227 ("[I]nsular trade and other policies, responsive to the demands of political majorities or special interest groups, may even be detrimental to the economic interests of many high income earners.").

143. *See id.* at 126-27 ("When persons are required to incur significant personal expenditure for security devices and insurance . . . the contention that high income earners particularly benefit from a safe society is not a compelling argument.").

144. *See id.* at 228 ("[H]igh income earners who do not avail themselves of the infrastructure may be required to incur substantial additional costs to obtain reliable, quality services; examples include Federal Express, UPS, e-mail, and private schools.").

145. Note, however, that this "value" is not the same as "value" from a market perspective. For a service to have value from a market perspective, there must be someone who is both willing and able to pay for the service.

income folks is the result of enormous effort and is, therefore, morally deserved. The notion that an organized society itself could be a contributor to the success of the successful is simply incompatible with such beliefs about entitlement to wealth.[146] The belief that success is the result of individual worthiness and effort is evident from the examples chosen to rebut the benefit theory. For example, a worker who works overtime and does good work is compared to a "slothful, sloppy" employee who performs at the "minimum tolerable level of quality."[147] Similarly a doctor who got where she was through "studying and suffering considerable self-denial" is compared to her less successful friends who spent their time "partying" and exhibiting a "lack of willpower and determination."[148] One scholar poses the question explicitly: "what if lack of achievement is largely ascribable to choice?"[149] Thus it is effort, and effort alone that is to be regarded as responsible for accumulation of wealth.

Notwithstanding the assumption that effort, and effort alone, gives rise to income, anti-redistributionists argue that one of the most important ways that the poor benefit more from government than the rich is that our strong national defense provides an "environment with opportunity."[150] At least formally, the lower-income classes in the United States have the opportunity to move up the economic ladder, a possibility that would be formally foreclosed in some societies.[151] The extent to which this opportunity exists in practice is much less clear.[152] Nevertheless, crediting the poor with a benefit in the form of opportunity while arguing simultaneously that the rich do not get rich

146. Professor Schoenblum addresses this point in one sense when he argues that there is "no demonstrable correlation" between the success of the wealthy and the accident of their being citizens or residents of the United States. Schoenblum, *supra* note 1, at 227-28. To the contrary, successful individuals would be successful anywhere and might even be more successful elsewhere with less governmental intervention. *Id. Compare* Schoenblum, *supra* note 1, *with* Rose, *supra* note 28, at 440 (a property regime makes everyone better off).

147. Schoenblum, *supra* note 1, at 261.

148. *Id.* Professor Schoenblum at least explicitly acknowledges that he is assuming equal intelligence and economic backgrounds in an effort to show that achievement due to effort deserves reward.

149. *Id.* at 263 (Schoenblum presenting the reader with situations where the diligent are rewarded and the lazy have rough lives because the determinate factor of success in society is the free exercise of autonomous choice).

150. *Id.* at 227. It seems, however, that Professor Schoenblum has failed to recognize the possibility that such defense of the system could be the preservation of the status quo where the top of society holds the vast majority of the wealth. This would be to argue that the poor benefit from having power structures protected that have roots in the institutions of racism, sexism, and classism.

151. *See id.*

152. *See* McMahon & Abreu, *supra* note 5, at 31 (citing evidence showing that "[t]op to bottom mobility is . . . quite rare, as is its converse, notwithstanding the emotional appeal of the American Dream").

because of greater opportunity in the U.S. seems at first to be inconsistent.

But these positions are quite consistent with a desert theory that treats all wealth obtained as the rewards to individual effort. If the state or society or luck had nothing to do with, say, Bill Gates or Ross Perot getting rich, then it is certainly not a benefit of government that there was the opportunity to become affluent. Gates and Perot, so the argument goes, would have gotten rich anywhere. On the other hand, someone who makes subsistence level wages must be too lazy, stupid, or busy partying to be troubled to go make a decent living.[153] The existence of the opportunity to acquire wealth is necessary to the view that essentially blames the individual for any measure of economic failure. It is a disguised way of assuming that individuals have equal capabilities. Those who are very sure that high-income people have high incomes because of their own efforts and that luck plays no role can thus confidently say that the benefit theory does not allow "unequal" taxation, and certainly not progressive taxation.[154]

## B. The Second Tax Theory Problem: Measurement

The second problem with the usual theories is one of measurement. Both are based on the value or amount of an intangible, subjective variable that is largely personal to the taxpayer. The benefit theory, even if we could agree on what "benefits" are benefits, depends on the "value" to the taxpayer of the benefit received.[155] There are several problems inherent in this concept of benefit. First, taxpayers may receive benefits they don't want. If the benefit theory is seen as taxpayers purchasing benefits with their tax dollars, the involuntary purchase presents a challenge. There is, generally speaking, no way

153. *But see* Jeremy Waldron, *Property, Justifictation, and Need*, 6 CAN. J.L. & JURISPRUDENCE 185, 204 (1993) (deriding the notion that poverty is the victim's own fault).

154. There is no need for a further, more philosophical, argument that would explain why the benefit theory as a theory is misguided. There is such an argument available, and Schoenblum mentions it. The benefit theory derives from contractarian notions of the state, according to which taxation is the price for having some central provision of defense and some other services, and presumably most individuals voluntarily would enter into such a "contract." But taxation is not voluntary; there is no real possibility of "opting out." Accordingly, a "contract" does not really exist between the individual and the state and regardless of the amount of benefit conferred, one should not be compelled to pay taxes for unwanted benefits. In other words, the state has no moral claim on part of an individual's wealth simply because it has provided some benefits. *See* Schoenblum, *supra* note 1, at 232.

155. Note that it is the value to the taxpayer and not the cost to government that matters, since the point of the benefit theory is to justify the contribution the taxpayer will make in return.

to opt out of the provision of government.[156] Even libertarian liberals recognize a role for some taxation to support government, whether the taxpayer approves or not.[157] Second, benefits that do not have a market price may nevertheless have value. In some cases the existence of government may increase the taxpayer's utility, for example, by providing a sense of security, clean air, transportation for employees or visitors. If so, any successful measure of total utility or satisfaction would also give a pretty good measure of benefit.[158] In other cases government provides benefits that should have market value, but that are almost impossible to measure, such as clear air and the sound of birds singing that result from pollution control measures.

The measurement problem applies even more clearly to the ability-to-pay/sacrifice theories. One of the reasons that we are still discussing progressivity after all of these years is that we insist on trying to justify a progressive structure with some sort of utility measure. This is like trying to make the trousers fit by sucking in your stomach. It seems to make some intuitive sense, and it would be great if it really worked, but in the final analysis it's not a good fit. There is no way to measure utility absolutely. Although we can rank an individual's preferences in order of priority, we have no way satisfactorily to assign absolute comparative rankings. Further, we cannot compare utility between taxpayers. Some theorists get around this problem by assuming it away. Others approach the problem as if only utility that is backed by market purchases counts.[159] But the parameter of utility can only be defined from the inside out, by the individual taxpayer. An individual without the means to participate in the market has little input into the assigning of values. Accordingly, utility does not provide a very good measuring stick for discussing tax rates with those who are generally opposed to taxation.

Thus even if one believes that respect for individuals is consistent with recognizing the role of luck and of society in producing wealth

156. Expatriation, being a hermit in the woods, joining a self-government religious community. All of these are imperfect.

157. *See generally* NOZICK, *supra* note 1.

158. Indeed, one of Professor Schoenblum's criticisms of the ability-to-pay theory is that it is the benefit theory in disguise. *See* Schoenblum, *supra* note 1, at 233.

159. Market prices do not even tell the whole utility story for market purchasers. Purchasers only pay the price that the seller asks. In many cases, a buyer would be willing to pay more than market price. For these inframarginal buyers, the market price understates utility. Similarly, some sellers may be willing to take less than the market price. In such cases the market price overstates the utility the seller attached to the item sold. Thus there is always consumer surplus and producer surplus. For example, in the movie *Pretty Woman*, Richard Gere and Julia Roberts agree that she will stay for a week in return for $3000. After the deal is closed, she proudly reports that she would have stayed for $2000. He smugly replies that we would have paid $4000. *See* PRETTY WOMAN (Touchstone Pictures 1990).

such that wealthy folks get more benefits from government or even if we accept one of the ability-to-pay theories as a theory, if only it could be measured, we are still doomed to the conclusion that the case for progressivity is uneasy at best. The problem here is that there is no externally measurable factor that determines fairness. There should be. Fairness inherently involves interpersonal comparisons and would seem to require some basis external to the person for making the comparison. That factor cannot be income or wealth alone. Somewhere we need to decide when it is fair to require that wealth be redistributed and when it is not.

## IX. TAX FAIRNESS FROM THE OUTSIDE

If we are trying to determine from the outside what is fair, then the measure that we use should also be somehow externally determined. Several possibilities suggest themselves. For example, personhood could be the sole criterion for imposing tax. If an individual is a person, then some amount of tax is expected. This criterion leads to Professor Schoenblum's lump sum head tax. A dog would not pay tax, but a human person would. Beyond that there is no basis for distinguishing between individuals. This is the approach that Schoenblum advocates. He argues that this is the only tax structure that would preserve our respect for individual autonomy. The problem with such an approach, of course, is that it is regressive with respect to income or wealth. Poor people would pay a higher percentage of their wealth than rich people would. The revenue raising potential of such a tax is compromised by its regressivity. To raise enough revenue, the amount of the tax would have to be so high that poor folks could not pay it.

A second alternative might be a straightforward income tax. Personhood is taken as a given and within the category of persons, those with more income would owe more tax, the amount of tax being proportionate to the amount of income; a flat tax. A flat income tax suffers from the same revenue raising limitation as the lump sum tax, only to a lesser degree. The rate imposed would have to be high to raise enough revenue. If we add a low-income exemption, we introduce progressivity, and we have to decide where to draw the line on the exemption. If a flat income tax were not tied to some underlying concept, it would seem arbitrary. If it were tied to some underlying concept such as utility, then we would have all the definitional problems that we have now. Why base the tax on income? Why not an increasing tax that is not proportionate to income? Although income presents the virtue of being measurable, without some elaboration, it is hard to see how it points to fairness.

Another alternative, and frankly, my favorite, would be to assign levels of deservedness to different levels of income. This approach would be theoretically similar to Justice Breitel's social increment of value approach in *Penn Central*.[160] It attempts to distinguish the role of effort from the roles of other factors in creating wealth.[161] Whether or not someone deserves income or shelter or anything else is surely a matter of opinion. But it is probably also the subject of some degree of societal consensus. Since it is a matter of external opinion, deservedness does not present quite the same difficulties that utility does. There is no need to look inside people's minds to determine the extent to which they deserve their income. Rather, perhaps we could agree on specific criteria for determining levels of deservedness. Income that is highly deserved should have more protection from tax than income that is barely deserved or that is a windfall.

For example, perhaps we would agree that everyone, even the lazy, deserves some subsistence level of income absolutely. Thus, rather than personhood as a criterion for tax liability, personhood would bestow a level of absolute deservedness of income. Many features of our existing tax system and welfare system lend support to the claim that agreement on this point would be possible. For example, the income tax has consistently allowed for some sort of zero bracket; the earned income tax credit has the further effect of exempting subsistence income from payroll taxes. Flat tax proponents base the fairness of the proposals partly on the presence of a large tax-free amount of income. Even Professor Schoenblum in advocating his "absolutely equal" tax, concedes that the tax should include an exempt amount for subsistence income. The subsistence amount then would have the highest level of deservedness and would be subject to the lowest level of taxation (or none).[162] All other income would be subject to tax. An extreme version of this approach would tax other income at 100%.

But if personhood were the only factor in determining deservedness and deservedness were the only basis for the imposition of tax, the result would be a strongly progressive tax—the personhood amount would be taxed at 0%; all other income at 100%, much like the equal marginal sacrifice tax, which also levels off income above a certain level. The difference is that a personhood exemption would be based on objective facts rather than on an assumption about levels of utility.

160. *See supra* notes 92 to 105 and accompanying text for a discussion of the *Penn Central* case and the social increment of value reasoning.

161. *See* Linda A. Malone, *The Future of Transferable Development Rights in the Supreme Court*, 73 Ky. L.J. 759, 785 (1984-85) ("The most innovative section of the . . . opinion . . . concluded that the base for computing a reasonable return should exclude the 'social increment' of value attributable to the government's activities rather than to private investment.").

162. The extent to which this level of deservedness requires public assistance is a separate issue from whether or not some basic amount of income should be exempt from taxation.

Personhood alone would be unsatisfactory as the sole determinant of deservedness, however, because it would take no account of effort. As studies have shown, people generally believe that the expenditure of effort creates desert. But effort as a basis for desert would not yield a minimum level of tax-free income. Rather, the amount of tax free income (or highly deserved income) would depend on the units of effort expended. This factor would create a flexible level of absolutely deserved income—flexible because the amount of wealth an individual deserves depends on the amount of effort the individual exerts. The deserved amount of wealth per unit of effort would be somewhat fixed, however, so that an hour of burger flipping in terms of effort should create the same level of desert as an hour of law review article writing. Basing entitlement to wealth on the number of hours of effort alone leaves some problems unresolved, however. What hours count? Is child-rearing counted? Or only market labor?[163] If non-market activities count, which non-market activities? Although these problems are significant, at least there is no need to fall back on the time-worn notion of "utility" with its inherent subjectivity.[164]

To take this hours-of-effort approach to another level, the effort consumed by time-consuming education and lifestyle sacrifices should be accounted for somehow, so it may be that the law review article-writing should carry a slightly higher level of desert than burger flipping.[165] The anti-redistributionist approach seems to be that education and forbearance together describe all the variation in incomes, and that no amount of accession to wealth is a result of anything but effort or forbearance. Although it may be difficult to make a distinction between rewards to effort and rewards to luck, it seems a necessary step.[166]

In reality, however, accession to wealth is often also a result of luck in the form of innate intelligence, childhood advantage, native talent, or pure serendipity. To the extent that wealth results from the existence of one or more of these forms of luck, people are much less likely to agree on the deservedness of that wealth. Initially, then, income resulting from luck would carry no additional deservedness, since the individual did not make any choices that created this source of wealth. Yet the individual does choose to apply the talent or intelligence in a way that produces wealth for society, and people do tend to believe that those with innate intelligence or talent deserve at least some of

163. *See generally* Nancy C. Staudt, *Taxing Housework*, 84 GEO. L. J. 1571 (1996).

164. Now is the time for some time physicist to come forward and say that hours are subjective.

165. The theory that bases desert on positive contribution to society would obviously arrive at the opposite result.

166. *See* Penn Cent. Transp. Co. v. New York City, 366 N.E.2d 1271, 1276 (N.Y. 1977) ("It is exceedingly difficult but imperative, nevertheless, to sort out the merged ingredients and to assess the rights and responsibilities of owner and society.").

the additional reward that flows to that talent in the presence of effort. Perhaps a talent premium is appropriate to induce people to apply their extra talents or intelligence. Accordingly, our deservedness scale could increase with the uniqueness of the intelligence or talent employed in making the effort. Because deservedness is a socially defined parameter, however, there is no reason that it would have to rise proportionate to intelligence or talent. Since innate intelligence and talent depend on luck, they should have less influence on absolute deservedness than does effort.

The practical result of a system based on deservedness would be a progressive tax schedule. Subsistence incomes, absolutely deserved as an incident of personhood would be exempt or taxed at the lowest possible level. Income beyond this minimum, to the extent it is the result of effort alone, say the number of hours worked times the minimum wage, would be very highly deserved and subject only to minimal taxation. The amount of income in the effort category would be increased somewhat to account for choices made along the way, such as lifestyle economy to acquire education and training. Finally, income in the luck category, to the extent it involves individual choice to apply windfall resources, would be subject to a higher rate of taxation, and income resulting from pure serendipity, brute luck (money falling out of the sky and the like) would be subject to the highest rates of taxation.

Presumably, extremely high incomes result from luck to a much greater extent than do lower incomes. For example, Bill Gates would deserve some subsistence amount just by virtue of being a person. He would deserve to be compensated for the eighty hours per week that he spends working, which would create a deservedness level twice as high as that of a forty hour per week burger flipper, and he would deserve some higher amount of income because he has chosen to employ his intellect in such a way that it produces income. But a large portion of his income would be subject to the highest level of taxation reflecting the elements of luck or serendipity that went into his success: being born with intelligence, being born to a part of society that would give him access to computers, having the good fortune to latch onto a hobby that could grow into something the rest of the world really needed, becoming a virtual monopolist.[167] All of these factors generate income beyond that resulting from application of effort, and

167. *See* Bill Gates et al., The Road Ahead (1996).

My argument is not that monopoly rents are immoral. Even antitrust law recognizes that a person can lawfully become a monopolist through superior vision, skill, ingenuity and industry. If so, and if the person does not unlawfully exploit the monopoly power, antitrust law does not object to the monopolist taking the profits the market will bear. My argument is that those profits carry a lower degree of deservedness and that, therefore, subjecting them to a higher rate of tax is not unfair.

it is thus fair to tax that high income at higher rates than we would tax a lower income.

This deservedness model has several advantages over the utility based systems, over Schoenblum's head tax, and over the Hall & Rabushka flat tax (a la Armey-Shelby). This system incorporates the philosophical position that effort and forbearance are meritorious and should be rewarded. It also incorporates the philosophical position that by virtue of personhood alone, each individual is equally entitled to something—a livelihood, respect, comfort. The deservedness model leaves relative holdings intact. There is no net penalty for making greater efforts. It does not rely on any internally determined factor such as utility. While deservedness is abstract, it is an externally abstract concept. Finally, people seem to believe that relative position should not be disturbed—the wealthiest should remain the wealthiest after imposition of tax. So our scale of absolute deservedness would start above zero (reflecting the personhood amount), would rise in proportion to effort (to reflect only the number of hours), and would rise somewhat with the level of talent applied (to induce people to apply unusual talent). With the deservedness model, then, the Lockean connection between labor and wealth is preserved. But the roles of factors other than effort are also recognized.

## X. CONCLUSION

What significance does deservedness have for the tax structure? Dollars that are deserved more should be taxed less. Some subsistence level of income should be free of tax, not because those dollars have the greatest utility where they are, but because as human beings, people absolutely deserve to have some minimum lifestyle.[168] The marginal deservedness of those first few dollars earned is very high. The tax burden on those dollars should be very light. Highly deserved dollars should generally not be taxed, or not much anyway. As income rises purely through effort and industry, the marginal deservedness of income may decline somewhat, reflecting a societal judgment that some balance is important. Or perhaps marginal deservedness does not decline with returns solely to effort and industry; perhaps we would agree that increased earnings that result

168. What that minimum should entail is also socially constructed. For example, Thomas Jefferson thought that every adult should be entitled to an appropriation of 50 acres in "full and absolute dominion." Stanley N. Katz, *Thomas Jefferson and the Right to Property in Revolutionary America*, 19 J.L. & ECON. 467, 470 (1976), *excerpted in* CURTIS J. BERGER & JOAN C. WILLIAMS, PROPERTY: LAND OWNERSHIP AND USE (4th ed. 1997). I heard on public radio once that in the Netherlands, a social minimum is defined as enough to provide shelter, food and a daily newspaper. Query whether a daily newspaper would be considered a bare necessity in other parts of the world.

purely from working more hours should be taxed somewhat more heavily. At some point, however, the role of increasing effort becomes *de minimis* and luck and circumstance or returns to innate intellect start to become more significant. A very low level of deservedness attaches to such income, yet these are the factors that produce huge earnings increases.

By starting from the right position on Locke and using a measurement that is externally determinable, the case for progressive taxation becomes much easier. The opponent of progressive taxation must now show first that the windfall of social increment of value is deserved (and should not be taxed), and second that deservedness is not a culturally derived norm.

# [6]

# NOZICK AND LOCKE: FILLING THE SPACE OF RIGHTS

By Jeremy Waldron

## I. The "Reverse" Theory

There is a passage in *Anarchy, State, and Utopia* (1974) where Robert Nozick voices the following general misgiving about the claim that people have affirmative rights *to* various things, such as social assistance or welfare:

> The major objection to speaking of everyone's having a right *to* various things such as equality of opportunity, life, and so on, and enforcing this right, is that these "rights" require a substructure of things and materials and actions; and *other* people may have rights and entitlements over these. No one has a right to something whose realization requires certain uses of things and activities that other people have rights and entitlements over. Other people's rights and entitlements to *particular things* (*that* pencil, *their* body, and so on) and how they choose to exercise these rights and entitlements fix the external environment of any given individual and the means that will be available to him. . . .
>
> There are particular rights over particular things held by particular persons, and particular rights to reach agreements with others, *if* you and they together can acquire the means to reach an agreement. . . . No rights exist in conflict with this substructure of particular rights. Since no neatly contoured right to achieve a goal will avoid incompatibility with this substructure, no such rights exist. The particular rights over things fill the space of rights, leaving no room for general rights to be in a certain material condition. The reverse theory would place only such universally held general "rights to" achieve goals or to be in a certain material condition into its substructure so as to determine all else; to my knowledge no serious attempt has been made to state this "reverse" theory. (*ASU*, 238)[1]

It may seem a nice idea to base some human rights on material needs, but Nozick is saying that, in the real world, the resources that would have to be used to satisfy these needs may already be owned by private individuals. And if all the relevant resources are privately owned, there is simply

[1] Here, and in what follows, "*ASU*" refers to Robert Nozick, *Anarchy, State, and Utopia* (New York: Basic Books, 1974). Accordingly, "*ASU*, 238" refers to page 238 of that work.

nothing to be done: the property rights that particular individuals have over particular things "fill the space of rights, leaving no room for general rights to be in a certain material condition."

Nozick's argument here assumes that claims based on need occupy a relatively superficial role in a general theory of economic entitlement. It is as though we first figure out who owns what, applying the principles that determine property rights, and *then* figure out whose needs are left unsatisfied and what is to be done about them. On this approach, welfare rights (if there are any) live only in the interstices of property. Some of what Nozick says suggests that this subordination of welfare to property is more or less unavoidable: "Things come into the world already attached to people having entitlements over them" (*ASU*, 160). He thinks this is clearest in the case of body parts: you may need these kidneys or this retina, but my entitlement to them is necessarily prior to yours, for we cannot even grasp my status as a person without comprising in that status a rightful claim to the limbs, cells, and organs that make me who I am (*ASU*, 206). Nozick thinks that the subordination of welfare to property holds for some external objects as well: "Isn't it implausible that how holdings are produced and come to exist has no effect at all on who should hold what?" (*ASU*, 155). The trouble with welfare rights, on this account, is that they "treat objects as if they appeared from nowhere, out of nothing" (*ASU*, 160). "[I]s *this* the appropriate model," he asks, "for thinking about how the things people produce are to be distributed?" (*ASU*, 198).

The virtue of the passage that I quoted at the beginning of this essay (*ASU*, 238) is that it forces us to confront issues of moral priority in the economic sphere. All sides to the debate can benefit from this. Often in philosophical discussions about welfare, we assume that it is already known who owns what and that the question is simply whether people can be forced to contribute out of their own wealth to relieve the needs of the poor. Nozick observes correctly that this way of arguing underestimates the challenge of welfare rights. The idea that a person's right to use or receive resources might be based generally on need, rather than on some proprietorial relation between *this* person and *this* thing, poses a threat to the conventional understanding of property. Property entitlements will never be secure if they are subject to challenge on this basis. So, he thinks, we have to choose: Either particular people have acquired property entitlements in particular things, in which case others cannot have welfare rights that can be enforced against them, or people in general have welfare rights to material and economic security, and others cannot have property rights that can be used to resist the demands of these welfare rights. One or the other of these statements can be true, but not both. We do not have to accept Nozick's resolution of this conflict in order to agree with him about the importance of confronting it honestly and explicitly.

Nozick's position is that "particular rights over things fill the space of rights, leaving no room for general rights to be in a certain material condition." He maintains that the alternative is to stipulate the general rights first, and then try to fit property entitlements around them. "[T]o my knowledge," he says, "no serious attempt has been made to state this 'reverse' theory" (*ASU*, 238). Is this right? Has no one made a serious attempt to use welfare rights to define the environment in which property rights operate? Has no one made a serious attempt to construct the mirror image of Nozick's view—that is, a conception in which welfare rights fill up most of the space of rights in respect of material things, leaving little room (or less room than one would intuitively think) for rights to private property?

In the "reverse" approach, rights based on needs would be *fundamental* in our theory of human access to and use of resources. And instead of making these rights the basis of a duty of charity incumbent upon existing property-holders, we would take them as a basis for calling property arrangements into question, so that the existence of unsatisfied need would become an objection not just to the way property rights are being exercised (e.g., selfishly, thoughtlessly, etc.) but to their very shape and distribution. In proclaiming welfare rights, we would not be begging property-holders to be a little more generous. Rather, we would be asking this question: By what right do they claim to hold something as exclusively their own in the face of others' needs? We would insist that property answer at the tribunal of need, not the other way round.

Philosophers have toyed with versions of such a "reverse" approach as part of the reaction to *Anarchy, State, and Utopia*. In "Property Rights and Interests" (1979), Virginia Held compares acquisitive economic activity to a game, "where winners and losers compete on friendly terms as if engaged in a sporting event." The idea is that winners are allowed to keep their winnings and "losers may prefer having had a chance to play the game and especially having a chance to play again and win, than to . . . be assured all along of an even apportionment of all proceeds."[2] But Held did not think that this game-playing could possibly trump the serious business of securing welfare rights:

> Economic justice is a serious matter. While those with moral rights to decent lives are deprived of these rights, playing games is not only frivolous but immoral. However, if such rights *were* respected . . . , and if, on utilitarian grounds, playing economic games could be justified in terms of the maximization of interests, well then there might be nothing wrong with capitalist games between consenting adults. But first, the children ought to be fed.[3]

[2] Virginia Held, "Property Rights and Interests," *Social Research* 46 (1979): 577.
[3] Ibid., 579.

Elsewhere she suggests, provocatively, that welfare rights are really the only property rights there are. People are entitled to what is needed for a decent life and adequate self-development. "Beyond this there are no moral rights to property." Held concedes that people do have property interests that go beyond this, but she denies that there is anything wrong (as there would be in the case of rights) with dealing with these in a utilitarian way.[4] This seems to me a fine example of what Nozick would call the "reverse" theory.

More notoriously, John Rawls's argument in *A Theory of Justice* (1971) has more or less exactly the structure that is required for the "reverse" theory. This should not be a surprise. Despite the "no serious attempt" rhetoric, Nozick criticizes Rawls's book on exactly this score, for relegating property entitlements to relatively superficial levels (*ASU*, 206):

> The nature of the decision problem facing persons deciding upon principles in an original position behind a veil of ignorance limits them to end-state principles of distribution. The self-interested person evaluates any non-end-state principle on the basis of how it works out for him; his calculations about any principle focus on how he ends up under the principle. . . . Rawls's procedure assumes that no fundamental entitlement view is correct, that . . . there is some level so deep that no entitlements operate that far down. (*ASU*, 201–2, 206)

Any attempt to generate anything like property entitlements based on original position premises would lead, says Nozick, to approximations at best: "It is difficult to see how such attempts could derive . . . the *particular* convolution of historical entitlement principles" (*ASU*, 202). This is what Rawls says too. Rawls's remarks on property are very sparse, but they indicate that property rights are relegated to an entirely derivative status in what is otherwise a well-developed theory of human claims in respect of material resources. It is true that Rawls's first principle of equal liberty comprises the right to hold personal property.[5] But like many such rights, this right to hold property has nothing to do with the existence-conditions for property entitlements. It is simply a right not to be excluded from the list of those who may hold property if there are any property rights to be held (as women and slaves sometimes have been excluded in the past).[6] Whether there are to be private property rights in significant resources is for Rawls an open question depending on how his principles of justice bear on the circumstances of a particular society. Though "[c]ertain insti-

[4] Virginia Held, *Rights and Goods: Justifying Social Action* (New York: Free Press, 1984), 190.
[5] John Rawls, *A Theory of Justice* (Cambridge, MA: Harvard University Press, 1971), 61.
[6] See Jeremy Waldron, *The Right to Private Property* (Oxford: Clarendon Press, 1988), chap. 1.

tutional forms are embedded within the conception of justice,"[7] private property is not one of them. Rawls does work with an example of "a property-owning democracy."[8] But this is just an illustration; it "is not intended to prejudge the choice of regime in particular cases."[9] A just society might be capitalist or socialist:

> Which of these systems and the many intermediate forms most fully answers to the requirements of justice cannot, I think, be determined in advance. There is presumably no general answer to this question, since it depends in large part upon the traditions, institutions, and social forces of each country, and its particular economic circumstances. The theory of justice does not include these matters. . . . The political judgment in any given case will then turn on which variation is most likely to work out best in practice. A conception of justice is a necessary part of any such political assessment, but it is not sufficient.[10]

The parameters of this assessment are the principles of justice, which include rights of exactly the sort that Nozick classified as general rights *to* various things (*ASU*, 238), such as equality of opportunity and the rights defined by the difference principle. Now, the difference principle—the Rawlsian principle that permits social and economic inequalities provided that they are to the benefit of those who are worst off[11]—may not specifically define rights to welfare. But it is a principle governing the manner in which the basic structure generates social and economic inequalities, and it insists that the structure must be arranged in a way that maximizes the expectations of members of the worst-off group. As legal scholar Frank Michelman insists—in a fine essay that examines exactly the extent to which Rawls's work makes welfare rights fundamental—the difference principle mandates "an outcome-oriented appraisal of the pattern and makeup of distributive 'shares' precipitated by economic, political, and other societal processes."[12] I do not mean to deny the procedural aspect of Rawls's conception.[13] But in the illustration that Rawls provides of the operation of such a system, institutions to secure the provision of

[7] Rawls, *A Theory of Justice*, 262.

[8] Ibid., 274.

[9] Ibid. Rawls adds: "Nor . . . does it imply that actual societies which have private ownership of the means of production are not afflicted with grave injustices. Because there exists an ideal property-owning system that would be just does not imply that historical forms are just, or even tolerable. . . . [T]he same is true of socialism" (ibid.).

[10] Ibid.

[11] Ibid., 75–83.

[12] Frank I. Michelman, "In Pursuit of Constitutional Welfare Rights: One View of Rawls' Theory of Justice," *University of Pennsylvania Law Review* 121 (1973): 962–63.

[13] Rawls, *A Theory of Justice*, 88 and 274–75.

a social minimum feature prominently.[14] Welfare institutions can operate procedurally too;[15] procedural justice is not associated exclusively with the operations of the market. As Michelman puts it, in Rawls's illustration market procedures (if there are any) must be complemented by procedures designed to secure a social minimum, "which must be provided in order that the residual market determination of distributive shares may be considered just."[16]

So I think that, viewed in this way, Rawls's argument answers exactly to Nozick's specifications for the "reverse" theory. The basic structure of a Rawlsian society is not adjusted to secure the integrity of anything like property entitlements. Instead, it is adjusted to respect the elementary claims that people have in regard to the material wherewithal for basic survival, flourishing (under conditions of equality), and self-respect. Then, given principles of this kind as parameters, we examine what room there is in the circumstances of any actual society for private property rights in goods of various sorts. The basic rights associated with welfare and equality fill up the space of rights first, and then property rights, if there are any, have to contort themselves to fit this Rawlsian substructure.

Did Nozick forget this when he said "no serious attempt has been made to state this 'reverse' theory"? I do not know. He certainly regarded Rawls's conception as "serious":

> *A Theory of Justice* is a powerful, deep, subtle, wide-ranging systematic work in political and moral philosophy which has not seen its like since the writings of John Stuart Mill, if then. It is a fountain of illuminating ideas, integrated into a lovely whole. Political philosophers now must either work within Rawls' theory or explain why not. (*ASU*, 183)[17]

Nozick thought indeed it *was* possible to explain why one should not work within Rawls's conception. He said that before we go ahead with a

[14] For Rawls's discussion of the social minimum, see ibid., 276–77 and 285. There is, further, the question of the relation between the provision of a social minimum and the broader work that the difference principle has to do (in the tax system, for example) to secure equality. For Rawls's critique of any social minimum approach that is not pursued within that broader egalitarian context, see ibid., 316–17. Michelman's comments on this connection (Michelman, "In Pursuit of Constitutional Welfare Rights," 974–77) are very helpful. Michelman relies mainly on the welfarist rather than the egalitarian strand of Rawls's account of the difference principle.

[15] Cf. William Simon, "Legality, Bureaucracy, and Class in the Welfare System," *Yale Law Journal* 92 (1983): 1198–1269.

[16] Michelman, "In Pursuit of Constitutional Welfare Rights," 976.

[17] Cf. the suggestion in the *New York Times* obituary for Rawls, which informed readers that "[t]he conservative philosopher Robert Nozick ... considered Dr. Rawls's argument egalitarian nonsense" (Douglas Martin, "John Rawls, Theorist on Justice, Is Dead at 82," *New York Times*, November 26, 2002, late edition-final, sec. C, p. 19, col. 1).

Rawlsian approach, we must be in possession of reasons for turning our backs on the concept of historical entitlement:

> [W]e do not need any *particular* developed historical entitlement theory as a basis from which to criticize Rawls' construction. If *any* such fundamental historical-entitlement view is correct, then Rawls' theory is not. . . . We would be ill advised to accept Rawls' theory and his construal of the problem as one of which principles would be chosen by rational self-interested individuals behind a veil of ignorance, unless we were sure that no adequate historical-entitlement theory was to be gotten. (*ASU*, 202-3)[18]

On the basis of the passage I cited at the beginning of this essay (*ASU*, 238), this seems right. Presumably, however, the epistemic burden is symmetrical. We would be ill advised to accept a Nozickian theory of historical entitlement (or to begin fleshing out principles that resonate with our proprietorial and libertarian intuitions) unless we were sure that no adequate theory of the Rawlsian kind—no adequate "reverse" theory—was to be gotten.

This last little exchange—"Don't go down the welfarist road until you are sure no entitlement theory is to be gotten," and "Don't go down the entitlement road until you are sure no welfarist theory is to be gotten"—suggests that it might be wise to develop a theory of entitlement and a theory of welfare hand in hand. We would try to ground property entitlements to vindicate our proprietorial intuitions, but we would do so in a way that also respected the impulse to assert welfare rights or rights to a social minimum. There would be no assumption that any one body of rights came into the arena first, to throw its weight around and fill up the space of rights, before the other was allowed to enter, to pick up the leavings. We would develop our property/welfare theory holistically.

Whether Nozick would regard this as a way of constructing the "reverse" theory, I do not know. It certainly has the characteristic of not permitting the construction or recognition of property rights to the extent that they conflict with certain imperatives of human welfare and survival. Whatever we call it, we do not need to look very far for instances of this kind of "reverse"/symmetrical approach. The first example I shall provide is the approach to property taken by John Locke. My second example is

[18] People sometimes attack Nozick for not having fleshed out his principle of justice in acquisition. The passage quoted above in the text provides an answer to that attack: "We are thus able to make this structural criticism of the type of theory Rawls presents and the type of principles it must yield, without having first formulated fully a particular historical-entitlement theory as an alternative to his" (*ASU*, 202-3). See also *ASU*, 230. Nozick is doing political *philosophy*, not setting out a political manifesto. I have discussed this further in Waldron, *The Right to Private Property*, 255-56, and in my article "What Plato Would Allow," in Ian Shapiro and Judith Wagner DeCew, eds., *Nomos XXXVII: Theory and Practice* (New York: New York University Press, 1995), 138-78.

Robert Nozick himself, in some of the features that his theory shares with Locke's.

Now citing these as examples might seem cheap or preposterous—preposterous because such imputations plainly contradict the tenor and the received understanding of these philosophers' works, and cheap if imputing this approach to Locke and Nozick were nothing but a provocation based on a throwaway line here and there. I am sensitive to these considerations. I shall try to show that the imputations are based on elements central to the arguments of Locke's *Two Treatises of Government* and Nozick's *Anarchy, State, and Utopia,* respectively. And I shall try to mitigate the outrageousness of these imputations by showing how they illustrate not only what I am calling the "reverse" position, but also the general importance of integrating claims about welfare rights with claims about property in the overall structure of a theory of justice.

## II. John Locke on Charity

No one will deny that John Locke was a believer in property,[19] and his theory of the acquisition of property rights has something like the structure of what Nozick calls a historical entitlement approach. I will not go into the details, for they are very well known. It is sufficient to cite the locus classicus of Locke on justice in acquisition:

> Though the earth, and all inferior creatures, be common to all men, yet every man has a property in his own person: this no body has any right to but himself. The labour of his body, and the work of his hands, we may say, are properly his. Whatsoever then he removes out of the state that nature hath provided, and left it in, he hath mixed his labour with, and joined to it something that is his own, and thereby makes it his property. It being by him removed from the common state nature hath placed it in, it hath by this labour something annexed to it, that excludes the common right of other men: for this labour being the unquestionable property of the labourer, no man but he can have a right to what that is once joined to, at least where there is enough, and as good left in common for others.[20]

This argument is applied to land as well as to objects.[21] It is supposed to establish entitlements that are resilient against expropriation by the state,

[19] James Tully comes close in Tully, *A Discourse on Property: John Locke and His Adversaries* (Cambridge: Cambridge University Press, 1980).

[20] John Locke, *Two Treatises of Government*, ed. Peter Laslett (Cambridge: Cambridge University Press, 1988), 287–88 (*Second Treatise*, chap. 5, sec. 27).

[21] Ibid., 290–93 (secs. 32–36).

that form the basis for a market economy, and that probably generate considerable inequality under modern conditions.[22]

However, Locke's account of acquisition is not unconditional. He says that appropriation by labor is permissible "at least where there is enough, and as good left in common for others."[23] This is commonly referred to as "the sufficiency proviso," or even just "the Lockean proviso" (and that is what I shall call it).[24] The Lockean proviso is plainly relevant to our discussion. However, since Nozick adopts a version of it, I shall postpone my consideration of it until Section III, below, where I consider Nozick's conception of historical entitlement as an instance of the "reverse"/ symmetrical theory.

Too much emphasis on the Lockean proviso belies a much more fundamental condition on his theory of property. This is what I shall call "the principle of charity."[25] The principle of charity requires property-owners in every economy to cede control of some of their surplus possessions, so they can be used to satisfy the pressing needs of the very poor when the latter have no way of surviving otherwise. I think the existence and importance of this condition shows that Locke held a version of the "reverse"/symmetrical theory: when considerations of desperate need are present, property rights must give way, because the fundamental definition of property rights is, in the last analysis, organized around the principle of satisfying need.

The principle of charity is not introduced in the *Second Treatise* chapter on property.[26] It is introduced in the course of Locke's argument against Sir Robert Filmer in the *First Treatise*. There Locke insists that anyone who is in desperate need has "a Title to so much out of another's Plenty, as will keep him from extream want where he has no means to subsist otherwise."[27] It is not an original doctrine: there are versions of it in Aquinas

[22] Ibid., 360–62 (secs. 138–40) and 299–302 (secs. 46–50).

[23] Ibid., 288 (sec. 27). Maybe this is not supposed to operate as a necessary condition on acquisition: Locke surely did not mean that no one should appropriate any resources if there is not enough for everyone. See Jeremy Waldron, "Enough and as Good Left for Others," *Philosophical Quarterly* 29, no. 117 (1979): 319–28. The proviso is better understood as a *sufficient* condition: Locke is saying that there is certainly no difficulty with unilateral acquisition (which satisfies the other provisos) in circumstances of plenty, but he is leaving open the possibility that some other basis might have to be found to regulate acquisition in circumstances of scarcity.

[24] The term "sufficiency proviso" was coined, I believe, by C. B. Macpherson in *The Political Theory of Possessive Individualism: Hobbes to Locke* (Oxford: Oxford University Press, 1962), 204 and 211. For "Lockean proviso," see *ASU*, 179.

[25] I am indebted to Virginia Held, "John Locke on Robert Nozick," *Social Research* 43 (1976): 169–82, and 171–75, for first bringing to my attention the significance of Locke's principle of charity in the context of an evaluation of Nozick's Lockean theory. See also Held, *Rights and Goods*, 132.

[26] What follows in the text is an abbreviated version of the discussion of the principle of charity in Jeremy Waldron, *God, Locke, and Equality: Christian Foundations in Locke's Political Thought* (Cambridge: Cambridge University Press, 2002), chap. 6.

[27] Locke, *Two Treatises*, 170 (*First Treatise*, chap. 4, sec. 42).

and in most natural law theories.[28] If it is taken at face value, it changes the complexion of Locke's theory of property quite significantly, mitigating the "disproportionate and unequal Possession of the Earth," which a market economy generates,[29] by providing in effect a right to a "safety net" for the poorest members of society.

The immediate context of Locke's introduction of the principle of charity is his attack on Filmer's claim that God gave the world and everything in it to Adam and his male heirs, and thus secured for them an entitlement to absolute political authority. Now Locke denied that there was in fact any such specific donation of resources by God to some humans at the expense of others.[30] But his strategy in the *First Treatise* is that of a lawyer—resisting each step in his opponent's argument by showing successively that even if the previous step is conceded, the next step does not follow, and so on.[31] So he insists that even if there was a donation, it was a donation of *property* not *sovereignty*. Property could become absolute power only if the proprietor of the world's resources were able to exploit his wealth to coerce political obedience. Locke dismisses this out of hand: "The most specious thing to be said, is, that he that is Proprietor of the whole World, may deny all the rest of Mankind Food, and so at his pleasure starve them, if they will not acknowledge his Soveraignty and Obey his Will."[32]

What are Locke's reasons for insisting that property rights cannot be exploited in this way? He offers a utilitarian argument,[33] but his main argument is based on elementary natural right:

[28] See, e.g., Aquinas, *Summa Theologiae*, ed. and trans. David Bourke and Arthur Littledale (New York: Blackfriars, 1969), II-II. q. 66, art. 7, concl.; Hugo Grotius, *The Rights of War and Peace* (New York: M. Walter Dunne, 1901), 92 (bk. 2, chap. 2, sec. 6). Again, see Held, "John Locke on Robert Nozick," 185. For a good general discussion, see Thomas A. Horne, *Property Rights and Poverty: Political Argument in Britain, 1605–1834* (Chapel Hill: University of North Carolina Press, 1990), chap. 1.

[29] Locke, *Two Treatises*, 302 (*Second Treatise*, chap. 5, sec. 50).

[30] Ibid., 161–62 (*First Treatise*, chap. 4, sec. 30).

[31] See ibid., 267 (*Second Treatise*, chap. 2, sec. 1) for a summary of his use of this strategy in the *First Treatise*.

[32] Ibid., 169–70 (*First Treatise*, chap. 4, sec. 41). Locke also argues that even if Adam *could* use his rights in this way, this would not show what Filmer wanted to show: "Should anyone make so perverse an use of God's Blessings poured on him with a liberal Hand;... yet all this would not prove that Propriety in Land, even in this Case, gave any Authority over the Persons of Men, but only that Compact might; since the Authority of the Rich Proprietor, and the Subjection of the Needy Beggar began not from the Possession of the Lord, but the Consent of the poor Man, who preferr'd being his Subject to starving" (ibid., sec. 43). Thus Filmer fails to dislodge political authority from its basis in the consent of the governed, and leaves as free as before the man who refuses (even suicidally) to be humbled by his needs in this way.

[33] Ibid. sec. 41. He argues that the inclusion of this power in the right of property would lead in practice to economic stagnation rather than "to promote the great Design of God, *Increase* and *Multiply*." A man with this sort of dominion is likely to exploit it inefficiently with all men as his slaves, rather than promoting a liberal economy: "He that doubts this, let him look into the Absolute Monarchies of the World, and see what becomes of the Conveniences of Life and the Multitudes of People" (ibid).

> God the Lord and Father of all, has given no one of his Children such a Property, in his peculiar Portion of the things of this World, but that he has given his needy Brother a Right to the Surplusage of his Goods; so that it cannot justly be denyed him, when his pressing Wants call for it.... As *Justice* gives every Man a Title to the product of his honest Industry, and the fair Acquisitions of his Ancestors descended to him; so *Charity* gives every Man a Title to so much out of another's Plenty, as will keep him from extream want, where he has no means to subsist otherwise....[34]

The language of this passage is interesting. In modern liberal theory, charity is not usually seen as a matter of right: to give of one's wealth to the poor is something one ought to do, but not something one owes to any assignable individual. It is often presented as a paradigm of a moral duty that ought not to be enforced.[35] Poor people should be grateful for charity, but they may not demand it or claim it or justify it as rightfully theirs. Some of what Locke says is suggestive of this tradition. He distinguishes the demands of charity from those of justice, drawing at least at a verbal level the distinction that modern liberals have made so much of. But, in order for his argument against Filmer to succeed, Locke needs to be able to show not only that it is wrong to withhold charitable assistance, but that *the rich man has no right to do so,* no right even to offer assistance subject to conditions such as political submission. For the most part, then, the Lockean language is emphatically stronger: though charity is contrasted with justice, still charity "cannot justly be denyed." If it cannot justly be denied, then anyone who denies it cannot claim to be exercising his property rights. The sin of uncharitableness simply vitiates the exercise of the rights in question. A man in need has "a Right" to another's surplus goods: indeed, Locke talks of his having "a Title," in a way that suggests that this too is to be regarded as a property entitlement.

What about the fact that charity is regarded by Locke as a specifically Christian virtue? Shouldn't this be a reason for not enforcing it in a liberal theory? Apparently not, according to Locke. He does make a point of saying that many aspects of religion cannot be enforced by the state.[36] The clearest example is Christ's commandment to believe in him as the Mes-

[34] Ibid., 170 (*First Treatise,* chap. 4, sec. 42).

[35] I have discussed this view of charity in Jeremy Waldron, "Welfare and the Images of Charity," *Philosophical Quarterly* 36, no. 145 (1986): 463–82; reprinted in Jeremy Waldron, *Liberal Rights: Collected Papers 1981–1991* (Cambridge: Cambridge University Press, 1993), 225–49. I also have discussed this view in Jeremy Waldron, "On the Road: Good Samaritans and Compelling Duties," *Santa Clara Law Review* 40 (2000): 1062–88.

[36] John Locke, *A Letter Concerning Toleration,* ed. James Tully (Indianapolis, IN: Hackett Publishing, 1983), 18. (See also Jeremy Waldron, "Locke, Toleration, and the Rationality of Persecution," in Waldron, *Liberal Rights,* 88–114.)

siah,[37] which, as Locke argues in *A Letter Concerning Toleration* (1689), cannot and should not be enforced. For that case, however, we have specific reasons for nonenforcement: (1) belief is not subject to the will, and coercion works only through the will; and (2) what anyone believes (e.g., about Jesus being the Messiah) does not affect the well-being of anyone else.[38] Neither condition applies to the principle of charity. Indeed, it is noteworthy that when Locke writes in *The Reasonableness of Christianity* (1695) about the difference between what Christ requires us to *believe* (where uncoerced sincerity is of the essence) and what he requires us simply to *do*, it is charity Locke mentions as an illustration of the latter.[39] The matter is complicated by one passage in *The Reasonableness of Christianity* which suggests that charity may be a virtue that state power *could* be used to uphold but should not: Jesus' commandment to the rich young man to "sell all you have and give to the poor."[40] But Locke reads this as Christ's test to see whether the young man in question really would be willing to follow his commandments, not as an imperative addressed to all of us:[41]

> [O]ur Saviour, to try whether in earnest [the young man] believed him to be the Messiah, and resolved to take him to be his king, and to obey him as such; bids him give all that he has to the poor, and come and follow him; and he should have treasure in heaven. This I look on to be the meaning of the place; this, of selling all he had, and giving it to the poor, not being a standing law of his kingdom; but a probationary command to this young man; to try whether he truly believed him to be the Messiah, and was ready to obey his commands, and relinquish all to follow him, when he, his prince, required it.[42]

Selling all you have and giving it to the poor would be a form of what I want to call *radical* charity—giving away what you actually have a moral right to keep, giving away enough to impoverish yourself—and that is not what Locke is arguing for in the *First Treatise*. Radical charity may be a particular requirement imposed on particular people, but it is not intended as a general command. Radical charity is not required by the principle we

[37] Locke spends most of *The Reasonableness of Christianity*, 1695 (Bristol: Thoemmes Press, 1997), 17–112, arguing that nothing else is necessary for salvation.

[38] Locke, *A Letter Concerning Toleration*, 46.

[39] Locke, *The Reasonableness of Christianity*, 127. He cites the charitable requirements of the sheep and goats story in Matthew 25:31–46 (feed the hungry, give water to the thirsty, shelter the homeless, etc.) as his prime examples of what we are commanded to do as opposed to what we are expected to believe.

[40] Matthew 19:21.

[41] It seems the young man failed the test: "[W]hen the young man heard that saying, he went away sorrowful: for he had great possessions" (Matthew 19:22).

[42] Locke, *The Reasonableness of Christianity*, 120.

are discussing. The principle of charity from the *First Treatise* affects the rich man only in "the Surplusage of his Goods."[43]

The doctrine of charity is set out in Locke's *First Treatise*, but it is not mentioned explicitly in the *Second Treatise*.[44] We know that the two treatises were written at different times.[45] Is there any reason to believe that the author of the famous chapter on property in the *Second Treatise* (chapter 5) intended the theory he set out there to be qualified by the doctrine I have been discussing?

It is tempting for modern theorists who claim Lockean inspiration in their thinking about property but oppose the principle of charity to insist on a separation between the *Second Treatise* doctrine and the *First Treatise* doctrine in this regard. The *First Treatise* doctrine—which, contrary to what its title may suggest, was produced later by Locke—they might treat as an aberration, unwarranted by the premises of his original theory.[46] In general, I think this approach to textual exegesis is quite unsound, motivated as it is more or less entirely by a desire to find a theory of a certain shape in Locke and by an irritation at having to consider aspects of his thought on these matters that indicate a more complex view. For there is nothing actually in the text of the *Second Treatise* that precludes the principle of charity. The textual evidence for the independence of the two treatises in regard to charity is just Locke's silence on the issue in the *Second Treatise* chapter on property: there are several places where one would expect him to mention such a proviso (if he believed in it), and he does not, at least not in so many words. But this is quite inconclusive. We do not take Locke's silence on inheritance and bequest in the *Second Treatise* chapter on property to indicate a belief that property rights were not inheritable or subject to passage by bequest; instead, we see that the very extensive discussion of inheritance and bequest in the *First Treatise* naturally adds to and complements the discussion in the *Second Treatise*.[47] The fact is that there was no particular need to discuss inheritance and

[43] Locke, *Two Treatises*, 170 (*First Treatise*, chap. 4, sec. 42).

[44] There are hints of it, however, in the announcement with which Locke opens chapter 5 of the *Second Treatise*: "Men, being once born, have a right to their Preservation. . . ." Ibid., 285 (sec. 25).

[45] The *Second Treatise* was composed in 1679–80; the *First Treatise* was added a little later. (See Laslett's introduction to Locke, *Two Treatises of Government*, 61–66). But the two were published together by Locke (though anonymously) in 1689. For the view that the date of publication matters more than the date of authorship, see Waldron, *God, Locke, and Equality*, 7n. Had the dates of composition been reversed, with the *First Treatise* written much earlier, then there might have been a case for saying that its doctrine of property, packaged together with the principle of charity, was superseded by the more "modern" theory presented in the *Second Treatise*. But the fact that the *First Treatise* was added later really undermines this suggestion.

[46] This view was urged on me in discussion with several of my fellow contributors to this volume and by one of the editors.

[47] See Locke, *Two Treatises*, 204–10 (*First Treatise*, chap. 9, secs. 86–93); see also Jeremy Waldron, "Locke's Account of Inheritance and Bequest," *Journal of the History of Philosophy* 19, no. 1 (1981): 39–51; and Waldron, *The Right to Private Property*, 241–51.

bequest in chapter five of the *Second Treatise,* but argumentatively it is required for Locke's account of heritable political authority in chapter 9 of the *First Treatise.* And similarly, there was no particular need to discuss the principle of charity in chapter five of the *Second Treatise,* though it could be deployed for political advantage in the attack on absolutism in chapter 4 of the *First Treatise.* In any other context, the fact that different doctrines are mentioned in different chapters would not be adduced as grounds for separating them from one another. It is only the fact that the principle of charity is seen as an annoyance for a certain sort of "Lockean" theory that requires me to spend time defending the claim that two consistent sets of propositions written by the same author and published in different parts of the same book should be regarded as parts of the same theory (unless very good reason is shown why they should not be).

I used to think there *was* a substantial difficulty in accommodating the charity doctrine with the *Second Treatise* theory of property. The basis on which Locke argues for individual acquisition is the idea of mixing one's labor with resources or land: "joyn[ing] to it something that is his own, and thereby [making] it his *Property.*"[48] On a literal interpretation of this argument, the laborer transfers to the object the inviolable right he has in his own person. Now, it is hard to see how that right can be overridden by the mere fact of another's need. Either the object contains the owner's labor or it does not: the other person's need cannot, as it were, drive the labor out. I used to think that what was going on here was that Locke was running two incompatible lines of argument to justify private property in the *Second Treatise*: one was entitlement-based, deriving from the exclusive right one has in one's person and one's labor,[49] and the other was based broadly on the notion of human need and what must happen in order for mankind to prosper.[50] The provisos and limitations seemed to make sense primarily in relation to the second of these lines of argument, and the same would be true of the principle of charity.

But I no longer think it makes sense to see the mixing of labor as a separate line of argument, less hospitable to modification by charity or the other provisos. I think the labor theory works only against a background of labor's significance in God's overall plan for the survival of the human beings he has created. Laboring is not just something we happen to do to resources, nor is being permitted to help oneself by labor just a divine indulgence of the self-interested inclinations of an acquisitive being. It is the naturally requisite next step following our creation, once we

[48] Locke, *Two Treatises,* 288 (*Second Treatise,* chap. 5, sec. 27).

[49] Ibid.

[50] Ibid., 285 (sec. 25): "Whether we consider natural Reason, which tells us, that Men, being once born, have a right to their Preservation, and consequently to Meat and Drink, and such other things, as Nature affords for their Subsistence: or Revelation, which gives us an account of those Grants God made of the World to Adam, and to Noah, and his Sons, 'tis very clear, that God, as King David says, Psal. CXV. xvi. has given the Earth to the Children of Men; given it to Mankind in common."

accept that we were created subservient to God's design "that Man should live and abide for sometime upon the Face of the Earth, and not that so curious and wonderful a piece of Workmanship by its own Negligence, or want of Necessaries, should perish again, presently after a few moments continuance."[51] If labor were not presented against this background, if it were just something I happen to own, there would be no answer to an embarrassing question that Nozick poses: "[W]hy isn't mixing what I own with what I don't own a way of losing what I own rather than a way of gaining what I don't?" (*ASU*, 174-75). Any account of the significance of labor rich enough to answer this question will have to hook up with the account based on need, and therefore will naturally be subject to the principle of charity.

Bearing this in mind, I think we can say that the substantive case for importing the *First Treatise* doctrine of charity into the *Second Treatise* theory of property revolves around the premises of Lockean natural law. The basic principle of the law of nature, said Locke, is the preservation of as many people as possible: "Everyone as he is *bound to preserve himself*, ... so by the like reason when his own Preservation comes not in competition, ought he, as much as he can, *to preserve the rest of Mankind*."[52] This sounds like a positive duty to do whatever will promote the preservation of as many people as possible. Locke makes it clear that it goes far beyond mere nonaggression. It includes the power to pardon offenders; it even includes a duty to infringe property rights in an emergency, like "pull[ing] down an innocent Man's House to stop the Fire, when the next to it is burning. . . ."[53] Anyway, it has never been clear to me that the duty of charity—at least as Locke presents it—*is* a positive as opposed to a negative duty. Paragraph 42 of the *First Treatise* denies that property owners have the right to *withhold* their surplus goods from the poor. Thus, Locke seems to be committed not to a view about *giving* but to the view that neither the rich person nor civil society on his behalf is entitled to *resist* the poor when the poor attempt to seize his surplus goods. It is not a question of forcing the rich to *do* anything: it is enough that they be compelled simply to stand back and let the poor take what (on account of their "pressing Needs") is rightfully theirs.[54]

More specifically, at the beginning of the chapter on property, Locke tells us in very general terms that "[m]en, being once born, have a right to their Preservation, and consequently to Meat and Drink, and such other things, as Nature affords for their subsistence. . . ."[55] Now, this might be construed as mere rhetoric, except that Locke quickly puts it in

[51] Ibid., 204-5 (*First Treatise*, chap. 9, sec. 86).

[52] Ibid., 271 (*Second Treatise*, chap. 2, sec. 6).

[53] Ibid., 374-75 (*Second Treatise*, chap. 14, sec. 159).

[54] This is the point of my argument about "charity" in Waldron, "Welfare and the Images of Charity."

[55] Locke, *Two Treatises*, 285 (*Second Treatise*, chap. 5, sec. 25).

play to do some rather important work. For when he defends the legitimacy of unilateral appropriation, he raises the specter of starvation as a basis for his rebuttal of any consent requirement:

> [W]ill any one say [that a man] had no right to those Acorns or Apples he thus appropriated, because he had not the consent of all Mankind to make them his? . . . If such a consent as that was necessary, Man had starved, notwithstanding the Plenty God had given him.[56]

The prospect of starvation simply short-circuits any complaint based on the illegitimacy of appropriation without consent. Since the rights that are rebutted in this way are real rights—each person's right to partake in God's original donation—Locke is saying, in effect, that the right to withhold consent can be trumped by desperate need. He cannot consistently maintain that without also maintaining what I have called the principle of charity.

One last hurdle remains. Those who want to portray an uncharitable Locke are fond of telling us about the John Locke who was the author of an essay on the poor law—a draft of a representation concerning methods of employing the poor. That draft certainly seems devoid of the sort of compassion that one would associate with a generous spirit of charity. Locke talks about "begging drones" and "superfluous brandy shops," and he suggests that the idle poor should be whipped and mutilated if they go begging instead of doing the work assigned to them. Even little children should be given two or three hours of labor useful to the parish per day.[57]

I want to say two things about this. First, we should bear in mind that the paper on the poor law *does* assume that the poor have a right to subsistence. "[E]veryone must have meat, drink, clothing, and firing."[58] Secondly, Locke took very seriously the injunction to labor, and a poor man with an offer of gainful employment was not a person who had no means to subsist (within the meaning of the principle of charity). We have already seen that Locke is in favor of charity being enforced, but not *radical* charity.[59] Well, now we have a *second* form of radical charity that Locke is not prepared to enforce: this would be charity to someone who refuses to work when he *could* work, charity to someone who does not

[56] Ibid., 288 (sec. 28).

[57] John Locke, "An Essay on the Poor Law," in Mark Goldie, ed., *Locke: Political Essays* (Cambridge: Cambridge University Press, 1997), 184, 186–87, and 190–92.

[58] Ibid., 189. Locke also says that "if any person die for want of due relief in any parish in which he ought to be relieved, the said parish [must] be fined according to the circumstances of the fact and the heinousness of the crime" (ibid., 198).

[59] See above, text accompanying notes 40–43.

make any efforts to provide for himself or work to subsidize the cost of his provision.

I hope this textual and historical account of Locke's principle of charity has not been tedious. What I want to establish is that Locke believed very strongly that human survival and flourishing (and indeed the increase of a surviving and flourishing population) were the basic moral imperatives of economic life. In Section I of this essay, I discussed which moral considerations come on stage first and establish themselves as the substructure, which other rights and principles must then work around. Well, in Locke's theory, the substructure comprises the principle of preservation and increase. No rights exist in conflict with this substructure, and the whole argument in favor of property entitlement and acquisition is predicated on these first principles:

> God having made Man, and planted in him, as in all other Animals, a strong desire of Self-preservation, and furnished the World with things fit for Food and Rayment and other Necessaries of his Life, Subservient to his design, that Man should live and abide for some time upon the Face of the Earth, and not that so curious and wonderful a piece of Workmanship by its own Negligence, or want of Necessaries, should perish again, presently after a few moments continuance: God, I say, having made Man and the World thus, spoke to him, (that is) directed him by his Senses and Reason . . . to the use of those things, which were serviceable for his Subsistence, and given him as a means of his *Preservation*. And thus Man's *Property* in the Creatures, was founded upon the right he had, to make use of those things, that were necessary or useful to his Being.[60]

If this is the foundation of property, then property cannot be used to oppose other consequences that flow from these first principles. Elementary rights to material assistance in conditions of urgent need flow directly, and they must condition the property rights, not the other way round.

## III. Nozick on Welfare

Now I want to return to the Lockean proviso and the work that it does in Robert Nozick's theory. Nozick is committed to the following proposition:

> A process normally giving rise to a permanent bequeathable property right in a previously unowned thing will not do so if the position

[60] Locke, *Two Treatises*, 204–5 (*First Treatise*, chap. 9, sec. 86).

> of others no longer at liberty to use the thing is thereby worsened. (*ASU*, 178)[61]

What is this, if it is not a statement of what Nozick called the "reverse" theory (*ASU*, 238)? It gives priority to the right not to have one's material situation worsened, whether that situation consists in holding property rights or just in having access of some kind to the resources needed for a decent life. It gives these rights priority in exactly the sense that the "reverse" theory is supposed to give priority to welfare rights: property entitlements must work around them; no property entitlements are recognized if they are incompatible with these rights.

One can quibble with this—does the Lockean proviso really generate *rights*?—and I will explore the quibbles in a moment. For now, just observe how strongly this condition operates in Nozick's theory. It applies to acquisition: if I want to be the first to take a given resource into possession as a private holding, I may do so (by engaging in whatever the principle of justice in acquisition says: labor, occupancy, whatever), but only so long as the situation of others is not thereby worsened. The condition also applies to the exercise of one's property rights in whatever one has appropriated: "a person may not appropriate the only water hole in the desert and charge what he will" (*ASU*, 180), for previously the situation was that other people could come to the water hole and drink for free. And the condition renders one's property rights and their exercise vulnerable to revision in the light of changing circumstances: "[n]or may he charge what he will if he possesses one [water hole], and unfortunately it happens that all the water holes in the desert dry up, except for his" (*ASU*, 180).[62] It also affects justice in transfer:

> A theory which includes this proviso in its principle of justice in acquisition must also contain a more complex principle of justice in transfer. Some reflection of the proviso about appropriation constrains later actions. If my appropriating all of a certain substance violates the Lockean proviso, then so does my appropriating some and purchasing all the rest from others who obtained it without otherwise violating the Lockean proviso. (*ASU*, 179)

Thus, the proviso affects property entitlements generally, even those at a great distance from the original acquisitions that got historical entitle-

[61] I follow Nozick in calling this "the Lockean proviso" (*ASU*, 179), though it differs somewhat from Locke's "enough, and as good left in common for others" proviso (Locke, *Two Treatises*, 288 (*Second Treatise*, chap. 5, sec. 27).

[62] Elsewhere I have argued that this affects not only acquisition, but also whatever we think we ought to do in the way of the rectification of injustice. See Jeremy Waldron, "Superseding Historic Injustice," *Ethics* 103, no. 1 (1992): 4–28; and Jeremy Waldron, "Redressing Historic Injustice," *University of Toronto Law Journal* 52 (2002): 135–60.

ment underway: "Each owner's title to his holding includes the historical shadow of the Lockean proviso on appropriation" (*ASU*, 180).

Despite this "shadow," Nozick believes that the Lockean proviso can be satisfied fairly easily. He argues against any interpretation of it that would limit acquisition to cases where there is no impact on other people's *acquisitive* opportunities (so that there is enough, and as good, left in common for others *to appropriate*).[63] If people are no worse off overall as a result of others' acquisitions, they have no ground for legitimate complaint (*ASU*, 176). This means we can appeal to "the various familiar social considerations favoring private property" on grounds of efficiency (*ASU*, 177)[64]—considerations that leave him confident "that the free operation of a market system will not actually run afoul of the Lockean proviso" (*ASU*, 182). I shall not quibble with this, though it is worth noting the honesty of Nozick's observation that the claim is an empirical matter and he may be wrong (*ASU*, 182). As we shall see, Nozick's objections to actually existing market economies have more to do with the brutal injustice associated with their establishment and with the particular property rights held by the rich than with any violation of the Lockean proviso (*ASU*, 230–31).

Does the ease with which the Lockean proviso can be satisfied in a market society based on property entitlements mean that we cannot use Nozick's embrace of the proviso as a ground for attributing to him what we have called the "reverse" theory? Not at all. A principle may be fundamental and it may define the substructure of rights, in Nozick's sense (*ASU*, 238), without being very demanding. All that is necessary to sustain the proposition that Nozick's theory is a "reverse" theory is to show that it is *not* the case that property rights fill up the space of rights leaving no room for rights such as a right not to have one's material condition worsened. The Lockean proviso shows this. Does it make any difference that the Lockean proviso is part and parcel of Nozick's conception of historical entitlement so that property rights (subject, admittedly, to that proviso) fill up the space of rights leaving no room for any

[63] See *ASU*, 176 and 178. Cf. Locke, *Two Treatises*, 288 (*Second Treatise*, chap. 5, sec 27).

[64] John Locke does something similar in his famous passage comparing the agricultural economy of England with subsistence economies of the Native Americans:

> There cannot be a clearer demonstration of any thing, than several Nations of the *Americans* are of this, who are rich in Land, and poor in all the Comforts of Life; whom Nature having furnished as liberally as any other people, with the materials of Plenty, *i.e.* a fruitful Soil, apt to produce in abundance, what might serve for food, rayment, and delight; yet for want of improving it by labour, have not one hundredth part of the Conveniencies we enjoy: and a King of a large and fruitful Territory there, feeds, lodges, and is clad worse than a day Labourer in *England*.

See Locke, *Two Treatises*, 296–97 (*Second Treatise*, chap. 5, sec. 41). This argument is based on maximin, though on a particularly strong version of it: Locke claims that the poorest participant in the English economy is better off than the *best*-off participant in the Native American economy.

*other* right to be in a given material condition? No, that is just being silly. At most it shows that Nozick is adopting what I referred to at the end of Section I as the "symmetrical" approach—developing his theory of historical entitlement hand in hand with a theory of people's rights to be in a certain material condition.

But does Nozick's version of the Lockean proviso actually enshrine *rights* to be in a certain material condition? There is certainly a difference between the proviso and Locke's principle of charity. The latter establishes that each person has a right to survive, and hence "a Title to so much out of another's Plenty, as will keep him from extream want, where he has no means to subsist otherwise. . . ."[65] Nozick's version of the proviso respects only a claim not to be shifted from a certain baseline of well-being. It is a baseline defined (rather problematically—*ASU*, 177) as the condition one would be in but for the appropriation(s) or holding(s) whose legitimacy is now called into question. Moreover, it is not a claim to be and to remain at that level of well-being (however it is defined): it is only a claim not to be moved down from it by an appropriation (or the equivalent of an appropriation). If one's well-being declines for other reasons, the Lockean proviso does not generate a claim to have it restored. These are important points. But they do not affect the underlying argument about the shape of Nozick's approach. His theory begins with the assumption that the formation and justification of property entitlements must be responsive to concerns about well-being that are not embodied in property rights. In this sense, it is not true that on Nozick's account only property rights define the "substructure" of rights.

The Lockean proviso is not an incidental accretion to Nozick's conception that he could easily abandon. Without such a proviso, any principle of justice in acquisition (and anything founded on it, such as a system of ongoing property rights in a market economy) becomes morally very problematic, since it involves the unilateral imposition of duties (albeit negative duties) on people without their consent.[66] Few are willing to say that the imposition of such duties can be justified utterly without reference to the interests or needs of those whom they exclude from access to resources.[67]

That is very general. More specifically in Nozick's case, we see the importance of the Lockean proviso in assimilating the justification of initial acquisition to the kind of justification used for principles of justice

[65] Ibid., 170 (*First Treatise*, chap. 4, sec. 42).

[66] The point is made most forcefully by Immanuel Kant: "When I declare (by word or deed), I will that something external is to be mine, I thereby declare that everyone else is under obligation to refrain from using that object of my choice, an obligation no one would have were it not for this act of mine to establish a right." Immanuel Kant, *The Metaphysics of Morals*, ed. and trans. Mary Gregor (Cambridge: Cambridge University Press, 1991), pt. 1, sec. 8, 77 (VI, 255 in the Prussian Academy Edition). See also Jeremy Waldron, "Kant's Legal Positivism," *Harvard Law Review* 109 (1996): 1535–66.

[67] See also the discussion in Waldron, *The Right to Private Property*, 266–71.

in transfer. In the latter case, we justify transfers on grounds related to their representing Pareto improvements: because the transactions are voluntary, no one thinks that he loses in a market transfer. Therefore, so long as the parties are rational, a market transfer (barring externalities) makes at least some better off without making anyone worse off. In initial acquisition, by contrast, it looks as though there will be losers: I acquire this field as my property; and since you are excluded, you no longer have the access that you had before. The Lockean proviso ameliorates this problem. Now we say that an acquisition is legitimate only if it leaves no one worse off, that is, only if it is a Pareto improvement. Acquisition is thus assimilated to transfer so far as the principle of its justification is concerned.

By the way, it is interesting to note how Nozick's use of the idea of Pareto improvement differs from that of scholars involved in the Economic Analysis of Law (EAL).[68] When a change is justified as an improvement according to EAL, it is because it is thought that although some people benefit and some suffer from the change, the gains of those who benefit are sufficient to compensate the losses of those who suffer. This is the famous Kaldor-Hicks criterion of social improvement: a change that improves the situation of some by worsening the situation of others, is permitted if the winners win more than enough to compensate the losers.[69] For EAL, this gives the change in question the respectability of a Pareto improvement. But although a Kaldor-Hicks improvement is *like* a Pareto improvement in certain respects (e.g., in the amount of wealth-gain required), it is not *relevantly* like a Pareto improvement in the respects that ought to matter when we think about justice. True, in a Kaldor-Hicks improvement, we ensure that the winner gains enough to compensate the loser, so that no one *need* be worse off. But this assessment is not associated, in any way, with a practical determination actually to assign the loser any portion of what the winner gains. The preferences of the losing party are certainly taken into account in considering whether the change is an improvement: it must be the case that the loser would prefer a portion of the winner's gain to what he could secure in the absence of the change. But justice is not interested in facts about preferences *per se*. Justice is interested in facts about the satisfaction of preferences, and with a Kaldor-Hicks change there need be no actual satisfaction of this preference of the loser. Similarly, the legal imposition of a Kaldor-Hicks improvement has none of the consensual respectability of a Pareto improvement. When we impose a Kaldor-Hicks improvement, we are not in any way honoring the voluntary consent of the losing party. That the loser

[68] Exemplars of EAL include R. H. Coase, "The Problem of Social Cost," *Journal of Law and Economics* 3 (1960): 1–44; Guido Calabresi, "Some Thoughts on Risk Distribution and the Law of Torts," *Yale Law Journal* 70 (1961): 499–553; and Richard A. Posner, *The Economics of Justice* (Cambridge, MA: Harvard University Press, 1981).

[69] Cf. J. R. Hicks, "The Rehabilitation of Consumers' Surplus," *Review of Economic Studies* 8, no. 2 (1941): 108–116.

*would* consent (under condition C) adds nothing to the respectability of a change that involves no actual consent (because condition C is *not* satisfied).[70] To oppose a Kaldor-Hicks improvement in the name of justice is therefore not to oppose justice to human welfare, nor is it to oppose justice to people's revealed preferences, nor is it to oppose justice to a scheme that makes everyone better off. It is, rather, to insist on the importance of respecting actual individuals with their actual preferences in the actual world; and it is to oppose the imposition on individuals of actual losses for which nothing but hypothetical compensation is envisaged. Now Nozick will have none of this. He famously rejected the utilitarian idea that some people's gains can make up for other people's losses: what happens is that some people gain and others lose; nothing more (*ASU*, 33). And he is insistent on this point specifically in connection with the Lockean proviso:

> Someone whose appropriation otherwise would violate the proviso still may appropriate provided he compensates the others so that their situation is not thereby worsened; *unless he does compensate these others,* his appropriation will violate the proviso of the principle of justice in acquisition and will be an illegitimate one. (*ASU*, 178; emphasis added)

This is a striking difference between Nozick and the EAL: Nozick's account has integrity, theirs does not.

This is but one example of the integrity of Nozick's argumentation in *Anarchy, State, and Utopia.* When the book appeared, left-liberals were so shocked that many of them complained the book was written simply to promote a political agenda. Brian Barry's review was typical and a now-famous passage of it ran as follows:

> [T]he intellectual texture is of a sort of cuteness that would be wearing in a graduate student and seems to me quite indecent in someone who, from the lofty heights of a professorial chair, is proposing to starve or humiliate ten percent of his fellow citizens (if he recognizes the word) by eliminating all transfer payments through the state, leaving the sick, the old, the disabled, the mothers with young children and no breadwinner, and so on, to the tender mercies of private charity, given at the whim and pleasure of the donors and on any terms they choose to impose.[71]

[70] In some cases, we legitimate action on the basis of hypothetical consent, but not when the difference between the hypothetical and the real world is the presence of one of the conditions on which the hypothetical consent is predicated!

[71] Brian Barry, review of *Anarchy, State, and Utopia, Political Theory* 3, no. 3 (1975): 331–32.

I think this sort of abuse is quite unwarranted. If Nozick were standing for office and these were his policies, I guess there would be reason to vote for some other candidate. In fact, he was not in a position to starve or humiliate anyone or to eliminate any transfer payments through the state, nor was he was aspiring to any office where his "proposals" to this effect would be a matter of political concern. He was, as Barry reminds us, occupying a professorial chair in a philosophy department. He was not in fact *proposing* anything, or *calling for* anything, or indeed *urging* anything, except this: that we might try thinking about justice in a slightly different way. As Nozick pointed out in his preface to *Anarchy, State, and Utopia*:

> My emphasis upon the conclusions which diverge from what most readers believe may mislead one into thinking this book is some sort of political tract. It is not; it is a philosophical exploration of issues, many fascinating in their own right, which arise and interconnect when we consider individual rights and the state. (*ASU*, xii)

Nozick's integrity probably explains why his work has had more influence on the Left than on the Right. For those of us on the Left, it was Nozick (rather than, say, F. A. Hayek) who undermined our confidence in simple formulae of equality and who convinced us that "no end-state principle or distributional patterned principle of justice can be continuously realized without continuous interference with people's lives" (*ASU*, 163). Nozick laid down the challenge that we thought we needed to answer. (I am not saying we succeeded in answering it, but it was Nozick's challenge that sharpened our wits.) However, Nozick argued too honorably to be of much use to the triumphant Right in the 1980s and 1990s. He was never prepared to say that the historical-entitlement critique of equality and welfarism in his book amounted to a defense of actually existing market institutions, nor would he pretend that a Lockean defense of property could go any distance toward legitimizing contemporary disparities of wealth in (for example) the United States. On the contrary, he thought it undeniable that contemporary holdings would be condemned as unjust by any remotely plausible conception of historical entitlement. (The point of Nozick's argument in chapters 7 and 8 of *Anarchy, State, and Utopia* was that egalitarians were condemning the existing distribution for the wrong reason—that is, simply as unequal—rather than on account of the violence, fraud, expropriation, ethnic cleansing, state corruption, and so on, involved in the history of most holdings of property in America.) Once actual historical injustice was established, then the burden fell on the part of his conception dealing with the rectification of injustice. And for Nozick, it was an open question whether the actual operation of (say) Rawls's difference principle might approximate the operation of a plausible process for rectifying historical injustice. That, Nozick thought (quite rightly), would involve addressing some very difficult questions about time, counterfactuals, second-best principles, and so on:

> These issues are very complex and are best left to a full treatment of the principle of rectification. In the absence of such a treatment applied to a particular society, one *cannot* use the analysis and theory presented here to condemn any particular scheme of transfer payments, unless it is clear that no considerations of rectification of injustice could apply to justify it. (*ASU*, 231; Nozick's emphasis)

This was not what defenders of free markets and opponents of welfare wanted to hear in the 1980s and 1990s.

## IV. Welfare and Justice

It is often said of welfare rights that they are impracticable or too expensive or too demanding. Some critics even argue that socioeconomic rights violate the logical principle "*Ought* implies *can*." Many nations, they say, do not have the resources to provide even minimal economic security for masses of their citizens, and since states differ considerably in this regard, it hardly makes sense to regard economic provision as a matter of universal human entitlement.[72]

In some cases, sheer scarcity will trigger the principle "*Ought* implies *can*." But the fact that this happens in some cases does not undermine the universalist thesis. The "ought" remains in the background, in all cases, commanding each country to do as much as it can in this regard, and its full force will be triggered for a given country whenever it acquires the ability to fulfill it. Moreover, in many cases, the alleged impossibility stems not from brute scarcity as such but from an assumption that the existing distribution of property is to remain largely undisturbed. When a conservative government in the West says in response to some plea for welfare provision, "The money simply isn't there," what is usually meant is that it would be either impolitic or improper to try and raise it from existing property-holders and income earners by taxation. On the one hand, if the objection is simply that raising the money would be impolitic, then really the "*ought*" of welfare rights is being frustrated, not by the "*can't*" of impracticability, but by the "*shan't*" of selfishness and political ambition. If, on the other hand, the objection is that the money is not the government's to distribute, then we are back where we began, with our question about the relative priority to be accorded to property rights as opposed to welfare rights. Either way, resting the matter simply on "*Ought*

[72] See, e.g., Maurice Cranston, "Human Rights, Real and Supposed," in D. D. Raphael, ed., *Political Theory and the Rights of Man* (London: Macmillan, 1967), 50–51.

implies *can*" underestimates the challenge posed by these rights to the underlying distribution of wealth and income.

Still, someone may press the question: Aren't these socioeconomic rights awfully demanding? They may say: The first generation of rights claims—civil and political rights—require only that we and our governments refrain from various acts of tyranny and oppression. They are "negative" rights correlative to duties of omission, whereas so-called second-generation rights—socioeconomic rights—are correlative to positive duties of assistance. An advantage of negative rights is that they never conflict with one another, for one can perform an infinite number of omissions at any given moment. With positive rights, by contrast, we inevitably have to consider the inherent scarcity of the resources and the services that are called for.

There are many things wrong with this argument. For one thing, the correlation of first- and second-generation rights with the distinction between negative and positive rights simply will not stand up. Many first-generation rights require the positive establishment and maintenance of certain frameworks, and all of them make costly claims upon scarce police and forensic resources. Even those first-generation rights that can be conceived in the first instance in terms of negative freedom—such as free speech and freedom of worship—still require more from a government than that it simply stay its hand. We set up a government to *protect* our rights, not simply to respect them. All serious political theorists recognize that protection is costly,[73] and that therefore first-generation rights as much as socioeconomic entitlements raise hard questions about priorities for us all.

It follows that where resources are scarce relative to human wants, *any* system of rights or entitlements will seem demanding to those who are constrained by it. If an economic system includes provision for welfare assistance, it may seem overly demanding to taxpayers. But if it does not include such provision, then the system of *property rights* in such an economy will seem overly demanding to the poor, requiring as it does that they refrain from making use of various resources that they may need. As usual, the question is not whether we are to have a system of demanding rights, but how the costs of the demands are to be distributed. That, of course, is why the question that Nozick raised in the passage cited at the outset of this essay is so important.[74]

Thinking about scarcity and practicability does have one important advantage: it forces proponents of second-generation rights to take seriously issues of distributive justice. It is an unhappy feature of the language of rights that it expresses demanding moral claims in a sort of

[73] See Henry Shue, *Basic Rights: Subsistence, Affluence, and U.S. Foreign Policy* (Princeton, NJ: Princeton University Press, 1980), 35–64.

[74] *ASU*, 238 (see above, text accompanying note 1).

"line-item" way, presenting each individual's case peremptorily, as though it brooked no denial, no balancing, no compromise. This feature of rights has always troubled those who are sensitive to the fact that individuals live in a social environment where the things that they may reasonably expect must be adjusted constantly to reflect similar claims and expectations on the part of others. If we want a framework that more adequately reflects the necessarily compromised character of rights claims (civil rights, property rights, welfare rights), we must turn instead to the modern discussion of justice. The theory of justice—not Rawls's theory necessarily, but theorizing about justice—is the proper matrix for reconciling conflicting claims of right. Modern theorists have not written nearly enough about the relation between liberal theories of rights and liberal theories of justice. Let me end with a gesture toward such an account.

Familiar claims of right will figure both as inputs and as outputs in our theorizing about justice. They function as *inputs* inasmuch as they help constitute our initial sense of the individual claims that need to be considered. That people are normally taken to have the right of freedom of worship, the right to participate in politics, and the right to work, helps us *frame* the problems of justice that a society of such persons gives rise to. We expect that many familiar claims of right will also figure among the *outputs* of an adequate theory of justice. We hope the institutional structure that is set up in this way is one that will be able to offer certain guarantees, though they may not be as strong or as unqualified as those we had in mind before we remembered the need to balance our own claims against those made by others. For example, we may go in with a sense that respecting a human being means respecting his freedom of worship, but come out (of the balancing process) with a religious guarantee that is perhaps somewhat modified by a recognition that children, for example, must be given an adequate education and not left at the mercy of their parents' convictions, and that certain aspects of religious practice must on occasion give way to independently grounded considerations of public administration.

The same is true in regard to socioeconomic claims. We go into the discussion of justice with the sense that people are not just the disembodied wraiths of liberal ideology, but needy individuals subject to vicissitudes of embodiment and materiality: we must have food and shelter, we must work, we get sick, we grow old, we are often dependent, and so on. A preliminary sense of the importance of all this—I mean its importance to each of us as individuals, not just its importance to society—is conveyed by provisions such as the second-generation rights we have been discussing.

However, things are less clear at the output end. Consider Rawls's theory, again, as an example. Rawls is anxious that the task of a theory of justice not be understood simply as an allocation of distributive shares: who gets what, when, and how? "We must not assume," he says, "that there is much similarity from the standpoint of justice between an administrative allotment of goods to specific persons and the appropriate design of society."[75] Thus, for example, the "difference principle" is not to be interpreted as dictating that the worst-off group be *given* a certain share of resources. The effect of the principle is that when we are designing or (more likely) evaluating and reforming the network of rules and procedures that constitute the institutional structure of society, we should do so in a way that is oriented toward the advantage of the worst-off group. The institutions should be designed to operate on the assumption that when the system is working, outcomes are evaluated purely procedurally. We are not to meddle with the outcomes of a just institutional structure even if we think that by doing so we could make the array of outcomes even *more* just from a distributive point of view.

Now, here is a curiosity. F. A. Hayek has taken the comments that I have just cited as grounds for claiming that the difference between Rawls's approach and his own approach is "more verbal than substantial."[76] Rawls's work, he says, has been "wrongly ... interpreted as lending support to socialist demands."[77] Hayek takes Rawls to agree with his own central claim that "[j]ustice is not concerned with those unintended consequences of a spontaneous order [such as a market] which have not been deliberately brought about by anybody."[78]

I think that Hayek is mistaken about this and that he exaggerates the implications of Rawls's refusal to consider the justice of particular allocations of goods. Rawls's position may be illuminated as follows. Suppose that, on one occasion, the institutions of our economy happen to yield a distribution of wealth, $D_1$, that is judged inferior in terms of the difference principle to another distribution, $D_2$. Should we immediately interfere and reallocate wealth so that we change $D_1$ into $D_2$? Rawls's answer, like Hayek's, is no. For Hayek the matter ends there. But for Rawls there is a further question to be addressed: Can we change the institutional structure (including the structure of property entitlements, if there are any) so as to render it more likely in the future that the normal operation of our economy will yield distributions like $D_2$ rather than $D_1$? The answer to this question may also be no, because the proposed change might be incompatible with institutional virtues such as publicity, stability, and the rule of law.[79] The new institutions that are being suggested may not, as it were, hold up, as institutions. Still—and this is what Hayek overlooks—the answer is not *necessarily* no. If change is possible and if the

[75] Rawls, *A Theory of Justice*, 64. See also ibid., 88: "If it is asked in the abstract whether one distribution of a given stock of things to definite individuals with known desires and preferences is better than another, then there is simply no answer to this question."

[76] Friedrich A. Hayek, *Law, Legislation, and Liberty*, vol. 2: *The Mirage of Social Justice* (London: Macmillan, 1976), xiii.

[77] Ibid., 100, and the footnote to that passage on 183.

[78] Ibid., 38, and the footnote to that passage on 166.

[79] See Rawls, *A Theory of Justice*, 54–60 and 235–43.

resulting institutional structure would be viable, stable, and so on, then we are *required* as a matter of justice to implement it, for the difference principle just *is* the requirement that we arrange (and, if necessary, rearrange) our institutions so that social and economic inequalities are to the greatest benefit of the least advantaged. So, for example, if we find ourselves in a market society that lacks basic welfare provision, we have to consider whether the institutional structure of a market economy would be wrecked qua institutional structure by the addition of what Rawls calls a "transfer branch," charged with administering a social minimum. Would that make it impossible for the economic structure as a whole to operate predictably, publicly, impersonally, and in accordance with other institutional virtues? Hayek has devoted a large part of his life to arguing that it would—that the modern regulated welfare state is incompatible with the rule of law.[80] It is pretty clear that Rawls disagrees with him about that. But the deeper disagreement is that Rawls thinks it is the job of a theory of justice to select principles for evaluating economic institutions along exactly these lines, whereas Hayek simply denies that this is a legitimate concern about justice.

I have taken this digression into the Hayek-Rawls misunderstanding because I want to stress that in a theory of justice such as Rawls's we cannot guarantee that socioeconomic rights will emerge in a familiar or predictable form. As an abstract matter we can say, with the drafters of Article 25 of the Universal Declaration of Human Rights, that everyone has "the right to a standard of living adequate for the health and well-being of himself and his family." But this may not necessarily emerge as a specific legal or constitutional guarantee: a just society may not have a *rule* to this effect, nor even any particular agency charged with administering this standard. There may be a variety of provisions and arrangements—tax breaks, educational opportunities, rent control (or its abolition), unemployment insurance schemes, etc.—all of which taken together may represent the best that can be done in an institutional framework to honor the underlying claim for the individuals in whose behalf it can be made.

This fact may upset welfarists who think it more important that a right be *proclaimed* than that it be secured. It may upset those who are uninterested in the viability of social institutions and in rule-of-law values. But people who strike these attitudes should reflect a little on the role that rights are supposed to play in our social and political evaluations. When we think about rights, we must do our thinking in political philosophy not just moral philosophy, and this means being willing to consider the embodiment of various moral concerns in the *institutional* arrangements of human society. Once we see this as the distinctive perspective of polit-

[80] See F. A. Hayek, *The Road to Serfdom* (Chicago, IL; University of Chicago Press, 1944); and F. A. Hayek, *The Constitution of Liberty* (London: Macmillan, 1960).

ical philosophy, we begin to see the inadequacy of the approach that leaves rights as simply programmatic claims, without considering how they fit together as a system and how the rights of one person might be made compatible (concretely, not just in theory) with the rights of another.

The approach I have suggested may upset those who want to maintain at all costs that each individual right is absolute, and who in consequence refuse to face issues of scarcity, conflict, and moral priority. (Some say this about property and some may say it about welfare rights.) This insistence is perhaps understandable: the modern preoccupation with rights is partly a response to the trade-offs that characterize utilitarian calculations; rights were supposed to express limits on what could be done to individuals for the sake of the greater benefit of others; but if rights themselves involve conflicts and balancing, it looks as though there is no getting away from the casuistry and complex moral calculations that were thought to be the hallmark of more blatantly consequentialist theories. I have some sympathy with this view. However, the insistence on absolutism does not make the conflicts go away; it does not make the situations that appear to call for trade-offs disappear. Those situations are not something that consequentialists and their fellow travelers have perversely *invented* in order to embarrass moral absolutists. There is a danger that, if we insist on the absoluteness of rights, we may end up with no rights at all—or no rights that embody the idea of real concern for the individuals whose rights they are.

The proper response to situations that pose conflicts and dilemmas is not to deny that they exist or to protect the term "rights" from being contaminated by them. It is to face up to the challenges they pose with the clearest sense we can get of the intrinsic worth of each individual's well-being and independence in a world that is also inhabited by others. Unless that sense becomes hopelessly attenuated, it is exactly what we should identify as our theory of rights. Rights are not to be thought of as moral absolutes, standing tragically unemployed, on the sidelines of a world riven by distasteful conflict and hard choices. On the contrary, they are supposed to be our best, most honest, and most respectful response to such a world.

Let me return, finally, to Robert Nozick. With his emphasis on rights as side constraints (*ASU*, 26 ff.), it is tempting to associate Nozick with the sort of absolutism I have just been attacking. And it is tempting to read his critical comments about welfare rights (*ASU*, 238) as an indirect consequence of this absolutism. I do not just mean that his absolutism about property leads him to reject welfare rights; I mean that he might be thought to reject welfare rights partly because of what they would have to amount to qua rights. In fact, I think Nozick has contributed immeasurably to our ability to think these things through carefully in a manner that is appropriate to justice and not merely to line-item claims of right. I hope I have been able to show in this essay that this is true of his discussion about "filling the space of rights" in *Anarchy, State, and Utopia* (238), and true also of his discussion of the Lockean proviso.

## V. Conclusion

We began with Robert Nozick's challenge to come up with a moral theory—a "reverse" theory—that gives priority to welfare rights (or something like them) and recognizes claims to private property only to the extent that such welfare rights leave room for them. I have argued that the outlines of such a theory can be found in Nozick's own work—specifically in his insistence that historical entitlements to property must be conditioned on the operation of what he called the Lockean proviso. And I argued, too, that another version of the "reverse" theory can be found in the work of John Locke, not only in his own use of the Lockean proviso, but also in his insistence that property rights are qualified by an elemental principle of charity that entitles individuals to the surplus of goods that would otherwise belong to others, when they have no other means to survive. The point of adducing these two cases, in response to Nozick's challenge, is not to annoy or embarrass those who continue to develop the libertarian strands of the Lockean/Nozickian heritage. Rather, my aim has been to demonstrate the richness of that heritage and—particularly in Nozick's case—to highlight both the integrity of his view and the challenge that is posed by his theory of historical entitlement.

*Law, Columbia University*

# Part III
# Abortion

# [7]

# THE PRIZE AND THE PRICE OF INDIVIDUAL AGENCY: ANOTHER PERSPECTIVE ON ABORTION AND LIBERAL GOVERNMENT*

*Kimberly Sharron Dunn*

In the wake of the recent Supreme Court decision in *Webster v. Reproductive Health Services,*[1] Americans likely face yet another prolonged political clash over the abortion issue. The dilemmas raised by unwanted pregnancies involve fundamental questions about the nature of American government and society, questions which the Supreme Court, state legislatures, and voters must again address. For example, what are the goals of the United States as a political community? What is the status of an individual in that community? What kinds of harm must the law prevent? And who may define a "harm"? With an eye to the political upheaval[2] surrounding the Supreme Court's recent abortion decision, this Note revisits the question whether political power should be used to prevent abortion.

---

* This Note follows a year and a half of serious study and several revolutions in my thinking about abortion and government. I spent the spring of 1989 involved in the Duke Students For Life, a pro-life group. My first paper, "Abortion and the Sovereignty of the People," took the extreme position that all fundamental rights derive from super-majority consent, and that no right, including the professed right to abortion, will be protected as fundamental until that consent is secured. The paper is published as a runnerup essay in the Sidney Lewine Essay Contest in HEALTH MATRIX, Summer 1989, at 53. After educating myself about natural rights philosophy and the United States' tradition of judicial review, I wrote a second paper, "The Responsibilities of Government Regarding Abortion," for Professors Ruth Grant and John Aldrich at Duke University. Relying on John Locke's theory of government as Judge when individual shortsightedness and partiality prevent just individual judgments, I took the position in that paper that government must ensure due weight is given to the fetus' life when abortion is considered—"due weight" meaning that abortion usually is not justified and usually should not be allowed. Still uncomfortable with advocating the use of coercive political power on the question, I delved further and came to the position presented in this Note.

1. 109 S. Ct. 3040 (1989) (Missouri's prohibition on use of public facilities or employees for abortion upheld; test for viability requirement also upheld). The opinions of both Justice Blackmun, dissenting, and Justice O' Connor, concurring, foreshadow the continued debate on abortion. Justice Blackmun says: "For today, the women of this Nation still retain the liberty to control their destinies. But the signs are evident and very ominous, and a chill wind blows." *Id.* at 3079 (Blackmun, J., dissenting). Justice O'Connor explains her limited concurrence saying, "[T]here will be time enough to reexamine *Roe.* And to do so carefully." *Id.* at 3061 (O'Connor, J., concurring).

2. *See* Ted Gest, *The Abortion Furor,* U.S. News & World Report, July 17, 1989, at 18; Merrill McLoughlin, *America's New Civil War,* U.S. News & World Report, Oct. 3, 1988, at 23.

Pro-life activists make the critical assumption that a fetus is a developing human life and, therefore, attempts to destroy it ought to be forcefully prevented.[3] Pro-choice activists make the equally critical, contrary assumption that *even if* a fetus is a developing human life, the political community should not value it the same as a born human being for purposes of forceful protection.[4] Although this fundamental conflict cannot be resolved through a single point of view, both sides of the debate could benefit by considering more seriously the methods and purposes of moral and political power.[5] Sensitivity to the difference between moral and political power may lead to more common ground than has appeared possible in the past—even, perhaps, to the opportunity for a peaceful political consensus in the face of deep moral disagreements.

This Note addresses the difference between moral and political power primarily from the vantage point of political theory. The Note maintains that the decision to have an abortion is an immoral rejection of a voluntarily acquired responsibility to nourish the fetus, and that abortions should be opposed with all the methods of moral power. ("Voluntarily acquired" excludes a pregnancy resulting from rape or incest.) However, because of the importance of moral and religious commitments in the perception of a responsibility to nourish the fetus, individuals should not be coerced by political power to fulfill that responsibility.

For purposes of this Note, "political power" includes the use of physical and economic punishments or constraints to coerce conduct.[6] "Moral power" operates by example, reasoning and persuasion but leaves

---

3. Bernard Nathanson, Aborting America 259-60 (1979); McLoughlin, *supra* note 2, at 27; Mary Meehan, *More Trouble Than They're Worth? Children and Abortion*, in Abortion: Understanding Differences 145, 146-48 (S. Callahan & D. Callahan eds. 1984).

4. Kristin Luker, *Abortion and the Meaning of Life*, in Abortion: Understanding Differences, *supra* note 3, at 25, 42; McLoughlin, *supra* note 2, at 25, 27.

For the purposes of this Note, I compare only two categories of human life—fetuses and born human beings. I do not discuss the important question at what point from conception to birth government should begin protecting life with political power. The Supreme Court presently allows, but does not require, coercive protection of fetal life after the point of viability when the fetus "presumably has the capability of meaningful life outside the mother's womb." Roe v. Wade, 410 U.S. 113, 163 (1973).

5. The idea that the legality and morality of abortion are distinct issues is an argument usually made to support a pro-choice political position in combination with varying degrees of moral condemnation of abortion. *See* Rosalind Petchesky, Abortion and Woman's Choice: The State, Sexuality, and Reproductive Freedom 348-49 (1985) ("[W]e need to distinguish between the *political question*—who should decide—and the *moral question*—whether abortion is right or wrong in a given instance."); Mary Mahowald, *Abortion and Equality*, in Abortion: Understanding Differences, *supra* note 3, at 177, 178 (noting that some "approve of the legality but not the morality of abortion"); Mary Segers, *Abortion and the Culture: Toward a Feminist Perspective*, in *id.* at 229, 233 ("fact that abortion is legal is not held to be conclusive of its morality").

6. John Locke contemplated a similar meaning of political power in his Second Treatise of Government § 3 (C. Macpherson ed. 1980): "*Political power*, then, I take to be a *right* of making

individuals free to act according to their own choices. "Political community" is a community that maintains its bonds by political power and consequently serves a limited purpose among the people or society generally.[7] "Society" includes the political community as well as communities bound together by common interests and commitments not appropriately coerced by political power. "Individual agency," or "individual liberty," refers to the right of individuals to govern themselves—to be the final judges of when and how to act on a particular matter.

Part I of this Note explores the capacity for individual agency as the foundation for the separation of moral and political power.[8] The first Part concludes, as did the Framers of the Constitution, that existence of this capacity requires respect for individual agency, even if many individuals do not use their liberty to develop morally good actions and attitudes.[9] Proper respect for individual agency sometimes requires restraint in the use of political power in favor of moral power.

The Note emphasizes that the goal of moral power need not be moral relativity or appreciation for diversity on all matters calling for political restraint. One can distinguish meaningfully between right and wrong on issues such as abortion, while recognizing that the responsibility to do right, and the responsibility for both personal and social consequences of right or wrong conduct, lies with the individual.[10]

Part II discusses the difficulty of judging whether moral or political power should be used to enforce right conduct on the abortion issue. The desire to protect the fetus and to maintain consistency in the political community's treatment of human life leads to the conclusion that political power should be used. However, the importance of individual religious and moral commitments in valuing the fetus relative to other values implies that moral power, not political power, should be used.[11] Further, because forbidding abortion does much more than prevent harm—it also coerces substantial sacrifices from pregnant women— the use of moral power is more appropriate than the use of political power.[12] Finally, the Note argues that full individual responsibility for family and sexual relations requires the exclusive use of moral power, although al-

laws with penalties of death, and consequently all less penalties . . . and of employing the force of the community . . . and all this only for the public good."

7. Locke articulates this meaning of political community. *Id.* §§ 126-31; *see also* Ruth Grant, *Locke's Political Anthropology and Lockean Individualism*, 50 J. OF POLITICS 42, 51 (1988).

8. *See infra* notes 18-23 and accompanying text.

9. *See infra* notes 24-45 and accompanying text.

10. *See infra* notes 46-65 and accompanying text.

11. *See infra* notes 66-106 and accompanying text.

12. *See infra* notes 107-16 and accompanying text.

lowing for individual responsibility on the abortion question also allows some adults to settle for less in their moral commitments.[13]

Since *Roe v. Wade,* state legislatures have not been allowed to use political power to coerce individuals in the abortion decision. In *Roe,* the Supreme Court determined that pregnant women, in consultation with their doctors, should be the final judges of how to act when faced with an unwanted pregnancy.[14] State legislatures cannot infringe individual agency[15] on the question until a fetus is viable, although a state can regulate the abortion procedure in the interest of the mother's health prior to viability.[16]

In a recent case, *Webster v. Reproductive Health Services,* several Justices—namely Chief Justice Rehnquist and Justices White, Kennedy, and Scalia—express discomfort with the level of protection *Roe* grants to individual agency at the expense of the democratic process.[17] Although they would not prevent a state from protecting individual agency on the abortion question, they also would not prevent a state from protecting fetal life with political power, at the expense of individual agency. These Justices believe that the values of life and liberty at stake in the abortion dilemma should be balanced in the democratic process. A legislative majority should decide which value is paramount and to what extent.

Most of this Note advocates a negative answer to the question whether political power should be used to prevent abortion, without suggesting which government institution should answer that question. The discussion about the use of political power applies to state legislatures as much as to the Supreme Court. However, the Note's conclusion briefly

---

13. *See infra* notes 117-26 and accompanying text.

14. 410 U.S. 113, 163 (1973).

15. The Supreme Court uses the label "right of privacy" for what I refer to as individual agency.

> This right of privacy, whether it be founded in the Fourteenth Amendment's concept of personal liberty and restrictions upon state action, as we feel it is, or, as the District Court determined, in the Ninth Amendment's reservations of rights to the people, is broad enough to encompass a woman's decision whether or not to terminate her pregnancy.

*Id.* at 153. *But see* John Hart Ely, *The Wages of Crying Wolf: A Comment on* Roe v. Wade, 82 YALE L.J. 920, 932 (1973) ("I suppose there is nothing to prevent one from using the word 'privacy' to mean the freedom to live one's life without governmental interference. But the Court obviously does not so use the term.").

16. *Roe,* 410 U.S. at 163.

17. Chief Justice Rehnquist, joined by Justices White and Kennedy, writes for the plurality: "[T]he goal of constitutional adjudication is surely not to remove inexorably 'politically divisive' issues from the ambit of the legislative process, whereby the people through their elected representatives deal with matters of concern to them." Webster v. Reproductive Health Servs., 109 S. Ct. 3040, 3058 (1989). Justice Scalia expresses the same concern more directly in a separate concurrence: "[O]ur retaining control, through *Roe,* of what I believe to be, and many of our citizens recognize to be, a political issue, continuously distorts the public perception of the role of this Court." *Id.* at 3065. Despite the overtures, *Webster* does not expressly overrule *Roe. Id.* at 3058.

addresses the debate revived in *Webster*: Whether state legislatures or the Supreme Court should set the bounds of political power on the abortion question. Although state legislatures should endeavor to avoid illegitimately infringing individual liberty, their actions are properly reviewable by the Supreme Court under the fourteenth amendment. Indeed, the Supreme Court has assumed responsibility since the passage of the fourteenth amendment, by virtue of the characteristics and powers granted it in the Constitution and in the tradition of judicial review, to prevent state governments from unduly infringing individual liberty. Although the Note suggests some improvements for the analysis in *Roe v. Wade*, it concludes that the Supreme Court's decision in that landmark case is consistent with the principles supporting our form of government: respect for individual agency and unwillingness to coerce more than a minimum level of morally good behavior.

The Note does not address the many other abortion-related dilemmas that state legislatures and the Supreme Court have faced and will yet face: Whether public funds, employees, or facilities acquired in part from persons deeply opposed to abortion can be used to fund abortions; whether notice of intent to abort must be given to fathers of the fetus; whether notice must be given to parents of pregnant minors; which regulations of the abortion procedure exceed a state's powers; and whether and to what extent the law should require pregnant women to refrain from drugs and alcohol that harm fetal development. All these issues require separate consideration of the purposes and powers of government in their resolution and are beyond the scope of this Note.

## I. The Separation of Moral and Political Power

### A. *Foundation for the Separation: The Capacity for Individual Agency*

If forcing moral conduct would assure right conduct[18] and still allow individuals to develop a sense of responsibility, society would lose nothing by forcing moral conduct. In fact, society would gain. Rather than a world where some do right and some do wrong, with varying degrees of aspiration to do right or wrong, we would have a world where almost all do right. Aristotle saw this potential and argued that compelling the young to do good would allow some individuals to develop good habits as they mature. Continuing that compulsion into adulthood

18. I am aware of the difficulty of establishing a consensus on what is "right conduct." For purposes of this Part, I am speaking to the individual reader as if we all agreed with her or his judgments of right and wrong to whatever extent she or he makes those judgments.

would not burden them and would control the unruly at the same time. Aristotle writes:

> For most people are swayed rather by compulsion than argument, and by punishments rather than by *a sense of* what is noble. This is why some believe that lawgivers ought to exhort and try to influence people toward *a life of* virtue because of its inherent nobility, in the hope that those who have made good progress through their habits will listen to them. Chastisement and penalties, they think, should be imposed upon those who do not obey and are of an inferior nature, while the incorrigible ought to be banished abroad.[19]

While many may object to Aristotle's proposal, few would contend that his description of human nature is wholly inaccurate. Punishments often do sway individuals more than a sense of what is noble. However, the important question remains whether some individuals fail to respond to what is noble because of an "inferior nature" (bestowed by bad genes or improper education)— that is, whether they are *incapable* of so responding—or because, for a variety of reasons, none of which absolves them of final responsibility, they do not develop the moral capacities possessed by normal, adult human beings.[20] If the former is true, requiring those adults with an inferior nature to govern their lives without the compulsion of external penalties is neither sensible nor kind. However, if the latter is true of adults, then force generally will not encourage the development of desirable attitudes and behavior. Force under such circumstances will do about as much good as moving another's limbs in an attempt to strengthen their muscles for them. Therefore, knowing if all normal adults have the capacity for responsible moral behavior, like knowing if a person has muscles, helps determine whether one encourages others to flex (uses moral power or persuasion) or does all the pulling herself (uses political power or coercion).[21]

19. ARISTOTLE, NICOMACHEAN ETHICS 296-97 (M. Osdwald trans. 1962); *see* Martin Diamond, *Ethics and Politics: The American Way*, in THE MORAL FOUNDATIONS OF THE AMERICAN REPUBLIC 75, 80-81 (R. Horwitz 3d ed. 1986) ("Human character, Aristotle argues, can be perfected only within . . . the political community, and through what it alone can supply, namely, good laws 'with teeth in them' . . . .").

20. By "normal, adult human being," I mean a not mentally retarded or otherwise severely mentally handicapped adult human being. Although adverse life circumstances will make the lack of moral behavior in normal adults more understandable, under a liberal theory of human nature nothing can deprive individuals of ultimate responsibility for a lack of wisdom, self control, and love.

21. Professor Ruth Grant points out in her book, JOHN LOCKE'S LIBERALISM 205 (1987), that "[a] just estimation of men's capacities must be the foundation for any theoretical effort that hopes to offer men practical guidance in managing the political problem." She thoroughly discusses John Locke's estimation of humankind's capacity to reason and its implications for the possibility of political theory as well as for individual agency. *Id.* at 12-51.

Whether individuals use individual agency in a manner compatible with others in the community, and whether they develop themselves well or poorly, are questions that differ from the question whether they have the capacity to do so. If they have the capacity, political power can alleviate and prevent damage from severely antisocial behavior, but only moral persuasion can alleviate or prevent damage from undeveloped abilities and lack of goodness.[22] Adverse life circumstances may make failures more understandable, but an adult individual ultimately cannot blame anyone or anything for immoral behavior under a liberal theory of human nature: Human beings are capable and therefore must be free and responsible. The prize of individual liberty is that some individuals will develop their moral capacities in difficult or relatively congenial circumstances, including their capacity for wisdom, care, and responsibility for their own and others' welfare. These individuals will feel and act responsibly to an extent that would not be possible without individual liberty. The price of individual liberty is that some individuals, out of bitterness, fear, ignorance, or love of other things, will not develop their moral capacities and will behave in self-aggrandizing or hurtful ways. The prize cannot be had without the price.[23] We may have morally right conduct without individual liberty, but not morally responsible human beings.

No one can prove empirically that individuals who abuse their own freedom of action by damaging themselves and others (in ways that political power may or may not alleviate) are capable of doing better. To assume that they do, contrary to Aristotle, is an experiment of faith in humankind. However, observation, introspection, and experience does give confidence in this assumption and supports the decision to respect individual agency with both its prize and its price.

Recognizing and accepting the price of individual agency should not invite feelings of superiority, separation, or contempt toward others. We owe to each other commitment, comfort, and patience, however undeserving of them we sometimes may be, as well as an occasional thought-

22. *See infra* notes 46-65 and accompanying text (discussing the different purposes of moral and political power). Mill writes, "It is not because men's desires are strong that they are ill; it is because their consciences are weak." JOHN STUART MILL, *On Liberty*, in UTILITARIANISM, ON LIBERTY AND CONSIDERATIONS ON REPRESENTATIVE GOVERNMENT 69, 127 (H. Arton ed. 1972).

23. *See* Robert Goldwin, *Of Men and Angels: A Search for Morality in the Constitution*, in THE MORAL FOUNDATIONS OF THE AMERICAN REPUBLIC, *supra* note 19, at 35 ("The morality most appropriate to the American way . . . is a morality that is moderate, that does not crusade, that accepts the fact that among human beings who are free there will be abuses . . . .").

ful rebuke. This moral duty arises from our equal worth, and our potential for developing voluntary moral behavior.[24]

### B. *The Separation of Moral and Political Power in the Founding of the United States*

In contrast to Aristotle, the original thirteen colonies based the legitimacy of their revolution partly on a belief, taken from John Locke's political philosophy, that when political power inappropriately intrudes on individual liberty the people have the right to abolish it.

> We hold these truths to be self-evident: that all men are created equal; that they are endowed by their Creator with certain unalienable rights; that among these are life, liberty, and the pursuit of happiness. That, to secure these rights, governments are instituted among men, deriving their just powers from the consent of the governed. That, whenever any form of government becomes destructive of these ends, it is the right of the people to alter or abolish it and to institute new government . . . .[25]

Obviously, "created equal" does not mean "created the same" in interest or ability. When discussing the cause of factions in society while defending the government described by the Constitution, James Madison expressly noted the varying interests and abilities among persons: "The diversity in the faculties of men, from which the rights of property originate, is not less an insuperable obstacle to a uniformity of interests. The protection of these faculties is the first object of government."[26] Rather, "equal" means equal in the possession of faculties suited to individual agency in ordering individual lives.

No matter how much individuals differ in interest and ability,[27] they do not differ so much that as a general matter some are able to exercise individual agency whereas others are not. As Locke emphasizes in his political theory, the most important implication of this assumption for

24. *See* J.S. MILL, *supra* note 22, at 144 ("Human beings owe to each other help to distinguish the better from the worse, and encouragement to choose the former and avoid the latter."). In contrast with my position, Mill does allow for separation from and expressions of contempt toward others. *Id.* at 146.

25. The Declaration of Independence para. 2 (U.S. 1776). Professor Mary Ann Glendon compares the American emphasis on individual rights and equality with the European leanings toward social responsibility and moral education in the civil law. Professor Glendon believes Americans have neglected the educational power of the law—that we need to incorporate more of Aristotle's vision into our lawmaking because "law is, among other things, the art of pursuing dignified living, of establishing meaning and constituting community . . . ." MARY ANN GLENDON, ABORTION AND DIVORCE IN WESTERN LAW 142 (1987).

26. THE FEDERALIST NO. 10, at 78 (J. Madison) (C. Rossiter ed. 1961).

27. Diamond, *supra* note 19, at 103 ("But the American political order nonetheless still presupposed that an inequality of virtues and abilities was rooted in human nature and that this inequality would manifest itself and flourish in the private realm of society.").

political government is that no one, however superior in intelligence, can claim a right to govern others without their consent.[28] Locke writes:

> To understand political power right, and derive it from its original, we must consider, what state all men are naturally in, and that is, a *state of perfect freedom* to order their actions, and dispose of their possessions and persons, as they think fit, within the bounds of the law of nature, without asking leave, or depending upon the will of any other man.
>
> A *state* also *of equality*, wherein all power and jurisdiction is reciprocal, no one having more than another; there being nothing more evident, than that creatures of the same species and rank, promiscuously born to all the same advantages of nature, and the use of the same faculties, should also be equal one amongst another without subordination or subjection . . . .[29]

Justice Douglas, concurring in *Roe v. Wade*, articulates the same principle of individual liberty, or individual agency, using the language of "privacy:"

> That right [of privacy] includes the privilege of an individual to plan his own affairs, for, "outside areas of plainly harmful conduct, every American is left to shape his own life as he thinks best, do what he pleases, go where he pleases."[30]

The government described in the United States Constitution rests not only on the assumption of equality in the possession of capacities suited to individual agency but also, as Madison suggests in the following example, on the fact that many individuals do not develop their capacity for morally good behavior:

---

28. Walter Berns, *Religion and the Founding Principle*, in THE MORAL FOUNDATIONS OF THE AMERICAN REPUBLIC, *supra* note 19, at 218 ("Being free and equal with respect to natural right, and however unequal they may be according to any religious doctrine or in any other respect, no man may justly rule another without his consent . . . ."); Diamond, *supra* note 19, at 103 ("American democracy . . . denied the ancient claim of excellence to *rule as a matter of right*. Now this denial is of immense importance because, in contrast with the ancient justification of the political claims of the few, it deeply popularizes the very foundation of political life.").

John Locke's liberalism envisions consent to any form of government, such as a democracy, oligarchy, or even an hereditary monarchy, that preserves the life, liberty, and property of individuals as all the natural equality of humankind requires. J. LOCKE, *supra* note 6, §§ 132-33; *see also* R. GRANT, *supra* note 21, at 123-36 (discussing the practical problem of knowing when individuals have consented to the form of government and knowing the extent of their obligation to obey once consent is secure). He does, however, proceed to recommend the separation of powers in a "well-ordered commonwealth," J. LOCKE, *supra* note 6, §§ 143-48, and to discuss principles of "fair and equal representation," *id.* §§ 157-58. He also emphasizes the residual right of the people to alter "the legislative" if the government violates their natural rights. *Id.* § 149.

29. J. LOCKE, *supra* note 6, § 4 (emphasis in original).

30. Doe v. Bolton, 410 U.S. 179, 213 (1973) (Douglas, J., concurring) (quoting Kent v. Dulles, 357 U.S. 116, 126 (1958) (holding that Secretary of State's denial of passports to persons associated with the Communist party without explicit authorization from Congress is due process violation)); *see supra* note 15.

> A zeal for different opinions concerning religion, concerning government, and many other points, as well of speculation as of practice . . . have, in turn, divided mankind into parties, inflamed them with mutual animosity, and rendered them much more disposed to vex and oppress each other than to co-operate for their common good.[31]

The debates in the Constitutional Convention of 1787 about almost every issue in the proposed Constitution reflected concern for the best way to prevent tyranny (or protect individual agency and representative democracy) and avoid anarchy (or avoid widespread abuse of individual agency uncontrolled by organized political power).[32] The government needed to be organized to protect itself and its citizens from animosity, selfishness, and abuse of power—inevitable consequences of individual liberty—without imperiling responsible care for others and the wise exercise of power—also impossible without individual liberty.

Because the government is founded on the principle that "[a]mbition must be made to counteract ambition"[33] rather than on principles that depend on public virtue in our leaders, some people have accused the United States of moral purposelessness. Professor Benjamin Barber writes, "The republic worked because it never tried to contrive a center; and thus, by eliciting the assent of the citizenry to this value default, acquired a center after all—in the acquiescence of the people to purposelessness."[34] The Anti-Federalists argued during the debates over ratification of the Constitution that the large republic created by the Constitution "dangerously ignored" the cultivation of virtue essential to the maintenance of liberty, which was only possible in smaller, homoge-

31. THE FEDERALIST NO. 10, at 79 (J. Madison) (C. Rossiter ed. 1961).

32. Examples of the delegates' pervasive awareness of the tyranny/liberty tension include: the first resolution in the Virginia Plan as proposed to the Convention—"Resolved that the Articles of Confederation ought to be so corrected and enlarged as to accomplish . . . 'common defense, security of liberty and general welfare,' " JAMES MADISON, NOTES OF DEBATES IN THE FEDERAL CONVENTION OF 1787, at 30 (A. Koch ed. 1987); the debate whether unity in the executive would lead to or protect against tyranny, *id.* at 46-47; Benjamin Franklin's warning of the need to guard against the "two passions which have a powerful influence on the affairs of men," the love of power and money, *id.* at 52; Mr. Sherman's argument against the executive veto "enabling any one man to stop the will of the whole. No one man could be found so far above all the rest in wisdom," *id.* at 62; and the observation that "[n]otwithstanding the oppressions and injustice experienced among us from democracy; the genius of the people is in favor of it, and the genius of the people must be consulted," *id.* at 64. *See also* THE FEDERALIST NO. 37, at 227 (J. Madison) (C. Rossiter ed. 1961).

33. THE FEDERALIST NO. 51, at 322 (J. Madison) (C. Rossiter ed. 1961). Madison says that "government itself [is] the greatest of all reflections on human nature" and if "men were angels, no government would be necessary." *Id.*

34. Benjamin Barber, *The Compromised Republic: Public Purposelessness in America*, in THE MORAL FOUNDATIONS OF THE AMERICAN REPUBLIC, *supra* note 19, at 53; *cf.* Joseph Cropsey, *The United States as Regime and the Sources of the American Way of Life*, in *id.*, at 172 (Thus far, there is "[n]o mitigation of modern man's dissatisfaction with the absence of any exaltation, vivacity or high-heartedness from official political modernity as laid down by Hobbes and Locke and, incidentally, embodied in our parchment regime . . . .").

nous, agrarian communities.[35] And Alexis de Tocqueville warns against the tendency toward materialistic individualism at the expense of generosity in the United States:

> Men living in democratic times have many passions, but most of their passions either end in the love of riches or proceed from it. . . . When all the members of a community are independent of or indifferent to each other, the co-operation of each of them can be obtained only by paying for it . . . .[36]

From a perspective that suffers the price of individual liberty by allowing morally wrong conduct, the U.S. political project does have lower sights than did Aristotle, who believed that "laws can make us good."[37] Ideally, government in the United States does not use political power to force a high level of moral virtue—only the minimum necessary for peaceful coexistence.[38] However, from a perspective that emphasizes the prize of individual liberty—responsible, wise, and caring individuals—the U.S. political project aims higher than did Aristotle. Our society is simply not satisfied with right conduct on many matters. We want *individually chosen* right conduct, or moral goodness.[39] As Professor Martin Diamond describes it, "the explanation of the puzzling American discrepancy—character formation, but not by use of the laws— will be found . . . in the American idea of what is advantageous and right for humans."[40] He further suggests that the founders were confident that at

---

35. HERBERT STORING, WHAT THE ANTI-FEDERALISTS WERE FOR 19-21 (1981); Robert Horwitz, *John Locke and the Preservation of Liberty: A Perennial Problem of Civic Education*, in THE MORAL FOUNDATIONS OF THE AMERICAN REPUBLIC, *supra* note 19, at 138.

36. 2 ALEXIS DE TOCQUEVILLE, DEMOCRACY IN AMERICA bk. 3, ch. XVII, at 228 (H. Reeve trans., P. Bradley ed. 1946); *see also* Cropsey, *supra* note 34, at 174 ("We are dissatisfied with ourselves because our regime and life are marked by private striving for the satisfaction of individual goals rather than seeking to attain our individual ends through the mediation of a perfectly social act of provision.").

37. ARISTOTLE, *supra* note 19, at 299.

38. Diamond, *supra* note 19, at 83 ("In place of the utopian end postulated by the ancients, the forced elevation of human character, the moderns substituted a lowered political end, namely, human comfort and security."); Richard Hofstadter, *The Founding Fathers: An Age of Realism*, in THE MORAL FOUNDATIONS OF THE AMERICAN REPUBLIC, *supra* note 19, at 65 ("One thing that the Fathers did not propose to do, because they thought it impossible, was to change the nature of man to conform with a more ideal system.").

For a discussion of harms the U.S. government does and does not alleviate or prevent with political power, see *infra* notes 68-72, 107-11 and accompanying text. For examples of arguable violations of the principle that government will not employ political power to force moral goodness, see *infra* notes 59-61 and accompanying text (discussing religion and politics, the prohibition amendment, and the recent efforts to prohibit flag-burning) and Bowers v. Hardwick, 478 U.S. 186 (1986) (holding that states may criminalize consensual homosexual sodomy).

39. *See* H.L.A. HART, LAW, LIBERTY, AND MORALITY 58 (1963) ("[W]hat is valuable here [in the domain of morality] is *voluntary* restraint, not submission to coercion, which seems quite empty of moral value.").

40. Diamond, *supra* note 19, at 105.

least among some people, "the full range of the higher human virtues would have suitable opportunity to flourish . . . from religion, education, family upbringing, and simply out of the natural yearnings of human nature."[41]

Further, the U.S. political project aims higher than any other modern form of government in the possibility for good community, despite the fact that the critics of liberal government often mistake individual agency for selfish individualism. Professor Lisa Cahill writes:

> In such [liberal] views, persons are seen essentially as free and autonomous agents who come into society to protect self-interest by a series of mutually advantageous agreements. Society or community is thus secondary to the existence of the individual; persons are not social by nature and have no natural obligations antecedent to their free consent.[42]

Professor Ruth Grant argues to the contrary:

> The opposite of Locke's political individualism, however, is not community, but hierarchy. He is opposing the equality and freedom of men to the idea that there is a natural or divinely ordained hierarchy among them. Lockean individualism therefore is not incompatible with the recognition of the importance of communal ties, family associations, and social norms, though it is a critique of authoritarian political communities.[43]

An autonomous individual need not give priority to individual values above community values, although he or she certainly is free to do so. The significance of autonomy is that all individuals, although influenced by their social environment, have the imagination and ability to choose what to value, including community, free of political coercion. People are ultimately responsible for what they do and do not become, individually and collectively, as a result of their choice of values.

With politically guaranteed freedom of religion, speech, press, and association, the United States is the best possible environment for the

41. *Id.* at 107.

42. Lisa Cahill, *Abortion, Autonomy, and Community*, in ABORTION: UNDERSTANDING DIFFERENCES, *supra* note 3, at 261, 266; *see also* Rosanne Kennedy, Feminist Legal Theory: Changing the Subject, at 2 n.5 (1989) (unpublished manuscript available from the author) ("The autonomous individual who gives priority to individual over community values is often called 'the liberal self.' "). Professor Ruth Grant, in her article, *Locke's Political Anthropology and Lockean Individualism*, *supra* note 7, at 43 n.2, lists other sources that reflect a similar interpretation of Lockean individualism.

43. Grant, *supra* note 7, at 51. Professor Grant writes further:

> My purpose is to show that at least one classical liberal [Locke] recognized fully the extent to which human beings are social beings, but did not believe that that fact dictated any particular political conclusions. . . . The challenge to the communitarians is to show either that a communitarianism that attacks liberal individualism can nonetheless produce nonauthoritarian communities, or that, if it can't, community is worth the price.

*Id.* at 43, 61 (footnote omitted).

development of wise, responsible, and caring individuals and communities.[44] If Americans fail in this opportunity, they fail not from insufficient use of political power, but rather from insufficient use of moral power and from an inability to reach a voluntary consensus on moral dilemmas, not from moral purposelessness in their government.[45]

### C. *The Different Methods and Purposes of Moral and Political Power*

1. *Political Power Can Stifle Individual Responsibility and Development.* Separating moral and political power and distinguishing the purposes of each, although the purposes sometimes overlap, rests on the assumption that normal, adult human beings are capable of moral responsibility that cannot be coerced; indeed, coercion on some matters stifles the development of responsibility. Beliefs regarding religious matters and commitments to morally good behavior such as generosity, honesty, and kindness provide examples of attitudes and behavior that do not develop as a result of the use of force. Although "right conduct" in some instances can be forced, the inner commitment that makes moral action meaningful must come from individual, voluntary affirmation.

Coercing adults who will not make morally good choices through their individual agency into making better choices usually does not make them morally good people. Rather, the coercion often drives them to rebel against the coercion, or submit without assuming any responsibility for the coerced action.[46] In either case, their judgment has not improved, and their inner commitment to the better choice has not been secured. John Locke's description of the inability to secure worthwhile religious commitment through coercion illustrates this point:

> [T]rue and saving Religion consists in the inward persuasion of the Mind, without which nothing can be acceptable to God. . . . [A]nd Penalties in this case are absolutely impertinent; because they are not proper to convince the mind. . . . It is only Light and Evidence that can work a change in Mens Opinions; which Light can in no manner proceed from corporal Sufferings, or any other outward Penalties. . . .

44. I write this with confidence and hope as a member of a community aspiring to those ideals—the Church of Jesus Christ of Latter-Day Saints (the Mormons). Although we have our difficulties, as does any community of free agents, I honor my fellow latter-day saints for the depth of their commitment to the complete well-being of others as well as themselves. My respect for the organization, composed of persons of widely-varying interests and abilities, has grown tremendously as I have participated with them in California, Washington, Utah, and North Carolina.

45. *See* text accompanying note 34. Robert Goldwin writes, "And that conviction, that we are truly a moral nation of moral men and moral women, is essential to our survival and happiness, because of the way we are constituted." Goldwin, *supra* note 23, at 39.

46. *Cf.* H.L.A. HART, *supra* note 39, at 21-22 ("The second aspect of legal enforcement bears on those who may never offend against the law, but are coerced into obedience by the threat of legal punishment. . . . [I]nterference with individual liberty . . . is itself the infliction of a special form of suffering—often very acute—on those whose desires are frustrated by the fear of punishment.").

> [M]en cannot be forced to be saved whether they will or no. And therefore, when all is done, they must be left to their own Consciences.[47]

Laws that extend too far into the domain of individual agency also deprive adults who would use agency to make morally good choices of the need to explore different possibilities and thereby develop good judgment. The fit of the laws with their natural inclinations and the ease of following without thinking deeply or discovering why can discourage growth. John Stuart Mill thoroughly discusses this observation in his essay, *On Liberty*:

> He who chooses his plan for himself, employs all his faculties. He must use observation to see, reasoning and judgment to foresee, activity to gather materials for decision, discrimination to decide, and when he has decided, firmness and self-control to hold to his deliberate decision . . . . It is possible that he might be guided in some good path, and kept out of harm's way, without any of these things. But what will be his comparative worth as a human being? It really is of importance, not only what men do, but also what manner of men they are that do it.[48]

Sometimes governments should refrain from using political power to force decisions on individuals when the state lacks confidence in the universality of the answers, but that is not the only occasion. Sometimes the state should refrain because the decisions require voluntary affirmation to be meaningful. When "right" entails individual commitments to concern for others or deference to God, for example, people cannot be forced to assume these commitments.[49] The individual, not family members, communities, or governments, should answer questions that require such commitments because the *most important* consequence in answering them, among other consequences, is an individual's acceptance or rejection of deeply binding obligations.[50]

2. *Moral Right Without Political Enforcement.* Refraining from the use of political power to force moral behavior does not always entail abandoning the truth of the moral principles. On some matters left to individual agency, such as career interests or musical tastes, appreciation for diversity is a good in itself.[51] On other matters, pluralism may not be

47. JOHN LOCKE, A LETTER CONCERNING TOLERATION 27, 38 (J. Tully ed. 1983).

48. J.S. MILL, *supra* note 22, at 127; *see also* R. GRANT, *supra* note 21, at 194 ("And to be truly free, he must be guided by his own reason. It is not enough to do the reasonable thing. A man must have reached the conclusion on his own that it is the reasonable thing to do.").

49. J.S. MILL, *supra* note 22, at 85, 134-35.

50. *See id.* at 151.

51. Mill distinguishes between moral and political power in the project of making human beings good, but also carves out a large domain of individual agency that should not be disturbed by coercion *or* moral condemnation. J.S. MILL, *supra* note 22, at 123-42.

the highest good. Professor Robert Goldwin writes: "[T]he first step [in practical or political morality] is to make the moral judgment, to recognize evil as evil, and not look the other way, or refuse to judge (on relativistic grounds), or shrug our shoulders and say we 'don't care.' "[52]

The variety of opinions notwithstanding, a person can believe in right and wrong answers to moral questions, including the question whether or not to abort a fetus. Individuals may struggle to discover the right answers since no moral code can account for all the variations in real circumstances, and they may struggle even more to adhere to the answers they have discovered.[53] However, this observation need not dissolve one's thinking into "ethical relativism," if that term means that whatever individuals may choose for themselves is right because of the struggle involved in choosing.[54]

Feminist scholar and theorist Rosalind Petchesky mistakes the moral position that abortion is wrong for a denial of individual responsibility on the abortion issue:

---

52. Goldwin, *supra* note 23, at 36. The second step is to decide whether to use moral or political power to address the evil. *See id.* Professor Gordon Wood expresses the hope of some of the Founders that the diversity of opinions colliding freely in society would lead to "the ultimate triumph of Truth." Wood, *The Democratization of Mind in the American Revolution*, in THE MORAL FOUNDATIONS OF THE AMERICAN REPUBLIC, *supra* note 19, at 133.

Rosalind Petchesky warns against the dangers of absolutism and states that it is "false to link *relativism* irrevocably with *amorality.*" R. PETCHESKY, *supra* note 5, at 329. She suggests that all "moral, legal, and philosophical questions" are subject to "historical and cultural variations." *Id.* While there is room to learn restraint and appreciation for context from her without abandoning moral truth on some matters, she ultimately disagrees that abortion is one of those matters. *Id.* at 366-67, 374.

53. R. GRANT, *supra* note 21, at 180 ("We cannot know all things with certainty, and the principles that we can know do not automatically govern our behavior."); *see* Petchesky, *supra* note 5, at 365 (citing recent attitude surveys showing the disjunction between abortion beliefs and practices).

54. *See* Segers, *supra* note 5, at 251-52 ("A commitment to the availability of legalized abortion need not bind one to a kind of casual ethical relativism. . . . I believe that feminists can and should define the moral standards and principles against which to measure our behavior with respect to abortion.").

Rosalind Petchesky describes the "morality of praxis" in her book, ABORTION AND WOMAN'S CHOICE: THE STATE, SEXUALITY, AND REPRODUCTIVE FREEDOM, *supra* note 5, at 364-74. A popular way of expressing the extreme form of the "morality of praxis," or contextual morality, on the abortion issue is that every individual must exercise moral judgment about abortion, but no one can tell another individual that their decision is right or wrong. *Id.* at 333 (quoting a Baptist clergyman) ("Abortion presents a matter for individual moral decision . . . ."); *see also* Luker, *supra* note 4, at 44 ("[P]ro-choice people tend to see ethical issues as matters of individual conscience, guided by moral principles, rather than as moral codes *per se.* Hence, the emphasis that pro-choice people put on abortion as an *individual, private* choice."); McLoughlin, *supra* note 2, at 29 ("It's a permanent decision . . . . I don't think that anyone has the right to say, 'You have to do it this way.' ").

Although she would never support references to general, categorical right and wrong, Rosalind Petchesky does recognize some limitation to private morality regarding abortion. For example, she writes that aborting "solely on the basis of gender preference" is "immoral." R. PETCHESKY, *supra* note 5, at 349.

> Abortion is wrong, in their view, not only because it "destroys innocent life," but even more because it rests on and validates a principle of morality that assumes that individuals must make choices for themselves and ought to do so in terms of the concrete situations in which they live.[55]

Not all pro-life individuals conclude that contextual morality is wrong as a matter of principle, although they conclude that aborting a fetus rarely is moral in any context. In the dilemmas people face every day, "right" and "wrong" are a function of a person's intentions, her judgments about how best to realize those intentions, and the effects of her resulting action on herself and others. Meaningful morality cannot be anything but contextual. Realizing this, family therapist Theodora Ooms aptly describes the difficulty of applying moral values to specific situations:

> Moral values—such as the need to preserve and protect life— are ideals to strive for. In concrete moral situations, they nearly always have to be weighed against other, conflicting moral values. They serve as principles to be applied differently to different situations, and the consequences of applying them also need to be taken into account.[56]

Although I agree with Ooms' assessment of the general difficulty, I do not share her view that the responsibility for beginning life and the moral claims of the fetus to continued life do not outweigh almost all other considerations. Some intentions and the means to accomplish them are universally better, in a moral sense, than others. I submit that accepting the possibility of pregnancy from heterosexual intimacy and determining to nurture the fetus should pregnancy occur is a better decision than engaging in sexual intimacy and then deciding to abort a fetus that may be conceived. Abortion is an immoral rejection of the mutual responsibilities of two individuals to a developing fetus, responsibilities that were voluntarily acquired.[57] I do not slight the gravity and difficulty of the struggle faced by women and men who deal with unwanted pregnancies, or the need to allow individuals to make their difficult choices free from political coercion, as discussed below. However, I contend that principles not appropriately enforced by political power may still be the right principles on which individuals should make their

55. R. PETCHESKY, *supra* note 5, at 379.

56. Theodora Ooms, *Commentary to Chapter 6*, in ABORTION: UNDERSTANDING DIFFERENCES, *supra* note 3, at 171, 172.

57. Unfortunately, the purpose of this Note will not allow a full defense of my moral position, but see *infra* text accompanying notes 97-99 for a slightly longer statement. Although she advocates coercive prevention of abortion, Mary Meehan provides a concise moral statement for valuing the fetus even in grave social, emotional, and financial circumstances, and even if the fetus is handicapped. Meehan, *supra* note 3, at 151-68.

choices regarding abortion. The individual and collective struggle to know and adhere to these principles is the domain of moral power.

Refraining from political coercion on moral questions should not also mean abandoning the public struggle over issues such as abortion. Moral power cannot operate properly, and individuals cannot develop fully, without using every channel available to persuade individuals to make right choices on moral issues, and this includes public speaking and writing. Mill offers insight concerning the importance of using persuasion as an aspect of moral power:

> In the case of any person whose judgment is really deserving of confidence, how has it become so? Because he has kept his mind open to criticism of his opinions and conduct. . . . No wise man ever acquired his wisdom in any mode but this; nor is it in the nature of human intellect to become wise in any other manner. . . . Instead of any diminution, there is need of a great increase of disinterested exertion to promote the good of others. But disinterested benevolence can find other instruments to persuade people to their good than whips and scourges, either of the literal or the metaphorical sort.[58]

3. *No Bright Lines Here.* Securing peaceful, purposeful human community depends on choosing well when political power is necessary to ensure that individuals live peaceably in political community and when the use of political power is inappropriate. Often persons' strong religious and moral commitments have spilled over into political activity in America.[59] Members of the First Congress believed religion was essential to the preservation of morality, which was, in turn, essential to the preservation of liberty. Consequently, they expected the states to continue to foster religion over non-religion by public assistance and ex-

58. J.S. MILL, *supra* note 22, at 88, 144.

59. In his dissent in *Poe v. Ullman*, Justice John Harlan reasons from an unexamined assumption that the State has some "rightful concern for its people's moral welfare":

> The right of privacy most manifestly is not an absolute. Thus, I would not suggest that adultery, homosexuality, fornication and incest are immune from criminal enquiry, however privately practiced. So much has been explicitly recognized in acknowledging the State's rightful concern for its people's moral welfare. But not to discriminate between what is involved in this case and either the traditional offenses against good morals or crimes which, though they may be committed anywhere, happen to have been committed or concealed in the home, would entirely misconceive the argument that is being made.

367 U.S. 497, 552-53 (1961) (citation omitted). For a discussion of the duty judges have to make the reasoning behind their assumptions explicit, see Katharine Bartlett, *Feminist Legal Methods*, 103 HARV. L. REV. 829, 862-63 (1990).

Ironically, Justice Harlan's emphasis in *Poe* on protecting private *marital* relations from government intrusion is ignored by the Supreme Court in later cases. These cases trumpet Justice Harlan's dissent in support of a general right to sexual and reproductive privacy for all individuals regardless of marital status. *E.g.*, Griswold v. Connecticut, 381 U.S. 479, 495 (1965) (Goldberg, J., concurring) (access to contraceptives); Roe v. Wade, 410 U.S. 113, 169 (1973) (Stewart, J., concurring) (abortion).

ample, while somehow remaining neutral among religions.[60] Current disagreements over matters such as school prayer, nativity scenes on public property, and tax exemptions for churches are evidence of the difficulty involved in judging when and how to use political power with respect to religion. Another example, the doomed prohibition amendment, partly stemmed from some individuals' aspiration to use political power to instill higher ideals in other individuals.[61] For some, the recent attempts to prohibit flag-burning represent a similar aspiration.

Part of the difficulty in judging when to use political rather than moral power stems from the realization that on some level, all laws regulate moral behavior. Laws regulate relationships between people that involve an obligation to do or refrain from doing certain things. Stealing money from a business partner, failing to pay taxes, driving over the speed limit, sexually abusing a child, or killing another person all involve immoral conduct that the political community refuses to tolerate without regard for the moral commitments, or lack of commitments, of the individuals involved.

Further, almost all behavior implicates moral concerns of some kind. Human beings are inescapably interdependent. Everything we do or fail to do affects the people with whom we live and work.[62] The same action may both benefit some and harm others, depending on the values and perspectives of those individuals affected by it. The political community must choose which harms it will prevent and alleviate with coercive political power and which should be left to the conscience and agency of individuals and their communities.

---

60. Berns, *supra* note 28, at 207-14.

Abraham Lincoln also teaches that American democracy needs civil religion, *see* Michael Zuckert, *Locke and the Problem of Civil Religion*, in THE MORAL FOUNDATIONS OF THE AMERICAN REPUBLIC, *supra* note 19, at 181, and Tocqueville writes that "provided the citizens profess a religion, the peculiar tenets of that religion are of little importance to [society's] interests." 1 A. DE TOCQUEVILLE, *supra* note 36, ch. XVII, at 303.

John Locke also was convinced that religious activity of some kind is necessary for peaceful coexistence in political community. He would have supported political intolerance of atheists in tandem with religious liberty to all believers. Locke, *supra* note 47, at 51. The United States political community disagrees with Locke on that point, U.S. CONST. amend. I; *e.g.*, Wallace v. Jaffree, 472 U.S. 38, 52-55 (1985) (reaffirming that individual freedom of conscience protected by the first amendment embraces the right to select any religious faith or none at all), but not because we all do or do not believe religion essential for knowledge of truth or the attainment of human excellence. We may believe religion is essential to these ends and yet agree that religion should not be coerced for two reasons: The coercion is not necessary for peaceful political coexistence, as Locke mistakenly thought (atheists can live up to their obligations as well as any religious individual), and because the attainment of human excellence demands freely-considered commitment. Therefore, forcing right conduct that prevents freely considered commitment will not do.

61. U.S. CONST. amends. XVIII, XXI.

62. J.S. MILL, *supra* note 22, at 148.

Clear rules that eliminate the need for continual reexamination and good judgment on this choice do not exist.[63] However, the two step analysis applied in *Roe v. Wade*[64] to decide whether abortion causes a harm that should be prevented with political power threatens a confusing polarization of individual interests, or "fundamental rights," against "compelling state interests." A liberal constitutional government such as we have in the United States *has* a compelling interest in the preservation of individuals in the appropriate exercise of individual agency.[65] The importance of agency in human development, as well as the gravity and nature of the potential harm threatened by the lack of political coercion, should guide the political community in making the choice whether to prevent or alleviate a given harm through the use of political power.

## II. The Abortion Debate

The importance of individual agency and assumptions about human potential and human responses to coercive power have guided the American government in its use of political power.[66] These same considerations should guide the debates about abortion. The abortion dilemma perhaps demands greater sensitivity to the difference between moral and political power than any other current issue because of the significance of

63. Professor Ruth Grant counsels government actors making such choices in her discussion of Locke's epistemology and political theory:

> [W]hile certain knowledge of true standards of behavior is possible, it is difficult and requires that we use our rational faculties well. And even then, such knowledge of abstract principle is not sufficient by itself. . . . Even when the principle or the rule is clear, a judgment must often be made as to whether it applies to the circumstances in question, whether a given thing or action belongs to the categories included in the rule.

R. Grant, *supra* note 21, at 49.

64. 410 U.S. 113, 155 (1973) ("fundamental rights" can be limited only by a "compelling state interest").

65. "Liberal" in this context does not mean the opposite of "conservative" as used in current political discourse. It refers to a government founded for the purpose of preserving individual liberty, such as Locke describes in his writings. Professor Ruth Grant explains: "Locke's is a dual standard. One element cannot be elevated above the other, and there is no need to choose between them. Both preservation and freedom are necessary conditions for legitimacy [in liberal government], while neither alone is sufficient." R. Grant, *supra* note 21, at 97-98. For a full discussion of the relationship between freedom (individual agency) and the preservation of individuals in liberal government, see *id.* at 88-98.

66. For example, in *Zablocki v. Redhail*, the Supreme Court strikes down Wisconsin's attempt to encourage the payment of child support by preventing remarriage until the parent provides evidence that the obligation is being met. The Court says a direct prohibition on marriage unreasonably infringes individual liberty. 434 U.S. 374, 389 (1978). In *Shapiro v. Thompson*, the Court reaffirms that "the nature of our Federal Union and our constitutional concepts of personal liberty unite to require that all citizens be free to travel throughout the length and breadth of our land uninhibited by statutes, rules, or regulations which unreasonably burden or restrict this movement." 394 U.S. 618, 629 (1969) (waiting-period requirement before new-comers receive state public assistance violates equal protection). For a discussion of the rejection of Good Samaritan laws in the American legal system, see *infra* notes 107-11 and accompanying text.

the values in tension: protection of life and protection of individual agency in deeply personal matters.[67] Whether to include the fetus in the political community and protect it with the same protection provided each human being who is born requires consideration of the nature of the harm caused by abortion, whether prohibiting abortion merely prevents harm or also coerces sacrifices in behalf of the fetus, and whether we desire morally responsible human beings or instead would settle for right conduct without regard for individual commitments on this matter.

## A. *The Nature of the Harm in Abortion*

John Stuart Mill writes that respect for individual agency ends when "there is a definite damage, or a definite risk of damage, either to an individual or to the public."[68] But if "damage" includes spiritual damage, and assuming the failure to worship spiritually damages individuals, then we would not have the first amendment. If it includes emotional damage to public figures, then our libel laws would look different. And if it includes symbolic damage to governmnet authority, perhaps we should curtail expressive freedom with a flag-burning amendment.

Respect for individual agency requires tolerance for some kinds of suffering brought about by wrong choices. "Definite damage" must have a more restricted meaning than general human suffering to work as an appropriate limitation on individual agency. Constitutional scholar Walter Berns paraphrases Thomas Jefferson's suggestion for the kind of damage the government should alleviate or prevent with coercive power: "Americans are not entitled to regard it as an injury—or an injury for which the law will provide a remedy—for their neighbors to say there are twenty gods or no God. Such religious opinions neither pick their pockets nor break their legs . . . ."[69]

Causing physical damage to persons and property has been a punishable crime in this country for centuries.[70] Some less tangible harms,

67. Researcher Gilbert Steiner writes: "Abortion can be counted on to be the dominant family-related public problem for the indefinite future, and the one the policy process is least likely to resolve, because neither side is comfortable with less than total victory, each side views its cause as sacred, and both are right." GILBERT STEINER, THE FUTILITY OF FAMILY POLICY 71 (1981) *quoted in*, M. GLENDON, *supra* note 25, at 40.

68. J.S. MILL, *supra* note 22, at 150; *see also* LOCKE, *supra* note 6, at 9 ("Every one, as he is *bound* to *preserve himself* . . . may not, unless it be to do justice to an offender, take away, or impair the life, or what tends to the preservation of the life, the liberty, health, limb, or goods of another.").

69. Berns, *supra* note 28, at 217 (paraphrasing 4 THOMAS JEFFERSON, THE WORKS OF THOMAS JEFFERSON 78 (P. Leicester Ford ed. 1904)).

70. Murder, assault, battery, rape, larceny, embezzlement, burglary, and robbery are some familiar examples.

such as harm resulting from racial segregation,[71] also have become punishable, and courts increasingly award civil damages for "intentional infliction of emotional distress."[72] One need not delve further into the always evolving legal definitions of punishable and compensable harm to recognize the difficult judgments required to decide whether political power should alleviate or prevent harm of one kind but not another.

Much of the abortion debate revolves around the nature of the harm done when a woman aborts a fetus.[73] Obviously, the damage to the fetus is complete and irrevocable: Abortion destroys something that would have developed into a born human being. However, this observation does not answer the question whether the political community should value the fetus to the same extent as a born human being and thus prevent its destruction with coercive power. The observation leaves open the question whether abortion causes a kind of harm that the political community should not tolerate.[74] This issue differs from whether *individuals* should value the fetus the same as a born human being because of the additional concern for individual agency that forms the foundation of our political community.

As discussed above, our common commitment in the political community necessarily falls far below our human potential for moral goodness. Indeed, because our political commitments are enforced by

71. Brown v. Board of Educ., 347 U.S. 483, 494 (1954) ("To separate [Blacks] from others of similar age and qualifications solely because of their race generates a feeling of inferiority as to their status in the community that may affect their hearts and minds in a way unlikely ever to be undone.").

72. *See* RESTATEMENT (SECOND) OF TORTS § 46(1) (1965). ("One who by extreme and outrageous conduct intentionally or recklessly causes severe emotional distress to another is subject to liability for such emotional distress . . . .") The evolution of this tort from special application in cases of assault or for conduct on a common carrier, as reflected in the 1934 version of the RESTATEMENT OF TORTS § 46, is described in GEORGE CHRISTIE, CASES AND MATERIALS ON THE LAW OF TORTS 905-24 (1983).

73. By "harm," I refer to the nature of the wrong, if any, in abortion, not the emotional or physical harm to women that pro-life advocates document, *see* Brief Amici Curiae on Behalf of Feminists for Life et al., Webster v. Reproductive Health Servs., 109 S. Ct. 3040 (1989) (No. 88-05), and pro-choice advocates dispute, *see* R. PETCHESKY, *supra* note 5, at 367.

74. I ultimately conclude that abortion is not one of the causes of suffering the political community should eradicate. *See infra* notes 103-06 and accompanying text. By "suffering," I mean the moral and emotional suffering of those persons who struggle with the realization that others actually would kill the unborn, and any suffering experienced by the fetus. By contrast, Professor Lisa Cahill uses the inescapability of suffering—the suffering borne by a pregnant woman—to conclude that abortion usually should not be allowed:

> The liberal ethos discourages making personal sacrifices and encourages at best a minimal appreciation of the virtue and even the necessity of constructive suffering. . . . [S]ome human situations have unavoidably tragic elements and that to be human is to bear these burdens. We cannot be freed from all infringements on our self-fulfillment, and to persistently demand that is to avoid moral agency in the complete sense.

Cahill, *supra* note 42, at 271-72.

coercive power, we must limit them in order to realize a greater degree of individual and collective moral goodness. Therefore, regardless of how we ultimately answer questions such as those posed by abortion, we must consider them carefully with the political/moral power distinction in mind.

Pro-choice advocates sometimes have emphasized that a fetus is not "human life" but rather the "potential" for human life. As such, they argue, it can be treated as no more than a tumor or a tissue growth and removed if desired.[75] According to this perspective, the "harm" (if any) in abortion is no concern for the political community. Some pro-life advocates, on the other hand, have gone to the opposite extreme and personified the fetus, acting as if it lacks only a voice, which they willingly provide, and calling abortion murder.[76]

Both extremes distort reality. On the one hand, a developing fetus with a unique genotype that will become a human being if undisturbed differs significantly from a tumor. Free-lance writer Mary Meehan posits:

> And there is a special unfairness in penalizing the unborn for not having size or abilities, which if left alone, they will surely develop. It is almost like saying, "In another few months, you will grow to the point where we cannot kill you because you will be too much like us. Therefore, we will end your lives now . . . ."[77]

On the other hand, until the point of viability, a developing fetus lacks not only a voice, but other mental and physical capacities that make an individual. Feminist theorist Rosalind Petchesky articulates this view:

> The most striking fallacy in the genetic arguments of anti-abortionists is their leap from the *fact* of genetic individuality . . . to the *value* of human personhood. This is a problem, in part, of confusing the self, the person, with her or his genetic basis, ignoring the enormously com-

75. *See* Jean Elshtain, *Reflections on Abortion, Values, and the Family,* in ABORTION: UNDERSTANDING DIFFERENCES, *supra* note 3, at 47, 50 ("Examples of discourse that aim to distance us . . . include arguments that construe the fetus, variously, as a 'parasite,' a 'tenant,' an air-borne 'spore,' or 'property.' "); Mahowald, *supra* note 5, at 179 ("[A] genuinely pro-abortion position emphasizes . . . the fetus is in reality an invasive growth, like a wart or a tumor.").

76. *See* JOHN NOONAN, JR., A PRIVATE CHOICE: ABORTION IN AMERICA IN THE SEVENTIES 171 (1979) ("When the mask is lifted from the liberty of abortion, it is seen that the liberty consists in a freedom to knife, poison, starve, or choke a human being differing only in his or her degree of helplessness . . . .") *quoted in* R. PETCHESKY, *supra* note 5, at 331; Meehan, *supra* note 3, at 147 ("It is a violent act, one that usually involves dismemberment of the human embryo or fetus. . . . But the violence of abortion, though important, is secondary to the fact that it ends a human life."). *Contra* R. PETCHESKY, *supra* note 5, at 328 ("idea that abortion is 'murder' and you are 'killing a baby' is a culturally generated one, not shared by many eras and peoples").

77. Meehan, *supra* note 3, at 150.

plex interaction between genes, environment, and development that ultimately determines who or what an actual person becomes.[78]

On the most basic level, a developing fetus differs significantly from a born human being in the complete symbiotic relationship with another body necessary for its survival.

Greater scientific evidence will not improve the lack of consensus on the fetus' relative value or on the gravity of the harm involved in abortion. We already know a lot. Even junior high school students are taught that from the moment one sperm penetrates the ovum, a series of rapid divisions begins a progression of development—heartbeat at eighteen days, brainwaves at forty-two days, all organs formed by the ninth or tenth week.[79] Unless disturbed by natural or artificial forces, this union of sperm and ovum will become a human being capable of existing outside the uterus. Some persons on both sides of the abortion debate are willing to agree that conception and implantation in the uterus is the most definite point to identify the beginning of human life. Nevertheless, both sides continue to disagree about the role of the government in forcefully preventing abortion.[80] As psychologist Sidney Callahan asks poignantly, "How can it be that so many wise and good people can know all the same facts, be familiar with all the same arguments, and yet reach different conclusions"?[81] Something more than biological reality affects one's evaluation of the harm involved in abortion. A value judgment, not a scientific determination, enables individuals to decide whether aborting a fetus is acceptable or not. Differences in individual commitment to religious or moral principles goes a long way in explaining the difference in value judgments. The following descriptions illustrate how different attitudes toward sex and pregnancy correspond to different evaluations of the fetus.

78. R. PETCHESKY, *supra* note 5, at 337. Rosalind Petchesky thoroughly discusses the importance of the consciousness of relationship in making us human. *Id.* at 344-46.

79. PREGNANCY RESOURCE CENTER, GRAND RAPIDS, MICH., MAKING AN INFORMED DECISION ABOUT YOUR PREGNANCY (1988) (pamphlet).

80. *Compare* R. PETCHESKY, *supra* note 5, at 337-38 ("It might be conceded that the fetus is a *form* of life insofar as it is alive (as established by EEG readings, heartbeat, and other biological responses) and it is human. . . . [But this] does not move us one step toward knowing what *value* to give the fetus . . . .") *with* Meehan, *supra* note 3, at 149, 151 ("Medical and scientific textbooks affirm that the life of each human begins at fertilization (conception). . . . If their right to life is not recognized and protected, then they are completely vulnerable to power and violence and death.").

81. Sidney Callahan, *Value Choices in Abortion*, in ABORTION: UNDERSTANDING DIFFERENCES, *supra* note 3, at 285, 287. Sidney Callahan, who is pro-life, asks that question from a unique vantage point. For over 30 years, she has been married to Daniel Callahan, who also speaks and writes regularly about abortion from the pro-choice perspective. Together they organized and edited the book, ABORTION: UNDERSTANDING DIFFERENCES. A dialogue between them is printed in *Friendly Persuasion*, U.S. News & World Report, Oct. 3, 1988, at 30-31.

If conception involves more than matter and natural forces, and a soul pre-exists conception and enters the developing body at some point before birth,[82] or if God spontaneously gives spirit to the developing body at some point before birth,[83] then we would need to know when that occurred to avoid the substantial harm caused by prematurely disembodying the soul. However, beliefs about ensoulment are inextricably bound up with religious beliefs,[84] which should not be enforced by political power.[85] Even if true, religious beliefs about human beginnings must be considered and accepted or rejected as premises for action by free individuals if they are to have any meaning or power in individual lives.

Juxtaposed with those who conclude that abortion is a sin almost as grave as murder, are those who say that abortion is more than the better of difficult alternatives—it is not a harm at all, but a positive good in many circumstances. Feminist theorist Rosalind Petchesky argues for this position:

> The view of abortion as a necessary evil born out of desperate circumstances is a liberal accommodation to recent waves of anti-abortion (and anti-feminist) ideology. . . . The "necessary evil" concept oddly forgets the spirit of buoyancy infusing not only feminists but masses of women after *Roe v. Wade*. . . . From this perspective, abortion conducted under safe, affordable, and stigma-free conditions is neither a necessary evil nor a matter of private choice. Rather, it is a positive benefit that society has an obligation to provide to all who seek it, just as it provides education and health benefits.[86]

82. Mormons, for instance, believe that each individual has existed forever as a conscious being; that similar to energy/matter, intelligence (or consciousness) cannot be created or destroyed, *see* DOCTRINE AND COVENANTS OF THE CHURCH OF JESUS CHRIST OF LATTER-DAY SAINTS 93: 29 (1981 ed.), but only improved by acquiring spirit bodies (fine matter) as literal children of a Heavenly Father and Mother before mortal life, and then bodies of flesh and bone as children of parents on Earth. They believe that although individuals temporarily "die" (their spirits return to their prebirth form) all individuals will eventually "resurrect" into tangible bodies of flesh and bone that can never die thereafter, such as those possessed by our Heavenly Father and Mother. *Id.* at 130: 22; *see also* Ezekiel 37: 11-14 (analogy between the regathering of Israel and the resurrection); 1 Corinthians 15: 51-54 (discussing resurrection).

83. The Catholic Church, for instance, teaches that God creates life: "Human Life is precious because it is the gift of a God whose love is infinite, and when God gives life, it is forever." Pope John Paul II, *Homily at Mass in Washington, D.C.*, N.Y. Times, Oct. 8, 1979, at B6, *quoted in* Meehan, *supra* note 3, at 148. For a discussion of historical changes in Catholic beliefs and teachings about ensoulment and abortion, see Webster v. Reproductive Health Servs., 109 S. Ct. 3040, 3082-84 (1989) (Stevens, J., concurring and dissenting in part).

84. R. PETCHESKY, *supra* note 5, at 329, 332; Cahill, *supra* note 41, at 270.

85. U.S. CONST. amend. I; Virginia Abernethy, *Children, Personhood, and a Pluralistic Society*, in ABORTION: UNDERSTANDING DIFFERENCES, *supra* note 3, at 117, 133 ("The debate, one finds, is not just about when biological human life acquires the rights associated with personhood. The debate is about whether this nation shall depart from its constitutionally designed heritage of separation of Church and State."). *But cf.* Cahill, *supra* note 42, at 263 ("I dissent from the proposition that abortion is a narrowly religious issue.").

86. R. PETCHESKY, *supra* note 5, at 386-87.

Still other people oppose abortion not for religious reasons, but rather because they place great importance on the life-giving potential of heterosexual sex.[87] In some circumstances, these people may refrain from sex to avoid altogether the possibility of pregnancy. Or if they engage in sexual intimacy, with or without using birth control, they do so fully prepared to assume responsibility for a pregnancy that might result.[88] People with these perspectives value a fetus as a living, developing human being and consider it an unjustified harm, with few exceptions, to cut off fetal development.[89]

People who assume this level of responsibility for the life-giving potential in sex do not necessarily appreciate the potential for pleasure in sex less than others, as is sometimes suggested.[90] Rather they seek inner peace and fulfillment by subordinating their uninhibited pleasures to the duties those pleasures potentially create. Psychologist Sidney Callahan supports this view:

> [I]n the synthesis proposed, sexual expression as an erotic manifestation of love and unity is equal in value to sexuality as procreative. Neither dimension can be denied or discarded or can displace the other in importance. . . . Excitement, love, and emotional fulfillment may be necessary for the good life, constant sexual expression is not. When human beings can have access to many other emotional joys and pleasures equal to sex, then it is possible to preserve the procreative dimension inherent in human sexuality by reserving sexual expression for procreative contexts of commitment and love.[91]

Others emphasize, sometimes under the anguishing weight of incompatible concerns in the event of an unwanted pregnancy, that conception is more appropriately attributable to natural forces or chance than to a deliberate decision to engage in sexual relations.[92] To them,

87. Callahan, *supra* note 81, at 287-93; *cf.* Meehan, *supra* note 3, at 149 ("Yet, the absence of religious belief does not remove all support from the notion of human rights. . . . Other people still exist, and their very existence imposes obligations on us, just as our existence imposes obligations on them.").

88. Callahan, *supra* note 81, at 288; Luker, *supra* note 4, at 33.

89. Callahan, *supra* note 81, at 291, 295 ("Stopping a pregnancy is in the same category of act as stopping any dynamic, ongoing human life."). *Contra* R. PETCHESKY, *supra* note 5, at 341 ("The doctrine of fetal personhood . . . . demeans pregnant women, who are treated in this perspective as the physical vessels for genetic messages rather than responsible moral agents. Motherhood in this sense becomes, not a socially determined relationship, but a physiological function . . . .").

90. Summarizing from her five-year study of pro-life and pro-choice activists, Kristin Luker says that for pro-life people "a commitment to amative sex [sexual activity whose goal is sensual pleasure and mutual enjoyment] is at odds with a primary commitment to mothering." Luker, *supra* note 4, at 33.

91. Callahan, *supra* note 81, at 289-90. Sidney Callahan accepts contraception and voluntary sterilization as "acceptable means to further the nurturing potential of a committed procreative pair." *Id.* at 289.

92. R. PETCHESKY, *supra* note 5, at 336.

conception is a happy or unhappy by-product of sex, but a by-product nonetheless. Although this view admits that a fetus deserves weighty consideration,[93] no one need feel unduly bound by the joining of sperm and egg which might occur even despite reliance on birth control. A sincere desire to avoid or postpone parenting, commitments to personal goals or to already-existing relationships (including other children), financial or emotional insecurity, and other factors could justify terminating an unexpected pregnancy under this view of the role of human agency in conception.[94] To some people, abortion enables them to abide by their original intention that the birth of a child not result from ongoing heterosexual intimacy. As Rosalind Petchesky points out, they feel that the risk of pregnancy should never prohibit women and men from engaging in the sex:

> A clear feminist vision, an alternative culture of sexuality embracing passion and play as well as love, . . . a revolution in women's social place and in the relations of reproduction is impossible without a "new morality" of sex and love. . . . Abortion . . . has to do with women's sexual and moral autonomy as much as their physical integrity. . . . [W]e may posit that sexual self-expression is itself a basic human need so allied to a person's physical and emotional well-being as to constitute an aspect of "health" in the widest sense.[95]

All of these attitudes emphasize only part of the life-giving process—either the role of human agency or the role of natural forces—as a premise for action. The degree of emphasis on human responsibility affects one's view of whether the fetus deserves primary, equal, or relatively minor weight when balanced with other concerns in the event of an unwanted pregnancy. It is difficult, if not impossible, to tell whether a person's attitude toward sex determines her view of the value of fetal life or vice versa. But a person's views on both subjects mutually reinforce the other view and together show a pattern of individual commitment. Individuals usually will feel "right" and "justified" in the commitments they accept, and they often find opposing views incomprehensible, if not foolish or irresponsible.[96]

In my mind, individuals should value human agency in conception enough that abortion is altogether unacceptable, except when pregnancy

---

93. *Id.* at 338, 348.

94. *Id.* at 365, 369; Callahan, *supra* note 81, at 292.

95. R. PETCHESKY, *supra* note 5, at 391, 392, 393; *see* Callahan, *supra* note 81, at 288; Luker, *supra* note 4, at 40.

96. *See* R. PETCHESKY, *supra* note 5, at 372 ("For the liberal it is not the woman who gets an abortion who is 'selfish' but the one who doesn't—when she is too young or too poor or too 'incompetent.' "); Cahill, *supra* note 42, at 272 ("The decision to continue a pregnancy might be construed as a decision by the stronger to assume burdens that would otherwise fall on the most defenseless."); Luker, *supra* note 4, at 33; Ooms, *supra* note 56, at 174-75.

endangers a woman's life or is the product of rape or incest. (Since the physical and psychological violation of human agency inherent in rape and incest is incompatible with attributing moral responsibility to a woman for the conception of a developing fetus, I cannot condemn her if she chooses to abort.[97]) For a woman to carry a fetus to term and for a man to share the burdens of pregnancy and childbearing is the better, more responsible, more fulfilling commitment for human beings to make.[98] However, if keeping the baby is not possible, the woman should plan to give the baby up for adoption rather than abort the fetus.[99] And we should employ all methods of moral power—writing, speaking, rebuking, listening, encouraging—to persuade others to act responsibly with regard for the beginnings of human life.

Individuals who value a fetus the same as a born human being often feel strongly that the political community should enforce their value. They point out the danger of valuing life differently because of its degree of dependency or level of development, and they discuss the distinction between liberty and license in society.[100] Some think that protecting the fetus with political power will reinforce the persuasive methods of moral power.[101] This view, however, fails to recognize that political enforcement interferes with the operation of moral power in the abortion decision because of the importance of individual agency in moral conduct. The pointed threat of coercion backing the expression of pro-life views in the United States today derails the moral debate, masks the insights of the anti-abortion perspective, and hampers its persuasive potential.

Some individuals who oppose abortion feel so strongly about protecting the fetus that they do not care about the possible lack of commitment of the fetus' father and mother to the creation of their child. These individuals would force a woman to give birth without regard to the adverse effect of coercion on individual moral responsibility because of their

97. *Contra* Meehan, *supra* note 3, at 163-64 ("These problems are not the children's fault; we should not blame the children or punish them for the failure or crimes of others.").

98. I would suggest further that confining sexual desires to the expression of attraction, care, and emotional commitment in a marriage relationship is a happier, healthier choice for human beings, all concern for pregnancy aside. Others disagree. *See supra* note 95 and accompanying text.

99. Although giving a baby up for adoption can be traumatic, it also offers many benefits for the child and the new family. As one commentator notes: "A nonfamilial, nonpossessive appeal to continue a pregnancy can be made in order to give a new innocent life its chance to join the human family and to be reared by those ready and able to enjoy the privilege." Callahan, *supra* note 81, at 288, 293. Unfortunately for all concerned, some minority women may not have the option to give their babies to eager, caring adoptive parents. I am hopeful such a situation is not prevalent and will not last.

100. M. GLENDON, *supra* note 25, at 37; B. NATHANSON, *supra* note 3, at 259-60; Callahan, *supra* note 81, at 296; Meehan, *supra* note 3, at 151-52.

101. M. GLENDON, *supra* note 25, at 62; Callahan, *supra* note 81, at 301.

confidence in the immorality of abortion. Mill describes (and criticizes) a similar attitude in his essay, *On Liberty*:

> It is the duty of governments, and of individuals, to form the truest opinions they can; to form them carefully, and never impose them upon others unless they are quite sure of being right. But when they are sure (such reasoners may say), it is not conscientiousness but cowardice to shrink from acting on their opinions, and allow doctrines which they honestly think dangerous to the welfare of mankind, either in this life or in another, to be scattered abroad without restraint . . . .[102]

Although one may agree fully with pro-life forces in the moral condemnation of abortion, it is not necessary to then agree that coercing birth is the appropriate response. The *perception* of abortion as a harm of the most abhorrent kind—equivalent to murdering a born human being—depends on religious or moral commitments[103] that emphasize the role of human agency in conception and value the fetus as a developing human being. Neither of these commitments can be coerced effectively; they are only meaningful if produced by careful, individual reflection and affirmation aided by private and public discussion. As Professor Mary Segers writes: "[I]t is not a departure from the values of liberalism to hold that individuals can be taught, encouraged, educated, exhorted, urged, entreated, and persuaded—but not legally compelled—to use their freedom (including reproductive freedom) wisely and with due care for others."[104]

The withdrawal of pro-life views from the political arena probably would not cause a revolution of moral consciousness and fewer abortions. Individual agency means the freedom to make both wrong and right choices. But individual agency also means that everyone recognizes where *full* responsibility for wrong choices lies—with the individual.

As previously discussed,[105] attitudes of superiority, contempt, or separation should not follow a judgment of right and wrong on the abortion issue. After explaining and encouraging an anti-abortion position, people who oppose abortion have "an obligation to respect the moral autonomy of individual women regardless of their final decisions."[106]

102. J.S. Mill, *supra* note 22, at 87.

103. *See* R. Petchesky, *supra* note 5, at 331; Abernethy, *supra* note 85, at 132; *supra* notes 82-96.

104. Segers, *supra* note 5, at 251.

105. *See supra* text accompanying note 24.

106. Segers, *supra* note 5, at 251.

### B. *Preventing Abortion Does More Than Prevent Harm*

American law declines to coerce individuals into making substantial sacrifices for others without sufficient evidence of a freely considered commitment to make the sacrifices. Unless a statute creates an enforceable duty to care for another, none exists without the voluntary assumption of a fiduciary or contractual relationship. In *Jones v. United States*,[107] a woman who had complete custody of her friend's baby for over ten months following the baby's birth was convicted of involuntary manslaughter when the baby died of severe malnutrition and neglect. The court of appeals overturned her conviction because the trial judge had not instructed the jury that they must find beyond a reasonable doubt that Mary Jones had a legal duty to supply food and necessities to the infant.[108] The court of appeals describes the circumstances under which individuals may be held to a legal duty to care for others:

> One can be held criminally liable: first, where a statute imposes a duty to care for another; second, where one stands in a certain status relationship to another; third, where one has assumed a contractual duty to care for another; and fourth, where one has voluntarily assumed the care of another and so secluded the helpless person as to prevent others from rendering aid.[109]

Because no legal duty to aid others attaches without evidence of individual commitment, an individual can pass a stranger bleeding in the gutter without lifting a finger to help and have committed no tort[110] or punishable crime, even if that injured person dies. Government does not fail to use political power to punish this kind of behavior because of uncertainty about what the individual should do or because of a diversity of opinions about whether the giving of aid is right. Almost everyone would agree that right conduct for the person passing by would be to do what ever she or he could to save the injured person's life. However,

107. 308 F.2d 307, 310 (D.C. Cir. 1962). I am indebted to Jay Brown's suggestions and the aid of his paper, Emergency Aid as a Claim of Right: A Criticism of Criminal Good Samaritan Statutes (1989) (unpublished manuscript available from the author), for the information regarding Good Samaritan statutes included in this section. After completing this Note, I discovered an excellent article discussing abortion restrictions as Good Samaritan laws. I recommend that much more thorough discussion to the interested reader. Donald Regan, *Rewriting* Roe v. Wade, 77 MICH. L. REV. 1569 (1979).

108. *Id.* at 311.

109. *Id.* at 310.

110. RESTATEMENT (SECOND) OF TORTS § 314 comment c (1965) ("[O]ne human being, seeing a fellow man in dire peril, is under no legal obligation to aid him, but may sit on the dock, smoke his cigar, and watch the other drown."). Two states, Vermont and Minnesota, have bypassed the common law with duty to aid statutes as follows: "A person who knows that another is exposed to grave physical harm shall, to the extent that the same can be rendered without danger or peril to himself . . . give reasonable assistance to the exposed person . . . ." VT. STAT. ANN. tit. 12, 519 (1973); *see also* MINN. STAT. § 604.05 (1988).

recognition of the importance of individual agency in assuming responsibility for others' welfare makes the futile nature of Good Samaritan laws apparent.[111] If an unfeeling passer-by could escape without detection, then she probably would, and a compassionate passer-by will act from genuine concern not fear of punishment.

Even assuming the harm in abortion is as grave as the harm in murder, one must recognize that preventing abortion involves much more than preventing murder—it coerces substantial, prolonged sacrifices in another's behalf.[112] A woman, in giving her body and its resources to the development of another body, makes a sacrifice that takes its toll on her physical, emotional, and often financial, health during pregnancy and afterward. If the mother alone or with the father[113] decides to keep the child, then they assume life-spanning responsibility for someone else's well-being to which they must attend regularly. The mother and father may need to make substantial changes in their relationship to each other and to others to meet this responsibility. Their sense of control over their lives will be permanently affected. Future plans and goals for personal development may be prolonged, if not permanently adjusted. If the option of adoption is available, and the parents choose to give up the baby for adoption, they will probably feel emotional loss and perhaps guilt for some time. Each parent may wonder for the rest of his or her life what has become of the child.[114]

111. *See* A.D. Woozley, *A Duty to Rescue: Some Thoughts on Criminal Liability*, 69 VA. L. REV. 1273, 1290 (1983) (four principled objections to Good Samaritan laws: "[1] concern with selective enforcement of the law, [2] fear that a legal sanction diminishes the moral virtue of rescuers, [3] concern with an infringement of civil liberties, and [4] fear of a 'slippery slope' once an omission is treated as a criminal act").

112. R. PETCHESKY, *supra* note 5, at 375 ("Maternity, if chosen, is not servitude; it is in many ways pleasant and satisfying, socially as well as personally. But it is at the same time a *service* that every childbearing woman performs for others . . . that requires an irreducible physical burden: the renunciation of bodily health and well-being for many months, perhaps with permanent physical consequences . . . ."); Callahan, *supra* note 81, at 297 ("In all pro-life positions, the problem remains that one is also going to inflict suffering by supporting the claims of the fetus to be protected by a change in the law."); Segers, *supra* note 5, at 231-32.

113. Giving the woman full agency to abort or not requires that the father be given a fair opportunity to renounce his responsibility to the child either during the period when the woman can safely abort or later when the baby can be adopted. As long as the woman has the choice to avoid parenting, she cannot fairly strap him to that responsibility without similar deliberation and consent on his part. If he does not consent, then the woman may still decide to give birth and have the baby adopted or keep the child herself.

114. R. PETCHESKY, *supra* note 5, at 346 ("The experience of going through a full-term pregnancy, bearing a child, and giving it up for adoption is punitive and traumatic for a woman because the relationship by then is real; it exists."); Callahan, *supra* note 81, at 293 ("The sorrow of seeing one's own flesh and blood, a family member, given away to outsiders and an unknown fate becomes too hard to face.").

Coercing birth resembles a Good Samaritan law, particularly when safe, effective, relatively inexpensive means for terminating a pregnancy exist as they do today in the United States. The majority in *Roe v. Wade* were well aware of the burdens of childbirth when they decided abortion could not be prevented appropriately with political power.[115] We simply do not coerce that level of commitment to others. We rely on caring, responsible impulses among people bound together by something other than coercion to bring out the best in us.[116]

However, anti-abortion regulations differ from a Good Samaritan law in some ways. Whereas an uncompassionate passer-by can avoid helping an injured person by doing nothing, a pregnant woman must destroy the fetus to avoid helping it. Also, a mother and father are directly responsible for the fetus' existence, whereas a passer-by did not create the injured individual. While these distinctions reinforce my conviction that abortion is not morally justified, they fail to persuade me that a pregnant woman should be forced to nourish the fetus.

Another natural objection to analogizing anti-abortion regulations to Good Samaritan laws follows from the recognition that we use political power to prevent or punish the abandonment or killing of a born infant, without regard for the beliefs of the offender and whether our actions will encourage or discourage a change in those beliefs.[117] All of the observations about dependency, sacrifice, commitment, and the effect of coercion that apply in discussions about unwanted pregnancies—except for the peculiar physical symbiosis between woman and fetus in pregnancy—apply to newborns and children. Yet none of us would say that a parent should be allowed to resort to the "safe, effective and relatively inexpensive" means of avoiding parental responsibility by abandoning or killing an infant.

115. 410 U.S. 113, 153 (1973) ("The detriment that the State would impose upon the pregnant woman by denying this choice altogether is apparent. . . . Maternity, or additional offspring, may force upon the woman a distressful life and future. Psychological harm may be imminent. Mental and physical health may be taxed . . . ."); *cf.* Callahan, *supra* note 81, at 298 ("However, when suffering cannot be relieved, or when it is *freely taken on* for the sake of others, the suffering will not be meaningless for those who live in basic trust.") (emphasis added).

116. Segers, *supra* note 5, at 231.

117. Rosalind Petchesky suggests using the capacity for conscious individuation from others as a moral touchstone to distinguish treatment of born infants from fetuses. R. PETCHESKY, *supra* note 5, at 345-47.

Justice Stevens wrote in *Thornburgh v. American College of Obstetricians and Gynecologists*:

> [I]t seems to me quite odd to argue that distinctions may not also be drawn between the state interest in protecting the freshly fertilized egg and the state interest in protecting the 9-month-gestated, fully sentient fetus on the eve of birth. Recognition of this distinction is supported not only by logic, but also by history and by our shared experiences.

476 U.S. 747, 779 (1986) (Stevens, J., concurring) (footnotes omitted).

One important difference between responsibility to a born human being and a fetus lies in the degree to which we can say the individual has *assumed* responsibility for the other's welfare. Some pro-choice persons believe that a conscious decision to continue a pregnancy, a choice more deliberate than simply conception, is required before a man and woman become subject to an enforceable moral obligation. As Professor Lisa Cahill describes, pro-life persons believe that conception brings with it enforceable obligations to nurture the growing life:

> Of particular relevance to the abortion dilemma is the fact that duties or obligations can bind humans to their fellows in ways to which they have not explicitly consented. Such obligations originate simply in the sorts of reciprocal relatedness that constitute being human. The mother-fetus relation is characterized by obligations of this sort, as are all parent-child relations.[118]

Pro-life persons may retain the importance of consent in creating legal obligations if they view the choice to engage in heterosexual relations as an assumption of possible parenting responsibilities. If the political community protects fetal life with political power, as it does with respect to born infants, then government sends a clear message to women and men that whenever they have sex, they assume the risk of responsibility for a third person's welfare. The political community sends the message that because it values fetal life the same as a born human being, the important choices regarding parenting concern when, with whom, and under what life circumstances to have sex, not whether or not to continue a pregnancy.

To most people who have a religious or moral commitment to respect the role of human agency above the role of natural forces in conception,[119] this message is self-evident.[120] But the truth of the message does not justify backing it with political power. To those who do not profess a strong religious or moral commitment to the life-giving potential in sex, the message sounds tyrannical. It threatens grave penalties for not changing their behavior about deeply intimate, life-spanning concerns—sex and family—without respect for a voluntary process of change in their attitudes. As Professor Virginia Abernethy posits:

> In the "abortion debate," adherents of the right-to-life movement are attempting to force the behavioral consequences of their beliefs on others. The debate exists because a moral insight apparent to just a

118. Cahill, *supra* note 42, at 265.
119. *See supra* notes 82-91 and accompanying text.
120. *See supra* notes 97-101 and accompanying text.

portion of the citizenry has been infused into the political process and is being proposed as the law of the land.[121]

As a political community, will we settle for right conduct on such deeply significant matters or do we want individually chosen right conduct? If we prevent abortion with political power, undoubtedly some women will continue to exercise their individual agency and procure abortions either at great financial cost or at great risk to their own lives and health.[122] Undoubtedly, other women will not be able to pay the price or will not take the risk, but instead will patiently or bitterly bear the child they would have aborted. However, no woman will have the opportunity to *voluntarily* reconsider whether they have assumed responsibility to give the fetus life when they conceived the fetus. True, some people might reconsider in spite of, or even because of, the coercion, but many people will blame the coercive arm for the birth.[123] As a result, the political community may have more infants born but will have sacrificed the moral growth of individuals in the process.[124]

More important than utilitarian considerations for the good lost to society in preventing abortion—perhaps as much can be said for the good gained[125]—is the false message sent to women with unwanted pregnancies. Inappropriate external rewards or punishments mask the truth about full individual responsibility for exercising or not exercising

121. Abernethy, *supra* note 85, at 133; *see also* R. PETCHESKY, *supra* note 5, at 378 ("Control over one's body . . . [is] a positive and necessary enabling condition for full human participation in social and communal life.").

122. Webster v. Reproductive Health Servs., 109 S. Ct. 3040, 3077-78 (1989) (Blackmun J., concurring and dissenting in part); Ooms, *supra* note 56, at 172-73.

123. *See* Ooms, *supra* note 56, at 173 ("The energies of the pro-choice movement would focus entirely on challenging, disrupting, or disobeying the law.").

Professor Hart writes:

> [T]here is very little evidence to support the idea that morality is best taught by fear of legal punishment. Much morality is certainly taught and sustained without it, and where morality is taught with it, there is the standing danger that fear of punishment may remain the sole motive for conformity.

H.L.A. HART, *supra* note 39, at 58. *But see* Callahan, *supra* note 81, at 301 (role of the law in educating and disciplining the emotions); *supra* note 25.

124. Segers, *supra* note 5, at 235 (We must have "a realistic sense of the limits of the criminal sanction . . . [for] recriminalizing abortion will not achieve their intended effect of reducing the incidence of abortion and will result in more harm than good."); *see also* R. PETCHESKY, *supra* note 5, at 350 ("[W]hat is going on here is a struggle, not over the contents of the womb, but over the meaning of maternity and the competence of adult women to exercise judgment.").

125. The positive educational effect of the preventive laws on some, *see* M. GLENDON, *supra* note 25, at 60, or the good saved in the lives of the born infants are possible examples of the good in preventing abortion. For recognition of the harm done by present permissive abortion laws, see *id.* at 34-35 ("filtered through the communications media to popular consciousness, the statement by the highest court of the land that a fetus is not a 'person' has great potential for being misunderstood"); Ooms, *supra* note 56, at 172 ("[U]ndoubtedly, such liberalization of the law did contribute to the rise in the number and the rate of abortion and has changed attitudes even further.").

the capacity to grow in wisdom, self-control, and love.[126] But if an individual is truly and fully responsible to her own conscience for her actions on a particular matter, the most important effect among other effects of right or wrong conduct will be internal. When the political community refrains from imposing external punishments on the abortion issue, it allows the truth about individual responsibility for morally good behavior in sexual and family relations to become real and powerful in individual lives.

Admittedly, the "individual responsibility" message subordinates the effect of abortion on the fetus to the woman's moral choice. That is, the message says that the political community values human agency on the abortion issue, with its prize and price, more than it values fetal life. I, for one, want the prize—full individual responsibility for family relationships with the moral development that individual responsibility brings—enough to suffer the price—that sometimes individuals will settle for less in their moral commitments and some fetuses will never be born.

## CONCLUSION

By refraining from using political coercion to prevent abortion, those who find abortion abhorrent do not participate in the sin of those who choose to abort. Rather, they make a judgment about the limits of political coercion and our common commitment as a political community, and about the extent of individual responsibility to conscience, to others, and to God rather than to government. Making this judgment enables pro-life advocates to commit themselves fully to the more difficult, but more worthwhile, task of winning hearts and minds to a better way of life.

Some Supreme Court Justices have revived the question of which government institution should make the judgment about the limits of political coercion in regulating abortion. In *Webster v. Reproductive Health Services,* four Justices express with varying degrees of conviction

126. Although concluding that laws will aid rather than hinder the process, Sidney Callahan recognizes the possibility for growth in wisdom, self-control, and love: "Educating and disciplining the emotions are seen as necessary to character development, for emotional growth is possible. A woman, for instance, who may not want a child can change her emotional reactions through reflection, self-mastery, and the power of love." Callahan, *supra* note 81, at 301; *see also* R. GRANT, *supra* note 21, at 45-48 (describing Locke's understanding of individuals' ability to "educate their desires" and "submit themselves to self-government" in the exercise of freedom).

Again, I emphasize that recognizing others' decision regarding abortion as wrong and damaging to their moral growth does not justify stereotyping them as "careless, immoral, and selfish." *See* R. PETCHESKY, *supra* note 5, at 370 (discussing inappropriate stereotyping of women who abort); *see also supra* notes 24, 105-06 and accompanying text.

their view that, contrary to the decision in *Roe v. Wade,* the state legislatures and not the Supreme Court are the appropriate institutions to decide the limits of abortion regulations.[127] Unlike the dissenting Justices, Chief Justice Rehnquist and Justices White, Kennedy, and Scalia, suggest (but do not expressly hold) that the Constitution does not put abortion "beyond the reach of the democratic process."[128]

However, the fourteenth amendment, in combination with the characteristics bestowed on the Supreme Court by article III of the Constitution[129] and the power bestowed by the tradition of judicial review, requires the Court to assume watchdog responsibilities in the federal system, ensuring that states do not "deprive any person of life, liberty, or property, without due process of law."[130] While some commentators, such as John Hart Ely, argue that "due process" means little more than procedural fairness in the operations of democratic government,[131] "liberty" is more than a word in the due process clause of the fourteenth amendment passed in 1868. Liberty, or individual agency, is one of the "unalienable rights" for which early Americans fought and died in a bloody revolution. They believed that "whenever any Form of Government becomes destructive of these ends, it is the Right of the People to alter or abolish it . . . ."[132] Liberty is a foundation principle in our form of government, a right we believe pre-exists government and survives its abolition. Alexander Hamilton defended the judiciary created by article III of the Constitution as a protector of liberty not only when faced with a specific violation of the Constitution, but also when faced with "unjust and partial laws."[133] Justice Douglas quotes a 1905 Supreme Court case

127. Webster v. Reproductive Health Servs., 109 S. Ct. 3040, 3040-58, 3064-67 (1989) (Rehnquist C.J., White, J., Kennedy, J.) (Scalia, J., concurring). For quotes of these Justices' opinions regarding the importance of the legislative process on issues such as abortion, see *supra* note 17. The dissenting Justices in *Roe v. Wade* express similar concerns about the relationship of the legislative and judicial processes: "[T]he conscious weighing of competing factors that the Court's opinion apparently substitutes for the established [rational relation] test is far more appropriate to a legislative judgment than to a judicial one." 410 U.S. 113, 173 (1973) (Rehnquist, J., dissenting); *see also id.* at 222 (White, J., dissenting) ("I find no constitutional warrant for imposing such an order of priorities on the people and legislatures of the States.").

128. *Webster,* 109 S. Ct. at 3058.

129. Article III grants life tenure and an undiminishable salary during their term in office to all Supreme Court Justices, as well as to judges of the lower federal courts. U.S. CONST. art. III, § 1.

130. U.S. CONST. amend. XIV, § 1.

131. Ely, *supra* note 15, at 935 ("But 'due process' generally guarantees only that the inhibition be procedurally fair and that it have some 'rational' connection—though plausible is probably a better word—with a permissible government goal.").

132. The Declaration of Independence para. 2 (U.S. 1776). For a longer inclusive quote from the Declaration of Independence, see *supra* text accompanying note 25.

133. Hamilton argues:

> But it is not with a view to infractions of the Constitution only that the independence of the judges may be an essential safeguard against the effects of occasional ill humors in the

suggesting a similar idea in his *Roe* concurrence: "There is, of course, a sphere within which the individual may assert the supremacy of his own will and rightfully dispute the authority of any human government, especially any free government existing under a written constitution, to interfere with the exercise of that will."[134] Recognizing the importance of liberty does not answer immediately the question whether women ought to be free to abort fetuses, but it does recommend greater consideration of the implications of political coercion on the question than suggested by a narrowly procedural interpretation of the due process clause.

James Madison expressed concern for the majority tyranny that can result from the (albeit procedurally fair) operations of democratic government. In *The Federalist No. 10,* he recommends a large republic to help alleviate the danger of majority tyranny.[135] Although a large republic may suffice to make majority tyranny difficult on the national level, the lessons of slavery, civil war, segregation, and racial discrimination demonstrate the dangers of majority tyranny on the state level. The fourteenth amendment was passed in response to these crises, and should be interpreted as conferring authority on the Supreme Court to prevent majority tyranny on the state level similar to its power to prevent majority tyranny at the national level.[136] Consequently, contrary to the plurality's intimations in *Webster,* the Supreme Court has a duty to consider whether state restrictions on abortion amount to majority tyranny.

The Supreme Court embraced that duty when in *Roe v. Wade* it thoroughly considered and negatively answered the question whether political power can be used appropriately to prevent abortion before fetal viability.[137] Political power cannot appropriately be used to prevent

> society. These sometimes extend no farther than to the injury of the private rights of particular classes of citizens, by unjust and partial laws. Here also the firmness of the judicial magistracy is of vast importance in mitigating the severity and confining the operation of such laws.

THE FEDERALIST No. 78, at 470 (A. Hamilton) (C. Rossiter ed. 1961).

134. Doe v. Bolton, 410 U.S. 179, 213-14 (1973) (quoting Jacobson v. Massachusetts, 197 U.S. 11, 29 (1905)).

135. THE FEDERALIST No. 10, at 83 (J. Madison) (C. Rossiter ed. 1961).

136. *See supra* text accompanying note 133. Robert Bork points out that "[m]ajority tyranny occurs if legislation invades the areas properly left to individual freedom," whereas "[m]inority tyranny occurs if the majority is prevented from ruling where its power is legitimate." Bork, *Neutral Principles and Some First Amendment Problems,* 47 IND. L.J. 1, 3 (1971). Apparently, on the abortion question some of the Justices fear minority tyranny at the hands of the Supreme Court more than majority tyranny at the hands of state legislatures.

137. 410 U.S. 113, 159-60 (1973). For a more thorough discussion of the legitimacy of *Roe*'s constitutional grounding, see Ely, *supra* note 15 (bad decision without adequate constitutional grounding), and Laurence Tribe, *Foreward: Toward a Model of Roles in the Due Process of Life and Law,* 87 HARV. L. REV. 1 (1973) (although *Roe* has its problems, it is a step in the right direction). *See also* Walter Dellinger & Gene Sperling, *Abortion and the Supreme Court: The Retreat From* Roe v. Wade, 138 U. PA. L. REV. 83 (1989) (*Webster* discounts *Roe*'s principles without adequate expla-

harms that without moral or religious commitments are not perceived as harms.[138] Further, even if all agreed that abortion causes a harm similar to murder, coercing involuntary sacrifices for others of the magnitude involved in a nine-month pregnancy has no precedent in our society.[139] The choice to adhere to the principle that sexual relations entail the risk of parenting obligations is a value judgment that requires individual reflection and moral commitment. Women should not be coerced into assuming the responsibility of giving birth to children if they reject the value judgment that enjoying sexual intimacy necessarily brings with it that potential responsibility.[140] With these minor adjustments in the analysis, the decision in *Roe* is mandated by our structurally limited form of government[141] and is enforced appropriately by the Supreme Court against the states through the due process clause of the fourteenth amendment.

*Kimberly Sharron Dunn*

nation); William Van Alstyne, *Closing the Circle of Constitutional Review from* Griswold v. Connecticut *to* Roe v. Wade: *An Outline of a Decision Merely Overruling* Roe, 1989 DUKE L.J. 1677 (responding to Dellinger and Sperling's defense of *Roe* as a necessary extension of *Griswold*).

138. *See supra* notes 82-104 and accompanying text.

139. *See supra* notes 107-16 and accompanying text.

140. *See supra* notes 118-21 and accompanying text.

141. Although he may not consider the analysis convincing, John Hart Ely suggested that the "system of government contemplated by the Constitution" might support a "constitutional right to an abortion" when he pointed out that the Court did not make use of that justification in *Roe*, as it had when it recognized a fundamental right to interstate travel. Ely, *supra* note 15, at 927-28.

# Part IV
# Constitutional Law

# [8]

# JOHN LOCKE'S DOCTRINE OF THE SEPARATION OF POWERS: A RE-EVALUATION

SURI RATNAPALA

THE ORIGINS OF THE MODERN DOCTRINE of the separation of powers are traced most often to the writings of John Locke and Baron de Montesquieu. Yet, despite their great political influence, the contributions of these writers to the separation doctrine have been vigorously questioned in academic circles. The most common charge directed at Locke and Montesquieu is that their theories of separation were based on misdescriptions of the successful English Constitution. As long ago as 1836, the German writer, Carl Ernst, referred to Locke as "the creator of the false theory of the English State."[1]

An equally important theme in academic discussions of Locke's political theory is that his reputation as an author of the separation doctrine is unwarranted, as he neither unequivocally recommended it nor conceived it in the modern tripartite form. There are two major reasons for this view of the Lockean theory. The first is that Locke appears to insist that "there can be but one *Supreme Power*, which is the *legislative*, to which all the rest are and must be subordinate."[2] Scholars have inferred from this and other statements that Locke regarded the separation of powers as a convenient arrangement, but not something vitally important.[3] The second reason is that Locke often treated judicial power as part of the executive power and that his threefold separation of legislative, executive, and federative powers does not correspond to the constitutional model which was eulogized by Montesquieu and adopted in modern constitutions to greater or lesser extents.

The broad aim of this essay is to examine Locke's theory of separation in its historical context in order to re-assess his contribution to the development of modern constitutionalism. Towards this end, I will examine firstly the historical antecedents of the Lockean theory. These antecedents show that Locke's theory represents, in many ways, the culmination of an historical process which linked medieval

1. J. Gough, *John Locke's Political Philosophy* (1973), p. 104.
2. J. Locke, *Two Treatises on Government* (P. Laslett, ed. 1970), p. 384.
3. *See ibid.*, p. 118; *John Locke's Political Philosophy*, p. 108; M. Vile, *Constitutionalism and the Separation of Powers* (1967), p. 61.

constitutionalism to the modern version. Secondly, I will examine Locke's theory in the context of the political events of the seventeenth century, to demonstrate its impact on the future shape of the English constitution. In doing so, I argue that his theory is a genuine theory of separation, which, far from misrepresenting the post-Revolution constitution, provided its essential ingredients.

## I. Historical Antecedents of Locke's Theory of Separation

It is evident that neither Locke nor Montesquieu invented the theory of the separation of powers. To regard them as having done so would be to ignore one of the recurring themes of European political history and the nature of the conflict between king and Parliament in England. The institutional division of powers in England, like that in the Roman Republic, was mainly the result of practical politics. Nevertheless, as in Rome, the nature of the political conflict and its ultimate resolution provided the ingredients for a theory of government. In the case of the Republic, the theoreticians were Cicero and Polybius and, in the case of England, the most influential, in the long term, were Locke and Montesquieu.

M.J.C. Vile notes that, by 1659, "the doctrine of a twofold separation of powers had become a commonplace" in England and that "John Locke's treatment of the powers of government must be seen in the light of an assumption that his readers were well acquainted with such a doctrine, rather than as if he were hesitantly presenting a new concept of government."[4] What was the nature of this twofold separation? In the early seventeenth century the common theory of the English constitution was that of mixed government. Since Charles' *Answer to the Nineteen Propositions*, the popular descriptions of the English constitution emphasized its mixture of monarchy (King), aristocracy (Lords), and democracy (Commons). However, as the controversialist Philip Hunton pointed out in 1643, there was an important qualification to the mixed nature of the constitution. Hunton drew the distinction between "power which is estated in a mixed principle" and power which "is solely entrusted and committed to the prince by the fundamental constitution of the state."[5] In the execution of laws, all subjects and the other estates were subject to the king, whereas in the exercise of power granted on the mixed principle, mainly the power to make law, each estate had a free

4. *Constitutionalism and the Separation of Powers*, p. 51.

5. *Political Ideas of the English Civil Wars (1641-1649)* (Sharp, ed. 1983), p. 153.

negative voice. We find in the distinction drawn by Hunton, the old separation between the power to make law, which belonged jointly to the three estates, and the power to conduct the government, including the administration of justice, which belonged solely to the king. It is this twofold separation which was commonplace in England at the time Locke embarked on his *Two Treatises*. In order to better appreciate Locke's contribution, it is instructive to take a closer look at the older doctrine of separation.

## II. The Medieval Separation of Powers

The twofold separation had its roots in the medieval constitutionalism of feudal Europe, specifically in the legal tradition of the Germanic and Frankish tribes. In his work, *Kingship and Law in the Middle Ages*, Fritz Kern identifies three cardinal principles of medieval constitutionalism, namely, the principle of legal limitation (king is bound to the law), the principle of popular representation (king's duty of obtaining consent), and the principle of responsibility (the right of resistance).[6] These principles were derived from the medieval concept of the law.

In the manner of most tribal communities, Germanic and Frankish peoples considered the law as a manifestation of the collective wisdom of the community. It was the wisdom by which the peaceful life of the tribe was carried on.[7] The law was to be found in the folkways and not in the expressed will of the rulers.[8] From this idea of the law as an abiding order, there followed certain important consequences. The first consequence was that law could not be made, but had to be discovered and declared. As the law could not be made by the rule, he was obliged to administer the law of the realm as it actually was and as ascertained by consulting immemorial practice.[9] The king, like subject, was bound to the law. This was the first principle of constitutionalism.

The second consequence was, since the law was the emanation from the people, its ascertainment and proclamation required the participation of the persons who traditionally spoke for them under

6. F. Kern, *Kingship and Law in the Middle Ages* (1968), pp. 181, 187, 194; *see* W. Ullman, *Principles of Government and Politics in the Middle Ages* (1966), p. 22.

7. G. Sabine, *A History of Political Theory* (1961), p. 200; *see* F.K. von Savigny, *System of Modern Roman Law* (W. Holloway, trans. 1867), pp. 12-17.

8. For recent anthropological evidence of such tribal perceptions of the law, *see* M. Gluckman, *Judicial Process Among the Barotse* (1967), pp. 230-39.

9. *Ibid.*, p. 207.

feudal arrangements. This second principle of constitutionalism was articulated in the enacting words of Charlemagne's laws:

> Charles the Emperor . . . together with the bishops, abbots, counts, dukes and all the faithful subjects of the Christian Church, and with their consent and counsel, has decreed the following. . . .[10]

The third consequence was that a king who breached the law *ipso facto* forfeited his right to rule.[11] The resistance of the community was declaratory of this fact.[12]

However, it is fanciful to think that these principles of constitutionalism were always realized in practice. The major causes for the divergence of theory and practice were the imprecision and uncertainty of the "unwritten" customary law and the lack of formal procedures and institutional checks for securing the observance of the law. Constitutional principle required the prince to harmonize his actions with the law and in cases of doubt to obtain the consent of the community. But, as Kern remarks, the practice was:

> Unless proof is brought forward to the contrary, all that is declared by the king is law, in the same sense as if it issued from the people, the community. Until proof was brought to the contrary, the monarch would be described as the standing representative of the people and its law. For this reason, the rules as to how the king attains agreement with the community, and at the same time his own harmony with the law, are exceedingly vague and undeveloped.[13]

There were three degrees of popular participation. In the first, the king acted alone with the tacit consent of the people. In the second, where doubts arose with respect to the law, he acted with the advice and consent of the representatives. In the third, with respect to individual cases, he obtained a judicial verdict. However, in the absence of institutional checks, the monarch effectively determined the appropriate form of consent. "Whether he settled the matter by personal decree, or after giving audience to, or even perhaps with the collaboration of counsellors, i.e., representatives of the community; or finally, by procuring the judgment of the high court or a court of princes, was decided entirely at his option."[14] So long as he was seen to be in harmony with the law, he avoided the ultimate sanction

10. *Ibid.*
11. *Kingship and Law in the Middle Ages*, p. 195.
12. *Ibid.*
13. *Ibid.*, p. 188.
14. *Ibid.*, p. 189.

of resistance, held to exist not only in the barons but also in every freeman.[15] This uncertainty of constitutional due process was lessened in the later middle ages when Estates became formally constituted with rights to be consulted in defined circumstances.[16]

The picture of medieval constitutionalism which emerges from history is that of a paradigm of government in which the function of ruling was clearly distinguishable from that of legislating. The king participated in both functions. The first was within his exclusive jurisdiction, but the second he performed by observing the cooperative procedures and forms involving the feudal tenants-in-chief. Whereas in the later theocratic conception of monarchy, the king's *voluntas* created law, "within the feudal framework there was no margin for the sovereign display of *voluntas*."[17]

The judicial power in the community was yet indistinct from the executive power, as the law was applied through the royal courts whose members had no independence through tenure or otherwise. It is not unusual that laws undergo alteration in the process of its judicial application to new situations. Hence customary law which was theoretically immune from royal amendment, nevertheless was in flux in the royal courts. But the modifications to the law effected through adjudication, resulted, not from the king's *voluntas*, but from legal rationality involved in the task of applying principles to particular circumstances. Development of the law proceeded along a "path unchartered by theory," a path strikingly illustrated by the development of the English common law.[18] Thus, although royal judges were still part of the executive, we see in the judicial method, a specialization which served as a foundation for the later separation and independence of the judiciary.

As noted, medieval constitutional practice often departed from theory. Yet, despite its partly mythical nature, and perhaps because of that nature, the medieval constitution remained a powerful influence on the community. It remained part of the popular culture, throughout the period of regal absolutism that followed. As Ullman avers, its ideas "provided a living bridge between the primitive European period and the new Europe."[19]

15. *Principles of Government and Politics in the Middle Ages*, p. 22.
16. *Kingship and Law in the Middle Ages*, pp. 198-99.
17. *Principles of Government and Politics in the Middle Ages*, pp. 150-51.
18. E. Lewis, *Medieval Political Ideas* (1974), p. 243.
19. *Principles of Government and Politics in the Middle Ages*, p. 24.

## III. Survival of Medieval Constitutionalism in England

It is common history that medieval constitutionalism in Europe was eclipsed by the theocratic conception of monarchy. According to this idea, the king derived his authority directly from God without human mediation. The theocratic view was the undisputed doctrine of the later Empire, receiving the explicit ecclesiastical endorsement in a pastoral rule of Pope St. Gregory.[20]

The scriptural authority for the rule was almost certainly found in the Pauline declaration:

> Let every soul be subject to the governing authorities. For there is no authority except from god, and the authorities that exist are appointed by God. Therefore whoever resists the authority resists the ordinance of God, and those who resist will bring judgement on themselves.[21]

Thus, according to the theocratic view, royal authority was derived, not from consensus, but from divine grace. The reversal of the legitimating doctrine (reflected in the royal title *Rex Dei gratia*) had the most profound consequence for the concept of law and the medieval separation of powers. The law was equated to the ruler's will (*voluntas principis*) and accordingly, the conceptual distinction between law and execution was obliterated from theory. The importance of folk laws diminished and their place was taken by the true *Konigsrecht*, the *capitularia per se scribenda*.[22] What the king willed was the law. Hence there could be no theoretical separation of the functions of law making and governing. As St. Thomas Aquinas later asserted, the ruler was entitled to "complete plenitude of power."[23] In his categorical opposition to any separation of powers, Aquinas also stated that "the interpretations of laws and dispensation from observance belongs to him who made the law"[24] and that "it pertains to the king to be over all human offices and to direct them through the authority of his rule."[25] Aquinas was deeply concerned about the possibility of absolute monarchy turning into tyranny. Unfortunately, his promise in *De Regimine Principum*, to discuss the precautions for preventing tyranny did not materialize,

20. R. Carlyle and A. Carlyle, 1 *A History of Medieval Political Theory in the West (1903-1936)*, p. 152.
21. *Romans* 13:1-2.
22. *Principles of Government and Politics in the Middle Ages*, p. 124.
23. *Commentaries on the Sentences*, IV, XXIV, 2, 1, ad 3.
24. *Summa Contra Gentiles*, III, q. 76.
25. *De Regimine Principum*, I, q. 15.

as he died before the completion of the work.[26] Tyranny, if established, may be resisted and overthrown "except perhaps in the case that it is accompanied by such disorder that the community suffers greater harm from the consequent disturbances than it would from a continuance of the former rule."[27] Thus, while the right of resistance persisted, under the theocratic conception of monarchy, there was an important difference between this and the older right of resistance. The right under feudal monarchy was exercisable when the king acted contrary to law. In the theocratic monarchy, as the king's will *was the law*, the right accrued only when *in fact* his conduct became unjust or tyrannical.

The absolutist view of monarchy, although challenged by the conciliar movement within the church and by Christian philosophers such as Marsilius of Padua,[28] remained dominant in the continent. However, the medieval constitutional tradition survived in England in the form of the Ancient Constitution, challenging the tide of absolutism and providing the foundation of modern constitutionalism. The two-fold separation of powers, which lay at the core of this tradition, was preserved in the Ancient Constitution in the form of the distinction between *gubernaculum*, the government of the realm, and *jurisdictio*, the capacity to determine the rights of the subject. This distinction entailed the denial of legislative power to the king in so far as it concerned the rights of the subject. In his outstanding work, *Constitutionalism, Ancient and Modern*, McIllwain captures the essence of this distinction in the following words:

> It is in *jurisdictio*, therefore, and not in "government" that we find the most striking proof that in medieval England the Roman maxim of absolutism was never in force theoretically or actually. For in jurisdiction, the king was bound by his oath to proceed by law and not otherwise. Although the judges were his, appointed and acting in his name alone, they were nevertheless bound by their own oath to determine the rights of the subject not according to the king's will, but according to the law; and any careful study of the masses of plea rolls which survive from this period must convince one that this was no mere pious theory, but on the whole the actual and general practice. When King John substituted his will for this law, in proceeding against vassals whose wrong had not been judicially proved, civil war and the Great Charter were

26. *Ibid*, I, VI.

27. *Summa Theologica*, II.II, q. 42, a. 2. Concerning particular unjust laws, *see* II.II, q. 96, a. 4: "Such laws do not, in consequence, oblige in conscience, except, on occasion, to avoid scandal or disorder."

28. Marsilius of Padua, *Defensor Pacis* (A. Gewirth, ed. 1956), p. 29.

> the result. The famous thirty-ninth chapter of *Magna Carta* contains merely the classic statement of the principle that was always insisted upon and usually enforced as a rule of positive coercive law, and not, as the Austinians would say, as a mere maxim of positive morality. . . .[29]

The ancient constitution, itself, may have been partly mythical, but its influence on law and politics was real. As Pocock notes, appeals to this constitution formed one of the chief modes of political argument in the seventeenth century.[30]

Under the Ancient Constitution *jurisdictio* belonged to the courts, and to Parliament. Parliament exercised *jurisdictio*, not as a general legislature, but as the highest court. The legislative power of Parliament originated from its authority as the supreme court, to supply a rule of law where none existed. As William Lambard wrote in 1591, "It hath jurisdiction in such cases which have need of helpe and for which there is no helpe by any Law, already in force."[31] However, the infrequency and brevity of Parliamentary sessions under the Tudors and the emergence of other courts, provided the major impetus to the conversion of Parliament into a mainly legislative organ.[32] With this development, the idea of law as immutable custom gave way to the still medieval idea that law is changeable, but only with the consent of the people assembled in Parliament. The king's assent was necessary for the making of new law, but he lacked independent legislative authority outside the sphere of his prerogative. Conversely, the legislative power of Parliament did not extend to the administration of the realm which remained exclusively in the hands of the king.

## IV. The Crisis of the Constitution

Locke's theory of civil government was formulated in the context of the great seventeenth century crisis of the constitution. The meaning as well as the significance of Locke's theory can be appreciated best, if the nature of this crisis is understood. The political events leading to the Glorious Revolution must surely comprise one of the most examined chapters of English history. Hence, these events need no repetition here. However, it is important for this discussion to look closely at the legal dimension of this crisis.

29. C. McIlwain, *Constitutionalism, Ancient and Modern* (1947), pp. 85-86.
30. J. Pocock, *The Ancient Constitution and the Feudal Law* (1967), p. 46.
31. *Constitutionalism, Ancient and Modern*, pp. 123-24.
32. *Ibid.*, pp. 131-33.

It appears from most historical accounts that the crisis was caused mainly by the absolutist ambition of the Stuarts and the parliamentary resistance to it. But if we look at this crisis through the prisms of constitutional theory, we may discern beneath the naked ambitions of the Stuarts and the idealistic pretenses of many parliamentarians, a real crisis of the constitution precipitated by the economic, social, and religious changes which accompanied the transition of the nation from the medieval to the modern era. These changes exerted immense pressures on the Ancient Constitution which was not designed to withstand them.

There were at least three destabilizing elements within the constitution itself. The first of these, which was the uncertainty of the limits of the prerogative, encouraged royal attempts to encroach on the sphere of rights (*jurisdiction*). The other two, namely, the Parliament's control over finance and its power of impeachment of placemen allowed it to interfere with the functions of government (*gubernaculum*). Often, incursions by one party into the domain of the other provoked retaliatory or defensive actions which infringed the rights of the first party. There was a major weakness in the constitution which made it incapable of resolving these conflicts between government and Parliament. It was the fact that the constitution was built on precedent rather than on abstract principle. The distinction between *gubernaculum* and *jurisdiction* did not correspond exactly to the distinction between law and its execution. It was an approximation to that distinction in the circumstances of medieval England. *Gubernaculum* was not merely the execution of the law but an area of discretionary government which by ancient precedent belonged absolutely to the king. Likewise, *jurisdiction* was not a general capacity to lay down the law, but was the power to determine matters affecting the ancient rights at common law. These rights were concerned predominantly with property. Property was considered to determine the subject's liberty. Medieval government, owing to its traditionally limited role, had no need to interfere frequently with medieval rights in property. Conflicts were, therefore, infrequent and manageable. However, the transition to the modern era had two very important consequences for the constitution. Firstly, the concerns of government, and with them, the expenses of government grew enormously. Secondly, the changing social, economic, and religious conditions expanded the areas of private interests which were considered inviolable without consent. These included not only legal or customary rights, but also new-found freedoms and interests relating to religion and commerce. The traditional distance between *gubernaculum* and *jurisdiction* was eroded at both ends to the point where the two realms were in constant conflict. The intensity of this conflict increased naturally when men of commerce entered political life and altered the composition and consequently, the concerns of parliament. The situation demanded a clearer demarcation of authority than was provided by uncertain and contentious precedents. A creative interpretation of the distinction between *gubernaculum* and *jurisdiction* may have yielded such a demarcation, leading to the recognition of a right in parliament to legislate generally, while reserving to the king the function of governing in the narrower sense. Under such a demarcation government would have been confined to the execution of the laws and the administration of the realm *subject to law*. This demarcation was eventually established by the revolution settlement, but only after a century of strife.

Many of the state trials of the early seventeenth century showed up the growing obsolescence of the ancient constitution, perhaps none more vividly than *Bates' Case*. John Bates, a merchant, was prosecuted for failing to pay the infamous impositions which were added to the traditional duties of custom charged at the king's harbors. In defense, Bates challenged the impositions on grounds that they were not authorized by parliament. The Court of Exchequer upheld the impositions as a valid exercise of the prerogative. The court acted on precedents which regarded foreign trade as a matter exclusively within the king's right on par with the right to conduct war. These precedents were in tune with medieval realities which, however, were being overtaken by the tide of change. The court stated:

> all customs be they old or new, are no other but the effects and issues of trades and commerce with foreign nations, but all commerce and affairs with forrainers, all wars and peace, all acceptance and admitting for currant forrayn coyn; all parties and treaties whatsoever are made by the absolute power of the kings, and he who hath power of causes, hath power also of effects. . . .[33]

The court's decision was compatible with mercantilism, but was out of step with emerging patterns of private commerce among nations. The expansion of foreign trade necessitated new outlays by government to facilitate trade and to protect traders. But these matters were no

33. *Bates' Case 2 State Tr.* 371, 389 (1606).

longer exclusively or even primarily of royal concern. They also concerned the vital interests of individuals who were now strongly represented in Parliament. In short, changed economic conditions had converted what was previously an "administrative" situation into a "rights" situation. However, the judges in *Bates' Case* were guided by concrete precedent rather than by abstract principle. Hence, despite their recognition that private interests were involved in this issue, they decided according to precedent, that the question was one determinable at the king's discretion. This case and others like *Darnel's Case*[34] and the *Ship Money Case*[35] made it clear that the prerogative was operating in areas and in ways which were incompatible with the expectations of the transformed society. The constitution was cast in a medieval mold and was anchored to the past by precedent. It needed nothing short of a revolutionary overhaul in order to remain relevant.

The abolition of the monarchy in 1649 and the ensuing rule by the Long Parliament (in effect the Rump) proved to be a cure almost worse than the disease. Parliament conducted the day to day administration of government through its own Council of State and other committees. It appointed all military and civilian officials. It tried people, confiscated property, and victimized opponents. It became evident that a parliament invested with both legislative and executive powers could be as tyrannical as any absolute monarch. Given this experience, "Englishmen resolved at the Restoration never again to be ruled by parliamentary committees, to always keep separate, executive and legislative powers."[36] The principle of separation became the official doctrine of the Protectorate. In defending the *Instrument of Government*, the authors of the *True State of the Case of the Commonwealth* called the separation of executive and legislative powers "the grand secret of liberty and good government."[37] It was, however, Cromwell who best expressed the rationale of separation. Speaking of the Long Parliament's sovereign power, he said, that if parliament is asked the question, "What are the rules you judge by," parliament's answer would be "Why we have none . . . we are supreme in legislative and judicature."[38]

---

34. 3 *State Tr.* 1 (1627). Darnel who was imprisoned for refusing to pay the forced loan, was denied *Habeas Corpus* on the ground that the court could not look behind the king's writ.

35. 3 *State Tr.* 825 (1637). Hampden was refused relief against the exaction of ship money in peace time on the ground that the court had no competence to question king's judgment that an emergency existed.

36. C. Roberts, *The Growth of Responsible Government in Stuart England* (1966), p. 145.

37. *Ibid.*, p. 150.

38. *Ibid.*, p. 148.

Cromwell was, in the older fashion, treating the judicial power as an aspect of the executive power. As Vile notes, by the time Locke began compiling his *Two Treatises of Government*, at least two authors, Charles Dallison and George Lawson, had distinguished judicial power from the general executive power.[39] The need to separate the judicial power from the executive became painfully clear in the seventeenth century, as disputes between king and parliament went before judges who served at the king's pleasure. The king was able and wiling to interfere in the judicial process to secure his political or personal interests. Learned and upright judges had precarious tenure,[40] as shown by the dismissals of Chief Justice Coke (1616), Crew (1627), Heath (1634), and Chief Baron Walter (1630). The insecurity of judicial office did not create the constitutional problem, but accentuated it by making the abuse of prerogatives less amenable to challenge. Hence, as the century progressed, it became increasingly evident that judicial independence was critical to the containment of power within constitutional bounds.

## V. Locke's Theory of Separation

Vile is substantially correct when he points out that all the elements of the separation of powers doctrine were in place when Locke commenced his *Two Treatises of Government*. But, while the writings of his predecessors faded into obscurity, Locke's work gained phenomenal fame and for more than two centuries stood as a foundation of western constitutionalism. How does one explain Locke's influence? Locke's impact on the immediate political scene was not surprising, considering his enormous influence on the Whig Party which came into ascendancy after the Revolution. Laslett states, "As a result of the Revolution the obscure exile became a man of political influence, with powerful friends in high places."[41] His writings became the celebrated vindication of Whig political ideas and a refutation of the patriarchal and royalist theories of Filmer and others. Although contrary to popular belief, the *Two Treatises* was written a decade before the Revolution.[42] It was received as an outstanding Apology for the Revolution. Yet, its lasting appeal, both in England and abroad, cannot be explained by these circumstances

39. *Constitutionalism and the Separation of Powers*, pp. 46, 55.
40. W. Holdsworth, VI *A History of English Law* (1924), p. 503.
41. *Two Treatises of Government*, p. 37.
42. *Ibid.*

alone. To understand this, the essential difference between Locke's inquiry and those of his English predecessors, must be examined.

Locke's reputation as "the creator of the false theory of the English State" has persisted in academic circles. Yet, what Locke sought to do in the *Two Treatises* was not to describe the English constitution but to formulate a theory of the free state, by which he hoped to influence the thinking of his age and possibly that of the future. The controversialists before him had, without exception, appealed to the letter or the spirit of the old English constitution and had sought to draw therefrom the principles regarding separation. Locke was unavoidably a creature of his time and there is no reason to doubt that the events that were shaping the constitution also shaped this thinking. The issues he addressed were the issues of Englishmen. The answers he provided were already present in the fabric of English custom and political thought. But Locke was not content to reconstruct a constitutional theory from precedent. He searched instead for first principles from which he could build a general theory of the free state which would justify the assumptions of the Whig political movement. These principles he found in his view of the state of nature and man's natural rights. Locke's anthropology is patently fictitious. Yet, the formulation of his constitutional theory on this basis gave it the level of abstraction which marks enduring ideas. Laslett states:

> Neither Machiavelli, nor Hobbes, nor Rousseau succeeded in making the discussion of politics so completely independent of historical example, so entirely autonomous an area of discourse, yet Locke has affected the everyday activity of practising politicians more perhaps than any of them.[43]

Locke made no appeal to the common law and almost none to the *Ancient Constitution*. The independence he gave himself and the premises from which he argued, enabled him to transcend the immediate controversy between King and Parliament and to place both institutions in a wider political scheme. This had crucial implications for his theory of government. It resulted in a focus on the nature of legislative power and its limitations, whereas the contemporary political focus was on the limitation of the monarchical power. It is true that, in the period of the Long Parliament, the question of government by Parliament had become the key issue. However, it was no longer the immediate issue, since executive power

43. *Ibid.*, p. 78.

had been restored to the king. The concern once again had become monarchial excesses, this time, of Charles II and James II. Locke was looking beyond the immediate controversy into the nature of civil government. His concern went much further than a desire to remove executive power from Parliament. It arose out of his theory of property and his theory of trust. Property, wrote Locke, included a man's "Life, Liberty and Estate"[44] and "the great and *chief end* . . . of Mens uniting into Commonwealths, and putting themselves under Government, *is the Preservation of their Property*."[45]

What is Locke's theory of the separation of powers? The popular view has been that Locke proposed the old division of legislative and executive powers with a further elucidation of the federative power which nonetheless is an aspect of executive power. This view, it is submitted, is essentially correct. However, considerable confusion has resulted from Locke's insistence that "there can be but *one Supream Power*, which is *the Legislative*, to which all the rest are and must be subordinate."[46] Some have seen this as a contradiction,[47] while others have concluded that, to Locke, the separation of powers was only a matter of convenience and not something vitally important.[48]

Locke's indiscriminate use of terms and his apparent inconsistencies do create problems. The overlapping senses in which he refers to legislative, executive, and judicial powers are particular troublesome to the modern mind. However, some of this confusion also results from trying to understand Locke's theory of separation of powers by working backwards from present day notions about the theory. Locke's theory can best be comprehended by tracing it from his own first principles.

Locke's theory commences with an idea of the state of nature which is at least as old as Plato's *Republic*.[49] Locke's state of nature (unlike that of Hobbes) was not nasty or brutish, but was a state governed by a benign law of nature.[50] In it, man has "Title to perfect Freedom, and an uncontrouled enjoyment of all the Rights and Priviledges of the Law of Nature, equally with any other Man, or Number of Men in the World, hath by Nature a Power, not only to preserve his Property, that is, his Life, Liberty and Estate, against

44. *Ibid.*, p. 341.
45. *Ibid.*, pp. 368-69.
46. *Ibid.*, p. 384.
47. *Constitutionalism and the Separation of Powers* (1967), p. 62.
48. *John Locke's Political Philosophy*, p. 108.
49. E. Barker, *Political Thought of Plato and Aristotle* (1973), p. 36.
50. *See* T. Hobbes, *Leviathan* (J. Plamenatz, ed. 1972), p. 143.

the Injuries and Attempts of other men; but to judge of, and punish the breaches of that Law in others, as he is perswaded the Offence deserves. . . ."[51] Unlike all other proponents of separation of powers, Locke begins, not by considering the consequences of concentrating power in a ruler, but by considering its concentration in individuals. "For in the State of Nature, to omit the liberty he has of innocent Delights, a Man has two Powers. The first is to do whatsoever he thinks fit for the preservation of himself and others within the permission of the *Law of Nature*. . . . The other . . . the *power to punish the Crimes* committed against that Law."[52] Man is thus his own legislator, judge, and executor. Locke examines this condition and finds it one "which however free, is full of fears and continual dangers."[53] By examining the reasons of this insecurity, he arrives, by a reverse process, at the very conclusions that others have reached from examining the absolute power of rulers. There are three things wanting in the state of nature.

First, there is no "establish'd, settled, known Law, received and allowed by common consent to be the Standard of Right and Wrong. . . . For though the Law of Nature be plain and intelligible to all rational Creatures; yet Men being biased by there Interest, as well as ignorant for want of study of it, are not apt to allow of it as a Law binding to them in the application of it to their particular Cases."[54] The deficiency Locke sees is none other than the lack of generality of the law which has been an immemorial concern of philosophers. "*Secondly*, In the State of Nature there wants *a known and indifferent Judge*, with Authority to determine all differences according to the established Law."[55] The problem here is that, even if parties are agreed as to the law of nature, its application will be tainted by the partiality and emotion that results from a man being a judge in his own cause. "Thirdly, In the state of Nature there often wants Power to back and support the Sentence when right, and to *give* it due *Execution*. They who by any Injustice offended, will seldom fail, where they are able by force to make good their Injustice. . . ."[56]

The three deficiencies of the state of nature which Locke outlines, correspond closely to the lack of differentiation between legislative,

51. *Two Treatises on Government*, pp. 341-42.
52. *Ibid.*, p. 370.
53. *Ibid.*, p. 368.
54. *Ibid.*, p. 369.
55. *Ibid.*
56. *Ibid.*

judicial, and executive powers in the state. It has been said Locke did not formulate a separate judicial power alongside the legislative and executive powers, or, more accurately, he did not divide the functions of the enforcement of the law into two independent "powers" as Lawson had done.[57] Plamenatz states:

> [Locke] though he distinguished between three governmental powers, the legislative, the executive and the federative (by which last he meant the control of relations with other states), the third is nowadays included in the second; and, in any case, he did not advise that it should be in separate hands. The only separation that seemed to him to matter was between the legislative and the other two powers. Locke did not even mention the judicial power, which he no doubt thought of as part of the executive.[58]

These remarks are true of the twelfth chapter of the *Second Treatise*, but not of the *Second Treatise* as a whole. In the twelfth chapter, Locke speaks, without distinction, of the power necessary "to the execution of the laws that are made and remain in force" and gives reasons why "the legislative and executive power come often to be separated." A close look at this chapter reveals that Locke is here concerned to distinguish powers in relation to their primary character. If executive power is taken to mean, only the power to "execute the law," then judicial power can be accommodated within it. For, the judicial function consists mainly of applying the law to the particular case or situation, which is a form of "executing" the law. However, executive function in the wider sense, means more than merely "executing" the law. It would include the general administration of the state, a function which may not, or may only remotely involve enforcing the law. Did Locke fail to perceive the distinction between the wider and narrower meanings of executive power? If he did, it may explain partially, his failure to clearly identify a separate judicial power. An alternative explanation may be found in Locke's assertion that coercive executive power should be employed at home "only in the execution of . . . laws."[59] By this statement, Locke seems to deny to the king any coercive power in administration which was not authorized by law. The non-coercive aspects of administration finds no place in Locke's division of powers as, strictly speaking, they involve no power. Thus, in Locke's scheme,

57. *Constitutionalism and the Separation of Powers*, pp. 59-60.
58. J. Plamenatz, 1 *Man and Society* (1963), p. 283.
59. *Two Treatises of Government*, p. 371.

the executive power means coercive power to execute the law, whether employed by the king's judges or by other officers.

The federative power identified by Locke relates to the management of the community's relations with alien nations and peoples. In Locke's time, these matters were rarely the subject of legislation, although Parliament did have a measure of control through its fiscal powers. Even now this is the area where, in the absence of legislation an inherent executive power is most readily conceded to the executive branch of government.[60] Here, Locke draws a distinction between matters which are properly within the area of legislative control and matters which by their nature are "much less capable to be directed by antecedent, standing, positive Laws, than the *Executive*; and so must necessarily be left to the Prudence and Wisdom of those whose hands it is in to be managed for the publick good."[61] Locke went on to say, "But what is to be done in reference to *Foreigners*, depending much upon their actions, and the variation of designs and interests, must be *left* in great party *to* the *Prudence* of those who have this Power committed to them, to be managed by the best of their Skill, for the advantage of the Commonwealth.[62] However prudent it might have appeared, the Whig philosophy could not concede a similar power in domestic affairs.

The distinctions drawn in the twelfth chapter are therefore, between the making of laws, the execution of laws and the conduct of government without recourse to law, where such is appropriate. It is also true that, in this chapter, Locke makes no positive recommendation that these powers be kept in different hands, although he stated that "legislative and executive power come often to be separated." The reason for this will be presently made clear. But first it is necessary to question whether the essence of Locke's doctrine can be gathered from the twelfth chapter alone.

Locke does not commence his theory by examining existing constitutions, although they would have provided much of his inspiration. Rather he sets out to demonstrate, from his own conception of nature, that absolute rule is irrational and that people will choose to have it only through shortsightedness. People unite into political societies for the protection of their property, which, in the Lockean sense meant life, liberty, and estate. In pre-society, these things are in jeopardy because each man is his own law giver, judge,

60. For a discussion of the Australian constitutional position, *see*, G. Winterton, *Parliament, the Executive and the Governor-General* (1983), p. 32.

61. *Two Treatises of Government*, pp. 383-84.

62. *Ibid.*

and executor. Society is advantageous precisely for the reason that it differentiates these functions. The fundamentals of Locke's theory are to be found in this reasoning and to understand them one must look at the portions of the text where he expounds them from first principles. It is however there, that we also come across the apparent contradiction in Locke's theory, which is said to arise from his insistence on the supremacy of the "legislative."

Locke writes of the supremacy of the legislative in two senses. One sense is clearly explained by Locke's own words:

> In all Cases whilst the Government subsists, the *Legislative is the Supream Power*. For what can give Laws to another must needs be superior to him and since the Legislative is no otherwise Legislative of the Society, but by the right it has to make Laws for all the parts and for every Member of the Society, prescribing Rules to their actions, and giving power of Execution, where they are transgressed, the *Legislative* must needs be the *Supream*, and all other Powers in any Members or parts of the Society derived from subordinate to it.[63]

Here, Locke is making the point that since all organs are subject to the law, the organ that makes the law is superior to the others. This idea of legislative supremacy, as Vile pints out, is perfectly consistent with the separation of powers, as "the legislative function is prior to the executive, and the latter must be exercised according to the rules which result from the exercise of the former."[64] In other words, it is a concomitant of the rule of law, or government according to law. But Vile appears to overlook another sense in which Locke refers to the supremacy of the legislative, one which must be comprehended in order that the true meaning and depth of Locke's doctrine be realized.

Although Locke regards the non-differentiation of legislative, judicial, and executive functions as the great deficiency of the state of nature, his account of the transition to political society strongly suggests that, in uniting into societies, men do not set up different institutions for the performance of these functions, but surrender *all their powers* to one supreme authority. The beginning of political society, according to Locke, is when people "give up all the power, necessarily to the ends for which they unite into Society, to the *majority* of the Community, unless they expressly agreed in any number greater than the majority."[65] Political society is established

63. *Ibid.*, pp. 385-86.
64. *Constitutionalism and the Separation of Powers* (1967), p. 63.
65. *Two Treatises of Government*, p. 351.

"where-ever any number of Men, in the state of Nature, enter into Society to make one People, one body Politick, under *one Supreme Government* . . . And this *puts Men* out of a State of Nature *into* that of a *Commonwealth*, by setting up a Judge on Earth, with Authority to determine all the Controversies, and redress the Injuries, that may happen to any Member of the Commonwealth; which Judge is the Legislative, or Magistrates appointed by it."[66]

In these marks Locke clearly is referring to the legislative, as the original repository of all power and as the embodiment of the composite power of the state. The important question is whether Locke thereby lost sight of the original purpose of men uniting into societies and, if not, how he reconciled the composite nature of the surrendered power with the separation of its parts. The answer to this question is to be found in the last paragraph of his ninth chapter entitled "Ends of Political Society and Government." This paragraph is so crucial to an understanding of Locke's theory of the separation of powers, that it must be quoted in full.

> But though Men when they enter into Society, give up the Equality, Liberty and Executive Power they had in the State of Nature, into the hands of the Society, to be so far disposed of by the Legislative as the good of the Society shall require; yet it being only with an intention in every one the better to preserve himself his Liberty and Property; (For no rational Creature can be supposed to change his condition with an intention to be worse) the power of the Society, or *Legislative* constituted by them, *can never be suppos'd to extend farther than the common good*; but is obliged to secure every ones Property by providing against those three defects above-mentioned that made the State of Nature so unsafe and uneasie. And so whoever has the Legislative or Supream Power of any Common-wealth, is bound to govern by establish'd *standing Laws*, promulgated and known to the People, and not by Extemporary Decrees; by *indifferent* and upright *judges*, who are to decide Controversies by those Laws; And to employ the force of the Community at home, *only in the Execution of such Laws*, or abroad to prevent or redress Foreign Injuries, and secure the Community from Inroads and Invasion. And all this to be directed to no other *end*, but the *Peace, Safety* and *publick good* of the People.[67]

In this paragraph, Locke cleverly reconciles the elements of trust, the supremacy of the legislative, and the limitation of its power. Men give up their individual powers to the society for the purpose of

66. *Ibid.*, p. 343.
67. *Ibid.*, p. 371.

preserving life, liberty, and estate. More specifically they do so in order that the condition which threatened lives, liberties, and estates, namely the non-differentiation of law, adjudication and execution be remedied. Thus, the duty to effect this differentiation is the key term of the trust upon which power was surrendered to the community as a whole. The reason for men "quitting" the state of nature is fundamentally this. The establishment and maintenance of this differentiation becomes the very essence of the duty of the state.

Laslett submits that in Locke's writing there is "no theory of the importance and desirability of the perpetual residence of these powers in separate hands in order to preserve liberty, guarantee rights, or keep the constitution in harmony, unison and health."[68] He is correct to the extent that Locke did not insist that powers be kept in separate hands. But he did insist that they be exercised by different processes. Laslett errs in stating that the "proper functioning and just exercise" of the powers of government were provided for by Locke "not by any doctrine of necessary separation . . . [but] by the concept of trust, which applies to the legislative in its fullest force, but also to the executive and federative."

There are two mistakes in this conclusion. Firstly, Laslett appears to lose sight of the purpose and the terms of Locke's "trust." Powers were given on trust to an authority because in the hands of individuals they are necessarily undifferentiated and concentrated. Precisely this condition made the state of nature unsatisfactory, and it was to bring about such a differentiation that powers were conceded to the state. Locke was clear in his view that where the differentiation ceased to exist in the conduct of government, there will be a return to the state of nature.

> For the *end of Civil Society*, being to avoide, and remedy those inconveniencies of the State of Nature, which necessarily follow from every Man's being Judge in his own Case, by setting up a known Authority, to which every one of that Society may Appeal upon any Injury received, or Controversie that may arise, and which every one of the Society ought to obey; where-ever any persons are, who have not such an authority to Appeal to, for the decision of any difference between them, there those persons are still *in the state of Nature*. . . . For he being suppos'd to have all, both Legislative and Executive Power in himself alone, there is no Judge to be found. . . . So that such a Man, however intitled, *Czar* or *Grand Signior*, or how you please, is as much *in*

68. *Ibid.*, p. 118.

> *the state of Nature*, with all under his Dominion, as he is with the rest of Mankind.[69]

Locke discusses the reversion to nature mainly in relation to monarchies. The reason is not that he regarded the differentiation of powers as dispensable where they are granted to representative bodies, but that he considered such bodies to be inclined by their representative nature to uphold such differentiation, hence, to honor their trust. Even so, Locke spared no effort to lay down limitations on legislative authority, which limitations, as presently noted, were calculated to prevent a reversion to the state of nature. Laslett's mistake is in treating Locke's concept of the trust as something unconnected to his idea of separating powers rather than as something calculated to give effect to it.

Laslett's second mistake is shared by many modern writers. The error lies in a failure to appreciate the distinction between the separation of powers and the mechanics of separating powers. The fact that Locke did not stipulate the separation of powers in distinct bodies does not detract from this position that the making of the law should be kept separate from its execution and the process of adjudication. Locke was aware that, in England, the king and placemen were an inextricable part of the legislature. Applied to the English Constitution, his theory meant, not that the king should have no part in the making of laws, but that the king could not legislate in his own right and could exclusively exercise only the executive and federative powers. Such a situation was perfectly possible and was largely achieved during Locke's lifetime. Locke was similarly conscious of the fact that the highest court in the land was Parliament itself, but he felt that it need not prevent adjudication of disputes by "indifferent and upright judges." He was also aware that, given those conditions, the legislature could be restricted to the making of general laws through the cooperation of the three estates. For Locke, as for Aristotle, the condition of liberty was not necessarily the separation of powers in different bodies, but the way in which the powers were differently regarded and differently exercised. This concern becomes clearer in Locke's treatment of "The Extent of the Legislative Power" in Chapter XI.

Locke regarded the legislative power to be limited by its original purpose, which is the preservation of life, liberty, and property such that the legislative "can never have a right to destroy, enslave, or

69. *Ibid.*, p. 344.

designedly to impoverish the Subjects."[70] Although the legislative may make laws for the regulation of property, it "can never have Power to take to themselves the whole or any part of the Subjects' *Property* without their own consent."[71] Government expenditure can be met by taxation only with the "Consent of the Majority giving it either by themselves, or their Representatives chosen by them." Locke also places two other limitations on the legislature which are based squarely on the separation of functions. "The *Legislative* or Supream Authority, cannot assume to its self a power to Rule by extemporary Arbitrary Decrees, but *is bound to dispense Justice*, and decide the Rights of the Subject *by promulgated standing Laws and known Authorised Judges.*"[72] This limitation is implicit in the trust "that they shall be governed by *declared Laws*, or else their Peace, Quiet and Property will still be at the same uncertainty as it was in the State of Nature."[73]

Locke's final limitation was that "The *Legislative cannot transfer the Power of Making Laws* to any other hands. For it being but a delegated Power from the People, they, who have it, cannot pass it over to others . . . when the People have said, We will submit to rules, and be govern'd by Laws made by such Men, and in such Forms, no Body else can say other Men shall make *Laws* for them."[74] It is possible to understand this limitation purely on the principle of "*delegata otestas non potest delegari.*" But it is almost inconceivable that Locke did not have uppermost in his mind, the consequences that would occur when the legislator is free to delegate his power. The trust placed in the legislative requires laws to be made not only "by such men" but also "in such forms." Delegation destroys the first condition and instantly imperils the second, that laws shall not be made for particular ends but shall be general.

The textual evidence is so overwhelming that Locke considered it fundamental to his theory that the making and execution of the law should be kept separate. Where locke differed from others was in his belief that an elected assembly could be entrusted with all powers on the condition that they be exercised differently. He sought to ensure the separation of powers, not by placing powers in diverse

70. *Ibid.*, p. 375.
71. *Ibid.*, p. 379.
72. *Ibid.*, p. 376.
73. *Ibid.*, p. 373.
74. *Ibid.*, p. 380.

hands, but by insisting upon the limitations on each power derived from the original trust.

There remains to consider Locke's position on the judicial power. The widely held view is that Locke treated the judicial power as part of the executive and hence failed to accord it the importance it received later.[75] This view is valid subject to the qualification that Locke did not always refer to the executive power in the modern sense. On several occasions Locke uses the term actually to mean the judicial power and employs a distinct expression such as the "force of the community" to denote the executive power in the coercive sense. In one instance Locke states:

> And herein we have the original of the *Legislative* and *Executive Power* of Civil Society, which is to judge by standing Laws how far Offences are to be punished, when committed within the Commonwealth; and also to determine by occasional Judgements founded on the present Circumstances of the Fact, how far Injuries from without are to be vindicated and in both these to imploy all the force of all the Members when there shall be need.[76]

Elsewhere he refers to the duty of the supreme power "to imploy the force of the Community at home *only in the Execution of such Laws*, or abroad to prevent or redress Foreign Injuries, and secure the community from Inroads and Invasion."[77] In keeping with Whig philosophy, Locke appears to require that the executive power when employed for the execution of the laws, should be judicially performed. In other words, when speaking of the execution of the laws he often meant the judicial function. For example he says:

> Tis this makes them so willingly give up every one his single power of punishing to be exercised by such alone as shall be appointed to it amongst them; and by such Rules as the Community, or those authorised by them to that purpose, shall agree on. And in this we have the original *right and rise* of both the *Legislative and Executive Power*, as well as of the Governments and Societies themselves.[78]

The Whig antipathy to discretionary government shows in Locke's reluctance to concede the use of "the force of the community" except for the purpose of supporting "the sentence when right" and for the purpose of conducting foreign policy. In his short but crucial ninth chapter, Locke clearly distinguishes the judicial power to be

75. *See Man and Society*, p. 283; *John Locke's Political Philosophy*, p. XXIII; *Constitutionalism and the Separation of Powers*, p. 59.
76. *Two Treatises of Government*, p. 343.
77. *Ibid.*, p. 371.
78. *Ibid.*, p. 379.

exercised by "indifferent judges" from "the force of the community" to be exercised in support of the law and judgment. The judicial power is ever present in Locke's scheme. Locke often included the judicial power within the executive power. But not infrequently, he uses "executive power" to mean, in fact, judicial power.

Locke's theory of separation of powers is not expressed with the terminological precision to which modern scholarship is accustomed. But in his confusing and sometimes discordant text, we can still see a clear differentiation between legislative, executive, and judicial powers. What was lacking in Locke's theory was a proposal to place each power in a different authority. The absence of this element, which found its way into later theories, is not hard to explain.

Although Locke consciously avoided arguments based on English history, there is no doubt that his theory was primarily intended to influence the course of constitutional development in England. The separation of powers by means of vesting different powers exclusively in different organs, meant denying the king any role in law making and the exclusion of placemen and judges from Parliament. Locke could not have failed to realize that the course of English history precluded the adoption of a wholly new constitution and that the likely resolution of the constitutional dispute lay in the eventual supremacy of Parliament. Locke says that men emerge from the state of nature by conceding their powers to the majority amongst them. *King in Parliament* did not represent a majority of the community, so long as the king and the Lords had equal voices with the Commons. But Locke carefully qualifies his position by also stating, "That the *beginning of Politick Society* depends upon the consent of the Individuals, to joyn into and make one Society; who, when they are thus incorporated, might set up what form of Government they thought fit."[79] The minimum condition for the establishment of a political society is the unity "under one supreme government," which the *King in Parliament* readily provided. It is evident that, in this respect, Locke tailored his thesis to suit the English political reality. But Locke's overriding concern was to keep powers separate in their actual exercise. To him, this was the basic condition which distinguished political society from the state of nature.[80] He had, therefore, to superimpose this theory of the separation of powers on

79. *Ibid.*, p. 355.

80. By stark contrast, Hobbes comes to the conclusion that man escapes the state of nature by granting to the sovereign plenary and inseparable power. *Leviathan*, p. 184.

the supremacy of the *King in Parliament* dictated by history. He had to reconcile the reality of a mixed and composite sovereign with his insistence upon the separation of powers in their actual exercise. He did so by prescribing limitations on the sovereign power. The supreme legislative power was subject to the natural rights of life, liberty, and estate. It could not rule by extemporary decrees. It had to dispense justice through known and authorized judges. And it could not delegate its power to others. The supreme legislature is effectively restricted to the making of general laws. The legislature having "put the Execution of the Laws they make into other hands" may resume it, but only "when they find cause, and to punish for any mall-administration against the Laws."[81]

The limitations on the supreme power arise from the terms of the trust. How were these terms to be enforced? It is apparent that Locke considered the representative nature of the supreme body to be the best assurance against the violation of the trust. Insofar as he had the English constitution in mind, there could hardly be any other guarantee. The subjection of Parliament to the supervision of an independent judiciary was precluded by historical circumstances. The king's prerogative had been extended and maintained through judicial decisions. The conflict between king and Parliament was often a contest between the jurisdiction of the prerogative courts and those of the High Court of Parliament and the common law courts. The nature of this conflict left no scope for resolution other than by the supremacy of Parliament. Given its bitter experience, Parliament could not be expected to yield any part of that supremacy to the judiciary, even as it sought to ensure judicial independence from the king.[82]

But Locke did not lay down his imitations for mere guidance. He regarded them as real and binding. Although "there can be but *one Supream Power*, which is *the Legislative* . . . yet the Legislative being only a Fiduciary Power to act for certain ends, there remains still *in the People a Supream Power* to remove or *alter the legislative*, when they find the *Legislative* act contrary to the trust reposed in them."[83]Where the legislature violates the trust, "the *trust* must necessarily *be forfeited*, and the Power devolve into the hands of

81. *Ibid.*, p. 389.

82. *See* C.H. McIlwain, *The High Court of Parliament and its Supremacy* (1910), pp. 295-96.

83. *Two Treatises of government*, pp. 384-85.

those that gave it, who may place it anew where they shall think best for their safety and security."[84]

For the sake of credibility and effectiveness, Locke's theory of separation of powers had to suit the emerging English Constitution. Yet he was conscious that there could be other mechanisms for separating powers, including that of reposing them in different hands. The makers of new constitutions, who were free of the historical constraints faced by Englishmen, were inevitably drawn to the purer form of separation which Locke was unable to propose for England.

## VI. Did Locke Misrepresent the Constitution?

Two facts need be remembered before we examine the charge that Locke authored a false theory of the English constitution. One is that Locke wrote the *Two Treatises* a decade before the revolution of 1688. The other is that Locke did not profess to describe the English constitution, in writing his treatises. Yet, it is worthwhile investigating the extent to which Locke's theory coincided with the form in which the constitution emerged from the revolution.

The greatest impediments to the realization of a Lockean type separation of powers was the existence of the legislative prerogatives and the non-existence of tenure for judges. In this situation, the Lockean requirements that the supreme authority "govern by establish'd *standing Laws* . . . and not by Extemporary Decrees" and that controversies be decided "by *indifferent* and upright Judges" could not be met. In his short reign, James II demonstrated the potency of the legislative powers which remained after the restoration, particularly the power of dispensation. Justice Powell, in the *Seven Bishops' Case* went so far as to claim that dispensation "amounts to an abrogation and repeal of all the laws."[85] The problem of the undefined prerogative was exacerbated by the insecurity of judges called upon to determine its limits.

The problem could not be solved by legislation. The king was unlikely to give his assent to an Act which impinged on his claimed prerogatives. Even if the king gave his assent, it was doubtful whether the Act could lawfully restrain the exercise of prerogatives sanctioned

84. *Ibid.*

85. W. Costin and J. Watson, *The Law and Working of the Constitution: Documents 1660-1914* (1961), p. 268.

by ancient usage. Certainly, James did not let legislation approved by his predecessors to stand in the way of his prerogatives. Because prerogatives and parliamentary power were both claimed from ancient custom, one body, arguably, could not abrogate the rights of the other. Any change in the situation had to be effected by a revolutionary political act. The forced departure of James and the enthronement on terms, of William and Mary, contrary to legitimist principles, achieved the break with the past. *The Bill of Rights*, and other Acts making up the settlement, marked a new constitutional beginning.

In its cumulative effect, this legislative package deprived the king of his legislative prerogatives and secured the tenure of judges. The *Bill of Rights* abolished the powers of suspension and dispensation.[86] The Court of High Commission (through which the king was able to interfere with clerical and academic appointments and the statutes of universities) and other special courts were declared "illegal and pernicious." The power to levy taxes without grant of Parliament had been abolished previously, but doubts always remained whether powers such as that recognized in *Bates' Case* could be taken away by Parliament under the ancient constitution. These doubts were finally laid to rest by the *Bill of Rights* which was enacted in revolutionary conditions. The limits of the prerogative could not be questioned safely even by humble petition or parliamentary debate. As demonstrated by the court's directions to the jury in the *Seven Bishops' Case*, such challenges were capable of being construed as treason by a court willing to apply strict precedent. The *Bill of Rights* declared the subject's right to petition the king without being prosecuted therefor and established the freedom of speech in parliament by making it unimpeachable "in any Court or Place out of Parlyament."

The other factor undermining the Lockean separation, namely the corruption of the judiciary, was addressed in a number of ways. The *Bill of Rights* required jurors to be duly impanelled and in cases of high treason, to be freeholders. It prohibited excessive bail (which was used to nullify the protection of the Habeas Corpus Act), excessive fines, and cruel and unusual punishments. The crippling procedural and evidentiary obstacles which served to secure convictions in treason trials were removed by the Trial of Treasons Act enacted in 1696. Finally, the Act of Settlement of 1701 conferred on judges immunity from royal ouster.

86. Section 11 of the *Bill of Rights* prohibited dispensations "except in such cases as shall be specially provided for by one or more Bill or Bills to be passed during this present Session of Parliament." As no empowering legislation was passed in that session, the prerogative was destroyed.

The cumulative effect of the enactments which formed the revolutionary settlement was to establish a separation of powers closely resembling the Lockean theory. Directly or indirectly, the provisions eliminated the king's power to rule in contravention of the law or in accordance with a law of his own making. In Lockean terms, he was prevented from ruling by "extemperory decrees." They sought to guarantee judicial independence and to abrogate ancient precedents which made political dissent treasonous. The settlement removed the legislative elements from the prerogative, but left the executive element intact. Parliament neither sought nor gained executive capacity. The king was pre-eminent in foreign policy, the province of Locke's federative power. In domestic affairs, despite losing the legislative prerogatives, the king remained "a real working, governing king—a king with a policy."[87] In both spheres he now needed parliamentary cooperation to finance his operations and to obtain warrant for actions which impinged on rights. But he still had significant means of securing this cooperation, the most valuable being his prerogative to appoint and dismiss officers of the state, which gave him enormous patronage with which to buy cooperation. Placemen continued to remain in parliament, and the king himself was part of the legislature. But a clear difference emerged between the king and the king in parliament, with the king in parliament resembling the Lockean supreme authority, the legislative.

Locke's theory looks back to the medieval, in its non-differentiation of the executive and judicial functions. But it also looked forward in its insistence that the law be administered through "indifferent *and upright judges*." The executive power, in the older sense, was both administrative and judicial. Under the settlement, this composite power notionally remained with the king. In administration, he was pre-eminent, and in judiciary, he acted through royal courts. However, in practice, the king lost the judicial part of his power. The division of power between king and his courts followed the distinction between *coercitio* (executive power in the narrower, administrative sense) and *iurisdictio* (judicial power) which was evident in the later Roman Republic.[88] The king was the sole repository of the former, whereas judges acted independently in the exercise of the latter.

87. F. Maitland, *The Constitutional History of England* (1911), p. 388.

88. The early consuls enjoyed *imperium* or comprehensive authority which encompassed *coercitio* (executive power), *iurisdictio* (judicial power), and *imperium* in the narrower sense, which was military command. However, in the late republic, *iurisdictio* was largely in the hands of the specialized magistrates, the *praetor urbanus* and the *praetor peregrinus*. *See* W. Kunkel, *An Introduction to Roman Legal and Constitutional History* (1973), p. 84.

Locke's separation of the legislative and executive powers was also intended to be secured by the principle of non-delegation of lawmaking power by the legislative.[89] Delegation of such power to the executive would have utterly defeated the results of a century of struggle. Such, precisely, was the feeling of parliament in the century following the revolution. Parliament showed reluctance to leave even matters of detail to the executive. It passed, among others, special laws to establish a workhouse at Havering, to license a playhouse at Margate, to pave the town of Cheltenham, to widen roads in Bodmin, to naturalize Andreas Emmerich, to let Cornelius Salvidge change his name, to authorize William Frye's guardians to grant leases, to dissolve the marriage between Jonathan Twiss and Franciss Dorrit, and to enclose this, that, and the other common. As Maitland observes, it was natural that parliament should look with suspicion on anything that would increase the influence and patronage of the crown.[90] Parliament, in its jealousy of the executive, contravened another Lockean principle, that of governing by standing laws and not by extemperory decrees. In time, parliament acquired the confidence to caste its laws in general terms leaving the particulars to the executive to work out subject to guiding principles set out in the statute. What is important to note is that until this century, parliamentary practice was firmly against leaving matters of policy (as opposed to detail) to the determination of the executive. In 1932, the Committee on Ministers' Powers reported, after extensive inquiry, that such delegations, when resorted to, were generally on account of the special subject matter and without the intention of creating a precedent.[91] The report establishes that the constitutional practice of parliament (at least in the two centuries following the revolution) viewed with disfavor, the delegation of primary legislative power to the executive.

## VII. Locke's Importance in Constitutional Theory

In many ways Locke's theory of separation appears to be the crucial intellectual link between medieval and modern constitutionalism. As observed before, it looks backwards to the medieval in its failure to distinguish clearly between the executive and the judicial powers. His recognition of the federative power, where the prince acts without parliamentary authority, is clearly a

89. *Ibid.*, pp. 29-30.
90. *The Constitutional History of England* (1911), p. 383.
91. Committee on Ministers' Powers, *Report*, Cmd. No. 4060, p. 31.

part of the medieval *gubernaculum*. Locke draws the idea of the trust under which the supreme authority is given power, from his mainly fictitious account of the original compact among persons living in the state of nature. However, something very similar, the idea of fealty, was central to medieval constitutionalism. The right of resistance, exercisable when the trust is broken, was also medieval. As Kern points out, "fealty, as distinct from obedience, is reciprocal in character, and contains the implicit condition that one party owes it to the other only so long as the other keeps faith."[92] If the king failed in the duty to keep the law, he automatically lost the right of "obedience" from subjects. thus, the main ingredients of Locke's theory were essentially medieval.

With these ingredients, Locke constructs a theory which reflects the Whig vision of the constitution, one where the king forfeits his legislative prerogatives while retaining the right to administer the realm, parliament becomes supreme legislator and independent judges police the arrangement. The theory looks forward to the emerging era of parliamentary superiority and representative democracy.

Locke's major contribution to modern constitutionalism was his persuasive argument that an adequate separation of the law making and law executing functions is a *sine qua non* of a constitution under which liberty is secure. Locke radically altered the theory of the mixed constitution which had dominated English political thought immediately before and after the *interregnum*. The theory of the mixed constitution laid faith in the distribution of powers among the three classes. According to this theory one class could not determine the direction of government and the content of the law without the cooperation of the other two. It produced a crude system of checks and balances. Locke, however, grasped the deeper problems of the English Constitution to which the mixed theory had no real solution. It is evident that he, like Hunton before him, realized that the mixture of the English Constitution was different to that of the Aristotelian concept. Aristotle praised the sharing, by all classes, of the deliberative, magisterial, and judicial powers. In England, the mixture (of King, Lords, and Commons) obtained with respect to the enactment of legislation, but the king alone was supreme in the monarchical functions. The problem was that the monarchical power included a substantial legislative component which, when exercised at sole discretion, negated the mixed principle. Therefore, the mixed principle could not be effective without the separation of legislative

92. *Kingship and Law in the Middle Ages*, p. 87.

power from the monarchical power. In other words, government by cooperation required the king to be subject to the laws made jointly by the three estates. The class based distribution of power could not operate without a further, function-based separation.

The conditions on which the theory of the mixed government operated were themselves being undermined by social change. The principle of mixed government is effective where classes and their interests are distinct. The changing society was confusing these distinctions. In particular the religious and commercial interests were transcending class boundaries and making the class based distribution of power increasingly irrelevant. It is evident that Locke realized, as Aristotle before him, that, in the final analysis, the rationale of mixed government lies in its tendency to keep powers functionally separated. Mixed government is said to secure liberty. But the object is achieved by making it impossible for one class to pursue its own particular ends. The negative voice of each class meant that laws had to satisfy all classes. To do so they had necessarily to be general. Where society is conveniently stratified into large and homogeneous interest groups, the consensus among group representatives ensures sufficient generality. When the community becomes individualized, class consensus dissipates to the point of irrelevance. Those who once spoke for segments of the society end up speaking for themselves. When this happens, liberty can be preserved only upon more abstract principles. Lawmaking has to be democratic and government must be subject to law. Locke projected both these ideas in his theory of the separation of powers. Above all, Locke resurrected the idea that the making and execution of the law must be kept separate for reasons more fundamental than the need to create political checks and balances. From his interpretation of the state of nature, Locke derived the ancient principle that, for the preservation of liberty, laws should be general and therefore be kept distinct from their application to particular circumstances. The proposal he made for maintaining such distinctions, were, to a large extent, determined by the possibilities afforded by English history. They consisted of limitations on power which were to be enforced, in the last resort, by the people themselves. One may fault him for not recommending judicial review and procedures for popular determination of constitutional disputes. But Locke wrote at a time when written constitutions were unknown and the efficacy of constitutional principles depended on the veneration of custom and the influence of theories. Judicial review and procedures for formal amendment are peculiar to written constitutions. Locke's theory undoubtedly inspired the substance of, and indeed the very desire for, written constitutions. But such constitutions (with the exception of the ill fated *Instrument of Government),* were beyond the pale of Locke's experience.

Many have criticized the makers of modern constitutions for having misread and misapplied Locke's principles. These criticisms are misconceived. It is true that Locke did not categorically propose the constitutional mechanisms which form the modern separation doctrine. But Locke was firm in his insistence upon keeping the making and execution of laws separate. He also clearly recognized an area of execution action involving the force of the community which was undictated by law. His declared faith in reposing all these powers in a supreme government appears to be a concession to English history. But his first principles clearly demanded the preservation, howsoever, of the distinctions among powers. It was by no means illogical to infer therefrom the eminent desirability of dividing powers among separate organs. The makers of modern constitutions were not subject to the constraints which history imposed on Locke. Therefore, they were at liberty to implement Locke's theory of separation of powers through constitutionally enforceable rules of government. But before this happened there were two developments which provided a decisive impetus to the institutionalization of the separation os powers as an enforceable doctrine. One was the publication of Montesquieu's *De l'esprit des lois* in which the writer advanced what was then an unprecedented empirical-sociological argument for the separation of powers. The other was the radical reassessment of the classical ideas of virtue and society, most notably by David Hume, which led to a revision of the role of government and a condemnation of power as intrinsically dangerous. These developments ushered in modern constitutionalism with its emphasis on the practical means of preventing despotism. That, however, is another historical chapter.

# [9]

# Reason to Ratify: The Influence of John Locke's Religious Beliefs on the Creation and Adoption of the United States Constitution

*David L. Wardle**

## I. INTRODUCTION

"We hold these truths to be self-evident, that all men are created equal."[1] "Life, liberty, and the pursuit of happiness."[2] "We the People."[3] Statements like these evoke powerful emotions and strong attachments from many modern Americans. Yet these sentiments are not uniquely American. They can be traced to the philosophies of a man who lived across an ocean and a century before our Constitution was even ratified: John Locke.

John Locke has been accused of being a Calvinist,[4] a Deist,[5] a Latitudinarian,[6] and a Socinian.[7] However one chooses to categorize Locke's beliefs, he was, at least, a Christian and a baptized member of the Church of England. He put a great deal of effort into personal

---

* J.D. J. Reuben Clark Law School, Brigham Young University. The author works for the San Diego office of Thomas D. Neelemen, Esq., L.C. The author would like to thank his father, Lynn D. Wardle, a law professor at Brigham Young University, for his help with this article.

1. THE DECLARATION OF INDEPENDENCE ¶ 2 (U.S. 1776).

2. *Id.*

3. U.S. CONST. pmbl.

4. One who accepts "the theological system of Calvin and his followers marked by strong emphasis on the sovereignty of God and esp. by the doctrine of predestination." WEBSTER'S NINTH NEW COLLEGIATE DICTIONARY 198 (1983). *See also* Herbert D. Foster, *International Calvinism through Locke and the Revolution of 1688*, 32 AM. HIST. REV. 475, 486–87 (1927).

5. One espousing Deism, "a movement or a system of thought advocating natural religion, emphasizing morality, and in the 18th century denying the interference of the Creator with the laws of the universe." WEBSTER'S DICTIONARY, *supra* note 4, at 335. *See also* Dewey D. Wallace, Jr., *Socinianism, Justification by Faith, and the Sources of John Locke's* THE REASONABLENESS OF CHRISTIANITY, 45 J. HIST. OF IDEAS 49 (1984).

6. "A person who is broad and liberal in his standards of religious belief and conduct." WEBSTER'S DICTIONARY, *supra* note 4, at 676. *See also* Wallace, *supra* note 5, at 50.

7. "An adherent of a 16th and 17th century theological movement professing belief in God and adherence to the Christian Scriptures but denying the divinity of Christ and consequently denying the trinity." WEBSTER'S DICTIONARY, *supra* note 4, at 1119 (1983). *See also* Wallace, *supra* note 5, at 63.

study of the Bible.[8] A graduate of Christ's Church at Oxford University,[9] Locke was also familiar with the writings of Christian reformists and associated with many influential religious leaders of his time.[10] Locke's personal religious philosophy was a major influence in the United States at the time that the Constitution was drafted. The pervasive influence of Lockean religious convictions motivated the framers of the Constitution to establish a new form of government, provided the theoretical basis for the document itself, and inspired its popular ratification.

Part II will lay the groundwork for this thesis by outlining Locke's life and sources of his religious beliefs. Part III will undertake a more substantive examination of Locke's opinions and the writings that memorialized them. Establishing how Lockean ideas of natural law, social contract, and reason are related to the inspiration, drafting, and acceptance of the Constitution takes place in Part IV, before the article's conclusion in Part V.

## II. Sources of Locke's Religious Philosophy

Locke's education and travels, both in and out of England, during the latter half of the seventeenth century provided a foundation of personal experience from which his religious philosophy would derive. Locke was formally educated at Oxford University, where he studied medicine.[11] Although it has been suggested that his coursework at Oxford did more to detract from Locke's education than it did to further it,[12] the Puritan ideals of his formal education at Oxford—the necessity of discipline in education and morals; the duty of men to use their God-given talents in furtherance of the public good; the desirability of a return to the primitive church and original government—stayed with him long after he earned his degrees.[13]

A large portion of Locke's professional life was devoted to the study and practice of medicine, chemistry, and physics,[14] and throughout his life Locke maintained relationships with intellectuals

8. *See* Wallace, *supra* note 5, at 49.

9. *See id.*

10. *See* Foster, *supra* note 4, at 478–86.

11. The son of a captain in the Parliamentary Army, Locke pursued his education first at Westminster School, then at Christ's Church at Oxford, where he received his Master of Arts degree in 1658. In 1674, Locke graduated as a Bachelor of Medicine, and was afterwards appointed to one of two medical studentships at Oxford. *See* LORD KING, THE LIFE AND LETTERS OF JOHN LOCKE 1–3 (Burt Franklin ed., Lennox Hill 1972) (1884).

12. *See id.*

13. *See* Foster, *supra* note 4, at 486.

14. KING, *supra* note 11, at 31.

and men of science.[15] Notably, many of these colleagues were also men of God.[16] Some of the most influential relations that Locke had were with Fellows of the Royal Society who were famous advocates of natural law.[17] Locke himself was a student of natural law and studied nature as though it were Scripture, believing the author of both Scripture and nature to be the same.

In addition to Locke's scientific approach to both nature and the Scriptures, his travels to France and Holland influenced his religious ideas by allowing him to observe the social effects of religious and political conflicts. After completing his studies at Oxford, Locke moved to France, where he befriended a community of French Calvinists, the Huguenots.[18] Locke shared the group's desire to return to the primitive church and its belief in the establishment of a church by voluntary contract.[19] The Huguenots had been guaranteed religious freedom by such a contract, the Edict of Nantes.[20] In 1685, however, Louis XIV violated the Edict, after which Locke, along with the Huguenots, began advocating resistance of tyranny based on breach of social contract and fundamental law.[21]

Locke also spent time in Holland where he made friends among the Dutch Calvinists.[22] Like their counterparts in France, the Dutch

---

15. Through the Fellows of the Royal Society, Locke developed a friendship with Robert Boyle. When Boyle died, Locke organized and substantially rewrote the work that was published as Boyle's *History of the Air* in 1692. HUYLER, LOCKE IN AMERICA: THE MORAL PHILOSOPHY OF THE FOUNDING ERA 69 (1995).

16. Locke exchanged many ideas with Sir Isaac Newton. Newton shared his work in mathematics with Locke for suggestions before publication. Likewise, Locke sent papers on the New Testament to Newton for his review and comment, which were later published (posthumously) as the *Paraphrases of St. Paul's Epistles*. Of Newton, Locke once wrote, "Mr. Newton is really a very valuable man, not only for his wonderful skill in mathematics, but in divinity also, and his great knowledge in the Scriptures, wherein I know few his equals." H. MCLACHLAN, THE RELIGIOUS OPINIONS OF MILTON, LOCKE, AND NEWTON 101 (1941); *see also*, HUYLER, *supra* note 15, at 69.

17. Fellows of the Royal Society were students and followers of the writings of Francis Bacon. Bacon believed that men should study "God's Work, as a supplement to his Word." HUYLER, *supra* note 15, at 115. Bacon wrote:

> God has revealed himself to man by means of two scriptures: first, of course, through the written word, but also, secondly, through his handiwork, the created universe. To study nature, therefore, cannot be contrary to religion; indeed, it is part of the duty we owe to the Great Artificer of the world.

*Id.* (quoting Bacon as quoted in BASIL WILLEY, THE SEVENTEENTH-CENTURY BACKGROUND: THE THOUGHT OF THE AGE IN RELATION TO RELIGION AND POETRY 30, 35 (1953)).

18. Locke stayed in France for about four years. *See* Foster, *supra* note 4, at 481.

19. *See id.*

20. *Id.*

21. *See id.*

22. Locke returned to England from France in 1679, but was forced to flee to Holland in 1683 because of his association with the Earl of Shaftesbury, who was found plotting to kill King

Calvinists were advocates of natural law and social contract.[23] But, while the Huguenots in France had suffered a tremendous blow, Locke encountered the Dutch as they were coming off of one successful revolution and were in the midst of planning another: the Great Revolution of 1688.[24] Locke supported their efforts to place Prince William on the English throne because he believed that the English court had violated its social contract with the people of England in many ways, including religious intolerance.[25] Locke believed that religious toleration was the key to social harmony and that Christians should unite on the essentials, and agree to differ on the nonessentials.[26] Due in part to Locke's influence, a religious toleration act was passed by the English parliament shortly after William and Mary took the throne in England.[27]

It was against a similar backdrop of political turmoil and feelings of social frustration that the colonists left England nearly a century later to find a New World. Locke's philosophies, memorialized in a legacy of writings and woven into generations of minds, emboldened this nation's founders in their quest for religious toleration and freedom from an oppressive government.

## III. LOCKE'S RELIGIOUS OPINIONS

As a product of his studies, life experiences, and associations with religious men, John Locke developed well-defined religious beliefs and a well-defined worldview. He shared these views in his writings, and influenced a generation of new Americans eighty years after his death by giving them the faith and understanding to create a new Constitution.

### A. *John Locke's Religious Beliefs*

John Locke believed that Christianity consists of merely one essential article of faith: belief in Jesus Christ as the Savior of the world.[28] He believed that anyone who confesses a belief in Jesus

---

Charles II. MAURICE CRANSTON, JOHN LOCKE, A BIOGRAPHY 184, 226–30 (1957). Locke lived in exile in Holland until 1689, returning after William of Orange invaded England in 1688. *Id.* at 304–11.

23. *See* Foster, supra note 4, at 482.

24. As a result of this revolution, William III, an admirer of Locke's, took the English throne and cleared the way for Locke's return to England. *See* Foster, *supra* note 4, at 482.

25. Lois G. Schwoerer, *Locke, Lockean Ideas, and the Glorious Revolution*, 51 J. HIST. OF IDEAS 531, 531–39 (1990).

26. *See* HUYLER, *supra* note 15, at 71.

27. *See* Schwoerer, *supra* note 25, at 544–45.

28. *See* HUYLER, *supra* note 15, at 70.

Christ as the Messiah is a Christian, "[f]or that this is the sole doctrine pressed and required to be believed in the whole tenor of Our Savior's and his apostles [sic] preaching."[29] Locke boiled Christianity down to two means by which persons could be saved: faith and repentance.[30] Alluding to the New Testament,[31] Locke explained:

> Though the devils believed . . . yet they could not be saved by the *covenant of grace*; because they performed not the other condition required in it, altogether as necessary to be performed as this of believing: and that is repentance. Repentance is as absolute a condition of the *covenant of grace* as faith; and as necessary to be performed as that.[32]

Locke understood the "covenant of grace" to be that by which God gave people agency and reason, and in exchange also gave them commandments for how they should act.[33] By agreeing to submit one's will to God's and keep the commandments, a man might sacrifice his agency in return for grace:

> The law of works makes no allowance for failing on any occasion. Those that obey are righteous; those that in any part disobey, are unrighteous, and must not expect life, the reward of righteousness. But by the law of faith, faith is allowed to supply the defect of full obedience; and so the believers are admitted to . . . immortality, as if they were righteous.[34]

Locke believed that a government of men should model the government of their Heavenly Father. Just as God's purpose is to promote the good of mankind, so also the end of government is the good of mankind.[35] Just as God refuses to take from man that portion of his will which he will not freely offer, so government has power over men

---

29. "This was the only gospel-article of faith which was preached to [men]." JOHN LOCKE, THE REASONABLENESS OF CHRISTIANITY (1695), *reprinted in* JOHN LOCKE, ON THE REASONABLENESS OF CHRISTIANITY ¶ 165, at 123 (Ewing ed., 1965) [hereinafter LOCKE, THE REASONABLENESS OF CHRISTIANITY]; *see also* HUYLER, *supra* note 15, at 70.

30. *See* LOCKE, THE REASONABLENESS OF CHRISTIANITY, *supra* note 29, ¶ 172, at 128.

31. *James* 2:19 ("the devils also believe, and tremble").

32. LOCKE, THE REASONABLENESS OF CHRISTIANITY, *supra* note 29, ¶ 167, at 125; HUYLER, *supra* note 15, at 70–71 (emphasis added).

33. God's instructions on how to act are found both in the Scripture (the word of God revealed to his prophets) and in nature (the works of God revealed to all mankind). "[T]he law of nature stands as an eternal rule to all men." *See* JOHN LOCKE, CONCERNING CIVIL GOVERNMENT, SECOND ESSAY: AN ESSAY CONCERNING THE TRUE ORIGINAL EXTENT AND END OF CIVIL GOVERNMENT (1690), *reprinted in* GREAT BOOKS OF THE WESTERN WORLD 25-28 (Mortimer J. Adler ed., 1994) [hereinafter LOCKE, CONCERNING CIVIL GOVERNMENT].

34. LOCKE, THE REASONABLENESS OF CHRISTIANITY, *supra* note 29, ¶ 22, at 13; HUYLER, *supra* note 15, at 70–71.

35. *See generally* LOCKE, CONCERNING CIVIL GOVERNMENT, *supra* note 33.

only to the extent that they give their consent to be governed.[36] Just as God gave men reason so that they could submit to his will, so must a man have reason before he can consent to be governed.[37] Just as a man may enter a covenant of grace with God in order to receive life and immortality in the next world, men of reason may enter into a covenant with each other, and agree to limit their agency—that is, submit their individual wills to the collective will of society—in order to preserve their lives in this world.

### *B. Locke's Writings*

These theories were not all uniquely Locke's, but his writings were certainly his own. Locke simply took the shared beliefs of his peers, Calvin, and other philosophers, incorporated his own thoughts, and organized them into well-articulated, rational theories. Locke shared his religious opinions in several influential texts published in his lifetime. Distinct political theories also come through in Locke's writings, including fundamental law, natural rights, contract and consent of people, popular sovereignty, and resistance to tyranny.[38]

Locke's most political texts were his *Two Treatises of Civil Government*.[39] Written while exiled in Holland, the influence of the Dutch and Anglican Calvinists is apparent.[40] In 1695, Locke anonymously published his most controversial, and arguably his most religious, piece, *The Reasonableness of Christianity*, which was so poorly received by some that Locke spent the next few years answering critics in the *Vindications*, published in 1695 and 1697.[41] Locke's *A Letter Concerning Toleration* was published in 1689, the same year his *Essay Concerning Human Understanding* was published in its entirety.[42]

Of all of Locke's works, his *Essay* was by far the most widely distributed in America at the end of the eighteenth century.[43] One study

36. *Id.* at 25–28.

37. *Id.*

38. *See* Foster, *supra* note 4, at 487.

39. Volume one was published in 1690, and the second shortly thereafter.

40. Nearly all of Locke's citations in the *Treatises* are Calvinistic. He cited Scripture seventy-nine times, Calvinists seven times, and a former Calvinist once. *See* Foster, *supra* note 4, at 478. Only once did he cite a reference that was not Calvinist, and that was when he cited Barclay, a Scottish Catholic who also advocated resistance of tyranny. *See id.*

41. *See* CRANSTON, *supra* note 22, at 389–92; A VINDICATION OF THE REASONABLENESS OF CHRISTIANITY, &C. FROM MR. EDWARDS'S REFLECTIONS (London, A. & J. Churchill, 1695); A SECOND VINDICATION OF THE REASONABLENESS OF CHRISTIANITY, &C., BY THE AUTHOR OF THE REASONABLENESS OF CHRISTIANITY, &C. (London, A. & J. Churchill & E. Castle, 1697).

42. CRANSTON, *supra* note 22, at 318, 326.

43. Between 1777 and 1790, 82 percent of the libraries searched had a copy of *An Essay Concerning Human Understanding*, which was well received in England at the time of its original

shows that the height of Locke's popularity, as judged by the percentage of libraries carrying his books, was from 1777 to 1790, a critical period for the Constitution.[44] Locke's political philosophy was important to these early Americans, but even more important were the principles that he taught about human nature.[45] Locke's views on natural law and his firm commitment to the existence and attention of God had a significant impact on those who read his books, especially at the time that the Constitution was penned.

## IV. LOCKE'S INFLUENCE ON THE CONSTITUTION

These philosophies contain ideals that resonated with the American colonists. John Locke's influence in early America has been most directly tied to the Declaration of Independence, portions of which Thomas Jefferson was accused of lifting almost verbatim out of Locke's *Treatises*.[46] Lockean principles are also found in the Bill of Rights, particularly the freedom of religion. The Federalist Papers are often criticized as being weak;[47] part of the reason that they are not stronger is that the Federalists and Antifederalists did not squabble over the fundamentals. Both the Federalists and the Antifederalists agreed on basic Lockean principles.[48]

The impact of Locke's work on the origins of the Constitution was in creating a political climate that encouraged the creation of such a document and, perhaps more importantly, its acceptance. Locke's influence on the Constitution was not as strong in the actual substance and form of the document as that of Montesquieu; rather, it was more indirect, creating an atmosphere in early America conducive to its creation and adoption.[49] Locke's ideas influenced the creation and adoption of the Constitution in three specific ways: they inspired the founding fathers to undertake the creation of a new government; they

publication, and 24 percent had a copy of the *Treatises*. *Reasonableness*, heavily criticized at the time of its first publication, was found in 7 percent of the libraries searched. *See* David Lundberg & Henry F. May, *The Enlightened Reader in America*, 28 AM. QUARTERLY 262, 273 (1976).

44. *See id.*

45. Assertion based on the showing that more libraries stocked the *Essay* than the *Treatises*. *See id.*

46. *See* Donald L. Doernberg, *"We the People": John Locke, Collective Constitutional Rights, and Standing to Challenge Government Action*, 73 CALIF. L. REV. 52, 65 (1985) ("Richard Henry Lee of Virginia complained that Jefferson had copied the Declaration from Locke.").

47. *See generally* HERBERT J. STORING, WHAT THE ANTI-FEDERALISTS WERE FOR (1981).

48. *See* HUYLER, *supra* note 15, at 251–73.

49. Daniel C.K. Chow, *A Pragmatic Model of Law*, 67 WASH. L. REV. 755, 761–62 n.16 (1992); *see also* HUYLER, *supra* note 15, at 251.

formed the foundation of the document; and they encouraged public ratification of the Constitution.

### A. *A Bold Undertaking*

Under the Articles of Confederation, the United States was weak, but there was little incentive to change. The states were wary of a strong central government because of the trouble they had suffered as colonies of a country with abusive central powers. Additionally, flawed as they were, the Articles of Confederation had already been accepted by states, and a Congress had been established to run the country.[50] To propose any other system, after one had already been set up, bordered on treason.[51] Even if one undertook to change the government, there were no assurances that the new system would be better than the last. The task was daunting, to say the least.

Nevertheless, change was necessary. The nation suffered from the problems that attend a country with no strong central authority: foreign relations suffered; interstate relations were hampered; moreover, the nation had debts to pay, but no satisfactory method of collecting taxes.[52] It was a precarious position for the country to be in, surrounded by other countries that were waiting for the new union to fail so they could loot the remains. Thus, the framers knew they could not fail, lest the very purpose of establishing a new government be destroyed.

The moral impetus for such a bold undertaking was well articulated in Lockean philosophy. Lockean ideals and Lockean reason moved the founding fathers to action. In the first place, the framers of the Constitution felt as though they had a right to establish a new government. Locke taught:

> The power that every individual gave the society when he entered into it can never revert to the individuals again, as long as the society lasts . . . . But if . . . it is forfeited . . . it reverts to the society, and the people have a right to act as supreme, and continue the legislative in themselves or place it in a new form, or new hands, as they think good.[53]

Since England had forfeited its privilege of governing the American people, it was the privilege of the framers to not only continue to govern themselves in the same way that they had been governing

50. *See generally* CATHERINE DRINKER BOWEN, MIRACLE AT PHILADELPHIA (1966).
51. *Id.*
52. *See* HUYLER, *supra* note 15, at 252–58.
53. LOCKE, CONCERNING CIVIL GOVERNMENT, *supra* note 33, ¶ 243, at 81.

themselves previously, but also to put the legislative power into new hands.

Armed with a belief in the right to set up a new government, the framers were not entirely certain they had the ability. Again, a firm foundation in Lockean ideals gave them the confidence to try. In Locke's view, rather than focus on obstacles, people should be encouraged to identify problem areas and then search for solutions, with the assurance that God would provide the way to accomplish what was required.[54]

With Lockean optimism, one of the most influential delegates at the 1787 Constitutional Convention, South Carolina's Charles Pinckney, identified the opportunities that the Convention presented, rather than focusing on the obvious obstacles:

> Our true situation appears to me to be this—a new extensive Country containing within itself the materials for forming a Government capable of extending to its citizens all the blessings of civil [and] religious liberty—capable of making them happy at home. This is the great end of Republican Establishments.[55]

Connecticut delegate Roger Sherman helped the other delegates at the Constitutional Convention internalize the import of what they were doing when he identified the "citizens" to whom Pinckney was referring: "We are providing for our posterity, for our children [and] our grand Children . . . ."[56] The delegates were securing the "comfortable provision for this life, and the way that leads to a better" not only as representatives of the body politic, but as fathers and grandfathers providing for their children and grandchildren.

Recognizing both the import of the task and the opportunity that was theirs, New York's Alexander Hamilton identified the issue the delegates had to consider: "The great question is what provision shall we make for the happiness of our Country?"[57] The delegates took four months to arrive at an answer, and the states even longer to accept it.[58]

---

54. Quoting the Apostle Peter, Locke wrote, "[God] has given [men] . . . 'whatsoever is necessary for the conveniences of life and information of virtue; and has put within the reach of their discovery, the comfortable provision for this life, and the way that leads to a better." JOHN LOCKE, AN ESSAY CONCERNING HUMAN UNDERSTANDING Intro. ¶ 5 (1690), *reprinted in* GREAT BOOKS OF THE WESTERN WORLD 94 (Mortimer J. Adler ed., 1994) [hereinafter LOCKE, HUMAN UNDERSTANDING].

55. JAMES MADISON, NOTES OF DEBATES IN THE FEDERAL CONVENTION OF 1787, at 185 (Ohio Univ. Press 1996) (1927) [hereinafter MADISON, DEBATES].

56. *Id.* at 288.

57. *Id.* at 130.

58. *See generally* BOWEN, *supra* note 50.

One reason for the delay and possible dissatisfaction with the Constitution was that "[a] republican, or free government, can only exist where the body of the people are virtuous, and where property is equally divided."[59] Afraid of encouraging the same type of abusive government from which they had only recently won independence, critics of the Constitution recognized that "every man, and every body of men, invested with power, are ever disposed to increase it, and to acquire a superiority over everything that stands in their way."[60]

To these fears, supporters of the Constitution replied, "If men were angels, no government would be necessary. If angels were to govern men, neither external nor internal controls on government would be necessary."[61] "Is it not time to awake from the deceitful dream of a golden age, and to adopt as a practical maxim for the direction of our political conduct that we, as well as the other inhabitants of the globe, are yet remote from the happy empire of perfect wisdom and perfect virtue?"[62] Like John Locke, the supporters of the Constitution seemed to believe that as humans we are not perfect, but we have been given the ability to think, reason, and devise ways to make a society operate smoothly.[63]

The framers addressed the issue of perfect virtue with Locke's rational sensibilities as well. Pennsylvania's Benjamin Franklin said, "[W]e [should] not depress the virtue [and] public spirit of our common people."[64] The framers felt that "[Americans] are . . . as active, intelligent [and] susceptible of good [government] as any people in the world."[65] Still, they recognized that "in a free [government] those who are to be the objects of a [government] ought to influence the operations of it."[66] To this end, it was suggested that "[i]n free Governments the rulers are the servants, and the people their superiors [and] sovereigns."[67] Salaries of government officers were also limited, because the framers thought that "[w]ealth tends to corrupt the mind [and] to nourish its love of power, and to stimulate it to oppression."[68]

Issues of a strong national government and public virtue were not the only obstacles to overcome in negotiating the document that would become the Constitution. "[T]he greatest danger," observed Conven-

59. THE ANTIFEDERALIST PAPERS NO. 47, at 134 (Centinel) (Morton Borden ed., 1965).
60. *Id.*
61. THE FEDERALIST NO. 51, at 322 (James Madison) (Clinton Rossiter ed., 1961).
62. THE FEDERALIST NO. 6, at 59 (Alexander Hamilton) (Clinton Rossiter ed., 1961).
63. Or, in other words, to preserve ourselves.
64. MADISON, DEBATES, *supra* note 55, at 404.
65. *Id.* at 187.
66. *Id.* at 291.
67. *Id.* at 371.
68. *Id.* at 323.

tion organizer James Madison, "[was] that of disunion of the States."[69] The States' different interests and different opinions about key issues threatened on more than one occasion to tear the Union apart. The issue that most cleanly split the debate along state lines was that of slavery.[70]

The debate about slavery and the related question of representation in the Senate was bitter. On one occasion, Connecticut delegate Oliver Ellsworth prophesied, with eerie accuracy, "This widening of opinions has a threatening aspect. If we do not agree on . . . middle [and] moderate ground . . . we should lose two States, with such others as may be disposed to stand aloof, should fly into a variety of shapes [and] directions, and most probably into several confederations and not without bloodshed."[71]

After a particularly difficult day for the Convention, when tempers were flaring and the delegates seemed ready to give up, Benjamin Franklin, the oldest and most respected delegate at the Convention, called the delegates back to their senses. He reminded them:

> To [the Father of lights] we owe this happy opportunity of consulting in peace on the means of establishing our future national felicity. And have we now forgotten that powerful friend? Or do we imagine that we no longer need his assistance? I have lived, Sir, a long time, and the longer I live, the more convincing proofs I see of this truth—*that God Governs in the affairs of men.*[72]

Franklin's plea for the delegates to remember that God would help them is reminiscent of Locke, who often referred to God as the "Father of lights" when explaining how God inspires men.[73]

---

69. *Id.* at 516.

70. *See* MADISON, DEBATES, *supra* note 55, at 503–12.

71. *Id.* at 508.

72. *Id.* at 209.

73. LOCKE, HUMAN UNDERSTANDING, *supra* note 54, book IV chap. XVIII. ¶ 11, at 387. Perhaps Franklin's plea rang true in the hearts of his fellow delegates in part because of their familiarity with this passage of Locke's:

> We shall not have much reason to complain of the narrowness of our minds, if we will but employ them about what may be of use to us; for of that they are very capable; and it will be an unpardonable as well as childish peevishness, if we undervalue the advantages of our knowledge, and neglect to improve it to the ends for which it was given us, because there are some things that are set out of the reach of it. It will be no excuse to an idle and untoward servant, who would not attend his business by candle-light, to plead that he had not broad sunshine. The candle that is set up in us shines bright enough for all our purposes.

*Id.* Intro. ¶ 5, at 94 ("the candle that is set up in us" references *Proverbs* 20:27, which says that "the spirit of man is the candle of the Lord.").

Even though Franklin was successful at averting disaster for a time and convincing the delegates not to forsake such an important undertaking, disagreement still existed over how the new government should be set up. The disagreement was so great that in September 1787, at the end of the Convention, some delegates were unwilling to put their names to the final document.[74] At this time, Franklin spoke again, assuring the delegates of his confidence that they had done the best they could and reflecting that it was time to resign themselves to the public's reaction.[75]

There is a Lockean thread running through such declarations.[76] To those who would refuse to act at all for fear of acting wrongly, Locke advised, "If we can find out those measures whereby a rational creature, put in that state which man is in in this world, may and ought to govern his opinions, and actions depending thereon, we need not be troubled that some other things escape our knowledge."[77]

Although the delegates recognized that the Constitution might not be perfect, Lockean ideals prevented them from shrinking from the task of drafting it.[78] It was the beginning of a new social contract.

### *B. A New Social Contract*

The foundational concepts of freedom and liberty contained in the Constitution are derived from Locke's teachings. The reason that the framers of the Constitution felt that a social contract is the basis of free government goes back to Lockean principles of natural law.[79]

---

74. *See generally* BOWEN, *supra* note 50.

75. Directing his comments to George Washington, the president of the Convention, Franklin opined:

> [The new government] is likely to be well administered for a course of years, and can only end in Despotism, as other forms have done before it, when the people shall become so corrupted as to need despotic Government, being incapable of any other . . . . I consent, Sir, to this Constitution because I expect no better, and because I am not sure, that it is not the best. The opinions I have had of its errors, I sacrifice to the public good.

MADISON, DEBATES, *supra* note 55, at 653–54.

76. Ellsworth had previously made a similar statement when he said of himself that he "was not in general a half-way man, yet he preferred doing half the good we could, rather than do nothing at all. The other half may be added, when the necessity shall be more fully experienced." *Id.* at 219.

77. LOCKE, HUMAN UNDERSTANDING, *supra* note 54, Intro. ¶ 6, at 95.

78. In the end, all but three of the delegates put their names to it. *See* MADISON, DEBATES, *supra* note 55, at 659.

79. Locke explained that laws of countries "are only so far right as they are founded on the law of Nature, by which they are to be regulated and interpreted." LOCKE, CONCERNING CIVIL GOVERNMENT, *supra* note 33, ¶ 12, at 27–28.

Natural law, according to Locke, is that "men, being once born, have a right to their preservation."[80] In order to effectuate that preservation, "as much as any one can make use of to any advantage of life before it spoils, so much he may by his labour fix a property in. Whatever is beyond this is more than his share, and belongs to others."[81] In a state of nature, then, man has rights to property to the extent that he uses that property for his preservation. In this state, man may also enforce his right to property. Each man is a government unto himself.

In a state of nature, all men are free.[82] Freedom, according to Locke, is the "power of acting or not acting."[83] It is the power of acting in accordance with our own judgment of what is good and what is evil.[84] To this extent, freedom seems to be synonymous with liberty:

> So that the idea of liberty is, the idea of a power in any agent to do or forbear any particular action, according to the determination or thought of the mind, whereby either of them is preferred to the other: where either of them is not in the power of the agent to be produced by him according to his volition, there he is not at liberty; that agent is under necessity.[85]

> In [the mind having a power to suspend the execution and satisfaction of any of its desires] lies the liberty man has; and from the not using of it right comes all that variety of mistakes, errors, and faults which we run into in the conduct of our lives, and our endeavours after happiness; whilst we precipitate the determination of our wills, and engage too soon, before due examination. . . . This seems to me the source of all liberty . . . .[86]

According to Locke, then, an individual's liberty hinges on his power of self-control, his ability to suspend the "steady prosecution of true felicity" until determining for himself "whether that particular thing which is then proposed or desired lie[s] in the way to their main end, and make a real part of that which is their greatest good."[87] This greatest good, "though apprehended and acknowledged to be so, does not determine the will, until our desire, raised proportionably to it, makes us uneasy of the want of it."[88] Therefore, a man's ability to

80. *Id.*, ¶ 24, at 30.
81. *Id.*, ¶ 30, at 31.
82. *Id.*, ¶ 4, at 25.
83. LOCKE, HUMAN UNDERSTANDING, *supra* note 54, book II chap. 21 ¶ 23, at 183.
84. *See id.*, ¶ 73, at 198.
85. *Id.*, ¶ 8, at 180.
86. *Id.*, ¶ 48, at 190.
87. *Id.*, ¶ 53, at 191-92.
88. *Id.*, ¶ 35, at 186.

choose good gives him liberty.[89] Liberty, consequently, belongs only to agents because the ability to choose good is "grounded on his having reason."[90]

In the state of nature, man "is to be free from any superior power on earth, and not to be under the will or legislative authority of man, but to have only the law of Nature for his rule."[91] The Antifederalists paraphrased this Lockean explanation of natural law when they wrote: "[A]ll men are by nature free. No one man, therefore, or any class of men, have a right, by the law of nature, or of God, to assume or exercise authority over their fellows."[92] A person can only be put out of the state of nature and subjected to the political power of another by his own consent, "by agreeing with other men, to join and unite into a community for their comfortable, safe, and peaceable living. . . ."[93] When people join a society, "they are thereby presently incorporated, and make one body politic, wherein the majority have a right to act and conclude the rest."[94] When they do this by express consent, men give up their powers of the state of Nature, namely, to punish crimes and preserve his life.[95] Not every compact puts an end to the state of Nature between people, "only this one of agreeing together mutually to enter into one community, and make one body politic."[96] Once a man has given his consent to be of any society, he is "perpetually and indispensably obliged to be, and remain unalterably a subject to it, and can never be again in the liberty of the state of Nature, unless by any calamity the government he was under comes to be dissolved."[97]

This was the concern of the Antifederalists in advocating a Bill of Rights. They were concerned that the American people would too easily part with the liberty of the state of Nature. The Antifederalists cautioned:

> So the government is committed, to establish laws for the promoting the happiness of the community, and to carry those laws into effect. But it is not necessary, for this purpose, that individuals should relinquish all their natural rights. Some are of such a nature that they cannot be surrendered . . . . Others are

89. *Id.*, book IV chap. 12 ¶ 11, at 361 ("morality is the proper science and business of mankind in general").

90. LOCKE, CONCERNING CIVIL GOVERNMENT, *supra* note 33, ¶ 63, at 38.

91. *Id.*, ¶ 22, at 30.

92. THE ANTIFEDERALIST PAPERS NO. 84, at 242–46 (Brutus) (Morton Borden ed., 1965).

93. LOCKE, CONCERNING CIVIL GOVERNMENT, *supra* note 33, ¶ 95, at 46.

94. *Id.*, ¶ 95, at 46.

95. *See id.*, ¶ 8, 97, at 26, 47.

96. *Id.*, ¶ 14, at 28.

97. *Id.*, ¶ 121, at 53.

> not necessary to be resigned in order to attain the end for which government is instituted; these therefore ought not to be given up. To surrender them, would counteract the very end of government, to wit, the common good. From these observations it appears, that in forming a government on its true principles, the foundation should be laid . . . by expressly reserving to the people such of their essential rights as are not necessary to be parted with.[98]
>
> . . .
>
> [P]ersons who attempt to persuade people that such reservations were less necessary under this Constitution than under those of the States, are willfully endeavoring to deceive, and to lead you into an absolute state of vassalage.[99]

According to Locke, once a man, by mutual consent between himself and the other members of the society, decides to join a society, he becomes subject to its laws.[100] Freedom in society consists of being at liberty to follow one's own will "in all things where that rule prescribes not" and not being subject to "the inconstant, uncertain, unknown, arbitrary will of another man."[101] One must know what the law is in order to be subject to it.[102] Lawmaking power is therefore vested in a legislative body that creates laws common to everyone in the society and makes those laws known to the people.[103]

This power of making and enforcing laws, political power, is limited to the extent that it is used to further the public good, the end of government being "the good of mankind."[104] "The rules that [a legislative body] make . . . must . . . be conformable to the law of Nature—i.e., to the will of God," which, according to Locke, "stands as an eternal rule to all men."[105] The "fundamental law of Nature," according to Locke, is "the preservation of mankind."[106]

Locke believed that the will of God is the preservation of mankind and that governments of men must conform to the will of God. The two essentials for Locke's "covenant of grace" were faith and repentance. By covenanting to repent and keep God's commandments, one can receive preservation, which is life and immortality in the next

98. THE ANTIFEDERALIST PAPERS NO. 84, *supra* note 92, at 243.
99. *Id.*
100. LOCKE, CONCERNING CIVIL GOVERNMENT, *supra* note 33, ¶ 122, at 75–76.
101. *Id.*, ¶ 22, at 30.
102. *See generally id.* at 46–59.
103. *Id.*
104. *Id.*, ¶ 229, at 78.
105. *Id.*, ¶ 135, at 56.
106. LOCKE, CONCERNING CIVIL GOVERNMENT, *supra* note 33, ¶ 135, at 56.

world. The social contract patterns the covenant of grace. By covenanting to keep the laws of society, one is entitled to preservation of his life, and property, which is used to preserve life in this world. In both the covenant of grace and the social contract, the purpose of the covenant is to effectuate God's will, the preservation of life, and the good of man.

Accordingly, the Antifederalists wrote: "The common good, therefore, is the end of civil government, and common consent, the foundation on which it is established."[107] And similarly, the Federalists wrote: "[T]he Constitution is to be founded on the assent and ratification of the people of America . . . [T]his assent and ratification is to be given by the people . . . as composing the distinct and independent States to which they respectively belong."[108]

When a government fails to preserve the natural rights, like lives and property, of the people it governs, it is no longer promoting God's will and the covenant is broken. In such a case, the relationship between the government and the governed is no longer consensual. Locke taught that in the absence of consent, "shaking off a power with force, and not right, hath set over any one, though it hath the name of rebellion, yet is no offence before God, but that which he allows and countenances."[109]

It was precisely to avoid this situation that the framers required ratification by the American people. As Maryland delegate John Francis Mercer said at the Convention:

> It is a great mistake to suppose that the paper we are to propose will govern the [United] States? It is the men whom it will bring into the [government] and interest in maintaining it that is to govern them. The paper will only mark out the mode [and] the form. Men are the substance and must do the business. All [government] must be by force or influence. It is not the King of France—but 200,000 janissaries of power that govern that Kingdom. There will be no such force here; influence then must be substituted . . . .[110]

Ultimately, it was the ratification by the American people that gave the Constitution its life.

107. THE ANTIFEDERALIST PAPERS NO. 84, *supra* note 92, at 243.
108. THE FEDERALIST NO. 39, at 243 (James Madison) (Clinton Rossiter ed., 1961).
109. LOCKE, CONCERNING CIVIL GOVERNMENT, *supra* note 33, ¶ 196, at 70.
110. MADISON, DEBATES, *supra* note 55, at 455–56.

### *C. Ratification*

One concern of those opposed to popular ratification of the Constitution was that the average American would not be able to understand or appreciate the political import of the Constitution. Said Delaware delegate John Dickinson on one occasion, "Experience must be our only guide. Reason may mislead us."[111] Others, however, like Massachusetts delegate Rufus King, urged, "We ought to be governed by reason, not by chance."[112] Although some of the framers were uneasy about entrusting ratification of the Constitution to the ability of the American people to reason, the founders decided that in order to secure an enforceable social contract, they would have to rely on the intellect of the American people.[113] This was quite a leap of faith, considering prevailing political opinions of the day, but the framers of the Constitution were able to make that leap because of a solid core of Lockean ideals.[114]

Locke defined reason as "nothing else but the faculty of deducing unknown truths from principles or propositions that are already known."[115] He said it is "natural revelation, whereby the eternal Father of light and fountain of all knowledge communicates to mankind that portion of truth which he has laid within the reach of their natural faculties . . . ."[116] The founders had faith that the American people would recognize true principles in the Constitution because Locke had assured them that "[God] has given [mankind] a mind that can reason."[117] This was not a case where God was going to communicate a set of new discoveries immediately. This was a case where a portion of truth had been laid within the reach of men's natural faculties. "God hath given [reason] to be the rule betwixt man and man,"[118] and in the case of the Constitution, those who subscribed to Locke's philosophies would rely on the operation of basic natural principles, like

111. *Id.* at 447.

112. *Id.* at 362.

113. When asked "Wh[e]ther then must we resort?" to ratification of the Constitution, delegate George Mason of Virginia answered, "[T]o the people with whom all power remains that has not been given up in the Constitutions derived from them." He noted that "it was of great moment . . . that this doctrine [of social contract] should be cherished as the basis of free Government." *Id.* at 348.

114. Locke once observed that "all peaceful beginnings of government have been laid in the consent of the people." LOCKE, CONCERNING CIVIL GOVERNMENT, *supra* note 33, ¶ 112, at 51.

115. LOCKE, HUMAN UNDERSTANDING, *supra* note 54, book I chap. I ¶ 9, at 97.

116. *Id.*, book IV chap. XIX ¶ 4, at 385.

117. *Id.*, book IV chap. XVII ¶ 4, at 373.

118. LOCKE, CONCERNING CIVIL GOVERNMENT, *supra* note 33, ¶ 172, at 65.

human reason, to inspire the American people to accept and ratify the new social contract.

Adopting a Lockean worldview, the members of the Constitutional Convention recognized that they had done all that they could do. In order to achieve the government by social contract to which they aspired, they had to take a step into the unknown and exercise faith, that first principle of Locke's covenant of grace. They had to trust that God, through the natural process of revelation known as reason, would reveal to the American public the wisdom of the Constitution and inspire them to put their hands to it. Fortunately, God did reveal His will to the Americans and they ratified the Constitution, thereby sealing the great American social contract.

## V. CONCLUSION

John Locke's religious beliefs were shaped by his extensive study of Scripture and science, his life experience, and his associations with other religious men. Locke conveyed his religious beliefs to a great generation of Americans who, inspired by his assurance that God blessed men with the power to govern themselves, boldly undertook the task of creating a new government at the Constitutional Convention of 1787. Sharing Locke's belief that the government of men should model God's plan for their salvation, the Convention delegates determined to create a government by social contract. Because they believed that a social contract was necessary and because they shared Locke's belief that God would inspire men through the gift of reason, they exercised faith and surrendered the Constitution to the American people for their ratification. Although John Locke's voice may be literally absent from the text of the United States Constitution, his writings and thoughts were in the minds of our nation's founders. The result is a document that contains ideals and freedoms infused with John Locke's spirit.

# [10]

# JOHN LOCKE'S POLITICAL PLAN, OR, THERE'S NO SUCH THING AS JUDICIAL IMPARTIALITY (AND IT'S A GOOD THING, TOO)

JOHN M. KANG*

## INTRODUCTION

The image of the impartial judge is one that consoles and inspires the liberal imagination. Indeed, while liberalism's worth might not be logically reduced to its insistence on impartial judges, it seems safe to say that liberalism would look downright incoherent without their presence. For impartial judges and their institutional domains represent perhaps the clearest symbols of those values that we routinely associate with liberalism: toleration of social differences; recognition of people's equality; and the denial of prejudice and bias. Judges would thus seem to embody formally those values which everyone in a liberal society is expected to practice to some degree. While the need for impartial judges in a liberal society seems rather undeniable, there is a question that attends the idea of these judges whose answer isn't so clear for liberalism. If we expect judges to be impartial, must they also relinquish or subordinate their partiality?

Intuitively, the answer might seem to be a resounding yes. For we would be appalled at the judge who purports to be impartial but secretly decides the case on the seductive wink of a party's lawyer, its implications for the local Democratic or Republican parties, or some other self-indulgent reason. On the other hand, the insistence that judges be impartial is fraught with theoretical difficulties: what would a "completely" impartial judge look like, and precisely what judgments would qualify as impartial for starkly normative issues like abortion or school prayer? I shall argue in this essay that instead of juxtaposing impartiality against partiality, it is better to clarify the ways in which the latter can be harnessed to underwrite the former. I develop my thesis in the following manner. I demonstrate some flaws with impartiality as conventionally understood by examining the

---

* Ph.D. Candidate, University of Michigan, Ann Arbor; M.A., University of Michigan, Ann Arbor; J.D., U.C.L.A.; B.A., U.C. Berkeley. The title of the article is a play on Stanley Fish's *There's No Such Thing as Free Speech (And It's a Good Thing, Too)*. The reader familiar with that rewardingly mischievous work will recognize, in the course of reading this essay, that I've chosen to invoke Fish's title because like Fish's book, this article attempts to challenge the view that concepts like judicial impartiality can be logically or practically divorced from their contexts.

I am grateful to Mark Brandon, Don Herzog, Kim Smith, and especially Arlene Saxonhouse for comments on various drafts. This article is for Jung Won Kwak, to whom I am never impartial. The author can be reached at johnkang@umich.edu for comments or questions.

American Bar Association's Model Code of Judicial Conduct—the paradigm by which legislators craft their rules for assessing judges' purported impartiality. I show that the Code presents to judges an ambivalent and potentially unstable set of instructions: at times, it daringly insists that judges embrace impartiality for its own sake, and other times, it guardedly admonishes judges to be sensitive to appearance and hence hide their partiality. The former instruction, I'll argue, suffers from some fatal problems while the latter, although rather limp and ambiguous in its ABA Code form, can be worked up into an attractive theory via the older and more rewarding account of judicial impartiality by John Locke. Contrary to some other liberals, Locke did not position impartiality's exclusive antithesis in its intuitive opposite of partiality. Instead, I suggest, he also juxtaposed it against absolute or arbitrary power. That substitution, I argue, permits us to explore the political uses of impartiality without being encumbered by needlessly difficult and perhaps ultimately unanswerable questions about its ontological character.

## I. THE ABA CODE

Before I proceed with the arguments, there is the business of defining terms. It seems intuitive to view impartiality as the antithesis of partiality. I'll have cause later to revise this relationship but given its intuitive resonance, it is worth exploring now. So I'll begin provisionally by stipulating that impartiality is the denial of one's partiality, understood as either "particularity" or "affective attachment or desire."[1] The latter refers to "being partial to something, as when one is partial to chocolate cake, or committed to the principles of liberty and equality, or attached to the philosophic life" while the former means "taking a partial view of some matter, seeing it narrowly or incompletely."[2] The two forms of partiality have porous boundaries, it seems to me: one's particularity may be conditioned by one's affective attachment or desire (I am partial to America because that is what I have been taught to love), and one's affective attachment or desire can be conditioned by one's particularity (I love America because it is the only country that I have known). My concern then is less to patrol the borders separating particularity from affect and desire than to invoke their properties for purposes of defining impartiality.

The ABA's Code of Judicial Conduct defines impartiality partly by its prohibitions against the indulgence of both forms of partiality. There is the

1. The terms are borrowed from Sharon Krause, *Partial Justice*, 29 POL. THEORY 315, 318–19 (2001).

2. *Id.* at 319.

reference to affective attachment or desire: "A judge shall not allow family, social, political or other relationships to influence the judge's judicial conduct or judgment."[3] There is also a warning against particularity: "A judge shall not be swayed by partisan interests, public clamor or fear of criticism."[4] And there are many more injunctions against partiality that might fall into either category or overlap between the two.[5] The structure of these prohibitions takes shape in a lengthy series of rules which are accompanied by interpretive "commentaries." Yet instead of clarifying issues regarding judicial impartiality, the ABA Code's constitutive parts merely reflect and duplicate, again and again, a troubling moral ambivalence latent in its subject, an issue to which I turn next.

### *A. Troubling Ambivalence*

At times, the Code solemnly implores a purity of heart whereby the judge acts impartially for impartiality's own sake. Commentary on Section A of Canon 2 says that a judge should "avoid all impropriety" and that she must "accept restrictions . . . that might be viewed as burdensome by the ordinary citizen and should do so freely and willingly."[6] Other times, the Code, exuding a skeptical instrumentalism, urges the judge to keep up appearances and thus hide her latent partiality. Commentary on Section B(5) of Canon 3 observes that "[f]acial expression and body language, in addition to oral communication, can give to parties or lawyers in the proceeding, jurors, the media and others an appearance of judicial bias. A judge must be alert to avoid behavior that may be perceived as prejudicial."[7]

There is nothing inherently wrong with such ambivalence, but instead of coming across as a knowing paradox about the inevitable tension between moral aspirations and professional realities, it reads more as unselfconscious banality. Section A of Canon 2 at once encapsulates the ambivalence and elides its tension: "A judge must avoid all impropriety and

3. MODEL CODE OF JUDICIAL CONDUCT Canon 2B (1990) [hereinafter ABA CODE].

4. *Id.* Canon 3B(2).

5. *See, e.g., id.* Canon 3B(6) ("A judge shall require lawyers in proceedings before the judge to refrain from manifesting, by words or conduct, bias or prejudice based upon race, sex, religion, national origin, disability, age, sexual orientation or socioeconomic status, against parties, witnesses, counsel or others."). *See generally id.* Canons 2–3.

6. *Id.* Canon 2A, cmt.; *see also id.* Pmbl. ("Intrinsic to all sections of this Code are the precepts that judges, individually and collectively, must respect and honor the judicial office as a public trust . . . in our legal system.").

7. *Id.* Canon 3B(5), cmt.; *see also id.* Pmbl. ("Intrinsic to all sections of this Code are the precepts that judges, individually and collectively, must . . . strive to enhance and maintain confidence in our legal system.").

appearance of impropriety."[8] Unfortunately, avoiding impropriety and avoiding its appearance aren't the same thing. Consider the following invented play on a familiar case. When law professors want to teach their students about what doesn't count as judicial impartiality, Justice Peckham's majority opinion in *Lochner v. New York*[9] is habitually summoned as the belabored whipping boy. In *Lochner,* New York passed a statute which stated that no employee shall "work in a biscuit, bread or cake bakery or confectionary establishment more than sixty hours in any one week, or more than ten hours in any one day."[10] Justice Peckham struck down the statute and justified his decision in the following way:

> There is no contention that bakers as a class are not equal in intelligence and capacity to men in other trades or manual occupations, or that they are not able to assert their rights and care for themselves without the protecting arm of the State, interfering with their independence of judgment and of action. They are in no sense wards of the State.[11]

Legal scholars have tended to ridicule these words, calling them a shameful example of what happens when judges set aside judicial impartiality for partisan politics, which in Justice Peckham's case was a purportedly excessive dedication to laissez-faire economics.[12]

But suppose Justice Peckham felt himself to be sincerely impartial. Let's say, hypothetically, that he felt his opinion to be free of any prejudice against a labor-sensitive welfare state and any bias towards a muscular capitalism, and that he sincerely meant every word when he said that "[t]his is not a question of substituting the judgment of the court for that of the legislature."[13] His sincerity, I suspect, wouldn't temper the contempt of his many critics. If anything, his sincerity might engender greater indignation

8. *Id.* Canon 2A, cmt.

9. Lochner v. New York, 198 U.S. 45 (1905).

10. *Id.* at 68–69.

11. *Id.* at 57.

12. *See, e.g.*, BERNARD H. SIEGAN, ECONOMIC LIBERTIES AND THE CONSTITUTION 23 (1980) ("*Lochner* . . . is one of the most condemned cases in United States history and has been used to symbolize judicial dereliction and abuse."); Cass R. Sunstein, *Lochner's Legacy*, 87 COLUM. L. REV. 873, 874–75 (1987) (noting that *Lochner* and modern cases based on similar reasoning involve excessive judicial activism); Cass R. Sunstein, *Naked Preferences and the Constitution*, 84 COLUM. L. REV. 1689, 1697, 1718 (1984) (explaining that *Lochner* was based on erroneous assumptions about laissez-faire economics). For a revisionist vindication of *Lochner*, see HOWARD GILLMAN, THE CONSTITUTION BESIEGED: THE RISE AND DEMISE OF LOCHNER ERA POLICE POWERS JURISPRUDENCE (1993).

13. *Lochner*, 198 U.S. at 56–57.

on their part, for it might then signal a bias and prejudice that would be so comfortably ensconced as to be unproblematically naturalized in his mind. At the very least, anyway, this depiction of a Justice Peckham who sees himself as sincerely impartial wouldn't, I take it, win meaningful moral approbation among his many critics.

By the same token, though, neither would they necessarily withhold such approbation from a judge who appears to be impartial but isn't sincerely so. Take an example (conveniently located in the same case containing Justice Peckham's opinion) that is conventionally applauded as a paradigm of judicial impartiality—Justice Holmes's celebrated dissent. Justice Holmes argued that *Lochner* "is decided upon an economic theory which a large part of the country does not entertain."[14] But for him, the "Fourteenth Amendment does not enact Mr. Herbert Spencer's Social Statics"[15] and as a judge, "[his] agreement or disagreement has nothing to do with the right of a majority to embody their opinions in law."[16] Law professors tend to commend the decision as marvelously clean of the rancid bias and prejudice of Justice Peckham's opinion. But suppose Justice Holmes's opinion was utterly insincere and that he himself could care less for protecting the operations of the democratic process. Let's say, hypothetically, he decided the case in order to serve ends that were grossly disconnected from his judicial opinion: to earn for himself an historic reputation as an impartial judge; to pay indirect homage to a social Darwinism that heroically inspires his worldview; to exact revenge against Justice Peckham for a public slight. If any or all of these were true motivations, we would be disappointed, perhaps, but would we want to formally extinguish Holmes's opinion too and all its legal progeny simply because it was born of partiality? If so, moral purity would seem to be purchased at the vengefully high price of a legally serviceable conception of impartiality and its incidental beneficiary of legislative autonomy. The ABA Code casually enjoins judges to "avoid all impropriety and appearance of impropriety[,]"[17] but the example that I've offered shows why compliance is a less than straightforward normative matter.

The ABA Code introduces, perhaps unknowingly, a logical tension yet does little to justify it nor even consciously recognizes its existence. In the morally complicated landscape of politics in which judges often operate, however, we need an account of judicial impartiality that explicitly addresses the tension and explains what to do about it.

14. *Id.* at 75.
15. *Id.*
16. *Id.*
17. ABA CODE, *supra* note 3, Canon 2.

### B. Political Justification

If the ABA Code stumbles and stalls in its internal operation, it also lacks a larger political justification for its entire enterprise. The ABA Code contains a Preamble that briefly outlines the larger political auspices that its numerous rules are to serve:

> Our legal system is based on the principle that an independent, fair and competent judiciary will interpret and apply the laws that govern us. The role of the judiciary is central to American concepts of justice and the rule of law. Intrinsic to all sections of this Code are the precepts that judges, individually and collectively, must respect and honor the judicial office as a public trust and strive to enhance and maintain confidence in our legal system. The judge is an arbiter of facts and law for the resolution of disputes and a highly visible symbol of government under the rule of law.[18]

The words are harmless because they are stitched together from the thin and well-worn platitudes that high school students encounter daily in their civics classes. And to be fair to the Code's drafters, perhaps this is all that is necessary, for the Code's formal task is to instruct judges in the pressing business of judicial conduct, not to brood over airy issues of political theory; the Preamble is philosophical boilerplate, its defenders may rejoin, but what of it? Still, judicial impartiality is a deeply political enterprise that deserves sustained discussion.

Specifically, in its explicitly political function, what do we make of the following tension in the Preamble between, again, being sincerely impartial versus being guarded and presenting only the appearance of impartiality. The Preamble implores the former: "Intrinsic to all sections of this Code are the precepts that judges, individually and collectively, must respect and honor the judicial office as a public trust . . . ."[19] However, the Preamble also silently subordinates impartiality for the promotion of public confidence: "Intrinsic to all sections of this Code are the precepts that judges, individually and collectively, must . . . strive to enhance and maintain confidence in our legal system."[20] Which imperative, if conflicting, is more important for purposes of liberal political philosophy? The Code provides no answers and indeed assumes a congenial overlap.

18. *Id.* Pmbl.
19. *Id.*
20. *Id.*

### C. Purity of Motive

But if the Code underestimates the political dimensions of judicial impartiality, it overestimates people's potential for impartiality, and in the process, makes its strongest insistence on impartiality as something that should be sincere. Section B of Canon 2 orders that "[a] judge shall not allow family, social, political or other relationships to influence the judge's judicial conduct or judgment."[21] The expectation comes across as quaintly archaic. It appears as an unintended and stubborn remnant of what the legal realists criticized in mechanical jurisprudence, the faith that judges merely consult their "reason," understood as at once disembodied and discernible, and eschew the silly whims of emotion.[22] An early precursor to the legal realists, Justice Holmes, offered the then relatively controversial declaration that:

> The life of the law has not been logic: it has been experience. The felt necessities of the time, the prevalent moral and political theories, intuitions of public policy, avowed or unconscious, even the prejudices which judges share with their fellow-men, have had a good deal more to do than the syllogism in determining the rules by which men should be governed.[23]

Worse than being the collateral target of a famous judge, read straightforwardly, the Code is impossible to follow, for no one including judges can avoid the influences of "family, social, political or other relationships." Without even rolling out the heavy artillery of communitarianism, we can say confidently that when judges consider inherently moral issues of abortion, euthanasia, gay marriage, and the death penalty, they necessarily bring to bear a worldview constructed from an elaborate web of relationships with other people. Of course, a legal positivist like H.L.A. Hart might say that while some legal issues belong to the "penumbra of uncertainty," those outside its purview can be perspicuously adjudicated according to the rules and without consulting one's emotions and their muddled subjectivity.[24] But that's not so clear.

Even apparently mundane categories of estate planning may present a judge with vexing moral issues that require her to draw on a set of beliefs

21. *Id.* Canon 2B.

22. *See, e.g.*, Roscoe Pound, *Mechanical Jurisprudence*, 8 COLUM. L. REV. 605, 605 (1908) (explaining the theory of mechanical jurisprudence).

23. OLIVER WENDELL HOLMES, JR., THE COMMON LAW 1 (Little, Brown & Co. 1949) (1881).

24. H. L. A. Hart, *Positivism and the Separation of Law and Morals*, *in* THE PHILOSOPHY OF LAW 17, 22–29 (Ronald Dworkin ed., 1977).

profoundly influenced by others. Consider Ronald Dworkin's use of *Riggs v. Palmer*[25] to criticize the naivety of Hart's legal positivism.[26] In that case, a named heir in a will murdered his grandfather.[27] A terrible crime to be sure, but what conventionally goes by the name of literal interpretation applied to the New York statute required the court to bestow upon the heir his murderously begotten inheritance.[28] The court refused to read the statute so literally, explaining that:

> [A]ll laws, as well as all contracts, may be controlled in their operation and effect by general, fundamental maxims of the common law. No one shall be permitted to profit by his own fraud, or to take advantage of his own wrong, or to found any claim upon his own iniquity, or to acquire property by his own crime.[29]

While formally the product of "the common law," the judge's decision reflects a worldview that was partly pieced together from those sources prohibited by the ABA Code: familial, social, political, and other relationships.[30] And we could say the same thing if the judge had decided to construe the statute "literally," for that, too, would be a psychological disposition shaped by relationships with others, including, say, a father who sternly drilled his young son about professionalism or an unpredictably emotional father inspiring in his son the opposite quality.

All of this leads to the subversive conclusion that the Code's injunction for judicial impartiality depends in its practical operation on the very thing that it resists in partiality. As I explained earlier, partiality falls into two categories, particularity (taking a partial view of some matter) or affective attachment (being partial to something). Morally knotty legal questions about abortion or euthanasia invite the judge to consult her affective attachments (this is what her mother's Catholic values taught her) and be guided by particularity (this is the only mother she has known and Catholicism the only religion), and that even in those instances when the judge appears to be removed from them, her professional posture is to an extent partially impelled or repulsed by them and hence partially influenced by them, too. The ABA Code implores a judge to be sincerely impartial,

25. Riggs v. Palmer, 22 N.E. 188 (N.Y. 1889).

26. Ronald Dworkin, *Is Law a System of Rules?*, *in* THE PHILOSOPHY OF LAW 38, 44 (Ronald Dworkin ed., 1977).

27. *Id.* at 189.

28. *Id.*

29. *Id.* at 190.

30. ABA CODE, *supra* note 3, Canon 2B.

but interpreted straightforwardly, the order appears impossible by which to abide.

A version of judicial impartiality that can meet this objection and the others that I've identified with the ABA Code is available in Locke's theory of civil society.

## II. JUDICIAL IMPARTIALITY IN LOCKE'S CIVIL SOCIETY

### *A. Equality and Freedom*

I'll begin with Locke's most famous work on politics, *The Second Treatise on Government*.[31] In the beginning of the *Second Treatise*, Locke suggests that there is nothing that makes government logically necessary or desirable and that, in theory, men may live together in a state of nature as long as they properly consult their reason. While the state of nature is also a "*State of Liberty*," it is "not a *State of Licence*."[32] Specifically, "[t]he *State of Nature* has a Law of Nature to govern it, which obliges every one: And Reason, which is that Law, teaches all Mankind, who will but consult it, that being all equal and independent, no one ought to harm another in his Life, Health, Liberty, or Possessions."[33] In general, reason, which Locke equates with the law of nature,[34] should in the state of nature "willeth the Peace and *Preservation of all Mankind*."[35] The natural state of liberty, then, is circumscribed by what reason allows and, conversely, the failure to exercise reason would not be a reflection of liberty but of an uninformed license incompatible with the law of nature.

The law of nature requires that men exercise their reason not just in its interpretation but in its execution. The law of nature presupposes a power of "*Execution* . . . whereby every one has a right to punish the transgressors of that Law to such a Degree, as may hinder its Violation."[36] The power of execution assumes that "there is no superiority or jurisdiction of one, over another," such that "what any may do in Prosecution of that Law, every one must needs have a Right to do."[37] The law of nature expects of men that in executing it, they will not punish the transgressor "according to the

31. JOHN LOCKE, TWO TREATISES ON GOVERNMENT (Peter Laslett ed., Cambridge Univ. Press 1988) (1690) [hereinafter TWO TREATISES].

32. *Id.* at 270.

33. *Id.* at 271.

34. *Id.*

35. *Id.*

36. *Id.*

37. *Id.* at 272.

passionate heats" or with "boundless extravagancy of his own Will, but only retribute to him, so far as calm reason and conscience dictates, what is proportionate to his Transgression, which is so much as may serve for *Reparation* and *Restraint*."[38]

Despite these injunctions for men to consult their reason with respect to the law of nature, there is no guarantee that they will or that if they do, they will lead to mutually compatible conclusions, for the condition of freedom and equality permits men to "be Judges in their own Case."[39] Therefore, the same equality and freedom that justify why men should not harm each other in the state of nature cause Locke to worry that injustice may ensue there as well, for "he who was so unjust as to do his Brother an Injury, will scarce be so just as to condemn himself for it."[40] Indeed, as a general matter, "it is unreasonable for Men to be Judges in their own Cases," for "Self-love will make Men partial to themselves and their Friends" while "Ill Nature, Passion and Revenge will carry them too far in punishing others."[41] Therefore, the freedom and equality of men in the state of nature produces a condition where a man's "enjoyment of the property he has . . . is very unsafe, very unsecure. . . . [He] is full of fears and continual dangers."[42] So "[t]he great and *chief end* therefore, of Mens uniting into Commonwealths, and putting themselves under Government, *is the Preservation of their Property*[,]"[43] for it is in government that men can hope to find what is lacking in the state of nature—"*a known and indifferent Judge*, with Authority to determine all differences according to the established Law."[44]

This is a familiar summary of Locke's narrative of the state of nature. What interests me is that all (or almost all) of it noticeably turns on juxtaposing the poison of partiality against the antidote of impartiality, a conceptual posture that calls to mind the ABA Code. It is also a summary that tracks with simply more detail a standard rehearsal of Locke's theory in law review articles. In the law review literature, there is an easy and sometimes almost perfunctory allusion to Locke's statements about judicial impartiality that tends to elide the disquieting tensions and paradoxes that require further explication. One finds the repeated and familiar observation that men in the state of nature are destructively partisan and require in civil

38. *Id.*

39. *Id.* at 276.

40. *Id.*

41. *Id.* at 275; *see also id.* at 351 ("Men being partial to themselves, Passion and Revenge is very apt to carry them too far . . . .").

42. *Id.* at 350.

43. *Id.*

44. *Id.* at 351.

society "a known and indifferent Judge."[45] But even on the face of it, this rendering is incoherent, for how could such irrationally partisan men suddenly invent an indifferent judge from amongst their midst? The answer, I'll suggest, is that Locke doesn't actually conceive partiality and impartiality as mutually resistant. He wants to encourage or at least provide theoretical space for governmental officials to exercise forms of partiality that are, somewhat unexpectedly, likely to contribute to impartiality.

### *B. Different Partialities*

Locke explains that impartiality is sometimes threatened by various psychological conditions in man. In the *Second Treatise*, these conditions, Ruth Grant observes, "are understood as failures of reason."[46] So too they tend to be examples of what I have called partiality, both affect and particularity. Sometimes the partiality takes the form of aggressive self-assertion: "Men being partial to themselves, Passion and Revenge is very apt to carry them too far, and with too much heat, in their own Cases . . . ."[47] Other times, partiality indulges in lax indifference: "negligence, and unconcernedness [make men] too remiss, in other Mens [cases]."[48] To passion and biased indifference, add interest as an additional obstacle to impartiality:

> For though the Law of Nature be plain and intelligible to all rational Creatures; yet Men being biassed by their Interest, . . . [they] are not apt to allow of it as a Law binding to them in the application of it to their particular Cases.[49]

These passages would seem to suggest that partiality viewed as passion, biased indifference, and interest would be impediments to the realization of impartiality.

Yet that general conclusion requires some qualification. These examples of partiality share a particular form and substance which do not

45. *E.g.*, Albert W. Alschuler, *The Descending Trail: Holmes'* Path of the Law *One Hundred Years Later*, 49 FLA. L. REV. 353, 377 (1997); Phillip A. Hamburger, *Revolution and Judicial Review: Chief Justice Holt's Opinion in* City of London v. Wood, 94 COLUM. L. REV. 2091, 2134 (1994); Matthew R. Kipp & Paul B. Lewis, *Legislatively Directed Judicial Activism: Some Reflections on the Meaning of the Civil Justice Reform Act*, 28 U. MICH. J. L. REFORM 305, 314–15 (1995); Douglas G. Smith, *A Lockean Analysis of Section One of the Fourteenth Amendment*, 25 HARV. J. L. & PUB. POL'Y 1095, 1161 (2002).

46. RUTH W. GRANT, JOHN LOCKE'S LIBERALISM 181 (1987).

47. TWO TREATISES, *supra* note 31, at 351.

48. *Id.*

49. *Id.*

encompass every kind of partiality. The partiality described by Locke can be distinguished from others in at least two respects.

First, Locke's examples of partiality are not entertained in private nor in silence. Partiality informs the way we see the world, as Locke argues, but we needn't logically share that perspective with others nor act on it. However, the forms of partiality sketched by Locke are projected onto the world where others are made to endure their effects, effects that are heedless of the law of nature. Locke specifically has in mind the partiality by a king or prince that causes "another's harm"[50] and that "makes use of the Force he has under his Command, to compass that upon the Subject, which the Law allows not."[51]

Second, the substance of the partiality described by Locke does not permit of mutual advantage; it is nakedly one-sided. Partiality becomes dangerous when "Princes . . . have distinct and separate Interests from their People."[52] But partiality as a general matter doesn't logically require such separation. One may be partial to those things that incidentally benefit others. In fact, Locke himself tells us that the reason that men create civil government is not so that they may realize a higher form of impartiality for its own sake, but because civil government's promise of impartiality is intended to better protect men's interests in their individual property. Hence, some forms of partiality, instead of being antagonistic to impartiality, may actually motivate men to realize it.

Locke doesn't seem to allow, at least not formally, partiality to be either mutually advantageous or harmlessly indulged in private, but the logic of his arguments appears more capacious. There are vague if suggestive intimations like the following:

> [W]hen *Ambition* and *Luxury*, in future Ages would retain and increase the Power, without doing the Business, for which it was given, and aided by Flattery, taught Princes to have distinct and separate Interest from their People, Men found it necessary to examine more carefully the Original and Rights of Government . . . .[53]

In the passage, Locke says that impartiality is impossible where "interests" between the people and the prince become "separate," thus suggesting that

50. *Id.* at 400.

51. *Id.*

52. *Id.* at 343.

53. *Id.* (adding italics for "Ambition" and "Luxury," and omitting italics for "the Original" and "Government").

impartiality is possible where interests converge. There is also in the passage Locke's reference to passion in "ambition." The ambition for office and prestige doesn't seem to be for Locke inherently antithetical to impartiality. Locke seems to suggest that ambition is dangerous only when it so blinds the governmental official to his duties, making the satisfaction of ambition an end in itself, "without doing the Business, for which [his power] was given."[54] Yet a limited form of ambition by politicians is inevitable. It is unrealistic to imagine a public official who is indifferent to ambition and its hunger for what Locke calls "luxury" and "flattery" (try to imagine a President who cares nothing for his place in history, for a lavishly decorated White House, or for the countless examples of formal deference).[55] Instead of trying to do the implausible by theoretically expunging such partiality from human nature, Locke tries to distinguish which of its forms are useful for his political enterprise and which aren't.

I can supplement this interpretation by turning to Locke's discussion of what kinds of power are justifiable for civil government to exercise. By doing so, I want to suggest that the antithesis of impartiality for Locke is better understood as "absolute" or "arbitrary" power than partiality per se. Locke argues that civil government should not exercise absolute or arbitrary power but only "political" power. The definitions for these terms are mutually constitutive, and I want to proceed by explicitly defining political power first and, in the process, obliquely defining arbitrary and absolute powers.

### *C. Political Power*

Political power is "*a Right* of making Laws with Penalties of Death, and consequently all less Penalties, for the Regulating and Preserving of Property, and of employing the force of the Community, in the Execution of such Laws, and in the defence of the Common-wealth from Foreign Injury, and all this only for the Publick Good."[56] Because political power must be "only for the Publick Good," it would seem to be devoid of partiality and reflective of a form of impartiality. There would seem to be support for that

54. *Id.* Locke worries that when "flattery prevailed with *weak* Princes to make use of this Power, for private ends of their own, and not for the publick good, the People were fain by express Laws to get Prerogative determin'd, in those points, wherein they found disadvantage from it . . . ." *Id.* at 376 (emphasis added). The worry here seems to be that *weak* princes will undermine impartiality by being overly preoccupied with flattery, not that flattery per se is a danger to impartiality.

55. For examples of how America's founding fathers, usually apotheosized as selflessly virtuous, were obsessed with their personal fame, see DOUGLASS ADAIR, FAME AND THE FOUNDING FATHERS (1998).

56. TWO TREATISES, *supra* note 31, at 268.

view in Locke's description of the state of nature. Locke introduced a law of nature that established grounds for what men ought (and ought not) to do, and hence suggested a standard for what constitutes a legitimate use of power. The law of nature "teaches all Mankind, who will but consult it, that being all equal and independent, no one ought to harm another in his Life, Health, Liberty, or Possessions"[57] and that men should generally "willeth the Peace and *Preservation of all Mankind.*"[58] It is true that these injunctions are not explicitly meant to guide *political* power since in the state of nature, there is no government and hence for Locke no politics to speak of. However, one would think that these injunctions should nonetheless be used to judge the government's use of power because the government was erected to do that which the people alone could not do: to better interpret and better enforce the law of nature.

Or, to define political power negatively, we may look to Locke's description of a slave. Locke says that "in the State of Nature, *one Man comes by a Power over another*; but yet [has] no Absolute or Arbitrary power" over him, for the law of nature forbids it.[59] Yet a slave's identity, for Locke, is defined by another having both absolute and arbitrary power over him. Locke makes that point by distinguishing an indentured servant from a slave. He says that a "Master" of an indentured servant cannot "kill him, at any time, whom, at a certain time, he was obliged to let go free out of his Service."[60] Nor does that master "so far from having an Arbitrary Power over his Life, that he could not, at pleasure, so much as maim him, but the loss of an Eye, or Tooth, set him free."[61] By contrast, the master of a slave has the "Absolute, Arbitrary Power of another, to take away his Life, *when he pleases*."[62] Accordingly, if political power is said to be for the "publick good," it must be something other than the governmental official's "Absolute, Arbitrary power" over men as if they were slaves.

We may say that political power, then, is subject to review by the people (and not absolute) and is, as required by the law of nature, directed to protecting the people's peace and their individual property (and not used by the government for the exploitation of the people). In this way, political power is meant to reinforce Locke's understanding of impartiality while arbitrary and absolute powers are destructive of it. Indeed, for Locke, political power is the only type of power that a legitimate, and hence

57. *Id.* at 271.
58. *Id.*
59. *Id.* at 272.
60. *Id.* at 285.
61. *Id.*
62. *Id.* at 284 (emphasis added).

impartial, government may justifiably exercise.

Another point about political power deserves attention. For Locke, political power isn't logically or practically contingent on being a good person; it's just contingent on good behavior. Locke doesn't seem to require of governmental officials that they be sincerely impartial but only that they act as if they are. So take for example a high-level judge who doesn't sincerely believe that he should act "only for the Publick Good," nor does he sincerely accept Locke's solemn democratic injunction that all men are "equal and independent." For Locke, the judge would still be said to act impartially if he can justify his decisions as exercises in political power by acting according to established procedures; by having his decisions ultimately subject to review by the people; and by persuading the people that his decisions are consistent with the law of nature. Locke's account of impartiality, then, is not necessarily resistant to a judge who is preoccupied with the social esteem that accompanies his office, his handsome salary, and the prospect of having some modest place in legal history. This private preoccupation wouldn't necessarily compromise the judge's capacity to appear impartial—it may very well be the thing that keeps him in line.

My suggestion that for Locke impartiality needn't be sincere to be effective gains support from his proposals for how best to ensure that governmental officials remain impartial. The proposals, I argue, reflect a keen skepticism for the view that judges are impartial because they sincerely want to be.

### *D. The Potential Insincerity of the People as Free and Equal*

What is to ensure, or intended to ensure, that governmental officials will act impartially by exercising political—and not arbitrary or absolute—power? In one place, Locke appears to bank his hopes on the virtuous character of the officials themselves when he states that government needs "*indifferent* and upright *Judges*."[63] Yet Locke, as I've suggested, remains skeptical about entrusting government to men of ostensible virtue or superior intelligence. Locke is interested in developing a theory that is more distrustful of governmental officials. That theory finds expression in his account of the people's right of resistance. Locke argues that "*Governments are dissolved* . . . when the Legislative, or the Prince, either of them act contrary to their Trust."[64] The language of a trust establishes a

63. *Id.* at 353.
64. *Id.* at 412.

fiduciary relationship between the people and their government where the latter is expected to act in the best interests of the former. That implies that political power, as opposed to arbitrary or absolute power, does not derive from the traditional model of an absolutely powerful patriarch and his absolutely obedient subjects. Being a fiduciary relationship, the people themselves may judge when the government has failed to exercise political power; by contrast, that assessment in a contractual relationship might require a third-party judge, something whose very existence Locke thinks may be in doubt by the people.

Locke leaves to the people to decide ultimately what is impartial. Much of what animates Locke's arguments is a reaction against what he calls Sir Robert Filmer's justification for "absolute Monarchy" as based on the belief "that *Men are not naturally free*."[65] Against Filmer, Locke argues that men are naturally free and each other's equals, and thus cannot subject themselves to an absolute monarchy. He begins making his case through a series of foundational assertions about men's natural equality and freedom. Sometimes he invokes religious authority: "For Men being all the Workmanship of one Omnipotent, and infinitely wise Maker . . . they are his Property, whose Workmanship they are, made to last during his, not one anothers Pleasure."[66] Notice the premise that men don't have a property right in each other, a claim that tends to escape the attention of some scholars who portray Locke as obsessed with individual property rights. Notice too how the condition of equality implies that men are equally free, a point made explicit elsewhere: "And being furnished with like Faculties . . . there cannot be supposed any such *Subordination* among us, that may Authorize us to destroy one another, as if we were made for one anothers uses, as the inferior ranks of Creatures are for ours."[67] In addition to these reasons, Locke's most sustained and theoretically powerful arguments come from his explication of the state of nature. Men in the state of nature live in "a *State of perfect Freedom*" whereby they "order their Actions, and dispose of their Possessions, and Persons as they think fit, within the bounds of the Law of Nature, without asking leave, or depending on the Will of any other Man."[68] It is also a condition of equality:

> [W]herein all the Power and Jurisdiction is reciprocal, no one having more than another: there being nothing more evident, than that Creatures of the same species and rank promiscuously born

65. *Id.* at 144.
66. *Id.* at 271.
67. *Id.*
68. *Id.* at 269.

> to all the same advantages of Nature, and the use of the same faculties, should also be equal one amongst another without Subordination or Subjection . . . .[69]

But this premise would seem intuitively implausible. For it is simply not true that men, strictly speaking, are "furnished with like Faculties." And there is nothing especially "evident" in the claim that men are "born to all the same advantages of Nature, and the use of the same faculties." If anything, the opposite seems true. "Faculties" aren't naturally distributed; men vary radically in all sorts of talents and failings. So in stipulating that men are by nature free and equal, Locke does not intend to make an observation about the social worth of men. It is a point he guardedly acknowledges: "Though I have said above . . . *That all Men by Nature are equal*, I cannot be supposed to understand all sorts of *Equality: Age* or *Virtue* may give Men a just Precedency: *Excellency of Parts and Merit* may place others above the Common Level . . . ."[70] Given these plain and familiar feelings that people are not equal in many respects, Locke's staunch invocation of equality and freedom must mean something else than a straightforward claim about social worth.

To begin to determine what they might mean, we need to look to Locke's repeated exercises in unmasking supposed social betters as insincerely extolling their own self-worth. One of the most telling passages comes from Locke's indictment of the arrogant professor:

> Would it not be an insufferable thing for a learned Professor . . . to have his Authority of forty years standing wrought out of hard Rock Greek and Latin, with no small expense of Time and Candle . . . overturned by an upstart Novelist? Can any one expect that he should be made to confess, That what he taught his Scholars thirty years ago, was all Errour and Mistake . . . ?[71]

Here, what normally goes by learning and the pursuit of truth is actually prompted by dire vanity, a theme that Locke rehearses elsewhere: "[T]he Philosophers of old . . . and the Schoolmen since, aiming at Glory and Esteem . . . found this a good Expedient to cover their Ignorance, with a curious and unexplicable Web of perplexed Words, and procure to

69. *Id.*

70. *Id.* at 304.

71. JOHN LOCKE, AN ESSAY CONCERNING HUMAN UNDERSTANDING 714 (Peter H. Nidditch ed., Oxford Univ. Press 1975) (1690).

themselves the admiration of others . . . ."[72] And again:

> If we could but see the secret motives, that influenced the Men of Name and Learning in the World, and the Leaders of Parties, we should not always find, that it was the embracing of Truth for its own sake, that made them espouse the Doctrines, they owned and maintained.[73]

Such injunctions for the people to be prepared to view as insincere the outward virtues of their social betters can be enlisted to interpret what I presented as Locke's assertions about men's equality. His airy declaration that all men are naturally free and each other's equals is meant to serve practical political ends. Recall Locke's observation that all men are "furnished with like Faculties" and that all men have "the use of the same faculties." What he meant in both instances was that all men should be presumed to possess the same faculties to reason about what is best for themselves in matters political and not to defer blindly to some ostensible superior. Locke thus prepares the reader for the argument that there is no natural distinction between rulers and subjects and that government and its rulers are neither inevitable through divine right nor natural as an extension of good birth. This premise expresses itself with the cutting rebuke that "notwithstanding these learned Disputants, these all-knowing Doctors, it was . . . from the illiterate and contemned Mechanick, (a Name of Disgrace) that they received the improvements of useful Arts."[74]

The presumption of equality justifies why "there cannot be supposed any such *Subordination* among us, that may Authorize us to destroy one another, as if we were made for one anothers uses, as the inferior ranks of Creatures are for ours."[75] Locke's biting criticisms of professors and governmental officials are meant to encourage the people to be partial to their own self-interests and not to surrender to those who claim to be their social betters. This doesn't mean that the premise of men's natural equality necessarily undermines all forms of political authority but does imply its normative limits. The most basic such limit is consent. If men are said to be naturally equal and free, government can only arise from their consent, not by individual invocations of divine right or good birth. Locke's language of freedom and equality is thus not intended to describe social variations and rank but to justify the people's authority to make

72. *Id.* at 494.
73. *Id.* at 718–19.
74. *Id.* at 495.
75. TWO TREATISES, *supra* note 31, at 271.

independent judgments about government.

But by urging people to believe that all are free and equal, Locke must be urging them to be insincere. After all, it simply can't be true that all men are free and equal in their ability to decide what is best for their political future. Some men are irresponsible, lazy, selfish, or, as the religious civil wars so hauntingly familiar to Locke evinced, zealous and dangerous. Accordingly, we wouldn't want *everyone* to decide what is best for himself. And Locke doesn't either. As already illustrated, he indicts entire categories of men in scholars and statesmen as stubbornly vain. Indeed, a significant problem in the state of nature for Locke is the presence of men who either ignore the laws of nature or interpret them badly. Therefore, Locke himself would hardly seem likely to believe that *all* men are naturally free and equal in their capacities for political judgments. By grandly asserting that all men are naturally "free" and "equal" to decide their political fate for themselves, Locke wants to prevent a judge from publicly presupposing what is best for them or from publicly treating them as evident inferiors who may be subject to arbitrary or absolute power.

In the next section, I will explore the institutional means by which Locke attempts to ensure that judges will remain impartial. His explanation reflects the view that judges may very well be motivated by considerations of partiality in their apparent impartiality.

## III. INSTITUTIONAL MEANS

In explaining Locke's arguments about how to establish judicial impartiality, I can revisit the tension between impartiality and partiality with which I began. Partiality per se, I've suggested, is not for Locke the only or the most heuristically useful antithesis of impartiality. Another antithesis is the exercise of absolute or arbitrary power. And thus, to realize governmental impartiality, the people must have the right to resist what they perceive as absolute or arbitrary power, and not partiality in some categorical sense. When we recognize that political leaders are potentially prompted to be impartial under Locke's account because they fear for their office, we realize too that their outward impartiality is motivated by reasons that are not themselves impartial. Ironically, then, what is potentially animating the impartiality is a most self-interested partiality; the governmental officials are responsive to the people because the latter are also responsive to their own professional and institutional interests. And therefore what passes for impartiality is potentially underwritten by partiality. In this sense, whereas impartiality cannot exist with absolute or arbitrary power, it potentially depends on a certain form of partiality.[76]

We may then define Locke's view of impartiality as follows: Impartiality is the outward responsiveness by governmental officials to the concerns of the people and is expected to be motivated ultimately by the officials' partiality in wanting not to be ousted from their offices. This is not to say that judges aren't or can't be prompted by principle or professionalism, but rather to suggest that neither alone is sufficient to erect and maintain a system of impartial judges.

Locke's institutional proposals for civil government evince a desire to reinforce governmental impartiality by impeding public officials' indulgence of those forms of partiality that lead to arbitrary or absolute power and by rewarding the forms of partiality by public officials that are responsive to the people's wishes out of concern for the officials' own professional interests. Consider Locke's most important institutional proposals which attempt to ensure that officials are bound by the rule of law. Locke is guided by the belief that "*Where-ever Law ends, Tyranny begins*, if the Law be transgressed to another's harm."[77] Law as the institutional embodiment of impartiality is therefore incompatible with the partiality that is insensitive to others' welfare, not partiality as a whole. To restrain those forms of partiality hostile to the rule of law, Locke argues that governmental officials must "govern by *promulgated establish'd Laws*, not to be varied in particular Cases, but to have one Rule for Rich and Poor, for the Favourite at Court, and the Country Man at Plough."[78] Furthermore, the legislature is "placed in collective Bodies of Men," such that "every single person became subject, equally with other the meanest Men, to those Laws, which he himself, as part of the Legislative had established."[79] The same legislators are also expected to hold limited terms so as to prevent them from exempting themselves from their own laws:

> [T]he *Legislative* Power is put into the hands of divers Persons who duly Assembled, have . . . a Power to make Laws, which when they have done, being separated again, they are themselves subject to the Laws, they have made; which is a new and near tie upon them, to take care, that they make them for the publick good.[80]

76. I would thus be inclined to modify Ruth Grant's observation that for Locke "there is no place for private interest in political judgment." GRANT, *supra* note 46, at 188.

77. TWO TREATISES, *supra* note 31, at 400.

78. *Id.* at 363.

79. *Id.* at 329–30.

80. *Id.* at 364.

Not even the king's order can exempt anyone from the law's reach, "[f]or the King's Authority being given him only by the Law, he cannot impower any one to act against the Law, or justifie him, by his Commission in so doing."[81] The logic of these institutional restraints assumes that governmental officials will be impartial not because they sincerely want to be, but because they are pressured to do so.

## IV. Revisiting the ABA Code

I can now revisit the objections related to the ABA Code that I posed earlier. I'll address the objections in the reverse order in which I presented them, as that structure leads to a more coherent explication. There was the objection from purity of motive. The ABA Code, I argued, overestimates the judge's potential for impartiality, understood as "not allow[ing] family, social, political or other relationships to influence the judge's judicial conduct or judgment."[82] The prohibition, interpreted straightforwardly, is impossible to follow for it is theoretically incomprehensible. By contrast, Locke doesn't forbid one from consulting those sources which I've identified as partial in particularity and affective desire, perhaps an implicit recognition that to be utterly devoid of such partiality is to be devoid of what makes us human. What preoccupies Locke isn't a purity of motive but the creation and maintenance of a judicial impartiality which underwrites civil society and distinguishes it from a state of war marked by arbitrary and absolute powers. His view of judicial impartiality thus isn't principally an exploration of ontology but a proposal for politics. The motives on the part of judges which animate this form of impartiality may themselves be rooted in interests and passions that are exquisitely self-serving, but for Locke, their moral character remains of subordinate concern for the enterprise of civil society. Indeed, Locke seems to urge judges to repress any bias or prejudice they may have about particular individuals or the people generally as incompetent and undeserving, for the political imperatives of civil society require that judges treat all men as presumptively equal.

That point leads us to the second objection. I stated that the ABA Code lacks a larger political justification for judicial impartiality. Perhaps this omission is unavoidable given the Code's formal task, but it would be useful to have a sustained answer. Locke's arguments provide one. Judicial impartiality for Locke is central to the creation of civil society and

81. *Id.* at 403.

82. ABA CODE, *supra* note 3, Canon 2B.

all its corollary benefits in peace and the stable protection of property. We value impartiality not simply because, as the ABA Code proclaims, "Our legal system is based on the principle that an independent, fair and competent judiciary will interpret and apply the laws that govern us" or because, "The role of the judiciary is central to American concepts of justice and the rule of law" or because, "The judge is an arbiter of facts and law for the resolution of disputes and a highly visible symbol of government under the rule of law."[83] It is rather because without impartial judges, we face the awful prospect of being at the mercy of a tyrant who can gleefully exploit, torment and ultimately murder us in the exercise of arbitrary and absolute powers.

Bearing this in mind, the response gleaned from Locke's theory to a third objection to the ABA Code shouldn't be a surprise. I argued that the ABA Code contains a troubling ambivalence: sometimes it requires judges to be sincerely impartial and sometimes it requires them simply to act impartially. Which is more important and why? Given the decidedly political uses to which Locke employs judicial impartiality, it appears that judges needn't be sincerely impartial (whatever that simplistic formulation might mean) but may be prompted by motives rooted in partiality. Indeed, Locke doesn't want judges to ruminate primarily over the purity of their motives but to be sensitive to the people's perceptions of their conduct as assessed in terms of the law of nature. This is why he empowers the people with the right of resistance. It is to make sure that the judges are responsive, however much they dread, to the people's understanding of the law of nature.

To illustrate Locke's views in idiom more accessible to our contemporary sensibilities, let me reexamine the play on *Lochner* with which I began. I depicted a hypothetical in which Justice Peckham sincerely regarded his widely criticized opinion as impartial while Justice Holmes insincerely delivered an opinion that is extolled as the paradigm of impartiality. The ABA Code provides no perspicuous answers for how to come to terms with these two, but Locke's account of judicial impartiality does. Justice Holmes's dissent shouldn't be applauded as impartial for meeting criteria that is cleansed of any trace of partiality. It should be regarded as impartial because it resonates with our contemporary cultural preferences for a certain degree of legislative autonomy and a degree of skepticism regarding the equality of bargaining powers between employees and employers. Like the authority of Locke's impartial judge, Justice Holmes's authority derives from being sufficiently responsive to what the

83. *Id.* Pmbl.

people believe to be fair in political terms. By contrast, Justice Peckham's majority opinion is derided as being biased and prejudiced because it seems to grate against the cultural preferences which vindicate Justice Holmes's dissent.

The same cultural dynamic seems to be applicable in explaining popular reactions that have greeted other landmark cases like *Plessy v. Ferguson*[84] and *Brown v. Board of Education.*[85] We all condemn *Plessy*, where Justice Brown for the Supreme Court interpreted the Fourteenth Amendment's Equal Protection Clause as permitting the doctrine of state-sponsored racial segregation.[86] We chastise it as an appalling demonstration of racial bias and prejudice. Yet we enthusiastically celebrate Chief Justice Warren's unanimous opinion in *Brown* which formally overturned some of Justice Brown's opinion and informally foreshadowed its entire demise by declaring that separate but equal racial schools violated the Fourteenth Amendment's Equal Protection Clause.[87] In counterpoint to Justice Brown, Chief Justice Warren, according to contemporary cultural accounts, admirably shunned any racial animus towards Black Americans and hence was more impartial. But it's not that Justice Brown missed the mark on some inherently impartial understanding of the Constitution awaiting him at some Archimedean point and that Chief Justice Warren got it right. It's instead that the latter's view of race, and not the former's, was more responsive to a strand of cultural ethos in America present at the time of *Brown* and far less influential at the time of *Plessy*.

Given this understanding of judicial impartiality, we can say that the requirement to be impartial needn't entail for judges a corresponding requirement to be sincere. It makes more sense to argue that judges who insist on the stark moral project of being sincerely impartial at all costs are politically dangerous because they needn't logically be responsive to the people's view of impartiality. Supreme Court justices themselves at certain moments appear to recognize this unmistakably political understanding of impartiality. The joint-plurality opinion authored by Justices O'Connor, Kennedy, and Souter in *Planned Parenthood v. Casey*[88] provides a revealing look. They write: "The Court's power lies . . . in its legitimacy, a product of substance and perception that shows itself in the people's acceptance of the Judiciary as fit to determine what the Nation's law means

84. Plessy v. Ferguson, 163 U.S. 537 (1896).
85. Brown v. Board of Education, 347 U.S. 483 (1954).
86. *Plessy*, 163 U.S. at 551–52.
87. *Brown*, 347 U.S. at 495.
88. Planned Parenthood v. Casey, 505 U.S. 833 (1992).

and to declare what it demands."[89] At one point, the joint-plurality opinion makes reference to the conventional dichotomy between principle and politics but even then people's perceptions remain significant:

> The Court must take care to speak and act in ways *that allow people* to accept its decisions . . . as grounded truly in principle, not as compromises with social and political pressures . . . . Thus, the Court's legitimacy depends on making legally principled decisions under circumstances in which their principled character is sufficiently plausible to be accepted by the Nation.
>
> The need for principled action to be perceived as such is implicated to some degree whenever this, or any other appellate court, overrules a prior case.[90]

In addition, the opinion contains language that uncannily echoes Locke's observation that while judges are bound to make some decisions that upset the people, the right of resistance should only be exercised if the legal abuses are sufficiently serious and prolonged:

> People understand that some of the Constitution's language is hard to fathom and that the Court's Justices are sometimes able to perceive significant facts or to understand principles of law that eluded their predecessors . . . . [T]he country can accept some correction of error without necessarily questioning the legitimacy of the Court.[91]

This statement implies that from the judge's perspective, impartiality isn't a sacrosanct subject that is somehow immutable. Rather, it is contingent and changing, and ideally, responsive to the people.

## CONCLUSION

What I've argued in this essay is that the attempt to define judicial impartiality as an ontological subject is needlessly difficult for the enterprise of civil society. It is better, I've suggested, for judicial impartiality to be understood principally as a political project whereby the judge responds, in a meaningful way, to what the people regard as

89. *Id.* at 865.

90. *Id.* at 865–66 (emphasis added).

91. *Id.* at 866.

sufficiently impartial behavior and refrains from arbitrary or absolute power.

# Part V
# Law and Society

# [11]

# Radical Evil in the Lockean State: The Neglect of the Political Emotions

MARTHA C. NUSSBAUM*

The University of Chicago Law School
1111 East 60th Street
Chicago, IL 60637, USA
martha_nussbaum@law.uchicago.edu

**All modern liberal democracies have strong reasons to support an idea of toleration, understood as involving respect, not only grudging acceptance, and to extend it to all religious and secular doctrines, limiting only conduct that violates the rights of other citizens. There is no modern democracy, however, in which toleration of this sort is a stable achievement. Why is toleration, attractive in principle, so difficult to achieve? The normative case for toleration was well articulated by John Locke in his influential *A Letter Concerning Toleration*, although his attractive proposal thus rests on a fragile foundation. Kant did much more, combining a Lockean account of the state with a profound diagnosis of 'radical evil', the tendencies in all human beings to militate against stable toleration and respect. But Kant proposed no mechanism through which the state might mitigate the harmful influence of 'radical evil', thus rendering toleration stable. One solution to this problem was proposed by Rousseau, but it has deep problems. How, then, can a respectful pluralistic society shore up the fragile human basis of toleration, especially in a world in which we need to cultivate toleration not only within each state, but also among peoples and states, in this interlocking world?**

Keywords: toleration; emotion; evil; liberal democracy; Locke; Mill; Kant; Rousseau

## The Fragility of Toleration

Toleration is an urgent preoccupation in all modern liberal democracies. All such democracies are based on an idea of equal respect for citizens. But all contain a plurality of religious and secular 'comprehensive doctrines'

* A longer version of this paper will appear in Thomas Banchoff (ed.), *Democracy and the New Religious Pluralism* (New York: Oxford University Press, forthcoming 2007). I am grateful to Thom Brooks and Thomas Banchoff for working out an arrangement that permits me to publish both versions. My thanks to those who helped me with comments will appear with the longer version, as will many further references, examples (including a discussion of Franklin Delano Roosevelt's use of the arts during the New Deal), and arguments.

(to use John Rawls's phrase), doctrines in terms of which people make sense of life to themselves and search for its moral basis and its ultimate meaning. It would seem that equal respect for citizens, in such circumstances, requires respect for their freedom and equality, as they pursue matters of such fundamental importance. All such democracies therefore have strong reasons to support an idea of toleration, understood as involving respect, not only grudging acceptance,[1] and to extend it to all religious and secular doctrines, limiting only conduct that violates the rights of other citizens. This norm is widely shared.

There is no modern democracy, however, in which toleration of this sort is a stable achievement. Toleration is always under siege from the forces of intolerance, and constant vigilance is required lest a powerful group impose its ways on an unwilling and relatively powerless minority. Examples are so numerous that it would be pointless to list them.

Why is toleration, attractive in principle, so difficult to achieve? The normative case for toleration was well articulated by John Locke in his influential *A Letter Concerning Toleration*, a work that has profoundly influenced all subsequent proposals in the Western tradition. But Locke made no attempt to diagnose the forces in human beings that militate against toleration; his attractive proposal thus rests on a fragile foundation. Kant, I shall argue, did much more, combining a Lockean account of the state with a profound diagnosis of 'radical evil', the tendencies in all human beings to militate against stable toleration and respect. But Kant proposed no mechanism through which the state might mitigate the harmful influence of 'radical evil', thus rendering toleration stable. One solution to this problem was proposed by Rousseau, but it has deep problems, as I shall argue. How, then, can a respectful pluralistic society shore up the fragile human basis of toleration, especially in a world in which we need to cultivate toleration not only within each state, but also *among* peoples and states, in this interlocking world? I shall argue that the problem cannot be resolved without careful thought about how a liberal state can cultivate emotions that support equal respect and a toleration that is more than grudging obedience to law.

## Toleration and Equal Respect: The Lockean State

John Locke's thought about toleration is complex, and it is impossible to understand the argument of his *Letter* fully without connecting it to the rest of his political thought. Let me, however, attempt a summary. Locke insists that in matters of religious belief and religious conduct (so long as it does not violate the rights of others) the state must strive to protect '[a]bsolute

1. I use the word 'toleration' because Locke and much of the tradition uses it, but the term was sometimes understood to involve only grudging acceptance, and it is therefore important to emphasize that my own use (like Locke's) builds in an idea of positive respect for persons.

liberty, just and true liberty, equal and impartial liberty'. Not only must the state refuse the use of coercion to compel religious homogeneity, it must strenuously protect all its citizens from coercion on the part of others. Moreover, no person is to be 'prejudiced in his civil enjoyments' because of religion. Magistrates must go beyond non-persecution to zealous protection of all citizens in their rights, so that 'the goods and health of subjects be not injured by the fraud or violence of others' (35).[2] The state must leave religion strictly alone, except insofar as it ventures into areas that the state rightly regulates, such as property.

For both citizens and state actors, the norm of toleration requires not only the grudging preservation of rights, but a spirit of 'charity, bounty, and liberality' (27). Church officials ought to advise their members of 'the duties of peace and good-will towards all men; as well towards the erroneous as the orthodox' (32). They should 'industriously exhort' their members and especially civic magistrates to 'charity, meekness, and toleration' (32).

Locke advances several different arguments for this norm. Some of these arguments rely on Christian texts and doctrines. Some rely on a skeptical attitude toward religious beliefs. One influential strand of argument relies on the Protestant idea of 'free faith': genuine religious belief cannot be coerced. What concerns me here, however, is a line of argument that I take to be both central to the work and more pertinent to modern debates than any other. Modern readers of Locke may justly feel that some of his arguments are too 'internal', requiring a framework of Protestant ideas for their success. But this criticism cannot be made against the line of argument that concerns me. This is, that all citizens have rights, that is, rightful claims over liberty, property, and other prerequisites of well-being. Moreover, these rights are equal. It is simply wrong for these equal rights to be undermined on grounds of religious difference. Summarizing his argument, Locke emphasizes the centrality of this strand in his argument, stating, 'The sum of all we drive at is, that every man enjoy the same rights that are granted to others' (69).

This argument is based on Locke's general political theory. I shall not pursue those connections further here. However we understand the origin of Locke's doctrine of rights, it is a powerful idea for modern pluralistic democracies, one that most of them already accept, however much they differ concerning the metaphysical grounding of rights-claims and the precise nature of the rights in question. I take the key idea in this Lockean argument to be an idea of respect for persons. To say that persons have rights is a way of saying that persons deserve respect from one another. With regard to the fundamentals of well-being they are all equally entitled, and their entitlements must not be interfered with, either by the state or, through state inaction, by one another.

Locke recognizes that people are not always generous and peaceable. Indeed, his insistence on the duty of churches to exhort their members to

2. Page references are to the edition by Prometheus Books, 1990.

toleration, generosity and peace acknowledges the presence of a problem: people are inclined to go against the Lockean ideal. Locke's political surroundings did much to illustrate such violations. But nothing is said about how a Lockean state can grapple with this problem, beyond asking people to be nice to one another. Perhaps Locke believes that the problem is only temporary, the artifact of recent religious strife and bad clerical behavior. Moral psychology cannot be said to be Locke's strongest point as a philosopher. He simply lacks interest in the psychological underpinnings of intolerance, tending to blame it, instead, on bad individuals who can be replaced by good individuals.

Locke thus leaves his own project in a position that is at best uncertain, at worst highly unstable. Without trying to figure out why intolerance is so ubiquitous, however speculative all such accounts are bound to be, it is difficult to justify a conception of the state. For surely part of justifying a political conception is showing that over time it can be stable, and stable, as Rawls puts it, 'for the right reasons', that is, stable not just as a grudging *modus vivendi*, but as something people can really endorse as good for their lives. Locke leaves us uncertain whether this condition has been fulfilled.

## Radical Evil

Kant is deeply influenced by the social contract doctrines of both Locke and Rousseau. His state is basically Lockean in structure, uses a roughly Lockean understanding of rights, and understands the limits of state action in roughly Locke's way. Kant does, however, feel the need to fill the gap in Locke's account by supplying a moral psychology of evil and intolerance that may explain why intolerance and other forms of evil are likely to remain a permanent problem in human societies. In *Religion Within the Boundaries of Mere Reason*,[3] Kant articulates his famous doctrine of 'radical evil', a doctrine closely related to Rousseau's moral psychology, but one that Kant develops in a powerful and original way.

Evil is radical, according to Kant, that is to say it goes to the root of our humanity, because human beings, prior to any experience, have a propensity to both good and evil, in the form of tendencies that are deeply rooted in our natures. We are such that we can follow the moral law, but there is also something about us that makes it virtually inevitable that under certain circumstances we will disregard it and behave badly.

What are those conditions? Animality itself is not the problem; animality is basically neutral (6.32; 6.57-58). Here is where Kant locates the error in Stoicism, which he portrays (wrongly[4]) as involving the doctrine that our

3. All quotations are from the version translated and edited by Allen Wood and George Di Giovanni in the Cambridge Texts in the History of Philosophy Series (New York and Cambridge: Cambridge University Press, 1998). Page numbers are those of the Akademie edition, which are given in the margins of the translation.

4. See my 'Equity and Mercy', in my *Sex and Social Justice* (Oxford: Oxford University Press, 1999); and also *The Therapy of Desire: Theory and Practice in Hellenistic Ethics* (Princeton,

moral struggle is against animal inclination alone (57-58). The tempter, the invisible enemy inside, is something peculiarly human, a propensity to competitive self-love, which manifests itself whenever human beings are in a group. The appetites all by themselves are easily satisfied, and animal need is limited (6.93). The human being considers himself poor only 'to the extent that he is anxious that other human beings will consider him poor and will despise him for it'. But a sufficient condition of such anxiety is the mere presence of others:

> Envy, addiction to power, avarice, and the malignant inclinations associated with these, assail his nature, which on its own is undemanding, *as soon as he is among human beings*. Nor is it necessary to assume that these are sunk into evil and are examples that lead him astray; it suffices that they are there, that they surround him, and that they are human beings, and they will mutually corrupt each other's moral disposition and make one another evil. (6.94)

Kant's account is powerful. Although he surely is too sanguine about the opportunity of many of the world's people to satisfy bodily need,[5] he is also surely right in holding that mere satisfaction is not the biggest cause of bad behavior. Even when people are well fed and housed, and even when they are reasonably secure with respect to other prerequisites of well-being, they still behave badly to one another and violate one another's rights. And even though an innate propensity is a difficult thing to demonstrate, Kant is surely right when he suggests that people require no special social teaching in order to behave badly, and indeed regularly do so despite the best social teaching.

Kant is offering a general explanation for the origins of bad behavior, not a particular explanation of intolerance. But it has an obvious relevance to Locke's problem. Wherever people are together, they form themselves into religious (and ethnic) groups and vie for superiority. This process, difficult to explain with reference to the ideologies of the religions, which may be strongly in favor of peace and compassion—as Locke pointed out for the case of Christianity—is well explained by Kant's positing of a propensity to competition that is activated by the mere presence of a plurality.

Kant's account of radical evil, while attractive in many respects, seems incomplete. It is all very well to say that there are tendencies in human beings such that the presence of others will elicit competition and aggressive behavior; but Kant says little about the nature of those tendencies. Perhaps he thinks that there is nothing more to be said: radical evil is just the disposition to manifest competitive and morality-defying behavior in the presence of

NJ: Princeton University Press, 1994), ch. 11. I suggest that Seneca locates the origins of evil in the 'circumstances of life', that is the competitive striving for good that human life as it is brings forth. His account is not exactly Kant's, because he does not hold that bodily appetite is easily satisfied; nor does he posit an innate tendency to competition. But the similarity of the two accounts is considerable.

5. Thus Seneca's account is in some ways stronger than Kant's.

others. It seems to me that we can say more. In two books on the emotions[6] I argue that understanding the roots of bad behavior requires thinking about human beings' problematic relationship to their own mortality and finitude, their desire to transcend conditions that are painful for any intelligent being to accept. The earliest experiences of a human infant contain a jolting alternation between blissful completeness, in which the whole world seems to revolve around its needs, and an agonizing awareness of helplessness, when good things do not arrive at the desired moment and the infant can do nothing to ensure their arrival. The expectation of being attended to constantly—the 'infantile omnipotence' so well captured in Freud's phrase 'His Majesty the baby'—is joined to the anxiety, and the shame, of knowing that one is not in fact omnipotent, but utterly powerless. Out of this anxiety and shame emerges an urgent desire for completeness and fullness that never completely departs, however much the child learns that it is but one part of a world of finite needy beings. And this desire to transcend the shame of incompleteness leads to much instability and moral danger. In writing about the role of shame and disgust in the process of group-formation and social intolerance, I have argued that the type of social bad behavior with which I am most concerned in this paper can be traced to child's early pain at the fact that it is imperfect, unable to achieve the blissful completeness that in certain moments it is encouraged to expect. This pain leads to shame and revulsion at the signs of one's own imperfection. And then, what most concerns me here, shame and revulsion, in turn, are all too often projected outwards onto subordinate groups who conveniently symbolize the problematic aspects of humanity, those from which people want to distance themselves.

Thus my account of prejudice and hatred, whether religious or ethnic or sex-based, is more complicated than Kant's, invoking not only mere plurality but also the hatred of weakness, helplessness, and (ultimately) death that is omnipresent in our relationship to our humanity.[7] And I argue that a primary reason why people form groups of the sort that engage in bad behavior toward others is an (ultimately futile) attempt to recover completeness and safety. By defining their own group as the good 'normal' one, lacking in nothing, and by surrounding themselves on all sides with such people, people gain the illusion of safety and control, projecting onto subordinate others the weaknesses that they wish not to accept in themselves. By stigmatizing and persecuting others, they conceal from themselves their own weakness and vulnerability.

Thus, unlike Kant, I think that radical evil is not a bare disposition to behave badly in certain circumstances. It has an underlying content and a narrative history. Radical evil concerns the pursuit of transcendence and the

6. *Upheavals of Thought: The Intelligence of Emotions* (Cambridge: Cambridge University Press, 2001), and *Hiding from Humanity: Disgust, Shame, and the Law* (Princeton, NJ: Princeton University Press, 2004).

7. See *Hiding from Humanity*.

hatred of finitude: it is about narcissism, we might say, and the fear of death that is a powerful prop to narcissism. Thus the remedy for radical evil will have to address this deeper problem—not curing it, for life is too painful for human beings ever to accept it as it is, but mitigating the role of narcissism in social life. This narrative history of radical evil has implications for the social treatment of evil that Kant's far more abstract account does not. For now, however, let me return to Kant's account, which is compatible with mine, although it does not entail it.

Whenever human beings are together, then, according to Kant, bad behavior is a likely outcome, and intolerance is one prominent form that such bad behavior typically takes, as one very prominent form of competitive self-love. Intolerance, then, is not an easily eradicated social condition. People will in general seek to violate the rights of others, and in particular will seek to establish the superiority of their own religious doctrines. Although Kant himself does not make this connection between his doctrine of evil and the specific problem of intolerance, it is strongly suggested by his argument.

To individual human beings, Kant gives extensive advice. To counteract the bad tendencies in their nature they have the duty to surround themselves with a group of people who are all working for the victory of the good tendencies over the bad. People are unlikely to achieve such a victory stably on their own, but in a group of like-minded strivers they have a better chance, forming a counter-society that will strengthen the moral disposition and protect it from the temptations that worldly society offers. That is the role Kant sees for religion: it is a social force that supplies a support structure for morality. Given that we are all morally weak and liable to error, we have an ethical duty to join such a society, leaving our ethical state of nature to join an ethical community. Kant argues that not just any ethical community will do: it has to be a religious one, meaning one that is united by the idea of a higher moral being. Much of the text is then devoted to distinguishing good religious communities from bad, asking what sort of religious community could actually do the job Kant has laid out. Most existing churches, Kant argues, are actually a bad influence, since they teach people to placate God in extraneous ways, and undermine the purity of the moral incentive. But any of the major faiths can become acceptable, if reconstructed in the right (moral, rational) way.

What, however, of the Lockean state? Given the ubiquity of the propensity to evil, what can such a state do to protect itself against the forces of bad behavior generally, and intolerance in particular? Well, it can certainly use coercion to protect people's property rights and other rights that they have under the social contract. Here Locke and Kant are in agreement. But I have suggested that this leaves equal respect in a fragile position. So it would be nice to think that the state could find some further ways of supporting good behavior in general, toleration in particular.

For Kant, the choice to enter a church must always remain a choice. He is just as averse as Locke is to the Hobbesian idea of state-based religious coercion. He argues against it on both moral and prudential grounds. '[W]oe to the legislator who would want to bring about through coercion a polity directed to ethical ends', he writes, 'for he would thereby not only achieve the very opposite of ethical ends, but also undermine his political ends and render them insecure' (6.96). Moreover, even when people make a bad choice and join a bad church, or even declare themselves atheists, Kant is convinced that respect for autonomy requires respecting their liberty. Like Locke, he insists that no person's civil liberties may be infringed on grounds of religious membership or practice; but he goes even further than Locke, protecting atheists as well as believers. The most the state can demand is that churches include nothing in their constitution that contradicts the duties of members as citizens of the state. So there is a problem: respect for autonomy requires us to tolerate bad churches, which is what Kant thinks most actual churches are. Such churches actually strengthen evil and thus undermine toleration. What, then, can the Lockean state do to protect itself?

Kant's answer, and the only answer he believes he *can* give, consistently with his defense of autonomy, is that the state can and should foster a vigorous critical culture, including strong protections for the freedom of speech and debate. Moreover, this state support should extend to generous funding for education and support for scholarship, especially critical religious scholarship. All that is fine, as far as it goes. But the same principle that protects the scholarship Kant likes also protects the scholarship that he detests. And the same public openness that creates the conditions for rational religion to come into existence also gives wide scope for the mobilization of prejudice and intolerance. This being the case, the state that Kant envisages remains in a fragile condition. He has to rely on the sophistication and rationality of a general public who are, as he himself knows, very much inclined to the emotional and rhetorical appeals of the bad churches. In his suspiciousness about the passions and sentiments, he seems unwilling to propose any emotional dimension to the public rhetoric in favor of rational religion and the good churches. To the extent that they do prevail, it must be because of good scholarship and enlightened argument.

The dilemma with which Kant's thought leaves us becomes more acute still when we consider the global society to which Kant's thought so powerfully pointed the way. As Kant knew and stressed, one of the worst expressions of radical evil lies in the conduct of nations toward other nations. Wars of conquest, colonial domination, all these are outgrowths of the competitive tendencies that Kant so well identified, and it is not surprising that intolerance of the different beliefs and ways of life of others is so often a part of these projects. But if the state seems to be impotent to stop threats to the stability of its own tolerant policies internally, it has a harder time still once we articulate the human goal in world terms, as that of respecting humanity wherever it is, and protecting the freedom to pursue one's own comprehensive doctrine, for all world citizens. Many people who can be led to behave with toleration to their own fellow nationals forget about this principle completely when they are abroad. Thus a tolerant world order will be far harder to produce than a stably tolerant Lockean state.

## A Civil Religion?

Because Kant's moral psychology is not altogether new, the problem that it raises for the liberal society is also not new. Rousseau, whose psychology is in essence the source of Kant's, understood that the state that is going to protect toleration needs to think about the moral emotions and needs to adopt some program for their cultivation. In the important section of *The Social Contract* on the 'civil religion', Rousseau argues that complete toleration in spiritual matters is of great importance, but that it needs to be undergirded by the promulgation of a 'civil religion' consisting of 'sentiments of sociability, without which it is impossible to be a good citizen or a faithful subject'. This religion, a kind of moralized Deism fortified with patriotic beliefs and sentiments, will hold the state together and create moral unanimity among citizens. Its dogmas include the existence of a powerful beneficent deity and a life after death; the happiness of the just; the punishment of the wicked; the sanctity of the social contract and the laws; *and* the unacceptability of intolerance.

Around all of these dogmas the sovereign will create ceremonies and rituals, engendering strong bonds of sentiment connected to morality and patriotic duty. The civil religion functions as the common moral core of all the acceptable forms of religion: people may add to this core various metaphysical and spiritual beliefs. But all must adhere to the core, both with respect to conduct and with respect to belief.

Rousseau believes that this device will solve the problem of stability in the tolerant state, giving people sources of motivation to behave well to one another. For Kant, respect for autonomy requires that the choice to enter a church be left entirely free. Rousseau, by contrast, permits the sovereign to enforce the civil religion by coercive means, including banishment and even capital punishment. State coercion applies not only to conduct harmful to others, but also to non-harmful conduct expressing lack of adherence to the civil religion; and it applies, as well, to nonconforming belief and speech. In particular, Rousseau insists on a belief not only in civil, but also in theological toleration. Thus state coercion extends to a great deal in the way of religious opinion, since Rousseau believes that '[i]t is impossible to live in peace with those one believes to be damned'. If we think about the actual doctrines of the major religions in his own time, we can see that in Rousseau's state Roman Catholics will not be tolerated, and many if not most forms of Protestantism will not be either.

Rousseau has taken the problem of evil seriously and made a proposal that may be sufficient to cope with it. Obviously, however, his solution would be unacceptable to Locke, Kant, and anyone who finds the idea of a Lockean state attractive. Such a state is built on the idea that respect for persons entails respect for their comprehensive doctrines. This starting point requires broad toleration of religious opinion, including theological opinions about the salvation of others, so long as these opinions do not issue in conduct that violates the civil rights of others. Rousseau has purchased stability at much too high a price. We may see Kant's emphatic insistence on freedom of speech, scholarship, and association as an implicit repudiation of Rousseau, as well as a comment upon his own situation under a series of different Prussian leaders.

Another grave problem with Rousseau's civil religion, as with all attempts at a civil religion based on patriotic sentiment and the idea of willingness to die for one's country, is that this religion provides a very bad basis for international relations. The very sentiments that cement the homogeneity of Rousseau's society make it suspicious and intolerant of foreigners, and conduce to warlike behavior against foreigners. Rousseau likes this consequence. Indeed, one reason why he feels the need for a civil religion to supplement Christianity is that he finds Christianity too passive, meek and mild. But anyone who finds Kant's idea of a peaceful and tolerant world community attractive will find here yet further reasons to take exception to Rousseau.

Rousseau's psychological insight, however, does not disappear once one rejects his solution. He seems right to insist that the state needs to take the problem of evil seriously and to devise some sort of public psychology to address it, a 'civil religion' if you will. And yet Kant seems right in his insistence that the problem of radical evil cannot be addressed by state coercion of free political and religious debate; this cure is worse than the disease. At the margins we may legitimately debate the legal regulation of some forms of hate speech, asking how immediate the threat to safety and stability must be in order for such speech to be legally regulable. But in general we should agree with Kant: the very value of respect for persons that leads us to want a Lockean state also prevents us from protecting it with a coercive civil religion of Rousseau's sort.

How, then, can a respectful pluralistic society shore up the fragile bases of toleration, especially in a world in which we need to cultivate toleration not only within each state, but also between peoples in this interlocking world?

Kant was surely right in thinking that one very important part of the solution is the vigilant protection of freedoms of speech, press and scholarship. Intolerance thrives in a situation in which opinion is curtailed, and we may observe that intolerant groups usually if not always seek the curtailment of these freedoms as a road to domination. One more thing that a society may certainly do, and that most societies do already, is to attach rituals and ceremonies to the basic freedoms protected by the society, inspiring citizens to love those values by linking the values to music, art and ritual. This strategem is dangerous, given the propensity of all forms of patriotism to lead to demonization of foreigners and local 'subversives'. Nonetheless, there are ways to institutionalize such ceremonies that do not buy into these dangers. Where toleration is concerned, a reasonable 'civil religion' would include, for example, a celebration of the diversity of traditions and comprehensive doctrines that are contained within a nation, as a source of its strength and richness. (The national anthem of India, written by Rabindranath Tagore, is a good example: it celebrates the diversity of India's regional and ethnic traditions, at the same time asserting that all are linked by reverence for moral principle.) In general, there is much that the tolerant state may do by way of persuasion and rhetorical undergirding, without infringing on the freedoms of speech, assembly and publication of those who think differently.

An attractive further proposal was made by John Stuart Mill in his essay on 'The Utility of Religion'. Here Mill, recognizing the importance of religious sentiments in giving force to moral motivation, suggests what (following Comte and others) he calls a 'The Religion of Humanity', a moral ideal that could be promulgated through public education.[8] According to this moral ideal, a good person is one who cares deeply about humanity generally. Her thoughts and feelings learn the habit of being carried away from her own parochial concerns; they are habitually fixed on this 'unselfish object, loved and pursued as an end for its own sake'. She learns to view helping others as a part of her own good: she identifies her good with that of humanity as a whole, and thinks of her afterlife as the life of those who follow her. She learns, in these ways and others, that helping others is not a sacrifice, but an intrinsic good.

These ideas are closely linked to some that I have tried to develop, in *Upheavals of Thought*, concerning compassion as a moral sentiment that can be cultivated by public institutions and public education. I have argued that a liberal society, without offending against respect for pluralism, can still employ a moral ideal of this sort, and promote a moral education aimed at underwriting it. This ideal would serve as a basis for public political culture, in connection with public norms of equality and respect.

How, more precisely, would this moral education be institutionalized? A good part of it, I argue, would in fact take the form of developing institutions that express the views of equal respect and due attention to the needs of all: a just tax system, a just healthcare system, a just welfare system. But institutions remain stable only when human beings have the will to sustain them, a fact that the collapse of social democracy in the United States, since the Reagan era, has made an all too vivid reality. Therefore, I argue, public education at all levels should focus on putting forward something like Mill's religion of humanity, conveying the sense that all human lives are of equal worth, and all worthy of being lived with dignity and a decent minimum level of well-being.

Where toleration is concerned, the 'religion of humanity' takes, in the first instance, an institutional form, in the form of strong protections for religious liberty and a support for the idea of equal respect for comprehensive doctrines. (A doctrine of non-establishment is one very usual and valuable means of promoting equal respect.) Enhanced penalties for crimes involving ethnic,

8. I am indebted to an unpublished paper by Daniel Brudney, which offers an attractive analysis of this essay.

racial and religious hatred would also be prominent parts of the institutional side of such a program, expressing society's very strong disapproval of intolerance and the actions to which it can give rise.[9]

Although my proposal is Kantian in the sense that no civil penalties attach to people who speak in favor of greed, inequality, and even intolerance, so long as they do no harm to others, it seems appropriate for public education and the media culture of a democratic society to focus on imparting norms that do support the values of a liberal society and a decent world culture. Thus, where toleration is concerned, I would support education at all levels aimed at conveying understanding of and respect for different religious and secular comprehensive doctrines[10] and different ethnic and national traditions. Although knowledge does not guarantee good behavior, ignorance is a virtual guarantee of bad behavior: stigmatization of the other is much easier when people know nothing, or nothing complicated, about a religious or cultural tradition. But education can surely go further, fostering a sense of respect for persons and of their equal entitlements to lives with human dignity, of which religious freedom is one big part.

Because my own understanding of radical evil is more complex than Kant's, I also argue, in my recent book on shame and disgust, that public culture needs to devote special emphasis to minimizing the negative effects of narcissism, and of the aggression that is so closely connected with people's unwillingness to tolerate their own neediness, finitude and embodiment. Many aspects of the inhibition of narcissism will, once again, be institutional. But much of the program must be informal and educational, devising ways to bring children up in a climate that fosters equal respect and minimizes the baneful social influences of disgust and stigmatization, and a positive attitude toward aspects of our embodied life, such as sexuality and aging, that are difficult to confront. There is no reason why a more psychologically complex version of Mill's 'religion of humanity' cannot be widely taught and promulgated by liberal democratic societies, together with support for a robust critical culture of the sort that Kant favors.

But because my program is more psychologically complex, more unsettling, than Mill's, it is going to need real artists to carry it out, not just well-intentioned public servants. Such artists can play a role in at least three different ways. First, they may participate in constructing emotions supportive of the political norms, for people who do not yet support them, or fully support them (especially children and young people). Second, they may give people a sense of how important the political norms are, again by attaching them to

9. For an argument that these penalties do not involve an illegitimate penalizing of political speech, see *Hiding from Humanity*, ch. 5.

10. Like John Rawls, I would insist that we must respect all *persons*, giving all the space in which to unfold their comprehensive doctrines, so long as they do not violate the rights of others; we need not respect all doctrines, however, but only those that join in society's 'overlapping consensus' concerning basic constitutional principles.

emotions that support them and embody a sense of urgency. As Rawls remarks, it is not enough that people support norms of toleration and equal respect: they must also think that these political goals are quite important, worth really trying hard to secure and maintain, because these political goals may sometimes require sacrifices of their own self-interest.[11] Emotions constructed by art and rhetoric frequently play a valuable role in such a process. Third, a 'public poetry' of the type I envisage can also support the efforts of those who already believe in the political norms, giving them hope (as they participate in the public celebration of their own values) that these good norms may eventually prevail and are not merely a foolish utopianism.

Now we must leave the realm of abstraction and turn to political history. For there are indeed examples of the good kind of civil religion in our recent history. If I were giving this paper in India, I would turn at this point to Rabindranath Tagore, who was the arch-entrepreneur of a public poetry of diversity and inclusion. In his songs, dance-dramas and poems, he celebrated the richness of a nation that derives from its diversity; at the same time, he celebrated the body, with all its complexity, its sexuality, its aging, as a source of joy. As an educational entrepreneur, he created a school that aimed at forming the imaginations of young citizens, through the arts, in accordance with these notions of the human.

But since I am in the US, let me now choose US examples of a 'civil religion' addressed to the formation of political emotions.

*Walt Whitman's Poetry*

Although I have written so much about this topic before, Whitman's effort to construct a public poetry supportive of democracy cannot be overlooked, since, unofficial though it is, it is a paradigm of what I have in mind, and it has deeply influenced most subsequent examples. I will simply ask you to excuse the poverty of detail in this account on the ground that *Upheavals of Thought* contains the details I think most important.

Whitman understood, and repeatedly asserted, that the civic fabric of a democracy cannot be held together by laws and institutions alone: 'To hold men together by paper and seal or by compulsion is no account' (In 'Blue Ontario's Shore', l. 130). What is needed is something 'which aggregates all in a living principle' (l. 131)—and that, he insists, can be supplied only by poets. Writing during the Civil War, he says that the US needs poets more than any other country does; 'Their Presidents shall not be their common referee so much as their poets shall' (l. 133).

Why are poets needed? This is a large topic, but the connection of poetry with the emotions is a central part of it. An insistent theme in Whitman's poetry is the relationship we have to minorities in our society: African-Americans, women, and homosexuals. Whitman understood that laws can *say* that

11. See, for example, John Rawls, *Political Liberalism* (New York: Columbia University Press, exp. edn, 1986), pp. 154-58.

all citizens are equal, but only poetry can construct sentiments that lead all citizens to acknowledge that equality, because only poetry can characterize the suffering of exclusion in a way that moves us to put an end to it, and only poetry can characterize what we stigmatize and hate in ways that make us see it differently. Crucial to this project is forging a new idea of the body. My own very Whitmanesque view about the nature of 'radical evil' is that a certain shame and disgust at our very humanity leads, under many social circumstances, to the stigmatization of others. Whitman saw his task, therefore, as creating a new relationship to the body, one of love and delight rather than shame and disgust. Like Tagore, Whitman understood that emotions supportive of respect for all the different citizens of a great nation, whatever their race, gender or religion, required working vigilantly against the tendency to stigmatize the different by portraying people or groups as disgusting, as bearers of some type of bodily contamination or dirtiness. This human tendency, which I call projective disgust, is a flight from something in ourselves; it therefore can be countered only by a reconstructed relation to ourselves and our bodily fluids, which Whitman again and again tries to forge—above all in 'I Sing the Body Electric', but throughout 'Song of Myself' and many shorter poems as well.

Public poetry is therefore likely to be unsettling, as Whitman's poems have always been found unsettling. And yet the sheer richness of language and image in them leads the reader in, until the difficult and challenging images prove acceptable—even images of the relationship between self and soul as one of homoerotic intercourse, images of women being freed to bathe and dance with naked men, images of black men eating with white men and even exchanging clothing with them. When one considers the extraordinary fact that a poet who frankly challenged all the sources of disgust and stigma in American society is beloved and is taught to every school child in the country, one can see the magnitude of the task that Whitman has accomplished.

*Martin Luther King, Jr's 'I Have a Dream' Speech*

This famous speech is read by all school-children. They cut their public-emotional teeth on it, so to speak, and in the process form emotions relating to race and the relationship between race and American ideals. The speech had, and has, two quite different goals: to portray as beautiful and attainable a world of racial equality; and to convince African-Americans that this goal must be attained through non-violence. The two goals are connected, since the portrayal of the goal as wonderful and attainable is a large part of what might convince someone to persist with King's Gandhian program; violence feeds on despair. But the first goal reaches more broadly: King addresses the white majority, as well as his supporters, and, within that majority, people not yet convinced that the goal is worth pursuing, as well as people who already grant is worth pursuing. So King has a very difficult rhetorical task. King's brilliant success in these tasks owes a great deal to his ability to draw on the rhetorical traditions of American history and, at the same time, on the Bible.

The first words of the speech are 'Five score years ago', words that immediately establish it as a commentary on Lincoln's Gettysburg address; its first reference is to Lincoln's signing of the Emancipation Proclamation. This proclamation's 'great beacon light of hope' is contrasted to the prior situation of Negro slaves, 'seared in the flames of withering injustice'. So already Biblical images of heaven and hell make their appearance, and life in the pre-Civil War South is compared to being consigned to hell unjustly—something that only flawed human beings could have done. The next paragraph, however, makes it clear that one hundred years later, the life of Negroes in America is still hell rather than heaven: they are 'crippled by the manacles of segregation and the chains of discrimination', and are 'exile[s]' in their own land. With the image of exile, King cleverly positions African-Americans within the Exodus narrative of slavery and freedom, evoking emotions connected with that narrative, with which small Jewish and Christian children are taught to identify at a very early age.

But then King sharply changes course, to evoke yet another American tradition: fiscal responsibility. We have come, he says, to 'cash a check'. The Constitution and the Declaration of Independence were a 'promissory note', on which America has 'defaulted...insofar as her citizens of color are concerned'. Instead, America 'has given the Negro people a bad check which has come back marked "insufficient funds". But we refuse to believe that the bank of justice is bankrupt. We refuse to believe that there are insufficient funds in the great vaults of opportunity in this nation'. This part of the speech is little quoted, but for me it is especially shrewd. Most of the speech relies on prophetic Biblical imagery, which most Americans will find resonant, but perhaps not all. Here King reaches out to the rather unpoetic and unreligious American who just has a sense of fiscal rectitude. He says that national ideals are like a promissory note, and justice is like a bank that surely has sufficient funds to pay that note. Instead of the common racist trope that black Americans are shiftless and lazy, we have an opposing image: white racists are like people who pass a bad check. Suffusing the images of servitude and freedom that follow are insistent reference to tactile bodily sensations: the 'sweltering summer of the Negro's legitimate discontent' (a phrase that alludes to the actual heat of the August day in Washington, but whose Shakespearean reference also implicitly contrasts the Negro's legitimate strivings with Richard III's crafty manipulations); the 'warm threshold which leads into the palace of justice', as if its comforting touch can even now be felt by the weary feet of the marchers; the bodies of Negro men and women which, 'heavy with the fatigue of travel, cannot gain lodging in the motels of the highways and the hotels of the cities'. Thus, in a Whitmanesque manner, King evokes a physical empathy with Negro bodies, which may transcend the disgust and stigmatization that usually made it impossible for whites to imagine how a Negro body feels.

Now we arrive at the most famous parts of the speech, as King remarkably mingles American ideals with prophetic rhetoric. It seems unnecessary to mention the parts that we all know, and have heard in the cadences of King's extraordinary voice. I have particular admiration for the Exodus-style characterization of Mississippi as 'a desert state, sweltering with the heat of injustice and oppression', but scheduled to become 'an oasis of freedom and justice'. It is so odd to think of Mississippi as a desert land that the metaphor forces thought: what is really desert, and what fertile oasis, in this country of ours? I also have particular admiration for the way in which the governor of Alabama is first characterized as a fairy tale witch, his 'lips...presently dripping with the words of interposition and nullification', but then the future of Alabama rises up out of the end of that same sentence, as a future where all children, black and white, 'walk together as sisters and brothers'. Although I am not sure, I believe that this sentence makes reference to 'Hansel and Gretel' where we first have the witch who has imprisoned the little children, and then, after she is gotten out of the way, the previously paralyzed children rise up, and join hands together—an image linked to German racism, now turned around to stand for a future of racial equality.

The famous ending of the speech, in which King evokes 'America the Beautiful', and urges freedom to ring from each state, is Whitmanesque for the way in which the states are personified, in quite sexy ways: the 'heightening Alleghenies of Pittsburgh', the 'curvaceous peaks of California'. And then, his sly humor comes back, as he says, let freedom ring 'from every hill and every molehill of Mississippi'. I am inclined to think that the sly humor in the speech is one of its great points, for it says to the audience, 'We are nobody's fools, we are no sentimentalists. We know a molehill when we see it. We also know a Richard III, we know a witch, when we see them. But we overlook that, to pursue the cause of freedom'. The path of nonviolence looks, then, like something smart people can embrace without feeling stupid.

The closing broadens the message of freedom, making it not just about the freeing of black people, but about the freeing of all people: racism enshackles us all, so it is all who need to be freed, 'black men and white men, Jews and Gentiles, Protestants and Catholics'. All, this time, will not just sing 'America the Beautiful' together, they will sing 'in the words of the old Negro spiritual, "Free at last! Free at last! Thank God Almighty, we are free at last!"'

How, more precisely, does King construct emotions in his audience? Let us focus on anger and hope. To make an audience angry, as Aristotle long ago observed, you need to make them feel that they—or someone they care about—have been wronged, in a way that is significant and not trivial, and that the wrong was not merely inadvertent or negligent, but willfully inflicted. Obviously enough, King's references to hell, to the bad check, to the weary bodies of people who can't stay in a hotel, and to the dripping mouth of the governor of Alabama, engender such beliefs. Could such beliefs have been summoned up without King's use of imagery and his references to the Biblical and literary traditions? Probably, in people who had them already, as most of the audience did. For them, the key aspect of King's manipulation of anger lies in the way in which, by connecting anger to hope, he defuses the urge to violence. But what about uncommitted members of the audience? And, since the speech was written for posterity and not only for a single occasion, what about school children who read it now to learn about the civil rights struggle? For those children, the vivid bodily depiction of fatigue and insult is crucial in getting the propositions involved in anger to be really believed, really taken in beneath the surface of the mind.

So too, I believe, with hope. To have hope, one must believe that an important future good is possible. One might have had a speech that said, 'There is an important goal we are pursuing, and we can achieve it if we work hard'. But who would really listen to that or believe in it, while standing with weary feet in Washington on a hot August day? King's depiction of the contrast between the 'dark and desolate valley of segregation' and the 'sunlit path of racial justice', his resonant use of the prophetic 'every valley shall be exalted' whose familiarity is one part of what makes it easy to take in beneath the mind's surface, the repetition of the phrase 'I have a dream', and the vivid depiction of a possible future time corresponding to that dream, the references to the familiar text of 'America the Beautiful', which surely must be possible and attainable, because we already sing it as if it *is* reality—all this positions the hoped-for goal as both glorious and available; no idle dream, but a dream that will become reality.

It is hardly necessary to mention the fact that high-minded philosophical sentiments compatible with this hope, if written as you or I would write them, or even as John Stuart Mill would have written them, could not on their own have moved large masses of people to support its cause. King's rhetorical genius played a key role in getting people to support the non-violent movement, and in getting still other people to understand what it was all about. In this way, rhetoric and emotion changed history. If King hadn't been this sort of poet, we can hardly say what would have happened next.

King advances a civil religion in the best sense. In its Gandhian vision of non-violence and its reliance on the tradition of Constitutional rights, it is a civil religion in a way that is compatible with the vision of Locke and Kant; it does not rely on Rousseauian coercion. Moreover, although the speech relies for some of its effects on familiarity with religious texts, it uses those texts in a non-sectarian way, as it also uses Shakespeare and 'America the Beautiful'. Its sentiments can be endorsed by people who do not belong to that religious tradition.

### *Millenium Park*

The poetry of great cities is a particularly powerful source of public emotion-construction in the American tradition. New York and Chicago, in particular, have given rise to a type of civic poetry and art that expresses a love of differences and celebrates the great energy that comes from difference when difference is respected and not feared. Here we must return to Whitman, whose public poetry of inclusiveness for all America, during and in the wake of the horror of the Civil War, was modeled on his love of New York and his sense of what New York stood for. 'Walt Whitman, a cosmos, of Manhattan the son', he announces himself early in 'Song of Myself', and immediately he juxtaposes to the idea of New York the key values of his ideal America: 'Whoever degrades another degrades me. / And whatever is done or said returns at least to me... By God! I will accept nothing which all cannot have their counterpart of on the same terms'.

What is the connection between these values and the idea of New York? Whitman shortly makes it explicit:

> Through me many long dumb voices,
> Voices of the interminable generations of prisoners and slaves,
> Voices of the diseas'd and despairing and of thieves and dwarfs,
> ... And of the rights of them the others are down upon,
> Of the deform'd trivial, flat, foolish, despised,...
> Through me forbidden voices,
> Voices of sexes and lusts, voices veil'd and I remove the veil...

New York is a metaphor for the turbulent diversity that is Whitman's America, and for the daring and energy of that diversity, all the forbidden people and things that dare to speak their names there. One can see that Whitman is addressing the roots of shame and disgust in a way that goes to the heart of intolerance as I understand it. He says that if we learn to love and celebrate what is noisy, messy, tumultuous—including, prominently, our own messy sexuality—then we will be less likely to hate and oppress others. It is not surprising that New York figures centrally in the climactic lines of Whitman's elegy to Abraham Lincoln, as the only place the poet calls his 'own': 'Lo, body and soul—this land, / My own Manhattan with spires, and the sparkling and hurrying tides, and the ships...'[12]

I am reminded of the painter Red Grooms, who said this, in an interview, about his great painting 'Ruckus Manhattan': 'What I wanted to do was a novelistic portrait of Manhattan from Battery Park to Grant's Tomb. I also felt it had to include the dark sides of life as well as the lighter ones: prostitutes, thieves and gamblers, tourists, shoppers, babies, moms and dads. I wanted to get it all in, it got quite busy'.

In both Whitman and Grooms, this poetry of diversity is not free from difficulty. The dark side of life is dark. But there is a kind of love undergirding the whole enterprise, and the suggestion is that this love, which is at bottom a love of the messier parts of ourselves, can carry us forward. When we don't like our fellow citizens, or approve of what they do, we can still love them as parts of the great city that we celebrate and are. The poetry of inclusion beckons to us, offering pleasure as we investigate corners of life we usually view with suspicion. These include, as Whitman knew so well, aspects

12. 'When Lilacs Last in the Dooryard Bloom'd', 12.89-90. Another great New York poem is 'A Broadway Pageant', which depicts a parade celebrating a treaty between the US and Japan, and, as the poet imagines himself blending into the dense and diverse crowd to watch the Japanese visitors, New York becomes a symbol of the whole nation: 'Superb-faced Manhattan! / Comrade Americanos! To us, then at last the Orient came'.

of human sexuality that we usually cordon off as forbidden territory, telling ourselves that what makes us uncomfortable is outside and 'other'. Thus Whitman's invitation to love the body provides a solvent for turbulent hatreds that grow out of our inability to tolerate ourselves.

But enough of New York. At this point, Chicago patriot that I am, I want to describe Chicago's new Millenium Park, opened by the city in the summer of 2004, which creates a public space that is its own poem of diversity. As you approach the park from Michigan Avenue, you encounter, first, the Crown Fountain, designed by Spanish artist Jaume Plensa. On two huge screens, 50 feet high and about 25 yards apart, one sees projected photographic images of the faces of Chicagoans of all ages and races and types. At any given time two faces are displayed, changing expression in slow motion, with wonderfully comic effect. Every five minutes or so, the faces spit jets of water, as if from out of their mouths, onto the waiting bodies of delighted children, who frolic in the shallow pool below and between the screens—often joined, at first shyly and gingerly, by parents and even grandparents. (My daughter, a cultural historian, calls this an 'ejaculatory aesthetic'. Well, yes. That is its charm. As Whitman said of the young men bathing, so of these faces: 'They do not think whom they souse with their spray'.)

If you watch all this from a certain angle, you will also see the sprouting plumes of the Frank Gehry band shell curling upward, a silver helmet, lying on its side, a relic of war that has decided to abandon aggression and turn into a bird. From yet another angle, you see the buildings of Michigan Avenue, and the clouds above, reflected as crazy curves in Anish Kapoor's sculpture, 'Cloud Gate', a huge inverted stainless steel kidney bean. The buildings look nice straight, and they look even more delicious curved or, I'm tempted to say, queered. People of all sorts lie on the ground underneath the sculpture to get a view, or walk around it looking, with laughter, at their own distorted reflections. Meanwhile, on Gehry's improbably curving bridge over the highway—a bridge that seems to go nowhere in particular—people meander, pause, talk to strangers. The interactive public space celebrates diversity together with astonishing beauty, and both together with the pleasures of the body, as young and old paddle contentedly, or stare at the reflected clouds.

What attitudes and emotions are constructed by this magical place? Well, certainly a love of diversity in one's fellow citizens, and a sense that diversity is a source of pleasure, not of anxiety. Then too, a delight in getting wet—for one of the features of the park least anticipated by its designers has been the extent to which not just children, but people of all ages, want to stand in front of those spewing fountains, enjoying an odd kind of sensuous, if not exactly sexual, intercourse with Chicagoans of many races and genders and ages. Also, not insignificantly, a sense of the ridiculous in oneself and others, a sense that when the body looks odd and funny, or when fluids suddenly shoot out from some part of the body, that is good rather than bad. Also, again not insignificantly, a kind of calmness, a willingness to lie around, to walk slowly, to pause and greet people.

Radical evil is not a piecemeal affair. What Kant and Mill rightly want is a wholly new view of human relations, not simply progress on this or that issue. And it is clear that radical evil is alive and flourishing in the US. Suspicion and mistrust of other peoples and groups are growing. Rather than being encouraged to see the world as an international society in which we must all support the aspirations of people everywhere to decent and dignified lives, we are all too often encouraged to think in terms of US pre-eminence, and to see other nations as looming threats to US power and safety. Domestically, the dominant religion increasingly asserts its hegemony over minority religions and non-religion, and public rhetoric too often gives sanction to this aim. In the proposed gay marriage amendment, we see deep-rooted anxieties about sexuality taking a stigmatizing and repressive form.

To counteract the influence of all this division, we need not only good liberal doctrines and arguments, and not *only* (though it is crucial) the vigilant protection of free speech. We need a poetry of the love of free citizens, and of their noisy, chaotic, sometimes shockingly diverse lives, constructing emotions that provide essential undergirding for good laws and institutions. Without this, liberal principles, as Whitman said, are just dead words on paper. Whitman and King understood, and Mayor Daley understands, this. If we are to survive as a pluralistic nation, we'd better hope that there are more like them.

# Part VI
# Punishment

# [12]

# Locke and the Right to Punish

A. JOHN SIMMONS

## I

Most philosophical discussions of punishment focus in one way or another on the question, "When is punishment just?" Even a brief glance at these discussions, however, reveals the many different ways in which that question may be understood. We might, for instance, take it to be a question about the *kind or amount* of punishment that is just in response to various offenses, or a question about *who* can be justly punished, or a question about *when* (if) punishment is the proper response to crime or wrongdoing at all. The array of possible answers to these three versions of the question, and observations about the ways in which these answers must be related to one another, are well displayed in contemporary philosophical literature on punishment. There is, however, a fourth way of understanding the question, which is not so often touched on in the literature on punishment because it places the question more squarely within the province of political philosophy. This interpretation makes the question one about authority and the "right to punish." What makes it just for a particular person or group to punish us, instead of some other person or group?

What is distinctive about this fourth interpretation of the question "When is punishment just?" is that the kinds of answers often given to the other three interpretations seem quite feeble when offered as answers to this one. While one may be convinced that the practice of pun-

This article is a shortened version of a chapter in my forthcoming book, *The Lockean Theory of Rights*, to be published by Princeton University Press. I am grateful to Nancy Schauber, George Klosko, Julian Franklin, and the Editors of *Philosophy & Public Affairs* for their very helpful comments on recent drafts of the article, and to audiences at many schools for their questions about much older drafts.

ishment is justified by its social utility (its deterrent value), it is much harder to believe that just *anyone* may rightfully punish (and so deter) others, or that the person or group that may rightfully punish another individual is that person or group whose doing the punishing would maximize total happiness (or most effectively deter crime). This latter position might entail that citizens of country A could be justly punished for their ordinary crimes by the government of country B, provided only that this arrangement would be maximally useful. And again, while one might be convinced that only those who deserve punishment may be justly punished, and only then to the extent deserved, it is much harder to believe that just anyone may rightfully punish those citizens who deserve it, or that those who most deserve to do the punishing are the ones entitled to do so. Neither one's general level of virtue nor one's particular talents in the area of punishing (e.g., special aptitude for being a judge, jailer, or executioner) are normally taken to establish any special claim to be the one who should punish others.

When we ask what makes it just for a particular person or group, rather than another, to punish some person, the answer that seems most natural concerns neither utility nor desert. It is not that our governments deserve to punish us, or that their doing so maximizes happiness; it is rather that they have authority or the right to do so. Locke put the point thus: "To justify bringing such evil [i.e., punishment] on any man two things are requisite. First, that he who does it has commission and power to do so. Secondly, that it be directly useful for the procuring of some greater good. . . . Usefulness, when present, being but one of those conditions, cannot give the other, which is a commission to punish."[1] The natural answer to our question makes central reference to authorization and rights, and it has been the natural rights tradition in political philosophy that has emphasized this point most forcefully. According to that tradition, one person (A) may justly punish another (B) only if either (1) A has a natural right to punish the crimes (wrongs) of B, or (2) B has alienated to A or created for A by forfeiture a right to punish B for B's

1. *A Second Letter Concerning Toleration*, in *The Works of John Locke* (London: Thomas Davison, 1823), 6:112. Locke seems to have the same point in mind when he distinguishes between the justifications of punishment on the separable grounds that "it is effectual" and "it is just" (Lord Peter King, *The Life of John Locke* [London: Colburn and Bentley, 1830], 2:113).

313 *Locke and the Right to Punish*

crimes (wrongs). This position cannot, I think, adequately be characterized as either purely utilitarian or purely retributivist.[2]

It will not be my purpose here to evaluate the entire natural rights position on punishment, or to explore its relations to other views (e.g., whether it is consistent with or even reducible to retributivist or deterrence views).[3] I wish to concentrate on only one aspect of natural rights theory's claims about punishment, a position shared by classical natural rights theorists (such as Grotius and Locke) and contemporary ones (such as Nozick and Rothbard). All persons in a state of nature, these authors claim, have a moral right to punish moral wrongdoers. This "natural executive right," of course, plays a central role in Locke's account of how a government can come to have the right to punish its citizens (as it must in any Lockean account of these matters), and Locke's defense of the executive right is the best known of the classical defenses. I will, accordingly, focus much of my attention on Locke's arguments and possible extensions or developments of them. But any theory of punishment must either accommodate or reject this right, so my discussion of Locke's views should prove of more than purely historical interest.

The motivation for defending the natural executive right seems reasonably clear. Locke and other philosophers in the natural rights tradition have normally wanted to claim that all political authority (or "power") is artificial, and so must be explained in terms of more basic, natural forms of authority. Governments have rights to limit our liberty, for instance, only insofar as they have been granted those rights by us; we, however, possess these rights naturally (or, rather, are "born to" a basic set of moral rights). Governmental rights, then, are simply composed of the natural rights of those who become citizens, transferred to government by some voluntary undertaking (e.g., contract, consent, or

2. By which I do *not* mean to claim that, e.g., utilitarians do not have alternative accounts of authority and the right to punish.

3. Ted Honderich, *Punishment: The Supposed Justifications* (Harmondsworth, Eng.: Penguin, 1971), pp. 158–62. I do not believe that rights theories of punishment collapse (as Honderich argues) into retributivism. I trust that my argument below (Section IV) will show why this need not happen, since fairness, not desert, is the central notion at work. Honderich now classes rights theories as "rights retributivism," one form of the "new retributivism," with another being "restorative retributivism" ("Punishment, the New Retributivism, and Political Philosophy," in *Philosophy and Practice*, ed. A. P. Griffiths [Cambridge: Cambridge University Press, 1985], pp. 117–47). The theory I outline below utilizes both "rights" and "restorative" elements. Contemporary defenders of rights theories of punishment include Alan Goldman, Thomas Hurka, Vinit Haksar, and Warren Quinn.

the granting of a trust). This transfer of rights may go unobserved by some (as when consent is "tacit" only), but it must take place if government is to have any *de jure* power. However beneficial and fair the practices and policies a government enforces, it has no right or authority to enforce them against an uncommitted "independent."[4]

The same story can be told about a government's right to punish criminals. This right, like all governmental rights, must be composed of the redistributed natural rights of citizens, rights that the citizens must therefore have been capable of possessing in a nonpolitical state of nature. It is hard to deny that governments do, at least sometimes, have (or are capable of having) the *de jure* authority or right to punish criminals. But if they do, the argument continues, persons in a state of nature must also, at least sometimes, have the right to punish wrongdoers. From what other source could a government have obtained its right?

Locke was surely correct when he guessed that this would seem "a very strange doctrine to some men."[5] Critics in Locke's own day were uncomfortable with the idea of a natural right to punish, and contemporary philosophers have been quite solidly against it. We naturally tend to think of the right to punish as something denied private persons and possessed only by special authorities within a carefully defined institutional framework. The "private application of force," at least in matters of punishment, seems both institutionally and morally indefensible.[6] But these views are mistaken, according to the natural rights theorist; they are true only of private punishment in *civil* society, where government must have a "monopoly on force."[7] Perhaps the view that *all* private pun-

4. John Hodson, *The Ethics of Legal Coercion* (Dordrecht: Reidel, 1963), p. 117.

5. *Second Treatise*, para. 9. Subsequent references to the *Two Treatises* will be by I or II, followed by paragraph number.

6. Hugo Grotius, *De Jure Praedae Commentarius*, trans. G. Williams and W. Zeydel (Oxford: Oxford University Press, 1950), bk. VIII (question VII, article I), p. 89. Grotius's purpose here is to explore the general justifications for the private use of force (i.e., in his terms, what "causes justly give rise to private wars"). In discussing "the fourth cause" of just private war, namely, wrongdoing, Grotius is led to a defense of the natural executive right. Parallel, but less complete, discussions of these matters occur in *De Jure Belli ac Pacis Libri Tres*, trans. W. Kelsey (Oxford: Oxford University Press, 1925), bk. II, chap. xx. Grotius's views were, of course, extremely influential within the natural rights tradition. See Richard Tuck, *Natural Rights Theories* (Cambridge: Cambridge University Press, 1979), pp. 62–63.

7. Note Locke's claim: "For all force (as has often been said) belongs only to the magistrate, nor ought any private persons at any time to use force unless it be in self-defense against unjust violence" (*A Letter Concerning Toleration*, in *"The Second Treatise of Civil*

ishment is indefensible arises solely from the fact of our constant exposure to institutionalized forms of punishment. Be that as it may, the institutional authority can be explained only by conceding the existence of a natural executive right. And further, when we really set our minds to the task, the idea of a nonpolitical or prepolitical right to punish seems less and less counterintuitive. For the early natural rights theorist, it was not at all implausible to point to the prepolitical authority to punish wrongdoers possessed by God and by fathers. And there are ample scriptural grounds for concluding that God intended all persons to have such authority, as the earthly executors of his law.[8] But even if we insist on a secular foundation for natural rights theory, "Is the general right to punish so counterintuitive? If some great wrong were committed in another country which refuses to punish it (perhaps the government is in league with, or is itself, the wrongdoer), wouldn't it be all right for you to punish the wrongdoer, to inflict some harm on him for his act?"[9]

Is Locke's "very strange doctrine" defensible after all? It is important to see from the start that, properly understood, the idea of a natural right to punish can have a strong intuitive appeal; it can seem hard to deny that free and equal persons would have a right (or be morally at liberty) to punish in at least certain kinds of states of nature (remembering now that persons can be in the state of nature not only *before* the institution of government, but also after its collapse or during the rule of a despotical government).[10] Imagine that, for whatever reason, your society "dissolved" into disorder and chaos. Once again in your natural state, unpro-

---

*Government" and "A Letter Concerning Toleration,"* ed. J. Gough [Oxford: Blackwell, 1947], p. 132).

8. Grotius, for instance, cites Judges 15 (Samson's punishment of the Philistines) and Genesis 9 ("Whoso sheddeth man's blood, by man shall his blood he shed") as supporting a natural executive right (*De Jure Praedae Commentarius*, bk. VIII, p. 90). Locke follows Grotius in citing Genesis 9:6 (along with Genesis 4:14) for support (II, 11). Neither author cites those passages that seem to support the view that only God has the right to punish: e.g., Romans 12:19 ("Vengeance is mine, I will repay, says the Lord") or Genesis 4:15 ("If anyone slays Cain, vengeance shall be taken on him sevenfold"). See Thomas Pangle, *The Spirit of Modern Republicanism* (Chicago: University of Chicago Press, 1988), p. 303.

9. Robert Nozick, *Anarchy, State, and Utopia* (New York: Basic Books, 1974), p. 137. The "wouldn't it be all right" formulation here suggests a liberty to punish, rather than a full claim right to do so. As we will see, however, Locke *disagrees* with Nozick about the rights of *citizens* in legitimate polities to punish alien citizens. Locke's claims (and mine) in fact concern only the rights of some individuals in the state of nature.

10. Some take such a denial to be "implausible on its face" (Charles Sayward, "Anarchism and Rights Violations," *Crítica*, April 1982, p. 110).

tected by the rule of law, you witness a man brutally robbing and murdering a defenseless victim. If it were within your power to do so, would you not feel justified in seeing to it that the murderer suffered for his crime? Would there be anything morally objectionable in your inflicting on him some harm, either to save others from his atrocities or (supposing you somehow know that he will commit no more) simply as a response to *what he did*? Would not anyone in that state of nature have a right to *punish* him for his moral crime? If you are in any way tempted to answer yes, there are obvious reasons to think more about the executive right. But even if your inclination is to say no, theoretical considerations may persuade you to excise this belief from your set of "considered judgments" about morality. And if you eventually accept the idea that there is such a right, as we will see, you will be hard-pressed to reject the natural rights tradition's account of the origin of the *state's* right to punish.

Now I would not want to appear to be placing too much weight on (as yet) undefended intuitions. They are, at best, only a provisional starting point. If there are sound theoretical grounds for rejecting the idea of a natural right to punish, then we must, of course, discount intuitions to the contrary. And contemporary philosophers have certainly argued that there are such theoretical grounds. Their criticisms of the natural right to punish can, I think, fairly be reduced to three main claims: (1) The very idea of a natural right to punish involves a fundamental confusion, or even incoherence; (2) One cannot, in any event, give a satisfactory account of the origin and nature of the natural right to punish; and (3) If we begin with a private right of punishment, we can give no persuasive account of how a just government can come to have an *exclusive* moral right to punish wrongdoers. I deal with the first of these criticisms elsewhere.[11] Here I will try to respond to (2) and (3), arguing that a Lockean theory of rights has available to it the resources to deal with these attacks.

In addition to these quite basic complaints, of course, it may seem that even those who *share* my intuitions in the case just described will probably also have intuitions about punishment that Locke and the natural rights tradition would seem to want to reject—for instance, that private citizens even in a just state would be justified in punishing a criminal

11. In chap. 3, sec. 3, of my forthcoming book, *The Lockean Theory of Rights*.

whose cleverness made legal punishment impossible, or that private citizens in one country might justifiably punish a criminal in another, if both governments refuse to punish him. I believe that none of the objections mentioned above is convincing and that there is good reason to take seriously the idea of a natural right to punish. I begin this task by examining the case for a natural executive right as it was presented by its most famous advocate.[12]

## II

In chapter II of the *Second Treatise*, Locke argues that in the state of nature all persons enjoy an equal right to punish violators of the law of nature, that is, those who "invade" the rights of others:[13] "The execution of the law of nature is in that state [i.e., the state of nature], put into every man's hands, whereby everyone has a right to punish the transgressors of that law to such a degree, as may hinder its violation" (II, 7).

While the exercise of this right in a state of nature is necessary to give force to natural law, it is also a great inconvenience. Because people will tend to be partial toward themselves and their friends, they will not always properly use this right to punish. They may punish excessively, or where there is no guilt at all, which will prompt a similar response from the ones punished, and "confusion and disorder" (or a state of war) will follow (II, 13). What is needed, of course, is a common judge standing over them all, and authorized to decide the proper remedy for conflicts between them.[14] If each surrenders his right to punish to such a judge, each will profit from the greater security and consistency of decision that will result. This, of course, is one of Locke's main arguments for the desirability of civil society, his main response to the anarchist. Life under government is preferable to life in a state of nature at least largely because of the improved procedures for the rightful punishment of criminals. Indeed, the transfer of the executive right from citizen to common

12. For a concise recent summary of Locke's views on punishment, see James Tully, "Political Freedom," *Journal of Philosophy* 87 (1990): 517–18.

13. Locke calls this right the "executive power of the law of nature" (II, 89).

14. This view—i.e., that the partiality of each in judging for himself is what makes government necessary—was already present in Locke's early *Two Tracts on Government* (Cambridge: Cambridge University Press, 1967). See *First Tract*, pp. 137–38.

judge (i.e., the state) is so important to Locke's justification of civil society that he at times seems to *define* political society in terms of this transfer having occurred. The citizens' executive rights, once entrusted to government, become the executive power of the state.

Locke's defense of a natural executive right, then, lies at the very heart of his political philosophy.[15] For this reason, if no other, we should be careful to understand his claims. First, Locke is not claiming that each person in a state of nature has an unlimited right to treat a criminal however he pleases. While "every man in the state of nature has a power to kill a murderer" (II, 11), "lesser breaches" of the law of nature must be punished less severely (II, 12). The executive right is a right "only to retribute to him, so far as calm reason and conscience dictates, what is proportionate to his transgression, which is so much as may serve for reparation and restraint" (II, 8). Locke seems unconcerned about having here identified the limits to rightful punishment at once in both retributivist terms ("retribute" what is "proportionate" to the crime) and consequentialist terms (what is sufficient for "restraint"). During the remainder of the chapter, Locke talks almost exclusively like a consequentialist; but later in the text, retributivist language seems to dominate.[16] Similarly, while we have seen Locke's claim (in the *Second Letter Concerning Toleration*) that punishment, to be justified, must "be directly useful for the procuring of some greater good," in other portions of the same work he talks like a pure retributivist.[17] It may be, of course, that Locke is simply—and not very carefully—following the lead of Grotius, who maintained that while punishment should "fit the crime" as far as possible, punishment that accomplishes no substantial good end, in

15. Richard Ashcraft characterizes Locke's defense of the executive right (and of the possibility of others assisting in enforcing natural law) as "the whole point of the *Second Treatise*," since it is this position that legitimizes popular resistance against the king (*Revolutionary Politics and Locke's "Two Treatises of Government"* [Princeton: Princeton University Press, 1986], p. 332). I would put the point slightly differently. Locke cannot give up his defense of the natural executive right without surrendering as well the right of the people to punish a deposed king.

16. As in his talk of crimes "which deserve death" (e.g., II, 23). See also II, 11 and II, 87: "Man . . . hath by nature a power . . . to judge of, and punish the breaches of [the law of nature] . . . as he is persuaded the offense deserves. . . ." These passages are hard to square with Daniel Farrell's claim that Locke "neither suggests nor needs" the idea that punishment should be proportionate to desert ("Punishment Without the State," *Nous* 22 [1988]: 452). Farrell's Locke seems to be a pure consequentialist.

17. E.g., *A Second Letter Concerning Toleration*, pp. 71, 105.

terms of future consequences, should be avoided as unjust.[18] But we should notice that when Locke *employs* the right to punish in the arguments of the *Treatises*, he employs it as if it were a right to punish *all* wrongdoing, *not* as if it were a right to punish only when punishment can be shown to be directly useful.

Second, we should be sure that we remember what Locke means when he says that each person possesses the executive right in a *state of nature*. The state of nature is, of course, that state in which prepolitical man existed, but it is also the state into which each of us is born today, and in which we remain until we consent to join some commonwealth. It is the state to which we return when our political society dissolves (as in times of civil war), and perhaps also when our political leaders overstep the bounds of their rightful authority (i.e., cases of tyranny). It is the state in which all political rulers stand with respect to one another, and in which all citizens of one state stand with respect to citizens of another state.[19]

Third, Locke's position is not really that *all* persons in the state of nature with respect to others have the natural right to punish those others for their crimes. Children (those below the "age of reason") do not possess this executive right in spite of being in the state of nature with respect to all persons. Presumably the same is true of idiots, madmen, warmakers, and any other "persons" who do not qualify for Locke as full right-holders. Perhaps more important, Locke believes that when we join together to form a political society we must be understood not only to be agreeing to allow a common judge to exercise our executive rights in conflicts between us. We must also be understood to be entrusting to government the right to punish transgressors of natural law who are *not* members of our commonwealth. That right, thus entrusted, becomes the state's *federative* power (II, 145–48). As members of a legitimate civil society, then, we have no right to punish anyone. Our natural right to punish certain persons (those who become our fellow citizens) is entrusted to government as its executive power, while the natural right to

18. *De Jure Praedae Commentarius*, bk. VIII, pp. 93–104; *De Jure Belli ac Pacis*, bk. II, chap. xx. I take Locke to be committed to a moral theory that is neither purely consequentialist nor purely deontological. I discuss this in *The Lockean Theory of Rights*, chaps. 1 and 2.

19. Defense and explanation of these claims is provided in my "Locke's State of Nature" *Political Theory* 17 (1989): 449–70.

punish all other persons is similarly entrusted as the government's federative power.[20] In short, we have a natural right to punish those who breach natural law only after we reach the age of reason (and while we remain committed to the law of reason), and during those times when we are not members of some legitimate political society.

We have seen one reason why Locke was so eager to defend the natural right to punish: it is difficult to understand how an artificial body like a state could possess the moral authority to punish unless it received this authority from persons who possessed it naturally.[21] But surely, it seems reasonable to respond, a government might receive the right to punish from citizens without it following that each person, prior to becoming a citizen, had a right to punish every wrongdoer. Locke's first reply to such concerns—that the state of nature is a state of equal rights, so that if anyone has a right to punish another, everyone must have that same right (II, 7)—will not suffice. For might it not be the case that we all equally possess a more *limited* right to punish—say, the right to punish criminals who victimize *us* (i.e., a right to punish held only by the victim of a crime, not all mankind)? There would then be equal natural rights, but no general right to punish just any violator of natural law; and by entrusting these more limited rights to government, we would still grant to our governors the right to punish any who violated the rights of a citizen of the commonwealth.

Locke's response to this proposal has two parts. To the suggestion that the victim has special rights against the criminal, Locke agrees, as we will see. But the victim cannot hold the sole right to punish a wrongdoer, for the victim is not the only one who suffers from a crime. In a sense, Locke claims, mankind as a whole is the victim of every crime; every offense is "a trespass against the whole species" (II, 8). Those who violate the rights of others cast aside reason as a guide to their actions, mak-

20. Locke earlier calls these two powers "the power of making laws" and "the power of war and peace" (II, 88), though the first of these must also incorporate some of the *legislative* power.

21. There is, of course, a clear sense in which *the state* for Locke is perfectly "natural"—i.e., there is every reason to suppose that persons (acting "naturally") will in fact create states where they do not exist (indeed, they will be "driven" into them). See M. Seliger, *The Liberal Politics of John Locke* (London: Allen and Unwin, 1968), pp. 221–23. But the *moral authority* of states is for Locke created or artificial, not natural. Against Robert Filmer, Locke argues that "governments must be left again to the old way of being made by contrivance and the consent of men" (I, 6).

321 *Locke and the Right to Punish*

ing themselves a danger to all persons. Every person has a stake in protecting himself and others from future attacks, so every person shares in the right to punish the criminal.

These claims may seem extravagant. In what way can a harmless petty thief (or even a local bully) be seen as a threat to all mankind? The idea that someone who commits any kind of wrong against another is therefore liable to do all manner of immoral things to people far and wide seems a bit farfetched. On the other hand, if your neighbor (the victim of a violent assault, say) had sole authority to punish his sadistic attacker, and chose to be lenient, you might well feel that the "public element" of the crime gave you a right to try to more effectively deter that criminal from future attacks. Much more needs to be said about Locke's claim that every crime is against all mankind, and I will return to it later.

No one but the most eager disciple of Locke would be persuaded by the arguments thus far advanced that there is a natural executive right, or that we can explain a government's right to punish only in terms of a transfer of the executive right. Locke's insistence that God must have intended each person to be executor of His law obviously requires further support. And there are, of course, other arguments in the *Second Treatise* designed to provide this support. While only one of these is prominent in the text, it might be reasonable to ascribe to him two others as well.

1. Locke's language (in II, 7) might suggest to one the following view (though Locke nowhere in the *Treatises* explicitly states it): the ideas of duty and right (and, more generally, of morality) imply the existence of law. But there can be a real law only where there are sanctions attached to disobedience, where violations of the law are rightfully punished: "Where the laws cannot be executed, it is all one as if there were no laws" (II, 219). If, then, the law of nature is to be a genuine law, and the duties and rights it defines genuine, the law must rightly be backed up by physical force. Since it *is* a genuine law, binding even in a man's natural state, Locke supposes, someone in the state of nature must have the right to enforce natural law (and if someone has that right, everyone must have it, as we have seen). The internal sanction of the pangs of conscience that sometimes accompanies wrongdoing is insufficient to constitute real enforcement of the law. While little of this is stated in the *Treatises*, Locke does say such things in the *Essay*: "What duty is, cannot be understood without a law; nor a law be known or supposed with-

out a lawmaker, or without reward and punishment. . . . Since it would be utterly in vain to suppose a rule set to the free actions of men, without annexing to it some enforcement of good and evil to determine his will, we must, wherever we suppose a law, suppose also some reward or punishment annexed to that law" (*An Essay Concerning Human Understanding*, 1.2.12, 2.28.6). The very idea of morality (and of law), Locke seems to be claiming, implies a natural executive right.[22]

2. It is clear from the text that Locke believes there to be a strong connection between the executive right and the right we have to preserve ourselves and others. The idea that a right to punish is somehow implied by our right to defend ourselves or others was neither new with Locke nor confined to philosophers in earlier centuries. Grotius, in the earliest systematic defense of a natural right to punish, argued in this way,[23] as do many of the most recent such defenses.[24] The idea they share, presumably, is that insofar as punishment can serve as a means for deterring future crime (both crime committed by the criminal punished and by others, suitably impressed by the example of his punishment), it is a way of defending ourselves against aggression by others. If we have a right to defend ourselves, then, certainly we have a right to employ one *means* of self-defense, namely, punishment of criminals.

It might be natural to respond to the line of argument suggested above as we earlier responded to the claim that every crime threatens all mankind. Surely it is *not* true that our right of self-defense could justify punishing just any violator of natural law, as the executive right allows; for some criminals seem to pose no real threat to our safety at all. Simple considerations of self-defense are insufficient to derive a general right to punish.

22. Leo Strauss has written as if this were Locke's *only* (or at least central) defense of the executive right (*Natural Right and History* [Chicago: University of Chicago Press, 1953], p. 222). The text, of course, does not support such an extravagant claim (if, indeed, Strauss intended to make it). But there are also reasons, as we will see, to doubt that Locke had any such argument in mind.

23. *De Jure Praedae Commentarius*, bk. VIII, p. 91: "The causes for the infliction of punishment are natural, and derived from that precept which we have called the First Law." (The First Law is: "It shall be permissible to defend [one's own] life and to shun that which threatens to prove injurious" [p. 369].)

24. See, e.g., Murray Rothbard, *The Ethics of Liberty* (Atlantic Highlands, N.J.: Humanities Press, 1982), p. 89 ("All rights of punishment derive from the victim's right of self-defense"), and Farrell, "Punishment Without the State," pp. 443–44. Farrell's case is actually (like Locke's) the more complicated view that self-defense is justified by the same principle that justifies defense of other innocents, and hence punishment.

323 *Locke and the Right to Punish*

Locke seems sensitive to this worry, for his position is more complicated than the one just summarized. He in fact distinguishes between two separate aspects of our executive right. Two legitimate aims of punishment, remember, are "reparation and restraint"; these two aims define distinct rights. All men have the natural right to punish transgressors of natural law for the purpose of restraining (deterring) criminals; this right, however, derives *not* from our right of self-defense but from our right of "preserving all mankind." From the narrower right of self-defense (or self-preservation) that each of us possesses, Locke thinks, we derive only a right to take reparation from a criminal when we have been his victim: "The damnified person has this power of appropriating to himself the goods or services of the offender, by right of self-preservation, as every man has a power to punish the crime, to prevent its being committed again, by the right he has of preserving all mankind" (II, 11).[25] Locke is not, then, committed to holding that considerations of self-defense justify my punishing just any criminal in a state of nature; such considerations do not, strictly speaking for Locke, justify *punishment* at all, but only the exacting of compensation. Whether this claim is defensible or not, the important point for our purposes is that the executive right *is* implied, according to Locke (and more plausibly, I think), by the more general right to preserve mankind.

3. We arrive finally at Locke's most prominently presented argument for the executive right. Unless there is a natural right to punish, Locke maintains, the ruler (government) of a state could never rightfully punish an alien who commits a crime in that state. Since rulers clearly *can* rightfully punish alien criminals when they break the laws of the countries they are visiting, there must be a natural executive right (II, 9). Locke's thinking here runs as follows: An alien is not bound by the laws of the states he visits; he has not consented to the authority of those states' governments. The alien remains in the state of nature with respect to those governments. If that is true, however, the government can rightfully punish the alien only if it could rightfully punish him in the state of nature (i.e., if the citizens who gave the government its rights

25. Note Locke's apparent claim that this second right cannot be transferred to civil authorities, so that they might remit the requirement of compensation (II, 11). Locke is, I think, better read here as saying that the transfer of this right is not to be *presumed* to be part of *any* contract of government than as saying that the right literally cannot be transferred.

could have punished him in the state of nature). Since we all believe that the government *can* legitimately punish in such cases, we must accept the natural executive right as the only possible explanation of this fact. In punishing the alien, the state is merely doing what its citizens would have been entitled to do had they not left the state of nature by entrusting their executive rights to their government.[26]

## III

We have now seen Locke's arguments for a natural right to punish. Let me examine them in turn.

1. Take first Locke's apparent argument that we cannot understand the idea of duty, or moral ideas generally, without supposing a natural right to enforce the duty (by punishing offenders). The argument really proceeds in three stages:

(a) Moral duty implies the existence of law.
(b) True law requires the likely application of rightful sanctions for breach of the law.
(c) The only possible sanction for natural (moral) law that is likely to be applied at all times is punishment by other men. For this punishment to be rightful, men must have a right to punish wrongdoers.

Even granting Locke the truth of (a) and (b) (and, of course, many of Locke's contemporaries would have done so), the truth of (c), the crucial

26. This argument will not, of course, convince anarchists or any who doubt that the state *can* legitimately punish aliens. Let me conclude this explanation of Locke's case for the executive right with a purely historical observation. In his notes to the argument just considered, Peter Laslett comments that Locke's language announced "that his doctrine of punishment was, or was intended by him to be, a novelty" (*Two Treatises of Government* [Cambridge: Cambridge University Press, 1963], p. 313n). On this point, see Wolfgang Von Leyden, "Locke's Strange Doctrine of Punishment," in *John Locke: Symposium Wolfenbuttel 1979*, ed. R. Brandt (Berlin: de Gruyter, 1981). Philosophers and political scientists have, by and large, accepted at least Locke's *arguments* for his "strange doctrine" as a novelty (see, e.g., Geraint Parry, *John Locke* [London: Allen and Unwin, 1978], p. 58). But it is worth noting that even Locke's last, central argument (concerning the punishment of aliens) was used previously by Grotius (*De Jure Praedae Commentarius*, bk. VIII, p. 92); and, as the earlier portions of my discussion have suggested, much of the rest of Locke's position seems also to have been borrowed from Grotius. Locke's original contribution on this subject lay not so much in the formulation or defense of the executive right as in his systematic presentation of its importance for political philosophy.

claim in the argument, still seems doubtful. Why is an appropriate sanction for natural law not the rightful sanction of divine punishment (or reward)? That God backs up natural law with sanctions "of infinite weight and duration" (*An Essay Concerning Human Understanding*, 2.28.8) is surely sufficient for it to count as "true law"; indeed, this seems to be *precisely* what Locke had in mind in the passages from the *Essay* quoted earlier. There is no need for the sanctions of a general executive right in order to explain the possibility of moral duty (and natural law), and Locke seems, rightly, not to insist that there is such a need in the *Treatises*.

What Locke *does* say in the *Second Treatise* is that "the law of nature would, as all other laws that concern men in this world, be in vain, if there were nobody that in the state of nature had a power to execute that law" (II, 7). While Locke is not holding that the sanction of the law is what *makes* it obligatory, he does hold that the law has no *point* without sanctions.[27] And God surely wants his law to have a point. But God's sanctions are not sufficient to compel widespread obedience, so the law of nature will not be effectively enforced in the state of nature. What we need is sanctions immediately applied in this life, not the next. Now Locke undoubtedly means all of this, but he *cannot* mean to conclude that there can be no "real" law of nature or true morality *unless* men enforce that law in the state of nature. For in the *Essay*, immediately after insisting that law requires sanctions, and that in the case of moral (divine) law the relevant sanctions are those applied by God, Locke comments that "the penalties that attend the breach of God's laws some, nay perhaps most men, seldom seriously reflect on: and amongst those that do, many, whilst they break the law, entertain thoughts of future reconciliation" (2.28.12). This observation that God's sanctions are insufficient to compel obedience does *not* lead Locke to doubt that the law of nature is a true law; quite the contrary.

The ineffectiveness of God's sanctions does not seem to force us to choose between accepting the executive right and rejecting natural law, on Locke's view. What Locke is thinking, I believe, is that where a good law is not being obeyed by those bound to do so, those to whom the law applies have a duty and right to assist in its enforcement. The only ap-

27. E.g., in *An Essay Concerning Human Understanding*, 2.28.6, and *Essays on the Law of Nature* (Oxford: Oxford University Press, 1965), p. 173.

parent basis for such a claim in the case of natural law, however, would be that since natural law promotes the well-being of those to whom it applies, our general duty and right to help preserve mankind requires and permits that we enforce that law. This, of course, brings us to the second of Locke's arguments for the executive right, and forces the conclusion that the first argument we considered neither has any independent force (as a defense of the executive right) nor was intended by Locke to have any.

2. I turn now to Locke's second argument for the executive right: that it is implied by our right and duty to preserve all mankind. This right is for Locke a particularly "fundamental" one, a trivial consequence of the fundamental law of nature (II, 6, 11). So let us accept it for the moment. Does a right to preserve mankind imply a natural executive right?

First, how are we to understand the idea of a right to preserve mankind? Presumably, like the right of self-defense, this right could be taken at least two ways. Construed narrowly, the right to preserve others might be viewed as a right only to help defend them when they are actually being attacked by others. More broadly, the right to preserve others could be taken to include not only the right to defend them, but also the right to protect them in other ways—such as by creating a "deterrent climate" or by preemptive attacks against those whose presence endangers them.

It is difficult to see how the former of these versions of the right to preserve mankind could naturally yield a right to punish, for punishment of a criminal involves far more than defending someone against his attacks; punishment begins where defense leaves off. Much more than the narrow right to preserve will be required to derive a right to punish. What about the broader version of the right? It would clearly justify more than simply punishment, since preemptive attacks on the dangerous might well include harming those who have not yet broken the natural (moral) law (in order to prevent their doing so in the future). But Locke's remarks elsewhere suggest that he might well be comfortable with this sort of consequence: people "have not only a right to get out of [tyranny], but to *prevent* it" (II, 220; emphasis mine). And while the broad version of our natural right to preserve mankind justifies *more* than punishment, it appears *also* to justify punishment. It will (sometimes) explain our right to harm in response to wrongdoing, since doing this will (sometimes) help to preserve mankind (by virtue of having, in many instances, beneficial deterrent effects).

327 *Locke and the Right to Punish*

Here, then, we have a first, Lockean argument for the natural executive right. This argument, of course, will not satisfy *secular* concerns about the right to punish without independent derivation of the right to preserve mankind (a derivation that may well be possible). But whether presented in its religious or secular form, this argument simply cannot account directly for *all* of what Locke wants in a natural executive right. Locke seems most often to want to defend a right to punish *any* wrongdoer, not a right to punish that is conditional on the direct usefulness of particular acts of punishing. But it is manifestly false that punishment of wrongdoers will *always* be causally related to effective deterrence. Some punishment neither advances nor can be reasonably believed to advance the preservation of mankind. Only by further employment of rule-consequentialist reasoning (i.e., by arguing that punishment *tends* to deter crime) will a Lockean be able to draw from the right to preserve mankind a right to punish every breach of natural law. And the appeal of this style of reasoning is clearly limited.

3. Now for Locke's third and most prominent argument: that we cannot explain the rightful punishment of aliens unless there is a natural executive right. What is striking about Locke's prominent presentation of this argument is his total failure to see how badly it fits the overall position he defends in the *Second Treatise* (indeed, it looks as if Locke may have simply taken the argument from Grotius without seriously considering its implications). For there seems to be an incredibly simple refutation of the argument available, one that can be found in Locke's own text. Locke is well known for his theory of tacit consent, according to which any person who has "any possession or enjoyment of any part of the dominions of any government" can be taken to have consented to the authority of that government over him, "whether this his possession be of land, to him and his heirs forever, or a lodging only for a week; or whether it be barely travelling freely on the highway; and in effect, it reaches as far as the very being of anyone within the territories of that government" (II, 119).

The implication of these passages is clear: any alien, merely by freely entering the territories of the state, can be taken to consent to its authority over him. The alien, we might say, has authorized the state to punish him should he violate its laws. We can, then, explain the government's right to punish aliens entirely in terms of Locke's own account of the tacit agreement between government and alien.[28] No reference to a natural executive right seems necessary. The state's laws do "reach" (i.e., bind) the alien, for he is not in a state of nature with respect to the state once he enters its territories. He is a sort of "temporary member" of the commonwealth, like any resident or visitor who has not *expressly* consented to be a full member (II, 121–22).

Even more embarrassing for Locke is the following question: if we can explain the state's right to punish aliens without reference to a natural executive right, can we not similarly explain its right to punish *citizens*? Instead of starting with the assumption that each citizen has a right to punish everyone else, which he entrusts to government, why not assume that each citizen begins with only a right to control his own life (as it were, he has a right only to "punish" himself). Each citizen then entrusts a portion of this natural right of self-government to the state, authorizing government to punish him (i.e., control his life) for violations of its laws. The net result of all citizens so authorizing government, of course, would be that the government had the right to punish all citizens. This is the conclusion that Locke wants to reach; but, contrary to Locke's suggestions, it seems possible to reach it without appealing to a natural executive right. We can explain the right of governments to punish both citizens and aliens without having to suppose that any "natural man" ever had the right to punish another. And we can explain it in a way that is consistent with Locke's desire to show that all governmental rights are derived (by transfer in trust) from the citizens of the state.

This alteration in Locke's program seems even more desirable when we remember that if the government's right to punish is merely its citizens' executive rights, suitably transferred, the government's power to punish must be limited to cases where the law of nature has been transgressed. This, after all, was all that the natural executive right allowed. And while much of the behavior that a state will want to make criminal surely violates natural law, some clearly does not—for instance, violation of at least some tax laws, drug and "morals" laws, traffic and parking laws, and many other regulatory statutes hardly seems naturally immoral. How can we explain the government's right to punish in such areas? It is easy to reply that in addition to giving the state the right to

28. This seems to be what Jeffrie Murphy has in mind in "A Paradox in Locke's Theory of Natural Rights," *Dialogue* 8 (1967): 267. Farrell also notes the availability of this argument to Locke ("Punishment Without the State," p. 451).

punish violations of natural law, each citizen also gives up some further portion of his right to control his life (justifying punishment in these additional areas). This seems to be what Locke has in mind (e.g., II, 128–30).[29] But surely, if we must appeal to transfers of our natural right of self-government to explain *parts* of the state's right to punish, it would be theoretically more elegant to explain *all* of its right to punish in these terms. We would also thus spare ourselves the effort of defending Locke's "strange doctrine" of the executive right, telling Locke's story entirely in terms of citizens entrusting to government portions of their rights to govern themselves.[30]

What is wrong with this simpler, more elegant, revised Lockean account I have just outlined? Why did Locke not choose this course, with all of its apparent advantages? We might speculate about his reasons. First, Locke seems to have confusedly supposed that if all governmental rights come from the citizens, and the government has the right to punish everyone, then some citizen must have had the right to punish everyone. And if any citizen had it, everyone must have had it. He seems not to have considered that the government's right to punish might be composed, piecemeal, from the many and much more limited rights of citizens to "punish" themselves only. Second, there seems to be a serious problem, on our revised account, about capital punishment. No person, according to Locke, has the moral right to kill himself (nor is this morally permissible) (II, 6). How, then, could government come to have the right to punish us with death, if this right must have come from each citizen?[31] The natural executive right, of course, included the right to punish *others* with death (where appropriate), not ourselves. It might thus be supposed to be transferred to government, justifying capital punishment, without Locke having to defend a right to commit suicide. I will

29. Contrary to C. B. Macpherson's apparent claim that Lockean government can do no more than enforce natural law (*The Political Theory of Possessive Individualism* [Oxford: Oxford University Press, 1962], p. 218).

30. This seems to be roughly the solution proposed by J.E.J. Altham (as a remedy to problems in Nozick, not in Locke). Nobody has a right to punish others in a state of nature; the government's right arises from individual contracts ("Reflections on the State of Nature," in *Rational Action*, ed. R. Harrison [Cambridge: Cambridge University Press, 1979], pp. 140–41).

31. See Cesare Beccaria's related difficulties in deriving the state's right to punish crimes with death from the individual transfer of rights in a contract of government (*On Crimes and Punishments* [Indianapolis: Bobbs-Merrill, 1963], pp. 45–52).

say about this problem only that there are quite general difficulties in Locke about capital punishment, of which this is only one.[32] Perhaps the proper resolution of them, within a broadly Lockean framework, will require the abandonment of Locke's prohibition on suicide (which seems to me, on independent grounds, a good idea). Third, Locke may have been concerned about the revised account's apparent inability to ground a *federative* right of government. Insofar as the federative right includes a right to punish noncitizens, it is unclear how this could in any way be derived from citizens' rights over themselves only.

There is, I think, a final and much more interesting problem with the revised account proposed above, one of which Locke may well have been aware (as I argue in Section VI). The revised account can succeed only if there is no natural right to punish. My remarks thus far have suggested only that the revised account obviates the need to defend a natural executive right, but the point must be put more strongly. It is not just that a defense of our revised account saves us the trouble of proving Locke's "strange doctrine"; the revised account cannot *be* defended, if there *is* a right of all to punish. I will elaborate on this point more fully and explain the shortcomings of the apparently superior revised account in Section VI.

## IV

Locke does not always talk of our natural right to punish as something derivable from our right to preserve mankind, itself a consequence of God's positive authorization. There is in Locke another line about the right to punish, one that he does not really distinguish from those we have considered thus far. Sometimes, particularly where he is concerned with war, Locke talks not as if the right to punish were a *general* right all persons have as agents of God, but rather as if it were a *special* right created by the criminal himself, in committing his crime. By breaching the law of nature, a criminal *forfeits* certain of his natural rights, lowering moral barriers that previously existed against the infliction of harm. This leaves others with a greater right to interfere in the criminal's life and makes legitimate the punishment they may impose upon him. This

32. On these problems, see John Dunn, *The Political Thought of John Locke* (Cambridge: Cambridge University Press, 1969), pp. 126–27.

seems, at first blush, a plausible story about how punishment might become morally lawful in a state of nature. What is, perhaps, especially attractive about this account is that it seems not to require any reference to God's authority, making it an explanation of a natural right to punish that would be consistent with even a purely secular theory of natural rights, and with the secular strain of Locke's own thought, as we will see.

Remarks about the forfeiture of rights are scattered through both of Locke's *Treatises*, but no careful formulation of the doctrine is ever given. In the *Second Treatise*, comments on forfeiture are most prominent in discussion of those cases where an individual forfeits *all* of his rights by some act that deserves death. Murderers, and those who unjustly put themselves into a state of war against others (by declaring a wrongful intention to take their lives), lose all of their rights (II, 85, 172–73). All moral barriers to harming them are lowered, making punishment even by death rightful. It is only thus that arbitrary, despotical power of one man over another is possible. (Locke also, however, keeps the fundamental law of nature always in mind, for he observes that "even the guilty are to be spared, where it can prove no prejudice to the innocent" [II, 159].) In the *First Treatise*, Locke speaks of less complete and dramatic cases of the forfeiture of rights, as when a father forfeits his rights over his children (I, 100). Presumably, the idea is that by performing acts contrary to natural law one forfeits that portion of one's own rights against others that will make an interference in one's own life, proportionate to one's interference in others' lives, morally permissible.[33] The most serious offenses leave a criminal altogether rightless, like some lesser animal, which may be used or killed at will.

This kind of account of the forfeiture of natural rights seems very much like what some contemporary libertarians have had in mind. Murray Rothbard, for instance, writes that "the criminal, or invader, loses his own right to the extent that he deprived another man of his."[34] And Robert Nozick puts it only slightly differently: "One might take a contract-

33. Locke does not have in mind (as we saw in Section II) that just *any* crime, no matter how small, results in a forfeiture of *all* rights. See, e.g., T. H. Green, *Lectures on the Principles of Political Obligation* (Ann Arbor: University of Michigan Press, 1967), sec. 177, and Alan H. Goldman, "The Paradox of Punishment," *Philosophy & Public Affairs* 9, no. 1 (Fall 1979): 44–45.

34. *The Ethics of Liberty*, p. 80.

like view of moral prohibitions and hold that those who themselves violate another's boundaries forfeit the right to have certain of their own boundaries respected. On this view, one is not morally prohibited from doing certain sorts of things to others who have already violated certain moral prohibitions (and gone unpunished for this). Certain wrongdoing gives others a *liberty* to cross certain boundaries (an absence of a duty not to do it); the details might be those of some retributive view."[35] There is one prominent difference between the views of Rothbard and Nozick on forfeiture, however. Rothbard believes that the victim of a crime has a special right, not shared by others, to punish the criminal; Nozick regards the right to punish as shared by "all mankind." This disagreement in fact reflects a fundamental inconsistency in Locke's theory. Locke seems to have not one doctrine of forfeiture, but two.

Sometimes Locke presents the simple picture of forfeiture described above: criminals lose their rights, making punishment by any other person lawful. The criminal's right(s) simply disappears—for a time, that is; it presumably returns to him when he has received his just punishment, or perhaps when he is forgiven. This seems to be Nozick's version of Locke, and a version consistent with Locke's insistence that *all* persons in a state of nature have the right to punish criminals. At other times, however (and, indeed, in the most prominent passages on forfeiture—e.g., II, 23, 172), Locke talks as if the criminal's right were not simply lost, but rather forfeited *to* or *with respect to* a particular party—namely, the victim of the crime. The victim is the only person with the right to punish, though he may, of course, enlist the aid of willing assistants. This seems to be something like Rothbard's view. It implies, among other things, that if Morton wrongs Swanson, and I attempt to punish Morton for this, I wrong Morton by doing so, even if the punishment I apply to Morton is the one he deserves (or the one that would otherwise be lawful in kind and amount). Morton's moral barriers have been lowered only with respect to Swanson, not the rest of mankind. Locke also talks as if the victim of the crime has the right *not* to punish the criminal if he so decides, which seems to make room for the virtue of *forgiveness*.[36]

35. *Anarchy, State, and Utopia*, pp. 137–38. Notice that W. D. Ross, like Nozick, characterizes the right to punish as a *liberty* (*The Right and the Good* [Oxford: Oxford University Press, 1930], p. 61).

36. "If [the criminal deserving death] be once allowed to be master of his own life, the despotical, arbitrary power of his master ceases" (II, 172; see also II, 24). Locke also talks

333

## Locke and the Right to Punish

However we may feel about forgiveness, it has to be admitted that this second line on forfeiture conflicts with many of Locke's most important claims about punishment. It is inconsistent with his view that the natural right to punish a wrongdoer is held by all persons, and it implies that one man may forgive (or be lenient in response to) what is a "trespass against the whole species." And it conflicts with Locke's claim that the victim's special right, entailed by his right to preserve himself, is a right to *reparation*. Nor is it a plausible position considered on its own merits. It has serious difficulty in cases where the victim is killed by the wrongdoer (who then has a right to punish?).[37] And, as Nozick has observed, punishment is "owed" to the criminal, not to the victim;[38] the criminal does not deserve to be punished *by the victim*. Locke, by noting the victim's special right to reparation, has already taken account of what is unique about the victim's position. We must, then, reject this second line of argument about forfeiture in Locke as perhaps implausible in its own right and as certainly inconsistent with more important features of Locke's theory.[39]

I have spoken approvingly of the first Lockean line about forfeiture, where rights are simply lost for a time. But much about this line of argument remains unexplained—and goes largely unexplained by Locke and most of the libertarian authors who have followed his lead. For instance, it should be made clear how heavily this account relies not only on a theory of natural *rights*, but on whatever theory is used to determine

as if magistrates (II, 11) or rulers (II, 159) may decide *not* to punish the guilty (and they are, after all, also only exercising the natural executive right). The possibility of forgiveness might seem to modify an essentially Old Testament conception of punishment with some New Testament sentiments.

37. Perhaps the solution might be that whoever inherits the other rights (i.e., property) of the deceased also inherits the right to punish his killer. But this solution seems to conflict with the general limits on inheritance Locke elsewhere discusses (see, e.g., I, 74, 98). Warren Quinn has suggested to me that we might understand the victim to have tacitly transferred the right to punish his murder in advance, as an obvious act of prudential rationality.

38. *Anarchy, State, and Utopia*, p. 138; Altham, "Reflections on the State of Nature," p. 142.

39. This is not to say that the second line is without advantages of its own. In addition to those mentioned below concerning exclusivity, for instance, the second line obviates some (but not all) concerns, also discussed below, about the *reasons* for which we may harm others. If the unjust aggressor simply forfeits rights (not *to* anyone), his *fellow* aggressors, who share his evil aims, may justly harm or kill him, for whatever bad reasons they may have. I try to show below that the first line can handle such worries.

what punishments fit the crime (a subject on which I will not even begin to comment here). As I have outlined it, the Lockean line on forfeiture makes central use of certain aspects of a retributivist theory of punishment; moral desert determines the degree of right-forfeiture that results from moral wrongdoing. Of course, this does not mean that the Lockean position just reduces to a pure retributivism, insofar as those who are rightly punishable are not simply those who *deserve* punishment, but only those who have also first violated the rights of another. (Thus, one who might seem to *deserve* punishment more than some minor violator of rights—such as one who constantly and deliberately humiliated others—might not be punishable on the Lockean account.) Desert determines only the extent of the forfeiture, by determining what constitutes an appropriate response to wrongdoing.[40] But only another's forfeiture of rights can give one (in Locke's language) a "commission" to punish him. Forfeiture makes it legitimate to give wrongdoers what they deserve.[41]

This may still leave us wondering, however, about *why* the violation of another's rights causes us to lose our own (to the extent deserved). The answer is surely not obvious, as defenders of the doctrine of forfeiture seem to assume. It is the "mystery" or apparent emptiness of the idea of forfeiture that has led critics in this century to reject it (e.g., critics of W. D. Ross and other intuitionists). When asked why punishment is justified, defenders of forfeiture say: because the criminal has forfeited his rights. But no account is forthcoming of *why* the criminal loses his rights on this occasion. As a result, it appears that saying the criminal forfeits his rights is saying nothing *more* than that punishing him is justified.[42] But we naturally want to be shown *why* this is justified, not simply have it asserted in a mysterious way.

Locke would appear to have several accounts available of why a criminal loses rights. One is that God has granted us our rights and chooses

40. This may, of course, be a more strongly retributivist view than Locke would have been happy with, given the consequentialist character of some aspects of his moral theory. It is possible to replace this retributivist account of the proper kind and amount of punishment with a consequentialist one, without altering the basic character of the Lockean program. But the result would, in my view, be a less plausible position.

41. Of course, to the extent that retributivism is taken to *include* the view that neither punishability nor the authority to punish is to be determined *simply* by considerations of moral desert, this is a "retributivist" stance.

42. Warren Quinn, "The Right to Threaten and the Right to Punish," *Philosophy & Public Affairs* 14, no. 4 (Fall 1985): 332–33.

to withdraw them when we violate his law.[43] Another is that rationality is a condition for being subject to natural law and a possessor of the rights that law defines. Since acting wrongly demonstrates some measure of irrationality (on Locke's view), it involves a loss of some part of the rights enjoyed by the fully rational. Neither line of argument is entirely persuasive. The first line, while it is clearly consistent with Locke's premises, will not help us in any attempt at a *secular* theory of forfeiture (and it retains a rather mysterious quality itself). The second line is unconvincing because wrongdoing is neither a necessary nor a sufficient condition for lack of full rationality.

But it is possible to give other accounts of forfeiture within a secular natural rights theory. Perhaps the most "natural" way to view forfeiture involves maintaining that any reasonable or fair system of protective, right-defining rules (laws, conventions) must specify that one's status under the rules depends on respecting them. Protection under the rules is contingent on our obeying them; any rights the rules may define are guaranteed only to those who refrain from violating them (independent, of course, of unanimous agreement to alternative arrangements). Surely no one could reasonably complain of being deprived of privileges under rules he refuses to live by. Indeed, to extend such privileges to those who break the rules would seem to involve serious and straightforward *unfairness* to those who limit their own liberty by obeying the rules. Of course, considerations of fairness also seem to dictate that a minor violation of the rules result in only a minor loss of status under the rules, and so on, so that the protection we enjoy under the rules will be proportionate to our own conformity to them. Insofar as there are objective *moral* rules (defining rights) under which all persons originally stand, and protection under the rules depends on others' obedience to them, then, a proportional forfeiture of moral rights may be a *necessary* consequence of infringing the moral rights of others.[44] Valid moral rules do not

43. If, as I believe, Locke thinks that rights are entrusted to us by God only for certain uses, it is perfectly natural that when abused, our rights return to God.

44. Thus no *consent* to loss of rights (as in Hegel) is necessary to explain the idea of rights-forfeiture. The moral work in the account is done instead by the idea of fairness. The Lockean can as a result avoid Hegel's problem of having to claim that any inalienable right must also be nonforfeitable. See Allen Wood, *Hegel's Ethical Thought* (Cambridge: Cambridge University Press, 1990), p. 121, on Hegel's problem. For a related forfeiture account of punishment, see Goldman, "The Paradox of Punishment," pp. 43–45. Goldman seems to be discussing legal rights in his account of forfeiture; it is not clear whether he would wish

extend protection to persons unfairly taking advantage of others' willingness to abide by them. Locke occasionally uses language that suggests an account of forfeiture based in natural fairness, as when he speaks of punishment as "the abridgement of anyone's *share* of the good things of the world."[45]

There is, of course, a "Kantian" rendering of this argument that would, I think, be quite unobjectionable to Locke. One formulation of Kant's categorical imperative of morality proscribes our using persons merely as means to our own ends, just as Locke argues that we are not "made for one another's uses" (II, 6). When we violate protective rules under which all stand in ways that deprive others of their rights (or violate their rights), we seem to be using others in a straightforward way. We use their compliance and forbearance (which is motivated by their recognition of our equal standing under the law) as a means of securing greater advantage for ourselves.[46] Rights forfeiture can thus be seen as what secures the possibility of natural fairness and what renders impossible ongoing but morally protected patterns of (ab)use of others.[47]

## V

Even if these sketchy suggestions about the ground of forfeiture are found convincing or suggestive, of course, it may seem that serious prob-

to extend his analysis to natural rights (along the lines I have suggested). Herbert Morris discusses punishment in terms of fairness in his well-known paper "Persons and Punishment." But he is not trying either to analyze *forfeiture* or to discuss *natural* punishment. See also Ross, *The Right and the Good*, pp. 60–64.

45. King, *The Life of John Locke* 2:110 (emphasis mine).

46. See Murphy's discussion of Kant's own views on the unfairness of not punishing the guilty (which is, of course, slightly different from the unfairness I describe here of persons enjoying full moral protection while breaching the rights of others), in "Three Mistakes about Retributivism," *Analysis* 31 (1971): 167–68. *Punishing* the guilty is *not* a case of using them as mere means to our ends, on this account; for punishment is both required by a moral principle of fairness (and hence is *not* justified simply by its consequences for us) and responds to the free choices of persons to violate binding rules with their preestablished sanctions.

47. It is worth noting another reason for suspecting that Locke might have been happy to subscribe to this account of rights-forfeiture—i.e., to an account that centrally utilizes the idea of "taking advantage" of others. Locke never suggests that those violations of natural law that involve only harm to *oneself* result in forfeiture of rights; only harm to *others* is said to have this consequence. But self-harming violations of natural law *are* contrary to reason and *do* endanger mankind (i.e., oneself as part of mankind), just like other-harming violations. The only feature of other-harming violations that self-harming violations seem to *lack* is their taking advantage of the sacrifices of others.

lems for this account will be caused by the fact that the right to punish as I have derived it can only be a "liberty right," not a full "claim right." If my right to punish arises from another's forfeiture of his own right, the right to punish must be only a permission, the absence of an obligation to refrain. It does not imply, as a claim right would, that others must not interfere with my actions. That is, though a wrongdoer's forfeiture of his right leaves me morally free to punish him, it does not obligate others to *allow* me to punish him. They, being also at liberty to punish, may "compete" with me to punish him first.

The situation would be slightly different on the second line about forfeiture, considered and rejected above. For on that account, only the victim has the right to (is at liberty to) punish; the victim's liberty right is thus an *exclusive* liberty, not in competition with the liberties of others. Others could not punish the criminal first (this would violate the *criminal's* rights), nor could they interfere with the victim's lawful punishment of the criminal (for that would infringe the victim's right of self-government—his right not to be hindered by others in his lawful pursuits except by their *competition*). Thus, the exclusive liberty the victim would have on the second (unsatisfactory) account of forfeiture would have moral consequences similar to the victim's having a full claim right to punish. It may seem a shame not to pursue this account further, for is not this kind of exclusivity of the right to punish (i.e., the guarantee of freedom from interference) exactly the property we wish our *government's* right to punish to have? Do we not believe that legitimate governments have a right, in the full sense, to lawfully punish criminals, a right that includes an obligation on citizens not to interfere or try to punish the criminal before the state does (this is the so-called monopoly on force that governments are supposed to claim and that excludes, among other things, vigilantism)? We need to explore the potential of the *first* account of forfeiture (the one I have chosen to defend over the second account) to provide a solution to this problem of explaining the exclusivity of the legitimate government's right to punish.

Suppose, as the first account maintains, that Butch commits crime (moral wrong) C, for which punishment P is appropriate, according to natural law. Butch forfeits certain of his rights, making it morally permissible for me or any other person to impose P upon him (subject to the limit that no more than a total punishment of P be imposed). Just how strong a "right" to punish does this liberty give me? Well, what kinds of justifications might another person, Chico, have for interfering with my imposing P on Butch? First, Chico might think Butch deserved punishment Q, instead of P, and as a result believe himself justified in imposing Q and resisting my imposition of P. Or he might think Butch innocent altogether, and feel justified in defending Butch against me. Or he might oppose punishment generally and argue that he was justified in stopping my punishment of Butch. Finally, Chico might want to punish Butch himself, and compete with me to impose P.

Only the last of these could be a successful defense of Chico's interfering with my punishing Butch with P; and even this would not justify Chico's physically impeding my punishing. Chico's only justification would be for *competitive* interference (where he rushed to Butch's home and punished him with P before I could get there). We must remember that we are not describing a Hobbesian state of nature, in which people have liberty rights *only*. In a Lockean state of nature, each person has a full claim right to freedom from (noncompetitive) interference, provided he acts within the constraints of the moral law. Since my imposing P on Butch would be within those constraints, any interference by Chico other than competitive interference is morally indefensible. My right to punish, then, when combined with my right of self-government, rules out most kinds of interference, and constitutes a reasonably substantial right.

My remarks above have already suggested that I think the proper solution to the problem of competitive liberties is an appeal to the principle "first come, first served." This answer for the system of "open punishment" I have been describing is similar to the Lockean solution for a system of "open property." Where land or natural resources are unowned, those who labor on them first (subject to certain provisos) "make a property" in them. All are initially at liberty to claim parts of the common, and may use only competitive interference (i.e., taking first) in exercising this liberty.[48]

Nozick worries that if we allow the first punisher to preempt the field, sadists will compete to arrive first at the scene of the crime, to get in

48. The well-known Lockean provisos on the creation of property (II, 31–33) are necessary in that case, but *not* in a system of open punishment, because obviously being deprived of access to natural resources endangers one's life, while being deprived of chances to punish criminals, as long as *someone* does it, does not—in fact, it may even enhance one's life prospects.

their licks while the getting's good. This possibility makes one uncomfortable, and not because (as Nozick supposes) the sadists will be hard to control (always imposing excessive punishment in the heat of passion). Sadists who thus lose control will also be punishable. What makes one uncomfortable is the prospect of punishing being done by rational, responsible sadists—who punish only the guilty, and only with the proper kind and amount of punishment, but who delight in doing so. This brings us squarely up against a difficulty I have thus far avoided facing. If the criminal simply forfeits his right not to be harmed in certain ways, then *any* way in which this harm is imposed appears morally acceptable, *any* reason a person has for imposing it is good enough. If Butch and his gang roam the state of nature, cutting throats at random just for the fun of it, and happen to cut the throat of a murderer (who deserves to be punished with a painful death, say), then that particular throat-cutting, but no other, might be morally acceptable. This seems a preposterous implication of the position I have been defending.[49]

We must remember first that punishment is the infliction of harm for (in response to, because of) wrongdoing.[50] At least *part* of what motivates one inflicting harm must be the belief that a wrong has been done and that the response he is making is morally (legally, conventionally) appropriate or deserved, or that infliction of harm cannot possibly count as *punishment*. Butch and his gang *punish* no one; neither do the rational sadists if part of their reason for acting is not the belief that punishment is appropriate. Punishers may have *additional* motives (beyond these beliefs)—anger, a desire to protect society, sadism, and so on. But these cannot be *all* that moves a person to inflict harm on another, if we are to count that infliction of harm as punishment.[51]

Of course, what we *call* the harm Butch and his gang cause is not very important or interesting. What is important is that it is not morally per-

49. Quinn, "The Right to Threaten and the Right to Punish," pp. 332–33.

50. On Locke's commitment to this view, see Von Leyden, "Locke's Strange Doctrine of Punishment," p. 121. For a recent general statement of this view of punishment, see Wood, *Hegel's Ethical Thought*, p. 108.

51. Where *institutional* forms of punishment are concerned, matters are not so simple. A criminal can properly be said to be punished, for instance, even if the motives of some judge, jury member, or executioner are purely sadistic. What remains true, however, is that what we might call the overall "institutional" motive must reflect the notion of a justified response to wrongdoing if we are to count the institutional process as one of punishing.

missible. We are permitted to harm wrongdoers only for certain reasons. The situation parallels that of taking reparation for injuries another has caused. If I take property from one who, completely unbeknownst to me, had previously stolen *my* property, my taking is still theft (and morally impermissible)—even though the property I took from him I might have been entitled to take, if I had taken it *as reparation*. Similarly, the throat-cutting Butch imposes is murder, not justifiable punishment, though he might have been entitled to kill if he had done so *as punishment*.

The main difficulty with this suggestion, as far as I can tell, is in motivating the revision it requires of the doctrine of forfeiture. Criminals must be said to forfeit not rights not to be harmed in certain ways (*simpliciter*), but rather rights not to be harmed in certain ways *for certain reasons*. The criminal, after such a forfeiture, has no right to complain about harms done him as punishment; he still has every right to complain (though we will no doubt be less sympathetic than usual) about other kinds of harming. These claims seem to me not unbearably awkward or ad hoc, for we often *voluntarily* transfer to others rights to act only for certain reasons (e.g., you may give your doctor the right to act during your upcoming surgery as he thinks best—but only when he acts for medical reasons, as opposed, say, to his acting for financial reasons or to enhance his professional reputation). If we may voluntarily create a situation where others have rights to act only for certain reasons, it seems plausible to suppose that nonvoluntary forfeiture might result, as I have claimed it must, in rights to harm another only for certain reasons. And the fairness account of forfeiture defended above seems to push us naturally in just this direction. For the unfairness to others that would be involved in allowing the criminal to *retain* his full complement of rights is unfairness only to those who themselves *obey* the relevant rules. Butch, with others who harm for the *wrong* reasons, is *not* obeying the rules in the relevant sense—that is, he is not prepared to deliberately limit his own liberty according to his view of what is required by fair rules. Indeed, he demonstrates his unwillingness to obey the rules in the very act of attempting to inflict the harm, since he *believes* the act *not* to be one of just punishment. There is thus no obvious unfairness to Butch in allowing a criminal to retain his right not to be harmed for Butch's reasons. Fairness (thus forfeiture) is at issue only in relation to those

341 *Locke and the Right to Punish*

who *do* obey the rules and attempt to harm others only for acceptable reasons.[52]

Again there is, I think, a Kantian (and thus, to the extent noted earlier, a Lockean) motivation for this restriction on rights forfeiture. Harming others (who deserve punishment) for the wrong reasons is morally wrong in the same way that disproportionate punishment of wrongdoers is wrong. Both fail to *respond* to the person and what he did, both fail to respect him and take him seriously. As Jeffrie Murphy puts the claim, "An autonomous person has a right that his punishment be *addressed* to that status—to those unique features of his individual, responsible conduct which occasion the punishment"; otherwise, he is "being *used*" for whatever the purposes are that motivate the excessive punishment (or, in my case, the wrongly motivated harming).[53] Respect or responsiveness is not determined just by the brute, physical description of our acts, but also by our beliefs and intentions. Since the possession of rights is premised on autonomy and moral agency, forfeiture of rights is similarly restricted—we forfeit rights by our misconduct only to the extent that makes possible *respectful* punishment. Only the total forfeiture of personhood affects this restriction for Locke.[54] The same style of argument that Locke could use to justify his insistence on proportionality of punishment (II, 8), then, can be used to justify this limit on the *reasons* for which we may legitimately harm wrongdoers.[55]

52. This argument provides as well, I think, a response to many who have criticized certain aspects of forfeiture theories of the right of self-defense. David Wasserman, for instance, has claimed (following George Fletcher) that there are "serious and well-recognized drawbacks to a forfeiture approach" to self-defense rights ("Justifying Self-Defense," *Philosophy & Public Affairs* 16, no. 4 [Fall 1987]: 361). Among these "drawbacks" is the alleged inability of forfeiture accounts to explain why aggressors' lives may not be taken for just any reason, why they may be taken only by those responding defensively, and then only if such force is necessary to repel the attack (see Judith Thomson's similar criticisms in "Self-Defense and Rights," in *Rights, Restitution, and Risk* [Cambridge, Mass.: Harvard University Press, 1986], pp. 33–37). The style of argument presented above suggests that forfeiture theory has ample resources to deal with such problems as these.

53. "Cruel and Unusual Punishments," in *Retribution, Justice, and Therapy* (Dordrecht: Reidel, 1979), p. 234.

54. Here Locke apparently disagrees with Gregory Vlastos, who claims that "the moral community is not a club from which members may be dropped for delinquency" ("Justice and Equality," in *Social Justice*, ed. R. Brandt [Englewood Cliffs, N.J.: Prentice-Hall, 1962], p. 48).

55. And Locke would here again be following Grotius, who restricts reasons for which one may punish (*De Jure Belli ac Pacis*, bk. II, chap. xx, p. 468).

If my claims to this point have been correct, a system of open punishment is a morally acceptable and morally well-motivated system.[56] But are there difficulties we have not yet considered for a system of open punishment (other than the obvious ones, like defending a theory of natural rights in the first place)? Admittedly, this account of the natural executive right leaves no room for a certain kind of mercy or forgiveness, understood as the right of any individual. While individuals can be forgiving in their hearts and can refrain from punishing, a criminal can be forgiven (in the performative sense, so that punishment is no longer rightful) only if everyone agrees to forgo punishing him. I accept this result without great discomfort. Perhaps someone might wish to argue that this is another reason for favoring civil society (where it will be easier for criminals to be forgiven); I do not.

It may, finally, seem that in spite of the "strength" of this version of a right to punish, in terms of making interference by others impermissible,

56. Nozick, in his discussion of open punishment, very quickly gives up trying to understand how it might work, and retreats instead to a view according to which everyone jointly holds the right to punish (or to empower someone to punish). No one *individually* has such a right (*Anarchy, State, and Utopia*, p. 139). But his apparent retreat turns out to be only a strategic withdrawal. Nozick has good reason to *want* a system of open punishment to be indefensible (which explains his haste in disposing of it). For if everyone jointly holds the right to punish, but people disagree about whom to empower to do their punishing, then the "dominant protective agency" operating in the state of nature has the best claim to do the punishing. For it represents a larger part of the "everyone" who jointly hold the right to punish than any competing agency or individual. And since no *individual* has the right to punish, held separately, no individual's rights are violated when the dominant protective agency does all of the punishing of criminals for us (i.e., for everyone). This is what allows Nozick to claim that the dominant protective agency has "some special legitimacy" and violates no individual's rights (ibid., pp. 139–40).

If, however, the best way to understand the right to punish in a state of nature is in terms of the system of open punishment defended above, Nozick's main argument appears to fail. He can argue neither that the dominant protective agency has a special legitimacy nor that the rights of individuals (who will be prevented by the agency from punishing in their own way) will not be violated by its practices. Even Nozick must have been uncomfortable about suggesting that the right to punish must be held jointly, since he observed that this would make it the *only* right in a state of nature "possessed by people jointly rather than individually" (ibid., p. 139). This has the appearance of a position designed only to produce the desired results. See Gerald Postema's interesting and much more complete discussion of the difficulties with Nozick's main argument in "Nozick on Liberty, Compensation, and the Individual's Right to Punish," *Social Theory and Practice* 6 (1980): 311–37. Some portions of my presentation in this section parallel Postema's work, though we reach quite different conclusions. See also Altham, "Reflections on the State of Nature," pp. 141–44.

343 *Locke and the Right to Punish*

it is still too weak a version of the right to punish to satisfy Lockean ambitions. I will consider two ways in which this might seem to be so.

First, it might be claimed that a mere liberty to punish, even if protected from all but competitive interference, fails to capture the sense (occasionally suggested by Locke) in which punishment in the state of nature is not merely morally permissible, but a *duty*.[57] If it is simply *permissible* to punish a thief, say, there seems to be no stronger moral reason to do so than there would be to hit an unruly dog (who also lacks the right not to be harmed). Punishment seems a matter of moral indifference. What this complaint overlooks is that in the case of the wrongdoer, but not in the case of the dog, the punishment is not only permissible but *deserved*. Where it is true both that someone deserves a certain treatment and that it is permissible for us to treat him in that way, we have good moral reason to act. Thus, punishing the wrongdoer is not a matter of moral indifference on this account (even if it is not, strictly speaking, a duty either), for the mere absence (through forfeiture) of rights is not the whole story.[58] I believe that the natural right to punish, understood as it has been described in this section, captures all of the force of the intuition expressed earlier (in Section I) about the justifiability of pun-

57. In the central sections on punishment (II, 7–13), Locke actually almost always talks of punishment as if it were permissible only, *not* a duty. His use of "may," "right," and "power" convey this sense. The quotation from Genesis (II, 11) stands out in quite dramatic contrast to this tendency. Punishment seems to be a duty at all only after government takes over and *agrees* to use the right to punish for the common good (making the duty in that case *consensual* in nature); and it is not always a duty even then, since the magistrate may rightfully *decline* to punish wrongdoers in some cases (II, 11) (see below, and note 36 above). Further, the idea that we have no *duty* to punish seems to be central to Locke's arguments concerning resistance to oppressive government. If there is no duty to punish in Locke, this is further reason to favor our first (simple) line on forfeiture as the best reading of Locke, since we can see now that it naturally yields no such duty. On the other hand, of course, the right to punish is derived by Locke from the right to preserve mankind—a right that is, as we have seen, also a *duty*. This strongly implies that punishment should also, at least often, be a duty. Perhaps Locke is attracted to a view like that of Grotius, for whom some punishment is required, while other is only permitted, so that forgiving the criminal is only sometimes acceptable (*De Jure Belli ac Pacis*, bk. II, chap. xx, pp. 489–91). But Locke seems never to take any explicit stand on this question.

58. This point provides a partial answer to one of Allen Wood's criticisms of Hegel's account of punishment—i.e., that Hegel shows how punishing is morally permissible, but can offer no positive moral reason *for* punishing the guilty. See *Hegel's Ethical Thought*, pp. 116–17. To the extent that we allow considerations of *deterrence* to function in the account, of course, there is a *further* reason (the preservation of mankind) for punishing the thief, but not the dog.

ishment in a nonpolitical state. But can it also be used to explain why a legitimate government has the *exclusive* right to punish, the other essential part of the Lockean project?

## VI

We can, I think, give a Lockean account of these matters (if not precisely Locke's own) that captures the main ideas Locke was concerned to defend: (a) that a legitimate government's right to punish can be understood only in terms of a redistribution of previously existing natural rights, and (b) that the natural right to punish *must* be sacrificed (i.e., freely alienated) by all members on entrance into civil society.

The Lockean account I have in mind proceeds as follows: As per the revised Lockean position outlined in Section III, each citizen must entrust to government that portion of his right to self-government that is necessary for effective government, if that government is to be legitimate. The government then holds against each of us a right to interfere (including, particularly, by punishing) in our lives in the designated areas. But the government *cannot* obtain from us in this way an *exclusive* right to punish those crimes that are *moral* wrongs. For our rights of self-government do not include the right of exclusive control over our lives when we violate the moral law. Our right to be free of interference is only a right to be free *within* the bounds of natural law. By our wrongdoings we forfeit the right of control over our lives in some measure, making the interference of any other lawful. The government can be given by each of us a right to interfere only where we are *not* violating moral law, for only in those areas do we begin with a natural right of self-government. In cases of *moral* wrongdoing, the government has (given what has been said thus far) only the same liberty to punish that other persons possess.[59] It is thus in competition with private citizens where it seeks to

59. Locke's sensitivity to these issues is best displayed in his early *Second Tract on Government*, where he carefully distinguishes between the magistrate's powers in the areas of morally obligatory conduct (covering crimes that are also moral wrongs) and "indifferent" conduct (covering those areas in which our right of self-government originally left us free). Locke worries that if the magistrate is not free to legislate concerning "things indifferent," then he could only re-command and enforce the requirements of natural law, in which sphere "the power of the magistrate seems to be no greater than that of any private citizen" (p. 228). This problem is solved by Locke in the *Second Treatise*, where both obligatory acts and indifferent acts bearing importantly on effective government are taken to be

punish acts that are *mala in se*. The simple transfer of our claim rights to noninterference cannot give the state an exclusive right to punish. This requires a remedy, if there is to be one judge over all citizens.

The obvious solution is that (in the Lockean spirit) each citizen must also surrender on entering civil society his natural liberty to punish wrongdoers. Each must agree not to *compete* with the state in punishing moral criminals.[60] In this way, and only in this way, can the government acquire an *exclusive* liberty to punish moral wrongdoers (the effective equivalent of a claim right), in addition to the claim right it receives from each consenting citizen to punish in other necessary areas.[61] The production of the exclusive liberty for government, of course, is in some ways analogous to Hobbes's account of the origin of the sovereign's right to punish and to Locke's own account of how a *father* can come to have title as a prince.[62] But because the Lockean version of man's natural con-

proper subjects for legislation. See also King, *The Life of John Locke* 2:109–10, and *A Letter Concerning Toleration*, p. 126.

60. More precisely, each citizen in his *private* capacity must renounce his natural right to punish, leaving citizens in their *public* capacities, possibly including himself, free to exercise a collectively exclusive liberty to punish. The renunciation is thus *conditional* on not occupying a public executive office.

61. Once the government *has* this right, citizens are no longer free to punish even those who somehow escape the punishment they deserve. This, however regrettable, must be understood as part of the price we pay for having one umpire over all citizens. If failure to punish the deserving is part of a deliberate, unjust program by government, of course, matters are changed.

62. "And this is the foundation of that right of punishing which is exercised in every commonwealth. For the subjects did not give the sovereign that right, but only in laying down theirs strengthened him to use his own as he should think fit for the preservation of them all; so that it was not given but left to him, and to him only, and (excepting the limits set him by natural law) as entire as in the condition of mere nature . . ." (*Leviathan*, chap. 28, para. 2). Locke similarly talks as if the father's children could simply "lay down" their rights to punish, leaving the father free to exercise his own executive right as an exclusive liberty (II, 74). The strategy I here suggest for Locke (and the Lockean) is similar to the "Hobbesian account" discussed and rejected by David Schmidtz in *The Limits of Government* (Boulder, Colo.: Westview, 1991), pp. 36–37. Schmidtz appears to reject the account because it cannot justify state punishment with reference to independents (nonconsenters, nonclients), since the state's liberty to punish is exclusive only with reference to those who have surrendered or laid down their similar liberties. But since I take the correct Lockean position on legitimacy to be precisely that standard state practices such as punishment typically *cannot* be justified except to those who freely consent to those practices, independents must simply be accepted by the Lockean as remaining in the state of nature and as being beyond coercive assimilation into the state (see note 63 below). The problem for the Lockean, then, is not with this account of the legitimate government's right to punish;

dition also includes full claim rights that may be transferred, none of the Hobbesian difficulties about the obligating force of the sovereign's laws arise.

The force of this account might be captured more simply as follows. If it is ever morally permissible to punish wrongdoers—that is, to coercively control them in certain ways—in the state of nature (and, of course, I have argued that, at least often, it is), then our natural rights of self-government must be taken (as Locke took them) to be limited to those areas of our lives where we operate *within* the bounds of natural law. The government cannot, then, obtain in the manner suggested in Section III (by a simple transfer of rights of self-government) an *exclusive* right to punish moral wrongdoers. If it tries to forcibly exclude attempts by private citizens to punish wrongdoers, it invades their natural liberty to use competitive interference in punishing. In the absence of a Lockean "contract" of government, in which this liberty to punish is laid aside by citizens, leaving their governors free to legitimately exercise their liberty to punish (and to force citizens *not* to punish wrongdoers), any government's claim to a "monopoly on force" within its territories must be morally indefensible.[63]

---

it is with the meaning of political consent and with the possible resulting truth of philosophical anarchism.

63. This conclusion does *not* follow, of course, if individuals can justifiably be deprived of or prevented from exercising their rights to punish *without* their consent (i.e., without actual wrongdoing on their part and without their free alienation or renunciation of those rights). Locke, of course, steadfastly opposes such "prescription" of natural rights (see my "Inalienable Rights and Locke's *Treatises*," *Philosophy & Public Affairs* 12, no. 3 [Summer 1983]: 178–79, 185). But Nozick has encouraged us to think instead about this question in terms of the *reliability* of methods of self-help enforcement of natural law, suggesting that the state (or a protective agency, or an individual) may justifiably prohibit and punish enforcement of natural law by others who use methods that are unreliable, thus legitimately eliminating any conflict between its right to punish and that of those independents whose private punishing threatens its clients (*Anarchy, State, and Utopia*, pp. 101–10). But Nozick really provides no justification for prohibiting independents from using *reliable* private punishing methods, or for doing any more than *monitoring* the use of even *unreliable* methods (and intervening only to prevent wrongful punishment). Since Locke's executive right is only a right to punish *correctly* (II, 13), the *proper* use of that right by independents cannot be justifiably infringed without their consent. Their agreement to give up their executive rights is thus still necessary to secure for government a legitimate monopoly on force. I think, then, that Farrell is mistaken in insisting that on Locke's own terms the consent of the governed is *not* really required for legitimate government (see, e.g., his "Punishment Without the State," p. 450, and "Coercion, Consent, and the Justification of Political Power," *Archiv fur Rechts-und Sozialphilosophie* 65 [1979]: 528–29, 532,

347

## *Locke and the Right to Punish*

However badly this account may fit with some of the details of Locke's own presentation, it surely captures the central spirit of his views. On the account I have sketched, the government's exclusive right to punish must be understood to be composed of its exclusive liberty to punish moral wrongdoers, plus its claim right(s) to control individual citizens (collectively) in other designated areas of their lives. Similarly, Locke insisted that governments could rightfully punish only if empowered in a fiduciary transaction between citizen and government—and that the rights transferred to government in this transaction must include *both* rights to control our lives and rights connected with the punishment of wrongdoers (II, 128–30). My agreement with Locke is, then, quite substantial. I agree that if there is a natural executive right (and if it is possible to defend the theories of natural rights and desert on which the executive right depends), then this Lockean transaction between government and citizens is necessary for the moral legitimacy of the common practice of punishment within political communities. Since I am further persuaded that there are good reasons to support the natural right to punish, Locke's beliefs about the necessity of this transaction may well be justified.[64]

---

536), both for the reasons suggested above and because the legitimate Lockean state can *at most* prohibit self-help enforcement of natural law, *not* coercively bring independents under the requirements of *civil* law. Similarly, I disagree with Schmidtz's conclusions that the right to punish should really be understood as the right to punish only by the method that is *least risky* to others, and that this may require that independents let the state punish for them (*The Limits of Government*, p. 38). For, in the first place, it is only *acceptably* risky methods of punishment that seem morally permissible, not the *least risky* method in use (which might, of course, be far *too* risky to be allowed). And independent punishment *may* be "acceptably risky." Second, while no individual can be sure that he is a "Charles Bronson type," as Schmidtz rightly claims (ibid., p. 46), state punishment methods can surely not be taken to be exactly risk-free either (given corrupt and overburdened police and courts, crowded and dangerous prisons, etc.). For criticisms of Nozick's approach related to those voiced above, see Sayward, "Anarchism and Rights Violations," pp. 106–9.

64. I have not yet commented on the international implications of the Lockean position—i.e., that, barring international covenants, each legitimate government has the right (i.e., liberty) to punish moral wrongs committed within the territories of other countries by citizens of those countries. This right is not, of course, a right to *interfere* with the legitimate processes of punishment that may be taking place within other countries, but only a right to punish alien wrongdoers who have gone unpunished. If even this limited right seems indefensible, remember the attitude of the Allies at the Nuremberg trials, where German war criminals were prosecuted for *moral* (not legal) crimes against German citizens, committed on German soil. Was it not within the rights of the Allies to punish the monstrous acts of these criminals? The Lockean view implies an affirmative answer. Le-

The results for which I have argued here seem to square well with the central intuition about the justifiability of "natural punishment" expressed in Section I. But what of the apparently conflicting intuitions (e.g., that private citizens *within* civil society might *also* be justified in punishing unpunished wrongdoers)? I suspect that such beliefs arise largely from skepticism about Locke's claims that we have in fact given up our natural right to punish to our government in the kind of transaction he describes. And this skepticism may well be warranted. The Lockean account I have just defended is an account of what must take place if legal punishment is to be *legitimate*. We must not confusedly suppose that it is a *descriptive* account of what in fact occurs in most civil societies (though Locke himself, of course, seems to have supposed just this). It may be true that punishment in many or most civil societies is *not* legitimate, and that private citizens in these societies *are* entitled to punish wrongdoers who go unpunished (either within or without their societies).[65] Lockean consent may be necessary for legitimate legal punishment, but not sufficiently in evidence in real political societies to justify our actual practices.

There are, obviously, many other details of the Lockean program on punishment that need elaboration.[66] But anyone, I think, who finds the

gitimate governments have exclusive rights to punish wrongdoers within their territories, but these rights are held only against their own citizens, not against the world at large. Other governments have the right to punish moral wrongs left unpunished by the responsible government, though exercising this right will be sensible and prudent only when (as in the case of Germany) the wrongs in question are serious and numerous.

65. If citizens retain their natural executive rights, of course, they may even have a right to punish wrongdoers *before* the state has a chance to institute legal proceedings. But there will often be good reasons for not doing so—e.g., reasons of prudence, or the fact that it is best (even if not obligatory) to allow more experienced and better-organized punishers to have the first chance to do the job.

66. For instance, it may seem to be an objectionable consequence of our Lockean account that legitimate governments have the right to punish *all* moral wrongs (including, for instance, those that are quite trivial and those that have not been made *legal* wrongs at all). The proper response to such worries is to note that the transaction necessary to create legitimate government involves not only a transfer of rights from citizens to governors. It also includes the specification of *limits* on the government's authority—most importantly, that it not violate the rights of any citizen and that it exercise its authority only for "the common good" (e.g., II, 131). The latter requirement (that it use its power only for the common good) can be understood to constrain the government's exclusive liberty to punish moral wrongdoers. It establishes that governments can rightfully punish only moral wrongs that have been made *legal* wrongs by "promulgated, established laws" (II, 142) ("Or else that law would have been of no use: it being to no purpose to lay restraint or give

Lockean intuitions about natural punishment compelling, who believes in the possibility of a defensible theory of natural rights, or who thinks the arguments of this essay not clearly defective will have reason to consider this program seriously. If it is not, in the end, an acceptable position, there is at least more to be said for it than most contemporary commentators have allowed.

privileges to men, in such general terms, as the particular person concerned cannot be known by" [I, 128]), that it should not *make* some moral wrongs (e.g., simple promise-breaking) into legal wrongs, and that it should not punish *trivial* moral wrongs. To do otherwise would be to exercise its authority in ways clearly at odds with the promotion of the common good. As Locke argued much earlier than the *Treatises* (in 1667), the magistrate may tolerate some vices if it is best for society that he do so (*An Essay Concerning Toleration*, in H. R. Fox Bourne, *The Life of John Locke* [London: King, 1876], p. 183). And the government violates no one's rights by *not* punishing certain moral wrongs (at least where it provides *equal* protection from wrongdoing for all of its citizens). Of course, the promotion of the common good requires that punishment be frequent and effective enough to secure a safe and decent life for citizens, but this in no way implies that all moral wrongs must be punished.

# [13]

# Locke on Punishment and the Death Penalty

BRIAN CALVERT

At the end of the opening chapter of his *Second Treatise of Government*, Locke describes political power in the following terms: 'Political Power then I take to be a Right of making Laws with Penalties of Death, and consequently all less Penalties, for the Regulating and Preserving of Property, and of employing the force of the Community, in the Execution of such Laws, and in the defence of the Common-wealth from Foreign Injury, and all this only for the Publick Good.'[1]

Words such as these, one would think, ought to be more than sufficient to whet the appetite of philosophers interested in the issue of capital punishment, and to some extent this has proved to be the case. Prominent authors with very different positions, such as Walter Berns[2] and Hugo Bedau,[3] make some reference to Locke, but they do not deal with his theory in any extended or detailed manner. Then again, in the many works devoted to Locke's moral and political thought there has certainly been some discussion of the topic; but nowhere, as far as I am aware, has there been an account which concentrates solely on Locke's defence of the death penalty. It seems to me that there is a gap which it would be useful to fill, and this paper is designed as one attempt to fill that gap.

In Locke's view, the political power which gives the state the right to impose the death penalty stems from the natural rights which all people

[1] Here, and throughout, I use the edition by Peter Laslett. Of course, in the context, one main reason why Locke begins in this way stems from his desire to distance himself from the position taken by Sir Robert Filmer and his followers. For Locke, the right to use the death penalty seems to be partly definitive of political power, and such power belongs only to the magistrate. This is why he argues at length that political power must not be confused with paternal power, and he denies that fathers have absolute power, especially the power of life and death, over their wives, children and servants. What is important about this is not simply that fathers/husbands/masters *do not* possess the power of life and death, but that magistrates *do* possess it.

[2] Walter Berns, *For Capital Punishment: Crime and the Morality of the Death Penalty*. (New York: Basic Books, 1979).

[3] Hugo Adam Bedau, *Death is Different* (Boston: Northeastern University Press, 1987).

possess in the state of nature. In that state the one who transgresses against the laws of nature departs from the rule of reason and puts himself into a state of war with other members of society. Consequently those other members have a right to protect themselves as well as others against the transgressor, and this right of self-protection includes the right to kill the transgressor. In political society, the right to punish a criminal is handed over to the state, and it now becomes the purpose of the state to function as the protector of the rights of its inhabitants. The justifications which govern the state's punitive activities derive from the powers individuals possess in the natural condition, and it is in the sections devoted to a description of those powers in the natural state that we get our fullest description of the justifications for imposing capital punishment, and clearly what Locke says in these sections merits close scrutiny.

Since Locke's day, most modern theories of punishment have been retributive, utilitarian, or some blend of the two. Though Locke does not describe his theory in any of these terms, what in fact we find is largely a tangled mixture of these traditions. The first task will be to distinguish and assess the various elements of retributivism and utilitarianism which are to be found in Locke's account, and then to suggest, in a very tentative manner, how he might think they should be combined together to form a coherent theory. Secondly, I want to argue that despite his apparently vigorous endorsement of the practice of capital punishment in response to a large number of different crimes, this initial impression is misleading, and his final position is that execution is only justifiable in a very restricted set of circumstances.

## Locke's Retributivism

Probably the best way to begin is to give an account of what Locke believes can be achieved by an appeal to the power of reason. In Section 6, he tells us that there are laws of nature discernible by reason, and that these laws lay down certain rules which are to govern human conduct—in particular, they forbid us 'to harm another in his Life, Health, Liberty or Possessions'. These same laws, he says later, stand as 'an Eternal Rule to all Men' (Section 135), and all our actions, including the laws of a political society, must conform to such a Rule. Similarly, the laws of nature lay down procedures which are to be followed in order to deal with those who refuse to obey these laws. The law breaker puts himself into a state of war with his fellows, abandons the 'Law of Reason' for that of 'Force and Violence' (Section 16), and by so doing 'makes a forfeiture of his Life' (Section 181, 23). Whether *any* breach of the laws of nature renders someone liable to forfeit his life is a matter we shall discuss later, but suffice it to say for now that just as reason can provide us with a knowledge of what rules we are to follow in our conduct, reason also provides us with a knowledge of what penalties are to be imposed upon law-breakers.

Locke refuses to go into any details about the content of these penalties—'it would be besides my present purpose, to enter into the particulars of the Law of Nature, or its measures of punishment' (Section 12). Nevertheless, he continues by insisting: '. . . it is certain that there is such a Law, and that too, as intelligible and plain to a rational Creature, and a Studier of that Law, as the positive Laws of Common-wealths, nay possibly plainer; As much as Reason is easier to be understood, than the Phansies and intricate Contrivances of Men, following contrary and hidden interests put into Words; For so truly are a greater part of the Municipal Laws of Countries, which are only so far right, as they are founded on the Law of Nature, by which they are to be regulated and interpreted'.

The framework which Locke presents us with seems clear enough, and gives a strong impression of what we might call ideal retributivism. The laws of nature and the corresponding measures of punishment for those who break the laws function as eternally existent and unchanging standards which are to guide legislators in their formulation of actual, positive laws and penalties. Though Locke gives no details of the just punishments which are supposed to be so plain and obvious to any rational creature, he is not entirely silent, and the more we explore some of what reason can discover, the more we see indications of retributive features in his account.

(i) In Section 7, Locke says that anyone may punish another in the state of nature 'for any evil he has done'. Though he does not dwell on what he may be assuming to be an obvious point, it is an important one none the less. What it could be taken to imply is that in order to be liable for punishment, someone must in fact have committed an evil deed which, as Locke explains, means to have broken one of the laws of nature. Non-retributive theories of punishment have often been criticized on the ground that they permit the punishment of the innocent; and while Locke, unlike Hobbes,[4] does not appear to place any great stress on ensuring that no innocent people are punished, it might be argued that he seems to take it for granted that those punished must be guilty of some crime.

However, some uneasiness about this may remain. One may certainly grant that, in this and succeeding sections in the early part of the work, Locke has plenty to say about the punishment of lawbreakers. At

[4] Thomas Hobbes, *Leviathan*. C. B. MacPherson (ed.), (Harmondsworth: Penguin Books, 1968), Part II, Chap. 26.

the same time, since he nowhere specifically excludes the punishment of the innocent, the evidence of these early sections can only be regarded as inconclusive.

Fortunately, there is further evidence from later in the work which, I believe, clinches the issue. In Section 179 Locke discusses the rights of the victorious in a just war. The unjust aggressors, as well as those who supported their aggression, have by their actions forfeited their lives. But what about their countrymen who neither participated in nor supported the unjust aggression? In their case, Locke makes it perfectly clear that they have done no wrong and must be treated as innocent. Those and only those who are actually guilty of unjust aggression are liable to punishment for their actions. Such a distinction, Locke recognizes, is one which victors seldom bother to make, but he is quite insistent that it ought to be made. Given this, it is surely reasonable to infer that in all cases he would say that only those who transgress the law are liable to be punished; furthermore, it would also seem reasonable to suppose that, perhaps as a preamble to his 'measures of punishment' it would be an 'eternal rule' that no innocent person must ever be punished.

(ii) A related feature: in order for someone to deserve punishment, it is necessary for that person not simply to have broken the law, but also to have done so consciously and voluntarily. In the *Second Treatise* Locke has little to say about this, apart from a passing reference in Sections 59–61 where capability of knowing the law is made a condition of responsibility. Excluded from this are children, lunatics, idiots, and madmen. However in *An Essay Concerning Human Understanding*, these issues are dealt with much more fully in chapters XXI and XXVII of Book II. While it may well be that his treatment of liberty and personal identity is fraught with difficulty, the conclusions he wants to arrive at are reasonably clear. In brief, Locke argues that in order to be held responsible for one's actions, one must be conscious of having performed them and have performed them voluntarily.

(iii) In section 87, Locke says that in the natural state a man has the power 'to judge of, and punish the breaches of that Law in others, as he is persuaded the Offence deserves, even with Death it self, in Crimes where the heinousness of the Fact, in his Opinion, requires it'. Similarly in Section 23 he talks of someone 'having by his fault, forfeited his own Life, by some Act that deserves Death'.

What we encounter here is a typical retributivist claim that criminal acts simply deserve to be punished, and the penalty to be imposed depends on the nature of the deed itself. No mention is made of the consequences of punishment; rather, what is deserved is determined solely by the seriousness of the crime, and the very worst of crimes deserve death. Nothing other than the responsibility of the agent (which is assumed here) as well as the enormity of the offence has any bearing on what is deemed to be the appropriate penalty.

On this view of the matter, there is an obligation to respond to crime and the appropriate authority has a duty to punish criminal acts. At other times Locke adopts a less stringent view and says that law breaking bestows a right rather than a duty to punish. So in Section 7 he tells us that in the state of nature 'everyone has a right to punish the transgressors . . .', and in political society the magistrate has the right not only to punish but also to remit punishment (Section 11).

(iv) Another feature typical of retributivism is the principle of proportionality, which maintains that the severity of the punishment must be proportioned to the seriousness of the offence, and that it is unjust to impose penalties which are not proportioned to the offence. One of the complaints retributivists level against utilitarians is that utilitarianism can justify penalties which are out of all proportion to the offence.

We have already seen some anticipations of this principle. In Section 89 the justification for imposing the death penalty seems to presume that death is an appropriately severe penalty which matches an especially heinous offence. Then again in Section 12 the notion of a variety of 'measures of punishment' for breaches of the laws of nature could be taken to imply that there would be a proportionate correspondence between the seriousness of the breach and the severity of the penalty.

However when Locke actually offers his own formulation of the principle, his version of it is tantalisingly ambiguous. In Section 8, he tells us that a man may not punish a criminal 'according to the passionate heats, or boundless extravagancy of his own Will, but only to retribute to him, so far as calm reason and conscience dictates, what is proportionate to his Transgression, which is so much as may serve for Reparation and Restraint. For these two are the only reasons why one Man may lawfully do harm to another, which is that we call punishment.'

How are we to interpret this passage? It could be taken to mean that if we make proper use of our reason we should consult the various precepts laid down in the 'measures of punishment' and so determine what penalty a particular offence deserves. The penalty will be determined by and be proportionate to the seriousness of the transgression. It also happens to be the case that a penalty which is decided primarily on retributive grounds may in addition serve certain important utilitarian purposes. But retributive considerations come first, and the amount of punishment which is determined by these considerations is what will also serve to fulfil the goals of restraint and reparation.

However it is also possible to give this passage a thorough-going utilitarian interpretation. Restraint and reparation are said to be what

## Brian Calvert

justify punishment, and these are to be the primary considerations. What is proportionate is what reason decides is necessary to secure these goals, and what is necessary will depend upon the circumstances of the particular case as well as the social climate of the time. Further confirmation for this view of the matter can be found in Section 7 where Locke says '. . . every one has a right to punish the transgressions of that Law to such a Degree, as may hinder its Violation'. Similarly in Section 12 he writes: 'Each Transgression may be punished to that degree, and with so much Severity, as will suffice to make it an ill bargain to the Offender, give him cause to repent, and terrifie others from doing the like.'

The ambiguity of this passage may simply be a symptom of what was mentioned at the outset, namely that Locke's theory contains both retributive and non-retributive features. Before trying to decide how these features are to be combined, let us first turn to his utilitarianism.

### Locke's Utilitarianism

(1) *Reform and Deterrence*

Locke's utilitarianism has two distinguishable dimensions. First, he sees punishment as a means of changing the attitudes and behaviour of the offender, and so in this respect it is directed toward the improvement of the offender. The second dimension aims at enhancing the good of society, and here the function of punishment is to deter potential evildoers other than the offender from acting likewise, as well as to offer protection to law-abiding citizens by confining or incapacitating the criminal.

In Section 8 Locke says that punishment is designed 'to bring such evil on any one, who hath transgressed that Law, as may make him repent the doing of it, and thereby deter him, and by his Example others, from doing the like mischief.' Then again, in Section 12 he writes that punishment will be as severe . . . as will suffice to make it an ill bargain to the Offender, give him cause to repent, and terrifie others from doing the like.'

While these two passages place considerable emphasis upon the importance of the reform[5] of the individual offender, the penalty imposed upon that offender is also intended to deter others from

[5] Modern theorists usually make a distinction here. If a person is reformed, this means that the person concerned has changed his values and does not commit similar crimes because he regards such activity as wrong. If a person is deterred, that person refrains from criminal activity simply out of fear of punishment.

criminal activity. In the same context we find a mixture of the two dimensions, one directed at the improvement of the individual, the other at the good of society. Locke seems to assume that both of these goals can be satisfied at the same time, and that no conflict will arise between them. In many cases this could well be true; but in one obvious instance a conflict does arise, and this is with the death penalty. While it may be reasonable to believe, as Locke does, that death deters potential criminals, death can hardly be a penalty which could reform an individual offender. How then are these two dimensions to be reconciled? Though Locke says nothing explicitly, it may be that he has in mind something like the following. Punishment is capable of reforming the behaviour of many offenders, and if it can succeed in doing this, an important and valuable goal has been achieved. Unfortunately, this reforming purpose does not work in all cases, because some people are simply incapable of being reformed, and so for the well being of society it is necessary that they be executed.

But if something like this represents the kind of balance Locke seeks to bring about, many problems still remain. For example, must a decision be made that an offender is beyond all possibility of reform before the death penalty is imposed? If so, how is such a decision to be made? Is someone who repeatedly engages in less serious criminal activity and who refuses to mend his ways to be a candidate for execution? We may also wonder how Locke's reformative theory is to be reconciled with his retributivism. As we have seen, sometimes he writes as if certain offences, by their very nature, are so heinous that the criminal simply deserves to die. Should he assume that such a criminal is beyond all hope of reform? Which is to be the prior consideration in this case? So despite the prominence given to the importance of reform, it is far from clear how it is to be fitted in with other aspects of his theory. Moreover the status accorded to reforming the individual will have obvious implications for capital punishment. The more the need for reform is stressed, the more capital punishment must retire into the background; whereas if reform, though important, is to play an essentially secondary and subsidiary role, the more room there is for capital punishment.

### (2) *Self Defence and the Protection of Society*

Locke's main argument to justify the use of capital punishment is based on the necessity of protecting society against dangerous criminals. The argument leans heavily on the use of two analogies.

The first of these re-introduces an ancient theme which is prominent in the defences of the death penalty in the writings of Plato and Aquinas. It depends upon viewing society as a living organism like a

**Brian Calvert**

human body, and just as a disease may threaten the health of a body and require the amputation of an infected limb, so too a society may be threatened, and it could prove necessary to execute a criminal who menaces the well being of society. Locke's version of this line of argument is to be found in Section 171. There he tells us that political power is '. . . a Power to make Laws, and annex such Penalties to them, as may tend to the preservation of the whole, but cutting off those Parts, and those only, which are so corrupt, that they threaten the sound and healthy, without which no severity is lawful.'

It is not necessary to think that Locke has to be fully committed to an organic view of the state in order for this argument to have force. It can be regarded simply as an analogy, where the main purpose is to defend the need to execute criminals who pose a serious threat to society. Then again, though the phrase 'without which no severity is lawful' might imply that only this justification for imposing the death penalty is satisfactory, it is probably safest to regard it as an exaggeration. Locke also thinks that other reasons suffice to justify execution.

Two further observations: firstly, if this line of argument is to be reconciled with his stress on reform, presumably it is required that every feasible attempt to 'cure' the unhealthy part will have been expended before a resort is made to execution. Secondly, it is worth noting that the term 'corrupt' is ambiguous, and it covers both those who pose a threat because of offences committed voluntarily and also those who are not responsible agents. If one places all reliance on an argument for the defence of society, then any threat to society must be countered, and the question of the degree of personal responsibility on the part of those who constitute a danger is irrelevant. However if we suppose that Locke intends what he says here to be consistent with his insistence that only voluntary acts are punishable, then the scope of those who might be candidates for execution will be restricted to responsible agents.

Though the organic analogy has an ancient heritage, it occurs but rarely in the *Second Treatise*.[6] A much more prominent analogy depends on comparing the criminal with a dangerously savage animal. Just as someone is entitled to defend himself against a wild beast which threatens his security or that of others, so too a person may kill a lawbreaker. In Locke's view, the one who breaks the law has abandoned the rule of reason and adopted another rule, that of force and violence; and since this is the rule of wild animals, we are perfectly entitled to kill

[6] It recurs in Section 212: ''tis in their Legislative, that the Members of a Commonwealth are united, and combined together into one coherent living Body. This is the Soul that gives Form, Life, and Unity to the Commonwealth.'

those who live by this rule to protect ourselves as well as others. One typical formulation is to be found in Section 16: 'And one may destroy a Man who makes War upon him, or has discovered an Enmity to his being, for the same Reason, that he may kill a Wolf or a Lyon; because such Men are not under the ties of the Common Law of Reason, have no other Rule, but that of Force and Violence, and so may be treated as Beasts of Prey, those dangerous and noxious Creatures, that will be sure to destroy him, whenever he falls into their Power.'

In brief, then, Locke's argument is that the right of the state to execute stems from the right we possess as individuals in the natural condition to defend ourselves against the assaults of those who transgress the laws of nature. However the right to kill in self-defence in the state of nature becomes extended to far more situations than those which are obviously life-threatening. On some occasions at least, Locke appears to think that any lawbreaker, whatever the nature of the offence, has necessarily abandoned the law of reason for the rule of force and violence and so may be destroyed. For example, in Sections 17–19 Locke says that it is permissible for him to kill a thief who tries to steal his horse or his coat (or, presumably, any article however trivial its value may be), even though he makes it quite explicit at the opening of Section 18 that the thief has no intent to make any threat against his life. Similarly, in Section 181, a person who steals something, refuses to return it, and is prepared to use force to retain the stolen item has, Locke maintains, put himself into a state of war with his fellows and forfeited his life. It almost seems as if in the state of nature every offence could become a capital offence.

However after the transition to political society, the scene changes. In the state of nature it is scarcely possible to distinguish punishing and acting in self-defence; but with the evolution of political society that distinction becomes clearer. The right to punish has been transferred from the individual to the state, and while the individual retains the right to kill in self-defence, that right is now intended to be restricted to situations which are genuinely life threatening and when it is not possible to look to the law for protection. Even so, as Locke tells us in Section 207, it is still legitimate to kill a thief who threatens to use force. But in contrast with Section 181, if a person refuses to return a sum of money which has been entrusted to him, there is now no justification for killing that person to recover the money. Rather, an appeal must be made to the appropriate legal authorities to punish the wrongdoer.

Nevertheless, though the right to punish clearly rests in the hands of the state, and punishment has been distinguished from individual self-defence, the same justification for the infliction of the death penalty remains. The criminal has abandoned the rule of reason, put himself

**Brian Calvert**

into a state of war with his fellows, and may, if necessary, be destroyed for the public good, in particular for the protection of society.

While the derivation of the right of the state to impose the death penalty from the individual's right to self-defence may seem persuasive, important differences become glossed over. In particular, there is an ignoring of the difference between the threat which a dangerous criminal may well pose when he is at large, and the much diminished threat after he has been arrested and safely placed in custody. Similarly, to cite Locke's favourite analogy, there is a difference between a savage animal on the loose which may prey upon innocent human beings and the same creature safely behind bars in a zoo. Or again, the enemy soldier on the battlefield presents one situation; the same soldier disarmed and a prisoner of war is quite different.

In each of these examples, there is an important difference in the level of danger before and after capture, but the argument from self-defence, as Locke deploys it, seems to overlook this difference and to presume that the same level of danger continues. In a state of nature, where there are no legally established punitive procedures and penal institutions, ignoring the difference would be understandable. But in a political society, where there are means other than execution to provide security, then in order for the use of the death penalty to be justified, it has to be presumed that none of these other means offers satisfactory protection.

Is it not the case, though, that there are some people who are simply so dangerous that they will always pose a threat, and who are so 'noxious' that they are a permanent menace to their captors and fellow prisoners? Perhaps so; but if the concern is simply that of the security of society, it is now a matter of whether it is possible, empirically, to provide sufficient safeguards by methods other than execution. In which case, what Locke probably should have said is that the argument from the defence of society furnishes no justification for capital punishment, unless it can be shown that it is not possible to provide adequate protection against a given offender by any other means. If the argument is set out in these terms, there would be relatively few occasions when the use of execution would be necessary.

## Locke's General Theory?

So far we have been considering the argument purely on its own merits. We might also wonder, of course, how it is to be tied in with various other themes we have looked at already, such as reform, deterrence and retribution. What we have seen to this point is that Locke's account contains a number of different elements. Some of these are clearly retributive, others clearly utilitarian, and at least one is hard to classify. That these elements are there seems beyond dispute.

What is more difficult to determine is how Locke thinks these various features should be combined together into a comprehensive theory. On this he provides us with no guidance,[7] except, perhaps, the implicit presumption that together they form a coherent whole. But given that tensions will arise if each of these features is accorded equal weight, some kind of compromise theory will have to be constructed. In what follows I shall sketch out two possibilities, but only briefly and tentatively. A fuller resolution of this matter would be the subject of another essay, and would divert us from our main goal.

(1) Locke emphasizes that the state has a right to punish rather than an obligation to do so, and the extent to which it actually exercises that right, if at all, is determined by the amount of good which is achieved in any particular situation. However, if punishment is inflicted it must be deserved; there must be no punishment of innocents, nor must the amount of punishment be out of proportion to the seriousness of the crime committed. Expressed in these terms, Locke's account has some similarity to the thesis put forward a few years ago by K. G. Armstrong. According to Armstrong, retributive justice gives 'the appropriate authority the right to punish offenders up to some limit, but one is not necessarily and invariably obliged to punish to the limit of justice.'[8] If the right is exercised, the principle of proportionality is interpreted as setting an upper limit to the severity of punishment which is permissible, but this having been said, utilitarian considerations can also play a role.

(2) Another alternative would be to put utilitarian features more clearly to the fore. At the very outset, Locke has insisted that the laws laid down by the state must be for the 'Publick Good' (Section 3). Later he tells us that the basic law of nature which is to be reflected in positive legal enactments is 'the preservation of Mankind' (Section 134–5). So, we might say, the general justifying aim is utilitarian. Some of the more particular features are also utilitarian—but what status is to be accorded to the retributive elements? Are they designed to provide some kind of check against potential excesses to which a purely utilitarian theory is prone? If so, is Locke's account to be seen as an early version of more

[7] Similarly, Locke provides no guidance on how to reconcile what have been perceived to be discordant features in his ethical theory. Is he a natural law theorist, a theological voluntarist, a hedonistic utilitarian? This issue has attracted considerable attention from commentators.

[8] K. G. Armstrong, 'The Retributivist Hits Back', in H. B. Acton (ed.), *The Philosophy of Punishment* (London: Macmillan, St. Martin's Press, 1969), 155.

**Brian Calvert**

modern attempts to reconcile retributivism with utilitarianism? With sufficient ingenuity, it might be possible to force Locke into a mould which would represent him as an early ancestor of, say, Rawls or Hart,[9] but we are given no real indication in the *Second Treatise* what kind of compromise Locke himself would find the most congenial. So apart from saying that some kind of compromise is necessary, I let this matter rest.

Next, I want to make a few comments on an issue which has only been touched on briefly so far, namely the relationship between punishment and reparation.

## Punishment and Reparation

In Section 8 Locke says that when one man punishes another in the state of nature he must 'only retribute to him, so far as calm reason and conscience dictates, what is proportionate to his Transgression, which is so much as may serve for Reparation and Restraint. For these two are the only reasons why one Man may lawfully do harm to another, which is that we call punishment.' Here we notice that reparation is described as one of the purposes of punishment.

Yet almost immediately after this, reparation and punishment are separated. Locke points out that one who offends against the laws of nature often does harm to another individual, and that individual 'who hath received any damage, has besides the right of punishment common to him with other Men, a particular Right to seek Reparation from him that has done it' (Section 10). This distinction is re-emphasized in the following section. The right of punishment belongs to all, the right of reparation only to the one who has been harmed. Moreover, in political society, the magistrate exercising the public right to punish may remit a sentence, but he has no power to deny an injured individual the right to compensation. So even if a magistrate decides that someone does not deserve to be punished for some act, if that act caused damage to another, that other person may still seek compensation (Section 11).

Now it certainly seems fair and reasonable to make a distinction between punishment and reparation. However at this stage, the problem is that while the one who demands and receives compensation may, as Locke says, appropriate 'the Goods or Service of the Offender,' (Section 11), there is no mention of any limit to be placed on that demand. Is each individual to be the sole arbiter of how much compen-

[9] John Rawls, 'Two Concepts of Rules', in Acton, op. cit., pp. 105–114. H. L. A. Hart, *Punishment and Responsibility* (Oxford: Clarendon Press, 1968), Chap. 1.

sation is due? When reparation and restraint were put together under the common banner of punishment in Section 8, at least there was the stipulation that 'calm reason and conscience' would determine the amount of reparation owing, proportionate to the transgression, that is, the damage inflicted by the offender. But once reparation has been cut free from punishment, it is not clear that the same governing criteria apply. There is also one further problem—what of the case of murder? Locke quite properly describes murder as being an injury 'which no Reparation can compensate.' (Section 11) Plainly, someone who has been murdered is in no position to seek compensation. But what of the dependents of the victim? Are any provisions to be made for them to seek compensation, and what form might this take?

In later sections, Locke does go some way to responding to the first difficulty. Once the state of nature has been superseded by political society, not only is the right to punish transferred to the state, but the state also determines what the appropriate level of compensation will be for those who have suffered loss. As we saw earlier in Section 181, Locke tells us that in the state of nature, if a criminal does another an injury, even by 'fraud' and 'quietly', and refuses to make reparation, the criminal's life is forfeited, and he may be killed in order that compensation be made. But in Section 207, after the establishment of a political state, the function of enforcing reparation clearly belongs to the appropriate magistrate. A person seeking compensation for a loss must do so by an appeal to the law. Similarly, in Section 89, Locke says that in political society a judge is set up 'with Authority to determine all the Controversies, and redress the Injuries, that may happen to any Member of the Commonwealth.'

Locke's final view on the matter appears to be this: the magistrate has two separate tasks to perform. He must determine the appropriate penalty for an offence, and he must also set the amount of compensation due to the victim of the offence. An injured individual has the right to demand compensation or he may waive his right; however he cannot determine what the level of compensation is to be. The magistrate may also exercise his right to remit punishment, but he has no power to decide whether compensation is to be made.

## Murder and the Death Penalty

Locke contends that the state has the right to inflict the death penalty, and in a number of places (e.g. Sections 23, 87) he alludes to crimes which are deserving of death, but at these places he does not specify which crimes he has in mind. However in Section 11 he does say that murder is a capital crime, and his reference at the beginning of Section

## Brian Calvert

12 to 'lesser breaches of that Law [of Nature]' suggests that he regards murder as the most serious breach of the law. Unlike lesser breaches, the harm it causes is one 'which no Reparation can compensate' (Section 11), and elsewhere Locke emphasizes this particular feature of killing, namely that the loss it causes is irreparable (Section 207). Given this, we might reasonably expect that the justification for the use of capital punishment will be strongest in the case of murder.

It would certainly be possible for Locke to attempt to justify the infliction of the death penalty for murder by an appeal to the retributive principles he has enunciated. Murder could be counted as a deed which is deserving of death (Sections 23, 87), where the murderer has forfeited his right to life, assuming that this is qualified by the condition that the killer is a responsible agent who committed his crime voluntarily. A purely retributive interpretation of the principle of proportionality would confirm that death is 'proportionate to his Transgression' (Section 8). Finally, in a biblical flourish, Locke appeals to the 'great Law of Nature, Who so sheddeth Mans Blood, by Man shall his Blood be shed' (Section 11).

But though such a mode of reasoning would have been possible, in the context we find that Locke makes his case on utilitarian grounds. Everyone in the natural state has the power to kill a murderer 'both to deter others from doing the like Injury, which no Reparation can compensate, by the Example of the punishment that attends it from every body, and also to secure Men from the attempts of the Criminal . . .' (Section 11). The murderer who has renounced the rule of reason may be destroyed, just as we may destroy a wild beast which threatens our security.

Why does Locke make no real use of the retributive justifications which he has available? The answer may be that since he thinks they coincide in their conclusions with his utilitarian arguments, it would be superfluous to mention them. Moreover, if the Biblical text at the end of Section 11 is to be counted as a retributive feature, it is not true that retributive considerations are entirely absent. But whatever the reason, we have already had cause to take note of potential tensions between these various lines of justification, some of which Locke lays the groundwork for, while there are others he may not have been aware of.

(i) We have seen already that retributive theory might require execution for every deliberate murder, and Locke may well have thought that this conclusion was also supported by the utilitarian considerations he cites. However, if our examination of his argument from self defence is correct, that argument ought to yield a much narrower conclusion, and restrict the use of execution to those against whom it is not possible to provide adequate protection.

(ii) More generally, a theme typical of retributivism maintains that crime deserves to be punished, and insists that it is unjust not to punish a crime which has been committed; hence if a capital crime is committed, it is also unjust not to punish this with the appropriate penalty.

On this issue, Locke seems to be much more thoroughgoingly utilitarian. In Section 11, he says that a magistrate 'can often, where the publick good demands not the execution of the Law, remit the punishment of Criminal Offences by his own Authority.' Similarly, in Section 159, Locke writes that 'a strict and rigid observation of the Laws may do harm . . .', and so ''tis fit, the Ruler should have a Power, in many cases, to mitigate the severity of the Law, and pardon some Offenders: For the end of Government being the preservation of all, as much as may be, even the guilty are to be spared where it can prove no prejudice to the innocent'.

It would be difficult to over-estimate the importance of these remarks. Locke makes it quite clear that one should set aside severe penalties justified on retributive grounds, if no good is served by their enforcement, or if no harm follows from their non-enforcement. Not only does this have an impact on his retributivism; it also affects his utilitarian reasons in favour of execution.

Firstly, it serves to reinforce the point about the restricted use of the death penalty under the rubric of the protection of society. While Locke may not have realized that his argument ought to have contained the restrictions, the passages just quoted confirm that they should be there. If Locke had incorporated the thoughts expressed in these passages into his formulation of the argument from protection, he should have seen that the argument committed him to a restricted application of the death penalty.

Secondly, to judge from the sentiments expressed in Section 11, Locke may well have thought that the death penalty provides the best deterrent against murder. But the insistence that real good flow from its enforcement, or that no harm ensue from its non-enforcement, opens the way for a reassessment. In the latter part of this century, a pressing question which has engaged the attention of investigators is whether execution deters more effectively than other penalties. Though it would be unfairly anachronistic to expect that Locke should have taken account of this question, I do not believe that it is unfair to ask what he would have thought if he had been exposed to modern empirical studies which seem to suggest that execution has no unique deterrent value. If he had been exposed to this evidence and found it convincing, there is every reason to suppose that his confidence in execution as a deterrent to murder would have diminished, or even disappeared completely.

(iii) We have seen that Locke's main case for the execution of murderers has been made to rest on reasons of deterrence and protection. In Section 11, no mention is made of reforming the offender, though reform is to be found as an ingredient of his theory in Sections 8 and 12. Now in one way it is not surprising, as we noted in an earlier discussion of reform, that there should be no mention of it in a context designed to justify execution. Still, it would be helpful to try to determine why any such mention is omitted. Is he simply assuming in Section 11 that the murderer is beyond all hope of reform, but for lesser breaches of the law (Section 12) it is appropriate to introduce the possibility of reforming the offender? If so, we may wonder why he should assume that every murderer is incapable of being reformed.

However if we consider the evidence concerning the prerogative of the magistrate, we can see that Locke may in fact have left himself with some room for manoeuvre. One of the reasons for giving the magistrate the opportunity of remitting the death penalty may be that the magistrate believes that the murderer is capable of reform. So despite the exclusion of all mention of reform in Section 11, it could be that Locke does not wish to rule out the possibility that at least some murderers are capable of changing their ways, and so obviously, in their cases, it would be best not to execute.

As far as the treatment of murderers is concerned, Locke seems to leave us with two different impressions. If we were to rely solely on the sentiments expressed in Section 11, we are given the picture of one who clearly advocates the execution of murderers, both to deter other potential murderers, and to rid society of those who have become like wild animals and adopted the rule of 'violence and slaughter.' But if we examine the implications of what is actually justified by his reasoning, and conjoin this with his insistence in Section 159 that life be spared as much as possible 'where it can prove no prejudice to the innocent', we get quite a different impression. While the state still retains the right to execute, the occasions on which it would actually exercise that right are few, being limited to those cases where the offender seems beyond all hope of reform and where his continued existence would pose an intolerable threat to the security of society.[10]

[10] Although it is even conceivable that the state might never impose the death penalty in practice, it is important to emphasize that it could not take the further step of deciding that it had no right to use it in principle. It remains an important part of Locke's argument that the magistrate possesses the power to put people to death. The right of nature (the right to judge in one's own case) which people give up in order to institute civil society necessarily includes the right to kill aggressors in appropriate circumstances (e.g. self-defence). In which case, it would not be possible to design a Lockean state which lacked the right to use the death penalty, even though that state might choose never to use it in practice.

I owe this point to my colleague Karen Wendling.

## Locke on Punishment and the Death Penalty

To conclude this part, I want to make a few more observations about reparation. Locke has drawn attention to one feature of murder, namely that it causes an irreparable loss to the victim, and one question which was left unanswered from the previous section was what kind of compensation, if any, he might wish to provide to the dependents of the victim. There is little that he says explicitly on this topic; however we can make some progress if we consider what his answer would probably be in response to two questions.

Firstly, let us consider a situation where the magistrate decides to remit the penalty of death, but the dependents of the victim object, because they contend that only the death of the murderer would provide adequate compensation and the magistrate has no right to deny them that compensation. As a desire for revenge, such a demand is understandable, and so what might Locke's response be? He would probably say two things. To begin with he would dissociate himself from the desire for revenge; in Section 8 he has said that we must not treat the criminal 'according to the passionate heats, or boundless extravagancy of [our] own Will, but only to retribute to him, so much as calm reason and conscience dictates, what is proportionate to his transgression, which is so much as may serve for Reparation and Restraint'. Considerations of calm reason rather than passionate emotion should determine the amount of reparation. In addition to this, if we go strictly by what we find in the text, Locke says that the person seeking compensation may make use of the 'goods and service' of the offender, not his life. In political society, only the state has the right to enact life or death decisions. A person's life is not part of the currency of reparation.

However there is an alternative and perhaps more intriguing possibility. Suppose a magistrate decides that a murderer deserves to die, but that this time the dependents of the victim object, on the ground that his execution would deny them access to the 'goods and service' of the murderer which they wish to use to compensate for their loss. What might Locke say here?

This is a situation which Locke does not seem to have anticipated, and so any remarks are bound to be speculative. But we can seek some guidance from what he says in a different context in Sections 182–3, where he discusses the rights of various parties in war. The victors in a just war have the right to take the lives of those who have engaged in an unjust aggression against them, but they also have the right to spare the aggressors' lives and make use of their 'Service and Goods' for purposes of reparation. While the decision to take or spare life rests solely with the victor, there are certain factors which indicate that the sparing of life should take precedence. The aggressor may have innocent dependants who also have a right to his goods and service for their support; in this case, in addition to involving the 'Fundamental Law of Nature . . . that all, as much as may be, should be preserved . . .', both the rights of the conqueror and those of the dependants of the vanquished have to be satisfied.

Although this context is admittedly different, there appear to be sufficient relevant similarities to enable some plausible applications to be made to the situation with which we are concerned. If compensation is to be given out, we must not only attend to the claims of the dependents of the victim; we must also recognize the needs of any innocent dependants of the murderer. He may have some possessions; if so, both sets of dependents have a claim on these. If he is allowed to live, he could make further compensation by performing some kind of labour, where, once again, both sets of dependents would have a legitimate claim. However, if he is executed this potential benefit is lost, unless ongoing compensation is provided from the revenues of the state. Assuming that concerns about security can be met, it seems that more good would ensue from having compensation paid from the labour of the offender, and there are indications that this might be Locke's own preference. If execution is to be restricted to those who pose an intolerable threat, the outcome for murderers who are not executed would not simply be that their lives are spared. Rather, their lives could be put to a more positive use if they were to make restitution for the losses they caused as well as to help to provide maintenance for their own dependants.

Nor need these remarks about reparation be restricted to the unusual possibility with which we began. They suggest a framework for all cases where compensation is to be made to the dependants of victims; nor are the innocent dependants of the criminal forgotten. While all this goes well beyond what Locke actually says, it seems a plausible extrapolation from his position. If so, there is at least the potential in Locke for an answer to be made to a complaint which is often heard, namely that theories of punishment seldom pay any attention to the victims of crime.

## Conclusion

Locke appears to hold two positions concerning the death penalty. His harsher position, which relies heavily on procedures in the state of nature, would apparently sanction execution not only for murder, but also for a wide variety of offences which are said to deserve death. In Section 181, as we have seen, it looks as if any illegitimate use of force entails a forfeiture of life and so becomes a capital offence. In Section 12, Locke says that 'Every Offence that can be committed in the State of

Nature, may in the State of Nature be also punished, equally, and as far forth as it may, in a Common-wealth.' Bedau takes this to be a faithful reflection of Locke's whole theory when he complains that virtually any offence can be treated as a capital offence; he also adds that Locke does not seem to give any thought to the question of how one decides if a given crime deserves death or a lesser penalty.[11]

But if my analysis is correct, such a view gives us an incomplete and distorted perspective of Locke's final position. Once the move has been made from the state of nature to political society and punishment has been distinguished from self-defence, his account of the occasions when the use of the death penalty is justified is much more narrowly drawn. Execution is to be restricted to the most desperate cases, where no adequate security can be provided against someone who poses a constant threat. If so, Locke does give some thought to the matter of who deserves to be executed—only the very worst menace qualifies. Finally, if we were right in supposing that Locke regards murder as the most serious breach of natural law and yet only wishes to make very restricted use of the death penalty in response to this crime, then any justification for its use in response to 'lesser breaches of that Law' would probably be more difficult, if not impossible, to provide.

*University of Guelph*

[11] Bedau, pp. 12–13.

# Part VII
# Tolerance and Civil Disobedience

# [14]

# "We the People": John Locke, Collective Constitutional Rights, and Standing to Challenge Government Action

Donald L. Doernberg†

The first three words of the preamble to the Constitution[1] suggest one element unique to the American Revolution: its outcome was a government created by the people, not one existing independently of them or, in some respect, over them.[2] Indeed, the preamble reads like a charge to the new government, as though the Framers had said "this is what you, the government, shall do," and then in the Constitution said "and here is how you shall accomplish it." The idea of popular sovereignty in the United States antedates the Constitution, appearing in its best known form in the Declaration of Independence's admonition that governments must be viewed as "deriving their just powers from the consent of the governed,"[3] and ultimately being attributed to the influence of both John Locke[4] and Jean Jacques Rousseau.[5]

One problem that the American legal system has encountered is the enforcement of the limits set by the Constitution and statutes on government operation.[6] Whether the government has exceeded its lawful

---

† Visiting Professor of Law, University of California, Hastings College of the Law, 1984-85; Professor of Law, Pace University. B.A. 1966, Yale University; J.D. 1969, Columbia University.

I gratefully acknowledge the thoughtful editing suggestions of Professors Burton Leiser and Donald H. Zeigler, and the research assistance of Steven Chananie, Jonathan Diamond, Veronica Hakim, Teri Shulman, Sarah Whalen, and the staff of the Pace University Law Library.

1. U.S. CONST. preamble:

> We the People of the United States, in Order to form a more perfect Union, establish Justice, ensure domestic Tranquility, provide for the common defence, promote the general Welfare, and secure the Blessings of Liberty to ourselves and our Posterity, do ordain and establish this Constitution for the United States of America.

2. Alexander Hamilton, arguing that the proposed adoption of a bill of rights was unnecessary and potentially harmful, relied heavily on the nature of the new American government. "Here, in strictness, the people surrender nothing; and as they retain every thing they have no need of particular reservations." THE FEDERALIST NO. 84, at 513 (A. Hamilton) (C. Rossiter ed. 1961). He also characterized the Constitution as "professedly founded upon the power of the people, and executed by their immediate representatives and servants." *Id.*

3. The Declaration of Independence para. 2 (U.S. 1776).

4. *See infra* note 41.

5. J. ROUSSEAU, THE SOCIAL CONTRACT AND DISCOURSES (D. Cress ed. 1983).

6. It is universally recognized that the United States government was intended to be one of carefully circumscribed powers, defined by enumeration. This limitation is, perhaps, most directly

bounds is a question for the judiciary to decide, as *Marbury v. Madison*[7] made clear. But who may ask the courts to decide? That question is ordinarily resolved by application of the doctrine of standing.[8] In recent years, questions of standing have been determined by application of a two-part test. First, the court must examine whether the party seeking relief has "such a personal stake in the outcome of the controversy as to assure that concrete adverseness which sharpens the presentation of issues upon which the court so largely depends for illumination of difficult constitutional questions."[9] Second, there must be "some connection between the official action challenged and some legally protected interest of the party challenging that action."[10] The first part of the test, commonly referred to as injury-in-fact,[11] is indispensable because it is viewed as part of the case-or-controversy requirement;[12] hence, it is jurisdictional.[13]

---

reflected in the 10th amendment: "The powers not delegated to the United States by the Constitution, nor prohibited by it to the States, are reserved to the States respectively, or to the people." U.S. CONST. amend. X.

7. 5 U.S. (1 Cranch) 137, 177-80 (1803).

8. The question of standing concerns whether "a party has a sufficient stake in an otherwise justiciable controversy to obtain judicial resolution of that controversy." Sierra Club v. Morton, 405 U.S. 727, 731 (1972). *See generally* L. TRIBE, AMERICAN CONSTITUTIONAL LAW §§ 3-17 to -29 (1978).

9. Baker v. Carr, 369 U.S. 186, 204 (1962). This first requirement, then, focuses on the party seeking relief rather than on the nature of the relief sought.

10. Jenkins v. McKeithen, 395 U.S. 411, 423 (1969). The phrase "legally protected interest" has been rejected by the Court as conveying too restrictive a view of this part of the test. *See infra* notes 217-26 and accompanying text. But current law still requires some nexus between the challenged official activity and a legally cognizable interest of the plaintiff. As Professor Tribe has explained:

> The nexus requirement bears a family resemblance to the "scope of the risk" doctrine in the law of torts. Thus, in tort law, it is not enough that the defendant's violation of the law caused injury to the plaintiff: the defendant also must owe the plaintiff some duty. Similarly, in the federal law of standing, it is not enough that the plaintiff be injured by some act or omission of the defendant; the defendant must additionally have violated some duty owed to the plaintiff. Applying this doctrine to challenges of official government action or inaction, the relevant question would not be simply whether the official or agency violated the law, but rather whether the official or agency violated any duty to the plaintiff.

L. TRIBE, *supra* note 8, § 3-22, at 98 (footnotes omitted).

11. *See, e.g.*, Valley Forge Christian College v. Americans United for Separation of Church & State, Inc., 454 U.S. 464, 472 (1982); Duke Power Co. v. Carolina Envtl. Study Group, Inc., 438 U.S. 59, 72-74 (1978). *See generally* L. TRIBE, *supra* note 8, § 3-20.

12. U.S. CONST. art. III, § 2, cl. 1.

13. The Court explained the jurisdictional nature of the injury-in-fact test in 1982:

> [A]t an irreducible minimum, Art. III requires the party who invokes the court's authority to "show that he personally has suffered some actual or threatened injury as a result of the putatively illegal conduct of the defendant," *Gladstone, Realtors v. Village of Bellwood*, 441 U.S. 91, 99 (1979), and that the injury "fairly can be traced to the challenged action" and "is likely to be redressed by a favorable decision," *Simon v. Eastern Kentucky Welfare Rights Org.*, 426 U.S. 26, 38, 41 (1976). In this manner does Art. III limit the federal judicial power "to those disputes which confine federal courts to a role consistent with a system of separated powers and which are traditionally thought to be capable of resolution through the judicial process." *Flast v. Cohen*, 392 U.S. [83, 97 (1968)].

Valley Forge Christian College v. Americans United for Separation of Church & State, Inc., 454 U.S. 464, 472 (1982) (footnotes omitted). In the same opinion, the Court recognized:

The second part of the test is commonly called the nexus requirement[14] and is not constitutionally mandated.[15] The nexus test, first announced in *Flast v. Cohen*,[16] requires examination of the substantive issues raised in a case "to determine whether there is a logical nexus between the status asserted and the claim sought to be adjudicated."[17]

Unfortunately, this two-part test proved extremely difficult to apply, leading the Court to observe in 1969 that "[t]he concept of standing to sue . . . 'is surrounded by the same complexities and vagaries that inhere in [the concept of] justiciability' in general."[18] The nexus requirement in particular has come under fire.

> The search for nexus . . . risks begging the vital question of whether the plaintiff is truly claiming injury to his own legally protected interest or whether the plaintiff, although claiming a material injury, is in fact asserting the interests of someone else but should nonetheless be accorded surrogate standing. Even when the nexus rule does not operate to deny standing, therefore, it may entail substantial disadvantages.
>
> Even more pointedly, the rule of nexus can induce denials of standing where a decision on the merits would be preferable.[19]

As a consequence, Professor Tribe has advocated dropping the nexus requirement in many circumstances, particularly where official action is

> [I]t has not always been clear in the opinions of this Court whether particular features of the "standing" requirement have been required by Art. III *ex proprio vigore*, or whether they are requirements that the Court itself has erected and which were not compelled by the language of the Constitution.

*Id.* at 471.

14. *See, e.g.*, Duke Power Co. v. Carolina Envtl. Study Group, Inc., 438 U.S. 59, 78-81 (1978); Flast v. Cohen, 392 U.S. 83, 101-02 (1968). *See generally* L. TRIBE, *supra* note 8, § 3-22.

15. *See, e.g.*, Duke Power Co. v. Carolina Envtl. Study Group, Inc., 438 U.S. 59, 78-81 (1978). "Unlike the 'injury in fact' requirement, the 'nexus' requirement is *clearly* not compelled by article III but represents only a prudential limitation upon the exercise of federal jurisdiction." L. TRIBE, *supra* note 8, § 3-22, at 97 n.2 (emphasis in original).

16. 392 U.S. 83 (1968). *Flast* was a taxpayer's challenge to government action that allegedly violated the first amendment's establishment clause.

17. *Id.* at 102. The nexus requirement thus stated has two components. First, the taxpayer must show a connection between his status as a taxpayer and the challenged activity. *Id.* Taxpayer standing therefore requires a challenge to some exercise of the government's taxing power. Second, the taxpayer must show that the exercise of the taxing power violates a specific constitutional restriction on that power, rather than that the challenged activity merely exceeds a more general restriction on governmental power. *Id.* at 102-03.

It was unclear in *Flast* whether the nexus requirement applied to suits not brought by taxpayers *qua* taxpayers. In Linda R.S. v. Richard D., 410 U.S. 614, 618 (1973), the Court applied the test in a nontaxpayer suit. *See infra* notes 117-19 and accompanying text. Five years later, however, in Duke Power Co. v. Carolina Envtl. Study Group, Inc., 438 U.S. 59, 78-79 (1978), the Court explicitly repudiated the test's applicability except in taxpayer suits. *See infra* notes 249-58 and accompanying text.

18. Jenkins v. McKeithen, 395 U.S. 411, 423 (1969) (quoting Flast v. Cohen, 392 U.S. 83, 98 (1968)).

19. L. TRIBE, *supra* note 8, § 3-27, at 110.

challenged as being lawless.[20] Professor Tribe's suggestion parallels that of Professor Davis, who observed:

> The natural system is that of the common law: If A and B are private parties and A hurts B, B has standing to get a determination of the legality of A's action. Why should not the law be the same, whether A is the government, and [sic] agency, an officer, or a private party, and whether the injury is to B's person, his physical property, or his intangible interests? Is not the natural system the simple one that injury in fact is enough for standing?[21]

Thus, Professor Davis, too, would leave only the injury-in-fact requirement for standing, noting that "[t]he only problems about standing should be what interests deserve protection against injury, and what should be enough to constitute an injury."[22]

This Article supports Professor Tribe's and Professor Davis' suggestion, but on a different basis. In addition to the problems outlined above, the Article suggests that the nexus requirement also overlooks one of the fundamental characteristics of American government foreshadowed in

---

20. Professor Tribe believes that challenges to governmental action do, and should, stand on special footing:

> When official action is challenged on grounds of illegality, values beyond those tangibly protected by the violated law or constitutional provision come powerfully into play. Both the value of legality as such, and the public respect which rests on it, may be seriously impaired whenever courts equipped to remedy an illegality at the behest of a factually injured party allow clearly illegal procedures or results to stand on the sole ground that all of the material interests required to be considered or "accommodated" by the statutory (or even constitutional) scheme were satisfied with the official action. To say in such circumstances that the "abstract concern for vindicating the bare words of statutes seems too attenuated a justification for disturbing mutually satisfactory arrangements struck by all of the relevant public and private interests," is to deprecate the "relevant public interest" in the rule of law. In any event, letting "mutually satisfactory arrangements" stand on such a ground requires assuming or finding that those who are silent are indeed "satisfied" rather than merely ignorant, impecunious, inadequately organized, or simply exhausted. At a minimum, the requirement for nexus should be dropped and surrogate standing allowed whenever a court has reasonable ground to believe that one of these alternative explanations has played a major role in the absence of any challenge by someone with direct standing.

*Id.* § 3-27, at 111-12 (footnotes omitted). Thus, Professor Tribe argues that "if government's overriding duty to act lawfully is accorded serious weight," the nexus requirement ought to be abandoned as a matter of sound policy. *Id.* § 3-28, at 113. Justice Powell has also suggested abandoning the nexus test. *See* United States v. Richardson, 418 U.S. 166, 180 (1974) (Powell, J., concurring). His views and *Richardson* are discussed *infra* in Part II.

21. Davis, *The Liberalized Law of Standing*, 37 U. Chi. L. Rev. 450, 468 (1970). In this respect, Professor Davis echoes Justice Frankfurter: "A litigant ordinarily has standing to challenge governmental action of a sort that, if taken by a private person, would create a right of action cognizable by the courts." Joint Anti-Fascist Refugee Comm. v. McGrath, 341 U.S. 123, 152 (1951) (Frankfurter, J., concurring). And indeed, Justice Brennan concurs in this suggestion. *See infra* text accompanying notes 221-25.

This Article suggests, however, that this injury-in-fact concept is underinclusive. Private parties, in their dealings with each other, are not bound by a charter by which one party creates the other and gives him or her legitimacy. Because of the nature of American government, the Davis tort metaphor fails at that point. *See infra* Part I.

22. Davis, *supra* note 21, at 468.

the writings of John Locke[23] and woven into the Constitution by the Framers: the concept that rights, in addition to being individually held, may also be held collectively by the body politic, which creates and provides the justification for civil government.[24] In Professor Davis' terms, there are additional interests, as yet unrecognized in the law of standing, that deserve protection against injury. The existence of collective interests has been widely recognized by courts and scholars,[25] but not in the context discussed here. Collective interests are most often discussed when they are perceived to be in conflict with rights or privileges asserted by an individual.[26] They are not evaluated in terms of their impact on the doctrine of standing. This Article suggests that there is a class of cases where individual and collective interests, far from being opposed, actually coincide—cases where the government is charged with violating the Constitution. Moreover, in a significant subclass of those cases, current standing doctrine makes impossible both judicial protection of such collective interests and judicial insistence that government operate only within the bounds of the Constitution. The effect is that certain constitutional provisions effectively exist only at the whim and during the good will of the government, because the collective interest in enforcement of such provisions will not be protected by the courts. This Article urges, therefore, that the existence and recognition of collective rights require a modification of standing doctrine so that such rights can be protected through judicial review.[27]

23. *See generally* J. LOCKE, TWO TREATISES OF GOVERNMENT *Second Treatise* (P. Laslett ed. 1960).

24. *See infra* notes 59-65 and accompanying text.

25. *See generally infra* Part III, Section *B*; *see also* Antieau, *The Jurisprudence of Interests as a Method of Constitutional Adjudication*, 27 CASE W. RES. L. REV. 823 (1977).

26. *See, e.g.*, Morris v. Slappy, 461 U.S. 1, 14-15 (1983) (public interest in protection of victim's rights balanced against individual's sixth amendment right to counsel); Gannett Co. v. DePasquale, 443 U.S. 368, 383 (1979) (public interest in open trials balanced against individual's 6th and 14th amendment rights to fair trial); Roe v. Wade, 410 U.S. 113, 153-54 (1973) (state's interest in the health of a prospective mother and in the potentiality of human life balanced against individual's constitutionally based privacy interests in making the abortion decision); Wisconsin v. Yoder, 406 U.S. 205, 213-15 (1972) (state's interest in universal compulsory education balanced against individual's first amendment right to free exercise of religion); Camara v. Municipal Court, 387 U.S. 523, 533 (1967) (public interest in enforcement of health and fire codes balanced against individual's fourth amendment right to privacy); Konigsberg v. State Bar, 366 U.S. 36, 49-52 (1961) (public interest in careful regulation of the fitness of attorneys balanced against individual's 1st and 14th amendment rights to free association).

27. Professor Berger has suggested that a broad concept of standing is consistent with our common law history in cases where illegal government action is challenged. His theory, however, is based on the ready availability of the prerogative writs to English citizens without requiring personal injury-in-fact and does not explicitly deal with more direct influences on the American process of creating a national government. Berger, *Standing to Sue in Public Actions: Is It a Constitutional Requirement?*, 78 YALE L.J. 816 (1969). Other scholars have also proposed broadening the doctrine of standing, effectively eliminating it in public actions, on the ground that it would be better policy to do so. *See, e.g.*, Jaffe, *Standing to Secure Judicial Review: Public Actions* (pt. 1), 74 HARV. L. REV.

The Article is presented in three Parts. Part I documents the enormous effect that Locke's political philosophy had on the Constitution's Framers and traces the idea of collective rights through Locke's *Second Treatise*,[28] showing how Locke viewed government as a trustee and society as the settlor-beneficiary that forms and gives legitimacy to the government. Part II reviews the development of the current doctrine of standing and demonstrates how the current standing model creates a class of cases where government may, with impunity, violate the Constitution. Part III demonstrates the anomaly of the Supreme Court's current doctrine in a society founded on the ideas of John Locke. It then explores the constitutional provisions where collective rights have already been recognized by the courts,[29] though not with respect to standing analysis. Finally, Part III proposes a revision of the current test for standing to ensure that vindication of society's collective rights is possible without creating universal standing and thus threatening the courts with a tidal wave of litigation brought by "officious intermeddlers."[30]

## I
## John Locke and the Framers of the Constitution

It would be difficult to overstate John Locke's influence on the American Revolution and the people who created the government that followed it.[31] One writer notes that most eighteenth-century liberal doctrines can be traced to Locke and his concept that community power

1265 (1961); Nichol, *Rethinking Standing*, 72 Calif. L. Rev. 68 (1984). *But see* Sedler, *Assertion of Constitutional Jus Tertii: A Substantive Approach*, 70 Calif. L. Rev. 1308 (1982) (personal injury-in-fact should be required for standing, and third parties should not be able to assert others' injuries in order to get standing). By contrast, this Article proposes that it is not necessary to discard standing doctrine entirely in public actions; it merely is appropriate to recognize the full range of interests—individual and collective—deserving protection under the Constitution.

28. J. Locke, *supra* note 23.

29. I have previously identified one such right that arises from the fourth amendment, Doernberg, *"The Right of the People": Reconciling Collective and Individual Interests Under the Fourth Amendment*, 58 N.Y.U. L. Rev. 259 (1983), but I focused on support of the collective fourth amendment right, implicit in the exclusionary rule, which is recognized by the Supreme Court itself. This Article demonstrates that the concept of collective rights has antecedents in the philosophical underpinnings of the American state.

30. *See* L. Tribe, *supra* note 8, § 3-22, at 99.

31. Locke can be regarded as the advance ideologist of the American Revolution.

> He developed a set of political ideas which has very largely served as the basis for American political values and for the institutional structure which American and British government has since assumed. His importance for American political thought can hardly be overestimated; indeed, there is probably no better short summary of the ideas of Locke than the American Declaration of Independence.

D. Minar, Ideas and Politics: The American Experience 47 (1964) (footnote omitted); *see also* L. Leder, Liberty and Authority: Early American Political Ideology 1689-1763, at 37-40 (1968).

resides in the majority.[32] To be sure, the colonists were influenced by other political philosophers as well, notably Blackstone, Hume, Montesquieu, Paine, Rousseau, Sidney, and Adam Smith,[33] "[b]ut Locke came nearest to the heart of the case. If an occasional criticism was passed on his [specific proposals], as was done by John Adams, . . . it was only to show how 'the most resplendent genius' may fail in practice."[34]

This is not to say, however, that the Framers accepted his theories completely and without question. In some ways, American political philosophy went beyond Locke's, as for example by its provisions for removal of officials and alteration of the form of government without political revolution.[35] But as a general matter, "the framers established their government in frank Lockean style upon the consent of the governed."[36] The Framers truly rejected only Locke's concept of absolute legislative supremacy over the executive and the courts, creating the "three coequal branches,"[37] which furnish the primary distinction between the American and English systems of government.[38] This distinction is important to the theory of standing presented in this Article. Before turning to the Supreme Court's development of the modern doctrine of standing, however, it is necessary to understand more of the phi-

32. Salvemini, *The Concepts of Democracy and Liberty in the Eighteenth Century*, in THE CONSTITUTION RECONSIDERED 105 (C. Read ed. 1938).

33. MacIver, *European Doctrines and the Constitution*, in THE CONSTITUTION RECONSIDERED, *supra* note 32, at 51, 52; *see also* Salvemini, *supra* note 32, at 105.

34. MacIver, *supra* note 33, at 52 (quoting 4 WORKS OF JOHN ADAMS 463-64 (C. Adams ed. 1865)). The extent of the early American response to that genius is reckoned by MacIver to be nearly universal. "Add to Locke's teaching Montesquieu's more explicit doctrine of division of powers, inject into it some republican fervor, and you have the whole substance of the Virginia Bill of Rights, and indeed all the preambles, manifestoes, and declarations of principle that followed." *Id.* at 53; *see also* E. DUMBAULD, THE DECLARATION OF INDEPENDENCE AND WHAT IT MEANS TODAY 20 (1950); A. RANNEY, THE GOVERNING OF MEN 152, 161-62 (1966).

Locke's influence on the American idea of separation of powers may have been as great as Montesquieu's. Daniel Minar notes that it was Locke's version of the doctrine that "later was to become so integral a part of the American political ideology and procedure." D. MINAR, *supra* note 31, at 52.

35. E. DUMBAULD, *supra* note 34, at 77; *see also infra* notes 70-100 and accompanying text.

36. Gabriel, *Constitutional Democracy: A Nineteenth-Century Faith*, in THE CONSTITUTION RECONSIDERED, *supra* note 32, at 247. Professor Mace notes, "Locke has long been considered the political theorist who exerted the greatest influence upon our natural-rights heritage. . . . Many go so far as to suggest his influence upon the American Founding Fathers was so great that the United States may be termed a Lockean nation." G. MACE, LOCKE, HOBBES, AND THE FEDERALIST PAPERS 9 (1979) (footnote omitted). Professor Mace disagrees with this, however, concluding that Hobbes' influence was more important. *Id.* at xii. The majority view, nevertheless, seems clearly to be on the side of Locke.

37. *See, e.g.*, United States v. Nixon, 418 U.S. 683, 707 (1974); Doe v. McMillan, 412 U.S. 306, 311 n.6 (1973).

38. MacIver, *supra* note 33, at 53.

losophy that so influenced the Framers and then to examine the specific reflections of Locke's ideas in American political thought.

### A. *John Locke's Philosophy*

John Locke is perhaps most commonly associated with the doctrine of government by consent of the governed. Throughout the *Second Treatise*,[39] Locke emphasized that civil government arises only when people remove themselves from the state of nature by combining to form a government.[40]

> Men being . . . all free, equal and independent, no one can be put out of this Estate, and subjected to the Political Power of another, without his own *Consent*. The only way whereby any one devests himself of his Natural Liberty, and *puts on the bonds of Civil Society* is by agreeing with other Men to joyn and unite into a Community, for their comfortable, safe, and peaceable living one amongst another. . . . When any number of Men have so *consented to make one Community* or Government, they are thereby presently incorporated, and make *one Body Politick*, wherein the *Majority* have a Right to act and conclude the rest.[41]

---

39. J. LOCKE, *supra* note 23.

40. "To those that say, There were never any Men in the State of Nature; I will not oppose the Authority . . . . But I moreover affirm, That all Men are naturally in that State, and remain so, till by their own Consents they make themselves Members of some Politick Society . . . ." *Id.* § 15, at 295-96; *see also id.* § 99, at 351, § 102, at 352-53, §§ 104-106, at 354-56, § 171, at 399-400.

41. *Id.* § 95, at 348-49 (emphasis in original). Moreover, because few people entering an established civil society affirmatively consent to its government, and to avoid the illegitimacy that would result from such a mass absence of consent, Locke constructed a theory of tacit consent, struggling to ensure that the theory was neither oppressive nor illusory:

> [E]very Man, that hath any Possession, or Enjoyment, of any part of the Dominions of any Government, doth thereby give his *tacit Consent*, and is as far forth obliged to Obedience to the Laws of that Government, during such Enjoyment, as any one under it; whether this his Possession be of Land, to him and his Heirs for ever, or a Lodging only for a Week; or whether it be barely travelling freely on the Highway; and in Effect, it reaches as far as the very being of any one within the Territories of that Government.

*Id.* § 119, at 365-66 (emphasis in original). Thus, Locke premised the entire existence of government on his theory of consent. Indeed, it has been noted that "[t]here is no point which Locke insisted upon more constantly and more forcefully than that all legitimate governments rest upon the consent of the governed." S. LAMPRECHT, THE MORAL AND POLITICAL PHILOSOPHY OF JOHN LOCKE 136 (1918). But Locke expanded the consent idea by hypothesizing a form of tacit consent embracing virtually all persons not actively engaged in forming the new state.

Students of civil procedure will recognize the genesis of two famous cases in the preceding quotation. Locke clearly foreshadows the declaration in Hanson v. Denckla, 357 U.S. 235 (1958), that, for in personam jurisdiction over the defendant to exist, "it is essential in each case that there be some act by which the defendant purposefully avails itself of the privilege of conducting activities within the forum State, thus invoking the benefits and protections of its laws." *Id.* at 253. And, though perhaps less emphatically, Locke's reliance on free travel upon the highway as a basis for inferring consensual submission to governmental power anticipated Hess v. Pawloski, 274 U.S. 352 (1927):

> [I]n advance of the operation of a motor vehicle on its highway by a non-resident, the State may require him to appoint one of its officials as his agent on whom process may be served in proceedings growing out of such use. . . . [This Court has recognized the] power of the State to exclude a non-resident until the formal appointment is made. And, having the

One reason this part of Locke's theory is so well known is its appearance in the Declaration of Independence.[42] Moreover, the concept is routinely referred to in cases where governmental action is challenged on constitutional grounds.[43] But one cannot properly understand Locke's political theory solely in terms of his idea of government by consent. Indeed, even the consent theory itself cannot be understood in isolation from the rest of the *Second Treatise*. Consent is, of course, the hallmark of a properly governed society. "The unmistakeable sign of civil society having come into being is when every individual has resigned up to the society or the public his individual power to exercise the law of nature and protect his property."[44] But several questions remain: How should the consented-to government exercise its power?[45] More important, what relationship should the government have to those who have consented to its existence, whether explicitly or tacitly?[46]

Government in a Lockean society is the product of a compact among people.[47] Government is, in fact, the creation of such a compact,

> power so to exclude, the State may declare that the use of the highway by the non-resident is the equivalent of the appointment of the registrar as agent on whom process may be served.

*Id.* at 356-57 (citations omitted).

42. *See supra* text accompanying note 3. The doctrine is also well known because it is ancient. *See, e.g.*, PLATO, *Crito*, in THE FOUR SOCRATIC DIALOGUES OF PLATO 112 (B. Jowett trans. 1903).

43. *See, e.g.*, Nevada v. Hall, 440 U.S. 410, 426 (1979); Schlesinger v. Reservists Comm. to Stop the War, 418 U.S. 208, 233 (1974) (Douglas, J., dissenting); Perez v. Brownell, 356 U.S. 44, 64 (1958) (Warren, C.J., dissenting).

44. Laslett, *Introduction* to J. LOCKE, *supra* note 23, at 106.

45. The manner in which a Lockean government is to exercise its power is beyond the scope of this Article. Locke considered this topic extensively in chapters IX through XIII of the *Second Treatise*. J. LOCKE, *supra* note 23, §§ 123-168, at 368-98.

46. Much has been written about Locke's concepts of individual rights and his limitations on the power of government in recognition of those rights. *See, e.g.*, R. LEMOS, HOBBES AND LOCKE: POWER AND CONSENT 103-08 (1978); Laslett, *supra* note 44, at 99-106. Professor Kendall has suggested, however, that Locke is properly viewed as an extreme majority-rule democrat, whose attention to individual rights is, at best, incidental to his main thrust. W. KENDALL, JOHN LOCKE AND THE DOCTRINE OF MAJORITY-RULE (1959). Professor Kendall is not alone in this view. Professor Macpherson suggests that Locke's view of individualism necessarily implies a collective view of society because Locke's political civil society is supreme over the individual.

> The wholesale transfer of individual rights was necessary to get sufficient collective force for the protection of property. Locke could afford to propose this transfer because the civil society was to be in the control of men of property. Under these circumstances individualism must, and could safely, be left to the collective supremacy of the state.

Macpherson, *The Social Bearing of Locke's Political Theory*, in LOCKE AND BERKELEY: A COLLECTION OF CRITICAL ESSAYS 227 (C. Martin & D. Armstrong eds. 1968).

Whether or not the Kendall view of Locke is entirely accurate, it begins to bring into focus the relationship of the people to government as developed in the *Second Treatise*. Each person in the state of nature is entitled to enforce natural law individually. *See* J. LOCKE, *supra* note 23, §§ 6-8, at 288-90, § 13, at 293-94. But in society the enforcement rights and power are collective.

47. *See* J. GOUGH, THE SOCIAL CONTRACT (2d ed. 1957). The idea of government as the product of a compact or contract is echoed in early American history. Jefferson accepted the contract theory as representative of an agreement among the states, *id.* at 236-37, and the contract idea in fact appeared in many state constitutions through the mid-1800's, *id.* at 231. Justice Story saw the

yet it is not a party to the compact. As Professor Laslett points out:

> If a contract is to be set up, or understood, it is necessary that the parties to it should each get something out of it, and applied to politics this would mean that the government got something out of governing which the subjects are bound to give. Now this is what Locke was most anxious to avoid. Although contractually related to each other, the people are not contractually obliged to government, and governors benefit from governing only as fellow members of the "Politick Body." They are merely deputies for the people, trustees who can be discarded if they fail in their trust.[48]

Thus, government may not properly insist upon any rights accruing to it from the people's compact. It is merely a functionary, "defined and limited by the end for which political society is established."[49]

Hence, the nature of the formative process of civil government gives rise to the concept of government-as-trustee—a political trust for the public good in which the people are at once settlors and beneficiaries.[50] Proper understanding of the trusteeship and the manner in which it differs from the social compact that creates civil government is essential to understanding Locke and his importance to modern American concepts of rights against the government and standing to enforce them. Locke distinguished the process of compact, which creates a community, from the further process by which the community entrusts political power to a government. In other words, Locke saw both a "contract of society" and a "contract of government," though for Locke, this second "contract" is not a contract at all—it is a trust.[51]

---

arrangement as an implicit contract between the community as a collective whole and each individual member, wherein the community agreed to protect its citizens on the condition that they obey its laws. *Id.* at 237. In Chisholm v. Georgia, 2 U.S. (2 Dall.) 419, 471 (1793), Chief Justice Jay describes the Constitution as "a compact made by the people of the United States." *See also* Munn v. Illinois, 94 U.S. 113, 124 (1876) (" 'A body politic,' as aptly defined in the preamble of the Constitution of Massachusetts, 'is a social compact by which the whole people covenants with each citizen, and each citizen with the whole people, that all shall be governed by certain laws for the common good.' "); J. LOCKE, *supra* note 23, § 97, at 350, § 99, at 351.

48. Laslett, *supra* note 44, at 113 (citations omitted).

> Although whoever holds legislative power is constitutionally supreme within the limits of the Constitution, they are nevertheless still only the fiduciary agents of the community. As such, they are subject to the supreme power of the community and subject to removal by the community if in its judgment they have violated their trust.

R. LEMOS, *supra* note 46, at 122.

49. Laslett, *supra* note 44, at 111.

50. The concept of government as trustee is not unique to Locke. "[T]he idea of trust was also very common in the seventeenth century, and while it is possible that eighteenth-century writers took it from Locke rather than from other authors, it is clear that it was already a political commonplace before Locke's time." J. GOUGH, JOHN LOCKE'S POLITICAL PHILOSOPHY 156 (2d ed. 1973). In fact, Gough traces the trust idea, at least with respect to the executive, back to the thirteenth century and the reign of Richard II. *Id.* at 165; *see also* Laslett, *supra* note 44, at 112. For a general discussion of the development of trust theory in English political thought, see J. GOUGH, *supra*, at 154-92.

51. *See* Laslett, *supra* note 44, at 112-13.

Several writers suggest that Locke's repeated resort to the trust metaphor[52] should not be taken to connote a trust in a literal or formal sense.[53] Yet it is clear in the *Second Treatise* that he uses the term as more than a synonym for "confidence," and that this heightened use of the trust concept is fully reflective of the political thought of his time.[54] For example, John Milton, having a view of the origins of civil society similar to Locke's, argued that "the power of Kings and Magistrates is nothing else, but what is [only] derivative, transferred and committed to them in trust from the people, to the Common good of them all."[55]

Locke's detailed discussion of trust demonstrates the existence of the trust and the collective nature of its creation. The legislature's supreme power

> is *not*, nor can possibly be absolutely *Arbitrary* over the Lives and Fortunes of the People. For it being but the joynt power of every Member of the Society given up to that Person, or Assembly, which is Legislator, it can be no more than those persons had in a State of Nature before they enter'd into Society, and gave up to the Community.[56]

Locke saw a two-step progression from the state of nature to civil society: first the combination of individuals into society, and second the vesting of power in the legislature as a trust.[57] Because the legislature's power is only derived from "a positive voluntary Grant and Institution" by the people, it cannot be transferred by the legislature to any other hands.[58] Thus, Locke's legislature functions within the trust metaphor.

In emphasizing that the transfer of power from community to legislature is a delegation rather than an alienation, Locke explicitly makes the legislature's power subordinate to the people's "*Supream Power* to remove or *alter the Legislative*, when they find the *Legislative* act contrary to the trust reposed in them."[59] Consequently, the legislature is

52. J. LOCKE, *supra* note 23, §§ 22, 110-111, 134, 136, 139, 142, 149, 155-156, 164, 171, 210, 221-222, 226-227, 231, 239-240, 242.

53. *See, e.g.*, J. GOUGH, *supra* note 47, at 175-78; Laslett, *supra* note 44, at 112.

54. *See infra* notes 56-65 and accompanying text.

55. Milton, *The Tenure of Kings and Magistrates*, in 40 YALE STUDIES IN ENGLISH 12 (A. Cook & W. Allison eds. 1911). Such thought was true in practice as well as in theory. During the trial of Charles I, the prosecutor explicitly presented his case to the court as a breach of trust matter, arguing that by reason of Charles' breach, he was required to answer to his superiors, the people who had established the trust. J. GOUGH, *supra* note 50, at 169 (citing J. MUDDIMAN, THE TRIAL OF CHARLES I (1928)). Gough also notes that the trust theory appeared, in some respects anticipating Locke's theory, in the work of Philip Hunton in 1643, *id.* at 171, and in R. FERGUSON, A BRIEF JUSTIFICATION OF THE PRINCE OF ORANGE'S DESCENT INTO ENGLAND (1689), where the executive powers of the king are described as having been delegated in trust. J. GOUGH, *supra* note 50, at 175. Further, "the accession of James I was soon followed by far-reaching constitutional disputes between king and parliament, in which the trust concept came to be freely used." *Id.* at 176.

56. J. LOCKE, *supra* note 23, § 135, at 375-76 (emphasis in original).

57. *Id.* § 136, at 376-77.

58. *Id.* § 141, at 380-81.

59. *Id.* § 149, at 384-85 (emphasis in original).

responsible to the body politic in a far more direct way than to any individual member of it.[60] The legislative power is explicitly "*limited to the publick good* of the Society,"[61] and it is to the society that the legislature is responsible.[62]

The theory of trust so explicitly applied to the legislative power also affects the executive. For example, the limited power to call the legislature into session is one of trust, to be exercised for the benefit of the people.[63] Moreover, even though the executive may be given certain prerogatives by the legislature to deal with unforeseen circumstances, the prerogatives themselves must be "imployed for the benefit of the Community, and suitably to the trust and ends of the Government."[64]

In all circumstances, therefore, Locke not only views the institution of government as a trust, but also as one created by the collective body of the people and responsible to it. "Locke suggests that the society as trustor assigns to the government as trustee a fund of power to be exercised on behalf of the safety (or pleasure) of the individuals of the community."[65] The obligation created by the trust is one way; the government-as-trustee is obligated to the people, not they to it.

The collective aspect of Lockean society extends even to the point where government ceases to function properly. Perhaps the most important demonstration of the community's collective voice is found in Locke's concept of the right of revolution. The *Second Treatise* discusses dissolution of government at length,[66] and explicitly considers the problem of a populace oppressed by its government.

> But if any one should ask, Must the People then always lay themselves open to the Cruelty and Rage of Tyranny? . . . I Answer: Self-defence is a part of the Law of Nature; nor can it be denied the Community, even against the King himself. . . . This therefore is the Priviledge of the People in general, above what any private Person hath; That particular Men are allowed . . . to have no other Remedy but Patience; but the Body of the People may with Respect resist intolerable Tyranny. . . .[67]

The collective right of revolution may be exercised whenever "tyranny"

60. In this respect, of course, the structure of Locke's political system supports the views of Kendall and Macpherson that Locke is a collective, majoritarian democrat. *See supra* note 46.

Locke's view of the legislature's responsibility to the collective body politic finds its ultimate expression in his right of revolution, discussed *infra* at notes 66-100 and accompanying text.

61. J. LOCKE, *supra* note 23, § 135, at 375-76 (emphasis in original); *see also id.* § 171, at 399-400, § 216, at 427, § 229, at 435.

62. Locke's view of the continuing responsibility of the legislature to the people contrasts sharply with Hobbes' insistence on the absolute rights of the sovereign once created by the social compact. *See* T. HOBBES, LEVIATHAN 113-20 (M. Oakeshott ed. 1960).

63. J. LOCKE, *supra* note 23, § 156, at 389-90.

64. *Id.* § 161, at 393.

65. D. MINAR, *supra* note 31, at 49.

66. J. LOCKE, *supra* note 23, §§ 211-243.

67. *Id.* § 233, at 438-39, (quoting (in translation) W. BARCLAY, DE REGNO ET REGALI POTE-

occurs, that is when government acts beyond purposes specified by the people.[68] Thus, the collective rights that underlie the formation of civil government also give rise to the collective right to dissolve the government when the people's trust is breached.[69]

This treatment of the right of revolution illustrates the pervasive effect that the method used to form a civil society has upon the society's relationship with the government it creates. It also exemplifies a corollary to the theory of trust: government is accountable to the people as a whole. The right of revolution Locke describes is no more than a method by which the accounting may be made; the accountability must be to the group, not to any individual member of it.[70]

### B. *The Influence of John Locke on American Political Thought*

Locke's direct influence on the formation of the new American government is evident in many places. The first statement of American governmental principles is the Declaration of Independence, and here Locke's impact is unmistakable.[71]

> Implicit in the Declaration is the "social compact" theory, that a people is a political organization of persons, who, having theretofore lived in a "state of nature" without being united by any political bonds, associate

STATI ADVERSUS BUCHANANUM, BRUTUM, BOUCHERIUM ET RELIQUOS MONARCHOMACHOS (1600)); *see also* S. LAMPRECHT, *supra* note 41, at 143.

68. J. LOCKE, *supra* note 23, § 199, at 416.

69. The right of revolution, however, was limited by Locke to cases where government had actually breached its trust.

> Locke . . . insisted that government was merely the bearer of executive power on trust for the community. But in Locke's case remnants of the belief in a contract between the community and the government had restricted the right of revolution against the government to occasions when government had betrayed its trust or failed in its proper task.

F. HINSLEY, SOVEREIGNTY 153-54 (1966). Moreover, the right of revolution was not exercisable in response to isolated acts of tyranny; resistance was authorized only when there was a calculated governmental design to subvert the law. J. FRANKLIN, JOHN LOCKE AND THE THEORY OF SOVEREIGNTY 95 (1978). On the other hand, government's failure to comply with the conditions for its existence created not merely a right, but a duty to overthrow the government. *See* R. AARON, JOHN LOCKE 286 (1937); R. LEMOS, *supra* note 46, at 121-22; A. RANNEY, *supra* note 34, at 151.

70. *See* S. LAMPRECHT, *supra* note 41, at 146, where the author notes that under Locke's theory, the majority of the people create the social compact, so only the majority may dissolve it. No minority is ever warranted in disturbing the peace of the community by resisting government. Thus, the right of revolution is designed, in Locke's view, to deal with the situation where government fails to rule within its proper boundaries. Professor Kendall compares the relationship to that of agent and principal.

> The relation between the government of the day in Locke's system and the society from which it derives its powers is, quite simply, assimilable to that between principal and agent in Anglo-American law; and for the government to claim *vis-à-vis* the society for which it acts powers which the society has not entrusted to it *would*, on Locke's showing, be as preposterous as for an agent to claim, *vis-à-vis* his principal, a freedom to do in the latter's name things which the latter does not wish [to be] done.

W. KENDALL, *supra* note 46, at 96 (emphasis in original).

71. *See* E. DUMBAULD, *supra* note 34, at 42; *see also* A. KELLY & W. HARBISON, THE AMERICAN CONSTITUTION: ITS ORIGINS AND DEVELOPMENT 90 (1948).

> themselves together and bind themselves by compact for the purpose of establishing government. It is the voluntary union of individuals that creates the "people" or state for secular political purposes, just as under the Puritan covenant theory it creates the church for religious purposes.[72]

The parallel to Locke's political theory is patent. One finds Locke's ideas, however, even more directly evidenced in the Declaration. "We hold these truths to be self-evident, that all men are created equal"[73] compares with Locke's "Men being, as has been said, by Nature, all free, equal and independent."[74] The Declaration's assertion of the people's right to "Life, Liberty, and the pursuit of Happiness"[75] is traceable to Locke's "Life, Liberty and Estate."[76] "[T]o secure these rights,"[77] referring to the trilogy of "unalienable" rights, reflects Locke's view of the state of nature as understood by Jefferson. Such rights are not "created" but rather are "secured" because they antedate government; they are rights people enjoy even in the state of nature.[78] Finally, the well-known phrase "deriving their just powers from the consent of the governed"[79] corresponds directly to Locke's assertion that "Men are naturally free, and the Examples of History shewing, that the *Governments* of the World, that were begun in Peace, had their beginning laid on that foundation, and were *made by the Consent of the People*."[80] Indeed, Richard Henry Lee of Virginia complained that Jefferson had copied the Declaration from Locke.[81] Locke's influence on Jefferson is certainly not surprising, since Jefferson spoke of Locke as one of the three greatest men of all time[82] and regarded Locke's work as one of the " 'elementary books of public right.' "[83]

Locke's influence did not stop with Jefferson or his Declaration of

72. E. DUMBAULD, *supra* note 34, at 31-32 (footnote omitted).

73. The Declaration of Independence para. 2 (U.S. 1776).

74. J. LOCKE, *supra* note 23, § 95, at 348.

75. The Declaration of Independence para. 2 (U.S. 1776).

76. J. LOCKE, *supra* note 23, § 87, at 341. Moreover, the phrase "pursuit of happiness" is said to appear in Locke's philosophical writings. E. DUMBAULD, *supra* note 34, at 60.

77. The Declaration of Independence para. 2 (U.S. 1776).

78. E. DUMBAULD, *supra* note 34, at 63; *see also* J. LOCKE, *supra* note 23, § 6, at 289.

79. The Declaration of Independence para. 2 (U.S. 1776).

80. J. LOCKE, *supra* note 23, § 104, at 354 (emphasis in original); *see also id.* § 119, at 365-66.

81. E. DUMBAULD, *supra* note 34, at 56. "The Declaration of Independence was almost pure Locke." Elliott, *The Constitution as the American Social Myth*, in THE CONSTITUTION RECONSIDERED, *supra* note 32, at 216. One author is kinder to Jefferson than was Mr. Lee: "[W]e would hardly know of [Jefferson's] familiarity with John Locke's *Two Treatises of Government* if he had not incorporated passages almost word for word in the Declaration of Independence, apparently unaware that he was doing so." E. MORGAN, AMERICAN SLAVERY, AMERICAN FREEDOM: THE ORDEAL OF COLONIAL VIRGINIA 375 (1975).

82. MacIver, *supra* note 33, at 52. The other two were Newton and Bacon. *Id.*

83. C. WILTSE, THE JEFFERSONIAN TRADITION IN AMERICAN DEMOCRACY 46 (1935) (quoting WRITINGS, XVI, 118-19 (May 8, 1825) (Thomas Jefferson to Henry Lee)).

Independence. Historian Clinton Rossiter notes that Samuel Adams can properly be regarded as an intellectual descendant of Locke,[84] and Locke's concept of the state of nature is implicit in Benjamin Franklin's views of the American Indians.[85] Moreover, "[i]n his natural-rights assumptions, his moderation, and his reasonableness, Locke was an intellectual godparent of James Madison, the Father of the Constitution."[86] Indeed, the builders of the American government routinely referred to Locke's writings with respect and reverence.[87]

Locke's flavor is found as well in documents other than the Declaration of Independence. His ideas were adopted by a 1774 resolution of the North Carolina Assembly asserting that governmental invasion of liberties was justification for revolution.[88] Locke's philosophy on revolution may well have contributed to the first amendment's provision of the right to petition for redress of grievances.[89] And while Locke's famous trilogy of life, liberty and estate[90] became transmuted to the more popularly known life, liberty and the pursuit of happiness in 1776,[91] it reappeared substantially in its original form in the fifth and fourteenth amendments.[92] Nor was Locke's influence limited to these three amendments. "The blended traditions of Coke and Locke were conveyed into the incipient stream of American constitutional law by the bills of rights of the early State constitutions and by judicial review, which soon after 1800 became a feature of all of them."[93] For example, Professor Elliott traces American constitutional structure directly to Locke, either as an intentional imitation or as a partial reaction to Locke's emphasis on majority rule.[94] Elliott notes that Locke drew directly from the Magna Carta,

---

84. C. Rossiter, 1787: The Grand Convention 68 (1966). But Adams went beyond Locke—he rejected the possibility of tacit consent to government by the governed, insisting instead that consent be explicit. MacIver, *supra* note 33, at 54.

85. MacIver, *supra* note 33, at 52.

86. L. McDonald, Western Political Theory, Part 2: From Machiavelli to Burke 326 (1968). Locke's theory of government was reflected in other colonial thought as well, notably the works of James Otis and John Dickenson. *See* D. Minar, *supra* note 31, at 72-76.

87. C. Becker, The Declaration of Independence 75-76 (1942). One even finds reference to the works of Locke as the subjects of specific testamentary bequests, as was done, for example, by Josiah Quincy in 1774. *Id.*

88. E. Dumbauld, *supra* note 34, at 104.

89. *See* U.S. Const. amend. I; E. Dumbauld, *supra* note 34, at 104-05.

90. J. Locke, *supra* note 23, § 87, at 341.

91. A. Kelly & W. Harbison, *supra* note 71, at 90; *see also* Elliott, *supra* note 81, at 216.

92. U.S. Const. amends. V, XIV. Actually, Locke's original form was reflected earlier in American thought. "The first resolution of the Declaration [of Rights published by Congress in 1774 was] an echo of John Locke [in providing that] all men are entitled to life, liberty, and property, and that they cannot be deprived of these rights without their consent." R. Rutland, The Birth of the Bill of Rights 1776-1791, at 27 (1955).

93. E. Corwin, Liberty Against Government 172 (1948). Professor Minar sees Locke's natural rights philosophy carried through the Declaration of Independence into its "most effective operational form in the American Bill of Rights." D. Minar, *supra* note 31, at 51.

94. *See* Elliott, *supra* note 81, at 217-18; *cf.* W. Kendall, *supra* note 46.

which the colonists used to justify the American revolution. Moreover, he traces the text of sections nine and ten of article I and all of the Bill of Rights directly to Locke's influence. Thus, the Constitution, as well as the Declaration of Independence, is traceable to Locke's natural rights philosophy—the concept that some rights cannot be alienated by individuals in forming a government. The Bill of Rights "built upon the ideas of that English philosopher whose pioneering work first grappled with the fundamentals of society in terms of the balancing of freedom and rights—John Locke."[95]

Wholly apart from Locke's traceable influence on particular documents, American society adopted Locke's view of the relationships between governed and government and among the governed themselves. Locke's contract analogy was used by eighteenth-century citizens to explain these relationships,[96] and the system of American government reflects Locke's concept of government as the product of a contract among people rather than between rulers and ruled.[97] Americans espoused a natural rights philosophy, which became the foundation of the American political system. "They endorsed the Lockean theory of a state of nature, inalienable natural rights, a social compact, a society rooted in popular sovereignty, the consent of the governed, and the right of revolution under conditions of intolerable oppression."[98]

The American political system has, however, modified Locke's model by developing two methods of governmental accountability other than revolution: the elective process and judicial review.[99] The electoral process allows the people to replace those exercising government's power when the people believe government action is unwise. The judicial process is explicitly reserved to correct governmental actions perceived to be unlawful.[100] Thus, when government violates the basic statements of

95. Shotwell, *Freedom—Its History and Meaning*, in FREEDOM: ITS MEANING 12-13 (R. Anshen ed. 1940).

96. G. WOOD, THE CREATION OF THE AMERICAN REPUBLIC 1776-1787, at 289 (1969).

97. *Id.* at 601; *see also supra* notes 46-49 and accompanying text.

98. N. RIEMER, THE DEMOCRATIC EXPERIMENT 101 (1967).

99. Locke himself emphasized that resort to extra-legal force was not justified so long as recourse to law remained. *See* P. MAIER, FROM RESISTANCE TO REVOLUTION: COLONIAL RADICALS AND THE DEVELOPMENT OF AMERICAN OPPOSITION TO BRITAIN, 1765-1776, at 32 (1972).

100. In fact, the courts explicitly refuse to consider whether governmental acts are wise or unwise. *See, e.g.*, South Carolina State Highway Dep't v. Barnwell Bros., 303 U.S. 177, 189-92 (1938); Village of Euclid v. Ambler Realty Co., 272 U.S. 365, 395 (1926); Jacobson v. Massachusetts, 197 U.S. 11, 30-31 (1905).

The Constitution "incorporated an instrument which was to reduce the supreme legislature of Locke's thinking (and Jefferson's) to the 'creature of the Constitution.' That instrument was, of course, the Supreme Court . . . through which the doctrine of judicial review developed." Elliott, *supra* note 81, at 218. The remaining question, however, concerns who shall speak for the collective society in the courts when government acts outside of its powers but not so far as to make revolution appropriate. That question will be considered *infra* in Parts II and III.

constitutional principle, the structure of the modified Lockean society suggests resort to the courts. In cases where government abuses cannot be corrected by resort to the polls, the right to government accountability can only be safeguarded by the courts. The next part of this Article, therefore, considers the Supreme Court's approach to the right of people to challenge unconstitutional government action, a concept dealt with in large part under the rubric of standing.

## II
## THE CURRENT DOCTRINE OF STANDING IN PUBLIC ACTIONS

In recent standing cases,[101] the Supreme Court has struggled to develop standards to determine which issues are appropriate for judicial resolution. Determining whether a particular matter is fit for judicial resolution embraces more than the doctrine of standing to be discussed here; it truly concerns the broader concept of justiciability. In *Flast v. Cohen*,[102] the Court noted:

> [T]he judicial power of federal courts is constitutionally restricted to "cases" and "controversies." . . . Embodied in the words "cases" and "controversies" are two complementary but somewhat different limitations. In part those words limit the business of federal courts to questions presented in an adversary context and in a form historically viewed as capable of resolution through the judicial process. And in part those words define the role assigned to the judiciary in a tripartite allocation of power to assure that the federal courts will not intrude into areas committed to the other branches of government. Justiciability is the term of art employed to give expression to this dual limitation placed upon federal courts by the case-and-controversy doctrine.[103]

Standing, like the judicial doctrines concerning political questions, advisory opinions, and mootness, was created to limit judicial power to cases in which adversarial presentation is possible and legislative or executive prerogatives are not infringed.[104] The exact contours of these doctrines limiting justiciability, however, are by no means clear;[105] they involve "a blend of constitutional requirements and policy considerations."[106]

Standing concerns whether the party seeking to invoke the judicial

101. For purposes of this Article, "recent" refers to cases beginning with Flast v. Cohen, 392 U.S. 83 (1968), after which, this Article suggests, the problems with traditional standing began to appear forcefully.

102. 392 U.S. 83 (1968).

103. *Id.* at 94-95.

104. *Id.* at 95.

105. *Id.*

106. *Id.* at 97; *see also supra* notes 11-18 and accompanying text.

power is the appropriate party to do so. "The fundamental aspect of standing is that it focuses on the party seeking to get his complaint before a federal court and not on the issues he wishes to have adjudicated."[107] Doctrines other than standing focus on the issues. Thus, though a plaintiff may have standing, the courts may decline to adjudicate his case because it raises a political question or is moot.[108] Conversely, the courts may refuse to adjudicate otherwise justiciable matters on the ground that the plaintiff lacks standing.[109] This Part will focus on the latter category of cases. Many of the cases falling into this category present the troubling prospect of issues that are, or should be, justiciable but for which no potential plaintiff exists. This Part will also compare these cases with contemporaneous cases in which plaintiffs were found to have standing to determine whether there are principled differences between the two groups.

### A. *Denials of Standing*

#### 1. *The Early 1970's*

In *Sierra Club v. Morton*,[110] the Supreme Court considered an environmental protection suit brought by the Sierra Club against the Secretary of the Interior challenging the proposed development and use of certain federal lands. While the Court found that aesthetic injury was sufficient injury-in-fact to confer standing,[111] it nonetheless dismissed the action for lack of standing because the Sierra Club, apparently for tactical reasons, chose not to allege harm to specific club members or individuals.[112] The Court required the party seeking standing to allege "more

107. *Flast*, 392 U.S. at 99; *see also* Sierra Club v. Morton, 405 U.S. 727, 731-32 (1972).

108. *See, e.g.*, DeFunis v. Odegaard, 416 U.S. 312 (1974) (declaring the controversy moot despite plaintiff's standing); Colegrove v. Green, 328 U.S. 549 (1946) (political question); Pacific States Tel. & Tel. Co. v. Oregon, 223 U.S. 118 (1912) (political question).

109. *See, e.g.*, Sierra Club v. Morton, 405 U.S. 727 (1972), discussed *infra* in notes 110-16 and accompanying text.

110. 405 U.S. 727 (1972).

111. *Id.* at 734. The Court treated the case as one of first impression, noting that its prior cases did not address "the question, which has arisen with increasing frequency in federal courts in recent years, as to what must be alleged by persons who claim injury of a noneconomic nature to interests that are widely shared." *Id.*

112. Thus, it is possible to read *Sierra Club* narrowly as a case involving a defect in pleading rather than announcing any new ideas about standing. While as a technical matter this may be correct, such a reading ignores what was truly going on in *Sierra Club*. Certainly a broad reading of the complaint, as encouraged by FED. R. CIV. P. 8(f), *see, e.g.*, Conley v. Gibson, 355 U.S. 41 (1957); United States v. White County Bridge Comm'n, 275 F.2d 529 (7th Cir.), *cert. denied*, 364 U.S. 818 (1960), would have permitted the inference that the required individualized injury existed, particularly in light of one paragraph of the complaint, which the Court felt compelled to quote before disregarding.

> "Plaintiff Sierra Club is a non-profit corporation . . . [with] approximately 78,000 [members] nationally . . . . For many years the Sierra Club by its activities and conduct has exhibited a special interest in the conservation and the sound maintenance of the national

than an injury to a cognizable interest . . . . [T]he party seeking review [must] be himself among the injured."[113] Although the Court recognized the public interest aspect of the Sierra Club's complaint,[114] it was unwilling to recognize such a "public action" unless the public's representative—the plaintiff—alleged personal harm.[115] In so holding, the Court made it clear that the concept of a plaintiff acting as the public's representative might still be viable, but not in the absence of some allegation of individual injury to the would-be representative.[116]

In 1973, the Court turned its attention from injury-in-fact and expanded the scope of the nexus test in *Linda R.S. v. Richard D.*[117] There, the mother of an illegitimate child challenged Texas' practice of refusing to enforce its penal statute addressing nonsupport of children against parents of illegitimate children. The plaintiff asserted that the state's practice denied her child equal protection. The Court affirmed the district court's dismissal of the case on standing grounds. Justice Marshall, writing for the majority, readily conceded that the plaintiff had satisfied the injury-in-fact requirement, but held that she had failed to satisfy the

> parks, game refuges and forests of the country, regularly serving as a responsible representative of persons similarly interested. One of the principal purposes of Sierra Club is to protect and conserve the national resources of the Sierra Nevada Mountains. Its interests would be vitally affected by the acts hereinafter described and would be aggrieved by those acts of the defendants as hereinafter more fully appears."

*Sierra Club*, 405 U.S. at 735 n.8 (quoting complaint at ¶ 3). At the same time, the Court specifically noted the possibility of the Sierra Club amending its complaint after remand to the district court. *Id.* at 736 n.8. Professor Nichol observes that the same sort of inversion of the normal pleading rules can be seen in Simon v. Eastern Ky. Welfare Rights Org., 426 U.S. 26 (1976), and Warth v. Seldin, 422 U.S. 490 (1975). Nichol, *supra* note 27, at 72 n.25. *Simon* and *Warth* are discussed *infra* in notes 159-78 and accompanying text.

Justice White is reported to have been especially exasperated with plaintiffs' failure or refusal to prepare themselves to meet the standing question. " 'Why didn't the Sierra Club have one goddamn member walk through the park and then there would have been standing to sue,' White remarked, before joining the four-member majority." B. WOODWARD & S. ARMSTRONG, THE BRETHREN 164 n.* (1979).

113. *Sierra Club*, 405 U.S. at 734-35.

114. *Id.* at 736-37.

115. The Court also noted, *id.* at 736 n.9, with apparent disapproval that the Second Circuit had recognized representative standing of the type asserted by the Sierra Club in Citizens Comm. for the Hudson Valley v. Volpe, 425 F.2d 97, 105 (2d Cir.), *cert. denied*, 400 U.S. 949 (1970).

116. The Court's reliance upon the injury-in-fact test reflected earlier standing decisions, notably Baker v. Carr, 369 U.S. 186 (1962), and Flast v. Cohen, 392 U.S. 83 (1968). *Flast*, in fact, sets out what is now taken as the basic framework of standing inquiry by delineating the two-part test for standing. *See supra* notes 10-17 and accompanying text. The Court insisted on an allegation of individual injury even though it favorably noted the emerging trend toward recognition of noneconomic injuries as appropriate predicates for standing.

> [T]he interest alleged to have been injured "may reflect 'aesthetic, conservational, and recreational' as well as economic values." But broadening the categories of injury that may be alleged in support of standing is a different matter from abandoning the requirement that the party seeking review must himself have suffered an injury.

*Sierra Club*, 405 U.S. at 738 (quoting Association of Data Processing Serv. Orgs. v. Camp, 397 U.S. 150, 154 (1970)).

117. 410 U.S. 614 (1973).

nexus test.[118] Specifically, the Court found that the plaintiff had not demonstrated either that the absence of support payments resulted from nonenforcement of the penal law section, or that enforcement, if ordered, would cause support payments to begin.[119] Thus, the majority was not satisfied that the plaintiff's injury resulted from violation of the constitutional right on which she based her complaint.

The Court next denied standing in *United States v. Richardson*[120] and *Schlesinger v. Reservists Committee to Stop the War.*[121] In *Richardson*, a taxpayer sought to have the Central Intelligence Agency Act[122] declared unconstitutional because it allegedly permitted a type of accounting for funds inconsistent with the requirements of the accountability clause.[123] The Court, in a five-to-four decision, ruled that Richardson had no standing.[124] Although the plaintiff sued as a taxpayer, he failed the nexus test[125] because his attack on the CIA's practice was not based on the taxing and spending power.[126] The Court, therefore, found that Richardson was "seeking 'to employ a federal court as a forum in which to air his generalized grievances about the conduct of government.' "[127]

The majority did not rest on the nexus ground alone; it went on to

---

118. *Flast*, 392 U.S. 83 (1968); *see supra* notes 9-17 and accompanying text.

119. *Linda R.S.*, 410 U.S. at 618. Justice White took issue with the majority's lack of faith in the salutary effect of threatened penal sanctions.

> I had always thought our civilization has assumed that the threat of penal sanctions had something more than a "speculative" effect on a person's conduct . . . . Certainly Texas does not share the Court's surprisingly novel view. It assumes that criminal sanctions are useful in coercing fathers to fulfill their support obligations to their legitimate children.

*Id.* at 621 (White, J., dissenting).

120. 418 U.S. 166 (1974).

121. 418 U.S. 208 (1974).

122. 50 U.S.C. §§ 403a-403j (1976 & Supp. V 1981).

123. U.S. CONST. art. I, § 9, cl. 7: "No Money shall be drawn from the Treasury, but in Consequence of Appropriations made by Law; and a regular Statement and Account of the Receipts and Expenditures of all public Money shall be published from time to time."

Before suing, Richardson had sought copies of the CIA's financial statements from the Government Printing Office, which referred his request to the Fiscal Service of the Bureau of Accounts of the Department of the Treasury. That office provided him some general records of expenditures, but reported that it had no information specifically relating to CIA expenditures. Richardson thereupon asked the Treasury Department to seek the Attorney General's opinion of the constitutionality of the CIA Act, and only upon the Department's refusal to do so was the action commenced. *Richardson*, 418 U.S. at 168.

124. The district court had dismissed the case for lack of standing, but the Third Circuit, sitting en banc, reversed with three judges dissenting. Of the majority in that court, three judges found that Richardson had taxpayer standing under Flast v. Cohen, 392 U.S. 83 (1968); and one judge found that he had citizen standing. Richardson v. United States, 465 F.2d 844 (3d Cir. 1972) (en banc), *rev'd*, 418 U.S. 166 (1974).

125. *See supra* notes 9-17 and accompanying text.

126. *Richardson*, 418 U.S. at 175; *see* U.S. CONST. art. I, § 8, cl. 1.

127. *Richardson*, 418 U.S. at 175 (quoting Flast v. Cohen, 392 U.S. 83, 106 (1968)).

explain that Richardson could not demonstrate injury-in-fact from the challenged practice.

> "It is an established principle that to entitle a private individual to invoke the judicial power to determine the validity of executive or legislative action he must show that he *has sustained or is immediately in danger of sustaining a direct injury* as the result of that action and it is not sufficient that he has merely a general interest common to all members of the public."[128]

The Court declined to recognize Richardson's interest as differentiable from that of any other member of the public. If there was any injury, the Court refused to find that Richardson was harmed more than anyone else.[129] Thus, the majority found that Richardson failed to satisfy any part of the test for standing. In this respect, *Richardson* echoed the insistence of *Sierra Club* that the plaintiff must plead and be prepared to prove injury to himself as an individual, obviously an impossibility in the sort of case Richardson brought. At the same time, the Court purported not to leave Richardson remediless. "In a very real sense," the Court held, "the absence of any particular individual or class to litigate these claims gives support to the argument that the subject matter is committed to the surveillance of Congress, and ultimately to the political process."[130] The plaintiff, therefore, was admonished to take his case to the ballot box,[131] an idea repeated in *Schlesinger v. Reservists Committee to Stop the War*.[132]

In *Schlesinger*, several members and former members of military reserve units who were opposed to the war in Viet Nam challenged the constitutionality of members of Congress holding commissions in the military reserves.[133] In an analysis similar to that in *Richardson*, a six-to-

128. *Id.* at 177-78 (quoting *Ex parte* Levitt, 302 U.S. 633, 634 (1937) (per curiam) (emphasis supplied by the *Richardson* Court)).

129. The Court relied explicitly on *Ex parte* Levitt, 302 U.S. 633 (1937). Levitt, a member of the Supreme Court Bar, challenged Justice Black's elevation to the bench on the ground that Justices' retirement benefits had been increased while Justice Black served as Senator from Alabama, and that his appointment therefore violated the ineligibility clause. U.S. CONST. art. I, § 6, cl. 2: "No Senator or Representative shall, during the Time for which he was elected, be appointed to any civil Office under the Authority of the United States, . . . the Emoluments whereof shall have been encreased during such time . . . ." The Court, per curiam, found Levitt without standing and declined to consider the matter further.

130. *Richardson*, 418 U.S. at 179.

131. There are several problems with the Court's suggested political substitute for judicial intervention. *See infra* notes 307-27 and accompanying text.

132. 418 U.S. 208, 227 (1974): "Our system of government leaves many crucial decisions to the political processes."

133. Specifically, the plaintiffs sought a declaration that a Congressman's membership in the reserves violated the incompatibility clause, U.S. CONST. art. I, § 6, cl. 2 ("[N]o Person holding any Office under the United States, shall be a Member of either House during his Continuance in Office"). In addition, the plaintiffs sought an injunction barring the Secretary of Defense from enrolling any member of Congress in the reserves and directing the Secretary to strike from the reserve rolls

three Court[134] found that the plaintiffs lacked standing. The majority affirmed the district court's finding that plaintiffs lacked standing as taxpayers,[135] but overturned its conclusion that they had standing as citizens.[136]

The Court focused upon the plaintiffs' inability to demonstrate any injury-in-fact or any individual interest differentiable from that of the citizenry generally.[137] The majority noted that recent cases had broadened standing by expanding the concept of judicially cognizable injury,[138] but declined to regard that trend as an abandonment of the injury-in-fact test.[139] " 'Abstract injury is not enough.' "[140] The Court concluded by discussing the policy reasons for refusing to recognize citizen standing:

> All citizens, of course, share equally an interest in the independence of each branch of Government. In some fashion, every provision of the Constitution was meant to serve the interests of all. Such a generalized interest, however, is too abstract to constitute a "case or controversy" appropriate for judicial resolution. The proposition that all constitutional provisions are enforceable by any citizen simply because citizens are the ultimate beneficiaries of those provisions has no boundaries.[141]

Therefore, as in *Richardson*, the Court found the political process was

---

any member of Congress then enrolled, to discharge any Reservist subsequently elected to Congress, and to recover any pay given to members of Congress as Reservists. *Schlesinger*, 418 U.S. at 211.

134. Justice Stewart moved from the dissent in *Richardson* into the majority in *Schlesinger*, explaining in the latter that the plaintiffs had failed to allege that the defendants had refused to perform an affirmative duty under the Constitution and that, in such circumstances, none of the petitioners could demonstrate injury-in-fact. *Schlesinger*, 418 U.S. at 228-29 (Stewart, J., concurring).

135. *Id.* at 215-16. The plaintiffs had asserted four bases for standing in the district court: as persons opposed to the United States' involvement in Viet Nam; as officers and enlisted personnel of the reserves who were not members of Congress; as taxpayers; and as citizens. The district court upheld standing only on the citizen theory. *See* Reservists Comm. to Stop the War v. Laird, 323 F. Supp. 833 (D.D.C. 1971), *aff'd mem.*, 495 F.2d 1075 (D.C. Cir. 1972), *rev'd sub nom.* Schlesinger v. Reservists Comm. to Stop the War, 418 U.S. 208 (1974).

136. *Schlesinger*, 418 U.S. at 224.

137. *Id.* at 217. The Court noted that this sort of generalized grievance had been rejected as a basis for taxpayer standing. *Id.* (citing Flast v. Cohen, 392 U.S. 83 (1968)). The Court has never explained why the fact that all citizens might wish to challenge governmental conduct inconsistent with the Constitution logically suggests a finding of no standing.

138. *Id.* at 218 (citing Association of Data Processing Serv. Orgs., Inc. v. Camp, 397 U.S. 150, 154 (1970)).

139. *Id.* at 218-19 (citing Sierra Club v. Morton, 405 U.S. 727, 738 (1972)).

140. *Id.* at 219 (quoting O'Shea v. Littleton, 414 U.S. 488, 494 (1974)). The Court also regarded *Ex parte* Levitt, 302 U.S. 633 (1937), as long-standing authority for this proposition. *See supra* note 129.

141. *Schlesinger*, 418 U.S. at 226-27 (footnote omitted). This Article suggests that citizen standing is appropriate in cases like *Schlesinger* and proposes a theory of standing that does have boundaries. *See infra* Part III, Section C.

the appropriate remedy.[142]

The *Richardson* dissenters were quick to note the implications of the Court's ruling. Justice Stewart, joined by Justice Marshall, argued that Richardson was a typical Hohfeldian plaintiff, seeking to exercise his right to receive information and to compel the government to fulfill its corresponding duty to supply it.[143] Indeed, Justice Stewart pointed out that if the government had owed Richardson money rather than information, no one would have questioned his standing. "I see no reason for a different result when the defendant is a Government official and the asserted duty relates not to the payment of money, but to the disclosure of items of information."[144] Justice Stewart, therefore, would have found that whenever government owes an affirmative duty under the Constitution, injury-in-fact is established by the nonperformance of that duty.

Justice Douglas, dissenting in *Schlesinger*, would also have found standing based on both citizenship and taxpayer status.[145] Referring to the injury-in-fact requirement, he noted:

> We have insisted that more than generalized grievances of a citizen be shown, that he must have a "personal stake in the outcome." . . . But that "personal stake" need not be a monetary one. In *Baker v. Carr* it was the right to vote, an important badge of citizenship. The "personal stake" in the present case is keeping the Incompatibility Clause an operative force in the Government by freeing the entanglement of the federal bureaucracy with the Legislative Branch.[146]

Justice Douglas, therefore, would have held each citizen's interest in the proper operation of government—an interest that the *Schlesinger* majority regarded as too abstract to be judicially cognizable—sufficient to support standing.[147]

Justice Marshall also would have found citizen standing in *Schlesinger*. Marshall noted that the incompatibility clause was intended

142. *See supra* notes 130-32 and accompanying text. *But see infra* notes 307-27 and accompanying text.

143. United States v. Richardson, 418 U.S. 166, 203 n.2 (1974) (Stewart, J., dissenting) (citing Hohfeld, *Some Fundamental Legal Conceptions as Applied in Judicial Reasoning*, 23 YALE L.J. 15 (1913) and Jaffe, *The Citizen as Litigant in Public Actions: The Hohfeldian or Ideological Plaintiff*, 116 U. PA. L. REV. 1033 (1968)). For Hohfeld, a plaintiff could bring suit only if he was vindicating a right for which there was a correlative duty *owed* him by the defendant.

144. *Id.* at 203 (Stewart, J., dissenting).

145. Schlesinger v. Reservists Comm. to Stop the War, 418 U.S. 208, 232 (1974) (Douglas, J., dissenting).

146. *Id.* at 234 (Douglas, J., dissenting) (quoting Baker v. Carr, 369 U.S. 186, 204 (1962)).

147. Justice Douglas distinguished *Ex parte* Levitt, 302 U.S. 633 (1937), the case challenging Justice Black's appointment to the bench, *see supra* note 129, on the ground that standing had been denied there because the injury claimed under the incompatibility clause was too speculative, since it involved retirement benefits that might never accrue rather than salary. He noted that Justice Black never received any retirement benefits. *Schlesinger*, 418 U.S. at 234-35 (Douglas, J., dissenting). Whether this distinction is persuasive is left to the reader.

to avoid conflicts of interest.[148] In his view, the plaintiffs' complaint did not necessarily reflect the interests of all citizens in having government abide by the Constitution. Rather, the complaint concerned the plaintiffs' first amendment right to petition the government for redress of grievances and to have a government free of conflicts of interest when it considered such petitions.[149] Thus, Marshall found injury-in-fact to be a specific constitutional right and distinguished this injury from the abstract complaint that the majority found to be insufficient to sustain standing.

Justice Brennan, in a dissent addressed to both *Schlesinger* and *Richardson*,[150] would have found standing in each. As to *Richardson*, Justice Brennan argued that injury-in-fact was established because Richardson had a personal right to receive the budget information concerning the CIA.[151] And in *Schlesinger*, he would have found injury-in-fact by reason of plaintiffs' taxpayer status.[152]

Addressing the nexus requirement, Justice Brennan argued that it was not properly a part of standing analysis:

> The Court's further inquiry, in each of these cases, into the connection between "the zone of interests to be protected or regulated by the statute or constitutional guarantee in question," . . . and the "interest sought to be protected by the complainant," . . . is relevant, not to "standing" but, if at all, only to such limitations on exercise of the judicial function as justiciability . . . or reviewability. . . .[153]

Justice Brennan thus viewed injury-in-fact as the only test for standing.

Thus, although a substantial minority of the Court had articulated preferences for a broader concept of standing in public actions, by the mid-1970's the Court had developed two distinct approaches using standing to restrict access to the courts. The first, exemplified by *Sierra Club v. Morton*[154] and *Schlesinger v. Reservists Committee to Stop the War*,[155] focused upon a plaintiff's failure or inability to plead sufficient injury-in-fact distinguishable from some generalized loss suffered by the public at large. The second, exemplified by *United States v. Richardson*,[156] denied

148. *Schlesinger*, 418 U.S. at 239 (Marshall, J., dissenting).

149. *Id.* at 239-40 (Marshall, J., dissenting).

150. *Id.* at 235 (Brennan, J., dissenting).

151. *Id.* at 236 (Brennan, J., dissenting). Thus, Justice Brennan agreed with Justice Stewart. *See supra* notes 143-44 and accompanying text.

152. *Schlesinger*, 418 U.S. at 236-37 (Brennan, J., dissenting). For that reason he declined to discuss whether the majority-rejected concept of citizen standing was appropriate. *Id.* at 237 (Brennan, J., dissenting).

153. *Id.* at 236 (Brennan, J., dissenting) (citations omitted). Justice Brennan did not indicate when he abandoned the *Flast* nexus requirement. In *Flast*, he had joined the Court's opinion. *See* Flast v. Cohen, 392 U.S. 83 (1968).

154. 405 U.S. 727 (1972); *see supra* notes 110-16 and accompanying text.

155. 418 U.S. 208 (1974); *see supra* notes 133-42 and accompanying text.

156. 418 U.S. 166 (1974); *see supra* notes 120-32 and accompanying text.

standing because the plaintiff failed to show a sufficient nexus between the harm he suffered and the constitutional right under which protection was claimed.[157] The distinction between these two approaches is important. By the Court's own analysis, a finding of no injury-in-fact is a constitutional bar to federal court jurisdiction, whereas failure to meet the nexus requirement establishes only a prudential impediment to federal court action.[158] The cases of the early 1970's focused far more on the first approach, a constitutional test that bodes ill for broader concepts of standing.

### 2. *Standing in the Mid-1970's*

In *Warth v. Seldin*,[159] the Court employed both the injury-in-fact and nexus tests, but it did so more restrictively than in *Sierra Club* or *Richardson*. *Warth* was brought by a kaleidoscope of plaintiffs[160] challenging a suburban zoning ordinance on the ground that it was tailored to exclude low- and moderate-income persons in violation of the Civil Rights Acts of 1870 and 1871.[161] A bitterly divided Court held that none of the plaintiffs had standing. With respect to the low-income plaintiffs, the Court noted that although they had pleaded deliberate exclusion of low-income racial and ethnic minority groups by the zoning ordinance, the plaintiffs had not pleaded that they had been personally excluded. The Court held that the complaint, therefore, failed to plead the individual injury required under the Constitution to confer standing.[162] The individual plaintiffs in *Warth* had pleaded injury to the group

157. *Richardson*, of course, involved both approaches; the Court found that the plaintiff had satisfied neither the injury-in-fact test nor the nexus test. *See supra* notes 120-29 and accompanying text.

158. *See supra* notes 9-15 and accompanying text. Thus, in cases where the Court finds no injury-in-fact, one must either take issue with the Court's definition and application of that term or dispute the theory that the injury-in-fact requirement is based on article III's case and controversy language and is therefore jurisdictional. This Article urges the first of these two approaches. *See infra* Part III. The nexus requirement, by contrast, may be opposed either, as Professor Tribe has done, on the ground that it serves to deny standing when a decision on the merits would be preferable, *see supra* notes 19-20 and accompanying text, or on other nonconstitutional grounds, *see infra* Part III, Section *A*.

159. 422 U.S. 490 (1975).

160. The plaintiff group included low-income individuals desiring to move to the suburb; urban taxpayers claiming that their taxes were higher because the zoning ordinance caused the city to have more low-income residents in need of municipal services; a not-for-profit corporation formed to foster low-income housing opportunities; and several builders and housing associations who asserted an interest in creation of low-income housing in the suburb. *Id.* at 493-97, 503.

161. *Id.* at 493; *see* Civil Rights Acts of 1870 and 1871, 42 U.S.C. §§ 1981-1983 (1982).

162. *Warth*, 422 U.S. at 502-05. The *Warth* plaintiffs had sued as representatives of a class, *id.* at 493 n.1, which presumably encompassed individuals who had been excluded. The Court, however, found that the absence of personal injury to the named individuals precluded them from relying upon injury to others, *id.* at 502-05 (citing O'Shea v. Littleton, 414 U.S. 488 (1974) and Bailey v.

of which they were members, unlike the plaintiff in *Sierra Club*,[163] but the Court still found the pleading insufficient because the plaintiffs had not pleaded injury traceable to particular individuals. *Warth*, therefore, seemed to deny standing in a situation in which the *Sierra Club* Court apparently would not have. The Court, though recognizing that the de-

Patterson, 369 U.S. 31 (1962)), and thus implicitly held that such plaintiffs would not satisfy the typicality requirement of FED. R. CIV. P. 23(a).

During the 1970's and early 1980's, the Court developed a variation on the *Sierra Club* and *Warth* theme of inability to show personal injury. Under the variation, the Court looked to the likelihood of future personal injury in cases where the plaintiff sought injunctive, as opposed to legal, relief. For example, in City of Los Angeles v. Lyons, 461 U.S. 95 (1983), the plaintiff had been stopped for a traffic violation. He asserted that though he had not resisted, he had been choked by the arresting officer, causing him to lose consciousness and to suffer damage to his larynx. *Id.* at 97-98. Evidence showed that Los Angeles police officers were trained in the use of two types of chokehold, *id.* at 97 n.1, that the officers were permitted to use chokeholds even when they were not threatened with injury or resistance, *id.* at 99, and that 16 persons had died from chokeholds applied by Los Angeles police officers. *Id.* at 115-16 (Marshall, J., dissenting).

The plaintiff sought damages and an injunction against future police use of such chokeholds. The Court held that the federal courts could not grant equitable relief because Lyons was unable to show any likelihood that *he* would be choked again, and therefore had not shown injury-in-fact. *Id.* at 105-06. Thus, the Court made clear that unless the government were to establish an unconstitutional policy in terms general enough to apply with certainty to any plaintiff, injunctive relief would never be available because a plaintiff would be unable to show a sufficient likelihood of future harm to *him*, even though it might be obvious that such harm would occur to large numbers of people. *See id.* This result, according to the majority, was not new doctrine; it merely reflected the Court's earlier decisions in Rizzo v. Goode, 423 U.S. 362 (1976), and O'Shea v. Littleton, 414 U.S. 488 (1974), both of which involved challenges to official practices alleged to be unconstitutional and racially motivated. *See Lyons*, 461 U.S. at 102-05.

Justice Marshall, joined in dissent by Justices Brennan, Blackmun and Stevens, charged that the majority's reliance upon *O'Shea* and *Rizzo* was misplaced because neither case had involved specific plaintiffs' allegations of past injury to themselves in addition to the need for prospective equitable relief. *Id.* at 113, 123-24 (Marshall, J., dissenting). Justice Marshall also assailed the Court for "fragmenting the standing inquiry and imposing a separate standing hurdle with respect to each form of relief sought." *Id.* at 127 (Marshall, J., dissenting). He argued that the Court should focus instead upon whether a plaintiff has standing to litigate a claim, as distinct from whether, having presented his claim, he is entitled to a particular form of relief. *Id.* Finally, Justice Marshall pointed out that the federal courts were powerless in a constitutional system restrained by a *Lyons* concept of standing:

> The Court's decision removes an entire class of constitutional violations from the equitable powers of a federal court. It immunizes from prospective equitable relief any policy that authorizes persistent deprivations of constitutional rights as long as no individual can establish with substantial certainty that he will be injured, or injured again, in the future. The CHIEF JUSTICE asked in *Bivens v. Six Unknown Fed. Narcotics Agents*, 403 U.S. 388 . . . (1971) (dissenting opinion), "what would be the judicial response to a police order authorizing 'shoot to kill' with respect to every fugitive?" His answer was that it would be "easy to predict our collective wrath and outrage." We now learn that wrath and outrage cannot be translated into an order to cease the unconstitutional practice, but only an award of damages to those who are victimized by the practice and live to sue and to the survivors of those who are not so fortunate. Under the view expressed by the majority today, if the police adopt a policy of "shoot to kill," or a policy of shooting 1 out of 10 suspects, the federal courts will be powerless to enjoin its continuation. . . . The federal judical power is now limited to levying a toll for such a systematic constitutional violation.

*Id.* at 137 (Marshall, J., dissenting) (citations omitted).

163. Sierra Club v. Morton, 405 U.S. 727 (1972); *see supra* notes 110-16 and accompanying text.

fendant's actions might have increased housing costs in the suburb, also refused to find a causal link between those actions and the plaintiffs' exclusion.[164] Finally, the majority characterized the harm to the individual plaintiffs as too speculative and remote.[165]

Regarding the taxpayer plaintiffs, the Court found that even were they able to satisfy the injury-in-fact test,[166] they would be relying upon violations of the rights of others who were discriminated against in housing rather than upon their own rights. The Court found that the taxpayers failed the nexus test.[167] Similar reasoning was used to deny standing to the associations claiming that the exclusion of certain groups from the suburb caused them economic injury.[168] Finally, the Court found that the builders association, which sought damages, alleged no pecuniary loss to itself and could not recover on behalf of its members. Its claim for prospective relief was barred because there were no allegations of current building projects being frustrated by the zoning ordinance.[169] Thus, the Court used the two-part test to deny standing to all of the plaintiffs.[170]

*Simon v. Eastern Kentucky Welfare Rights Organization*[171] continued the Court's increasingly restrictive view of standing by requiring that the causal link between government's wrongful act and plaintiff's injury be precisely pleaded. The plaintiff, a coalition of indigent individuals seeking hospital care and organizations representing indigents' interests,

164. *Warth*, 422 U.S. at 504-07.

165. *Id.* at 507.

166. *Id.* at 509. The taxpayer plaintiffs asserted that the exclusion of low- and middle-income residents from the suburb placed a greater burden on the municipality to provide tax abatements for low- and moderate-cost housing. This, in turn, was alleged to increase the tax burden of city residents in order to finance essential public services. *Id.* at 508-09.

167. *Id.* at 509-10.

168. *Id.* at 512-14.

169. *Id.* at 515-17. In this respect, the Court paralleled its treatment of Sierra Club's claim in Sierra Club v. Morton, 405 U.S. 727 (1972). *See supra* notes 110-16 and accompanying text.

170. Justice Brennan, dissenting, argued that three of the groups of plaintiffs clearly had standing. *Warth*, 422 U.S. at 521 (Brennan, J., dissenting). First, he would have granted standing to the low-income and minority plaintiffs because their complaint alleged sufficient, specific instances of concrete injury suffered as a result of the exclusionary practices of defendants. *Id.* at 523-26 (Brennan, J., dissenting). Second, with respect to the two organizational plaintiffs, he would have found their "allegations of past injury, which members of both these organizations have clearly made, and of a future intent, if the barriers are cleared, again to develop suitable housing" sufficient to demonstrate the "requisite personal stake in the outcome of *this* controversy." *Id.* at 530 (Brennan, J., dissenting) (emphasis in original).

Justice Brennan then pointed out that in order to deny standing, the majority had demanded first, that the low-income and minority plaintiffs plead an unprecedented, "unachievable specificity" in showing the nexus between defendants' actions and plaintiffs' alleged injury, *id.* at 528 (Brennan, J., dissenting), and second, that the organizational plaintiffs "allege the (economically) impossible"—specific concrete injuries with respect to a particular, current project, *id.* at 530 (Brennan, J., dissenting). Justice Brennan concluded that the Court's disposition of the case reflected its unexpressed feelings on the merits more than it reflected any principled analysis of standing concepts. *See infra* note 263.

171. 426 U.S. 26 (1976).

challenged a newly modified Internal Revenue Service ruling that allegedly encouraged hospitals to refuse care to indigent patients while allowing the hospitals to retain their status as charitable organizations. The organization argued that the ruling violated congressional intent embodied in the Internal Revenue Code's provision exempting charitable organizations from taxation. The Court held that the organization lacked standing on the narrow but significant ground that it had failed to establish that the revenue ruling had caused the hospitals to deny treatment to its members.[172] The plaintiff was, therefore, unable to demonstrate that a favorable judgment would redress the harm that its members had suffered.[173]

Justice Brennan concurred in the judgment on the ground that the plaintiff had failed to show that the hospitals denying the plaintiff coalition's members treatment were within the ambit of the modification wrought by the challenged ruling.[174] But he sharply criticized what he viewed as an addition to the injury-in-fact test by the majority:

> Nothing in the logic or policy of constitutionally required standing is added by the further injury-in-fact dimension required by the Court today—that respondents allege that the hospitals affecting them would not have elected to forgo the favorable tax treatment and that this would "result in the availability to respondents of" free or below-cost medical services.[175]

Thus, Justice Brennan repudiated the heightened causality requirement used by the Court in *Linda R.S. v. Richard D.*[176]

172. *Id.* at 41-43. "It is purely speculative whether the denials of service specified in the complaint fairly can be traced to petitioners' 'encouragement' or instead result from decisions made by the hospitals without regard to the tax implications." *Id.* at 42-43.

The problem in *Simon* was not one of pleading, as Justice Brennan made clear in his concurring opinion. Defendants sought summary judgment on the question of standing, specifically attacking the causation question. *Id.* at 53 (Brennan, J., concurring). As Justice Brennan noted,

> At this point in the litigation, it was clearly incumbent upon the respondents to make a showing sufficient to create a material issue of fact whether there was any connection between the hospitals affecting them and the Ruling alleged to be illegally "encouraging" tax-exempt hospitals to withdraw the provision of indigents' services, thereby injuring respondents' "opportunity and ability" for such services. . . . No such showing was made. There is absolutely no indication in the record that the contested Ruling altered the operation of these hospitals in any way . . . .

*Id.* at 53-54 (Brennan, J., concurring) (citation omitted).

173. In this respect, the Court echoed its opinion in Linda R.S. v. Richard D., 410 U.S. 614, 617-18 (1973). *See supra* notes 117-19 and accompanying text.

174. *Simon*, 426 U.S. at 47-50, 53-54 (Brennan, J., concurring).

175. *Id.* at 56 (Brennan, J., concurring). Justice Brennan was referring to the majority's assertion that:

> [i]t is equally speculative whether the desired exercise of the court's remedial powers in this suit would result in the availability to respondents of such services. So far as the complaint sheds light, it is just as plausible that the hospitals to which respondents may apply for service would elect to forgo favorable tax treatment . . . .

*Id.* at 43.

176. 410 U.S. 614 (1973); *see supra* notes 117-19 and accompanying text.

It is unclear in the aftermath of *Simon* whether the new twist to the injury-in-fact test that Justice Brennan criticized has actually become a permanent part of constitutional concepts of standing. Certainly the new factor was not necessary to the decision in *Simon*, and therefore it may be regarded as dictum.[177] If so, however, it was the dictum of at least six members of the Court,[178] and thus it may play a role in future decisions.

### 3. *Standing to Raise Fourth Amendment Claims*

Beginning in 1978, the Court decided a series of fourth amendment cases that radically changed the concept of standing in that area. The seminal case was *Rakas v. Illinois*,[179] where passengers in a vehicle that was stopped and searched were held to lack standing under the fourth amendment to challenge the search. The Court eviscerated a doctrine under which anyone legitimately on searched private premises had standing to challenge the search.[180] Instead, the Court said that the standing inquiry was whether the defendant's own fourth amendment right of privacy had been invaded by the search.[181] At the same time, the majority, led by Justice Rehnquist, announced that the vocabulary of standing would no longer be used in fourth amendment cases.

> [T]he question necessarily arises whether it serves any useful analytical purpose to consider this principle a matter of standing, distinct from the merits of a defendant's Fourth Amendment claim. . . . [W]e think the better analysis forthrightly focuses on the extent of a particular defendant's rights under the Fourth Amendment, rather than on any theoretically separate, but invariably intertwined concept of standing.[182]

Despite this language, Justice Rehnquist insisted that the new approach would result in no doctrinal change.[183] Nonetheless, *Rakas* had the effect of denying standing to a defendant who clearly would have had it in prior years.

---

177. The plaintiffs failed to show that the hospitals had refused service because of the ruling and not because of other factors. Since they made no such showing of causality, plaintiffs lacked standing. Therefore, the Court never had to examine, under some heightened causality requirement, whether the hospitals would actually provide the services if the ruling were overturned rather than deny the services and forgo the tax advantages. *See also* Allen v. Wright, 105 S. Ct. 51 (1984), in which the Court reiterated the reasoning of *Simon*, again as dictum, in denying standing to parents of black school children seeking to challenge Internal Revenue Service tax-exempt status conferred upon allegedly discriminatory private schools.

178. Justice Marshall joined Justice Brennan's concurrence. Justice Stevens did not participate in the case. *Simon*, 426 U.S. at 28.

179. 439 U.S. 128 (1978).

180. Jones v. United States, 362 U.S. 257, 265-67 (1960), *overruled by* United States v. Salvucci, 448 U.S. 83, 85 (1980).

181. *Rakas*, 439 U.S. at 138-40.

182. *Id.* at 138-39.

183. *Id.* at 139.

The trend begun in *Rakas* continued in *United States v. Salvucci*,[184] *Rawlings v. Kentucky*,[185] and *United States v. Payner*,[186] each of which denied defendants standing to challenge fourth amendment searches that they would have been able to attack before *Rakas*.[187] Review of these cases makes it clear that Rakas, Salvucci, Rawlings, and Payner all had demonstrated injury-in-fact: the government proposed to introduce material seized in contravention of the fourth amendment in evidence against the defendants. The Court denied standing, however, because it found that the defendants were asserting someone else's fourth amendment privacy interest, not their own.[188] In essence, the Court raised the same objection to standing in the fourth amendment context as in *Warth v. Seldin*:[189] defendants in the fourth amendment cases were said to lack standing because they could not connect the injury they unquestionably suffered with a personal constitutional right. In this sense, they failed to satisfy the nexus test.[190] Close reading of the fourth amendment standing cases reveals that the Court has retreated to use of the legally-protected-interest test, which it had repudiated explicitly in 1970 in *Association of Data Processing Service Organizations v. Camp*.[191] Indeed, this may be the reason that Justice Rehnquist was so eager to abandon standing terminology in fourth amendment standing cases; to do otherwise would have made the inconsistency clearer.[192]

#### 4. *The Decision in* Valley Forge

The Court's most recent consideration of taxpayer and citizen standing came in *Valley Forge Christian College v. Americans United for Separation of Church and State, Inc.*[193] The Court denied standing to a nonprofit taxpayer organization and four of its employees who argued

184. 448 U.S. 83 (1980).

185. 448 U.S. 98 (1980).

186. 447 U.S. 727 (1980).

187. For a detailed description of these cases, see Doernberg, *supra* note 29; *see also* Burkoff, *The Court That Devoured the Fourth Amendment: The Triumph of an Inconsistent Exclusionary Doctrine*, 58 OR. L. REV. 151 (1979); Mickenberg, *Fourth Amendment Standing After* Rakas v. Illinois*: From Property to Privacy and Back*, 16 NEW ENG. L. REV. 197 (1981).

188. Rawlings v. Kentucky, 448 U.S. 98, 105 (1980); United States v. Salvucci, 448 U.S. 83, 95 (1980); United States v. Payner, 447 U.S. 727, 732 (1980); Rakas v. Illinois, 439 U.S. 128, 133-34 (1978); *accord* Alderman v. United States, 394 U.S. 165, 174 (1969) ("What petitioners appear to assert is an independent constitutional right of their own to exclude relevant and probative evidence because it was seized from another in violation of the Fourth Amendment.").

189. 422 U.S. 490 (1975); *see supra* notes 159-70 and accompanying text.

190. *See supra* text accompanying notes 9-10.

191. 397 U.S. 150, 153-54 (1970); *see infra* notes 214-26 and accompanying text. Justice Brennan interprets Flast v. Cohen, 392 U.S. 83 (1968), as having abandoned this legally-protected-interest test. *See infra* note 225 and accompanying text.

192. *See generally* Burkoff, *supra* note 187; Doernberg, *supra* note 29; Mickenberg, *supra* note 187.

193. 454 U.S. 464 (1982).

that conveyance of a parcel of land by the federal government to Valley Forge Christian College violated the establishment clause. The five-to-four majority held that, although plaintiffs had alleged " 'depriv[ation] of the fair and constitutional use of [their] tax dollar,' "[194] they nonetheless had failed to demonstrate injury-in-fact.[195]

The Court based its conclusion on two grounds. First, the Court seemed to return to the limitation on taxpayer standing first announced in *Frothingham v. Mellon.*[196] It limited *Flast v. Cohen*,[197] a case allowing taxpayer standing, to challenges of congressional, rather than executive, action.[198] Second, the Court found that the plaintiffs, as taxpayers, were not challenging any exercise of power under the taxing and spending clause[199] (as was the case in *Flast*), but rather were objecting to the subsequent disposition of property that the plaintiffs conceded the government had lawfully acquired through expenditure of tax funds.[200]

The majority also attacked the lower court's decision to allow the plaintiffs standing as citizens. The Third Circuit had noted that the plaintiffs' real interest was not as taxpayers, but as persons interested in maintaining the rigorous separation of church and state.[201] The majority sharply criticized the assertion that the plaintiffs had shown sufficient violation of personal constitutional rights rather than generalized citizen grievances, which the Court in the past had found insufficient to confer standing.

194. *Valley Forge*, 454 U.S. at 476 (quoting Respondent's Amended Complaint at app. 10).

195. *Id.* at 485.

196. 262 U.S. 447 (1923).

197. 392 U.S. 83 (1968).

198. *Valley Forge*, 454 U.S. at 479. In dissent, Justice Brennan took sharp issue with this reading of *Flast*, accusing the majority of "wrenching snippets of language from our opinions," and of creating "tortuous distinctions . . . [that] are specious, at best: at worst, . . . pernicious to our constitutional heritage." *Id.* at 510 (Brennan, J., dissenting). He went on to rebuke the Court for artificially limiting *Flast* to challenges of Congressional power, noting that in *Flast*, the plaintiffs challenged executive action of the Department of Health, Education and Welfare pursuant to authority granted by Congress, precisely as in *Valley Forge*. *Id.*

199. U.S. CONST. art. I, § 8, cl. 1.

200. *Valley Forge*, 454 U.S. at 480 & n.17.

201. Americans United for Separation of Church & State, Inc. v. Department of Health, Educ. & Welfare, 619 F.2d 252, 261 (3d Cir. 1980), *rev'd sub nom.* Valley Forge Christian College v. Americans United for Separation of Church & State, Inc., 454 U.S. 464 (1982). The Supreme Court majority relied upon the Court of Appeals' own opinion to support the majority's argument that the plaintiffs were not entitled to standing as taxpayers. The Court of Appeals had analyzed plaintiffs' true interest, cutting through the verbiage imposed upon them by previous standing cases to deal explicitly with their actual concern.

> Plaintiffs have no reason to expect, nor perhaps do they care about, any personal tax saving that might result should they prevail. The crux of the interest at stake, the plaintiffs argue, is found in the Establishment Clause, not in the supposed loss of money, as such. As a matter of primary identity, therefore, the plaintiffs are not so much taxpayers as separationists . . . .

619 F.2d at 261.

> This reasoning process merely disguises, we think with a rather thin veil, the inconsistency of the [lower] court's results with our decisions in *Schlesinger* and *Richardson*. . . . [A]ssertion of a right to a particular kind of Government conduct, which the Government has violated by acting differently, cannot alone satisfy the requirements of Art. III without draining those requirements of meaning.[202]

At the same time, the majority recognized the possibility that under its analysis, cases might arise in which no one would have standing.

> Respondents' claim of standing implicitly rests on the presumption that violations of the Establishment Clause typically will not cause injury [to anyone] sufficient to confer standing under the "traditional" view of Art. III. But "[t]he assumption that if respondents have no standing to sue, no one would have standing, is not a reason to find standing."[203]

This Article suggests, contrary to the Court's implication, that the absence of standing for any possible plaintiff is indeed a matter for concern. Such an absence of possible plaintiffs may not, of course, by itself be a reason to allow standing. It is, however, a matter of some gravity if situations exist where the government may, with impunity, violate the Constitution because no one is able to challenge the government's action in court.[204]

Justice Brennan's vehement dissent traced the development of taxpayer standing doctrine and then argued that rights under the establishment clause are personal rights specifically designed, at least in part, to protect taxpayers.[205] Brennan also criticized *Frothingham v. Mellon*,[206] the seminal taxpayer standing case. He questioned its "obscure" reasoning and implicitly challenged *Frothingham*'s reliance upon the indirectness of the connection between the taxpayer's remittance and the government's expenditure.[207] "*Frothingham* also stressed the indirectness of the taxpayer's injury. But, *as a matter of Art. III standing*, if the causal relationship is sufficiently certain, the length of the causal chain is irrelevant."[208]

In fact, Justice Brennan noted that *Frothingham* contained an "unstated premise," which had been identified in Justice Harlan's *Flast* dissent: the notion that taxpayer standing, if it existed at all, should be based on citizens' generalized grievances concerning government actions,

202. *Valley Forge*, 454 U.S. at 483.

203. *Id.* at 489 (quoting Schlesinger v. Reservists Comm. to Stop the War, 418 U.S. 208, 227 (1974)).

204. *See generally infra* Part III.

205. *Valley Forge*, 454 U.S. at 500-05 (Brennan, J., dissenting). "It is clear . . . that one of the primary purposes of the Establishment Clause was to prevent the use of tax moneys for religious purposes." *Id.* at 504 (Brennan, J., dissenting).

206. 262 U.S. 447 (1923).

207. *Valley Forge*, 454 U.S. at 496 (Brennan, J., dissenting).

208. *Id.* at 497 (Brennan, J., dissenting) (emphasis in original) (footnote omitted).

rather than on some mythical injury-in-fact attributable to an individual taxpayer.[209] In support of that notion, Brennan argued that *Flast* was a special case, applicable only to taxpayer claims involving the first amendment religion clauses and not to standing generally.[210] Justice Brennan then argued that establishment clause cases themselves are special cases for taxpayer standing purposes.[211]

> It may be that Congress can tax for *almost* any reason, or for no reason at all. There is, so far as I have been able to discern, but one constitutionally imposed limit on that authority. Congress cannot use tax money to support a church, or to encourage religion. That is "*the* forbidden exaction." . . . In absolute terms the history of the Establishment Clause of the First Amendment makes this clear. History also makes it clear that the federal taxpayer is a singularly "proper and appropriate party to invoke a federal court's jurisdiction" to challenge a federal bestowal of largesse as a violation of the Establishment Clause. Each, and indeed every, federal taxpayer suffers precisely the injury that the Establishment Clause guards against when the Federal Government directs that funds be taken from the pocketbooks of the citizenry and

209. *Id.* at 498 (Brennan, J., dissenting). Indeed, Justice Harlan's entire dissent was based upon that unstated premise:

> [The] taxpayer's complaint can consist only of an allegation that public funds have been, or shortly will be, expended for purposes inconsistent with the Constitution. The taxpayer cannot ask the return of any portion of his previous tax payments, cannot prevent the collection of any existing tax debt, and cannot demand an adjudication of the propriety of any particular level of taxation. His tax payments are received for the general purposes of the United States, and are, upon proper receipt, lost in the general revenues.

Flast v. Cohen, 392 U.S. 83, 128 (1968) (Harlan, J., dissenting). Earlier in the opinion, Justice Harlan had discussed this problem in more explicit terms:

> [T]axpayers' interests in the expenditure of public funds [are not] differentiated from those of the general public by any special rights retained by them in their tax payments. The simple fact is that no such rights can sensibly be said to exist. . . . The national legislature is required by the Constitution to exercise its spending powers to "provide for the common Defence and general Welfare." Art. I, § 8, cl. 1. Whatever other implications there may be to that sweeping phrase, it surely means that the United States holds its general funds, not as stakeholder or trustee for those who have paid its imposts, but as surrogate for the population at large. Any rights of a taxpayer with respect to the purposes for which those funds are expended are thus subsumed in, and extinguished by, the common rights of all citizens. To characterize taxpayers' interests in such expenditures as proprietary or even personal either deprives those terms of all meaning or postulates for taxpayers a *scintilla juris* in funds that are no longer theirs. . . . We must recognize that these non-Hohfeldian plaintiffs complain, just as the petitioner in *Frothingham* sought to complain, not as taxpayers, but as "private attorneys-general." The interests they represent, and the rights they espouse, are bereft of any personal or proprietary coloration. They are, as litigants, indistinguishable from any group selected at random from among the general population, taxpayers and nontaxpayers alike.

*Id.* at 118-20 (Harlan, J., dissenting) (footnote omitted).

This Article does not disagree with Justice Harlan's characterization, but argues instead that in certain circumstances it is appropriate to adopt a broader concept of standing, consistent with the existence of such collectively shared interests, as the only effective available means to correct governmental wrongs. *See infra* Part III.

210. *Valley Forge*, 454 U.S. at 507-08 (Brennan, J., dissenting).

211. *Id.* at 509 (Brennan, J., dissenting).

placed into the coffers of the ministry.[212]

Thus, Justice Brennan realized that some claims of government misbehavior are not amenable to adjudication under traditional standing doctrine. But instead of insisting in procrustean fashion, as the majority did, that cases should be made to fit the standing doctrine, Justice Brennan implicitly suggested that the doctrine should be modified to fit the cases so that the judiciary could redress government wrongs. By the time *Valley Forge* was decided, however, a decade of Supreme Court standing decisions had made it clear that access to the federal courts in constitutional cases was far more limited.[213] Yet the trend toward narrower standing was not without its interruptions, as the next Section demonstrates.

### *B. Grants of Standing*

The Court began the 1970's by distinguishing questions of standing from questions involving the merits. In *Association of Data Processing Service Organizations, Inc. v. Camp*,[214] the Court considered a private corporation's challenge to a ruling of the Comptroller of the Currency that permitted banks to make nonbanking data-processing services available to other banks and bank customers. The plaintiff alleged that the ruling violated the Bank Service Corporation Act[215] and permitted banks

212. *Id.* (emphasis in original) (citations omitted) (quoting Everson v. Board of Educ., 330 U.S. 1, 45 (1947) (Rutledge, J., dissenting) and Flast v. Cohen, 392 U.S. 83, 103 (1968)). At the same time, Justice Brennan noted the practical impossibility of a taxpayer challenge at the time of collection of the funds, rather than when they are disbursed. This, he argued, militates in favor of a subsequent establishment clause challenge even though a successful challenge may not directly benefit the taxpayer-plaintiff's pocketbook. *Id.* at 509-10 (Brennan, J., dissenting).

213. Standing is not the only device that the Supreme Court used to narrow the availability of a federal forum for consideration of constitutional challenges during the 1970's. In a series of cases beginning in 1971, the Court announced the reemergence of a federal abstention doctrine based on considerations of comity, equity, and federalism. Under the doctrine, federal courts could not consider constitutional questions arising in state criminal proceedings, except at the Supreme Court level pursuant to 28 U.S.C. § 1257 (1982), when such questions could be decided by the state tribunals themselves. The doctrine's purpose was to avoid undue interference with state criminal justice systems. Younger v. Harris, 401 U.S. 37 (1971). As the decade progressed, this bar to federal action expanded to cases where the state proceeding was only quasi-criminal, *see* Huffman v. Pursue, Ltd., 420 U.S. 592 (1975), to some cases where the federal proceeding commenced before the state criminal proceeding, *see* Hicks v. Miranda, 422 U.S. 332 (1975), to cases where there was no state criminal proceeding pending at all, *see* Rizzo v. Goode, 423 U.S. 362 (1976), and finally to cases where the state proceeding was clearly civil, *see* Moore v. Sims, 442 U.S. 415 (1979); Trainor v. Hernandez, 431 U.S. 434 (1977). The *Younger* doctrine and the Supreme Court's reluctance to permit the federal courts to enforce federal constitutional guarantees have been sharply criticized. *See, e.g.*, Zeigler, *A Reassessment of the* Younger *Doctrine in Light of the Legislative History of Reconstruction*, 1983 DUKE L.J. 987. In all of the *Younger* line of cases, the plaintiffs clearly had standing, but the Court employed other justiciability doctrines in order to deny them access to the federal courts.

214. 397 U.S. 150 (1970).

215. Bank Service Corporation Act, 12 U.S.C. § 1864 (1962) (significantly amended 1982): "No bank service corporation may engage in any activity other than the performance of bank services for banks."

to compete unlawfully with nonbanking organizations. The district court dismissed the action for lack of standing and the court of appeals affirmed.[216]

The Supreme Court used *Camp* to clarify the injury-in-fact requirement. The Court easily found that the plaintiff had demonstrated injury-in-fact. The anticipated loss of future business to competing banks, plus the plaintiff's allegations that present customers had been lured away by a particular bank, constituted sufficient injury. In so holding, the Court rejected the court of appeals' requirement of injury to some legally recognized interest of the individual—an interest conferred by statute or contract—or to some public interest where the plaintiff's standing was congressionally recognized.[217] "The 'legal interest' test goes to the merits. The question of standing is different."[218] The plaintiff need only show that he was in the "zone of interests" protected by the statute. The unanimous Court went on to emphasize that the interest need not be economic, but that it might reflect " 'aesthetic, conservational, and recreational' as well as economic values."[219] The Court thus took an expansive view of the injury-in-fact test and did not require that the plaintiff allege a violation of a law designed for his protection, as required by the nexus test. In these respects, the *Camp* Court was far more liberal than

216. Association of Data Processing Serv. Orgs., Inc. v. Camp, 279 F. Supp. 675 (D. Minn. 1968), *aff'd*, 406 F.2d 837 (8th Cir. 1969), *rev'd*, 397 U.S. 150 (1970).

217. *Camp*, 397 U.S. at 153. Thus, under the legally-protected-interest test, the plaintiff would have had to show that the Bank Service Corporation Act's restriction, *see supra* note 215, was intended to protect its members from increased competition or that they had some common law or constitutional right to be free from such competition. *See* Note, *The Supreme Court, 1969 Term*, 84 HARV. L. REV. 1, 177-81 (1970). The absence of such a right would have deprived the plaintiff of standing. Under the test adopted in *Camp*, it was sufficient that the plaintiff was injured by defendant's failure to require banks to operate within the restrictions of the Act, since such operation would have, as a practical matter, relieved the plaintiff of the burden of competition from banks.

218. *Camp*, 397 U.S. at 153. In Barlow v. Collins, 397 U.S. 159 (1970), decided with *Camp*, the Court reiterated the disutility of the legal interest test. *Barlow* was brought by tenant farmers challenging an amendment to a Department of Agriculture regulation that dealt with assignments of funds received pursuant to the Soil Conservation and Domestic Allotment Act, 16 U.S.C. § 590h(g) (1982). The lower courts ruled that the plaintiffs lacked standing because no legally protected interest had been invaded. *Barlow*, 397 U.S. at 163-64. The Court rejected this narrow view of standing, and held that the plaintiffs were "within the zone of interests protected by the Act," *id.* at 164, because there clearly had been congressional intent to benefit tenant farmers. *Id.* at 164-65. The Court did not, however, elaborate on the extent to which the "zone of interests" concept was broader than the "legally protected interests" concept.

219. *Camp*, 397 U.S. at 154 (quoting Office of Communication of United Church of Christ v. FCC, 359 F.2d 994, 1000-06 (D.C. Cir. 1966); Scenic Hudson Preservation Conference v. Federal Power Comm'n, 354 F.2d 608, 616 (2d Cir. 1965)). Interestingly, the Court noted in dictum that "[a] person or a family may have a spiritual stake in First Amendment values sufficient to give standing to raise issues concerning the Establishment Clause and the Free Exercise Clause." *Id.* (citing Abington School Dist. v. Schempp, 374 U.S. 203 (1963)). The assertion is clearly at odds with the Court's subsequent disposition of Valley Forge Christian College v. Americans United for Separation of Church & State, Inc., 454 U.S. 464 (1982). *See supra* notes 193-212 and accompanying text.

the Courts that later decided *Valley Forge*, *Schlesinger*, and *Richardson*.[220]

Justice Brennan concurred in the results of *Camp* and the companion case of *Barlow v. Collins*,[221] but disagreed with the Court's standing analysis. He noted that the Court used a two-step inquiry in *Camp*, asking first whether plaintiff had suffered injury-in-fact and second whether the interest asserted was within the zone of protected interests.[222] But, he argued, the second step was inappropriate to standing analysis since it looked to the merits of the controversy or to its general justiciability.[223]

> I had thought we discarded the notion of any additional requirement when we discussed standing solely in terms of its constitutional content in *Flast v. Cohen* . . . . By requiring a second, nonconstitutional step, the Court comes very close to perpetuating the discredited requirement that conditioned standing on a showing by the plaintiff that the challenged governmental action invaded one of his legally protected interests.[224]

Justice Brennan's reading of *Flast* finds some support in his quotation of that case. The *Flast* majority had declared that " 'when standing is placed in issue in a case, the question is whether the person whose standing is challenged is a proper party to request an adjudication of a particular issue' and not [according to Justice Brennan] . . . whether on the merits, the plaintiff has a legally protected interest that the defendant's action invaded."[225] *Flast* was not as clear, however, as Justice Brennan's assertion made it seem. The Court's exclusion of the legally-protected-interest test in *Flast* was implicit rather than explicit.

Nonetheless, *Camp* initiated two liberal trends in the standing area: repudiation of the legally-protected-interest test in favor of the zone-of-interest analysis, and Justice Brennan's strong assertion that the only appropriate inquiry was directed to injury-in-fact. Professor Davis regards *Camp* as a watershed opinion.

> In *Data Processing* . . . the Supreme Court unanimously superceded a large batch of law [holding] . . . that something in the nature of a "legal right" or "legal interest" was necessary for standing. That shift is a great accomplishment and it deserves strong emphasis, for federal law of standing now has a new and better orientation. But that much is no

220. *See supra* notes 120-49, 193-212 and accompanying text.

221. 397 U.S. 159 (1970); *see supra* note 218.

222. *Barlow*, 397 U.S. at 167-68 (Brennan, J., concurring and dissenting).

223. *Id.* at 168-69 (Brennan, J., concurring and dissenting).

224. *Id.* at 168 (Brennan, J., concurring and dissenting) (footnote omitted) (distinguishing Associated Indus. v. Ickes, 134 F.2d 694, 700 (2d Cir. 1943) (relying upon the legally protected interest test)).

225. *Id.* at 171 (Brennan, J., concurring and dissenting) (quoting Flast v. Cohen, 392 U.S. 83, 99-100 (1968)).

longer a live issue, for it has been fully resolved by a unanimous Court.[226]

The Court seemed to reaffirm its liberal movement two years later in *Trafficante v. Metropolitan Life Insurance Co.*,[227] in which residents of a housing complex charged that the landlord had violated the Civil Rights Act of 1968[228] by discriminating against nonwhite applicants. The lower courts dismissed the complaint on the ground that only victims of discrimination had standing.[229] A unanimous Court reversed, finding that the statute defined an aggrieved person as one "who claims to have been injured by a discriminatory housing practice."[230] The *Trafficante* plaintiffs claimed to have suffered loss of social and business opportunities and imposition of a stigma by being residents of a "white ghetto."[231] The Court found that these claims constituted injury-in-fact and that they were sufficiently pleaded to establish the individualized injury[232] absent in *Sierra Club v. Morton*.[233] The Court also noted that Congress had broadened the concept of "persons aggrieved," making them private attorneys general—a classification the Court regarded as "not uncommon in modern legislative programs."[234] Finally, the Court noted how broad a concept of standing it was willing to consider, at least in civil rights cases: "The person on the landlord's blacklist is not the only victim of discriminatory housing practices; it is, as Senator Javits said in supporting the bill, 'the whole community.' "[235]

In *Trafficante*, the Court implicitly propounded several notions about standing. First, it reaffirmed the *Camp* view that injury-in-fact might be noneconomic.[236] Second, its reversal of the lower courts' dis-

226. Davis, *supra* note 21, at 457 (footnote omitted). Professor Davis' view that *Camp* settled the issue, however, now appears to have been overly optimistic, at least in the fourth amendment area, where the Court has *sub silentio* returned to the old standard. *See supra* notes 179-92 and accompanying text.

227. 409 U.S. 205 (1972).

228. 42 U.S.C. §§ 3601-3619 (1982).

229. Trafficante v. Metropolitan Life Ins. Co., 322 F. Supp. 352, 353 (N.D. Cal.), *aff'd*, 446 F.2d 1158, 1164 (9th Cir. 1971), *rev'd*, 409 U.S. 205, 208 (1972). The lower courts viewed the plaintiffs as asserting third-party rights, perhaps anticipating the Court's position in Warth v. Seldin, 422 U.S. 490 (1975). *See supra* notes 166-67 and accompanying text; *see also Warth*, 422 U.S. at 514.

230. 42 U.S.C. § 3610(a) (1982).

231. *Trafficante*, 409 U.S. at 208.

232. *Id.* at 209.

233. 405 U.S. 727 (1972); *see supra* notes 110-16 and accompanying text.

234. *Trafficante*, 409 U.S. at 211 (citing Perkins v. Matthews, 400 U.S. 379, 396 (1971); Allen v. State Bd. of Elections, 393 U.S. 544, 556 (1969); Newman v. Piggie Park Enters., 390 U.S. 400, 402 (1968); J.I. Case Co. v. Borak, 377 U.S. 426, 432 (1964)). The applicability of the private-attorney-general concept to the problems of standing is discussed *infra* in notes 367-73 and accompanying text.

235. *Trafficante*, 409 U.S. at 211 (quoting 114 CONG. REC. 2706 (1968)). The Court stated, "We can give vitality to [the Act] only by a generous construction which gives standing to sue to all in the same housing unit who are injured by racial discrimination in the management of those facilities within the coverage of the statute." *Id.* at 212.

236. *See supra* note 219 and accompanying text.

missal implied that an individual might be injured for standing purposes by unlawful conduct directed at someone else. Third, and most important, it explicitly recognized that a legislative enactment might consider the whole community to be the benefited class, and that in such circumstances, members of the benefited community ought to have standing to challenge a violation of the enactment.[237]

The Court expanded its consideration of standing related to alleged noneconomic injury in *United States v. SCRAP*,[238] in which an environmental group challenged an Interstate Commerce Commission ruling permitting railroads to levy a surcharge for transportation of recyclable commodities.[239] The plaintiff organization alleged that the ruling discouraged use of recyclable goods, and thus had an adverse impact on the environment. Unlike the plaintiff in *Sierra Club v. Morton*,[240] the *SCRAP* plaintiff had pleaded a threat to its members' own enjoyment of the environment.[241] At the same time, the Court recognized that the injury alleged in *SCRAP* was not nearly so limited in scope as that involved in *Sierra Club*.

> But we have already made it clear that standing is not to be denied simply because many people suffer the same injury. . . . To deny standing to persons who are in fact injured, simply because many others are also injured would mean that the most injurious and widespread Government actions could be questioned by nobody. We cannot accept that conclusion.[242]

Thus, the Court specifically acknowledged that the existence of widespread public noneconomic injury might suggest the absence of standing under the rubric of "generalized grievances" mentioned in *United States v. Richardson*.[243] At the same time, the Court deliberately affirmed the necessity of finding standing in such cases.

In *Craig v. Boren*,[244] the Court went a step further in a case involv-

237. The Court reaffirmed the *Trafficante* decision in Gladstone, Realtors v. Village of Bellwood, 441 U.S. 91 (1979), again giving an extremely broad reading to the word "aggrieved" in Title VIII of the Civil Rights Act of 1968, 42 U.S.C. §§ 3601-3619 (1982). In that case, the Court found that members of the community, not themselves discriminated against, nevertheless had standing to challenge Gladstone's actions, 441 U.S. at 111-15, and further noted that "[a]s we have said before, '[t]here can be no question about the importance' to a community of 'promoting stable, racially integrated housing.' " *Id.* at 111 (quoting Linmark Assocs. v. Willingboro, 431 U.S. 85, 94 (1977)). The importance of this observation to the concept of collective rights will be discussed *infra* in Part III.

238. 412 U.S. 669 (1973).

239. *Id.* at 672-78.

240. 405 U.S. 727 (1972); *see supra* notes 110-16 and accompanying text.

241. "Here, by contrast [with *Sierra Club*], the appellees claimed that the specific and allegedly illegal action of the Commission would directly harm them in their use of the natural resources of the Washington Metropolitan Area." *SCRAP*, 412 U.S. at 687.

242. *Id.* at 687-88.

243. 418 U.S. 166, 175 (1974); *see supra* note 127 and accompanying text.

244. 429 U.S. 190 (1976).

ing widespread injury to constitutional rights: it allowed a third party to assert them. The plaintiffs challenged an Oklahoma statute that prohibited the sale of 3.2% beer to males but not to females in the same age group, charging that it constituted gender-based discrimination. The case was brought by a male in the restricted age group and by a licensed vendor of beer, but the Supreme Court heard the appeal only from the vendor.[245] The Court upheld the vendor's standing to sue, noting that she clearly satisfied the injury-in-fact requirement.[246] The majority recognized, however, that on the merits, the vendor was relying upon an equal protection claim based on unequal treatment of other people. With respect to the nexus problem, the Court stated:

> [O]ur decisions have settled that limitations on a litigant's assertion of *jus tertii* are not constitutionally mandated, but rather stem from a salutary "rule of self-restraint" designed to minimize unwarranted intervention into controversies where the applicable constitutional questions are ill-defined and speculative. . . . These prudential objectives, [generally] thought to be enhanced by restrictions on third-party standing, cannot be furthered here, where the lower court already has entertained the relevant constitutional challenge and the parties have sought—or at least have never resisted—an authoritative constitutional determination. In such circumstances, a decision by us to forgo consideration of the constitutional merits in order to await the initiation of a new challenge to the statute by injured third parties would be impermissibly to foster repetitive and time-consuming litigation under the guise of caution and prudence. Moreover, insofar as the applicable constitutional questions have been and continue to be presented vigorously and "cogently," . . . the denial of *jus tertii* standing in deference to a direct class suit can serve no functional purpose.[247]

*Craig* thus demonstrates the Court's recognition that there may be circumstances where third-party representation of constitutional rights is appropriate, and reaffirms that problems with third-party standing are not constitutionally based.[248]

245. Craig, the young male plaintiff, had exceeded the upper age limit of the affected group following the Court's determination of probable jurisdiction of the appeal, mooting the case as to him. *Id.* at 192 & n.2.

246. *Id.* at 194. In fact, the defendants conceded her standing. *Id.* at 193.

247. *Id.* at 193-94 (citations omitted).

248. *Craig* was not a unanimous decision; Chief Justice Burger and Justice Rehnquist dissented. Only the Chief Justice's opinion mentioned the question of the vendor's standing. Justice Rehnquist, who wrote exclusively on the merits, apparently acquiesced in the majority's treatment of the standing issue.

In Carey v. Population Servs. Int'l, 431 U.S. 678 (1977), a strong majority of the Court relied on *Craig* and allowed vendors of contraceptive devices, on behalf of themselves and potential purchasers, to challenge a New York statute limiting access to and advertisement of contraceptives. Seven members of the Court explicitly joined the portion of the Court's opinion allowing standing. Justice Rehnquist, as in *Craig*, dissented on the merits without mentioning standing. The Chief Justice dissented without explanation.

In 1978, the Court clarified some of the limitations of the two-part standing test. In *Duke Power Co. v. Carolina Environmental Study Group, Inc.*,[249] environmental groups and individuals challenged the Price-Anderson Act's[250] liability limitation for private developers of nuclear power plants. The defendants, the Duke Power Company and the Nuclear Regulatory Commission, argued that the plaintiffs failed to satisfy either prong of the standing test. The Supreme Court disagreed. The Court found the plaintiffs' injury-in-fact in the "environmental and aesthetic consequences of the thermal pollution of the two lakes in the vicinity of the disputed power plants."[251] Certainly, the Court said, this is "the type of harmful effect which has been deemed adequate in prior cases to satisfy the 'injury in fact' standard."[252] Apart from the plaintiffs' fear of nuclear accidents, therefore, the Court found their allegations of injury sufficiently nonspeculative to justify standing.

The Court flatly repudiated the nexus test's applicability to cases other than taxpayer suits. "We . . . cannot accept the contention that, outside the context of taxpayers' suits, a litigant must demonstrate something more than injury in fact and a substantial likelihood that the judicial relief requested will prevent or redress the claimed injury to satisfy the 'case or controversy' requirement of Art. III."[253] The Court went on to state explicitly that the other limitations on standing were prudential only, referring specifically to its concerns about the proper role of the courts in American society,[254] its rejection of the courts as a forum for airing generalized grievances,[255] and its limited approach to third-party standing.[256] The Court noted: "Where a party champions his own rights, and where the injury alleged is a concrete and particularized one which will be prevented or redressed by the relief requested, the basic practical and prudential concerns underlying the standing doctrine are generally satisfied when the constitutional requisites are met."[257] Thus, the Court seemed almost to merge its prudential concerns into the constitutionally based injury-in-fact requirement, at least for some purposes. To the extent that this occurred, it clearly indicated a liberalization of the

249. 438 U.S. 59 (1978).

250. 42 U.S.C. § 2210 (1982).

251. *Duke Power*, 438 U.S. at 73.

252. *Id.* at 73-74 (citing United States v. SCRAP, 412 U.S. 669 (1973); Sierra Club v. Morton, 405 U.S. 727 (1972)).

253. *Id.* at 79 (footnote omitted).

254. *Id.* at 80 (citing Warth v. Seldin, 422 U.S. 490 (1975); Schlesinger v. Reservists Comm. to Stop the War, 418 U.S. 208 (1974)).

255. *Id.* (citing United States v. Richardson, 418 U.S. 166 (1974)).

256. *Id.* (citing Warth v. Seldin, 422 U.S. 490 (1975); United States v. Raines, 362 U.S. 17 (1960)).

257. *Id.* at 80-81 (citing Arlington Heights v. Metropolitan Hous. Dev. Corp., 429 U.S. 252 (1977)).

Court's view on standing.[258]

The Court's approach to standing throughout the past fifteen years has clearly been inconsistent.[259] The apparently liberal trend of the Court in *Camp*, *SCRAP*, *Craig*, *Carey*, and *Duke Power* led to expansions in the concept of injury-in-fact and the availability of third-party standing, as well as a corresponding limitation of the prudentially based nexus test as a restrictive factor in standing. At the same time, in *Sierra Club*, the Court took an extremely restrictive approach to the requirements for properly pleading injury-in-fact. Moreover, the Court clearly refused to recognize that any taxpayer or citizen (or, one supposes, all of them[260]) might have a sufficient particularized interest in lawful government conduct to give rise to injury-in-fact when government acts unlawfully.[261] And in *Warth v. Seldin*,[262] the Court took an extremely restrictive view of both injury-in-fact and third-party standing, refusing to reach the substantive issues[263] while insisting on a degree of pleading exactitude and third-party interest not seen prior to that time and certainly inconsistent with its decision a year later in *Craig*. Finally, in *Valley Forge*, the Court made clear its hostility to citizen claims of unlawful government conduct unless such claimants were able to show some injury more concrete than damage to their interest in having government abide by the social compact.[264]

### *C. Problems with the Current Standing Model*

Wholly apart from the inconsistencies in the Court's positions on standing, the majority's increasingly restrictive view of standing poses

258. The *Duke Power* Court's view of standing was not unanimous. Justice Stewart, concurring in the result, questioned whether the plaintiffs had shown sufficient injury-in-fact to cross the constitutional threshold. *Id.* at 95 (Stewart, J., concurring).

259. *See, e.g.*, Nichol, *supra* note 27, and the authorities cited at 68 n.3.

260. *See infra* Part II, Section *C*.

261. *See, e.g.*, Schlesinger v. Reservists Comm. to Stop the War, 418 U.S. 208 (1974); United States v. Richardson, 418 U.S. 166 (1974); *see also supra* notes 120-49 and accompanying text.

262. 422 U.S. 490 (1975); *see supra* notes 159-70 and accompanying text.

263. Indeed, Justices Douglas and Brennan attributed the Court's decision to something less than dispassionate judicial reasoning. "With all respect, I think that the Court reads the complaint and the record with antagonistic eyes." Warth v. Seldin, 422 U.S. 490, 518 (1975) (Douglas, J., dissenting).

> [T]he opinion, which tosses out of court almost every conceivable kind of plaintiff who could be injured by the activity claimed to be unconstitutional, can be explained only by an indefensible hostility to the claim on the merits. I can appreciate the Court's reluctance to adjudicate the complex and difficult legal questions involved . . . . But courts cannot refuse to hear a case on the merits merely because they would prefer not to, and it is quite clear, when the record is viewed with dispassion, that at least three of the groups of plaintiffs have made allegations, and supported them with affidavits and documentary evidence, sufficient to survive a motion to dismiss for lack of standing.

*Id.* at 520-21 (Brennan, J., dissenting).

264. *See* Valley Forge Christian College v. Americans United for Separation of Church & State, Inc., 454 U.S. 464 (1982); *supra* notes 193-213 and accompanying text.

substantial problems for a nation that, on the Lockean model, proceeds on the basis that government results from a social compact and is the trustee of the powers settled upon it by the citizens whose consent gives it legitimacy. Many of the problems can be illustrated by extensions of some of the Court's recent standing cases themselves. For example, suppose that Congress passed a joint resolution declaring that the legislative branch could not properly consider the military budget unless each of its members became a general or admiral in the armed forces. Suppose further that the President, as Commander-in-Chief, acceded to the request and commissioned each member. The nation would then be faced with a wholesale, deliberate violation, by Congress and the President, of the incompatability clause.[265] Yet under the rationale of *Schlesinger v. Reservists Committee to Stop the War*,[266] no judicial remedy would exist because no one would have standing. Indeed, this hypothetical merely confirms the recognition by the *Schlesinger* Court that the judicial system provides no remedy for certain types of governmental conduct that violate the Constitution.[267]

Cases like *Valley Forge*[268] present similar problems. Assuming that the conveyance to Valley Forge Christian College constituted a prohibited establishment of religion, one may legitimately ask who would have had standing to challenge it. Taxpayer standing was ruled out as a basis,[269] as was citizen standing,[270] and the Court explicitly recognized that this created a situation where no conceivable plaintiff could have standing.[271] Taken to its logical extreme, the reasoning of *Valley Forge* can, like *Schlesinger*, lead to utterly absurd results. Suppose Congress conveyed Fort Hood, Texas, to a fundamentalist religious group so that it could establish a center of religious worship. Clearly such a transfer would violate the establishment clause;[272] yet under the rationale of *Valley Forge*, no one would have standing to seek judicial redress.

In fact, many establishment clause cases raise standing problems under the *Valley Forge* rationale, problems ordinarily ignored by the

265. U.S. CONST. art. I, § 6, cl. 2.

266. 418 U.S. 208 (1974); *see supra* notes 133-49 and accompanying text.

267. *Schlesinger*, 418 U.S. at 227.

268. 454 U.S. 464 (1982); *see supra* notes 193-213 and accompanying text.

269. *See supra* notes 197-200 and accompanying text.

270. *See supra* notes 201-02 and accompanying text.

271. *See supra* text accompanying note 203.

272. U.S. CONST. amend. I; *see, e.g.*, Committee for Pub. Educ. & Religious Liberty v. Nyquist, 413 U.S. 756, 779-80 (1973) (invalidating state funding for maintenance and repair of sectarian schools, tuition grants for private school attendance, and tuition tax credits); Tilton v. Richardson, 403 U.S. 672, 682-84 (1971) (upholding federal construction grants to private postsecondary educational institutions only to the extent the funds were used for nonsectarian facilities); Lemon v. Kurtzman, 403 U.S. 602, 625 (1971) (invalidating state salary supplement for teachers in private schools).

courts deciding such cases. For example, in *Zorach v. Clauson*,[273] the plaintiffs challenged a New York program involving released time for public school students to attend religious instruction. The instruction program was not on school premises and received no state financial support, direct or indirect.[274] The Supreme Court upheld the program without any mention of standing. Yet, viewed in terms of *Valley Forge*, it is difficult to pinpoint any injury-in-fact to the plaintiffs, whose children remained in the secular schools for instruction during the released time period, other than some injury to their "spiritual stake" in the abstract concept of separation of church and state.[275] Similarly, in *Board of Education v. Allen*,[276] a case challenging a New York program to lend textbooks to religious schools for instruction in secular subjects, the Court also proceeded to the merits without any mention of standing.[277]

Possible cases of government lawlessness in which no one would have standing are not limited either to establishment clause cases or to situations like those in *Richardson* or *Schlesinger*. Indeed, the Court's insistence that "generalized grievances" cannot be the basis for standing[278] raises the spectre of all sorts of abuses by government where no one would have standing to seek judicial intervention.[279] Clearly, the prospect of a standing doctrine so restrictive as to prohibit the courts from restraining even the grossest types of governmental misconduct is not an enticing one. Yet the Court has warned that recognition of a substantially broader standing doctrine, or one based on an altered concept of injury-in-fact, would eviscerate the constitutional requirements relating to standing.[280] But the Court's response to the article III prob-

273. 343 U.S. 306 (1952).

274. In this respect, the program differed from the program the Court invalidated in Illinois *ex rel.* McCollum v. Board of Educ., 333 U.S. 203 (1948).

275. This interest was noted by the Court in dictum in Association of Data Processing Serv. Orgs. v. Camp, 397 U.S. 150, 154 (1970). *See supra* note 219 and accompanying text.

276. 392 U.S. 236 (1968).

277. This is not to suggest that the plaintiff will be unable to demonstrate injury-in-fact in any establishment clause case. For example, in McGowan v. Maryland, 366 U.S. 420 (1961), the plaintiff challenged Sunday closing laws. Traditional injury-in-fact was easily demonstrated; enforcement of the laws resulted in plaintiff's loss of revenue from either closing on Sundays or paying fines for being open. *Id.* at 430-31; *see also* Larkin v. Grendel's Den, Inc., 459 U.S. 116, 120-27 (1982) (plaintiff had standing to challenge Massachusetts law permitting churches to veto issuance of liquor licenses to establishments within 500 feet).

278. *See supra* notes 120-41, 201-03 and accompanying text.

279. For example, in the early 1970's, it was rumored that then Vice President Spiro Agnew had discussed suspending the 1972 general elections. *See* J. DEAN, BLIND AMBITION 32-33 (1976). Suppose that the Nixon administration had done so, using national security as a pretext to attempt to remain in office. Taking the Court's analysis to its logical extreme, no one would have standing to challenge the suspension except, perhaps, persons who could make a sufficiently concrete showing that they would have been candidates in those elections. Everyone else's interest would have been indistinguishable in character from the plaintiffs' interest in *Valley Forge* or *Schlesinger*.

280. *See supra* note 202 and accompanying text.

lem does not follow ineluctably from this premise. In the next Part, this Article proposes a new approach to "stake in the outcome" which leads to a broader, yet still manageable, standing doctrine consistent with our philosophical history.

## III
## Collective Constitutional Rights and Their Implications for the Doctrine of Standing

The Court's approach to standing has been inconsistent in two important ways. First, the Justices have not settled on a single concept of injury-in-fact, with reference to how individualized or generalized it must be.[281] Second, they have inconsistently applied the nexus test, relying heavily upon it in fourth amendment cases[282] while refusing even to acknowledge it as part of standing doctrine in other than taxpayer suits.[283] This Part of the Article explores a new approach to standing that eliminates the inconsistencies in current standing doctrine and permits suits involving serious governmental trespasses that currently appear immune from judicial remedy.[284]

This Part first sets out an additional kind of interest in constitutional cases, supplying a new predicate for the constitutionally required "stake in the outcome":[285] collective rights. Second, the compatibility of a collective stake in the outcome with our Lockean constitutional heritage is demonstrated. Third, areas where collective rights have already been or ought to be recognized are noted and discussed. Finally, this Part proposes a new theory of standing in constitutional cases that is consistent with the foregoing analysis yet does not create universal standing.

### *A. The Interest To Be Protected and the Lockean Model*

The classic statement of the case-or-controversy requirement in the area of standing is that plaintiffs must have "alleged such a personal stake in the outcome of the controversy as to assure that concrete adverseness which sharpens the presentation of issues upon which the court so largely depends for illumination of difficult constitutional questions."[286] The difficulty, of course, has occurred in applying the concept of "a personal stake in the outcome" to particular fact patterns. The

281. *Compare* Trafficante v. Metropolitan Life Ins. Co., 409 U.S. 205, 211-12 (1972) *with* United States v. Richardson, 418 U.S. 166, 176-78 (1974). *See also supra* notes 128, 227-37 and accompanying text.

282. *See supra* notes 179-92 and accompanying text.

283. *See* Duke Power Co. v. Carolina Envtl. Study Group, Inc., 438 U.S. 59, 78-79 (1978); *see also supra* notes 249-57 and accompanying text.

284. *See supra* pp. 92-94.

285. *See* Baker v. Carr, 369 U.S. 186, 204 (1962).

286. *Id.*

Court insists that if an individual's interest in a controversy is undifferentiated from the rest of the citizenry's, he has not demonstrated a sufficient personal stake in the outcome.[287] But this doctrinal approach leads to an anomaly: if government broadly and nonspecifically violates the Constitution, no individual has a sufficient stake in the outcome to pursue a judicial remedy. In short, the Court tells us that, for purposes of standing, no one has a sufficient stake to keep government behavior within constitutional limits.

In a Lockean society, this is the ultimate contradiction. The citizenry's compact and consent create the government and give it legitimacy. Citizens' inability to challenge actions that violate the charter of government's existence make the charter unenforceable.[288] It becomes the constitutional analog of the unenforceable contract that declares, "I will if I want to."[289] In fact, however, the Lockean model provides a solution to the dilemma. Because the society creates the government, and because the government is responsible to its creator—not as one contracting party to another but rather as trustee to settlor[290] or agent to principal[291]—there is a clear collective societal interest in having the government behave in strict accord with the Constitution. When government violates the Constitution, the stake in the outcome of the controversy is society's stake, and is the most fundamental interest possible: the interest in government functioning as agreed upon by its creators.

The collective interest concept is certainly not new, as Part I demonstrates. Locke conceived of the civil state as one in which government is responsible to society as a whole, rather than to any particular individual.[292] That concept was echoed in the Declaration of Independence[293] and subsequent American thought.[294] Both legal relationships suggested

287. *See, e.g.*, Valley Forge Christian College v. Americans United for Separation of Church & State, Inc., 454 U.S. 464 (1982); Schlesinger v. Reservists Comm. to Stop the War, 418 U.S. 208 (1974); United States v. Richardson, 418 U.S. 166 (1974); *supra* notes 120-58, 193-213 and accompanying text.

288. The only possible enforcement mechanism is the electoral process, but that is ill-suited to resolution of constitutional questions. *See infra* notes 312-21 and accompanying text.

Professor Nichol has noted that the Court's approach to standing in cases like *Valley Forge* means that the Constitution cannot always be enforced. "The Court . . . views some constitutional provisions as enforceable and others not." Nichol, *supra* note 27, at 92.

289. In the law of contracts this is referred to as an illusory promise. "Such an illusory promise is neither enforceable against the one making it, nor is it operative as a condition for a return promise." Corbin, *The Effect of Options on Consideration*, 34 YALE L.J. 571, 574 (1925) (footnote omitted).

290. *See supra* notes 48-56 and accompanying text.

291. *See supra* note 70.

292. *See supra* notes 58-62 and accompanying text.

293. The Declaration of Independence para. 2 (U.S. 1776).

294. For example, James Madison specifically spoke of "the permanent and aggregate interests of the community," THE FEDERALIST NO. 10, at 78 (J. Madison) (C. Rossiter ed. 1961), in arguing

by the Lockean model of civil society connote collective rights. First, the people whose consent gives rise to government may be regarded as a principal, and government as the agent.[295] The agency is created by the people acting as a collective unit, not by any individual; hence the responsibility of the governmental agent is to the collective principal. Second, Locke spoke of government as a trustee of powers given to it by the people,[296] and the people thus become both the settlors and the beneficiaries of the governmental trust.[297]

Two analogies from the law of trusts demonstrate these relationships. The beneficiaries of a trust have standing to challenge the malfeasance of the trustee, though the beneficiary must show that the trustee's conduct has harmed the beneficiary's interest under the trust.[298] The law of standing in the trust area, therefore, appears to parallel the Supreme Court's injury-in-fact analysis in constitutional adjudication. The Supreme Court has failed to recognize, however, that under the American constitutional model, the beneficiary's interest is the *performance* of the governmental trustee, not the receipt of more tangible benefits. The settlor of a trust for public benefit also has standing to challenge the misbehavior of his trustee if the settlor retains a beneficial interest in the performance of the trust.[299] In this respect, Locke's trust metaphor suggests a different concept of standing in constitutional cases, one that recognizes the citizenry as the source of the fiduciary power lodged in government. When a trustee violates the terms of the trust, the settlors and beneficiaries have standing to enforce the terms of the trust through the courts. Why should not the same be true when the governmental trustee violates the terms of the trust expressed in the Constitution?

Of course, one of the terms of this governmental trust is that judicial challenges may be raised only within the limits of the trust agreement—the Constitution. However, the Constitution requires only that a case or controversy exist for the judicial power of the United States to be exercised. It is the Supreme Court that has interpreted the case-or-controversy clause as requiring the individual plaintiff to have a stake in the outcome,[300] insisted that such a stake can be demonstrated only by plaintiff's injury-in-fact,[301] and declared that the government's violation of the

for a republican form of government that could "break and control the violence of faction." *Id.* at 77. Two years later he commented on "the general principle, that laws are unconstitutional, which infringe the rights of the community." 1 ANNALS OF CONG. 458 (J. Gales ed. 1789).

295. *See supra* note 70.

296. *See supra* notes 48-50, 57-61 and accompanying text.

297. *See supra* note 50 and accompanying text.

298. A. SCOTT, THE LAW OF TRUSTS §§ 199.1-.3 (3d ed. 1967).

299. *Id.* § 200.1.

300. *See, e.g.*, Baker v. Carr, 369 U.S. 186, 204 (1962).

301. *See, e.g.*, Barlow v. Collins, 397 U.S. 159, 164 (1970); Association of Data Processing Serv. Orgs. v. Camp, 397 U.S. 150, 152 (1970).

Constitution, without more, can never give rise to the sort of injury that satisfies the case-or-controversy requirement.[302] The Court's belittling references to "generalized grievances" imply that government's obedience to the Constitution is too meager an interest to deserve judicial attention. In fact, in a society based on the Lockean model, there can hardly be a greater interest, or one more worthy of judicial attention. The question whether the government has complied with the Constitution goes to the civil society's continuing right to exist as an organized unit.[303]

One must remember that society, acting as a unit, creates the government. No individual, standing alone, may properly be regarded as the settlor of the governmental trust. As Locke made clear in discussing society's formation and dissolution, it is the collective body of society that stands in direct relationship to government. For example, recall Locke's description of the two-step process that forms civil society: first, individuals combine into a society, and second, the community vests its power in government as a trust.[304] Similarly, the right retained by society to dissolve itself and to do away with civil government—the Lockean right of revolution—is also collective.[305] Thus, the interest in government's proper performance is primarily collective[306] because of the processes of government formation and dissolution. To the extent the judiciary regulates government on behalf of the people, the scope of adjudication should be affected by the collective model of society upon which the nation is established.

The Supreme Court has not been blind to this sort of collective interest. On occasion, the Court has specifically recognized it. In *United States v. Richardson*,[307] the Court admitted that its developing standing doctrine might create circumstances in which no one would have standing to sue. It did not, however, regard that as a problem with its doctrine; rather, it viewed that situation as supporting its argument that such controversies should be remitted to the political process for resolution.[308]

> [T]hat the Constitution does not afford a judicial remedy does not, of course, completely disable the citizen who is not satisfied with the

302. *See, e.g.*, Valley Forge Christian College v. Americans United for Separation of Church & State, Inc., 454 U.S. 464, 488-90 (1982); Schlesinger v. Reservists Comm. to Stop the War, 418 U.S. 208, 226-27 (1974).

303. *See supra* notes 66-70 and accompanying text.

304. *See supra* notes 57-58 and accompanying text.

305. *See supra* notes 66-70 and accompanying text.

306. That is not to say, of course, that there is no individual interest in proper government functioning. Locke recognized such interests when he described government as existing to protect individuals' property rights, J. LOCKE, *supra* note 23, § 138, at 378-79, and the American Bill of Rights was also designed in part to enhance individual interests.

307. 418 U.S. 166 (1974).

308. *Id.* at 179; *see also supra* notes 130-31 and accompanying text.

> "ground rules" established by the Congress for reporting expenditures of the Executive Branch. Lack of standing within the narrow confines of Art. III jurisdiction does not impair the right to assert his views in the political forum or at the polls. Slow, cumbersome, and unresponsive though the traditional electoral process may be thought at times, our system provides for changing members of the political branches when dissatisfied citizens convince a sufficient number of their fellow electors that elected representatives are delinquent in performing duties committed to them.[309]

Similarly, in *Valley Forge Christian College v. Americans United for Separation of Church and State, Inc.*,[310] the Court reiterated that "even when the plaintiff has alleged redressable injury sufficient to meet the requirements of Art. III, the Court has refrained from adjudicating 'abstract questions of wide public significance' which amount to 'generalized grievances,' pervasively shared and *most appropriately addressed in the representative branches*."[311] Thus, the Court relied upon what it characterized as a "slow, cumbersome, and unresponsive" process for vindication of rights sufficiently significant to merit specific constitutional mention.

There are four shortcomings in the majority's reliance on the political process to correct constitutional violations. First, as the Court itself has recognized, the political process is notoriously slow. Moreover, it is particularly unresponsive to single-issue candidacies, especially at the national level.[312] The more diverse the electorate and the more complicated the issue facing it, the less any single issue is likely to be dispositive in the electoral process.[313]

Second, the Court in effect makes constitutional decisions a matter

309. *Richardson*, 418 U.S. at 179. The Court did not explain why its treatment of standing in *Richardson* compels the conclusion that such disputes should be handled politically.

310. 454 U.S. 464 (1982); *see supra* notes 193-213 and accompanying text.

311. 454 U.S. at 474-75 (emphasis added) (quoting Warth v. Seldin, 422 U.S. 490, 499-500 (1975)).

312. *See* Jaffe, *supra* note 27, at 1286-87 ("Formal majorities register judgments only occasionally, and then as a rule not on specific issues but on total performance."). The phenomenon Professor Jaffe refers to is merely a general reflection of American voting patterns. "The role that any specific issue may play in ultimate partisan choice is limited in several directions. Only rarely does a single policy belief comprise the sole force in the psychological field as the voting decision is made." A. CAMPBELL, P. CONVERSE, W. MILLER & D. STOKES, THE AMERICAN VOTER 97-98 (abr. ed. 1964).

313. The Third Circuit has noted the difficulties of the political process in the context of broadening standing: "[U]nless individuals averring an encroachment of their legal rights have some recourse other than the political process for the vindication and protection of those rights, the proud claim that individual citizens have rights against the government may be emptied of significance." Americans United for Separation of Church & State, Inc. v. Department of Health, Educ. & Welfare, 619 F.2d 252, 265 (3d Cir. 1980), *rev'd sub nom.* Valley Forge Christian College v. Americans United for Separation of Church & State, Inc., 454 U.S. 464 (1982).

of majority vote.[314] The Court not only remits certain constitutional questions to the political process for resolution, but it also implicitly declares that the answers are not to be found in the Constitution itself. Rather, they are to be determined by the electoral process—a process against which the Constitution was to provide some insulation.[315] For example, in *Valley Forge*, the majority would apparently have the constitutionality of the conveyance be an issue in the next national election, after which, by tallying the vote, one would know whether the conveyance did or did not violate the establishment clause. To the extent that this is the Court's implicit suggestion, it prescribes a form of constitutional relativism that poses substantial difficulties; stare decisis may be less than immutable, but its mood swings certainly cannot compare with those of the American electorate.

The third problem stems from the limitations of the electoral process. Many constitutional questions avoided by the Court on standing grounds cannot be resolved by the electorate, no matter how speedy, consistent, and rational its behavior. For example, in *Ex parte Levitt*,[316] the plaintiff argued that Justice Black's appointment to the Supreme Court violated the ineligibility clause.[317] The political process provided no possible remedy for the allegedly unlawful actions of the President and the Senate that had placed Justice Black on the Court. Federal judges are not subject to recall; they can be removed from office only by impeachment, and then only for conduct not amounting to "good behavior."[318] Thus, the allegedly unconstitutional appointment was immune to electoral correction. Similarly, there is no apparent political remedy for the conveyance of federal land to Valley Forge Christian College. Even if the electorate were to unite to vote out of office those responsible for the conveyance, that would provide no mechanism by which to set the con-

314. The Court has previously made a similar suggestion in the fourth amendment context by leaving to the states the question of whether to adopt the exclusionary rule. In Irvine v. California, 347 U.S. 128 (1954), the Court declined to reverse the holding of Wolf v. Colorado, 338 U.S. 25 (1949), *overruled by* Mapp v. Ohio, 367 U.S. 643 (1961), that the exclusionary rule had no application to the states, though they were bound by the fourth amendment through the 14th amendment. The plurality in *Irvine* explained that "to upset state convictions even before the states have had adequate opportunity to adopt or reject the rule would be an unwarranted use of federal power." 347 U.S. at 134 (Jackson, J.). The Court did not explain why state courts' use of evidence seized in violation of the fourth amendment should become more or less constitutional according to how many states repudiated the practice, nor did it explain how, if the rule were not constitutionally required, the Supreme Court would have any basis for imposing it on the states.

315. Indeed, James Madison noted at some length that the then-proposed Constitution was structured to prevent, to the extent possible, tyrannies of the majority. THE FEDERALIST No. 51 (J. Madison); *see also* Whitney v. California, 274 U.S. 357, 376 (1927) (Brandeis, J., concurring) (specifically recognizing that the first amendment was intended to limit such tyrannies).

316. 302 U.S. 633 (1937) (per curiam); *see supra* note 129.

317. U.S. CONST. art. I, § 6, cl. 2.

318. U.S. CONST. art. III, § 1.

veyance aside.[319] It is, therefore, a bit too facile for the Court to assert, as it did in *Richardson*,[320] that questions that the federal courts refuse to address on standing grounds may be resolved through the political process.[321]

The fourth problem concerns the role of the federal courts in the constitutional system. Since *Marbury v. Madison*,[322] the established principle has been that the responsibility for evaluating the constitutionality of congressional and executive actions is lodged in the judiciary.[323] Even before the Constitution was adopted, James Madison recognized the judiciary's role in restraining government,[324] and the Supreme Court itself has been unequivocal in its support of this quintessentially judicial function. "[I]t is established practice for this Court to sustain the jurisdiction of federal courts to issue injunctions to protect rights safeguarded by the Constitution and to restrain individual state officers from doing what the 14th Amendment forbids the State to do."[325] The Burger Court has recognized that under the Constitution, "the judiciary is clearly discernible as the primary means through which [constitutional] rights may be enforced."[326] The Court's assertion, therefore, that the judiciary must yield to the political process when certain constitutional questions arise is in-

319. Indeed, once title became vested in the college, an argument could be made that a subsequent attempt to legislatively undo the conveyance would constitute a taking without just compensation in violation of the fifth amendment.

320. *See supra* note 309 and accompanying text.

321. That is not to say that no problem presented in a standing case is addressable in the electoral forum. It certainly is true that, upon rejection of his plea in the courts for a declaration that the Central Intelligence Agency Act was unconstitutional, Richardson could have mounted a nationwide campaign to elect a Congress and, if necessary, a President who would effect a repeal of the challenged statute. Some, of course, might view this as impractical. *See supra* notes 312-13 and accompanying text.

322. 5 U.S. (1 Cranch) 137 (1803).

323. *See id.*; *accord* United States v. Nixon, 418 U.S. 683 (1974) (power to review intrabranch dispute between President and special prosecutor); Powell v. McCormack, 395 U.S. 486 (1969) (power to review congressional decision whether to seat a duly elected Member of Congress); Kilbourn v. Thompson, 103 U.S. 168 (1881) (power to review exercise of congressional power to punish uncooperative witnesses).

324. Justice Brennan tried unsuccessfully to bring this part of American history to the Court's attention:

> As James Madison noted, if a bill of rights were "incorporated into the Constitution, independent tribunals of justice will consider themselves in a peculiar manner the guardians of those rights; they will be an impenetrable bulwark against every assumption of power in the Legislative or Executive; they will be naturally led to resist every encroachment upon rights expressly stipulated for in the Constitution by the declaration of rights."

Valley Forge Christian College v. Americans United for Separation of Church & State, Inc., 454 U.S. 464, 494 n.6 (1982) (Brennan, J., dissenting) (quoting 1 ANNALS OF CONG. 439 (J. Gales ed. 1789)).

325. Bell v. Hood, 327 U.S. 678, 684 (1946) (footnote omitted) (jurisdiction over claim for damages suffered from federal agents' violation of fourth and fifth amendment rights).

326. Davis v. Passman, 442 U.S. 228, 241 (1979) (implied cause of action for due process violation).

consistent with its own stated view of its role in the constitutional system.[327]

Thus, although the Court recognizes the collective interest in restraining government within the confines of the Constitution, it generally characterizes that interest as insufficient to give rise to a case or controversy within the meaning of article III.[328] Yet in several areas, the Court has recognized collective rights as part of the constitutional structure, and several Justices frequently speak of rights and remedies in collective terms.

### *B. The Court's Recognition of Collective Rights*

Explicitly or implicitly, the Supreme Court[329] has identified collective rights in the first, second, fourth, sixth and thirteenth amendments,[330] as well as in some of the provisions of article I.[331] In the first amendment area, the collective interest has manifested itself in two ways. First, the Court has clearly demonstrated its recognition of collective interests in public and press access to judicial proceedings. For example, in *Richmond Newspapers, Inc. v. Virginia*,[332] the Court specifically noted "a guaranteed right of the public under the First and Fourteenth Amend-

327. Chief Justice Marshall might have viewed the Court's current position more harshly, in light of his assertion in Cohens v. Virginia, 19 U.S. (6 Wheat.) 264 (1821), that for the Court to refuse to exercise power conferred on it by the Constitution is "treason to the Constitution." *Id.* at 403. And, as Justice (later Chief Justice) Charles Evans Hughes said, "We are under a Constitution, but the Constitution is what the judges say it is . . . ." D. PERKINS, CHARLES EVANS HUGHES AND AMERICAN DEMOCRATIC STATESMANSHIP 16 (1956).

328. *See, e.g.*, Schlesinger v. Reservists Comm. to Stop the War, 418 U.S. 208 (1974); United States v. Richardson, 418 U.S. 166 (1974); *supra* notes 120-53 and accompanying text.

329. One of the most vocal members of the Court in invoking community imagery is Chief Justice Burger, who argues that the community's collective interest must be given greater weight when balanced against the individual's than has heretofore been the case. But while he adopts the concept of community, the Chief Justice seems to apply it far more to limit assertion of individual constitutional rights than to aid in restricting unlawful governmental actions. *See generally* Chesler, *Imagery of Community, Ideology of Authority: The Moral Reasoning of Chief Justice Burger*, 18 HARV. C.R.-C.L. L. REV. 457 (1983).

330. In addition, Justice Marshall made fleeting reference to a "social interest in preserving [fifth amendment] liberties and in the integrity of the criminal justice system" in Jenkins v. Anderson, 447 U.S. 231, 254 (1980) (Marshall, J., dissenting), but neither he nor the Court has pursued this idea.

331. Both Schlesinger v. Reservists Comm. to Stop the War, 418 U.S. 208 (1974), and United States v. Richardson, 418 U.S. 166 (1974), characterized the plaintiffs' interests under the ineligibility clause and the accounts clause as no more than generalized grievances, implicitly placing these constitutional provisions in the realm of collective, not individual, interests. A similar argument may be made with respect to *Ex parte* Levitt, 302 U.S. 633 (1937) (per curiam).

332. 448 U.S. 555 (1980). *Richmond Newspapers* involved a press challenge to a Virginia trial court order closing a defendant's fourth murder trial to the press at the request of defense counsel. The press' motion to vacate the closure order was denied. The Supreme Court had held a year earlier that there was no public sixth amendment right to attend preliminary court proceedings in criminal cases. Gannett Co. v. DePasquale, 443 U.S. 368 (1979). By contrast, *Richmond Newspapers* presented the issue whether the first amendment allowed closure of criminal trials. The

ments to attend the trial."[333] Justice Brennan, concurring in the judgment, explored the nature of the public right at greater length and argued for more explicit recognition under the first amendment of such a public right to receive information.[334] In these respects, *Richmond Newspapers* echoed dicta from earlier cases that suggested recognition of a public constitutional right.[335] Thus, the Court has clearly recognized an interest held by the public under the first amendment to attend criminal trials.[336]

Individual Justices have also argued on the basis of collective first amendment rights. For example, Justice Black, joined by Chief Justice Warren and Justice Douglas, dissented in *Barenblatt v. United States*,[337] a decision that affirmed a contempt of Congress conviction entered against a teacher who refused to answer questions of the House Un-American Activities Committee. Justice Black specifically referred to "the interest of the people in having [first amendment rights] exercised."[338] Later in the same opinion, he sharply criticized the majority's approach:

> [The Court] balances the right of the Government to preserve itself, against Barenblatt's right to refrain from revealing Communist affiliations. Such a balance, however, mistakes the factors to be weighed . . . [and] completely leaves out the real interest in Barenblatt's silence, the interest of the people as a whole in being able to join organizations, advocate causes and make political "mistakes" without later being subjected to governmental penalties for having dared to think for themselves. . . . It is these interests of society, rather than Barenblatt's own right to si-

Court declined to extend *Gannett*, but explicitly based its holding on the first, rather than the sixth amendment.

One remarkable aspect of *Richmond Newspapers* is its unarticulated assumption of the petitioner's standing where the interest invoked was no less undifferentiated from that of the general citizenry than that in *Valley Forge*. *See infra* notes 388-92, 396-97 and accompanying text.

333. *Richmond Newspapers*, 448 U.S. at 580. Though the Chief Justice's opinion was only for a plurality of the Court, this aspect of it was joined by Justices Brennan, Stewart, White, Marshall, Blackmun and Stevens. *Accord* Globe Newspaper Co. v. Superior Court, 457 U.S. 596, 603 (1982) ("Richmond Newspapers firmly established . . . that the press and general public have a constitutional right of access to criminal trials. . . . [S]even Justices recognized that this right of access is embodied in the First Amendment, and applied to the States through the Fourteenth Amendment."); *see also* United States v. Chagra, 701 F.2d 354 (5th Cir. 1983) (access to pretrial criminal proceedings, specifically bail reduction hearing); United States v. Criden, 675 F.2d 550 (3d Cir. 1982) (access to pretrial suppression, due process, and entrapment hearings).

334. *Richmond Newspapers*, 448 U.S. at 585-98 (Brennan, J., concurring in judgment); *see also id.* at 598-601 (Stewart, J., concurring in judgment).

335. *E.g.*, Estes v. Texas, 381 U.S. 532, 541 (1965) ("[T]he public has the right to be informed as to what occurs in its courts . . . ."); Craig v. Harney, 331 U.S. 367, 374 (1947) ("A trial is a public event. What transpires in the court room is public property.").

336. The Third Circuit recently recognized that the public and press have a first amendment right of access to civil proceedings as well. Publicker Indus. v. Cohen, 733 F.2d 1059 (3d Cir. 1984).

337. 360 U.S. 109 (1959).

338. *Id.* at 143 (Black, J., dissenting).

> lence, which I think the Court should put on the balance against the demands of the Government, if any balancing process is to be tolerated.[339]

Thus, the three Justices recognized both the existence of a cognizable collective interest in the first amendment and the importance of considering the possible antagonism between the collective, societal interest and the government's interest. The collective interest not only exists as a constitutional concept, but also requires protection from the government itself; the government cannot be assumed to represent it.[340]

The Court's recognition of collective rights in the first amendment area has not been limited to questions of public access to courts. In *Scripps-Howard Radio, Inc. v. FCC*[341] and *FCC v. Sanders Brothers Radio Station*,[342] which concerned disputes over FCC licenses to operate radio stations, the Court expressly recognized the status of radio stations as representatives of the public interest. In *Scripps-Howard*, the petitioner contested a modification of a competitor's license. In reviewing the petitioner's standing, the Court noted that the Communications Act of 1934[343] was designed to protect "the public interest in communications."[344] The Act conferred a right of appeal on aggrieved persons, but the Court noted the limitations of that right. "[T]hese private litigants have standing only as representatives of the public interest. . . . That a court is called upon to enforce public rights and not the interests of private property does not diminish its power to protect such rights."[345] Thus, the Court recognized that Congress had created a statutory collective right in this area because of communication's public importance.

Regarding the second amendment, courts have been even clearer about the nature of the right guaranteed. Case after case has considered whether the right to bear arms is an individual or a collective right. The Sixth Circuit, for example, stated unequivocally that "[i]t is clear that the Second Amendment guarantees a collective rather than an individual right,"[346] a view apparently reflected by every court to have considered

339. *Id.* at 144 (Black, J., dissenting).

340. *See also* Bursey v. United States, 466 F.2d 1059, 1083 (9th Cir. 1972) (public interests in the first amendment may be more important than personal interests).

341. 316 U.S. 4 (1942).

342. 309 U.S. 470 (1940).

343. 47 U.S.C. §§ 151-610 (1982).

344. *Scripps-Howard*, 316 U.S. at 14.

345. *Id.* at 14-15 (citing FCC v. Sanders Bros. Radio Station, 309 U.S. 470, 477 (1940); National Licorice Co. v. NLRB, 309 U.S. 350 (1940)). The Court's remarkable position that the petitioner had standing not as a private entity but only as a public representative stands in stark contrast to the Court's more common assertion that to represent the public interest a litigant must demonstrate a private right. *See, e.g.*, Sierra Club v. Morton, 405 U.S. 727 (1972); *see supra* notes 114-16 and accompanying text. This apparently lenient position might be thought to result in part from the holding's statutory, rather than constitutional, basis. *But see infra* note 365.

346. United States v. Warin, 530 F.2d 103, 106 (6th Cir.), *cert. denied*, 426 U.S. 948 (1976).

the issue specifically.[347] The courts have adopted this position because of the introductory phrase of the second amendment, referring to the right to bear arms in the context of maintenance of a militia.[348] Nonetheless, it is significant that the courts have explicitly recognized that the Framers of the Constitution intended to create at least one collective right. It is also noteworthy that this recognition came in consideration of an amendment that speaks of rights held by a plural entity, the people, rather than by an individual. Compare the rights of "the people" referred to in the first, second, fourth, ninth, and tenth amendments with those of "the person" and "the accused" safeguarded in the fifth and sixth amendments. The second amendment joins the first as a provision in which collective rights have received a judicial imprimatur.

In the fourth amendment area, the Supreme Court has been less forthright about recognizing collective interests, but it has nevertheless done so in cases considering application of the exclusionary rule. Through the 1970's, the Court emphasized that the exclusionary rule exists to protect the collective, societal interest in deterring fourth amendment violations, and not to make whole the victim of an unlawful search or seizure.[349] Moreover, the Court used that societal interest concept as a predicate for refusing to apply the exclusionary rule in cases where the individual would have benefited by its application but the deterrent effect—the benefit to society generally—would have been more tenuous.[350] The collective interest is, therefore, now clearly recognized in the fourth amendment area, though in the cases where the Court has commented

347. *E.g.*, United States v. Johnson, 497 F.2d 548 (4th Cir. 1974); United States v. Tot, 131 F.2d 261 (3d Cir. 1942), *rev'd on other grounds*, 319 U.S. 463 (1943); Burton v. Sills, 53 N.J. 86, 248 A.2d 521 (1968), *appeal dismissed*, 394 U.S. 812 (1969); *see also* United States v. Miller, 307 U.S. 174 (1939). *But see* Levine & Saxe, *The Second Amendment: The Right To Bear Arms*, 7 HOUS. L. REV. 1 (1969) (suggesting that the second amendment guarantee is individual as well as collective).

348. "A well regulated Militia, being necessary to the security of a free State, the right of the people to keep and bear Arms, shall not be infringed." U.S. CONST. amend. II.

349. *See, e.g.*, United States v. Calandra, 414 U.S. 338 (1974):

> The purpose of the exclusionary rule is not to redress the injury to the privacy of the search victim: "[T]he ruptured privacy of the victims' homes and effects cannot be restored. Reparation comes too late." Instead, the rule's prime purpose is to deter future unlawful police conduct and thereby effectuate the guarantee of the Fourth Amendment against unreasonable searches and seizures . . . . In sum, the rule is a judicially created remedy designed to safeguard Fourth Amendment rights generally through its deterrent effect, rather than a personal constitutional right of the party aggrieved.

*Id.* at 347-48 (quoting Linkletter v. Walker, 381 U.S. 618, 637 (1965)); *accord* United States v. Janis, 428 U.S. 433, 453-54 (1976); United States v. Turk, 526 F.2d 654 (5th Cir.), *cert. denied*, 429 U.S. 823 (1976).

A contrary suggestion appears in Harrison v. United States, 392 U.S. 219 (1968), which mentions that one of the exclusionary rule's benefits is that it "restores the situation that would have prevailed if the Government had itself obeyed the law." *Id.* at 224 n.10. *Harrison* has not been followed.

350. *See, e.g.*, United States v. Janis, 428 U.S. 433 (1976); United States v. Calandra, 414 U.S. 338, 349-52 (1974).

upon the societal interest, it has used that interest as a reason for refusing to punish unconstitutional government behavior. Despite that unusual twist, this development of fourth amendment jurisprudence is important because of the emergence of the collective interest analysis.[351]

The collective, public interest in the fourth amendment was specifically mentioned in Justice Harlan's dissent in *United States v. White*.[352]

> [T]he issue here is whether to interpose a search warrant procedure between law enforcement agencies engaging in electronic eavesdropping and the public generally. By casting its "risk analysis" solely in terms of the expectations and risks that "wrongdoers" or "one contemplating illegal activities" ought to bear, the plurality opinion, I think, misses the mark entirely. [By not requiring warrants to eavesdrop, the Court] does not simply mandate that criminals must daily run the risk of unknown eavesdroppers prying into their private affairs; it subjects each and every law-abiding member of society to that risk.[353]

It was the public interest that Justice Harlan felt had been given insufficient consideration by the *White* plurality. But because *White* was written in Justice Harlan's last year on the bench, it is impossible to tell whether his collective-interest interpretation would have swayed other members of the Court in the 1970's standing cases had he been there to urge it.[354]

The Court has also implicitly recognized a public interest in the sixth amendment guarantee of a jury trial in all criminal cases.[355] Some defendants, however, prefer to be tried to the court. The Federal Rules of Criminal Procedure permit a defendant to waive a jury and be tried to the court, provided the judge and prosecutor agree.[356] In *Singer v. United States*,[357] the Supreme Court upheld this restriction on the waiver of a jury trial. The *Singer* Court did not discuss why the waiver limita-

351. For a detailed argument in favor of recognition of a collective fourth amendment right, see Doernberg, *supra* note 29.

352. 401 U.S. 745 (1971). Justice Harlan opposed reaffirmation of the Court's rule permitting warrantless electronic eavesdropping with the consent of any party to a conversation. That rule had been adopted by the Court in On Lee v. United States, 343 U.S. 747 (1952). The Court had occasion in *White* to reconsider *On Lee* because the Seventh Circuit had reversed White's narcotics conviction on the ground that *On Lee* had been overruled by Katz v. United States, 389 U.S. 347 (1967). *Katz* had ruled that wiretapping or eavesdropping could constitute a fourth amendment violation despite the absence of physical trespass into an area in which the search victim had a reasonable expectation of privacy. In *White*, the Court declined to extend *Katz* to the situation where one of the parties to a conversation has consented to the electronic intrusion.

353. *White*, 401 U.S. at 789 (Harlan, J., dissenting).

354. *See supra* text accompanying notes 179-92.

355. The Supreme Court now reads the word "all" in the sixth amendment to mean "some," permitting a nonjury trial over the defendant's objection where the offense charged is "petty": i.e. carries a possible penalty of less than six months imprisonment. *See* Baldwin v. New York, 399 U.S. 66, 69 (1970); Duncan v. Louisiana, 391 U.S. 145, 159 (1968).

356. FED. R. CRIM. P. 23(a).

357. 380 U.S. 24 (1965).

tion had been instituted, but at least one reason may be inferred from the opinion. The Court noted that "[t]rial by jury has been established by the Constitution as the 'normal and . . . preferable mode of disposing of issues of fact in criminal cases.' "[358] But to whom is this mode of adjudication preferable? The preference is obviously not the defendant's, since Singer sought to waive the jury trial. The *Singer* Court's statement must reflect, therefore, the existence of an unarticulated public interest in the sixth amendment right to jury trial.[359]

The thirteenth amendment[360] also indirectly implicates collective rights. Titles VIII and IX of the Civil Rights Act of 1968,[361] which concern fair housing practices, were enacted as enforcement measures in order to eliminate one of the remaining badges of slavery in American society.[362] In both *Gladstone, Realtors v. Village of Bellwood*[363] and *Trafficante v. Metropolitan Life Insurance Co.*,[364] the Supreme Court explicitly noted the community interest embodied in the Act and seized upon congressional recognition of that interest as a reason to find standing for plaintiffs against whom there had been no discriminatory action. Such plaintiffs' interest in integrated community living surely was undifferentiated from anyone else's similar interest; yet the Court, affirming the community interest, found standing.[365] This is significant for two reasons. First, it acknowledges another judicially cognizable collective right—a thirteenth amendment right to reside in a community the composition of which is not determined by race. Second, it casts grave doubt on the Court's repeated assertions[366] that generalized grievances—those shared by the community at large—cannot meet the requirements of the case-or-controversy provision. If that were so, congressional recognition of such interests would do nothing to alter or satisfy the constitutional minima. *Gladstone* and *Trafficante* are the Court's implicit recognition

358. *Id.* at 35 (quoting Patton v. United States, 281 U.S. 276, 312 (1930)).

359. The rule might be seen merely as an attempt to ensure that defendants' waivers of this constitutional right are knowing and intelligent within the meaning of Johnson v. Zerbst, 304 U.S. 458 (1938). But such paternalism would be anomalous given that other constitutional rights under the fourth, fifth, and sixth amendments may be waived unilaterally.

360. U.S. CONST. amend. XIII, § 1: "Neither slavery nor involuntary servitude, except as a punishment for crime whereof the party shall have been duly convicted, shall exist within the United States, or any place subject to their jurisdiction."

361. 42 U.S.C. §§ 3601-3619, 3631 (1982).

362. Williams v. Matthews Co., 499 F.2d 819, 825 (8th Cir.), *cert. denied*, 419 U.S. 1021 (1974); United States v. Hunter, 459 F.2d 205, 214 (4th Cir.), *cert. denied*, 409 U.S. 934 (1972).

363. 441 U.S. 91 (1979).

364. 409 U.S. 205 (1972); *see supra* notes 227-37 and accompanying text.

365. The fact that a statute explicitly provided standing is unimportant. If undifferentiability of the plaintiff's injury from the injury suffered by the public generally meant that no case or controversy existed, as the Court suggested in *Schlesinger* and *Richardson*, then the congressional attempt to grant standing through the statute would be ineffective. It is the nature of the interest asserted vis-a-vis the Constitution that is important, not the source from which the interest springs.

366. *See supra* notes 137-41, 201-03 and accompanying text.

that the community can have a stake in the outcome sufficient to have its interest represented by one of its members without running afoul of article III.

There are, in addition, two procedural analogs to the substantive collective rights that the courts have recognized. Generalized interests have been vindicated in the courts by representatives from the private and public sectors. When such representation is by a private individual, the courts refer to him as a private attorney general. When the public sector is involved in the representation, the concept of parens patriae is employed.

Private attorneys general have been explicitly recognized in a variety of contexts. For example, in *Newman v. Piggie Park Enterprises*,[367] the Court specifically approved of individuals acting as private attorneys general to enforce provisions of the Civil Rights Act of 1964.[368] The private attorney general theory was also used in *Trafficante v. Metropolitan Life Insurance Co.*,[369] with respect to the Civil Rights Act of 1968,[370] and it has been used to enforce the 1965 Voting Rights Act[371] and the Social Security Act.[372] It appears, however, that plaintiffs have never been accorded standing as private attorneys general in constitutional cases.[373] Nonetheless, the concept of collective interest clearly inheres in the concept of private attorneys general, and it would be difficult to argue that policies more important than those contained in the Constitution exist.

Parens patriae involves state action on behalf of its citizens pursuant to its duty to safeguard the general welfare of the people. The Supreme Court has accepted the principle of parens patriae suits.[374] In *Georgia v. Pennsylvania Railroad*,[375] the Court permitted the state to bring a parens

367. 390 U.S. 400 (1968) (per curiam).

368. 42 U.S.C. §§ 2000a to a-6 (1982) (as amended).

369. 409 U.S. 205 (1972); *see supra* notes 227-37 and accompanying text.

370. 42 U.S.C. §§ 3601-3619, 3631 (1982) (as amended).

371. *Id.* §§ 1971, 1973 to 1973b-4 (as amended); *see* Allen v. State Bd. of Elections, 393 U.S. 544 (1969).

372. 42 U.S.C.A. §§ 301-1397f (West 1983); *see* National Welfare Rights Org. v. Finch, 429 F.2d 725 (D.C. Cir. 1970).

373. In United States Parole Comm'n v. Geraghty, 445 U.S. 388 (1980), the Court analogized the right of class certification to the concept of the private attorney general in cases where the class representative's individual claim became moot or was otherwise resolved. *Id.* at 403. This analogy was dictum, however, as the Court ruled that appellate courts may review denial of a class certification motion even though the proposed representative's claim has become moot. The representative has standing to appeal because he has a "personal stake" in obtaining class certification within the traditional meaning of that language.

374. Hawaii v. Standard Oil Co., 405 U.S. 251, 258 (1972) (citing New York v. New Jersey, 256 U.S. 296 (1921); Kansas v. Colorado, 206 U.S. 46 (1907); Missouri v. Illinois, 180 U.S. 208 (1901); Louisiana v. Texas, 176 U.S. 1 (1900)).

375. 324 U.S. 439 (1945).

patriae suit to obtain injunctive relief against railroads allegedly violating the antitrust laws. And, in *Hawaii v. Standard Oil Co.*,[376] the Court reaffirmed the parens patriae principle, though it refused to permit the state as parens patriae to seek damages on behalf of its citizens.

But here too, the Court has explicitly denied states the use of parens patriae suits to challenge federal government actions on constitutional grounds. In *Massachusetts v. Mellon*,[377] the Court stated:

> It cannot be conceded that a State, as *parens patriae*, may institute judicial proceedings to protect citizens of the United States from the operation of the statutes thereof. While the State, under some circumstances, may sue in that capacity for the protection of its citizens . . . it is no part of its duty or power to enforce their rights in respect of their relations with the Federal Government. In that field it is the United States, and not the State, which represents them as *parens patriae*, when such representation becomes appropriate . . . .[378]

One must remember, though, that *Massachusetts v. Mellon* and the cases that followed it were decided by a Court that had not focused its attention on the concept of collective rights under the Constitution and the implications of their existence. Moreover, *Mellon* itself seemed not to question the existence of collective interests so much as it disputed whether the state was the appropriate representative to enforce them in this particular case.[379] What is significant is that the parens patriae doctrine represents an additional judicial recognition of circumstances in which collectively held rights may be vindicated by a litigant who cannot show the type of individualized injury normally required by the Court to confer standing.

The courts, therefore, have frequently given express or implied recognition to collectively held rights under the Constitution. Indeed, the idea of collective rights is not only consistent with the United States' constitutional and philosophical heritage, it is virtually compelled by it. What the courts have never done, however, is to synthesize these concepts with the doctrine of standing so that the doctrine permits protection of such rights rather than functioning as a barrier to their assertion and vitality. It is therefore necessary to develop a new theory of standing that permits representation of collective rights without simultaneously threatening to inundate the courts with suits that are frivolous, duplicative or both. The next Section addresses this problem.

---

376. 405 U.S. 251 (1972).

377. 262 U.S. 447 (1923).

378. *Id.* at 485-86 (citation omitted); *see also* Oklahoma v. Atchison, T. & S.F. Ry., 220 U.S. 277 (1911) (parens patriae concept will not support original Supreme Court jurisdiction when the state in fact seeks to represent citizens' interests but not its own). *See generally* Note, *Standing of States to Represent the Interests of Their Citizens in Federal Court*, 21 AM. U.L. REV. 224 (1971).

379. *See Mellon*, 262 U.S. at 485.

### C. *Standing to Vindicate Collective Rights*

As the law of standing exists today, collective interests in constitutional provisions cannot be effectively protected. Collective rights are vindicated from time to time when they fortuitously appear in cases in which a litigant can demonstrate individual standing, but there is no systematic way for these rights to receive their due. The difficulty with current standing theory lies in its restrictive view of the case-or-controversy requirement. It is the Court, not the Constitution, that has defined a case in terms of the plaintiff's stake in the outcome and further defined that stake in terms of personal injury-in-fact. But as the Court itself has recognized, there exists a collective interest in government behavior constrained by constitutional limits—an interest the Court disparagingly refers to as "generalized grievances."[380] What the Court fails to realize is that, in any society founded on the Lockean model, the citizens have an enormous collective stake in the governmental trustee acting within its powers and limitations.[381] When government violates the Constitution, society's interest is implicated, and that interest should be addressable in the courts.[382]

Who is to represent the societal interest? Possible cases may be divided into two groups based on the constitutional provisions and governmental actions involved. In the first group, government actions violating the Constitution necessarily produce an injury-in-fact traceable to a specific individual. For example, government suppression of speech in violation of the first amendment produces two types of injury. One is collective; society's rights both to hear what the speaker would have said[383] and to have government act according to the Constitution suffer when government becomes censor. The second injury is to the would-be speaker; his constitutional right to speak is impaired. This case presents a situation where judicial vindication of an individual's rights and redress of his injury a fortiori protects the public right simultaneously.[384] Similarly, when the government conducts a search without probable cause or

380. *See supra* notes 137-41, 201-03 and accompanying text.

381. *See supra* notes 286-91 and accompanying text.

382. *See supra* notes 322-27 and accompanying text. In American society, three methods are available to address government's constitutional violations: through the political process, through the courts, and through exercise of the Lockean right of revolution. For most purposes, the first is both impractical and inappropriate, *see supra* notes 312-21 and accompanying text, and the last is impractical and undesirable. Locke himself made clear that the right of revolution is to be exercised only in cases of the grossest government malfeasance. *See supra* notes 66-70 and accompanying text. The true alternatives, therefore, are acquiescence in constitutional violations or resort to the courts.

383. *See supra* notes 332-45 and accompanying text.

384. By contrast, if the individual chooses to acquiesce in the violation of his constitutional right to speak, current standing doctrine leaves no one to protect the collective interest since the right to receive information has not been accorded explicit first amendment status by the Court. *See, e.g.*, Richmond Newspapers, Inc. v. Virginia, 448 U.S. 555, 584-89 (1980) (Brennan, J., concurring).

a warrant in violation of the fourth amendment, the criminal defendant's subsequent motion to suppress the fruits of the search also serves to invoke the judicial power to protect the collective privacy interest embodied in the fourth amendment.[385] In a series of cases,[386] however, the Court has ruled that though the government might have violated the fourth amendment and though the defendant might have been directly injured thereby, he is without standing to complain of the government's illegal conduct. In such circumstances, the collective right cannot be vindicated under current standing doctrine, despite the presence of an individual injured in fact as a direct result of the constitutional violation. The difficulty arises because the Court has silently substituted the legally-protected-interest test for the injury-in-fact test of standing.[387] It has created a subgroup of cases where collective rights could be vindicated by individuals injured in fact, but where such individuals are refused standing either to represent the collective interest or to seek redress of the injury-in-fact they have suffered as individuals.

In the second group of cases, a governmental constitutional violation cannot produce individualized injury-in-fact as that term has been interpreted by the Court. *Valley Forge Christian College v. Americans United for Separation of Church and State, Inc.*,[388] *Schlesinger v. Reservists Committee to Stop the War*,[389] *United States v. Richardson*,[390] and *Ex parte Levitt*[391] are examples of cases in this group. In these cases, it was impossible for the plaintiffs to demonstrate any injury-in-fact attributable to them individually; yet, if their allegations could have been proved, the government would have been guilty of violating the Constitution. Nonetheless, in *Valley Forge*, *Schlesinger*, and *Richardson*, the Court recognized the possibility that no conceivable plaintiff would have standing.[392]

The two groups of cases suggest different tests for standing. Where the government's unconstitutional act can give rise to individualized injury-in-fact, it seems appropriate to insist that the one who challenges the action be one of those injured. But at the same time, the test of injury should remain faithful to the injury-in-fact standard that the Court has developed and should not retreat to the legally-protected-interest test unanimously repudiated by the Court.[393] Thus, in the fourth amend-

385. *See supra* notes 349-54 and accompanying text.

386. *See supra* notes 179-92 and accompanying text.

387. *See supra* notes 190-92 and accompanying text.

388. 454 U.S. 464 (1982); *see supra* notes 193-203 and accompanying text.

389. 418 U.S. 208 (1974); *see supra* notes 133-42 and accompanying text.

390. 418 U.S. 166 (1974); *see supra* notes 128-30 and accompanying text.

391. 302 U.S. 633 (1937) (per curiam); *see supra* note 129.

392. *See supra* note 203 and accompanying text.

393. *See* Barlow v. Collins, 397 U.S. 159 (1970); Association of Data Processing Serv. Orgs., Inc. v. Camp, 397 U.S. 150 (1970); *supra* notes 214-26 and accompanying text.

ment context, the use of illegally seized evidence would constitute injury-in-fact to the defendant. He would therefore qualify as a representative of society's interest in privacy reflected in the fourth amendment. Similarly, a member of the public or a reporter who is excluded from the courtroom is injured in fact and is the appropriate person to represent the public's first amendment interest in open judicial proceedings. The Supreme Court has recognized this sort of vicarious representation of the public interest claimed by plaintiffs. As the court said in *Sierra Club v. Morton*,[394] once a plaintiff has standing, he may argue the public interest in support of his claim that the government has exceeded its lawful authority.[395]

The second group of cases, where the unconstitutional government action cannot result in injury-in-fact to an individual, poses a more difficult problem for standing purposes. The Court has declared that such cases present "generalized grievances." Plaintiffs fail to present an article III case or controversy in these cases because their stake in the outcome is indistinguishable from that of anyone else.[396] The result is that the collective right involved is left unprotected and unenforceable. Therefore, I propose that individuals be accorded standing, much as private attorneys general,[397] to present constitutional challenges to unlawful government action on behalf of the collective public interest. There can be no question that the citizenry has a stake in the outcome of a constitutional case where the issue is whether the government has violated its charter. The conflict between the collective interest in constitutionalism on one hand and government's unlawful behavior on the other should be found to meet the case-or-controversy requirement of Article III. There is, accordingly, no constitutional impediment to the concept of citizen standing in the kind of case described here, provided that one does not view all possible interests atomistically, each having no possible connection to the others.

Citizen standing as proposed here would, however, present two potential problems. First, if unregulated, it might open the doors of the federal courthouses to a flood of constitutional litigation from persons who would lack standing under current doctrine. Second, it raises the possibility that the citizens who undertake to represent the public interest may not be fit to do so. Both difficulties can be overcome through the use

394. 405 U.S. 727 (1972).

395. *Id.* at 737 (footnote omitted) (citing Scripps-Howard Radio, Inc. v. FCC, 316 U.S. 4 (1942); FCC v. Sanders Bros. Radio Station, 309 U.S. 470 (1940)).

396. *See, e.g.*, Valley Forge Christian College v. Americans United for Separation of Church & State, Inc., 454 U.S. 464 (1982); Schlesinger v. Reservists Comm. to Stop the War, 418 U.S. 208 (1974); United States v. Richardson, 418 U.S. 166 (1974).

397. *See supra* notes 367-73 and accompanying text.

of a single device in citizen standing cases: the class action.[398] Courts have always determined the appropriateness of prospective class representatives in class actions. The Federal Rules of Civil Procedure require both that the representative party assert a claim typical of the class[399] and that he "fairly and adequately protect the interests of the class."[400]

---

398. The standing proposal advanced here requires no modification of the class action device itself. Once the existence of judicially cognizable collective interests is recognized, established class action principles permit appropriate invocation of the judicial power to protect such interests.

399. FED. R. CIV. P. 23(a)(3). The claims of named plaintiffs are typical of the class' claims when they are based on the same legal and remedial theories and when there is no adversity between the named plaintiffs and unnamed class members. 7 C. WRIGHT & A. MILLER, FEDERAL PRACTICE AND PROCEDURE § 1764 (1972); *see also* Mersay v. First Republic Corp. of America, 43 F.R.D. 465, 468-69 (S.D.N.Y. 1968). Clearly, when a single governmental act or pattern of acts is challenged as unconstitutional, a citizen's claim will be typical; the constitutional theories asserted will be common to all. It is possible, of course, that the class representative may not raise all of the possible constitutional objections to the challenged government activity. The failure of the representative and his counsel to raise and vigorously to pursue all nonfrivolous constitutional arguments goes directly to the representative's fitness to represent the class. *See infra* note 400. If the court feels that the named class representative overlooks or rejects appropriate arguments, certification of the class should be refused or, if already granted, should be withdrawn pursuant to FED. R. CIV. P. 23(c)(1). "The district court may decertify a class after trial if plaintiff's trial performance showed him or her to be an inadequate class representative." Payne v. Travenol Laboratories, Inc. 673 F.2d 798, 811 (5th Cir. 1982) (citing Johnson v. Uncle Ben's Inc., 628 F.2d 419 (5th Cir. 1980)), *vacated and remanded on other grounds*, 451 U.S. 902 (1981). It has been argued that the district court has an affirmative duty to decertify a class where the representative is unsuitable. Sessum v. Houston Community College, 94 F.R.D. 316, 322 (S.D. Tex. 1982) (citing DeGrace v. Rumsfeld, 614 F.2d 796 (1st Cir. 1980)). *But see* Carpenter v. Steven F. Austin State Univ., 706 F.2d 608, 617-18 (5th Cir. 1983) (suggesting that after trial, a new class representative should be appointed in preference to decertifying the class).

There is also no possibility of judicially cognizable adversity among the class members. It is, of course, conceivable that some members of the citizen class might not wish the government to correct its allegedly unconstitutional behavior. For example, supporters of Valley Forge Christian College might applaud the land grant even if it violated the first amendment. This would not make plaintiffs' claims any less representative of the claims of the class. "Whether all the members desire to exercise these rights is not relevant to the issues in the litigation. The possibility that some might not, at this time, wish to exercise their right . . . does not preclude a class action." Cortright v. Resor, 325 F. Supp. 797, 808 (E.D.N.Y.), *rev'd on other grounds*, 447 F.2d 245 (2d Cir. 1971), *cert. denied*, 405 U.S. 965 (1972). Moreover, one would hesitate to assert that there is a judicially cognizable interest in having government continue to violate the Constitution. Accordingly, though as a practical matter there may not be unanimity among members of the citizen class with respect to any particular action, its absence does not undermine the propriety of the device.

Similarly, class members may have divergent views on whether the government's action is constitutional, wholly apart from their feelings on its desirability. Such a difference of opinion does not, in this sort of public action any more than in any class action, constitute adversity among members of the class. It is the function of the courts, not the class members, to decide the constitutional issue. Indeed, to allow differences of opinion among class members to defeat the representativeness of the named plaintiff would make it impossible for anyone to raise the constitutional challenge at all. Thus, to allow diversity of opinion to preclude a public class action of the type advocated in this Article would be to recognize a theory of constitutional relativism similar to that discussed *supra* in notes 314-15 and accompanying text. In this case, however, diversity of public opinion would be the cause of the judiciary's decision not to resolve the controversy rather than a result of judicial abstention.

400. FED. R. CIV. P. 23(a)(4). Courts generally focus on two factual questions in determining whether the named plaintiffs will fairly and adequately protect the interest of absent class members:

The federal courts certainly have not been reluctant to refuse to certify classes where the representative or counsel has been found to be inadequate.[401] When the plaintiff asserts citizen standing, and therefore purports to represent the public interest, this inquiry will be crucial.

The threat of multiple actions dealing with identical constitutional issues can also be met by the class action device. The federal courts should establish a nationwide central indexing system to catalog ongoing class actions invoking the collective-right, citizen-standing principles discussed here. Once a citizen class is certified,[402] all other district courts should refuse to entertain similar suits since the plaintiffs before them would already be parties in another case presenting the same question. Duplicative actions can be stayed, enjoined, or dismissed.[403] In this manner, only one citizen-standing challenge to a particular governmental action could be maintained. It is precisely this sort of economy of judicial and litigative effort that the class action was in part designed to achieve.[404] Appropriate use of the class action device, therefore, suggests a solution to the two practical problems associated with the proposal for citizen standing in constitutional cases suggested here.[405]

Therefore, both the conceptual structure and an appropriate proce-

whether the named plaintiffs can present a strong case on behalf of the entire class, Mack v. General Elec. Co., 329 F. Supp. 72, 76 (E.D. Pa. 1971), and whether the attorneys representing the class will vigorously pursue the action. Mersay v. First Republic Corp. of America, 43 F.R.D. 465, 469 (S.D.N.Y. 1968). Counsel must be qualified, experienced and adequate to conduct the litigation. Eisen v. Carlisle & Jacquelin, 391 F.2d 555, 562 (2d Cir. 1968), *rev'd on other grounds*, 417 U.S. 156 (1974). The litigants must not be involved in collusive litigation, nor may named plaintiffs have interests antagonistic to those of the rest of the class. The named plaintiffs' interests must be coextensive with those of the remainder of the class. *Id.*; Weiss v. Tenney Corp., 47 F.R.D. 283, 290 (S.D.N.Y. 1969). Finally, the court must be satisfied that the named plaintiffs will protect the due process rights of absent class members. *Eisen*, 391 F.2d at 562.

401. *See, e.g.*, Green v. Carlson, 653 F.2d 1022 (5th Cir. 1981) (per curiam), *cert. denied*, 454 U.S. 944 (1982); *In re* Folding Carton Antitrust Litig., 88 F.R.D. 211 (N.D. Ill. 1980); Tomkin v. Kaysen, 69 F.R.D. 541 (S.D.N.Y. 1976).

402. "As soon as practicable after the commencement of an action brought as a class action, the court shall determine by order whether it is to be so maintained." FED. R. CIV. P. 23(c)(1).

403. The mere pendency of a class action does not preclude parallel individual actions by class members. 3B J. MOORE & J. KENNEDY, MOORE'S FEDERAL PRACTICE ¶ 23.92 (2d ed. 1984). Nevertheless, "a court having in personam jurisdiction over a class suit [under Rule 23(b)(1) or (b)(2)] should have the power to enjoin competing actions that are vexatious and oppressive." *Id.* (footnote omitted). For the government to have to litigate the same constitutional question repeatedly is oppressive, hence sound policy dictates the availability of injunctive relief.

Moreover, if a central index of citizen standing cases were established, all other courts would be able to stay duplicative suits pending judgment in the class action, thus avoiding judicial inefficiency. *See, e.g.*, Blinder, Robinson & Co. v. SEC, 692 F.2d 102, 106 (10th Cir. 1982); Leisner v. New York Tel. Co., 358 F. Supp. 359 (S.D.N.Y. 1973).

404. *See* Hohmann v. Packard Instrument Co., 399 F.2d 711, 715 (7th Cir. 1968); Kainz v. Anheuser-Busch, Inc., 194 F.2d 737, 740 (7th Cir.), *cert. denied*, 344 U.S. 820 (1952).

405. The other requirements of Rule 23 are easily satisfied by any case of the type described here. When the citizenry is the plaintiff class, the numerosity requirement of Rule 23(a)(1) is satisfied. In addition, the constitutionality of a government action is a question common to the class, as

dural device exist to permit recognition of a new type of standing in certain constitutional cases. The availability of citizen standing would have changed the results in some, but not all, of the standing cases from the 1970's.[406] *Sierra Club v. Morton*[407] provides an interesting example of how the limited citizen-standing theory would work. If one regards dim-

---

required by Rule 23(a)(2). The other two criteria of Rule 23(a) have already been discussed. *See supra* notes 399-401 and accompanying text.

With regard to Rule 23(b), citizen-standing actions would be maintainable under subsections (1)(A), (1)(B) or (2). With respect to Rule 23(b)(1)(A), separate individual actions against a single government action or policy alleged to be unconstitutional could certainly result in inconsistent judicial interpretations establishing wholly incompatible standards of conduct for the government. Moreover, judgments in individual cases would have stare decisis value for future litigation and thus, within the meaning of Rule 23(b)(1)(B), would tend to conclude the interests of other individuals not party to the action.

As for Rule 23(b)(2), an unconstitutional government act or policy that by its nature is incapable of producing individuated injury-in-fact, *see supra* notes 388-92, 396-97 and accompanying text, clearly constitutes an act generally applicable to the citizen class. In such cases, injunctive or declaratory relief is, as a practical matter, the only appropriate remedy. The courts have interpreted the rule to require that "the party opposing the class has acted either in a consistent manner toward members of the class . . . or has established a regulatory scheme common to all class members." 7A C. WRIGHT & A. MILLER, *supra* note 399, § 1775, at 19-20 (footnote omitted). Thus, Rule 23(b)(2) is the section best designed for management of the type of class action proposed here.

In recent years, the Supreme Court has restricted the use of the class action device to some extent. In Zahn v. International Paper Co., 414 U.S. 291 (1973), the Court held that in a diversity case, each member of the class (named or unnamed) must satisfy the jurisdictional amount requirement of 28 U.S.C. § 1332 (1982). Thus, the plaintiffs' claims may not be aggregated to satisfy the amount-in-controversy requirement. Accordingly, *Zahn* makes it more difficult for persons with small individual claims to pursue them as a class in the federal courts.

In Eisen v. Carlisle & Jacquelin, 417 U.S. 156 (1974), the Court ruled that each class member whose name and address was readily ascertainable had to be individually notified of the action's pendency pursuant to FED. R. CIV. P. 23 (c)(2). The Court also held that the proponent of the class was required to bear the entire cost of the notification. *Eisen* thus erects some substantial barriers to individuals' ability to undertake class action litigation.

Finally, Coopers & Lybrand v. Livesay, 437 U.S. 463 (1978), sharply restricted the appealability of orders denying class certification, finding them inappropriate bases for interlocutory appeals. At the same time, the Court acknowledged that denial of certification might well be the death knell of such litigation because the individual plaintiff would find it uneconomical to pursue litigation in the absence of class certification. *Id.* at 469-71. Nonetheless, the Court declined to permit interlocutory appeals despite the potential "incremental benefit" in situations where litigation would be ended by denial of class action certification. *Id.* at 473.

The factor which unites these cases and distinguishes them from the type of public action proposed here is that they are all actions brought pursuant to FED. R. CIV. P. 23(b)(3). Such actions are characterized by the separable individual interests of the class members; typically such actions seek money damages which may vary according to the individual's involvement in the controversy. It is for this reason that the Court has strictly interpreted the requirement of FED. R. CIV. P. 23(c)(2) that individual notice be given to each member of the (b)(3) class if practicable. Eisen v. Carlisle & Jacquelin, 417 U.S. 156 (1974). The public actions supported by this Article, however, would be certified under FED. R. CIV. P. 23(b)(1) or (b)(2) and by definition do not involve injuries differentiable according to class member. Hence, there is no individualized interest allocable to absent class members. Recent Supreme Court cases simply do not address such actions.

406. *See supra* Part II, Section *A*.

407. 405 U.S. 727 (1972); *see supra* notes 110-16 and accompanying text.

inution of one's enjoyment of the environment as an injury-in-fact,[408] then the result of *Sierra Club* would not change. Because individualized injury-in-fact would be possible, citizen standing would not be available.[409]

On the other hand, both *United States v. Richardson*[410] and *Schlesinger v. Reservists Committee to Stop the War*[411] would be decided differently under a doctrine of citizen standing. In *Richardson*, the Court denied standing precisely because the plaintiff had failed to allege an interest distinguishable from that of the public generally,[412] a finding echoed by the *Schlesinger* majority.[413] The concept of citizen standing urged here would seize upon that generalized public interest as a reason to find standing, not a reason to deny it. Without recognition of such a collective right to lawful government behavior, and standing to insist upon it, some provisions of the Constitution are unenforceable, dead-letter law. Similarly, the result in *Valley Forge Christian College v. Americans United for Separation of Church and State, Inc.*[414] would be different. A broader standing doctrine, recognizing a collective "right to a particular kind of Government conduct, which the Government has violated by acting differently,"[415] would make the alleged constitutional abuse in *Valley Forge* subject to judicial review, precisely in order to vindicate society's generalized, but nonetheless fundamental, interest in government behavior consistent with its trust.

Finally, there remains the question of the nexus requirement. To the extent that it reflects the idea that the governmental action must not only harm the plaintiff, but must also violate some duty owed to him,[416] then the recognition of the government's duty to act constitutionally as a duty owed to all citizens would satisfy the nexus requirement. That duty is breached whenever government violates the Constitution, and the nexus requirement is automatically satisfied under the collective-right citizen-standing proposal advanced here. To the extent that the nexus requirement is, in Professor Tribe's words, "an attempt to reduce the risk

408. *See* United States v. SCRAP, 412 U.S. 669 (1973); *see supra* notes 238-42 and accompanying text.

409. If, however, the Supreme Court were to reverse its view of environmental damage expressed in *SCRAP*, declaring it insufficient to give rise to individual injury-in-fact, then invocation of the citizen-standing doctrine would be appropriate. In that case, the result of *Sierra Club* would be reversed by the new standing concept.

410. 418 U.S. 166 (1974).

411. 418 U.S. 208 (1974).

412. *See supra* notes 122-28 and accompanying text.

413. *See supra* notes 133-42 and accompanying text.

414. 454 U.S. 464 (1982); *see supra* notes 193-203 and accompanying text.

415. *Valley Forge*, 454 U.S. at 483.

416. *See* Jaffe, *Standing Again*, 84 HARV. L. REV. 633, 636 (1971). *See generally* L. TRIBE, *supra* note 8, § 3-22, at 98.

that federal judges will unintentionally divert the central thrust of constitutional and statutory policies by allowing 'officious intermeddlers' to invoke federal claims under provisions designed to benefit persons who may be entirely satisfied with the action challenged,"[417] then the requirement is unnecessary under this new concept of standing. If the "intermeddler" can show injury-in-fact, then he should be entitled to invoke the judicial power. If he cannot make such a showing, then he is without standing unless no one else could suffer injury-in-fact either. The fact that some citizens may be satisfied with or unperturbed by the government action should not be a bar to standing; no one has the right to enjoy the perceived benefits of illegal government action.

In short, the nexus requirement diverts attention from the public's collective interest in having its government operate with the consent of the governed. On a day-to-day basis, that consent is manifest in the Constitution, statutes, and other regulations—the rules for conduct of government. Perhaps that is why the Court so sharply restricted the nexus requirement in *Duke Power Co. v. Carolina Environmental Study Group, Inc.*,[418] declaring its inapplicability except in taxpayer suits.[419] Professor Tribe has suggested that even in taxpayer suits the requirement be abandoned because it is "misguided," "unnecessary," and "unwarranted."[420] This Article supports that suggestion, but for an additional reason. Taxpayer standing was suggested, though repudiated, in *Frothingham v. Mellon*[421] and later adopted in *Flast v. Cohen*[422] to deal with a class of cases in which there could be no injury-in-fact under traditional doctrine. Citizen standing as suggested here, with appropriate recognition of the collective rights under the Constitution, would render taxpayer standing superfluous. Moreover, because the nexus requirement invariably operates, when applied, to foreclose standing in cases in which the collective interest of society clearly calls for the availability of judicial intervention, it is inconsistent with our Lockean foundation. The nexus requirement must be abandoned because it forecloses needed judicial review, not merely because, as Professor Tribe argues,[423] it functions poorly as an empirical matter.

## Conclusion

This Article has proposed a bifurcated standing doctrine in constitutional cases. In cases in which the challenged governmental action can

417. L. Tribe, *supra* note 8, § 3-22, at 99.
418. 438 U.S. 59 (1978).
419. *Id.* at 78-79; *see supra* notes 249-53 and accompanying text.
420. L. Tribe, *supra* note 8, at Supp. 12 (1979).
421. 262 U.S. 447, 486-88 (1923).
422. 392 U.S. 83 (1968).
423. *See* L. Tribe, *supra* note 8, §§ 3-26, 3-27.

cause individualized injury-in-fact, the collective interest in lawful government behavior is sufficiently protected if enforcement is left to the individuals directly suffering the harm. But in cases where the assertedly unlawful action cannot give rise to individual injury, the collective interest can only be adequately protected if individuals are given standing to represent the public interest. The public, the collective body, has a stake in the outcome whenever the issue is whether government has violated its charter. Each person in our society is one of the settlors and beneficiaries of the trust which is civil government under the Lockean model. When the trustee violates the trust, each person is aggrieved. A standing doctrine consistent with the political philosophy so important to our constitutional system cannot fail to permit judicial challenge when the trust is broken.

# [15]

## POLITICAL FREEDOM*

JAMES TULLY

THREE hundred years after the publication of the *Two Treatises of Government* and *A letter concerning Toleration,* one aspect of John Locke's thought continues to stand out in sharp contrast to the prevailing conventions of both seventeenth- and twentieth-century political theory. This is his hypothesis that institutionalized forms of government are derived from and perpetually rest upon the prior freedom of the people to exercise political power themselves (summarized at 2.171).[1] Locke had no doubt that it would "seem a very strange Doctrine to some" in his own time (2.9). It is no less unconventional today. In the current debate between liberals and civic humanists, for example, the leading participants share the assumption that political freedom is derived from and rests upon basic institutions and traditions.[2] The aim of this paper is to enable readers to understand Locke's strange doctrine by drawing attention to its distinctive features, first by means of a synopsis and then by a series of contrasts with more conventional views.

### I

Prior to the establishment of institutionalized forms of government, people are capable of exercising political power themselves in an ad hoc manner: "the *Execution* of the Law of Nature is in that State, put into every Man's hands" (2.7). The exercise of political power comprises the abilities to know and to interpret standards of right (natural laws), to judge controversies concerning oneself and others in accordance with these laws, and to execute such judgments by punishments proportionate to the transgression and appropriate for purposes of restraint and reparation (2.7–12). Individuals are free to order their actions within the bounds of natural laws and are equal in the "Power and Jurisdiction" to govern the actions of those who transgress these bounds (2.4, 2.6).

Since "every one is Judge, Interpreter, and Executioner," this ad

* To be presented in an APA symposium on John Locke after Three-hundred Years, December 30. John W. Yolton will be co-symposiast, and Vere Chappell will comment; see this JOURNAL, this issue, 510–6 and 524–5, respectively, for their contributions.

[1] The numbers in parentheses throughout refer to treatise and section numbers of Locke, *Two Treatises of Government,* Peter Laslett, ed. (New York: Cambridge, 1970).

[2] John Rawls, "Justice as Fairness: Political Not Metaphysical," *Philosophy and Public Affairs,* XIV (1985): 223–252; Richard Rorty, "The Priority of Democracy to Philosophy," in *The Virginia Statute of Religious Freedom,* M. Peterson and R. Vaughan, eds. (New York: Cambridge, 1987); Michael Sandel, *Liberalism and the Limits of Justice* (New York: Cambridge, 1982); Charles Taylor, *Philosophical Papers, Vol. 2* (New York: Cambridge, 1985), pp. 185–339.

hoc form of self-government, or individual popular sovereignty, does not run smoothly in practice (2.136). People disagree on a "common measure to decide all Controversies between them" and they are reluctant to concede that a law is binding in their own case (2.124). They lack the motivation to participate in the ad hoc adjudication and prosecution of disputes when the case does not concern them, and they tend to participate with passion and revenge when it does (2.125–6).

To overcome these difficulties, people set up institutionalized forms of government by uniting into a community and conditionally placing their political powers in the hands of designated legislators and executives (2.87–9, 95, 132, 144). Accordingly, political communities and governments not only derive from, but also perpetually rest on, the abilities of the citizens to judge and act politically. The members entrust their political power on the condition that the governors will exercise it in accordance with the public good. If the people find that their trustees (either the executive or legislators) abuse the power given to them and "act contrary to the trust reposed in them," the bond of obligation between governors and governed is forfeited, political power devolves "into the hands of those that gave it," and they may use it to remove them. "And thus," Locke emphasizes, "the *Community* perpetually retains a *Supream Power* of saving themselves from the attempts and designs of any Body, even of their Legislators, whenever they shall be so foolish, or so wicked, as to lay and carry on designs against the Liberties and Properties of the Subject" (2.149). As he explains in more detail in the final chapter, when political power devolves to the people, they exercise it in the form of a revolution to remove their untrustworthy governors, just as they would proceed against lawbreakers prior to the establishment of legislative and executive institutions, and "the People have a Right to act as Supreme, and continue the Legislative in themselves, or erect a new Form, or under the old form place it in new hands, as they think good" (2.243).

Who has the right to judge when the trust has been forfeited and government dissolved? Locke's answer is that "*The People shall be Judge*" and by this he means "*every Man* is *Judge* for himself" (2.240–1). Then, the "Body of the *People*" should execute this judgment by forcefully removing the unjust rulers. If this fails, each person who so judges has the right to act as best one can (2.242–3; cf. 2.168). Locke stresses that "*this Doctrine* of a Power in the People" will not lay "a *ferment* for frequent rebellion" (2.224–230) because people will not actually engage in a revolutionary contest until oppression touches the majority, or touches only a few but seems to threaten all (2.208–210, 2.230, 2.168).

The final claim Locke advances is that his account, in addition to being an explanation and justification of resistance to oppression, is also the best means of hindering oppression in the first place. Under any institutionalized form of government, those in power will be tempted in various ways to abuse the power entrusted to them: to develop an interest separate from and in violation of the good of the people (2.209–210, 2.228). This theme is emphasized even more emphatically in *A Letter concerning Toleration*[3] where he analyzes the post-Reformation case of government imposing a uniform religion and persecuting religious dissenters. The "properest way to prevent the evil, is to show them the danger and injustice of it"; that is, to confront power holders with a citizenry who know the popular basis of government, who constantly judge the public actions of their trustees, and who are always ready and willing to exercise political power themselves when it is abused (2.226; cf. 2.228).

II

The distinctive features of Locke's portrayal of political freedom can now be thrown into clear relief by contrasting them with a number of seventeenth-century alternatives. First, the conventional means to check the abuse of institutionalized forms of political power are all found by Locke to be insufficient. The argument, advanced by proponents of mixed and balanced government, that representative institutions, the division of powers, and the rule of law constitute sufficient checks was falsified in practice by the ability of seventeenth-century absolute monarchs to override these limitations (2.107, 2.111–2, 2.163). Further, these institutional arrangements, while important, are not always sufficient to stop an oppressive representative body (2.138, 2.149, 2.221–2). Locke is skeptical of the republican belief that participation in government fosters citizens oriented to the public good and impervious to the temptations of power (2.156, 2.223). He also rejects the claim that, as long as citizens are free to appeal to courts and parliaments, they will be able to hinder oppression and thus render revolution unnecessary. Locke learned from the unsuccessful attempts by religious Dissenters in the 1660s and 1670s to gain civil and religious liberties by legitimate means that those in power could block the Dissenters' appeals, stigmatize them as "seditious," and introduce repressive legislation (2.218). In *A Letter concerning Toleration,* he argues that the separation of church and state, and a clear distinction in law between politics and religion, along with representative institutions and a Bill of Rights, while necessary, are not sufficient to defend a free and tolerant society from oppression. The ultimate guardian is again said

[3] James Tully, ed. & intro. (Indianapolis: Hackett, 1983).

to be the ability of the people to judge if their governors are ruling in accordance with the public good and to be ready to remove them if they are not (*ibid.*, pp. 52–5).

Second, Locke's location of political power in the people contrasts sharply with the customary beliefs of his contemporaries. The rebellions of early modern Europe were standardly understood to be nonpolitical acts of self-defense by the people against a ruler who had attacked them. They were not thought of as political acts, because, on the conventional view, political power was never originally in the hands of the people and, consequently, could not devolve back to them. In addition, the "people" was interpreted as either a single person acting in self-defense or an established representative of the people (usually a parliament or an estate) defending them against an attack by a monarch. Theorists of mixed and balanced government could not claim that the representative bodies, let alone the people, exercised political power in a rebellion without undermining their theory that political power always exists in a mix or balance between monarch and representative bodies. Republicans could not say that the people exercise political judgment and power outside of political institutions, because they held that political judgment and power come into being with the establishment of an authoritative political community. And all these authors agreed that the worst conceivable basis for government would be the judgment of the multitude.

These commonplaces began to appear questionable in the light of the English Civil War. In the latter phase, the people took up arms against their own representatives and they presupposed the right to exercise political power, not just to defend themselves, in trying and executing Charles I and in setting up a new form of government. Either one held to the conventional understanding, and thereby deemed this exercise of popular sovereignty illegitimate, as Kant was classically to do, or one reconceptualized the power of the people, and thereby deemed this judicial proceeding legitimate, as Locke did. Furthermore, Locke wrote and published the *Two Treatises* to justify revolt against the persecution of religious Dissenters during the Restoration. Since the Dissenters were excluded from public office and lacked sufficient support in Parliament, he needed to ground the right to judge, initiate revolt, and reform government in the people themselves. The extent to which Locke deviated from orthodoxy can be measured by the widespread repudiation of the *Two Treatises* in 1690 because it presented an unacceptably radical interpretation of the Glorious Revolution.[4]

[4] See Julian Franklin, *John Locke and the Theory of Sovereignty* (New York: Cambridge, 1978); Richard Ashcraft, *Revolutionary Politics and Locke's Two Treatises of Government* (Princeton: University Press, 1986); Mark Goldie, "The

III

A contrast with the current debate between liberals and civic humanists can now be used to complete this survey of Locke's understanding of political freedom. Both sides start from the assumption that the foundation of a modern democratic society is the basic structure of post-Reformation institutions of representative government, the rule of law, religious toleration, and civil liberty. Accordingly, the role of the political philosopher, as John Rawls typically states, is to explicate or articulate the "basic intuitive ideas that are embedded in the political institutions of a constitutional democratic regime and the public traditions of their interpretation" (*op. cit.*, p. 225). This consists in making explicit the implicit consensus on conceptions of political agency and social cooperation which underlie surface disagreements and accord with the basic institutions. Despite their disagreement on what forms of political agency and cooperation best serve to support and enhance a democratic society, civil humanists are just as concerned to grant priority to political institutions, practices, and communities. Political institutions and public traditions of their interpretation, one might say, are taken to be sovereign.

The leading writers in the debate have not considered Locke's opposite hypothesis that political institutions and traditions rest upon the political freedom and popular sovereignty of the people. Instead, they have misinterpreted Locke from within their very different conceptual framework and, as a result, assimilated him to either Hobbes or Benjamin Constant, both of whom share their premise of institutional sovereignty. With Locke's hypothesis elegantly disposed of in this preemptive fashion, the conventional institutional theories, which Locke found insufficient to explain how concentrated political power can be held in check, have been recirculated as the solutions to contemporary problems.

This anti-Lockean consensus can be partly explained by the theoretical sources of the debate. Liberals draw on Kant, who lays it down that the basic structure of law and its agents is sovereign, not the consent of the governed, and can never rightfully be disobeyed.[5] Civic humanists draw on Aristotle, Cicero, Machiavelli, Rousseau, and Hegel, all of whom concur that the necessary precondition of

---

Roots of True Whiggism 1688–94," *History of Political Thought,* I, 2 (1980): 195–236; Mark Goldie, "The Revolution of 1689 and the Structure of Political Argument," *Bulletin of Research in the Humanities,* LXXXIII (1980): 473–564; and my "John Locke," *The Cambridge History of Political Thought: 1450–1700,* James Burns, ed. (New York: Cambridge, 1990).

[5] John R. Wallach, "Liberals, Communitarians, and the Tasks of Political Theory," *Political Theory,* XV, 4 (November 1987): 581–611, esp. pp. 587–8.

and limitation on political judgment and action is an established and authoritative political community. Moreover, ever since the Reaction to the French Revolution and the attack on Lockean popular sovereignty by Burke and Bentham, there has been a widespread tendency to take political, social, and economic institutions as foundational and then to ask what forms of freedom are compatible with them. Constant,[6] for example, set forth this picture of the relation between freedom and institutions in a form that has become the "horizon" of modern political thought for many liberal thinkers. Revolution as well has been reconceptualized as a social movement caused by the underlying social and economic institutions of the modern world, rather than as a political action in response to misgovernment.

The main theoretical argument against Locke is that the abilities to judge and act politically are acquired through practice, and practice presupposes and takes place in the context of practices—political institutions and communities. Therefore, to rest these institutions on the prior abilities of the people to judge and act politically is a philosophical mistake as well as a recipe for anarchy and confusion in practice.

Since Locke wrote extensively on how abilities to judge and act are acquired by practice in practices, it is difficult to believe that he overlooked this point when he came to write the *Two Treatises.*[7] Rather, the mistake may lie with his opponents. Their assumption appears to be that political abilities are acquired in *canonical* political institutions: namely, exactly those political institutions occupied by members whose overlapping consensus of judgments and actions is said to be authoritative. So, the judgments and actions of those who are outside these institutions, or are critical of them, will be, by definition, unreliable and illegitimate. Locke was, of course, familiar with this form of argument, used for example by Anglican royalists against Dissenters, and he devoted most of book one of *An Essay concerning Human Understanding*[8] to exposing its self-validating circularity.

The argument is mistaken because people are able to acquire and exercise political abilities outside the canonical institutions and traditions. Indeed, they often acquire them through the experience of

[6] "The Liberty of the Ancients Compared with That of the Moderns," in *Political Writings,* Biancamaria Fontana, ed. (New York: Cambridge, 1988).

[7] See my "Governing Conduct," in *Conscience and Casuistry in Early Modern Europe,* E. Leites, ed. (New York: Cambridge, 1988); and John Dunn, "Bright Enough for All Our Purposes: John Locke's Conception of A Civilized Society," *Notes and Records of the Royal Society in London,* XLIII (1989): 133–153.

[8] Peter Nidditch, ed. (New York: Oxford, 1975), 1.3.20–2; cf. 1.4.22–6. Rorty has carried this form of argument further in "Thugs and Theorists," *Political Theory,* XV, 4 (November 1987): 564–580.

exclusion from and oppression by these institutions. The Dissenters' struggle for religious toleration and political enfranchisement and the European women's movements are well-known examples of this. Further, according to Locke, the faculty of judgment, even though it is always developed in the context of a practice, involves the reflexive ability to suspend and examine the authoritative traditions of that practice itself.[9] Finally, unlike Locke's hypothesis, this form of argument cannot explain how political institutions are set up or changed. Either they must be taken for granted, as in the current debate, or a mythical legislator is required, as in the republican tradition.

The major pragmatic argument against Locke is that members of modern societies are shaped and constituted by the massive and complex institutions of power and authority. Therefore, from a sociological point of view, their judgments and actions derive from and rest upon these institutions rather than vice versa. The absence of revolutions in Europe since 1850 is often said to support this and to falsify the theory of popular sovereignty.

In reply, one might point to the remarkable revolutions that occurred in Eastern European countries over last winter. These outbreaks of popular sovereignty were neither predicted by, nor did they conform to, the social and economic theories of revolution available in the social sciences. The people involved did not have the background representative institutions that are said to be necessary to foster political freedom and judgment. Nor did they have the experience of participating in republican institutions in order to develop civic virtue and discern the common good. Their activity of civil dissent prior to the revolutions was also insufficient to reform their governments. Yet, for all that, their revolts were not simply acts of self-defense. The people claimed to respond to political oppression by governments whom they judged to have forfeited their trust (often in these terms). They proceeded to overthrow their governors, to put them on trial and punish them, and went on to set up new forms of government and new governors, as they thought good.

JAMES TULLY

McGill University

[9] For one way of working out this line of argument, see my "Wittgenstein and Political Philosophy," *Political Theory,* XVII, 2 (May 1989): 172–204.

# [16]

# Locke, Sincerity and the Rationality of Persecution

Paul Bou-Habib

*University of Bristol*

According to the most influential contemporary reading of John Locke's *Letter Concerning Toleration* (1689), his main argument against religious persecution is unsuccessful. That argument holds that coercion is ineffective as a means of instilling religious beliefs in its victims. I propose a different reading of the *Letter*. Locke's main consideration against persecution is not the unsuccessful belief-based argument just outlined, but what I call the *sincerity argument*. He believes that religious coercion is irrational because it is ineffective as a means of inculcating the right intentions in people. Once this alternative argument is placed at its centre, the *Letter* is seen to be a more fertile source of political argument than is suggested by alternative readings. In particular, the sincerity argument gives us a powerful reason for rejecting state moral paternalism, the doctrine that the state may use coercion to make people morally virtuous. If moral virtue depends upon people having the right intentions, and if coercion is ineffective as a means of instilling the right intentions in people, then state moral paternalism is ineffective and hence irrational.

There is a passage in John Locke's *Letter Concerning Toleration* (1689) in which he summarises what he considers to be 'the principal consideration' that weighs against religious persecution (Locke, 1993, p. 410):

> How great, soever, in fine, may be the pretence of good-will and charity, and concern for the salvation of men's souls, men cannot be forced to be saved whether they will or no; and therefore, when all is done, they must be left to their own consciences.

Most readings of the *Letter* assume that the reason Locke believes that 'men cannot be forced to be saved' is that force is ineffective as a means of instilling true religious beliefs in people. Although I believe that this is one line of argument that runs through the *Letter*, I suggest that it is not the one which is referred to above as the 'principal consideration' against persecution. His principal argument against persecution is what I call the *sincerity argument*: men cannot be forced to be saved, because salvation depends upon men having the *right intentions*, and force cannot make people have the right intentions.

If this interpretation is correct, we have reason to resist an objection that has been levelled against Locke by Jeremy Waldron and that has influenced much of the secondary literature on the *Letter*. In a remarkable article, Waldron claims that it is the belief-based argument against persecution that is the 'main line of argument' in the *Letter*, and he finds it 'an inadequate and unconvincing argument, one that in the last resort radically underestimates the complexity of the problem it addresses' (Waldron, 1991, p. 98). The implication is that the *Letter* falls outside the canon of important texts from which we might draw intellectual resources to bolster the contemporary defence of religious toleration, and that we must look elsewhere for such resources – say, to John Stuart Mill's insistence upon the value of diversity in *On Liberty*. However, as I will propose, this implication can only be drawn on the mistaken assumption that the *Letter*'s main line of argument is indeed the belief-based argument on which Waldron focuses. Once we notice that the 'principal consideration' for Locke is that people have the right intentions, as opposed to holding true beliefs, the *Letter* becomes a far more fertile source of argument against persecution than Waldron suggests.

## Locke's Aim in the *Letter*

While I am mostly interested in defending the view that the *Letter* contains a potentially powerful argument against persecution of relevance today, it may be helpful to preface the ensuing discussion of Locke's sincerity argument with a more specific description of the conclusion he intends it to support. His aim in the *Letter* is to reject one particular justification for why the state should withhold religious toleration. Several such justifications might be proposed. There is, for example, the realpolitik consideration that religious toleration may open the door to factional disputes, and eventually weaken the people as a fighting force against external adversaries. Another reason for withholding toleration is that of self-defence: to allow religious dissenters the time to flourish is to allow potential domestic enemies the time to gather in strength. The justification Locke is most concerned to discredit is different from these two. His attention is focused on the reason of compassion that motivates 'loving persecutors' – people who persecute the dissenter for the dissenter's own sake, or, more precisely, for the sake of the dissenter's spiritual welfare. He characterises this third reason as follows (Locke, 1993, p. 391):

> It be out of a principle of charity, as they pretend, and love to men's souls that they deprive them of their estates, maim them with corporal punishments, starve and torment them in noisome prisons, and in the end even take away their lives.

The principal aim of the *Letter*, then, is to show that a concern for the spiritual welfare of others never justifies such things.

As expected, the *Letter*'s fundamental claim, that it is irrational, because ineffective, to use force out of compassion for someone's spiritual welfare, has an important implication for Locke's political philosophy – specifically, for his views concerning the ends of government and the civil rights of individuals. He defined 'government' as an agent that acts only through force.[1] Since the use of force for the sake of promoting another's spiritual welfare is, in Locke's view, irrational, it follows for him that the government may not seek to promote the spiritual welfare of his subjects. The ends of government must therefore be restricted, he believes, to securing the 'temporal good and outward prosperity of the society' (Locke, 1993, p. 423).[2] The magistrate (or indeed any other government official) may still use persuasion in order to promote the people's spiritual welfare, but in that case he would not be acting in his capacity as a government official, and would be exercising a prerogative that is common to all.[3]

It is easy to mischaracterise this conclusion about the limited ends of government with terms that describe seemingly similar but actually different ways of conceiving the relation between government and religion. One such way of conceiving that relation is the doctrine we know today as the 'separation of church and state'. The doctrine of separation requires that government abstain from any kind of favourable treatment towards religion, that it may not offer financial support for religious institutions or activities, or sponsor any form of religious symbolism. Locke, however, is not necessarily committed to this doctrine, and it is important not to automatically assume that he is. There may be cases in which the government must support religion in order to protect everyone's earthly goods. Indeed, Locke believes there was such a case: he insists that the government must not tolerate atheists because their good intentions towards others cannot be trusted: 'Promises, covenants, and oaths', he wrote, 'can have no hold upon an atheist' (Locke, 1993, p. 426).

A second way in which we might be tempted to describe Locke's aim in the *Letter* is to say that he intends to defend the 'right to religious freedom'. Here, we must be especially careful, since the 'right to religious freedom' could mean several things. It might refer to a right that guarantees a person only a freedom from persecution – from burdens *intentionally* imposed upon his religious conduct. More generously, it might refer to a right that guarantees also a freedom from *unintentional* burdens upon religious conduct, and possibly even *assistance* with religious conduct. As is illustrated by an example Locke provided himself, his aim is to defend just the first of these rights.

Locke's example involves a man by the name of Meliboeus, whose religion requires him to sacrifice a calf as part of his worship – clearly a deviant religious practice in Locke's context and therefore, potentially, the target of persecution. Under ordinary circumstances, Locke said, Meliboeus may not be prevented by law from performing this sacrifice, since this is an action that causes no injury to other people or to their civil goods, and thus deserves the same freedom under law that all other harmless activities deserve. But suppose it were the case, Locke then went on to suggest, that the stock of cattle in the land falls drastically due to a widespread disease, and that, in order to prevent further depletion, the government prohibits the slaughter of cattle (Locke, 1993, p. 415):

> Who sees not that the magistrate, in such a case, may forbid all his subjects to kill any calves for any use whatsoever? Only 'tis to be observed that in this case the law is not made about a religious but a political matter; nor is the sacrifice but the slaughter of calves therefore prohibited.

The example shows well how Locke interpreted the right to religious freedom only as a right to non-persecution. Meliboeus has a right not to be made the *intentional* target of mistreatment on account of his deviant religion, but he has no right to be free also from the law's *unintentional* burdening of his religious conduct. This is the very point Locke makes in the last clause of the above passage. Since it is not 'sacrifice' but 'slaughter' that the law is prohibiting – since it is no part of the law's intention to prevent Meliboeus from practising his religion – Meliboeus has no right to be free from the burden this law may happen to impose on his religious conduct.

This conclusion may strike us as puzzling. If Locke cares about religious freedom, we might wonder why he should draw a line at protecting just a right to be free of religious persecution. After all, religious conduct will be as unfree when it is unintentionally prevented as it will be when it is intentionally prevented. To put this from Meliboeus's point of view: why should it make a difference to his interests whether the law intends to prevent 'slaughter' rather than 'sacrifice', if, given either intention, the law is equally burdensome to him? The answer to this question has to do with the particular nature of Locke's justification for the right to religious freedom. He does not justify the right to religious freedom on the grounds that there is something intrinsically valuable about Meliboeus's religious conduct, but on the grounds that religious persecution is irrational. That is why the scope of Meliboeus's right reaches no further than to a freedom from persecution.

## Two Arguments against Religious Persecution

What argument does Locke offer for the claim that justifies these political implications about limited government, the claim that religious persecution is irrational? He makes, not one, but three arguments against religious persecution in the *Letter*. I will concentrate on the first two of these, which can be summarised as follows (I will provide the relevant textual evidence for these two arguments later):

1. *The sincerity argument*: force cannot make an individual practise his religion sincerely, and sincerity is necessary for salvation.
2. *The belief argument*: force cannot make an individual believe something, and believing is necessary for salvation.[4]

Two observations about these two arguments will help sharpen the focus of my discussion. First of all, it is worth noting that they share the same form: both arguments denounce the use of force as irrational, insofar as the latter is aimed at achieving a certain effect.[5] According to Waldron, for an argument to take this form is a shortcoming: arguments that stress the instrumental irrationality of persecution fail to tell us why persecution is *morally* wrong. Here, focusing on Locke's belief argument, Waldron suggests that it lacks 'a sense of any deep concern for the *victims* of persecution or the moral insult that is involved in the attempt to manipulate their faith' (Waldron, 1991, p. 120). In other words, it appears as if Locke is mostly concerned with preserving the rational agency of the persecutors – with showing persecutors what they must do in order to act rationally – rather than with showing them what they must do in order to show concern and respect for those they are about to persecute.

In my view, this objection to Locke's two instrumentalist arguments is not entirely persuasive. It is not clear why Waldron believes that, in showing that persecution fails to achieve the persecutor's aim, Locke necessarily fails to show that persecution is morally wrong. For it is possible that Locke is assuming that the persecutor's aim is moral in character, insofar as it is focused upon the (spiritual) well-being of the persecuted. If that is the case, Locke's showing that persecution fails to achieve the persecutor's aim would amount to his showing that to persecute is to deviate from those actions a person ought to take in order to promote another's (the persecuted's) spiritual well-being and to inflict harm upon another for no good reason. In this vein, consider the following passage from the *Letter*: 'I appeal to the consciences of those that persecute, torment, destroy, and kill other men upon pretence of religion, whether they do it out of friendship and kindness towards them, or no?' (Locke, 1993, pp. 390–1). When Locke here castigates persecutors for believing that persecution is a mark of friendship and kindness, he reveals that he is addressing those persecutors who are interested in showing friendship and kindness to others. So while it is true that he focuses our attention upon the instrumental irrationality of persecution, he does this as part of an effort to show what it would mean, or rather not mean, to show friendship and kindness to others. In that case, it is misleading for Waldron to suggest that Locke is somehow not engaged by 'a sense of any deep concern for the *victims* of persecution'.

I will make a second observation in regard to Locke's first two arguments. While they share the same form, they differ in substance, and specifically over their statement of the effect that they claim force is incapable of producing. The first argument says force cannot make people practise their religion sincerely, whereas the second argument says it cannot make people acquire true religious beliefs. It is this difference that I wish to explore. In the next section, I will discuss Waldron's objection to Locke's belief argument, as well as several attempts at rescuing that argument from his objection. The reason these attempts fail, and why the belief argument is beyond rescue, will prove instructive in helping us eventually to see the strengths of the sincerity argument.

## The Belief-Based Argument

Locke's belief argument holds that persecution is wrong because belief, be it religious or otherwise, cannot be coerced (Locke, 1993, p. 395):

> True and saving religion consists in the inward persuasion of the mind, without which nothing can be acceptable to God. And such is the nature of the understanding that it cannot be compelled to the belief of any thing by outward force.

Belief is not subject to the will, and, since coercion influences only the will, people cannot accept one belief over another as a result of having their will subjected to coercion. Central to this argument is the psychological insight that the endeavour of believing is not captured in voluntarist terms: it is not 'a matter of choice', or a 'decision', and so it cannot be swayed one way or another by reward or threat. People cannot surrender their beliefs, say, in the holy trinity or in purgatory, the same way they can surrender their money at gunpoint. It is only by the route of better reasons that they can escape the conclusions to which their deliberations have taken them.

As Waldron has argued, Locke's belief argument is not as strong as it might initially appear to be. Public officials may well accept that using violence upon people will have no influence on their beliefs, but, rather than making them refrain from persecuting people altogether, this insight might only encourage them to search for less direct and more effective means of persecution. Waldron gives the following example: 'religious authorities know that there are certain books that would be sufficient, if read, to shake the faith of an otherwise orthodox population' (Waldron, 1991, p. 116). So, while coercion might not influence belief directly, 'those who wield political power can put it to work indirectly to reinforce belief by banning everyone on pain of death from reading or obtaining copies of these heretical tomes' (p. 116). In addition to *reinforcing* people's beliefs, force, when skilfully used, can also make people abandon a belief in favour of new ones. If beliefs are not influenced by violence, they are surely influenced by evidence, and evidence can be brought to people's attention through coercive means. We can imagine that the government might coerce people to read books aimed at undermining their heretical beliefs.[6] The cunning persecutor will thus refrain from beating people into the official belief system and opt instead for the more subtle approach of controlling the outlets of information, and ensuring that only one system of belief is disseminated. As Waldron concludes: 'Such means may well be efficacious even though they are intolerant and oppressive; and Locke, who is concerned only with the rationality of persecution, provides no argument against them' (pp. 116–17).

It may be instructive to consider three ways in which we might propose to defend Locke's belief argument against Waldron's objection, and which I will present here in order of increasing plausibility. The first line of defence is one that Waldron himself refutes. This is the suggestion that, while persecution might be effective in getting people to hold certain beliefs, what matters is that people stand in the right way to their beliefs – or, as we might also say, that they will have 'genuine' beliefs.[7] Genuine beliefs, this defence continues, arise in people only as the result of the free and autonomous activity of the mind, and cannot arise, then, as the result of the subtler forms of persecution to which Waldron refers. As he explains, this line of defence is not a very persuasive one, because it relies upon the false assumption that free mental activity is a necessary condition for genuine belief. To illustrate that this is in fact not a necessary condition, he gives the following example (Waldron, 1991, p. 118):

> If I am forced at the point of a bayonet to look at the colour of snow, is my consequent belief that snow is white likely to function differently from the corresponding belief of someone who did not need to be forced to take notice of this fact?

This shows quite convincingly that the beliefs that arise in people as the result of having their sensory apparatus coerced are not in any way deficient compared with beliefs that arise in people through free mental activity. So long as there are some beliefs that can be coerced in this way, Waldron's objection against Locke's belief argument stands.

At this stage, we might propose a second defence of Locke's belief argument: persecution is irrational because it cannot *guarantee* that people will acquire genuine beliefs. Susan Mendus suggests, for example, that persecution can only ever guarantee putting a person through a causal story, at the end of which he utters a belief in something (Mendus, 1991). These two conditions – being put through a causal story and utterance – are not sufficient, however, for this person to have a genuine belief. To see her point, consider the following example: the government might bombard its population for a long period of time with literature defending racial equality, at the end of which many people might utter their belief in racial equality. But the fact that these people have been put through this causal story and that they utter this belief is not sufficient for us to conclude that they genuinely believe in racial equality. As she writes: 'People who sincerely claim not to be racially prejudiced may nevertheless act out their true beliefs in such a way as to undermine the professed belief' (Mendus, 1991, p. 153). Note that her claim here is not that it is still possible, after the two above-mentioned conditions are satisfied, for people to *lie* about their racism. Rather, her point is that, even though the two conditions are satisfied, people may still *unintentionally misreport their state of mind,* both to themselves and to others, because – and this is the important claim – they may still harbour racist beliefs of which they are unaware. Even subtler forms of persecution, therefore, will not necessarily be successful in making people attain a genuine belief in racial equality.

While Mendus's suggestion is intriguing, and points to something of interest for the question of what counts as genuine belief, it seems, in the final analysis, to fall short of rescuing Locke's belief argument from Waldron's objection. In order to reply to Waldron's objection, Mendus must identify a necessary condition for 'genuine belief' that persecution cannot ensure. She does not do this. Instead, she argues that the use of force cannot always *guarantee* the effect of producing genuine belief in someone. If we stop there, however, we will not have closed the door to all forms of persecution. All Waldron needs to show in order to discredit Locke's belief argument is that there are *some* forms of persecution that are likely to produce genuine belief, and this does not seem difficult.

We are left with a third and final strategy for rescuing Locke's belief argument. While Waldron is correct in saying that coercing someone's sensory apparatus may eventually get this person to acquire *some* genuine beliefs, the class of beliefs that can arise in this way is very restricted. In other words, Waldron's objection may discredit Locke's belief argument as an argument against *all* forms of persecution, but not as an argument against *most* forms of persecution. For instance, while Waldron may be correct to say that persecutors are able to coerce people to see that snow is white, and consequently to believe it, there does not seem to be anything that persecutors can force people to look at in order to ensure that they will immediately infer more complex theological beliefs, such as, for example, the belief in the holy trinity. To be sure, the government can force people to read theological treatises, but it is questionable whether this will be a productive way to convert them: people who are coerced into considering evidence for complex beliefs are likely to suspect that this evidence has been fabricated, or that evidence unfavourable to the persecutors has been withheld. In short, Waldron's objection only manages to enforce a rather insignificant qualification to Locke's belief argument.

However, even this last strategy for rescuing Locke's belief argument is only a partial success. To see why, we must distinguish between persecution intended to make people embrace a belief and persecution intended to make people avoid acquiring a belief. The last line of defence shows that indirect persecution aimed at getting people to embrace a belief will be successful only in an insignificant class of cases. But it does not show that indirect persecution aimed at getting people to avoid acquiring a belief is similarly unsuccessful, and this would be a difficult thing to show. After all, there do seem to be very effective methods by which persecutors can extinguish beliefs that run contrary to the official orthodoxy: they can burn 'heretical' tomes, imprison dissident writers, prohibit societies that encourage free and open debate, and so on. Such methods will surely have a great effect in diminishing, if not eliminating, opposing religions or ideologies, and in doing so, they will remove alternatives to the persecutor's favoured belief system. There does not seem to be anything in Locke's belief argument that gives persecutors a reason to reject such methods.

Having considered a few lines of defence against Waldron's objection to Locke's belief argument, we may now be in a better position to see why that argument is beyond rescue as an argument against the rationality of persecution. An argument that shows why force is irrational when aimed at helping people achieve salvation must identify a necessary condition for salvation that people cannot meet as the result of being subjected to force. If Locke identifies this necessary condition to be that of belief, he fails to discredit the use of force because, as Waldron shows, belief can arise in people as the result of being subjected to force. We need only notice a distinction between *direct* and *indirect* persecution to see why this is the case. Both forms of persecution aim to coerce people into embracing or abandoning a particular belief, but whereas direct persecution aims to achieve this as the direct result of force, indirect persecution aims to achieve this by coercing people to take a series of intermediate steps towards that destination. The problem with the belief argument, then, is that it shows that direct persecution is irrational, but does not provide us with an argument against indirect persecution.

## The Sincerity Argument

We can now turn to the *Letter*'s first argument, the argument from sincerity, and ask whether it succeeds where the belief argument fails. The sincerity argument states that people would not rationally consent to a government that aims to coerce them into its favoured religion, since they would be unable to practise their religion sincerely under such a government, and practising their religion sincerely is their duty. Before considering the textual evidence for this argument in the *Letter*, I will briefly explain what it means for someone to practise a religion *sincerely*.

It may be helpful to begin by noticing how, in our ordinary language, we tend to use the term 'sincerity' in two different senses. According to the first and most familiar sense, we use it to refer to the expressive quality of an action – in order to point out that the action in question accurately expresses a person's state of mind or feelings. For example, we might say of someone that his expressions of regret are sincere, and by this mean that his speech and demeanour do really reflect a feeling of regret on his part. 'Sincerity' in this first sense is similar in meaning to 'truthfulness'. A second sense in which we use the word is truer to its etymological origins. The Latin *sincerus* was first used in order to describe objects as clean, sound or pure. It brought this meaning with it when it first entered the English language in the early sixteenth century: people would speak, for example, of 'sincere wine', and mean by this that the liquid was unadulterated, free of foreign substances.[8] In this second sense, 'sincerity' means something akin to 'purity'. When used to describe an action, it now refers to the *motivational* quality of that action – to the fact that the motives from which that action is performed are good, or at least not bad. Locke provides an example of this second usage of 'sincerity' in a passage from the *Essay Concerning Human Understanding* (1690), to which I will return below. He states that someone who 'seeks sincerely to discover the truth ... will not miss the reward of it', referring here to the divine reward of salvation. What he means is that a person will be rewarded provided he seeks in good faith – out of proper motives – to discover the truth (which, for Locke, is the desire to possess the truth for its own sake, or, as he also puts it in the *Essay*, the 'love of truth') (Locke, 1975, p. 688).[9]

This distinction between sincerity as truthfulness and sincerity as purity helps to illuminate Locke's concerns in the *Letter*.[10] When we turn to the sincerity argument as it is stated in the *Letter*, it may at first sight appear as if Locke is interested only in the first of the two senses in which someone might be said to practise a religion 'sincerely' – that is, by practising it 'truthfully'. It looks as if his reason for why it is irrational for people to consent to a government that coerces them into its favoured religion is that such a government would prevent them from performing religious actions that accurately express their beliefs. In fact, as I will argue, there is room for interpretation here, and I will propose that Locke is primarily interested in the second sense in which people might practise their religion 'sincerely'. In my view, the reason he believes it is irrational for people to consent to a government that coerces them into its favoured religion is that this would prevent them from practising their religion out of the right motives.

With this in mind, we can now consider the sincerity argument as it appears in the text of the *Letter*. The first occasion on which Locke makes the sincerity argument occurs in the section that immediately follows the *Letter*'s long prologue, a section that opens with the phrase, 'the commonwealth seems to me to be a society of men constituted only for the procuring, preserving, and advancing of their own civil interests'. The reason government may not also protect spiritual interests is one that Locke then states as follows (Locke, 1993, pp. 394–5):

> [1] The care of souls is not committed to the civil magistrate ...

And this holds because:

> [2] Whatever profession we make, to whatever outward worship we conform, if we are not fully satisfied in our own mind that the one is true, and the other well pleasing unto God, such profession and such practice, far from being any furtherance, are indeed great obstacles to our salvation. For in this manner ... we add unto the number of our other sins, those also of hypocrisy, and contempt of his divine majesty.

Passages 1 and 2 are the two main claims of the sincerity argument. Locke is arguing, in other words, that people cannot rationally consent to a coercively religious government (as passage 1 states), because people who allow the government to coerce them into its favoured religion do not practise their religion sincerely, and it is their duty to practise their religion sincerely (as passage 2 states).

Locke returns to the sincerity argument on two other occasions in the *Letter*. On those occasions, he restricts himself to re-stating its second component only (Locke, 1993, p. 410):

> [2a] Although the magistrate's opinion in religion be sound, and the way that he appoints be truly evangelical, yet if I be not thoroughly persuaded thereof in my own mind, there will be no safety for me in following it. No way whatsoever that I shall walk in, against the dictates of my conscience, will ever bring me to the mansions of the blessed ... Faith only, and inward sincerity, are the things that procure acceptance with God.

A few pages later, Locke re-states the second claim as follows (Locke, 1993, p. 413):

> [2b] He that worships God, does it with design to please him, and procure his favour. But that cannot be done by him, who, upon the command of another, offers unto God that which he knows will be displeasing to him, because not commanded by himself. This is not to please God, or appease his wrath, but willingly and knowingly to provoke him by a manifest contempt.

In exploring the sincerity argument further in what follows, I will leave aside an examination of its first claim concerning rational consent as a basis for setting the ends of government. It seems to me that this is the least interesting component of the sincerity argument. Arguments that settle the scope of political authority according to 'what people would rationally consent to' are purely formal and need to be conjoined with a substantive claim about the objective ends of individuals and about the kind of government that is necessary as a means for helping individuals achieve those ends. To be sure, appeals to rational consent in political philosophy are not entirely without significance, for they constrain us to think of the ends of government as ends of *individuals*, rather than as ends of some supra-individual entity, such as, for example, the 'nation', the 'church', the 'race', and so on. Nevertheless, it seems most appropriate for our purposes to leave this appeal in Locke aside and focus our attention upon the substantive claim that lends his sincerity argument its distinctiveness.

In what follows, then, I will investigate the second claim of the sincerity argument stated in the three passages above (2, 2a and 2b). It is pretty clear that in all three passages Locke is propounding the same basic view – that one ought not to profess and worship as others dictate, but only as one believes oneself. In other words, he seems to be holding to the view that one ought to practise one's religion sincerely in the first sense I distinguished above – that is, truthfully. The question now arises of why Locke believes that one has such a duty of sincerity: should we take him to simply assume that there is this duty, or can he enlist some further reason for insisting that one ought not to worship as others dictate? In the next two sections, I will distinguish between two possible reasons for why he might insist upon truthful worship, one of which will provide us, so I will argue, with a convincing case against persecution.

## The Weak Reading of the Sincerity Argument

Why does Locke hold the view that one ought not to profess or worship as others dictate, but only as one believes? The first of two answers that I will examine is as follows: he believes that, in failing to worship according to one's own lights, one shows oneself willing to disobey God. Even if one happens to hold mistaken beliefs about how God is to be worshipped, the fact that one fails to follow one's own mistaken beliefs about this matter is sufficient to demonstrate that one is willing to disobey God. That this is Locke's reason for insisting upon truthful worship might be inferred from his concluding statements in passages 2 and 2b, in which he says that worshipping as others dictate is to show 'contempt' for God.

However, if this were the only reason Locke insists that people must worship according to their own lights, then it would turn out that his argument is not powerful enough to provide a conclusive case against religious persecution. To see why this is the case, recall that a successful argument against *all* forms of persecution must identify a condition of salvation that will be violated by *any* form of persecution. If the only reason he believes that people must worship according to their own lights is that they must not show themselves willing to disobey God, then he faces the following problem. He might be able to show why persecutors ought not to prevent people from worshipping as they please, but he will not be able to show why persecutors ought not to use more subtle forms of persecution. For after all, it seems possible for a government to persecute its people without undermining their ability to worship as they believe they should. The government can refrain from interfering with their religious worship while exerting pressures upon their conduct outside of that sphere of action. Suppose, for instance, that the government makes it legally compulsory for people to read official religious propaganda. Such a policy controls the evidence that people consider in forming their religious beliefs, but it does not force people to practise a different form of worship from the one they believe they should practise. The first version of the sincerity argument thus fails to rule out this form of persecution.

We can imagine defences of the sincerity argument, as I am currently interpreting it, that are as unsuccessful as the ones considered above in support of the belief argument. Recall, for instance, Mendus's suggestion that persecution cannot guarantee that people will acquire genuine beliefs, since all it does is to subject them to a particular causal process at the end of which they might utter, but not genuinely hold, a particular belief. In a similar vein, a proponent of the weak sincerity argument might insist that indirect persecution may to some extent change people's beliefs about how they ought to worship, so that they willingly worship as others tell them to, but that this change will not be complete, and they will not therefore, when indirectly persecuted, worship truthfully after all. Even the most skilful persecutor might not be able to use force effectively, such that his victims will come to genuinely and completely believe they should practise the persecutor's preferred form of worship. Consequently, in worshipping according to their new but half-hearted beliefs, rather than their prior beliefs about how God is to be worshipped, they will show themselves willing to disobey God.

However much plausibility there is to this defence of the sincerity argument, it will not provide us with a conclusive case against all forms of persecution, for it can be replied, correctly, that it does not rule out uses of force that *can* succeed in leaving people fully confident in their religious beliefs. We can imagine, for instance, that the government might successfully prevent evidence from circulating amongst a population without the population's being aware of this fact. In such a case, no feelings of uncertainty would arise in the population about the validity of the beliefs they have come to form on the basis of the available evidence, and in proceeding to worship on the basis of those beliefs, they will worship according to their own lights. The problem with the first version of the sincerity argument, in short, is that the condition for salvation it identifies – worshipping according to one's own lights as a sign of obedience to God – is a condition that it is not impossible for some forms of persecution to respect.

## The Strong Reading of the Sincerity Argument

Is there alternative answer to the question of why Locke insists that one ought not worship as others dictate, but only as one believes? I will suggest that the reason is that he believes that people have a duty to practise their religion sincerely in the second sense I distinguished above – that is, *out of the proper motives*. Seen in this light, the three sincerity passages (2, 2a and 2b) reflect a worry on Locke's part that people will assume they have discharged their religious duty so long as they practise their religion in the manner that others command them to practise it, when in fact their duty is to search for the truth about God's wishes for themselves.[11] If this *is* his thinking behind his sincerity passages, then his sincerity argument does provide a powerful argument against persecution. For he can now say to persecutors that people who come to practise their religion only as the result of having been persecuted will not have met the condition they need to meet to obtain salvation. This argument shows why *all* forms of religious persecution are irrational. While there is no *conclusive* evidence in the *Letter* that this *is* his reasoning in the sincerity passages, I believe that we can plausibly attribute this argument to Locke on the basis of a sympathetic reconstruction of what he says in the *Letter*, as well as some of his remarks on sincere religion in other texts. I will say something more about the main claims of this argument, before turning to substantiate my view that it can be attributed to Locke.

To persecute someone is to use coercive means against that person and move him with fear. People who search for the truth about God's wishes only out of fear do not search for it out of the proper motives. If a necessary condition for salvation is that people search for the truth about God's wishes out of the proper motives, they will not be able to obtain salvation as the result of persecution. Seen in this light, religious persecution becomes the pointless infliction of harm, and hence irrational. This, it must be noted, applies to *any* form of persecution. Any action a person undertakes solely in response to another person's force, whether that action takes place in the context of his worship, or in any other context, is an action for which he cannot claim moral credit with God, as it were. Indirect persecution, as well direct persecution, will thus *necessarily* fail to help people meet the condition for their own salvation.

Evidence for this line of reasoning in Locke can be found, I believe, in some of his other texts – in two significant passages in particular. The first, which was briefly touched upon above, occurs in the *Essay Concerning Human Understanding*. He insists that people have a duty to limit and condition their religious faith by their use of natural reason (Locke, 1975, p. 688):

> He that does not [do] this [use his mental faculties] to the best of his power, however he sometimes lights on truth, is in the right but by chance; and I know not whether the luckiness of the accident will excuse the irregularity of his proceeding ... he that makes use of the light and faculties GOD has given him, and seeks sincerely to discover truth by those helps and abilities he has, may have this satisfaction in doing his duty as a rational creature: that, though he should miss truth, he will not miss the reward of it.

We find here Locke's commitment to the view that it is a necessary condition for salvation that one searches for the truth out of the proper motives, and that just ending up with the truth will not, by itself, get the reward of salvation. If one ends up with the truth without having searched for it out of the proper motives, then he doubts whether the 'luckiness of the accident will excuse the irregularity of the proceeding'.

The second passage occurs in a minor essay entitled 'Error'(Locke, 1997, p. 346):

> He that examines, and upon a fair examination embraces an error for a truth, has done his duty, more than he who embraces the profession (for the truths themselves he does not embrace) of the truth without having examined whether it be true or no ... For he that takes up the opinions of any church in the lump, without examining them, has truly neither searched after, nor found truth, but has only found those that he thinks have found truth ...

These two passages provide powerful evidence for attributing to Locke the stronger version of the sincerity argument. The reason he believes that one must not worship as others dictate is that, in doing so, one 'has truly neither searched after, nor found truth'.

## Concluding Remarks

I will conclude with some reflections about the significance of Locke's sincerity argument for us, his interpreters, some centuries on. A question that lurks in the background of any interpretation of his political thought is that concerning the extent to which the conclusions he reaches necessarily depend upon his religious premises. The issue presents itself as much with respect to Locke's sincerity argument as it does with respect to other parts of his thinking. At the beginning of chapter five of the *Second Treatise* (1690), for instance, he makes the important assumption that God granted the Earth to mankind in common (Locke, 1988, pp. 285–6). Just as we might wonder whether the conclusion he reaches in that chapter regarding the right and limits to private property necessarily relies on that assumption, so we might wonder whether his conclusion regarding the irrationality of religious persecution in the *Letter* necessarily relies upon his assumption that salvation depends on sincerity. It is beyond the purposes of this paper to treat the difficult question of whether and how we can draw intellectual resources from texts that are embedded in controversial theological foundations. However, I will put forward some suggestions about how we might go about answering the question of whether the sincerity argument might be a source of valid arguments against persecution, despite its theological foundations. It seems to me that the argument *can* be such a source, and that Waldron's implicit assessment of the *Letter* as obsolete in this regard ought to be revised.

To see the fruitfulness of the sincerity argument, it will be helpful to have it before us in its main steps:

1. salvation is the reward of a just God;
2. rewards are just when they go to agents who act from the right intentions;
3. therefore, to receive salvation (a just reward), one must act from the right intentions – one must act sincerely;
4. one cannot force someone to act sincerely; and
5. therefore, forcing someone to achieve salvation is irrational.

It is apparent that the above argument has religious and non-religious premises. Premise (1) is religious in nature, at least if we understand a 'religious premise' to be a statement the truth of which depends on the existence or nature of a god or gods. Until someone comes up with a conclusive proof of God's existence and of his nature as just, it seems obvious to me that this premise renders the sincerity argument, as Locke presents it, irrelevant for a pluralistic society such as our own of. Premises (2) and (4), however, are not religious in nature, and can be wholeheartedly embraced by atheists. One way in which Locke's sincerity argument may be a source of valid arguments, then, is that its non-religious premises may provoke us to find new arguments for toleration, arguments in which these non-religious premises combine with more defensible premises than (1) above. Here, I will suggest the outlines of an argument that draws, in this partial way, from Locke.

The argument I have in mind is one that shows the irrationality of moral paternalism. The doctrine of moral paternalism holds that one may, to the extent that it is practicable, use force in order to make people more virtuous.[12] To argue against this form of moral paternalism, then, we might draw upon Locke's sincerity argument as follows. We could argue that, since people being virtuous depends on them having the right intentions, and since force cannot make them act out of the right intentions, force aimed at making people virtuous is irrational. The argument is not precisely the same as the one seen in the *Letter*. It does not hinge, as Locke's does, on the claim that there is a just God who dispenses with the reward of salvation. But this anti-paternalist version of the sincerity argument is analogous to his by virtue of the fact that both share a common, non-religious claim to the effect that virtue is intention-dependent, and that force aimed at instilling virtue must therefore be irrational.

This is, of course, just the outline of a Lockean argument against moral paternalism. Many objections can no doubt be moved against it from within the paternalist camp, and there may be several ways in which the sincerity argument might be refined in order to meet those objections. My present concern has been simply to show that we have in the *Letter* a potentially promising point of departure for arguments in favour of toleration. Indeed, we have more than that. Locke's sincerity argument gestures towards no less than a different kind of liberalism from the Millian and Kantian varieties that tend most often to spring to mind nowadays. This is a form of liberalism according to which individual liberty is justified as providing the only context in which virtue can arise.

(*Accepted*: 21 May 2003)

## About the Author

**Paul Bou-Habib**, Department of Philosophy University of Bristol, 9 Woodland Road, Clifton, Bristol BS8 1TB, UK; email: *paul.bou-habib@bristol.ac.uk*

## Notes

I would like to thank Amy Gutmann, George Kateb, Serena Olsaretti, Paul Safier, Simon Stacey, the members of the Cambridge Political Theory Workshop and three referees for valuable comments on previous drafts of this paper.

1 As Locke writes: 'the care of souls cannot belong to the magistrate, because his power consists only in outward force' (Locke, 1993, p. 395).

2 The sorts of interests that constitute a person's 'temporal good' include 'life, liberty, health, and indolency of body; and the possession of outward things, such as money, lands, houses, furniture, and the like' (Locke, 1993, p. 393).

3 In Locke's words: 'Every man has commission to admonish, exhort, convince another of error, and by reasoning to draw him into truth: but to give laws, receive obedience, and compel with the sword, belongs to none but the magistrate' (Locke, 1993, p. 395).

4 Locke's third argument can be called the *universalisation argument*: if everyone were permitted to use force in religious matters, fewer people would attain salvation than if force in such matters were proscribed. It has been treated extensively by Richard Vernon (1997) and Alex Tuckness (2002).

5 In contrast, the third argument has an altogether different form: it holds that one is not permitted to pursue certain actions if terrible consequences would follow were these actions permitted to all. For further discussion, see Vernon (1997) and Tuckness (2002).

6 I am grateful to an anonymous referee for pressing me to clarify this distinction between the aims of reinforcing people's existing beliefs and making people abandon some beliefs in favour of others.

7 For an account of the distinction between beliefs and belief-like states, which is similar to the distinction I am drawing attention to here, see Williams (1973).

8 For the etymological origins of 'sincerity', see Trilling (1972, pp. 12–13).

9 In organising my thoughts about the concept of sincerity, I have benefited from reading Hampshire (1971) and Walker (1978).

10 The distinction may in fact be deceptive, however, for sincerity as truthfulness might actually be a particular instance of sincerity as purity. When we use 'sincerity' to mean something similar to 'truthful' (for example, when we say, 'he spoke sincerely', or 'his smile seemed sincere'), we seem to mean that a particular action was performed out of good motives, or at least not out of bad motives. When we say of someone that 'he spoke sincerely', or that 'his smile seemed sincere', we mean, in other words, that one particular bad motive behind those actions was absent – the motive to deceive. I think this is a plausible suggestion, but, in line with common usage of the notion of sincerity, in what follows I take it that the distinction is a real one. This should not affect the substance of the arguments I develop here.

11 Here, I take it that to practise one's religion includes searching for the truth about God's wishes.

12 For a powerful defence of moral paternalism, see George (1993).

## References

George, R. (1993) *Making Men Moral: Civil Liberties and Public Morality*. Oxford: Oxford University Press.

Hampshire, S. (1971) 'Sincerity and Single-Mindedness', in *Freedom of Mind, and Other Essays*. Princeton NJ: Princeton University Press, pp. 232–56.

Locke, J. (1975) *Essay Concerning Human Understanding* (1690), ed. P. Nidditch. Oxford: Oxford University Press.

Locke, J. (1993) *Letter Concerning Toleration* (1689), in D. Wootton (ed.), *Political Writings of John Locke*. London: Penguin, pp. 390–436.

Locke, J. (1997) 'Error' (1698), in M. Goldie (ed.), *Political Essays*. Cambridge: Cambridge University Press, pp. 345–8.

Locke, J. (1988) Two Treatises of Government (1690), ed. P. Laslett. Cambridge: Cambridge University Press.

Mendus, S. (1991) 'Locke: Toleration, Morality and Rationality', in J. Horton and S. Mendus (eds), *John Locke: A Letter Concerning Toleration in Focus*. London: Routledge, pp. 147–62.

Trilling, L. (1972) *Sincerity and Authenticity*. Cambridge MA: Harvard University Press.

Tuckness, A. (2002) *Locke and the Legislative Point of View*. Princeton NJ: Princeton University Press.

Vernon, R. (1997) *The Career of Toleration*. Montreal: McGill-Queen's University Press.

Waldron, J. (1991) 'Locke: Toleration and the Rationality of Persecution', in J. Horton and S. Mendus (eds), *John Locke: A Letter Concerning Toleration in Focus*. London: Routledge, pp. 98–124.

Walker, A. D. M. (1978) 'The Ideal of Sincerity', *Mind*, October, pp. 481–97.

Williams, B. (1973) 'Deciding to Believe', in *Problems of the Self*. Cambridge: Cambridge University Press, pp. 136–51.

# Name Index

For Product Safety Concerns and Information please contact our EU representative GPSR@taylorandfrancis.com
Taylor & Francis Verlag GmbH, Kaufingerstraße 24, 80331 München, Germany

www.ingramcontent.com/pod-product-compliance
Lightning Source LLC
LaVergne TN
LVHW080802011026
849160LV00015B/1509
* 9 7 8 1 1 3 8 3 7 8 4 5 2 *